THE CENTURY PSYCHOLOGY SERIES

Richard M. Elliott, *Editor*

Kenneth MacCorquodale, *Assistant Editor*

Developmental Psychology

DEVELOPMENTAL
PSYCHOLOGY

AN INTRODUCTION TO THE STUDY OF
HUMAN BEHAVIOR

Florence L. Goodenough

EMERITUS, UNIVERSITY OF MINNESOTA

Leona E. Tyler

UNIVERSITY OF OREGON

THIRD EDITION

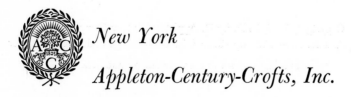

New York

Appleton-Century-Crofts, Inc.

Growth may be conceived as the creative function of the nervous system, not only with regard to the form of the behavior pattern but also with regard to its control. The creative component of thought, upon this hypothesis, is growth.

Man is more than the sum of his reflexes, instincts, and immediate reactions of all sorts. He is all these, plus his creative potential for the future. . . . The real measure of the individual, accordingly, whether lower animal or man, must include the element of growth as a creative power. Man is indeed a mechanism, but he is a mechanism which, within his limitations of life, sensitivity, and growth, is creating and operating himself.—From G. E. Coghill. *Anatomy and the problems of behavior.* Cambridge: The University Press, 1929.

Preface

MORE THAN TWO DECADES have passed since the publication of the first edition of this book in 1934. During that time changes have taken place in psychological thought and in the objectives of psychological research. Among these changes, one of the most striking is the increased interest in the developmental aspects of behavior; in the growing tendency to look upon behavior as a continuously growing and changing process in which no single phase can be properly considered by itself. We need to know the phases which preceded it, those which are likely to follow it, and the factors by which its course is influenced. Behavior, like life itself, is not static but dynamic.

Since the publication of the second edition in 1945, so much new material has appeared in the literature of the field that a new edition seemed compulsory. Unfortunately, however, almost complete loss of vision made it impossible for me to prepare the new work myself. In this emergency, my friend and colleague, Dr. Leona Tyler, of the University of Oregon, kindly consented to take over the task and this choice of a co-author has proved to be a very happy one.

In the present edition two features of the second edition have been retained. The orientation questions at the beginning of each chapter which have been found a useful guide to direct the student in his reading have been repeated in the third edition, though the wording of many of them has been changed, some have been omitted, and new ones added. The substitution of a short review of a single book that concludes each chapter for the longer list which is but rarely used is another feature of the second edition that we have thought worth retaining. Several completely new chapters have been added and others omitted or combined so that the total length of the book is approximately that of the second edition.

For the work of revision, Dr. Tyler has been entirely responsible. Not only such rewriting as was needed to bring the material up to date but also such changes in basic organization as have been made have been her work. My own share has been only to listen and approve as the successive chapters were read to me. Dr. Tyler has performed her task with zeal and understanding. Whatever success this book may enjoy will largely be due to her efforts.

F. L. G.

>> >> >> >> >> >> >> >> >> >>

Foreword

THE REVISION OF this book has been a challenging and rewarding task. My research activities in the field of individual differences, especially differences in interest patterns, have led me increasingly to a search for the developmental roots of individuality. My efforts in the counseling field have generated a firm conviction that developmental psychology constitutes the "basic science" for our work with individuals. Whatever else it may have accomplished the writing for this book has enabled me to organize my own thoughts on these matters.

As much as possible I have tried to keep the original structure, content, and "flavor" of Dr. Goodenough's book. Again and again I have been impressed with the soundness and the readability of the previous editions. Besides bringing the material up to date, however, I have made a few major changes in orientation and structure. These necessitated a rewriting of considerable portions of the text. First of all, I have adopted a consistent emphasis on *developmental tasks* as the distinguishing features of the successive life stages. Secondly, I have placed considerable emphasis on Piaget's theories, particularly his more recent ideas. Thirdly, I have included in the appropriate sections the ideas and research findings of psychoanalysts and of the psychologists who have based their work on Freudian theory. And finally, I have placed more emphasis than before on the development that occurs during the adult years.

As in its previous editions, this book is designed to be used as a textbook for students who have had no previous work in psychology. It presents all the concepts usually covered in general psychology, but approaches them from the developmental point of view. Instructors who use the text in more advanced classes may wish to omit the chapters on psychology as a science, heredity, and physiological psychology, if their students have already encountered these ideas in their elementary course. Instructors who use the text for child psychology courses may omit the chapters on the later periods of life. It seemed better to err on the side of overinclusiveness rather than underinclusiveness.

It would be impossible to list the many persons whose ideas have influenced me strongly. Besides the work of Piaget, mentioned above, that of E. H. Erikson and R. J. Havighurst has had a considerable effect on the basic structure of the book. The opportunity afforded me during a year spent in Berkeley to become thoroughly familiar with the work of H. E. Jones and his co-workers at the Institute of Child Welfare, University of California, was invaluable. The work of D. E. Super and his associates on vocational development has contributed much to my thinking about adolescence and the adult years. Acknowledgments of the sources of the new illustrations I have added are included with the illustrations themselves. I should like also to register my gratitude to Mr. C. J. Dunkleberger who helped with these illustrations and to Mrs. Betty Crosley whose ability to whip a manuscript into shape goes far beyond ordinary typing skill.

L. E. T.

Contents

PART I

Principles and Methods of Developmental Psychology

Why do people differ?—Growth is more than an increase in
size—Upon what does development depend?—The hereditary
component of development—The effect of learning on development—The effect of the psychological situation on development—The development of the self-concept—Developmental
stages—Psychology in the study of development

The field of psychology—Changing points of view—How psychology secures its facts—Methods of improving the accuracy
of psychological observation and of reducing the likelihood of
error in interpreting the subject's responses

PART II

The Person's Equipment for Living

How does human life begin?—What is given by heredity?—
The physical basis of heredity—The determination of sex—
Sex-linked traits—The protective effects of biparental heredity

PART III

The Principal Life Stages

PART IV

Developmental Deviations

»»»»»»»»»»»

List of Figures

»»»»»»»»»»»

List of Tables

Principles and Methods of Developmental Psychology

CHAPTER 1

Why do different people behave so differently under the same conditions?

In the same situation, why do not all persons have the same or similar experiences?

What does growth involve besides increase in size?

Does personality depend mainly on the maturing of natural tendencies or on the kind of training a child receives?

Why are self-concepts important in development?

With what is the study of psychology chiefly concerned?

»»»»»»»»»»

The Developmental Approach to Psychology

WHY DO PEOPLE DIFFER?

MODERN PSYCHOLOGY IS FOUNDED on experiment. The psychologist of a century ago hoped to learn how the human mind worked by sitting quietly in his armchair and, as an irreverent student once put it, "listening to hear himself tick." But the introspective method, which is the scientific name for the study of mental activity by means of self-observation, is no longer looked upon with much favor. Nowadays when we wish to learn how human beings think and act, we set them a problem to do and then record what happens. So your introduction to this fascinating subject of human behavior will be made by way of an experiment. Get a pencil and sheet of paper. Are you ready? Then turn to Figure 1.

Here you have a series of six ink blots. Most people find that each of these blots reminds them of something—an animal, perhaps, or a person doing something, or it may be a bird or a flower or something quite different from any of these. Look at each blot and write down the first thing it suggests to you. Work quickly and be sure to put down your *first* association for each blot.

Now show the page to some of your acquaintances and have them write their impressions. How many of them agree with yours?

Look at the blots again, more carefully this time. See how many different things you can see in each. Turn the page to different positions

3

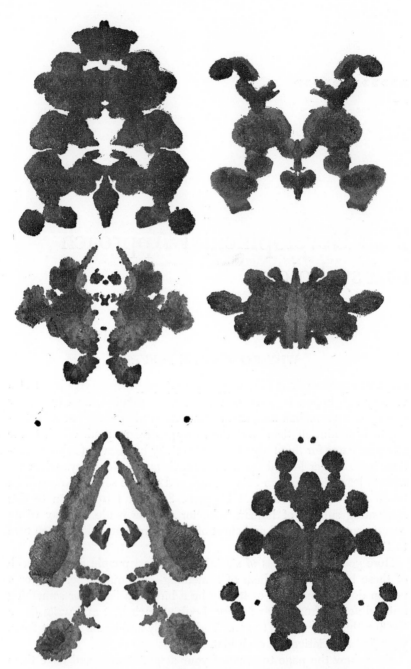

FIGURE 1.   What do these blots make you think of?

so as to get as many different associations as possible. Have your friends do the same and once more compare results.

This simple experiment affords a nice illustration of the fact that every one lives in a perceptual world of his own that is to some extent different from all other worlds. No two people interpret what they see in exactly the same way. Yet the external facts remain the same; the differences, evidently, are in the people who deal with these facts. Because people differ from each other, they regard the world from different points of view, and so the same facts take on different meanings for them. It is not surprising, then, that under the same external situations they often behave very differently.

The next time you go to the theater or to the movies, notice how the other members of the audience act. A joke is told. Most of the people laugh, some merely smile, others look bored; a few, perhaps, make audible comments of a disparaging nature. Observe their postures. Unless the play is unusually thrilling, most people assume an attitude of easy attention, sitting well back in their chairs with muscles partially relaxed in a position calculated to combine an unobstructed view of the stage with a maximum of bodily comfort. If it is impossible to get a good view and at the same time sit comfortably, some content themselves with such glimpses as they can easily get while others continually twist and wriggle about in their efforts to see more. Some, regardless of the location of their seats, lean forward with set faces and tensed muscles; others loll back with half-closed eyes and seem hardly aware of what is going on. A parcel is dropped with a loud thud. Several persons start visibly, others crane their necks to see what happened, still others continue to watch the stage with no outward sign of distraction.

But these, you say, are only trifles. Turn, then, to matters of greater importance. Here are five men, each forty years old. As babies you could have hardly told them apart. Today one is a distinguished statesman, another a farm laborer, the third a convicted murderer, the fourth a college professor, and the fifth a garbage collector.

Try to recall the children you played with at the age of eight. Even then, as you will recollect if your memory is fairly good, their behavior was not alike. Some were quick in their movements, others slow; some were fond of companionship and active sports, others were always slipping off by themselves with a book. Some did well in school, others poorly; some usually took the lead in play, others were satisfied to follow; some were always in mischief, others were "good boys" who rarely got into trouble. What are these children like now? Would you say that on the whole the differences between them have increased or diminished as they have grown older? If you had tried to predict from their behavior at the age of eight what they would be like at the present time, in how many cases would your guess have been approximately right? Are there any who have turned out very differently from the way that might formerly have been expected? If so, do you know of anything in their experience or training that might account for the change?

Abilities, habits, attitudes, ways of looking at things and ways of doing them do not come full-grown into the possession of their owners like garments bought from a ready-to-wear clothing store. Like the bodily organs, they grow and develop with age. As with the body, their growth and development are determined by laws. As yet these laws are not completely understood, but enough is known to show that, as is true of the laws of physics and chemistry, their action is relatively fixed and inevitable. Although we cannot change these laws, we can nevertheless make use of them if we learn what they are and how they operate. The differences, little and great, significant and trifling, that you see in the behavior of your friends and in yourself are not the result of chance but have come about through the combined action of growth and experience. To understand them you must know something of the laws of growth and of the factors by which its course is determined.

GROWTH IS MORE THAN AN INCREASE IN SIZE

All living beings grow. With this growth comes change, not only in size and appearance but in behavior. The baby does not look like a grownup and he does not act like a grownup.

He is different. We sometimes say of an acquaintance, "What a babyish face he has!" We do not mean that his face is small; it may even be larger than the average. But the contour of his features reminds us of a baby. Likewise, when we say that some adult is "acting like a baby" we do not necessarily mean that his behavior is simpler, more naïve, less elaborately organized than that of other adults. It is not simply a matter of doing less than we expect, but of doing something different.

Growth, whether physical or mental, is something more than a mere increase in size or an added ability to do things. The adult is not just a big baby, either in body or in mind. He has grown bigger, it is true, and his mental powers have improved. But he has also changed in many other ways that have nothing to do with size or with amount of ability. His bodily proportions have changed. His arms and legs make up a greater part of his body than they did in infancy; his head is smaller in proportion to his trunk. The composition of his bodily tissues has changed. His bones are becoming more brittle, his muscles less resilient. His features have become more clear-cut; the chin and lower jaw have increased in size and firmness. As age advances, the layer of fat directly underneath the skin gradually disappears, and wrinkles result.

Mental growth, like the growth of the body, is more than a gain in quantity. It is not just a matter of being able to do more things or of being able to do them better. It also involves changes in the way we think and act, in the emotions, interests, and desires that influence all our conduct. These changes are just as truly a part of mental growth as are gains in the ability to memorize, to form correct judgments, or to see relationships, and they merit quite as careful study.

UPON WHAT DOES DEVELOPMENT DEPEND?

To avoid some of the ambiguity that comes from viewing growth as primarily a change in size, we have increasingly come to use the word *development* for the more inclusive process. Many kinds of scientific workers have studied it. Biologists are interested in finding general laws that will apply to all living things. Physicians are on the lookout for deficiencies that if not corrected will retard growth and produce temporary ill health or lifelong handicaps. Teachers wish to promote mental and social development in the children for whom they are responsible. Most of all, parents wish to make sure that their children are developing normally.

With so many practical problems clustering around this concept of development it is not strange that there has been a large amount of research devoted to it. Different workers approached the problem from different directions and thus came out with varying conclusions about what factors were of crucial importance. It is only in recent years that it has been possible to get away from the controversies that have divided the hereditarians and the environmentalists, the advocates of maturation and of learning, the biologically- and the socially-oriented psychologists. We have come to see life as a series of stages. At each stage the developmental changes that will occur in a person depend upon several kinds of factors that interact with one another: the hereditary potentialities, the learning that has occurred at previous stages, and the present psychological situation.

It is simple enough to *say* that these are the factors that determine at each stage what an individual will be like at the next. The analysis of the ways in which specific determiners are operating in any case is, however, a very complicated business. Teachers, parents, and child therapists often come to have a great deal of skill in making such analyses on a somewhat intuitive basis. The aim of child development research centers has been to make the knowledge that leads to such skill more explicit. Psychologists hope that a better understanding of the complexities of the developmental process as it affects behavior and inner experience will allow more people to come to maturity with the kinds of skills and attitudes that constitute real assets for living.

THE HEREDITARY COMPONENT OF DEVELOPMENT

At any stage in his life history, what a person can do is limited by hereditary factors. The most obvious of these are the species differences that we see as we look at the world of living things around us. For each species there is a typical developmental pattern. A guinea pig is ready to walk when it is born. A human child must wait for about a year before the necessary structures of his body have matured sufficiently to make walking possible. For each species there are stages in the unfolding of behavior. There may be individual variations in the number of days or weeks required to reach a given stage, but the order of the stages is fixed.

Psychologists have studied these hereditary patterns characteristic of the human species under the general heading of *maturation*. They have identified, for example, the sequence of changes in the characteristic movements infants make during their first fifteen months of life, movements that finally result in the typical walking motion of the toddler. The transition from babbling to meaningful speech has been similarly studied. Much of this research, to be considered in more detail later, was designed to demonstrate that there are some kinds of behavior that do not need to be learned or taught—that will develop in any normal child at the appointed time simply because he is human and the machine his heredity gives him is designed to change its functioning in just these ways. As suggested above, this idea is too simple to explain the facts the maturation studies have uncovered. Maturation is a factor that operates at the same time as do other factors rather than as a substitute for them.

The other kind of hereditary factors involved in development at any stage are those specific to the individual. There is good evidence that the particular combination of genes a child starts with influences his development throughout his whole life. His level of general intelligence, his temperamental characteristics, and probably his talents and special aptitudes depend to a considerable extent on his individual heredity. In this area of research as in the previous one the bitter controversy that once raged around the heredity-environment issue has subsided. Potentialities arising from an individual's specific gene pattern, like the maturational changes characteristic of the species, never operate in isolation from other determiners. What happens in the individual case depends upon the *interaction* of the several kinds of factors, not upon any one kind alone.

THE EFFECT OF LEARNING ON DEVELOPMENT

The second main kind of factor which helps to determine the pattern of development that an individual person will follow is the diverse group of changes we classify under the term *learning*. What characterizes them is that they depend upon what the person *does* rather than upon his age or developmental stage, as the maturational changes do. Because a child sits down to the piano for a few moments each day and strikes the keys in an order he has been shown, he gradually acquires the ability to produce intricate and beautiful music. This would never have come spontaneously as his muscles and glands developed, even if he had been endowed with the genes of a long line of musical ancestors. Practice is necessary. Skills like these must be learned.

Most of the behavior and experience of each human being at any stage of life except the very earliest is determined to a large extent by what he has learned at previous stages. This is obvious when we consider such matters as playing the piano or solving arithmetic problems. It is not so obvious that the way one sees and hears the world around him is also dependent on learning. A girl from a small town who has never visited a museum or looked at an art book will not *see* the same thing in a Picasso painting as a more sophisticated fellow student does. The unmusical listener does not really *hear* a symphony. It is learning that organizes the tremendous complexity of the physical energies that are continually acting upon delicate nerve endings and gives them stability and pattern.

Furthermore it has become increasingly clear that the development of feelings and emotions also depends upon learning. From his first moment of life the child begins to form his basic attitudes toward people and toward life as a whole. Each successive experience, with its effect on the way he acts and the way he sees and organizes the world around him, leaves also its residue of feeling. As he grows up he will be responsive or sullen, friendly or suspicious, cautious or impulsive, because of what these experiences have added up to for him. Love for some kinds of people, rebellious hostility toward others, is learned in the schoolroom along with spelling and arithmetic.

Learning is not just the opposite of teaching, but a much broader, more fundamental thing. We learn all sorts of things we have never been explicitly taught. The essence of the learning process is that the person finds himself in a situation to which he must react in some way. The schoolroom is only one of innumerable such situations, and the tasks the teacher assigns are by no means the most important ones set before him. It has become increasingly clear that the most influential learning of all occurs in the years before the school begins its systematic efforts to educate. And learning in some form continues throughout all the adult years and makes for changes in great-grandmothers of 80 as well as in children of 8.

Nevertheless, the influence of learning on development, while it is very great, is not unlimited. The famous behaviorist J. B. Watson, in 1925, made the extreme statement:

> Give me a dozen healthy infants, well-formed, and my own specified world to bring them up in, and I'll guarantee to take any one at random and train him to become any type of specialist I might select—doctor, lawyer, artist, merchant, chief, and yes, even beggarmen and thief, regardless of his talents, penchants, tendencies, abilities, vocations, and the race of his ancestors.[1]

No responsible psychologist would say such a thing today. The progress of research has shown us the fallacy of this point of view. We know now that a child prodigy cannot be produced by parental coaching, no matter how skillful. An ordinary child does not have the hereditary equipment to develop the mental capacity that would make it possible for him to learn Latin grammar at the age of six. The intellectual performances that astonish us in the more spectacular of the child prodigies could not occur in the absence of a tremendous amount of learning. But this learning itself would not have occurred if an exceptional gene combination had not expanded the limits of what it is ordinarily possible for a child of this age to learn.

Similarly, anyone, prodigy or ordinary child, cannot learn complex new ways of doing, seeing, or understanding before he reaches the maturity level appropriate for such learning. The most brilliant teacher cannot make the most gifted six-month-old baby learn to talk intelligibly. The average two-year-old who has mastered the fundamentals of speech successfully still cannot at this stage learn to read. Heredity develops the potentialities. Learning must occur if they are to be actualized.

THE EFFECT OF THE PSYCHOLOGICAL SITUATION ON DEVELOPMENT

It has become increasingly evident that in order to understand the process of development we must study also the complex situations to which individuals are reacting. Child psychologists have always paid

---

[1] J. B. Watson. *Behaviorism.* New York: Peoples Institute, 1925, p. 82.

some attention to environmental influences. At first they took account of socio-economic level and the general adequacy of the homes from which children came. As work proceeded, it became apparent that there were more subtle variables that needed to be evaluated. It is the child's inner picture of his surroundings that affects his life, not those surroundings as they appear to an outsider. Furthermore, relationships to other persons constitute far more important features of the psychological situation than physical appearances do. This change in emphasis has led to the development of scales for rating parent behavior with regard to such qualities as warmth, severity, and possessiveness. It has led also to methods of ascertaining how children—even very young ones—perceive their homes and the larger world around them. What a three-year-old does with dolls and furniture may tell us much about what his psychological situation is.

The characteristics of his environment to which a person is sensitive affect his development through both the other factors that have been mentioned above. Hereditary potentialities, those of the species and of the individual, require certain conditions for their unfolding. Anthropologists have taught us much about what happens to the distinctively human traits in the psychological situations provided by different cultures. The man with all of the kinds of genetic endowment necessary for musical achievement of a high order will not compose a symphony if he is a native of central Africa never touched by European influences. On the other hand, a similarly gifted European may not be able to grasp the intricacies of the drum beats he hears on a visit to central Africa. In different surroundings different potentialities of an individual become actualized.

Within our own society evidence has been accumulating that the kinds of developmental sequences we have identified for motor skills, such as sitting and walking, and language skills, such as talking, listening, and reading, do not proceed normally in institutional settings or homes where children do not get the attention and stimulation from adults that are a child's customary birthright. The kinds of abilities we measure in our intelligence tests develop optimally in the intellectual environment a good school furnishes. If a child is cut off from this by poverty, isolation, or his own attitudes, his mental development may be stunted along the way, or proceed in unanticipated directions.

The influences of the psychological situation on the learning process is obvious. Often it is impossible to separate it, even in thinking about the matter, from the influences on maturation that we have been considering. A person learns by reacting to a stimulating situation in which he finds himself. If he has books and pictures to examine he learns to make the perceptual responses that enable him to get meaning from a picture. If he has space to run around in and companions to teach him the rules of the game he learns basketball and other athletic skills. If he spends his first ten years on a lonely farm where he seldom encounters other children, he learns to engage in solitary pursuits and does not become proficient in social skills. If he is reared by parents who show their love for him but encourage him to do things himself rather than to wait for someone to do them for him, he learns to proceed with confidence and feel independent. The process of growing up involves so many kinds of learning that examples of this kind could be extended indefinitely. From birth to death, a person is always a part of some situation. He cannot really be understood apart from his surroundings.

THE DEVELOPMENT OF THE SELF-CONCEPT

In an abstract, logical way the three kinds of factors we have been discussing—heredity, learning, and psychological situation—account for what each person is and does. To identify all of the specific factors of all three types that have produced any one individual is an almost impossible task. But there is an aspect of the developmental process itself that provides a kind of short cut for us in our attempts to understand a person. As he moves through the experiences that arise from his particular combination of genetic potentialities, maturation, and learning, a sense of self gradually emerges, an answer to the question "Who am I?" As this becomes more mature, it seems to steer the rest of his development. It helps him answer such urgent questions as "Where do I belong?" "What occupation shall I go into?" and "What do I believe?"

For the kind of understanding of other people that is needed by a counselor or teacher, mother or father, it is often more useful to get a glimpse of this picture the person has of himself than to know all the facts of his previous life. Thus if psychologists are to increase their knowledge of the developmental process as a whole, they must learn how this sense of self develops. At any point along life's journey, it constitutes a sort of integration of everything that has occurred up to this point. It shows not just what has happened, but the *pattern* in terms of which the person is interpreting what has happened. And at any point it indicates more about what an individual is likely to do next than do the facts about the experiences that helped to determine it.

Children sense very early, long before the school years begin, the implications of sex differences. The statement, "I am a boy," or "I am a girl," is probably one of the earliest manifestations of the emerging self-concept. As time passes the boy may be able to say "I am an athlete," and the girl to say "I am a pretty, popular girl." Such statements, though not made consciously, limit the number of environmental situations to which the person responds, and make for the practicing and learning of some skills rather than others. Thus, little by little, the individuality of the person develops.

DEVELOPMENTAL STAGES

Development throughout life is not a continuous, unbroken process in which the same kinds of changes are occurring all along the way. We shall be closer to the truth if we conceive of it as a series of stages differing to some extent from one another in a *qualitative* manner. Several lines of research substantiate this idea. Embryologists find that there are critical periods for the development of each organ. At one time the heart grows most rapidly, at another time the eye or the ear. If something happens to arrest progress during this particular period, the deficiency is never completely overcome.

Psychoanalysts whose work with neurotic patients made them aware of the importance of development in infancy have written much about oral and anal stages in the development of the young child, and much of this analytic theory has been incorporated into the main body of child psychology. According to this theory, in the earliest months the mouth is the child's most important organ and the gratifications and frustrations that come to him in connection with eating will produce some of the basic patterns of response to his surroundings throughout life. In the next period, where the anal cavity comes into prominence as a focus of attention, other basic patterns are laid down.

The idea of developmental stages appears in another guise in the work educators have done with regard to "readiness" for different kinds of school learning. The supporting evidence is most plentiful in the reading area, but it seems probable that the same concepts apply to other school subjects. There seems to be a period in which a child is ripe for reading, intellectually and emotionally. Instruction given before this stage is reached produces little effect, except perhaps to discourage the child and set up attitudinal barriers to later learning. On the other hand, if we delay reading instruction too long, we may find that other kinds of activities have been learned during the period, and that they serve as substitutes for reading, thus reducing the motivation to learn it. The popular notion of "the psychological moment" takes on new meaning with regard to development.

As early as 1933 Charlotte Bühler wrote of developmental stages characterizing life as a whole rather than just the years before maturity. While this idea is at least as old as Shakespeare, it seemed to have little influence in psychology until the 1950's. Renewed interest in the special problems of the very old in our society has made people aware that old age constitutes a definite developmental stage with its own challenges that must be met. Increased emphasis on the psychology of occupational choice and the part that work plays in personality adjustment has led to the identification of stages in careers. Thus the way has been paved for a developmental psychology that will encompass the whole life span. A significant step in this direction was the shift from *Child Psychology* to *Developmental Psychology* as a title for the chapter in *Annual Review of Psychology* in 1957.

Another kind of shift that has occurred in the thinking psychologists do about development is an increasing emphasis on *challenges* and *tasks* characterizing each period rather than on *influences* and *effects*. In a very real sense each individual shapes his own development by the choices he makes at each successive stage. The habits he forms, his perceptions of the world around him, and, above all, the picture he has of himself do not depend directly on circumstances but rather on the *responses* he makes to them.

The study of the choices or decisions of human beings made slow progress as long as the problem was approached from the standpoint of the age-old controversy over determinism vs. free-will. It has become apparent that it is more profitable to consider choice to be a kind of *spontaneous* activity, as contrasted with reactions determined in a mechanistic way by exterior circumstances. There is abundant evidence that such spontaneous activity occurs in all organisms, not just in man alone. Such behavior, determined by inner needs rather than by prodding from the outside, is not capricious and unlawful, nor is it unscientific to study it.

When we make this shift in our thinking about human behavior we find room for more optimism about the possibility of bringing about change. If it were true that the behavior of a person was completely determined by the events of his early life, the prospects for education or psychotherapy would be dim. It is obviously impossible to change the events themselves years after they happened. But if we recognize an intermediate process, an interpretation of life adopted by the person as a consequence of these events, and a pattern of behavior that followed in a spontaneous way from this interpretation, then our efforts to help him can be focused on these interpretations and the choices they generate.

This is not at all the same thing as to say that *any* change at any time of life is possible. Choices made at each developmental stage place limitations on the next stage. Because at the time of the death of his father, Jerry chooses to remain with his grandparents in a little Nebraska town instead of moving with his mother to New York, the things he knows and the interests he develops make it possible later on for him to decide to be an engineer but not to decide to be an interior designer. When a man of thirty who has been retiring and shy all through his high school and college years because he felt that he was basically stupid and unattractive becomes a successful scientist, marries a beautiful girl, and shapes his self-concept into a more appealing pattern, he is still not likely to be the life of any party, because all of his habits and interests are solitary rather than social.

Developmental psychology, then, can be seen as a study of the successive stages in the life of a human being. Each stage presents its particular challenges, and there are individual differences in the way in which the challenges are met. The way in which the person will interpret and respond to the challenges of any stage depends to some extent on how he has met those of the previous stages. Some change in the *interpretations* that have been made of earlier experiences are always possible, and some changes in spontaneous choices, or behavior determined from *inside* the person, will occur when such interpretations are modified.

PSYCHOLOGY IN THE STUDY OF DEVELOPMENT

It is simple enough to grasp what the growth process in general entails, but a real understanding of the specific processes that are involved in it requires a knowledge of many kinds of facts, the products of painstaking research. We must consider what is the usual or most frequent course that behavior patterns follow and the extent and nature of deviations from this pattern that occur in individual cases. We need to know how such variations come about, to study them in relation to family history, race, and sex, as well as to the personal experiences of the persons who exhibit them. We wish to know how our own behavior, or that of others, can be modified. To answer this question we shall have to look at the research psychologists have done on the learning process. We need to think in terms of physiological factors that influence behavior. Thus we must consider such specialized problems as the mechanism through which heredity works, the structure and function of the nervous system, and the part played by the glands of internal secretion.

At all times we shall need to remember that the activities we observe in human beings of all ages have their inner representations we call "mental activity" as well as their outer visible manifestations. Psychology is concerned with both the behavior and the "mental" processes. We should remember, however, that much that goes on inside the organism is not directly reportable. We do not really "know our own minds" very well.

Some would say that it is fruitless to consider learning by itself or perception by itself or physiological processes by themselves. The person acts as a whole, and in the situations of real life, these things are all going on at once. Even so simple an act as reaching for a pencil involves a complex combination of many kinds of process. First there is some kind of inner physiological change, probably in the brain, from a state of indifference to one of dissatisfaction or tension. Along with this is a mental state which the person recognizes as the need for a pencil. Somehow the physiological excitation spills over into some muscle groups, and the legs move, thus propelling the person to the place where pencils are kept. The image of the pencil appears on the retina of the eye, nerve fibers running to the brain are activated, and other nerve fibers to muscles of the arm and hand carry an electrical impulse that contracts just the right muscles to allow the hand to grasp the pencil. Simple as such an act is, it includes observable and nonobservable, physical and "mental," electrical, chemical, and mechanical processes. If we had to plan such sequences of happenings one by one, life would be a difficult business!

It is quite true, therefore, that one cannot be too analytical about what he is doing and still keep the smooth sequence of acts co-ordinated. However, in studying human behavior so as to be in a better position to anticipate and direct it, a study of the part processes is essential. Just as we may examine the electrical system or the cooling system of an automobile without paying much attention to the rest of the machine, so we have found it profitable to study part processes in the human organism by themselves, recognizing at all times the existence of the other processes we are ignoring temporarily.

Early psychologists defined psychology as the study of *consciousness*. Another generation of scientific workers, concerned over the fact that a person's conscious experience is private and unobservable by anyone but himself, reacted vehemently against this definition and insisted that psychology is the study of *behavior*. As time has passed, we have become less concerned with such controversies. Furthermore we have come to realize that inner experience is more than consciousness; unconscious processes must also be considered. And behavior is more than the muscle movements that the early behaviorists wished to study. *Experience* is a better word than consciousness for our purposes, and *activity* is a better word than behavior.

As age advances and experience increases, both the internal and the external phases of activity are constantly changing. It is the aim of psychology to learn how these changes take place, how to predict them, and how, when possible, to control them. To do this we must begin early, for actions are not independent of each other but form a continuous series, the completion of one giving rise to the next. Nor are they independent of the growth of the organism, for acts that would be im-possible at one stage emerge at later stages and exert new effects upon subsequent behavior. *The study of psychology may therefore be de-fined as the study of the development of activity, including both its in-ternal and its external phases.*

SUMMARY

It is through a process of development that people come to differ from one another in their perception of situations, their emotional re-sponses, their attitudes and habits. Growth involves a qualitative change as well as an increase in size. At each developmental stage the changes that occur depend upon hereditary potentialities, previous learning, and psychological situation.

The integration of these complex interacting factors is brought about primarily through the person's self-concept. Developmental stages can be differentiated in various ways. One of the most useful is based on an analysis of the special tasks or challenges that face the developing self at each period.

Psychology has emerged from controversy over whether it should study consciousness or behavior. It can be defined as the study of *activity,* including both internal and external aspects.

THE MAKING OF A DEVELOPMENTAL PSYCHOLOGIST

PIAGET, Jean. In E. G. Boring and associates [Eds.],
A history of psychology in autobiography. Vol. IV.
Worcester, Mass.: Clark Univ. Press, 1952. Pp. 237-256.

One of the most interesting ways to begin thinking about the psychology of human development is to read the account a psychologist gives of the developmental stages through which his own life has progressed. This volume is the fourth in a series. Psychologists who have achieved eminence in their profession are asked to tell their own stories in any way they like.

While you may find many of these stories interesting, that of Piaget is perhaps the one that will stimulate most thought on the processes of development themselves. He tells of his childhood in Switzerland and the way in which his early scientific interests began. He explains how the im-pact of philosophy on these scientific interests during adolescence stimulated a tremendous outburst of thinking about life and its basic principles. Out of that seething mental activity came a general orientation toward science and a program of work in psychology that he could follow for the rest of his life.

We shall often be referring to Piaget's work in later chapters of this book. You will enjoy knowing something about the man himself and what sort of person he is when you encounter a discussion of his books or ideas.

CHAPTER 2

With what kinds of facts is psychology concerned?

How do psychologists obtain these facts?

How do methods used in psychological studies differ from the common observations made by the man in the street?

What does it mean to be scientific?

»»»»»»»»»»»»

Problems and Methods of Modern Psychology

THE FIELD OF PSYCHOLOGY

IN THE EARLY STAGES of any science a great deal of spadework has to be done in the way of describing, arranging, and classifying the material with which it deals. During this time there is likely to be some friendly wrangling among the workers about what kinds of material should be included, what names should be given it, whether this or that bit of data is significant or worthless.

Since psychology is so young a science, it is not surprising that up to the present time there has been much discussion among psychologists about what kind of facts should be regarded as suitable material for the psychologists to handle. The German psychologists led by Wundt were at first very insistent that the field of psychology stopped with the study of sensations and their attributes. They also held that the aim of psychology was to discover general principles and trends only, that it had no concern with the individual person as such, nor with questions about how differences between persons were brought about. In spite of Wundt's lack of sympathy with the problem, however, Cattell, who was one of the pioneers among American psychologists, began his work on individual differences while he was an assistant in Wundt's laboratory, and it is in large measure due to his efforts that the study of differences in the abilities and personality of individuals has become such an important part of psychology today.

19

But the rising interest in differences between people has in no way lessened the significance of knowing what principles hold good for people in general, and while it is true that there are many respects in which people differ, it is also true that there are many psychological laws that hold good for practically all normal persons. The following are just a few of them: To persons with normal color vision, red colors look darker and blues look lighter when seen in twilight than when viewed under full daylight. Children become able to draw a circle from copy before they can make a square, and the square can be copied at a considerably earlier age than they can copy a diamond. Straight lines terminating in obtuse angles are judged to be longer than lines of the same length that terminate in acute angles. (See Figure 2.)

Psychology, therefore, is concerned with two kinds of knowledge: that which tells us *how people in general react to different kinds of stimulating conditions,* and that which has to do with *differences in the responses of individual persons when the external conditions remain*

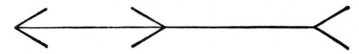

FIGURE 2.   The Müller-Lyer illusion. The horizontal line on the left is the same length as the one on the right. If you don't believe it, measure them.

the same. Only a very narrow-minded person could insist that one of these is more important than the other. Both kinds of information are needed for the understanding of human behavior.

As an example of the way in which work in psychology makes progress simultaneously in both directions, let us look at a kind of performance that has been extensively studied over a long period—reaction time. The ability to react quickly and correctly when a stimulus is given is a matter of rather obvious practical import, and it has a number of theoretical implications as well. Common observation tells us that some people are quick to respond, whereas others are slower, and it is reasonable to suppose that certain kinds of stimuli are likely to evoke more rapid responses than others. But these statements are too indefinite to be serviceable. Specifically, we need to know just what conditions make for speedy reactions and what significance may be attached to individual speed of response. Casual observation is not exact enough to answer these questions, but the laboratory has provided us with information about some of them. For example, psychologists interested mainly in questions of the first type have conducted experiments to find out whether people react more quickly to a visual stimulus or to an auditory stimulus. The usual method of conducting the experiment is to have the subject seated comfortably at a table with his finger resting on a telegraph key which is connected with an electrical timer that records time in small fractions of a second. In the experiments on visual reaction time he is told to watch for a light that will appear at a specified point and to press the key the instant he sees the light. In the same experiments on auditory reaction, the instructions

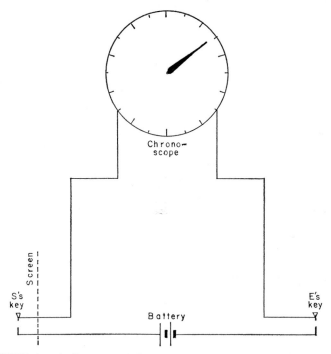

FIGURE 3.   A diagram of the experimental situation for a reaction time experiment. (Adapted from J. F. Dashiell, *Fundamentals of general psychology.* Boston, 1949, p. 37. Courtesy of Houghton Mifflin Co.)

are the same except that he is told to listen for a specified sound. Both the giving of the stimulus and the recording of the response are mechanically controlled. The general setup is shown in Figure 3.

This experiment has been tried many times by different investigators and always with the same result: the response to the auditory stimulus will be decidedly more prompt than that to the visual stimulus. The time required for response to a touch on the skin is about the same or perhaps a trifle slower than that required for an auditory stimulus, and the responses to taste and smell are the slowest of all.

Whatever the sense organs stimulated, there is a direct relationship between the intensity of the stimulus and the speed of the response. A loud sound or a bright light will induce a quicker response than will a faint sound or a dim light. [1]

There are other changes in the conditions of experiment that affect the speed of reaction. A Danish psychologist, Lange, is credited with having been the first one to point out (in 1888) that if the instructions are given to the subject in such a way as to lead him to direct his efforts chiefly toward watching for the stimulus, his responses will be slower than if he fixes his attention upon the part of his body that is to make the response. The first is usually spoken of as the *sensorial reaction* because the attention is fixed upon the stimulus that affects the sense organ; the second is known as the *muscular reaction.*

Other psychologists have studied the question of reaction time from a different point of view. Their interest has centered around the reacting individuals, rather than the conditions of reaction. Some people, they found, were consistently slow in their reactions, others quick, and still others were variable, reacting now quickly, now slowly, and never seeming to settle down to a reasonably uniform rate. What, they asked, do these differences signify? Is quick reaction a sign of superior intelligence, of a particular type of personality, or is it a kind of special ability that is mainly important for success in certain skilled acts, such as driving an automobile? Does speed of reaction vary with sex? How does it change with age?

These and other similar questions have also been put to experimental test by many investigators, and while the findings have not always shown complete agreement, the general trend may be summed up about as follows: On the average, persons of superior intelligence react to a stimulus more quickly than do those of less ability, but the difference is so small and there are so many individual exceptions to the general rule that it is unsafe to judge the intelligence of any person on the basis of his speed of reaction. Measures of reaction time have also been included as parts of standard tests for predicting ability to learn certain trades or special skills such as automobile driving. The results indicate that while the "simple reaction time" described in an earlier paragraph has not much value in predicting these abilities, "discrimination time" in which a number of different stimuli are presented in irregular order and the subject is told to press the key only when a certain one—say, a *red* light—appears, may be more meaningful. The problem is sometimes made still more complicated by providing the subject with two keys and telling him to press the left-hand key

---

[1] This is true only within limits. A stimulus that is so intense as to be disorganizing may block the response instead of accelerating it.

in response to one kind of stimulus, the right-hand key for another. This is known as "the choice reaction."

Some of the reaction time experiments used in tests for automobile drivers have been made very realistic by placing the subject in a stationary apparatus like the driver's seat of an automobile, with steering wheel, pedals, and gear shift all connected to a recording device so as to give a graphic record of all his responses, thus making it possible to know just what he does and how quickly he does it. Before his eyes is a screen on which a moving picture is projected of the "highway" along which he is supposed to be driving. Various emergencies occur at unexpected intervals. Traffic signals change, a dog leaps suddenly out of a ditch, a child runs from behind a parked car. These tests have distinct value in showing what a prospective driver can do when he puts his mind to it; they do not, unfortunately, guarantee that he will be equally careful when on the road!

Most investigators have found a very slight superiority of males over females in average speed of reaction, but this, too, is a rule that has many exceptions. The reactions of children are slower and much more variable than those of adults, and in old age the pattern of childhood gradually returns with a slow decrease in speed and a more rapid increase in variability.

In clinical settings, a special kind of reaction time, often referred to as "association time," has been used by psychologists to uncover emotional "sore spots" in persons coming to them for help. A prepared list of words [2] is read to the subject, one at a time, and he is instructed to respond to each one with the *first* word that comes to his mind. The time required for each response is noted. It has been found that words having a strong emotional connotation require a longer time for response than do words of indifferent meaning. Thus, by noting where the long delays occur, a clue to the patient's difficulties may often be obtained.

It would be possible to devote many more pages to the description of reaction time experiments, but the examples that have been given are probably sufficient to show how a kind of behavior can be studied in various ways so as to produce usable knowledge about the stimulating conditions that influence it and the differences between persons with regard to it. Which kind of knowledge we come out with depends upon the way in which we set up the experiment. If we wish to compare the responses to two different kinds of stimuli—such as buzzer

[2] Sometimes a standard list is used, but if the psychologist has any inkling about the probable nature of the difficulty, a special list is often made out in which words that are likely to have special associations for the subject are interspersed at irregular intervals with other words that are not likely to have particular emotional significance.

and light, "emotional" and "neutral" words—we must use the same subjects or closely similar groups of subjects under both conditions. If we
are primarily interested in comparing the performance of each person
with the others, we must use the same stimulating conditions for all
subjects. Generally speaking, experimenters have varied only one thing
at a time, though progress in statistics has increasingly been making it
possible to draw conclusions from more complex situations where several conditions vary simultaneously.

We could have used any one of a number of other examples of lines
of research in psychology that have produced integrated bodies of
knowledge about some special kinds of behavior. There has been a
tremendous number of experiments on *learning* focusing on the change
in behavior that occurs when a person or animal is placed repeatedly in
the same stimulating situation. There has been a large group of experiments focused on the question of how human beings *perceive* a
three-dimensional world when all that comes to them from the outside
is the impact of light rays on the flat, two-dimensional surfaces inside
the eyeballs. There has been much work on emotional behavior, problem-solving, and social attitudes. Even a catalogue of the main topics
of research in psychology over the three quarters of a century in which
it has existed as a special field of scientific knowledge would require
far more space than we wish to give it here. We shall, however, be referring to this research throughout the book in connection with the
developmental stages where the behavior with which it was concerned
is especially important.

CHANGING POINTS OF VIEW

For a time psychologists were much occupied with the study of so-
called mental faculties, such as memory, imagination, and attention.
These, they believed, were distinct and special powers of the individual, to be observed and studied independently. They were accordingly
regarded as the central facts under which psychological material should
be classified. Since then we have grown to realize that factors such as
these are not distinct from each other, that one cannot, for example,
"reason" without at the same time remembering, imagining, and paying attention. We can take the same behavior and classify or describe
it in a dozen different ways, depending upon which of its many aspects
we choose to observe. We may notice the movements of our subject's
arms and hands and describe or classify these movements according
to their speed, their accuracy, their force, their gracefulness. Or we
may ignore the arm movements and center our attention upon those
of his legs and feet, or upon his facial expression, or upon his speech,

and here we may give attention either to what he says or to how he says it. Speed, accuracy, grace, memory, persistence, and so on are nothing more than descriptive terms that we sometimes find useful in classifying behavior as it is shown at any particular time. A complete picture of psychology as it is today cannot be given in these terms any more than we can take the qualities they are supposed to represent and by putting them together like the pieces of a jigsaw puzzle turn out a real likeness of a human being.

Many other important questions have arisen in the course of psychology's attempts to define its field of interest. One of the most significant of these is the question whether or not verbal reports about such private and unverifiable data as feelings, sensations, or thought processes have any real scientific value or whether the psychologist might not better confine his attention to the later stages of activity, the external features that are open to general observation. This battle between the "behaviorists" and the "introspectionists" was hard fought for a number of years, but most psychologists now seem committed to a middle ground where data of both kinds are accepted if they seem likely to be useful. If, for example, we are interested in studying food preferences among a group of intelligent adults, it would be unsafe to generalize very far from their behavior, because Smith may be very fond of griddle-cakes but consistently refrain from eating them because they give him indigestion, while Brown may manfully swallow his portion of the rice pudding he detests in order not to disappoint his hostess. If we want to know what foods our subjects like best, we should select a suitable time and place and ask them. But if we are interested in finding out what they eat, the way to do it is to observe them and keep a record. Observation of behavior gives us one set of facts; verbal reports by the subjects themselves give us another. Sometimes one method is to be preferred, sometimes the other. It depends on what we want to find out.

More recently still another school of thought has arisen, which, as was the case with "behaviorism," may be looked upon as a reaction against an extreme and restricted point of view. This new psychology is known as the psychology of Gestalt (from the German word, *Gestalt* which means *form* or *shape*). Just as the advocates of behaviorism criticized those who put too much trust in the data obtained by introspection, so the supporters of Gestalt theory criticize the behaviorists for concerning themselves only with fractional bits of behavior which lose their essential character when viewed out of their natural setting. A musical tone, they point out, is one thing when heard by itself; it is quite a different thing when it is part of a melody. If you arrange sixteen dots to form a square as in Figure 4, and then look at the square intently for a minute or two, you will find that some of the dots appear to stand out from the others to form patterns, and that these patterns shift themselves about from time to time but always maintain some kind of internal organization. They are patterns, figures, and not just haphazard arrangements. So with things in general. We respond, not to simple isolated features of the world around us but to patterns, to groups of objects or conditions that stand out from moment to moment as unified wholes, as *gestalts*[3] that cannot be divided further without destroying their essential character. And these patterns or gestalts are individual matters. They do not depend entirely upon the external conditions surrounding the person, nor are they merely the constructs of his own fancy. Rather they represent the special ways in which every person organizes the objects and events of his life as he lives it.

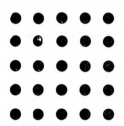

FIGURE 4. Dots illustrating the tendency to perceive forms or figures. Look intently at these dots for a moment or two. What organized arrangements or figures do you see?

Both the individual and his physical surroundings play a part in determining the pattern of an experience, and it is the pattern, the design, rather than the parts of which it is composed that determines his behavior. The error of those who carried behaviorism to an extreme, so say the Gestalt psychologists, was that they looked upon behavior and the conditions that stimulate it as something on the order of a physical additive compound like hash, whereas it is more nearly analagous to a chemical compound like water.

These and other points of controversy that have arisen in the past have served a useful purpose, not only in defining more exactly what psychology is and does, but in suggesting new ways of attacking psychological problems and in correcting extreme and restricted points of view. As time passes and our knowledge increases, other questions will doubtless arise and be debated as hotly as their predecessors have been. The student who finds that the authorities in his subject sometimes hold conflicting views should be neither disappointed nor alarmed. A reasonable amount of controversy is a sign of health. It is only in death that scientists never disagree.

There is some indication, however, that the kind of theorizing that divided all of psychology into distinct schools is on the decline. Theo-

---

[3] The German plural is, of course, *Gestalten* but now that the term *Gestalt* is rapidly becoming a part of the psychological vocabulary of English-speaking people, the Anglicized plural is frequently used.

ries about which controversy has been centered in the 1950's have to do with limited areas. There are alternative theories of learning, of perception, and of personality dynamics. Some of them are formulated in rigorous mathematical or logical terms rather than in words, to make possible the testing of hypotheses derived from them. This shift from broad general theories based on inadequate evidence to more limited theories that are testable is perhaps a sign of increasing maturity.

HOW PSYCHOLOGY SECURES ITS FACTS

Before psychology can give an organized account of mental activity and of the effect of growth and experience upon the manner in which human beings respond to their environment, it must first of all gather a great many facts. We have already seen how the exact study of such an apparently simple form of behavior as reaction time can yield significant information about a wide variety of different problems. But these problems do not by any means indicate the scope of modern psychological interest, which extends into every realm of human conduct. Psychology today is concerned not only with the classical problems of sensation, perception, memory, and the like, but with the morals and manners of individuals and of social groups, with their talents and defects, their beliefs, conflicts, and goals. We want to know how learning takes place and what are the conditions under which people learn fastest and retain longest. We want to know what causes the mind to become diseased, what makes the alcoholic patient see snakes where there are none, and why some psychotic persons think they hear the voices of angels or of devils urging them to great deeds. Why do perfectly normal people see and do such fantastic things in dreams? Whence come our motives, our interests and desires, and why are people so different in their interests? Why does John like books and school, while Jerry who is in the same class plays truant on every possible occasion? Why is Mary so popular while her sister is shunned and disliked?

To make any headway in the investigation of problems so diverse and complex, it has been necessary to develop many kinds of special procedures. The one thing that all of them have in common is an emphasis on *observation as the source of data*. The reaction time experiments discussed in a previous section are examples of observations made in the laboratory under carefully controlled conditions. But not all aspects of human life can be studied in such circumstances. At the other extreme from the laboratory experiment is the kind of observations that a psychotherapist makes of the clients he serves in the course of his daily work. Some of the most important ideas about development have originated in this way. Freud and his fellow psychoanalysts were impressed with the fact that what had happened at certain crucial stages in early childhood seemed to be affecting the functioning of personality years later in the lives of the troubled adults they were analyzing. It is desirable that the ideas and hypotheses arising in settings like the psychotherapy situation be checked by other kinds of observation made under conditions where it is possible to control more of the sources of possible error. This has been done with many of the psychoanalytic theories, and we will be concerned with some of this research in later chapters. But it is important to remember that the methods of psychology range all the way from the observations and inferences of psychotherapy to the exact laboratory experiment.

In between the two is a wide range of methods which could be described as an attempt to extend the laboratory into the larger world outside its walls. Controlled observation can be carried on in the home, the street, the classroom, and the factory. The condemned criminal in his cell, the commuter on the 5:15, the newborn baby in the hospital, the genius and the idiot, the butcher, the baker, and the candle-stick maker, all furnish their grist for the psychological mill. Armed with a stop watch and a mechanical counter, the psychologist today studies the attention value of various window displays as indicated by the number of people who stop to look at each, and the length of time they stay. Tomorrow we find him in the schoolroom conducting experiments in learning or giving psychological tests to discover the special aptitudes and weaknesses of the children in order that their training may be more wisely directed. On other occasions he may observe and record the social reactions of children or adults toward each other, or, back in his laboratory, he may busy himself with photographing the eye-movements of good and poor readers, or with studying changes in heart rate or in the electrical resistance of the skin during strong emotion. Whether they are collected in seclusion of the formal laboratory or under the more flexible conditions of everyday life, the data of modern psychology are the observed and recorded facts of actual behavior. The psychology of today bears slight resemblance to the philosophy from which it sprang.

METHODS OF IMPROVING THE ACCURACY OF PSYCHO- LOGICAL OBSERVATION AND OF REDUCING THE LIKELIHOOD OF ERROR IN INTERPRETING THE SUBJECT'S RESPONSES

Every one, no matter how carefully he tries to observe, is likely to make mistakes. He may overlook important features of the behavior he is studying, or be led by suggestion to record events that never occurred. He may make errors in counting, in timing, in measuring. Even more common are the errors of interpretation due to failure to recognize what it is to which his subject is giving attention or to what stimulus he is responding. A mother was greatly impressed by the rapt attention with which her small son listened to the sermon at church. He sat motionless with eyes fixed on the minister, apparently drinking in every word. As they left the church, however, he inquired earnestly, "Mother, did you know that Dr. Brown's back teeth are made of gold? Every time he opened his mouth I could see them shine!"

Whenever a number of different stimuli are presented at the same time, there is danger that an observer may not be able to tell which one is determining the subject's behavior. If the small boy just mentioned had been listening to the sermon given on a phonograph concealed from his sight by a screen, it would have been easier to judge from his behavior whether or not the sermon itself interested him. One of the main advantages of the formal laboratory experiment as compared to casual observation lies in the possibility of safeguarding interpretation by reducing the number of stimulating conditions to a minimum.

It is interesting to know that experiments in psychology had their beginning in the important discovery that no human being can observe and record with absolute accuracy. In 1796, Maskelyne, an astronomer at Greenwich, found that Kinnebrook, his assistant, was observing and recording the time of stellar transits almost a second later, on the average, than Maskelyne himself did. This was a very serious error indeed, since upon these observations depended the calibration of the clock by which the world's time was regulated, as well as all astronomical calculations about time and space. Although Kinnebrook strove to correct the error after his attention was called to it, he was unable to do so. If anything it grew worse. Maskelyne therefore decided that Kinnebrook could not be following the accepted method of observation but must have "fallen into some irregular and confused method of his own." Kinnebrook was accordingly dismissed.

Several years later, Bessel, the astronomer at Königsberg, became interested in the matter and decided to find out whether the Maskelyne-Kinnebrook affair was a unique case or whether other astronomers might not also disagree in their observations if put to the test. In 1820, he found an opportunity to compare his own observations with those of Walbeck. It was found that Bessel always observed a transit earlier than Walbeck and that the average difference between their observations was even greater than that found between Maskelyne and Kinnebrook. This discovery led to a number of further investigations from which it became evident that the time required to observe and report any external event will differ from person to person, even when the utmost efforts to secure accuracy are made. This difference came to be known as the "personal equation," and while it was first considered a problem of interest chiefly to astronomers, its wider significance soon became recognized, and many important investigations aimed at determining its physiologcal and psychological attributes were undertaken.

Since that time, psychologists have been devoting much time to the question of errors of observation, and many important discoveries about the peculiarities of human nature have had their origin in attempts to account for the prevalence of certain kinds of mistakes. Early psychological experimentation was largely concerned with questions of sensation and its attributes. Careful investigations were made of the extent and manner in which color qualities as perceived by us are dependent upon such matters as lighting, position with reference to other colors (contrast), and whether the colors are seen in direct or marginal vision. As a result of these and many other investigations in the field of the senses, it became evident that small changes in the surrounding conditions may bring about large differences in the appearance of any external object, and that accordingly, unless the external conditions are carefully controlled, the difficulty of interpreting behavior is vastly increased. More recently we have come to see that the internal state of the subject himself, his emotional and physical condition, his level of mental development, and his past experiences also exert a great influence upon the way the world looks to him. Although matters such as these are not easy to deal with, their importance at least is recognized and attempts to control them are being made.

In psychological investigation, although ideal conditions of experiment are never reached, research workers are continually trying to find ways by which the conditions under which experiments are carried on can be kept under better control, and to develop instruments for refining observation and for making records in a more uniform and exact fashion. In the psychological laboratory are to be found chronoscopes for measuring time in units as small as the thousandth part of a second, photographic apparatus of many kinds for making permanent records of behavior that would otherwise be over before it could fairly be seen, galvanometers for measuring electrical changes in the skin, and apparatus for studying other bodily functions such as heart rate, blood pressure, and changes in the distribution of blood. There are special arrangements for controlling lighting, and soundproof rooms to prevent distraction from outside noises. There are machines for presenting the stimuli to which the subject is supposed to respond, so arranged that such factors as the intensity of the stimulus, its duration, and the intervals between successive trials are kept exactly the same from one trial to another. There are other instruments for recording the responses made by the subject, thus keeping the results free from the effects of unconscious bias or imperfect observation on the part of the experimenter.

Even when the psychologist leaves his laboratory and sallies forth into the outside world to learn what he can of behavior as it is shown there, he cannot afford to ignore the question of scientific technique. He may not be able to control conditions as he does in his laboratory, but he can and does select from the wide variety of circumstances open to him certain ones in which the conditions that have a bearing on his particular field of investigation are sufficiently uniform for his purpose. Stop watches, moving-picture cameras, and the like can be carried with him and used where he happens to be, and other pieces of apparatus can often be set up temporarily in the home, the school, the factory, or other places as they are needed. Psychological equipment, moreover, is not confined to pieces of mechanical apparatus but includes also printed blanks for various kinds of tests, questionnaires, rating scales, and standardized interview forms. Even the humble pad and pencil in the hands of one who knows what to observe and how to record his observations in a systematic fashion may yield information of greater scientific value than the most elaborate apparatus will furnish to those unskilled in its use.

There are many important aspects of behavior that cannot be studied by means of any mechanical devices now known to us but must be observed and recorded as they naturally occur in everyday life. Social behavior is an example. We cannot weigh it or measure it. Yet social behavior can be studied, though not as easily as other forms of behavior that are more amenable to control. By making repeated observations under different circumstances, comparing the results, and checking the facts for accuracy in as many different ways as possible, even behavior that at first thought appears to be so fluctuating and uncertain as to fall completely outside the field of possible experiment can often be reduced to some form of order by means of a carefully organized system of records. When this is done, it is often found that behavior that appears irrational or unpredictable is consistent enough, once we have got hold of the right key for understanding it.

Even from the very incomplete account given in this chapter, you can see how great is the variety of problems that the psychologist of today is attempting to solve, and how absurd it would be for him to confine himself to any one method for studying them. Methods and techniques do not spring up in a vacuum; they are the tools we construct as we feel the need for them. We find out their inaccuracies and inadequacies by using them, not by letting them lie idle in the hope that by some miracle they will perfect themselves. The method is always the outgrowth of the problems that it is designed to solve. It is the aim of every science to perfect its techniques, but no science would progress far if it refused to use imperfect tools when no others were available.

SUMMARY

Psychology is concerned with two kinds of knowledge—how people in general react to differences in stimulating conditions and how individuals differ in their response to the same stimulating conditions. The many variations of the reaction time experiment typify these two concerns.

Psychologists were concerned first with "mental" faculties such as perception, attention, and memory. During the first quarter of this century behaviorists brought in the study of observable actions rather than sensations or ideas, and Gestaltists stressed the study of *wholes* or organizations of experience rather than separate parts. All of these theoretical approaches have become part of modern psychology.

The basic method by which psychology secures its facts is observation. The difference between experiments in a laboratory and other kinds of observation is primarily one of control over possible sources of error. Many special methods and many kinds of equipment have been devised to improve the accuracy of observation in the laboratory and in life situations.

A BOOK ABOUT PSYCHOLOGICAL EXPERIMENTS

GARRETT, Henry E. *Great experiments in psychology.*
(3rd Ed.) New York: Appleton-Century-Crofts, 1951.

This book gives an account of some experiments that have made psychological history. It tells how the idea of measuring intelligence originated and what intelligence tests are like. It describes the many different ways by which psychologists have tried to find out how people and animals learn, and tells you what modern science has discovered about many practical questions in the field of learning. For example, is it true, as many people think, that learning one thing "strengthens" the mind so that it then becomes easier to learn something else? Do animals think or reason in solving problems or learning tricks? Is there any advantage in going over a lesson again after it has once been thoroughly learned?

The book also includes a fascinating chapter on methods of studying personality and another that describes the changes that take place in the body during strong emotion. It shows how experiments on animals and young children have helped us to understand the behavior of human adults and why people differ from each other. An account of one of the earliest experiments in reaction time will interest you, as well as the story of how Weber and Fechner discovered the mathematical relation between a change in the physical magnitude of an object and our perception of that change, a law that is perhaps the most famous in all psychology. A number of other topics of equal interest are discussed.

The book is easy to read and contains many helpful illustrations. Your college library probably has a copy.

PART II

The Person's Equipment for Living

CHAPTER 3

What do we mean by heredity?

Why are children sometimes like one parent, sometimes like the other, and sometimes like neither?

Why do some plants and animals not breed true to type?

How and when is sex determined?

Why are men more likely than women to be color-blind?

What are the biological advantages of having two parents instead of one?

Will a hereditary trait always show itself in any environment?

Do we inherit habits formed by our parents?

If a mother is badly frightened during pregnancy, is the baby likely to be affected?

What can be said about the relative importance of heredity and environment in bringing about the mental differences we see in our friends?

Our Hereditary Background

HOW DOES HUMAN LIFE BEGIN?

WHEN PEOPLE SPEAK of the beginning of life, they usually refer to the time of birth. But the life of any person goes back further than birth. In one sense it may be said to begin with the fertilization of the egg cell, but even this is not strictly its beginning. Life is continuous from one generation to another. The egg cell at the time it is fertilized is a living bit of tissue that is changing and developing according to its own laws of growth. The sperm by which it is fertilized is also alive. Each was originally part of a living body, one of the vast numbers of cells of which that body was composed. However, these germ cells, as they are often called, differ from the other body cells in several important ways, one of which is their ability to detach themselves from the tissue in which they have grown and to live an independent life within the body for a short period of time. But this perod of independent life is limited unless something happens to change the course of development and to give to the individual germ cell a new impetus for growth. If a male germ cell or spermatozoon meets and fuses with a female cell or ovum, the single cell that results from the fusion takes on a new lease of life. Had they remained apart, both ovum and sperm must soon have died; combined they live and in time develop into a new individual who in his turn will pass on to others the life that has been given him.

In all the higher animals and plants, sexual reproduction is the rule. Even among the lower forms of life that commonly reproduce by simple division of a mature cell to form two new individuals, occasional re-production by the fusion of two parent cells is seen in the greater number of species. In these cases, the generations immediately follow-ing the sexual reproduction commonly exhibit greater vigor than those that preceded it. An increase in vitality thus seems to result from the conjunction of the parent cells even in those organisms that are able to reproduce themselves independently for many generations.

Sexual reproduction has other advantages. Since each new individual represents the convergence of two lines of ancestry, greater possibility of variation is afforded than would be the case if reproduction took place by the division of a single parent cell. As we shall see later, the number of "traits" (by which we mean tendencies to grow and develop in certain ways rather than in others) handed down by each parent is very great, and these may be recombined in the offspring in a vast number of different ways. The likelihood that any two persons will receive exactly the same combination is very small unless the parents, to begin with, are exactly alike, and in the human race this is never true. Biparental ancestry thus makes for differences between the indi-vidual members of the species, and as a result of these differences a complex form of social organization develops. People with special abilities perform certain tasks for which they are particularly fitted, and are repaid by having other kinds of work done for them by per-sons whose abilities excel along those lines. Modern civilization has in large measure been built up by utilizing the differences between people in the formation of co-operative social groups.

WHAT IS GIVEN BY HEREDITY?

Many people think of heredity as some kind of vague "force" or "influence" that the parent in some unknown way exerts upon the child. This is just as inexact as it would be to think of the reaction that occurs when two chemicals combine to form a new substance as some mysterious force acting upon the chemicals from without. The laws of heredity are simply the rules to which the behavior of the physical substances contained in the germ cells conforms. Although these laws are not as yet completely understood, much is known con-cerning them, and the way to further study has been cleared. Just as a chemical reaction consists of the breaking up of the original mole-cules into the atoms of which they are composed and the recombination of these atoms into new molecules with different atomic arrangement and composition, so when two germ cells meet and fuse certain chem-ical substances called *genes,* half of which were originally contained in the sperm and half in the ovum, combine to form a new cell with a *genetic composition* different from either of the parent cells.

We cannot say as yet whether the process is essentially the same as that of the ordinary chemical reaction or whether it belongs in a separate class, but at any rate the two reactions have many points of similarity. One important difference, however, is found in the fact that whereas the chemical reaction is "touched off," as it were, when the two original substances meet, the genetic reaction begins before the union of the cells. At the proper stage in its development, something in the growth process provides the initial stimulus that causes the dormant cell to grow and change, to reorganize its internal structure, and finally separate itself from the glandular tissue in which it originated and start out on an independent career where it may find the mate without which it must soon die.

THE PHYSICAL BASIS OF HEREDITY

In each sex the germ cells originate in paired organs known as the *gonads.* The male gonads are called the *testes,* the male germ cells the *spermatozoa;* the female gonads are called the *ovaries,* the female germ cells the *ova.* The ovum or egg cell differs greatly from the sperm cell in form and size. In its free state, that is, after it has been extruded from the ovary, the human ovum is a sphere about one tenth of a millimeter in diameter, just visible to the naked eye under favorable conditions. It has no means of locomotion within itself. Its movements are determined solely by the contraction of the tissues by which it is surrounded. The greater part of its bulk is composed of a protoplasmic material known as the *cytoplasm.* The cytoplasm provides the material —for convenience we may call it nutriment, though it is really more than that—by which the first stages of development are made possible. Within the cytoplasm is a denser part known as the *nucleus,* which is made up almost entirely of strings or bundles of the genes to which we have already referred.

The spermatozoa, on the other hand, are fashioned for free locomotion under their own motive power. They are microscopic in size, since they contain very little cytoplasm, and in form are not unlike the tadpoles that you have seen wriggling about in warm, stagnant water in the early summer. There is an ovate head, consisting chiefly of the nucleus, which, like the nucleus of the ovum, is composed mainly of bundles of genes. Back of the head is an elongated portion called the body, to which is attached a fine hairlike "whip" or *cilium* that lashes back and forth and so enables the sperm to swim forward through the milky fluid or semen in which they are released.

If the developing germ cell, either sperm or ovum, is viewed under a microscope, certain very interesting changes can be observed. In the early stages of development the nucleus is seen as a kind of network within which are long-drawn-out chains of minute particles of material like tangled strings of beads. It is important to remember that the genes in each string are arranged in a definite linear order that is always the same from one cell to another within a given species.

Later the strings contract and fold into thick bundles of definite size and form. These bundles are known as *chromosomes*. Examination of the chromosomes shows that they are always arranged in pairs. The two members of each pair are exactly alike in size and appearance. Each one contains the same number of genes, arranged in the same order, so that if the bundles were to be unfolded and the two sets of strings laid out side by side, the genes of each pair would correspond exactly in number and position. Moreover, any two corresponding

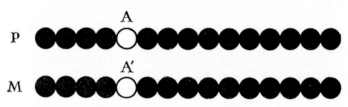

FIGURE 5.　Diagram illustrating linear arrangements of genes.

genes affect the same part of the body or its function, but they do not always affect it in the same way.

The reason for this is very simple. It is known that every cell is the product of two parents. One of the two chromosomes in each pair was received from the father, one from the mother. Throughout all the complicated process of growth and development, throughout the countless number of cell divisions and multiplications, the basic substances received from the two parents have maintained their separate identity in the cell. Now that the time has come when they, in their turn, are ready to play a part in the production of a new individual, they are still distinct. Each individual chromosome passes on as a whole.

Examine Figure 5. Here we have represented diagrammatically two chromosomes belonging to the same pair. The upper chromosome came from the father, the lower one from the mother. The genes are shown as beadlike structures joined in a string.

Let us assume that the fifth gene from the left (A/Á) produces some particular trait. One that has been intensively studied because it seems to depend on a single pair of genes is the ability to taste phenylthiocarbamide (usually abbreviated PTC). While the ability to taste this rather rare chemical substance would not seem to be a very essential part of a person's equipment for living, the clear-cut differences between persons with regard to it have made it of considerable importance to science. Such a difference suggests that instead of maintaining generation after generation that "there is no accounting for tastes," we may be able eventually to account for many of them when we understand better how the more complicated combinations of genes work.

Suppose that the upper chromosome of the pair shown contains only the A variety of gene which produces tasters. The lower one is that of a mother with a gene that makes her a nontaster. When the two chromosomes come together in the production of a new individual and the genes for tasting and nontasting combine, the individual produced will himself be a taster, because the taster genes are *dominant* over the other variety. But this individual's children may be either tasters or nontasters, depending upon the way in which the two kinds of genes combine with those obtained from the other parent. Each of us carries such *recessive* genes for traits that do not show at all in us but may appear in our children if they happen to come into combination with other recessive genes of the same kind.

If the cell in its present condition with its full complement of paired chromosomes were to mate with another in the same state, it is evident that the offspring would have double the number of chromosomes possessed by either of its parents. We know, however, that the number of chromosomes is always the same for a given species, although it varies from one species to another. For example, the common fruit-fly, *Drosophila melanogaster,* has four pairs of chromosomes. In man there are twenty-four pairs. [1] This constant number is maintained without increase by a process known as *meiosis,* which takes place before fertilization, during the process of development in the individual cell. At a certain stage of development the chromosomes separate, one member of each pair passing to one side of the nucleus, the other to the opposite side. As far as we know, chance alone determines the nature of the division. One of the resulting groups may be made up entirely of paternal, the other maternal, chromosomes, or each group may contain half of each kind or any other combination.

After the chromosomes have separated, the cell divides in such a

[1] There seems now to be considerable doubt as to whether 48 is the correct total number. Several investigators have reported 46 and some have indicated that the number varies from cell to cell, some showing 46, others 47, and still others 48. The problem is undergoing active investigation by geneticists. See M. Kodani. Three diploid chromosome numbers of man. *Proceedings of the National Academy of Sciences,* 1957, 43, 285-292.

way that each one of the new cells formed from the division has one member (and only one) of each pair of chromosomes. Each of these single chromosomes now divides lengthwise so that half of each of the "beads" or genes is contained in each part. The halves then move to opposite sides of the cells and the cells again divide as before. From these divisions there result in the case of the spermatozoa four cells where but one was previously, but the new cells differ from the parent cell in having but half the original number of chromosomes. In the ovum a similar process of reduction takes place but with this difference, that at each division most of the cytoplasm remains with one of the newly formed cells while the other half of the divided nucleus with its freight of chromosomes passes off as a microscopic bit of protoplasm known as a *polar body*. The polar bodies are soon absorbed or excreted. In the ovum, therefore, only one functional cell results from the reduction division, and this cell, like the newly formed sperm cells, contains only one member of each of the original pairs of chromosomes.

Fertilization consists in the penetration of the outer membrane of the ovum by one of the spermatozoa, which then passes directly to the nucleus, where the chromosomes range themselves with the half-set remaining in the ovum so that the cell again has its full complement of genes.

What are the consequences of meiosis and the recombination of genes that comes with fertilization? What this process does is to produce a tremendous *variety* of individuals, because the number of possible kinds of *paired genes, or alleles*, is far larger than the number of genes themselves. The science of genetics has developed out of the work of an obscure Austrian monk named Gregor Mendel (see Figure 6) who in 1865 published a paper on the experiments he had been doing on the breeding of peas. He was the first to discover the basic principles with regard to *dominance* and *recessiveness* in gene pairs. While his ideas were not noticed until about 1900, long after he was dead, these principles of what is now called *Mendelian* inheritance became the foundation of modern genetics. A great deal of experimental research has been done on plants and on the fast-breeding fruit-fly, *Drosophila melanogaster*, which has served to clarify and supplement the original Mendelian theory.

The basic idea of the *dominance* concept is very simple. We can understand it by considering what happens when a husband and wife try to decide whether to go to the mountains or to the seashore for their vacation (assuming that the vacation is not long enough for them to do both). The idea of one *or* the other person determines the outcome, and in general we say that the *dominant* partner wins. Seeing this couple walking on the beach, we would never guess that one of them was harboring a secret longing for the mountains. If he were to meet another mountain lover, however, it might well become apparent. So with dominance and recessiveness in gene pairs. With a pair made up of a *dominant* and a *recessive* gene, like the taster, nontaster combination mentioned above, the dominant trait is the one that shows. With a gene pair made up of two recessive genes, like a nontaster, nontaster combination, the recessive trait will be apparent in the person.

FIGURE 6.   Portrait of Mendel. (From *J. Hered.*, 1940, 31, p. 258. Courtesy of American Genetic Association.)

In practice, of course, we do not know what genes the individual is carrying with regard to any trait. We work backward from the *phenotype*, the characteristic that shows up in the individuals we are studying, to inferences about the *genotype* that produced it. This is done by analyzing the possible varieties of gene combination and calculating what the ratio of one to the other phenotype would be in the descendants of parents with such a combination. If the observed ratios match those we expect as a result of our logic and computation, we conclude that our guess about the genotype was correct. For example, if we had hypothesized that John's genotype with regard to the tasting of PTC was AÁ and his wife Mary's genotype ÁÁ, we would expect that tasters and nontasters among their children would occur equally often. The children's genotype, if our hypothesis about the parents is correct, must be either AÁ or ÁÁ, and since at meiosis it is a matter of chance how the division goes, our best guess would be that the two types would occur with equal frequency. If John and Mary have twelve children, and six of them turn out to be tasters, six nontasters, our hypothesis is supported. Even if the division were seven to five we would still be willing to accept it as a chance deviation from the expected frequency. Had we formulated another hypothesis with regard to the parents' genotypes it would have led to a different expected ratio.

To set up such hypotheses and see whether the results of breeding experiments support them has been a standard method in genetics. Naturally it has had to be applied to plants and simple animals rather than to human beings. Since each mating pair produces large numbers of offspring, it can readily be determined whether or not the proportions showing or not showing a trait conform to the expected ratios. Work in human genetics requires more complicated hypotheses about what would be expected over a period of many generations as a result of a certain combination of genotypes.

There is a rare type of short wooly hair that occurs in some Norwegian families (see Figure 7). A pedigree for this family is shown in Figure 8. The rectangles represent males, the circles females. The black symbols represent wooly-haired individuals, the white ones individuals without the trait. The evidence suggests that this trait is transmitted as a dominant characteristic. Because this kind of hair is of rare occurrence, we should expect that the genes for it would in past generations have been combined with the more common variety, so that genetically the persons showing the characteristic would be of the Ww rather than of the WW type. (Remember that there is no way of determining for certain what kinds of genes a human being has.) Assuming this to be true, we should expect that approximately half of the offspring of parents, one of whom was wooly-haired, would show the trait themselves. Figure 8 indicates that this hypothesis fits the data very well. Of twenty marriages involving one affected parent, there were thirty-eight wooly-haired and forty-three non-wooly-haired children. (The three squares with question marks inside them represent deceased members of the family for whom no information was available.) This distribution is close to the 1:1 ratio we should expect if our hypothesis held. (We expect some chance deviation from the logical expectation.)

As so often happens with the development of knowledge in any area, the laws of heredity have turned out to be considerably more complicated than Mendel's original work suggested that they would be. First of all, when two genes are located in the same chromosome rather than in different ones, we would expect that they would always occur together. What apparently happens, however, is that there is some exchange of segments of chromosomes during meiosis, so that some genes "cross over." Thus new combinations of genetic characteristics may occur. Second, dominance has not turned out to be an all-or-none af-

FIGURE 7.   **Picture of Norwegian family.** (From O. L. Mohr. Wooly hair: a dominant mutant character in man. *J. Hered.*, 1932, 345-352. Courtesy of American Genetic Association.)

fair. In the case of some gene pairs, the characteristic produced by the combination of two unlike genes will be *intermediate* between the two pure types instead of conforming to one of them. A botanical example is found in one of the four-o'clocks in which the first generation resulting from the breeding of a pure-bred white variety with a pure-bred red variety bears pink flowers.

A third complication in genetic studies is that there is considerable variation in the extent to which a genetic trait comes to expression in different individuals, all of whom are known to carry the gene for it. The surroundings and influences during one's developmental period,

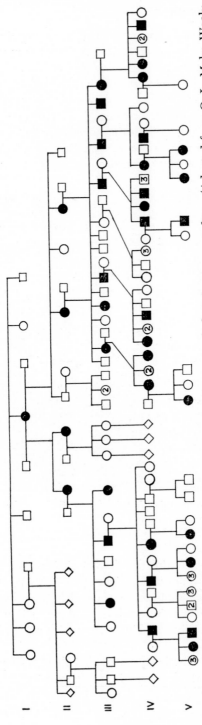

FIGURE 8. Pedigree of Norwegian family showing hereditary wooly hair in some members. (Adapted from O. L. Mohr. Wooly hair: a dominant mutant character in man. *J. Hered.*, 1932, 23, 345-352. Courtesy of American Genetic Association.) In pedigree charts of this kind, each line after a Roman numeral represents a generation. Circles represent females, squares males. In cases where information about the sex of the individual is not obtainable from the records, a diamond is used. Black entries represent persons who show the trait being studied—in this case wooly hair. A number within a square or circle means that this entry represents that number of children who are not listed separately. This particular chart shows at a glance that about half the descendants of the one wooly-haired woman in line I had wooly hair.

from the prenatal period on, modify the "expressivity" of genes. Furthermore, there even seem to be genes whose function is to modify the expressivity of other genes.

Finally, it has become increasingly clear that almost all the human traits in which psychologists are interested are determined by many genes acting in combination with one another rather than by one gene pair alone. While there is one rare type of mental defect, phenylketonuria, associated with a recessive gene that prevents an essential metabolic process in the body from occurring, intelligence as it is ordinarily manifested depends on large numbers of genetic determiners. Stern [2] has used the analogy of the starting mechanism of an automobile to make clear how hereditary mechanisms work. It is a complicated piece of equipment in which many parts must function smoothly if it is to work efficiently. One minor defect in any one of these parts may in some cases make the *difference* between starting and not starting, but we cannot for that reason say that it is responsible for the whole mechanism. Appearance, intelligence, temperament, health, longevity—these are all dependent on many genes whose functioning is tremendously complicated.

THE DETERMINATION OF SEX

"Is it a boy or a girl?" is likely to be the first question when a new baby is announced. This is not surprising, for few things are more important than sex in shaping the later careers of any person. When and how is the sex of the developing ovum determined?

Shortly after the discovery of the paired arrangement of the chromosomes, an important exception to the general rule that every chromosome has its mate was noticed. In every species in which sexual reproduction is the rule, one chromosome pair in males is made up of two chromosomes that do not match. It has become customary to call the chromosomes making up this pair X and Y. A female has two matching X's, so that this pair of chromosomes is like the others. But in males, the X is accompanied by Y, a smaller one of different shape. Thus when a male cell divides, half of the spermatozoa thus produced contain an X, the other half a Y. When fertilization occurs, these X chromosomes will unite with the mother's X's to produce girls; the Y's will unite with the mother's X's to produce boys. Since there are the same number of X's as there are of Y's, it follows that on the average about as many of one sex as of the other will be born. [3]

[2] C. Stern. *Principles of human genetics.* San Francisco: Freeman, 1949, p. 57.
[3] The actual sex ratio at birth is 105 males to 100 females, and there is evidence that at the time of conception the excess of males is even greater. A number of possible explanations for this imbalance have been proposed by geneticists, none entirely satisfactory.

SEX-LINKED TRAITS

Recessive traits that develop from genes carried in the X (or sex-determining) chromosome show a pattern of transmission that differs from the ordinary Mendelian heredity in certain ways. The principle involved is exactly the same, but the fact that one sex has only a single X chromosome causes the principle to work out differently. In man, a number of sex-linked hereditary characteristics are known, and two have been studied extensively. There is a hereditary defect known as hemophilia in which the mechanism that causes the blood to coagulate when exposed to the air is so defective that the affected person is likely to bleed to death from a very slight wound. There is another condition in which the mechanism in the eye for perceiving certain colors is defective. Persons having this defect are said to be color-blind. Color-blindness is of several types and occurs in various degrees ranging all the way from "color-weakness," in which there is greater than normal difficulty in distinguishing certain colors, to very rare cases of complete color-blindness when all colors are seen merely as differing shades of gray as they appear in an ordinary photograph. The most common form is red-green blindness, in which red cannot be told from green. This was not a very great handicap a century ago, but it is one that may have serious results under modern conditions of traffic regulation. [4] Both hemophilia and color-blindness are carried by genes in the X chromosome and are completely or almost completely recessive to the normal gene that accompanies them in the female. Their pattern of inheritance will be easily understood if it is remembered that the male has only a single X chromosome and that this chromosome always comes from the mother, for if the father had also supplied an X chromosome, the child would not have been a male.

Sex-linked traits thus *occur* most commonly in males, but are *caused* by females. It is always possible that a man who is color-blind because he has a certain kind of X chromosome will mate with a non-color-blind woman, one of whose X chromosomes is of the variety making for color-blindness. The trait may then appear in either boy or girl

---

[4] In order to lessen the hazards from this source, a test for color vision is usually made a part of the examination for drivers' licenses required in most states. Moreover, the actual color of the standard traffic lights is such that a color-blind person can distinguish them, since the red will appear darker to him than does the green. But because the difference in the lights is far less apparent to him than it is to the person with normal color vision, it is of great importance that every color-blind driver shall be made aware of his defect and of the need to compensate for it by greater attention to the traffic signals. Surprisingly enough, most partially color-blind persons reach maturity without ever finding out that their vision differs from that of other people.

children of such a mating. But in the more frequent combinations, in which the father is not color-blind himself, the mother's recessive genes for the condition can affect only her sons (and only about half of them, on the average).

THE PROTECTIVE EFFECTS OF BIPARENTAL HEREDITY

It is fortunate for the health and welfare of human beings that heredity works as it does. All sorts of defects and disadvantages that might arise if all of our hereditary tendencies were derived from one parent are prevented from occurring by the simple fact that the other parent transmits a different kind of determiners. A small girl who had been forbidden to go swimming until she had mended her bathing suit came running into the house to explain to her mother that it would now be quite all right for her to go in without stopping to mend her suit. What she had done was to find another suit of nearly the same color that she could wear outside the torn one. It too had holes in it, but no two holes happened to coincide in position, and Ann thus considered the combination to be entirely adequate. Similarly in our hereditary make-up, the "holes" in the contributions from the two parents seldom coincide.

Most of us carry in our germ plasm a fairly large number of defective genes of one kind or another. Some of the defects that would result from these genes might be fairly serious if they were allowed to come into being. But so long as a defective gene is balanced by a normal gene received from the other parent, the individual is protected in the great majority of cases, since the normal characteristic usually dominates over the defective one. As with the child and her bathing suits, it is only when the defects from both lines of ancestry coincide that harm results. This protection, to be sure, extends only to the individual himself. His children will receive the defective genes unchanged, ready to show themselves for what they are as soon as the protective effect of the normal gene is removed through mating with another who carries the same defect. It is not within our province here to debate whether or not this all-determining effect of the dominant gene, which protects the individual from the influence of a recessive defect but in so doing conceals its presence without affecting its likelihood of being transmitted to further generations, is in the long run desirable for the race. We can say confidently, however, that because of the protection afforded by having two genes provided for each trait when one would be sufficient, defects of all kinds occur much less frequently than would be the case if we had but one parent instead of two. The latter condition is well exemplified in the cases already described of hereditary defects that are carried in the X chromosome. So far as these traits are concerned, males may be said to have only one parent, for their only X chromosome comes from the mother. If any of the genes in this chromosome are defective, nothing can protect the sons from the consequences. They will always exhibit the defect. But the daughters may receive the same defective genes and yet be normal if the corresponding genes in the second X chromosome that comes to them from the father are normal. Only when both lines of descent are defective will the daughters be affected, while a defect in the maternal line alone is sufficient to bring about the defective condition in the sons.

MUTATION: THE MECHANISM BY WHICH NEW TRAITS APPEAR

In animals and plants that have been bred under controlled conditions for many generations and whose ancestry is therefore well known, it occasionally happens that a change of unknown nature occurs in one of the chromosomes by which a new gene, affecting some part of the body or its functions in a way not previously observed, comes into existence. In the fruit-fly a number of such changes in genetic constitution are on record. They affect such factors as eye-color, length and form of wing, and abdominal bands. These changes are called *mutations*. Once they occur, they are inherited in exactly the same way as other traits. Most of the mutations on record have proved to be recessive, but a few dominant genes have also appeared in this way.

Mutations probably occur in the human race as well as in the lower animals, but unless their frequency in terms of generations born is far greater than has been found for organisms such as the fruit-fly, they take place only at exceedingly long intervals. The fruit-fly produces a new generation every ten or twelve days. Counting three generations to a century, it will take more than a thousand years to trace the ancestry of a human family as far as that of a fruit-fly can be followed in the course of a single year. When further allowance is made for the enormous difference in the number of offspring produced by each individual in the human race as compared to the fruit-fly, the absence of authentic records of the occurrence of genuine mutations in human beings is not surprising. If we had any laboratory records of human heredity equaling those available for the fruit-fly in length and accuracy, much that is now uncertain about the inheritance of specific traits in man would be made clear.

One of the principal reasons for the tremendous interest among scientists in the biological effects of radiation is that it is known that mutations can be produced by such means. Unfortunately, most of the mutations that have been experimentally studied seem to produce *defects* rather than improvements in the new generations. Thus the increase in the radiation to which all human beings are being exposed since World War II is a matter about which we must all be concerned

HEREDITY IN RELATION TO ENVIRONMENT

The question is often asked whether a particular characteristic is due to heredity or to environment. The answer must always be that it is due to both. It is not a matter of heredity *or* environment, but of heredity *and* environment, for neither can operate without the other. From the beginning, growth and development proceed by interaction between the hereditary substances—the genes—that the individual receives from his ancestors, and the new environment in which these genes find themselves. Different genes react in diverse ways to the same environment; the same genes will grow and develop differently if the external conditions under which they develop are changed. In our old friend the fruit-fly there is a gene known as "abnormal abdomen" the effect of which is to cause the abdominal segments to be irregularly shaped, not sharply marked off from each other. This is a recessive gene found in the X chromosome and therefore shows sex-linked inheritance. It appears in males whose mothers carry the defective gene, whenever the flies are reared under adequate conditions of food and moisture. But if the food becomes dry and scanty the trait no longer appears, even in males known to carry the defective gene. The production of the abnormal abdomen is therefore dependent both on the presence of the defective gene and on the supply of food and moisture. As Jennings[5] puts it, "When grown in a moist environment, the difference between normal and abnormal individuals is due to a gene difference, or, as it is usually put, to heredity. If the defective gene is present in all the individuals compared, the difference between normal and abnormal individuals is due to an environmental diversity; to moisture or dryness. The same difference that is produced in some cases by diversity of genes is produced in others by alteration of the environment."

A number of similar cases have been noted in the study of the fruit-fly. There is a gene for reduplicated legs that exerts its effect if flies carrying the gene are reared in a cold atmosphere but not otherwise. There is another that causes the number of facets in the eye to be reduced, making the eye imperfect. This condition is also dependent upon temperature as well as upon the presence of the defective gene, but in this case the colder temperatures favor normal development. As

[5] H. S. Jennings. *The biological basis of human nature.* New York: Norton, 1930.

the temperature under which the flies develop is increased, the number of perfect facets in the eye decreases.

Two principles of major importance may be inferred from these examples. An inherited defect is not always the inevitable, inescapable thing that some people imagine. What is inherited is not the defect itself but a tendency, a constitution that under certain conditions will produce the defect but may not do so if the conditions are changed. Secondly, we cannot tell by any *a priori* process of reasoning what conditions will favor normal development in individuals with defective genes. Take the examples just cited for the fruit-fly. In the case of flies bearing the gene that makes for abnormal abdomen, normal development is favored by the very conditions that a modern social worker among flies would probably try to change, that is, by a scanty supply of food and moisture. Flies having an inherited tendency to reduplicated legs are more likely to be normal if they are reared in warm temperatures, but those with a tendency to imperfect eyes are more likely to escape when reared in the cold. Experimental breeding has proved these things to be true, but we do not know the reason for them, and they do not tell us how the environment should be modified to prevent other defective genes from exercising their effect.

CAN ACQUIRED CHARACTERISTICS BE INHERITED?

Few questions in the field of genetics have aroused more heated controversy than the one just stated. To put it concretely, if parents for many generations are trained to perform a given act, will their children be able to learn it more easily because of the skill acquired by the parents? After their ancestors have lived for centuries under the rays of a tropical sun, will the babies born to fair-skinned Northern races have swarthier complexions than their progenitors if there is no intermarriage with dark-skinned races during that time?

Many experiments have been conducted in an attempt to answer this question, with results that have upon the whole been negative. Often it has seemed for a time that the results pointed to some effect of parental experience upon the abilities or physical characteristics of the offspring, but in all cases that have been investigated so far, it has later been shown that the effects could be explained in terms of selective breeding or other factors making for imperfect control. Social custom has also provided us with many experiments of this kind, and here too the results seem to be negative. The feet of Chinese women have been bound for centuries, but neither the size nor the shape of the feet of Chinese babies has been altered thereby. Generations of fox terriers have had their tails cut short, but the length of the puppies' tails has not lessened by an inch. Babies whose ancestors for many generations have spoken only German nevertheless have no special predisposition toward speaking German rather than any other language. If adopted at birth into English-speaking homes, they learn English as readily as they would have learned German, and speak it without an accent. If they attempt to learn German later on, say in high school or college, the knowledge acquired by their forebears does not give them an hour's advantage over their classmates of English or American stock.

A special phase of this question that has given concern to many expectant mothers is the matter of "prenatal influence." Even intelligent women sometimes believe the popular superstition that it is possible for an unborn child to be "marked" by some terrifying experience of the mother's, or that its abilities and character can be influenced by the mother's physical and mental regimen during pregnancy. Without going into details, it may be said that the tales reported in this connection are usually just nonsense. Dozens of them have been investigated and found to have no basis in fact, or to be easily explainable in terms of other well-known factors, such as physical injury or a genetic defect that has skipped one or more generations. Furthermore, since there is no nerve-connection between mother and child, the mechanism for transmitting a mental experience of the mother to the child is lacking. There is a possibility that some of the *chemical* effects of a strong emotional experience may get through to the child in its mother's womb. But they would not be the kind of influence that could produce a birthmark of a bear or an innate fear of the animal.

THE INHERITANCE OF BEHAVIOR

Until recently, most of our knowledge concerning the possibility of the transmission of behavior-tendencies from parent to offspring was inferential rather than scientifically proved. True, stock breeders have for many years succeeded in producing strains of fast-trotting horses, but these animals usually differ from the generality of horses in build as well as in performance on the race track. And fond mothers, for countless generations, have assured each other that all Johnnie's naughtiness was inherited from his father! (Their hearers have not always agreed!) The fact that certain special talents such as musical ability or special defects like feeble-mindedness often seem to "run in families" does not always provide incontrovertible evidence that heredity is the cause, since the children from musical families are likely to be reared in a musical environment and to receive special training in music, and the children of feeble-minded parents typically come from homes where there is little intellectual stimulation. Is there, then, any

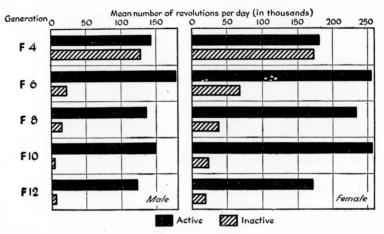

FIGURE 9.   The effect of selective breeding for activity in the white rat.
Because of the greater activity of the female rats, the sexes have been kept
separate in the tabulation of results. For the first three generations (not
shown here) the selection of active and inactive rats for breeding purposes
was made from the entire group without reference to the degree of activity
in the ancestors of the selected rats. Only a very slight difference in the
activity of the offspring was brought about in that way. Beginning with the
fourth generation (F_4) the two strains were kept separate. Active rats for
breeding were selected only from the active strain; inactive rats from the
inactive strain. The rapid differentiation of the two groups after this plan
was followed is a neat illustration of the fact that heredity goes back for
many generations and does not depend only upon the immediate parents.

Rundquist points out that the results shown above suggest that activity is a
dominant trait and that inactivity is recessive to it. The discussion on pages
42-44 of this book give you the basis for his thinking. Application of these
principles to the data of Figure 9 provides a good test of your understanding
of the basic theory involved. (The data for this figure are taken from E. A.
Rundquist. Inheritance of spontaneous activity in rats. *J. comp. Psychol.*,
1933, 16, 415-438.)

clear evidence that behavior-tendencies as well as differences in bodily
form may be passed on as a biological inheritance from parent to
offspring?

At the University of Minnesota, psychologists have applied the principles of selective breeding in the development of two strains of rats,
one characterized by great physical activity, the other by lethargy. The
method employed was to measure the activity of each rat in each
successive generation by placing him in a special cage to which a
recording device for registering movement within the cage was attached. From the records so obtained the most active rats were selected
for breeding Strain A and those showing least activity for breeding
Strain B. This was repeated in each new generation with the results
shown in Figure 9.

A similar experiment has been carried out at the University of California by Tryon. In this case, however, the separation was made on the basis of a special manifestation of rat "brightness" as shown by the animals' ability to learn the pattern of a complicated maze so that they could run through it quickly from entrance to food compartment without entering any of the blind alleys that were set to confuse them. Animals who showed unusual aptitude for learning the mazes were selected for breeding the superior strain; those who learned only with difficulty or were unable to learn at all became the parents of the inferior strain. As in the case of the Minnesota experiment, the two groups became increasingly different with each successive generation until eventually a race of rat "geniuses" had been evolved from the first strain in contrast with a group of "mental defectives" from the other. (See Figure 10.)

These results show that the differences in the nervous system that lie at the base of differences in behavior are subject to the same laws of heredity as differences in external structure and form. They do not show, as the careless reader might perhaps think, that acquired tendencies may be inherited, but only that superior stock tends to reproduce its kind and inferior stock does likewise. By continually selecting the most able members of a group for purposes of breeding, advantage is taken of all favorable variations, whether they result from mutation in the desired direction, from elimination of undesirable genes from the stock, or from unusually favorable recombination of the genes already present.

Many years ago, Darwin pointed out the effect of "natural selection" in changing the characteristics of man and animal. But natural selection works slowly because the selective process is so uncertain. When man steps in to control the selection, the number of generations necessary to effect a major change is vastly reduced. And this man has done, to the great improvement of many breeds of plants and animals. He alone remains untouched. Do we hear a whisper, *Physician, heal thyself?*

MENTAL INHERITANCE IN MAN

The fruit-fly of the biological laboratory, reared in bottles under conditions that can be kept the same from generation to generation or varied at the will of the experimenter, with its thirty or more generations a year and every mating carefully controlled and recorded, affords possibilities for the study of inheritance that in man can hardly be approximated. Yet the close agreement of the facts of human heredity, as far as they have been learned, with those obtained by the experimental breeding of plants and animals leaves little doubt that the fundamental

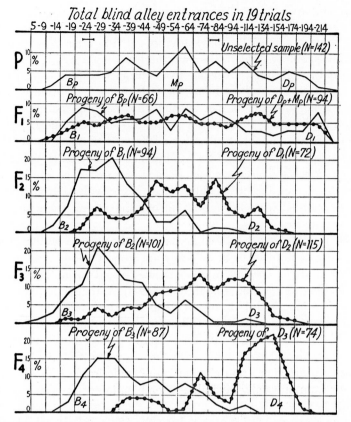

FIGURE 10.   The effect of selective breeding on maze learning in the white rat. The first curve (*P*) shows the distribution of errors (blind-alley entrances) made by an unselected sample of laboratory-reared white rats in learning to find their way through a maze to a food box at the end. You will notice that the rats differed greatly in their ability to learn. Some smart (or lucky) animals made fewer than 10 errors in 19 trials; others made as many as 200.

From this parental (*P*) generation, the brightest (*B*) and the dullest (*D*) animals were chosen for breeding. In the first filial (*F₁*) generation, not much difference between the bright and the dull strains can be noted, but by the

principles are the same for both. Specific facts, however, such as the question of which of two companion genes is dominant over the other, which genes are carried in the same chromosome and therefore tend to be inherited together, and how environment operates to modify inherited tendencies, must be determined separately for each individual trait in man and animal alike. Few of these facts are known with certainty yet; nevertheless the problem of heredity is one of the most important in the entire field of human behavior. We cannot ignore it, for it underlies every reaction shown by the individual in later life. But

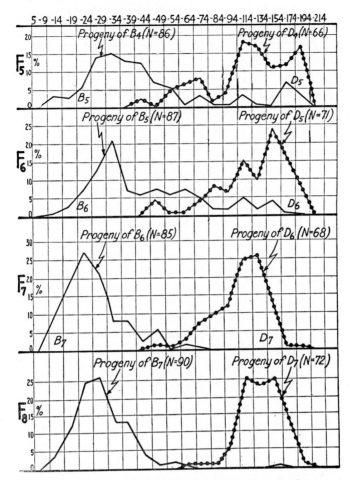

second (F_2) generation the separation begins to be clearly apparent. By the eighth (F_8) generation, two distinct strains have been developed in which the smartest rat of the dull strain does only a little better than the most stupid rat of the bright strain. (Reproduced by courtesy of the author and the publisher from Individual differences, by Robert C. Tryon, Chapter 13, in *Comparative psychology*, F. A. Moss [Ed.], Prentice-Hall, Inc.)

we must not be dogmatic in asserting either its powers or its limitations in any given instance. The same genes in different environments may produce very different effects; under the same environment different genes may develop in diverse ways. If this is true of the physical characteristics of the fruit-fly, how much more likely it is to be true of the mental traits of man in the development of which learning plays so important a part.

The difficulty of studying mental inheritance in man is greatly increased by the fact that most children are reared by their own parents, and, as we all know, experience and training have much to do with determining what people learn to do. Yet experience is not the only factor. The idiot remains an idiot, no matter in how cultured a home he is reared or how careful training is given him. The person with little musical ability may be trained to play and sing after a fashion, but he will not become a real musician. On the other hand, talent that is not cultivated may never display itself well enough to be recognized for what it is. Since parents of superior ability are more likely than others to provide superior advantages for their children, it becomes hard to say to what extent the children's accomplishments are due to native ability and how much of a part has been played by opportunity and training. For this reason the genealogical record as a means of studying the heredity of mental traits is rapidly falling into disuse, though a generation ago it was very popular.

Two methods of distinguishing the mental differences between persons that result from dissimilar heredity—different genes—and those that result from dissimilar environments are commonly employed. One method consists in comparing the resemblances between parents and children who are reared in their own homes with those between foster parents and their foster children adopted in early infancy. Similar checks have been made by comparing brothers and sisters reared apart with those brought up together or by comparing the resemblances of unrelated children reared in the same home with those of true brothers and sisters.

These studies have shown that parent-child resemblance does not disappear when children are brought up from early infancy in foster homes where they have no further contact with their parents. This is true not only of their physical traits but of their mental characteristics as well. Environment undoubtedly exerts some effect, but just how great this effect is likely to be is still a matter of controversy. It is reasonable to suppose that some characteristics can more readily be changed by environmental factors than others, and this seems to be the case. It is unlikely that the color of a child's eyes or hair will be affected by taking him away from his family at birth and rearing him among strangers. Probably his mental abilities will not be greatly changed, though of this we are less certain. But his conduct, the use that he makes of whatever abilities he may possess, is likely to depend very largely upon the conditions under which he has been reared and the particular kind of training he has received. One person of exceptional mental powers may become a great scientist; another, equally gifted, may become a master criminal. Equal ability in no way ensures similar accomplishment.

Another method often used for studying the relative effectiveness of heredity and environment in producing mental differences among individuals is by means of a comparison of the resemblances of identical and fraternal twins. It is now generally conceded that there are two kinds of twins. Among human beings, as a rule, only one ovum matures at a time, and consequently there is only one child at a birth. Sometimes, however, two or more ova may develop simultaneously and both be fertilized at the same time. When the chromosomes of each ovum separate during meiosis, it is unlikely that the grouping will be the same. One ovum may receive a preponderance of chromosomes that came from the maternal grandfather of the child-to-be; in the other the grandmother's chromosomes may be in the majority. In like manner the sperm-cells by which they are fertilized will in most cases carry different assortments of chromosomes as a result of dissimilar grouping at the time of the reduction division. The children who develop from these fertilized ova will then, as a rule, carry genes of which some are alike (because by chance it is likely that some of the chromosomes will be the same for each) and others unlike. They will resemble each other in those hereditary traits that develop from similar genes, but may be very unlike each other in traits that arise from unlike genes. This is exactly what happens in the case of ordinary brothers and sisters. We have all noticed that some brothers and sisters are much more alike than others. This is quite to be expected, because it will sometimes happen that the chromosomes divide in much the same fashion on the two occasions, so that both receive about the same assortment of genes, while in the other cases the division may take a very different pattern.

Twins that result from the simultaneous fertilization of two different ova are therefore no more closely related than are ordinary brothers and sisters. They may be of either the same or of different sex. Their heredity may be fairly similar or very different; in rare cases it may be completely different. Because they are only brothers or sisters born at the same time, they are commonly known as *fraternal twins.*

Twins sometimes originate in another way. After the usual single ovum has been fertilized by a single sperm, it begins to develop by a process of cell division. Normally, however, the new cells formed by this division do not separate but remain attached to each other, and in this way the body of the new child is formed. At each cell division every chromosome divides itself lengthwise, so that every new cell receives a portion of each gene. Now it occasionally happens that at the time of the first division, when the newly fertilized ovum divides to form two, these new cells do not remain together; they separate, and each part develops into a complete individual. Twins formed in this way are known as *identical twins* because they have exactly the same assortment of genes and therefore resemble each other very closely in all their hereditary traits. Identical twins are always of the same sex.

By comparing a large number of such minute physical characteristics as palm and sole prints, form of ear, color and texture of hair, and so on, it is possible to distinguish between identical and fraternal twins with considerable accuracy. Now by noting the mental resemblances found in each group, we can measure roughly the extent to which identical heredity plus very similar environment[6] can increase resemblances between individuals beyond that which results when the environment is similar but the heredity is only partially similar.

A number of studies of this kind have been made, with results that upon the whole agree very closely. In most tests of mental ability, identical twins reared together resemble each other about as closely as two tests of the same person on different occasions, while the resemblance of fraternal twins is about the same as that of ordinary brothers and sisters. In social and emotional characteristics, temperament, and such personality traits as persistence, effort, energy, and so on, the difference between the two groups is usually less marked, a fact which suggests that traits such as these are more strongly influenced by experience and training than is mental ability. However, in every trait studied, identical twins usually resemble each other somewhat more closely than fraternal twins.

An important study of twin resemblances reported from the University of Chicago[7] includes one section that is of special interest because it combines the two techniques we have mentioned—the study of twins and the study of foster children. This study gives a very detailed report of the later resemblances of nineteen pairs of identical twins who were separated in infancy and brought up under different surroundings. Although in four of these pairs, for whom the environmental differences were very marked, the differences in intelligence and personality were somewhat greater than was true of the other

---

[6] Even in the matter of environmental similarity, however, the two types of twins differ to some extent. Just because they are more likely to differ in ability, fraternal twins are the more likely to make unequal progress through the school grades, and because they are then in different classes they are less likely to have the same playmates. Differences in size and strength may lead them to prefer different games; differences in special talents make for differences in interests that lead to differential choice of surroundings and playmates. Here we have one more illustration of the close interaction between heredity and environment; a change in one almost inevitably means a change in the other. Even in childhood the relationship appears, and as with advancing age the individual becomes more free to choose his own environment and more dependent upon his own abilities in making a place for himself in the world, the association, at first slight, becomes increasingly stronger and more apparent.

[7] H. H. Newman, F. N. Freeman, and K. J. Holzinger. *Twins: a study of heredity and environment.* Chicago: Univ. of Chicago Press, 1937, p. 369.

members of the group, in the remaining fifteen cases the resemblances in mental ability were almost (though not quite) as close as has usually been reported for identical twins reared together. In such matters as temperament and personality, greater divergences appeared. Upon the whole, however, the resemblances were decidedly closer than is usually found for brothers and sisters reared in the same household. We may separate a child from his family after he has been born, but we cannot separate him from the genes with which he was born.

What shall we conclude from all this? Is our destiny packed up in our germ cells, fixed and inevitable from the time of our birth? Will heredity alone make from this infant a genius, from that one a criminal? Or, on the other hand, are all men created equal, with similar talents, similar potentialities, equal ability to learn by experience, to persist in spite of difficulties, to foresee consequences, and stand fast in the face of temptation?

Neither the one nor the other. No one above the rank of imbecility need be a helpless victim of his hereditary defects, if he has any, nor can he depend on his native gifts to take him on his way unaided by his own efforts or without recourse to the advantages offered by education and training. But people are not alike, and those who wish to make the most of themselves will recognize the fact frankly and try to plan their lives in such a way that their natural abilities will be given the fullest opportunity for expression and the defects or weaknesses from which no one is entirely free will be as little of a handicap as possible. We no longer insist that the man with weak lungs shall try to brave the rigors of a New England winter; we send him to a climate that he can stand. We do not try to make an opera singer from the girl who cannot distinguish one note from another, but instead we try to find out where her talents lie and to direct her training along lines where it seems likely to be most effective. No one need be discouraged because he has weaknesses, nor should he hesitate to look his weak points squarely in the face. Whether they have a hereditary basis or not, they can often be improved if it seems worthwhile to do so; if they cannot, the thing to do is to adjust one's mode of living so that they will interfere with it as little as possible. We cannot change our genes, but to a great extent we can determine for ourselves which of them shall be the governing forces in our lives.

SUMMARY

For the human individual, life begins with the fusion of two germ cells, an ovum and a spermatozoon. This kind of biparental reproduction makes for the diversification of human characteristics upon which complex forms of social organization rest.

Hereditary characteristics are determined by minute particles called *genes,* combined into larger units called *chromosomes.* Corresponding chromosomes from the two parents are paired in the new individual. Sex is determined by one of these pairs. One gene in each gene pair is ordinarily dominant, the other recessive, though intermediate kinds of combination are known. Sex-linked traits are transmitted through the X, or sex-determining, chromosome. Most human traits depend upon a large number of gene pairs rather than on one alone. Changes in the genes themselves are called *mutations.*

Heredity and environment work together in the production of human traits. It is not possible to say that some are determined by heredity, others by environment. Acquired characteristics of parents cannot be inherited by their children.

Animal breeding studies have shown that tendencies to behave in certain ways can be transmitted through heredity. Studies of human heredity have made extensive use of foster children and identical twins. They have shown that heredity does help to determine mental characteristics and temperamental qualities, as it does size and shape.

A BOOK YOU WILL ENJOY READING

FULLER, John L. *Nature and nurture: a modern synthesis.* Garden City, New York: Doubleday, 1954.

A brief but very adequate treatment of the principal implications of the research that has been done on heredity for our thinking about human nature in general, and a number of specific human problems, is given in this monograph.

CHAPTER 4

Why should psychologists be interested in the development that occurs before birth?

Into what three periods can prenatal life be divided? What is the chief characteristic of development in each?

Are the separate parts of the body—the arms, legs, trunk, head, and internal organs—present in miniature from the start? If not, how do they come into existence?

How does the nervous system develop?

How does activity begin?

How does behavior develop during the early months of life?

What general laws or principles of development have arisen from the study of embryology?

Prenatal Development

IMPORTANCE OF EMBRYOLOGY FOR PSYCHOLOGY

IF WE REALLY WISH to understand the way a human being acts and thinks and feels, we must begin by considering the nine months of life that come before the day he celebrates as his birthday. The most important changes that occur in his makeup during the entire course of his life have already taken place during that brief period. The structures that must form the basis of all his later growth and activity have already taken shape.

One of the reasons why the psychologist studies this prenatal period is that he needs to understand the nature of these *structures*. A knowledge of the way in which they develop contributes much to such understanding. Especially is this true with regard to the nervous system, so essential to all kinds of mental activity.

The other reason why the psychologist concerns himself with the prenatal period is that he hopes to come upon general *laws* with regard to the developmental process itself—laws that will guide him in his study of the development of the human individual throughout his whole life span.

PHYSICAL DEVELOPMENT DURING THE
PRENATAL PERIOD

On the basis of the type of growth most characteristic at the time, embryologists commonly divide prenatal life into three periods. The first week or two [1] after fertilization comprise the germinal period. During most of this time the ovum remains a free organism, existing within the body of the mother but not attached to it, and so far as we know, not obtaining any sustenance from it. It does not increase in size during this time, but changes greatly in internal structure. The single fertilized cell divides into two, then each of these cells divides again to make four, and so on until a globular mass of cells has been formed. At each of these and of all subsequent cell divisions each chromosome splits lengthwise so that every new cell formed has a complete assortment of genes.

The first indication of a change in form is the development of a small cavity in the interior of the mass. This cavity is formed by the death of some cells and a rearrangement of others. The cavity gradually increases until two parts are formed: an outer membrane and an inner mass of cells. Two further cavities then form in the inner mass. Between them is a small disk, known as the *germinal disk*. From this disk the child is ultimately formed.

At the end of about two weeks, the ovum attaches itself to the uterus. The outer layer of cells has the power of cutting away the uterine surface, and in this way the ovum becomes completely imbedded in the uterus and surrounded by the blood stream. Only the outer membrane, however, is in contact with the maternal organism. The child now exists as a parasite, taking its nourishment from the mother but living a separate life of its own and growing according to its own nature. (See Figure 11.)

The period between the time the ovum attaches itself to the mother and the time when the general form and structure of the body parts have all been laid down is known as the *embryonic period*. It lasts from about the end of the second to the end of the sixth week. During this period, growth in size proceeds at a tremendous rate, and differentiation of the bodily parts is brought to about 95 per cent of completion. Thus within the short period of four or five weeks, the tiny disk that can be seen only under the microscope changes into an unmistakable human being. To be sure, this human being still differs greatly in appearance from the adult or even the newborn baby. Its head is enormously large in proportion to the rest of the body. (See Figure 11.) The eyes are large and far apart; the arms and legs are tiny, and the fingers and toes are not yet completely separated from each other. Nevertheless it is a baby, a human being, and not a bird or a puppy. To the trained

---

[1] The reader may be puzzled as to why the time is given in this inexact, approximate fashion. The fact is that for a human individual it is impossible to be certain just when the real beginning of life, the moment of fusion of the nuclei of the two parent cells, occurs. There are a number of ways of estimating this beginning, but all are only approximations.

eye it is not even a monkey, though you and I might have some difficulty in making the last distinction.

The rapid growth in size is quite as remarkable. By the end of the embryonic period the embryo has increased in mass about 2,000,000 per cent. It is then approximately two inches in length and weighs from one-half to one ounce. A waggish mathematician has figured out that if the organism were to continue to double itself in size at the embryonic rate, it would be as large as the whole solar system by the age of twenty-one years. It is just as well that this tremendous rush of growth soon begins to slow down.

The third and last period of prental life is known as the *fetal period*. It includes about the last thirty-two weeks before birth. Fetal development is characterized chiefly by growth in size, or perhaps we had better say by growth in "absolute" size, since the time required for doubling either the weight or the length of the fetus is far greater than the corresponding time during the embryonic period. During the first part of the fetal period, growth is accomplished mainly by increase in the number of cells through cell division; during the later part of the period the rate of cell division slows down and growth takes place chiefly through increase in the size of the individual cells.

DIFFERENTIATION OF THE BODY INTO PARTS

The fertilized ovum bears little resemblance to the child into which it will develop later on. The most powerful microscope cannot enable us to distinguish within it anything resembling a human body. Nevertheless from it a human body will grow. But how?

The differentiation of the body into parts cannot well be accounted for solely on the basis of the genes, since each cell contains all the genes and yet, as the body grows, the cells in different regions grow to be very unlike each other both in form and in arrangement. The brain is not like the stomach; the liver is not like the teeth; the bones are not like the muscles. Nevertheless, all these different parts develop from the single fertilized ovum. If they were not there in miniature at the start, how did they come into existence?

The answer, at least in part, is to be found in the environmental conditions under which the cells develop. At first thought it may seem to you as though the environment of all the cells is the same. But a moment's consideration will convince you that it is not. The cells on the outside of the child's body have not the same environment as those on the inside, and there are other regional differences as well. Some cells are crowded close together; others have plenty of room to grow. Some receive ample nourishment; others get relatively little. These are

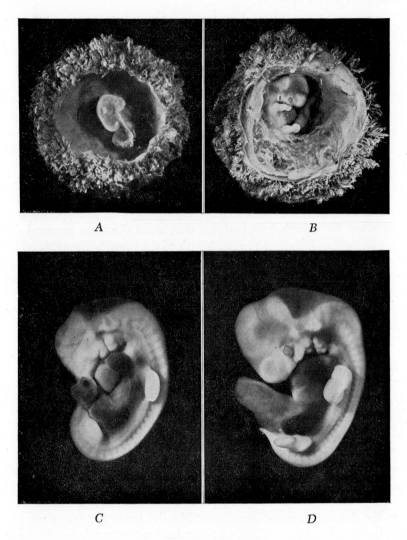

A   B

C   D

FIGURE 11.   Embryos and fetuses of different ages. *A.* Human embryo
about six weeks old. Here the surrounding membranes of the placenta to
which the embryo is attached by the umbilical cord are shown in cross-
section. Note the many thousands of finger-like processes by which the
placenta is embedded in the lining of the uterus.

B. Human embryo about nine weeks old. By this time arms and legs can
be clearly distinguished as well as many other organs and structures.

C and *D.* Enlarged photographs, showing embryos about six and seven
weeks old without the surrounding membranes. Note the very large size
of the head and its relatively advanced state of development as compared to
the lower parts of the body. At this stage the embryo is about ½ inch in
sitting height.

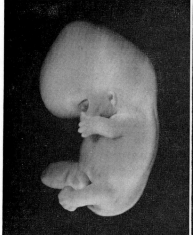

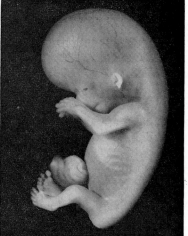

E   F

E. Embryo about eight weeks old. Sitting height at this age is about ¾ inch. Note the development of the limbs, the eyes and the opening of the ear, which at this time is located toward the base of the neck. Note, too, that the "finger buds" are further advanced than the "toe buds," a fact that provides another example of the rule that development of the upper regions of the body is more precocious than in the lower regions.

F. Embryo about ten weeks old. Sitting height about 1½ inches. The ear lobe can now be seen, and the position of the ear, as a result of more rapid growth of the lower part of the neck and face, is more nearly that which it will take later on. Growth of the

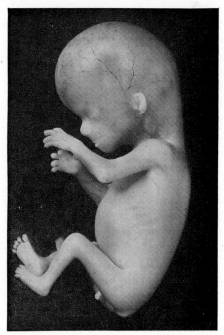

G

skeleton is shown in the outlining of the ribs. Both arms and legs have increased markedly in length.

G. Embryo about twelve weeks old. At this age the sitting height is about 2¾ inches, and the total height from crown to heel is nearly 4 inches. The usual weight is a little less than half a pound. Sex can usually be determined by external inspection. (Courtesy Department of Embryology, Carnegie Institution of Washington, Baltimore, Md.)

just a few examples of the differences in cell environment that are found from one region of the growing body to another.

Experiments carried on with lower animals during the very early stages of development have shown how completely the body as a whole controls the development of its parts. By transplanting certain cells to other regions of the growing body, that is, by changing their environment, almost any cells can be made to transform into almost any part, provided only that this is done early enough, before the transformation into a particular kind of cell is too far advanced. Primitive cells that would normally have become skin cells can be made to develop into the spinal cord if placed in the appropriate region; those that would have become eyes can be made to give rise to brain and so on. Thus we see that the cells which make up the body are never independent units. The single cell from which the child develops need not, in any physical sense, "contain" all the parts that later appear. All that it need contain is a single kind of protoplasm that is capable of developing in various ways according to the influences or "environment" in which it is placed. As the cells multiply, those in certain regions become unlike those in other regions because they are not subject to the same influences from without the organism or from within it. Certain cells are compressed more than others; some receive a more abundant food supply; in others waste matter accumulates in greater amounts, and so on. Thus the growth and development of one part of the body directly affects the growth and development of other parts. The body, not the individual cells of which it consists, is the fundamental living unit.

Such a highly organized system as the human body can work effectively only if there is communication from one region to another. The hand must work in co-operation with the eye; the internal organs must co-ordinate their activities if the organism is to survive. This highly important function of supplying a means of communication from one region of the body to another so that all parts may work together harmoniously is taken care of primarily by the nervous system. The development of the nervous system is therefore of particular interest to the psychologist in his studies of behavior. In this chapter we shall not attempt to give more than a very brief account of its growth but will merely call attention to some of the main features.

DEVELOPMENT OF THE NERVOUS SYSTEM
AS A WHOLE

In the development of the child from the germinal disk, the first marked differentiation that can be seen is the formation of a ridge or thickening on the surface. This fixes the axis of the body. Gradually this thickened portion lifts itself above the germinal disk, carrying with it part of the surrounding surface. Eventually the whole thing pinches off except for a small attachment that later becomes the umbilical cord. Along the center of the original ridge the outer layer of cells now begins to proliferate more rapidly than the remainder, thus forming a thickened row of cells running down the center of the back of the developing embryo. This *neural plate,* as it is called, marks the beginning of the nervous system. A little later on, the center of the neural plate begins to fold in, as shown in Figure 12. The groove thus formed is called the *neural groove;* the edges of the groove, where the developing nervous tissue joins the non-nervous surface layer of the cells, is called the *neural crest* or the *neural fold.* The infolding con-

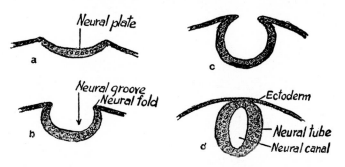

FIGURE 12.   **Successive stages in the infolding of the neural groove.** (From H. E. Jordan and J. E. Kindred. *A textbook of embryology.* D. Appleton-Century Co.)

tinues until in about a week's time the edges of the groove meet and join to form a tube. Successive stages in this process are seen in Figure 12.

The *neural tube* formed by the closure of the sides of the infolded neural groove is the starting point of the spinal cord and brain. Very soon the head end of the embryo can be distinguished from the caudal end[2] by the faster growth of this part of the neural tube. The spinal cord develops from the caudal portion of the tube by a gradual and regular thickening of its walls. The brain results from a much more rapid but uneven thickening of the forward end of the neural tube.

In the course of this uneven growth of the part of the tube that will later become the brain, two bulges soon appear, one on each side of its foremost portion. These mark the beginning of the *cerebral hemispheres.* Their growth is the most conspicuous feature of brain development during the embryonic period, though all the other main divisions

---

[2] From the Latin word meaning "tail."

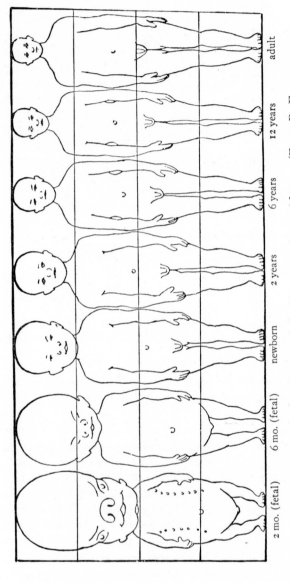

FIGURE 13. Changes in bodily proportions with age. (From R. E. Scammon. Developmental anatomy. In Morris's *Human anatomy.* (6th ed.) Courtesy P. Blakiston's Son & Co.)

of the brain are also laid down during this time. The enormous size of the embryo's head as compared to the rest of its body is almost entirely due to the rush of brain development, particularly cerebral development, during the embryonic period. When we remember that the most conspicuous differences between the human brain and that of the lower animals is to be found in the enormous development of the cerebral hemispheres in man, the significance of this precocious growth of the cerebral portion of the brain becomes apparent. In the early embryonic stages the head includes about half of the total body mass. (See Figure 13.) It is made up almost wholly of the brain and sense organs, since the jaws and other parts of the head are little developed at this time. The neural tube as a whole represents about 75 per cent of the body mass. From the very start, the nervous system, which is the chief co-ordinating and integrating mechanism of the body, takes the lead in growth.

Few new cells form in the central nervous system after birth. The increase in size that occurs is brought about principally by an increase in the size of the individual cells, by the lengthening of fibers, and by the addition of a protective sheath of a white fatty substance called *myelin.* Figure 14 shows how completely developed the cerebrum of a newborn infant appears to be.

One important fact that should not be overlooked is that growth of the fibers making up the nervous system continues not only until adulthood but throughout the life span. Thus new connections can be made, new concepts developed, new skills learned as long as life lasts.

At the same time that the individual is developing a highly differentiated nervous system that will serve to co-ordinate and integrate his activity and experience throughout life, he is acquiring a complex chemical system that also plays its part in such integration. This is made up of the *endocrine glands,* designed to discharge into the blood stream minute amounts of complex biochemical substances called *hormones* that have marked effects on the state of the organism. The embryology of the hormonal system has been less thoroughly studied than that of the nervous system, but its importance is being increasingly recognized.

It is through this medium that it may be possible in some instances for the emotional state of the mother to affect the biochemical characteristics of the fetus upon which later temperamental characteristics are to some extent based. The extent to which this occurs is still far from clear. Obviously it is quite a different sort of phenomenon from the superstitious belief that the child of a mother frightened by a dog during her pregnancy will have a dog-shaped birthmark or that the child of a mother who listens constantly to music will be musical. But in the fact that general emotional characteristics depend to some extent on hormones and that some hormones diffuse through the placenta, there is at least a basis for research on this important problem.

THE EMBRYOLOGY OF BEHAVIOR

The psychologist's field of study is *behavior*. As we use this word in our ordinary speech, it does not need to be defined. We all know what we mean by it. But when we are considering the earliest period of life, it is not so apparent just what the term signifies. Psychologists have agreed for convenience sake to take as the origin of true behavior the point where the organism first *responds* to a *stimulus*. In order for this to occur there must have been developed receptor organs to register the stimulating energy, nerve cells to pass it along, and muscle cells to carry out the movement.

One of the interesting findings of embryological research is that behavior, defined in this way, is not the first activity that the organism shows. Movement itself is more fundamental than response to stimulation. The three kinds of element listed above—receptor cell, nerve cell, and muscle cell—do not develop at exactly the same rate. Thus it has become necessary to distinguish between *myogenic* movements (originating in the muscle cells themselves) and *neurogenic* movements (originating in nerve cells). Of the kinds of structures necessary for behavior, it is the muscles that are ready for action first.

The first movement that can be detected in any kind of developing organism is the beating of the heart. In the chick this has been observed as early as the second day of incubation, before anything that remotely resembles a chicken can be seen in the egg. In the human embryo the heart begins to beat during the third week, long before any of the features that make it look human have been differentiated. The initial movement is produced by metabolic processes in the muscle cells themselves, and the basic rhythm that is set up is self-perpetuating. Later, nerve fibers do become connected with the muscles of the heart, so that its functioning is influenced by stimulation from outside itself, but the rhythmic beating is more fundamental, in this developmental sense, than anything we call behavior.

One implication of this fact is that from the beginning the embryo is a separate individual, attached to the maternal body but not really a part of it. It has its own circulatory system, able to carry food and oxygen to all parts of its growing body and remove the waste products.

As noted above, studies of lower animals having embryos more accessible and available for experimentation than those of man have shown that, in general, muscle cells are ready to function at a considerably earlier stage of development than are the nerve cells or the

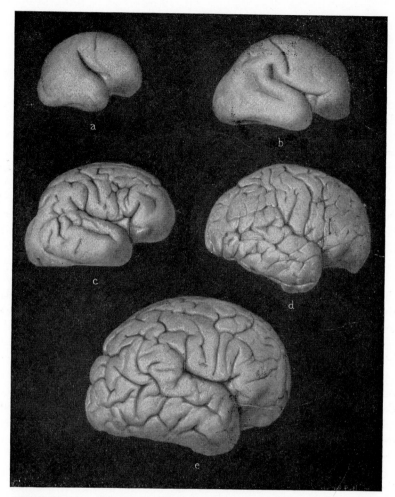

FIGURE 14. Changes in the external appearance of the cerebral hemispheres from the sixth to the tenth lunar month of prenatal life. Anatomists commonly reckon ages during the prenatal period in terms of lunar months of four weeks (28 days) each in order to avoid the irregularities resulting from the unequal length of the different calendar months. The figures show the developmental changes at monthly intervals from the sixth to the tenth lunar month (168 to 280 days of age) which is the usual age at birth. Except for the increase in size, little further change in the appearance of the cerebral hemispheres takes place between birth and maturity, but microscopic examination shows that at birth many areas are still unmyelineated and other differences in cell structure exist. (Courtesy of Dr. R. E. Scammon.)

receptor cells that are necessary to rouse them to activity. The growth
of differentiated behavior from then on depends upon the maturation
of the nervous structures and receptor organs that make it possible to
stimulate and innervate the muscles and to co-ordinate their separate
movements. It has been chiefly the developmental sequence of movements that can be elicited in response to various kinds of stimulation
that psychologists have studied. In a number of animal species, the
sequences are understood fairly accurately. Human behavioral development during the prenatal period has been more difficult to study. The
only subjects available for many kinds of testing are infants who for
medical reasons are delivered prematurely, and the difficulties of
maintaining normal environmental conditions in such cases are very
great. But by generalizing wherever possible from carefully controlled
animal studies and by taking advantage of every opportunity to study
human subjects, scientists have been able to accumulate a considerable
body of knowledge about early behavioral development.

Many of our fundamental ideas about development have come from
the brilliant and long-continued research of the biologist Coghill [3] on
the common salamander, *amblystoma*. His special research problem
was the relationship of the progressive development of behavior to the
neurological development that paralleled it. By the use of motion
pictures he was able to make permanent records of the behavior shown
by an animal at any given stage of development and then, by means of
post-mortem examination, to determine the degree of neurological
development corresponding to that stage. He found that the first movement that can be detected is a simple coil of the trunk, which later
develops into a double coiling movement something like the letter S,
from which the swimming movements are derived. (See Figure 15.)
Later still the limbs participate, first the forelimbs, and later the hind-
limbs. In the case of salamanders that become able to live either in
water or on land, the walking movements develop directly out of the
swimming movements displayed at an earlier stage of development.
Walking is a more advanced stage in the sequence than swimming,
however, because in walking the leg movements are more important
than trunk movements. It is the undifferentiated trunk movements that
come first. The neurological studies indicated that the capacity for
carrying on the kind of activity shown in each successive stage depends
upon the growth of nerve fibers outward to the developing muscle
fibers.

The major idea or principle that arose from Coghill's work was that
developmental processes making for unified activity of the whole

[3] G. E. Coghill. *Anatomy and the problems of behavior.* Cambridge, Mass:
Harvard Univ. Press, 1929.

organism are more fundamental than processes producing limited movements of smaller parts. In order to understand the effect that this generalization had on scientific theories, the student must know something of the history of psychological and physiological thinking about these matters. Perhaps because the atomic theory had been so useful

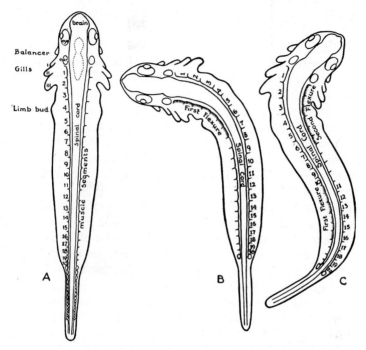

FIGURE 15.   Development of swimming movements in amblystoma. From the resting position (*A*) a flexure (*B*) begins in the head region and proceeds tailward as if, according to its earlier habits, the animal were going to throw itself into a tight coil but instead of doing this it reverses the flexure in the anterior part before the first flexure has passed through the entire length of the animal. There are now two flexures in progress at the same time, one to the right and the other to the left, both of them progressing from the head tailward (*C*). (From G. E. Coghill. *Anatomy and the problems of behavior.* Courtesy Cambridge University Press.)

in chemistry, workers in the biological fields made a determined effort to organize their material into a system based on something like elements and compounds. In psychology the first widely influential theory was *structuralism*, in which the basic unit was the sensation, and all complex mental life was derived from combinations of these elementary "particles." The next widely influential theory was the "chain

reflex theory" favored by behaviorists. According to this way of thinking little bits of behavior, automatic responses of separate muscles to
the stimulation of specific sense organs, were the elements that became
linked together into the complex activities psychologists study. What
Coghill was saying was that instead of the independent development
of the separate parts of an act which are later linked together into a
whole, the mass movements appear first and the finer movements
develop out of them. We may liken it to the growth of a tree. First
there is the main shoot. As it grows, offshoots or branches arise; as
these grow, smaller branches proceed from them. So in the development
of behavior during the fetal period, movements of the trunk precede
movements of the limbs; movements of the arms and legs precede independent movements of the fingers and toes, and so on. There seems,
moreover, to be a tendency for movements of the upper parts of the
body to precede those of the lower parts, just as in physical growth the
head portions of the body are precocious in development as compared
to the legs. The whole is not built up from its parts, but the parts
develop out of the whole.

Research on a number of species seems to support Coghill's generalization with regard to the direction of development. Frogs, turtles, opos-
sums, guinea pigs, rats, and a number of varieties of birds have been
among the species to which the Coghillian principles apply. Thus there
seems to be enough evidence to warrent adopting the principle as a
guide in our thinking about development. It is natural for the activity
of a living organism, at whatever level of development it has reached, to
be integrated and organized. Behavior does not develop piecemeal.

As in so many other fields, however, the progress of research has
shown that the whole situation is more complicated than it was thought
at first to be. Not all experiments have confirmed the whole-part
developmental sequence in detail. Particularly in the case of the human
fetus, there is considerable evidence for some quite specialized kinds of
responses fairly early in the individual's development. These differences
between species, however, provoke less theoretical controversy than
they did when first encountered. They seem to be related to another
kind of characteristic in which species differ—namely, the stage of
development at which specific *parts*, such as the limbs, appear. It has
been shown that the rapid growth of the differentiated structures making up the limb is accompanied by rapid growth of nerve fibers making
specific responses of the limb possible. In amphibians, limb structures
develop late, in mammals early, relative to the rest of the ongoing
development. The soundest conclusion now seems to be that continuous
integration of all kinds of activity is the rule in all species, though the
means of producing such integration may vary.

Any systematic study of developmental stages in the activities of the human fetus is, of course, exceptionally difficult because it must be done with fetuses that for medical reasons have been removed from the uterus by Caesarian section or delivered prematurely. Possible sources of abnormality in the responses such a subject makes, arising from the effects of drugs, anesthetics, or the abrupt change in surroundings, must always be considered. The first extensive study was published by Minkowski in 1922, and it was doubtful how well these sources of error had been controlled. The most thorough study so far is the one by Hooker[4] in which fetuses ranging in age from seven weeks up to practically full term infants have been tested for their response to tactile stimulation. Motion pictures were used to make permanent records of the responses, records that could be used for later study. Since the respiratory apparatus is not yet functional in these very young organisms, they do not survive for more than a very brief period after delivery, and the advantage of securing durable records that can be examined repeatedly and at leisure is very great. Hooker also exercised exceptional care in his experimental technique. Many investigators of fetal activity have employed relatively coarse instruments such as a horsehair, a cactus thorn, or a fine needle, any of which, unless handled with extreme care, is likely to penetrate the very delicate skin of the young fetus and induce direct muscular activity which may be mistaken for true reflex activity. Hooker used a human hair, mounted in a handle. The degree of resistance of this hair was determined by finding how many milligrams of pressure had to be exerted against its end to cause it to bend. He found that many human hairs were too coarse and stiff to be safe, especially when experimenting with the smaller fetuses.

All of the fetuses examined by Hooker that were under eight weeks of age proved to be nonmotile. The first response was obtained in a fetus 1.18 inches in length, whose estimated age was just over eight weeks. When the neck of this fetus was stimulated with the point of a hair, there was a slow bending of the body toward the side away from the stimulus. Two other fetuses, estimated to be about nine and one-half weeks old, exhibited a kind of movement that Minkowski had previously described as "worm-like." The body was bent away from the stimulus with rotation of the hips, a downward movement of both arms, and rotation of the head. At eleven and one-half weeks the movements were elaborated and more rapid. The arms were first separated and then brought forward "as if to clap the hands." By the age of fourteen weeks many new responses had appeared. Even mimetic facial grimaces occurred if the lips or cheeks were touched.

Almost every one has observed that if a finger is placed in the hand

[4] D. Hooker. Early fetal activities in mammals. *Yale J. Biol. and Med.*, 1936, 8, 579-602.

of a young infant, the baby's fingers will close about it. This is known as the *palmar or grasping reflex*. Minkowski reports the beginning of this reflex at ten and one-half weeks; Hooker observed it at eleven and one half weeks, at which time "a light stimulation of the palm, if repeated, induced a barely perceptible flexion movement of the fingers accompanying a slight flexion of the wrist. At thirteen weeks the flexion was more pronounced. At fourteen weeks a fairly respectable 'fist' was made, but it was not of a closed type, nor did the thumb play much of a role in the flexion. The grasp does not hold an object placed within it until twenty-two weeks, and then but feebly."[5]

Hooker's results show that by about the fourteenth week the human fetus is capable of producing almost all of the reflex responses of the new-born infant. At this stage there is a change in the quality of movements, both reflex and spontaneous, as well. They lose their earlier stereotyped character and become more "graceful and flowing." From then on until birth, the process of development is largely a matter of maturation of activities already present. Because all movements become stronger and more vigorous, the mother begins to feel them, usually at about the eighteenth week. They also become more complex and involve more parts of the organism in response to a single stimulus. Preliminary breathing movements occur at eighteen weeks, and one fetus was able to breathe and cry at twenty-two weeks. No premature infant younger than twenty-seven weeks, however, survived for very long.

Hooker's studies and others, less extensive, that corroborate them demonstrate "that there is a normal, progressive evolution of behavior in the human fetus. Furthermore, the development of fetal behavior lays a necessary foundation for the later development of postnatal behavior, so that the latter is not merely imposed upon the former, but arises from it by a process of further maturation of already existing activities."[6]

GENERAL PRINCIPLES OF DEVELOPMENT

One of the most important contributions that biological research on prenatal development has made to the thinking of psychologists is to direct their attention to processes that are somewhat different from those that would ordinarily be noticed in psychological research on more mature organisms. This leads to an effort for synthesis and thus to a modification and reformulation of concepts and working hypotheses. It should be emphasized that such applications of principles from another scientific field are no substitute for research in our own. Before

[5] Hooker, *op. cit.*
[6] *Ibid.*

we can conclude with any certainty that the laws of prenatal development apply to development throughout all the life stages, we must demonstrate that they do. But in an area so complex as that of human behavior, it is helpful to have ideas that serve as guides to research—that suggest what we should look for. Let us look, then, at some of these broad generalizations about the developmental process in the earliest period of life.

The broadest of all of the statements that can be made is that development is a process of *actualizing potentialities.* This inevitably involves progressive limitations on what is possible. The process begins with fertilization itself. Of the millions of sperm cells, each with the genetic basis for the development of a unique individual, only one succeeds in fertilizing an ovum and thus getting the developmental process started. At the time of the first cell division and for a little while after that, each cell has the potentiality for development in any specialized direction. Within a few days this equipotentiality has disappeared, and specialization has set in. By the time of birth, the inexorable ongoing process of patterned change has given the person a unique neurological and chemical structure which will limit in all later years the kind of psychological traits he can acquire. From infancy to old age, each developmental period in postnatal life can be viewed as part of the process of progressive limitation of the individual that must occur if potentialities are to be transformed into realities.

The second broad general principle that can be drawn from studies of prenatal life is that development involves progressive *differentiation of parts,* each of which has an increasingly specific function. Coghill's studies and the others that corroborate them have stressed the fact that differentiation is always matched by integration. The unity of the organism is maintained throughout all the successive changes, and the differentiation consists in the emergence of partial patterns within the total pattern. The parts of a living creature, either its structures or its functions, are never independent of one another. They are always organized. The structure that is primarily responsible for maintaining such organization is the central nervous system. There is a pattern in even the earliest developmental stages that insures the predominance of the central nervous system. The well-established "anterior-posterior" gradient, the tendency of the "head end" to develop most rapidly, can be seen as a means of keeping development organized.

The third principle deserving of some emphasis is that activity rather than inertness is what an organism is designed for. Coghill called this concept *intrinsic motivity* and expressed the principle in brief form when he said, "The individual *acts* on its environment before it *reacts to it."* (Italics added.) The muscle cells and the nerve fibers leading to

them are ready for use well before the sense organs necessary to stimulate them come into existence. The most fundamental activity of all, the
beating of the heart, is initiated by factors intrinsic to the organism
before there is any means of activating the heart muscles from outside.
Many kinds of chemical and mechanical changes can lead to apparently
"spontaneous" movements in the fetus. In simple terms, it is natural for
a living creature to be active.

For psychologists who study behavior, a grasp of this principle leads
to a clearer understanding of the effects of extrinsic or environmental
influences on "natural" motivity. It is not simply a matter of presenting
a clear-cut stimulus and observing a definite, invariable response, as
the reasoning centering around reflexes had suggested. At any instant,
what an immature organism will do when we present a stimulus depends upon many things—its level of development, chemical and
physical influences within and external to it, the nature of the stimulus,
how strong it is, and just where it is administered. "Intrinsic motivity"
does not mean that the organism is unaffected by its environment. What
it does mean is that environment supports, maintains, or modifies processes occurring in the organism, but it does not initiate them. The
significance of this kind of thinking for the study of later stages of
human development is something we will return to in subsequent
chapters.

A fourth principle related to this one has to do with the crucial importance of timing in developmental change. During the early period
when change is most rapid, even a few hours may make a tremendous
qualitative difference in what happens as a result of some environmental change. In vertebrates at the critical stage when the development
of the neural tube shown in Figure 12 is the center of the most rapid
growth processes, X-rays, changes in temperature, chemical poisons,
or mechanical interference result in the production of organisms with
a defect called spina bifida, divided spine. The same influence, coming
at a later stage when the front part of the brain is the center of rapid
development, does not affect the spine at all but produces instead the
defect called cyclopia, a single abnormal eye in place of the two normal
ones. Experimental study of all kinds of developmental abnormalities
in the lower forms of life has made it abundantly clear that when
an environmental change is introduced is as important as what the
change is.

The other more positive aspect of this time principle is what Carmichael has called the law of anticipatory function. "Functional capacity may be demonstrated experimentally in many action systems of the
growing organism well before the time when the function in question
is normally called upon to play an active and significant part in the

vital economy of the organism." [7] In the case of the human individual, all of the structures needed to carry on the essential activities after birth are completely shaped by the twenty-fifth week of prenatal life, fifteen weeks before the fetus must normally meet the challenge of independent existence. Experiments have shown that a fetus is able to move in response to a touch on the skin by the eighth week. Normally it does not use this capacity until the fourteenth, and the mother does not feel movement occurring until the eighteenth week. Similar findings characterize the other systems of the body that have been studied.

The psychologist interested primarily in the later developmental periods might well ponder these principles with regard to timing. In thinking about the effects of environmental change on the course of psychological development, the matter of *when* the change occurs should always be considered. It may make a difference, for example, whether an enrichment of the environment designed to stimulate intellectual growth comes at the preschool or at the high school years. We need to know much more than we do about *optimum* time relationships in postnatal development. What the awareness of the importance of this timing principle in prenatal life can do is to alert us to possibilities we might otherwise miss in the planning and interpretation of research.

This excursion into the complex field of prenatal development has been designed to remind us that life does not begin at birth, to show us how the structures and physiological systems on which all experiences and activity depend come into existence, and to make us aware of general developmental principles that may be applicable to the subsequent stages as well as the early ones. There is perhaps one other purpose it can serve. One who considers the course of development can hardly fail to be impressed with the patterned orderliness in all of its complexity. It is such patterns for which we are searching in scientific psychology. Consideration of them gives us hope that order and intelligibility can be achieved in all of the sciences concerned with human life.

SUMMARY

Prenatal life can be divided into three periods—germinal, embryonic, and fetal. Most of the essential structures are formed during the embryonic period which lasts through about the sixth week.

Differentiation of identical cells into separate parts arises through

[7] L. Carmichael. Ontogenetic development. In S. S. Stevens (Ed.), *Handbook of experimental psychology*. New York: Wiley, 1951, p. 292.

environmental changes that occur inevitably as cells grow and multiply. The body is an organized system in which the development of one part affects all the others. The nervous system, the principal structure by means of which integration is accomplished, originates in the neural plate that develops into the neural tube. The brain begins to develop very early and very rapidly.

The basis of behavior, or response to stimulation, is spontaneous activity. The muscles are the first part to develop of the system on which actions are based. The heart begins to beat spontaneously during the third week. Nerve cells and sense organs become connected with muscle cells at a later stage. Integrated activity of the whole organism is more fundamental than specific activities of single parts.

Even by the fourteenth week the human fetus is capable of a wide variety of behavior, although the mother does not ordinarily feel the child's movements until the eighteenth week, and an infant born younger than twenty-seven weeks usually does not survive.

General principles of development useful to psychologists as a source of hypotheses are: (1) progressive limitation as potentialities are actualized; (2) progressive differentiation; (3) intrinsic motivity; (4) the importance of timing; and (5) anticipatory function.

AN EMBRYOLOGIST'S VIEW OF LIFE AND ITS MEANING

CORNER, George W. *Ourselves unborn: an embryologist's essay on man*. New Haven: Yale Univ. Press, 1944.

Each year Yale University invites some eminent scientist to give the Terry lectures, a series set up to attempt to build the "truths of science and philosophy into the structure of a broadened and purified religion." The three lectures Dr. Corner gave are what make up this beautifully written volume. The first gives a much more detailed account of prenatal development, particularly the very earliest stage of it, than we have presented in this chapter. The second explains in detail what happens in cases where something goes wrong with the natural course of development and an abnormal specimen is produced. The third considers the characteristics that make man human and the nature of his relationship to other species.

CHAPTER 5

*What three main kinds of structure are needed to make possible the adjust-
ment to conditions in the outside world?*

What does a muscle do that produces a movement?

What is the general function of a sense organ?

What is the physiological basis for sensations of warmth? cold? pain?

In what ways is the eye like a camera? How is it different?

*Why can a faint star often be seen better if you look a little to one side of
it rather than directly at it?*

How can a person tell the direction from which a sound comes?

How does a person distinguish between different colors? different tones?

»»»»»»»»»»»

Basic Structures and How They Work

IT IS AN AWE-INSPIRING thought that the tiny, seven-pound newborn baby already has in his small body the basic structures that he will need to carry him through the seventy or more years of his life. In the nine months inside the uterus, cells have divided and redivided, changing their specialized characteristics as they multiplied. One system of related parts after another has been readied for use. The heart beats, the lungs are prepared to begin their unceasing inhalation and exhalation, the digestive organs are in place, and the mouth structures are ready to suck and thus pull in nourishment.

A full account of all the basic anatomical structures and physiological systems upon which life depends is far beyond the scope of a text in psychology. The structures upon which psychologists concentrate their major attention are those that are involved in the two aspects of life which constitute their special field of study—experience and activity. Thus their special interest is in the muscular and glandular structures needed for bodily responses, the sense organs by means of which energies from the outside world impinge upon the person, and, above all, the nervous system that is the body's complex communication system.

EFFECTOR ORGANS—MUSCLES AND GLANDS

As has been explained in the previous chapter, the parts of the body needed to produce movement develop very early. What are the essen-

87

tial features of these *effector* organs (so-called because they are the ones that produce the *effects* on other structures, things, or people)?

Muscles are of three kinds. *Striped* or *striate* muscles are attached to the bones. They are made up of fibers all of which run in the same direction. Because fibers made of a darker substance alternate with those of a lighter substance, the whole muscle has the striped appearance that gives it its name. These are the muscles we can see beneath the skin, and can contract voluntarily. They are often arranged in pairs

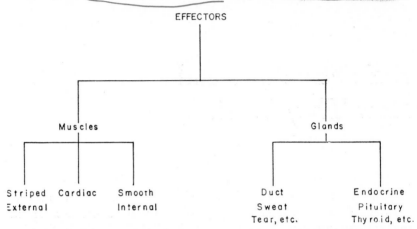

FIGURE 16.   Diagram showing main types of effector organs.

called *antagonistic* muscles in such a way that a contraction in one is accompanied by a stretching of the other. The biceps and triceps muscles of the upper arm with which most of us are familiar constitute such a pair. When one flexes his arm at the elbow and contracts the biceps muscle, the triceps stretches accordingly. When both antagonistic muscles are contracted at once the state we feel as muscular tension is produced.

The second group consists of the *smooth* muscles of the internal organs and blood vessels. They are made up of much smaller fibers that form a compact network capable of a more elaborate pattern of contraction than that of the striped muscles. An organ like the stomach, that carries on its job of reducing food to a semiliquid condition by means of a combination of chemical and mechanical action, would be greatly handicapped if it were equipped only with muscles like the biceps where all the fibers run the same way so that the muscle as a whole can contract in only one direction. These smooth muscles in the wall of the stomach and other internal organs have their fibers arranged in a way that enables them to contract in a circular fashion in order to carry on their special work.

The third kind, _cardiac muscles_, are of less importance to psychologists, as they are found only in the heart. They look like striped muscles but function like smooth muscles. As has been mentioned in the previous chapter, these muscles begin to function spontaneously before there are any nerve fibers through which they can be stimulated. After such nerve fibers have developed and made contact with them, the heart-beat may be quickened or slowed by stimulation from the outside, but the basic rhythmic beating is self-stimulated.

Muscles are designed to produce alternate contraction and relaxation. The most obvious effect of the contraction is to shorten the muscle and produce a movement of some part of the body. It is possible, however, for a muscle fiber to contract without shortening. When this happens the effect is like that of a stretched piece of elastic or violin string, an increase in _tension_. A certain level of tension needs to be maintained in order to make skilled movements of the striate muscles possible.

The other broad class of effector organs consists of the glands. These are little organs whose function is to manufacture and secrete various chemical substances that the body needs. Glands are of two kinds, the _duct glands_ that have special outlets and serve a comparatively local function, and the _ductless_ or _endocrine glands_ that discharge secretions called _hormones_ directly into the blood stream. Thus they are carried all over the body, where they exercise a widespread effect upon growth and behavior.

Among the most familiar of the duct glands are the _sweat glands_, with their outlets leading to the surface of the skin; the _salivary glands_, with ducts opening into the mouth; the _tear glands_ that provide moisture for the eye; the _kidneys;_ and the _sex glands_, as well as many glands in the stomach and intestines by the action of which the chemistry of digestion is carried on. Since each of these glands has a highly specialized work that is carried on in a circumscribed area of the body, they are, by comparison, easy to study and their functions are fairly well understood.

But the ductless glands which make up what is often called the _endocrine system_ are in a very different category. Only during recent years has science begun to grope its way toward some fragmentary and not-too-certain knowledge of the part played by these glands in the regulation of growth and behavior. That their role is both extensive and profound is evident when something happens to interfere with or change their normal functioning. The results of such a defect may be so dramatic or so bizarre that it is not surprising to find writers of sensational fiction developing fantastic plots of the Dr. Jekyll and Mr. Hyde variety by unwarrantably exaggerating some new development in glandular therapy. Nevertheless, in this case the truth may be even

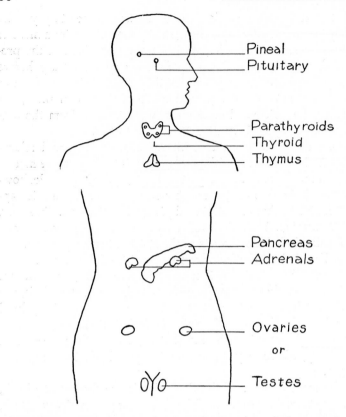

FIGURE 17.   Diagram showing the location of the most important endocrine glands.

stranger than fiction. Let us consider just a few of the physical anomalies resulting from malfunction of these glands. There is the midget who at maturity may be no taller than the normal infant of six months, or the giant who may reach a height of well over eight feet. Both these conditions are believed to be mainly due to malfunctioning of the anterior lobe of the *pituitary gland* (see Figure 17), the former resulting from lack of the normal amount of the secretion, the latter from an excess. The bearded lady of circus fame is in all probability suffering from excessive activity of the *cortex* or outer surface of the *adrenal glands* situated, as shown in Figure 17, just above the kidneys. The fat lady in the next booth likewise owes her pay check to her glands. In her case, several different glands are likely to be involved.

Occasionally an infant is born in whom the *thyroid gland* at the top of the larynx in the throat is largely or wholly inactive. If nothing is done about it, such a child will develop into what is known as a *cretin*.

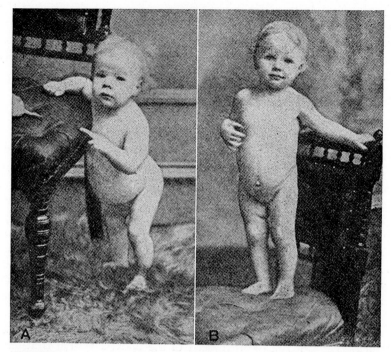

FIGURE 18.   A cretin before and after four months' treatment with thyroid powder. (From H. O. Nicholson, *Archives of pediatrics*, Vol. 17, 1900.)

Its mental level will be that of an idiot, its body stunted and malformed. (See Figure 18.) But if thyroid extract is administered in the proper dosage early enough an amazing transformation may be brought about. The pot-bellied, helpless dwarf becomes a normal, active child and remains so as long as the treatment is continued. But deprive him of his daily allotment of thyroid and in a very short time the magic will have departed and the child will again become a misshapen idiot.

The endocrine glands are important to psychology in two ways. For one thing, they constitute a complicated chemical system by means of which the functioning of the whole organism is regulated and integrated. The *relations between* the activity of the different glands has come to seem more and more important as research has progressed. In particular, the pituitary gland has a complex influence on all of the others. Many medical and psychological conditions that were once unintelligible can now be understood in terms of some malfunctioning of the glandular system as a whole, even where the specific symptoms are not so obvious as in the case of the bearded lady or the fat lady in the circus mentioned above.

In the second place, glandular differences may underlie some of the more or less persisting individual differences in personality or temperament that we encounter in people. Evidence on both these topics —the integrative action of the endocrine system and the personality differences correlated with glandular differences—will be considered in later chapters.

RECEPTOR ORGANS—THE SPECIAL SENSES

Along with the effector organs by means of which actions are carried out, the human being has a large number of specialized receptors. As would be inferred from this name, these are designed to receive or pick up different kinds of energy and transform it into nerve impulses. Anatomically, each sense organ consists of the finely branched endings of a sensory nerve together with the specialized cells in which these nerves usually terminate. Each sense organ can be aroused by one, and as a rule by only one, kind of physical event. We cannot see with our ears or hear with our eyes or smell with the taste buds in the mouth. Since each sense organ has its own particular set of afferent neurons which run to a particular part of the brain or spinal cord and there make synaptic connections with association neurons and with the motor nerves that run to other parts of the body, a system is at once provided for making a kind of preliminary classification of neural activity in terms of the particular sense organ in which it originated. For example, if the nerve impulse comes in to the central nervous system over the nerves that run from the touch receptors in the skin on the back of the left hand, the only thing that can have happened to produce that effect is a touch on the skin at the point in question. But if those sense organs could be stimulated by any one of half a dozen different things, if they were sensitive alike to touch, to light, to sound waves, to pin prick, to cold, or to heat, the organism could not make useful adaptations to changes in the world about it because it would have no way of distinguishing them. The limitation of sensitiveness in a given sense organ to a particular kind of external condition is thus a very great advantage to the organism as a whole because it provides a means by which appropriate responses can be made in terms of the particular nerves over which the stimulus was received. The sensory apparatus as a whole may thus be looked upon as a very elaborate and delicate sorting machine by means of which events going on both without and within the body are classified.

In addition to the sensitive tissue and the neuron endings within it, many of the sense organs are also equipped with special parts or accessories that serve to bring them into better contact with the environmental conditions to which they respond. The eye, with its eyelid to protect it from injury, its muscles for turning it about, and its many other special parts which will be described later, is an outstanding example. The amount of accessory apparatus varies greatly from one organ to another. Moreover, the whole organism may respond to a faint or confusing sensation by doing certain things that bring a particular sense organ into better relationship to the outside stimulus. We walk toward the source of a faint sound, we pick up a small object and hold it at the distance at which it can be seen most clearly, we move our fingers over objects in order to intensify and clarify the touch sensations. Almost any part of the body can be temporarily drafted into the service of one or more of the sense organs.

Sensations are aroused by *changes* or *differences* rather than by constant conditions. As long as the oxygen supply in the air does not vary beyond a certain limit, we are not conscious of its existence. But reduce it below this limit, and sensation definitely begins. We do not feel the circulation of blood as long as it proceeds in a normal fashion, but let some local area be constricted, so that there is interference with the circulation in that area, and the resultant pressure of the accumulating fluid upon the surrounding tissues is immediately perceived. If all light waves were of the same length we should not know color.

The fact that a change in the stimulating condition is necessary for the arousal of sensation is demonstrated in many phenomena with which we are all familiar. There is, for example, the principle of *adaptation,* whereby we become so used to a condition that we no longer notice it or make overt reactions to it. There is also the principle of *contrast* whereby a given sensation seems to be much stronger or more noticeable if it occurs in close proximity to another that is very different. The change from prenatal to postnatal life is essentially a change from an environment of great constancy and few demands for sensory and motor adjustments to one of great variability with many demands for adjustment.

There are sense organs that are stimulated by conditions within the body as well as those that are sensitive to conditions in the external world. If this were not so, we should not have aches and pains to warn us of indigestion or fatigue; we could not tell when our jaws were moving or whether our elbows were straight or bent without looking to see or touching them with our fingers.

All the organic senses—hunger, internal pain, and so on—seem to function actively from the time of birth, and we may infer from this that their sense organs reach complete or nearly complete functional development before birth. The receptors for these senses are sometimes grouped together under the name *interoceptors.* They consist chiefly of sensitive nerve-endings located in the internal membranes. They require little accessory apparatus. If we may judge from his behavior, the newborn baby feels stomach-ache as keenly as we do, the chief difference being that he has not learned to know what is the matter with him.

A second group of internal receptors are known as the *proprioceptors*. These consist of nerve-endings located within the muscles, tendons, and joints. They are stimulated by movements of these parts. Through them we have what is commonly known as the "muscle sense" by which

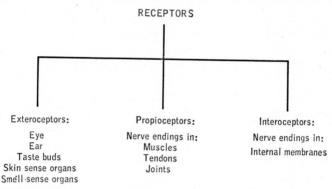

FIGURE 19.   Diagram showing main types of receptor organs.

we know the position of the different parts of the body without having to look. These, too, probably reach complete or nearly complete development before birth, but, as with other sensations, the baby has to learn to interpret them. He probably gets much the same sensation from crooking his elbow that we do, but he does not know what it means or from what part of his body it comes.

The third group of sense organs, known as the *exteroceptors*, are sensitive to environmental conditions outside the body. They include a series of "skin senses" located within the skin all over the surface of the body, the senses of smell, taste, hearing, and sight, and the less well-recognized sense of head-position through which we are able to maintain bodily balance.

THE SPECIAL SENSE ORGANS

1. The Cutaneous Senses

Until the latter part of the nineteenth century, scientists as well as laymen used to speak of the "five senses" as making up all the sense-equipment of the body. Under the "sense of touch" they grouped all four of the cutaneous senses—cold, warmth, pain, and touch—as well as the organic and muscular sensations. We now know that the four cutaneous senses are just as distinct as sight and hearing. They have different sense organs whose activity is transmitted to the central nervous system over different nerve fibers, and they do not feel the same to us. A cool breeze yields a very different kind of sensation from a pin-prick; a feather touching the skin does not feel like a hot iron. The reason the skin senses were formerly confused is that their sense organs are not conspicuous like the eye, and are so near together in the skin that they are often stimulated simultaneously. Thus the separate sensations are often hard to distinguish. It can be shown that the skin senses really are separate from each other if the skin is explored with instruments so small that they are not likely to come into contact with more than one sense organ at a time.

One interesting finding is that the temperature senses, both for warmth and for cold, have variable thresholds (points at which sensation begins to be aroused) dependent on the temperature of the skin. Hold your right hand for a few minutes in a basin of very cold water, your left in a basin of hot water. Then plunge both into a basin of tepid water. To the right hand the water will feel warm; to the left hand, cold. "Cold," as we experience it, really means "colder than the skin"; "warm" means "warmer than the skin." The condition that stimulated the temperature senses is not absolute warmth or cold as shown by a thermometer but a difference between the skin temperature of the moment and the temperature of the air or the object that comes into contact with the skin. In most parts of the body, a difference of as little as 1° Fahrenheit will arouse one or the other of the temperature senses. If the skin is the warmer of the two, the sense organs of cold will be stimulated; if the skin is cooler, the warm spots will be aroused to action.

This concept of *adaptation level*, as it affects many kinds of judgments a person makes about the characteristics of the world around him, has come to seem increasingly important in other areas also as psychological research has continued. In order to understand how a stimulus appears to a person, we must know something about the kind of experience that has *preceded* the one in which are interested. For some kinds of judgment, much previous experience is involved in the person's adaptation level.

For the most part, the organs of the cutaneous senses consist of finely branching nerve-endings in the layer of the skin just below the cuticle or outer skin. There has been a good deal of research effort devoted to a search for other structures in the skin and tissues below it that serve as receptors for the separate senses. If there are such specialized organs in addition to the nerve-endings themselves, as yet there is no agreement as to just what they are.

2. Smell

The receptors for smell are located in a small cavity far back in the nose. They are stimulated by tiny gaseous particles of certain substances dissolved in the air. In spite of long effort, no psychologist has yet succeeded in working out a wholly satisfactory system for classifying odors, although Henning's grouping into six main classes—fragrant, etherial, resinous, spicy, putrid, and burned—has attracted most attention. Undoubtedly, a large share of our adult liking or disliking for certain odors is based mainly upon experience, and in our attempts to classify olfactory sensations we are hampered by an unconscious effort to associate the odor with the thing to which it usually belongs and to make our classification conform to what we know about odors, rather than just the qualities of the odor itself.

In many lower animals, smell is the most highly developed of the senses. But in man it is of much less importance than vision or hearing. This is perhaps the main reason that much less is known about it. It is not clear as yet just how the receptors in the nose are activated or what the primary odors are.

3. Taste

The organs of taste are called *taste buds*. They lie near the bottom of little pits extending down from the surface of the tongue. In the adult and in the older child the taste buds are chiefly confined to the extreme tip, the edges, and the rear part of the tongue, though there are a few on the soft palate and in the back of the throat. The early distribution of taste buds is very different. At birth and during the latter part of fetal life they are found on the inner surface of the cheeks, all over the tongue, in the throat, on the lips, and even in the larynx. Later on they become localized and increase in number within the areas in which they occur. Thus a much larger area of the infant's mouth is sensitive to taste stimuli than is that of the adult. Whether or not the infant's taste is more acute we cannot say, but experiment has shown that the taste buds are sensitive at birth.

Taste sensations are much fewer in kind than most people suppose. Most of what we regard as taste is really smell. Blocking the nasal passages so that no air can pass through them causes most of the characteristic flavors of food to disappear. Every one has noticed that a bad cold in the head which produces partial obstruction of the nasal passages makes all food taste very much alike. This is not a direct effect of the cold, but occurs because the cold interferes with the sense of smell. Careful investigation has shown that there are only four distinct taste sensations: sweet, sour, salty, and bitter. In the adult or older child sweet tastes come chiefly from the tip of the tongue, sour from the sides, salty from the tip and from the sides, and bitter from the upper surface of the back part of the tongue.

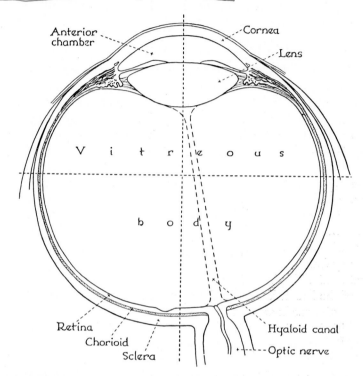

FIGURE 20.   Transverse section through the equator of the left eye seen from above.

4. Sight

The senses that have the most elaborate apparatus are sight, hearing, and the apparatus in the inner ear by which we maintain balance. All these are very precocious; their development is well-nigh completed at birth.

The eye, which, as we all know, is the organ of sight, is constructed much like a camera. (See Figure 20.) The sensitive nerve-endings in the *retina* correspond to the sensitized plate or film on which the image is projected. In the front of the eye are two strong lenses, the *cornea* and (back of this) the *crystalline lens,* which bend the rays of light as they enter the eye and bring them to a focus on the retina. In the ordinary camera it is necessary to adjust the focus for near and distant objects by changing the distance between the lens and the sensitive plate; in the eye this is done automatically by means of a little muscle, called the *ciliary* muscle, that changes the curvature of the lens as needed.

On the outside, the eyeball is covered with a strong white membrane called the *sclerotic coat* or *sclera;* it is this that we ordinarily speak of as the "white of the eye." The sclerotic coat is lined with a second membrane whose purpose is to absorb any stray light rays that may happen to penetrate the eye except through the pupil. This coat is black in color and is known as the *choroid coat.* The sclerotic and the choroid coats extend all the way around the eye except for the region in the front that is occupied by the transparent cornea, underneath which the choroid coat is replaced by the *iris,* or colored portion of the eye. The iris is like a colored curtain with a circular hole in the middle, known as the pupil of the eye, through which light is admitted. The cornea in front of the pupil and the crystalline lens behind it together focus the rays of light so that an image of the object from which they are reflected is formed on the retina. Without the lenses we could distinguish light from darkness, but we could not see the forms of objects. It would be like exposing a photographic plate outside the camera. The whole thing would be darkened but there would be no picture.

The eyeball is filled, both before and behind the lens, with a transparent semifluid substance that keeps it in shape. The part that lies in front of the lens is known as the *aqueous humor,* that which lies back of it the *vitreous humor.*

The iris is equipped with a series of little muscles that regulate the size of the pupil and hence control the amount of light that enters the eye. They correspond to the diaphragm of a camera. You have all noticed how the size of the pupil enlarges after having been in the dark for some time and how it contracts on exposure to strong light.

In the retina are the sensitive cells that react to light. These cells are of two kinds, called from their shape the *rods* and the *cones.* (See Figure 21.) They lie at the back of the retina. The layer of retinal cells which is just beyond the rods and cones, next to the choroid coat, contains pigment, and it is thought that the incoming light produces some chemical change in the pigment which stimulates the rods and cones. The endings of the sensory nerve fibers (the optic nerve) enter the bases of both the rod cells and the cone cells.

You know that you see an object most clearly when you look directly at it, although you also see the objects near it fairly well. This is because the part of the retina that lies directly back of the pupil of the eye (called the *fovea*) contains very many cones and no rods at all. The cones are the most sensitive cells; they respond best both to form and

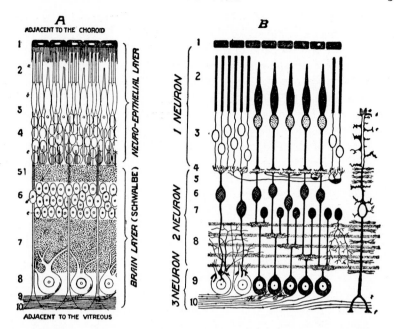

FIGURE 21. Diagram of the human retina, showing the relationships to each other of the retinal neurons and their disposition in the different layers of the retina. The retina may be said to be formed by an expansion of the fibers of the optic nerve which enters the eye from the back, pierces the sclerotic and the choroid coats and spreads out over the inner surface of the eyeball. Ten separate layers can be distinguished under the microscope. These layers are composed of three neurons which form synapses with each other as shown above. The inner layer of the first neuron is the pigmented layer. The second layer is the layer of rods and cones. Synapses between the neurons are made at the fourth and the eighth layers. The tenth layer consists of the fibers of the optic nerve which pass back to the brain. These layers are numbered from the back of the retina inward toward the center of the eyeball. (After Fox's *Opthalmology*.)

color. As you go out from the fovea an increasingly greater number of the cones are replaced by rods. The rods are entirely insensitive to color; however, they respond to changes in light and shade (that is, to form), though not as well as the cones. They have one great advantage over the cones, which is that they become adapted to very dim lights better than the cones do. In deep twilight we cannot distinguish colors at all, because the rods and not the cones are functioning at that time. Color-vision is purely a function of the cones.

The physical basis of visual sensation is the activity incited in the visual apparatus by light waves. Generally speaking, differences in the apparent brightness of light correspond to differences in the energy of these waves as they strike the eye, but other factors, both in the character of the waves and in the organism itself, also affect brightness sensations. Not all the waves known to exist, but only those falling within the range of 380 to 780 millionths of a millimeter (commonly written as 380 $\mu\mu$. to 780 $\mu\mu$.) in length, are seen by us as light. The human organism has no sense organs that respond directly to the waves immediately outside this range, but man's ingenuity has nevertheless turned some of them to practical use and in so doing has greatly extended the effective range of our sensory powers. An outstanding example of this is seen in broadcasting, which makes use of waves too long to affect the visual organs or to be felt as heat and even longer than the atmospheric waves that constitute the physical basis for hearing. At the other extreme we have the ultra-violet waves that we neither see nor feel but which affect the pigmentation of the skin, causing it to tan, and produce other changes in the organism making for better general health and resistance to infections. Still shorter than these are the X-rays that have been made to serve so many valuable purposes in physical and medical science. In spite of the fact that all these waves fall outside the range of our unaided perception, they may nevertheless be reckoned among the most valuable of our "natural resources," although their very existence would forever have remained unknown to us were it not for that greatest of all resources, the mind of man.

Ordinary uncolored light (as daylight) consists of a mixture of waves of all lengths within the visible spectrum. When this mixture is broken up into groups of more nearly uniform length, we see color. The longest visible rays (780 $\mu\mu$.) give a sensation of red; the shortest (380 $\mu\mu$.) a sensation of violet. The other colors are spread out between them in the order in which they appear in the rainbow or *spectrum*.

In all studies of color sensations it is important to distinguish between the color of objects, which is due to reflected light, and the color of radiant light itself. Object-color results from the absorption of light rays of certain lengths by the surface of the objects so that only those *not* absorbed are reflected back to the eye. It is therefore a subtractive process. The direct mixture of light rays of different lengths is an additive process. It is possible to take light waves of known length and, by combining them in the proper proportion, make white light out of a number of colored lights. One cannot do this by mixing the corresponding pigments because the two processes, although at first thought they may seem the same, are actually very different.

There is a vast literature on all aspects of the visual process. Physicists, physiologists, and psychologists have all made contributions. We shall consider some of the special problems that have interested psychologists, problems centering around visual *perception,* in later chapters.

5. The Senses of Hearing and Bodily Equilibrium

Sound is caused by waves or vibrations in the external air (or other mediums, such as water). Roughly, we perceive as sounds vibrations that occur at the rate of 20 to 20,000 per second, the slower vibrations with longer wave lengths producing sounds that are low in pitch, and the faster, shorter vibrations producing the high pitches.

The difference between musical tones and noises is due to differences in the character of the sound waves. Musical tones come from waves that are regular and even; noises, from waves that are broken and irregular in sequence. Pure tones result from waves that have a simple and uniform pattern, with each wave like the preceding one; complex tones from waves that have a more complicated though rhythmic pattern, with little waves superimposed upon or interspersed between the larger ones. But strictly pure tones are rarely heard because any material substance tends to vibrate not only as a whole but also in parts. Careful observation of a violin string when it is lightly bowed will reveal this tendency to vibrate in halves or thirds in addition to the fundamental vibration of the whole string. These partial vibrations produce faint complementary sounds which are higher in pitch than the fundamental and hence are known as overtones. The differences in tonal quality, or timbre, by which we are able to distinguish one musical instrument from another, are the result of the variations in the form of the sound waves caused by the number and character of the overtones.

The ability to localize sounds depends in part upon the relative intensity of the sounds at the two ears and in part upon differences in phase, that is, the fact that the crests of the sound waves entering the two ears will not exactly coincide in time, hence the successive stimulations of the auditory sense organs will occur at different intervals. We learn to translate these differences in intensity and in phase into terms of localization at the right or left of the body. If our own positions in space were fixed, if we could not turn our heads or move our bodies, we should only be able to tell when a sound was at the right or at the left. We could get no information about whether it came from above or below, from the front or from the rear. But by moving our heads in various ways we are able to vary the sound effects so as to receive a very complex system of cues by which the direction of the sound waves can be judged. Children learn to do this very early in life. Before the end of the first year the infant will promptly turn toward the unseen source of a sound or cock his head this way and that in attention to a faint or unusual sound. Through repeated experiences of this kind the art of localizing sounds is learned.

Like the eye, the ear accomplishes most of its growth before birth. This is particularly true of the parts of the ear that lie inside the head. The shell-like structure on the outside is not an essential part of the

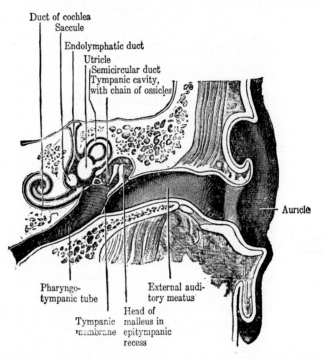

FIGURE 22. **Diagram of parts of the human ear.** (Reproduced in Olof Larsell, *Anatomy of the nervous system.* New York: D. Appleton-Century Co., Inc., 1942, from Cunningham, *Textbook of anatomy.* London: Oxford University Press.)

ear but only an accessory that in many animals is useful for collecting and directing the sound waves inward toward the real hearing apparatus. In man the external ear has lost most of its usefulness except as a partial protection from dirt and insects.

Within the head are the real organs of hearing. Extending inward from the external ear is the canal leading to them. In the adult, this canal is a little more than one inch in length. Across the inner boundary of the canal is stretched a membrane known as the *tympanic membrane* or eardrum. When the sound waves reach this membrane, they cause it to vibrate, and this vibration is passed on to the nerve cells in the inner ear by means of a chain of three little bones known as the ossicles that are hung across the middle ear in such a way that the vibration is concentrated upon a small opening between the middle and inner ears. (See Figure 22.) The inner ear is filled with a salty fluid, and this fluid is set in vibration by the vibration of the ossicles.

Besides the special apparatus for hearing, the inner ear contains the apparatus for the sense of static equilibrium or, as it is sometimes called, the sense of head-position. This apparatus consists of three semicircular canals lying nearer the outside of the head and somewhat higher up than the part of the inner ear in which the sense cells for

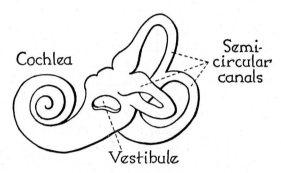

FIGURE 23.   A second view of the inner ear, showing arrangement of the semicircular canals and the cochlea.

hearing are located. As can be seen in Figure 23, these canals lie in three different planes, corresponding to the three plane surfaces that make up a solid right angle like that on the corner of a cube. In addition to the canals there is a rounded cavity called the *vestibule* from which the canals open. Both the vestibule and the canals are filled with fluid and are equipped with receptor cells that end in fine hairs sticking up into the fluid. When the head is turned in any direction the hairs bend and the fine sensory nerve-endings that lie at their bases are stimulated. The fact that the canals lie in three different planes means that it is impossible to move the head even slightly in any direction without setting up a flow of liquid in one canal or another, and thus stimulating the nerve-cells. Sensations of this kind are rendered even more acute by reason of the fact that in the vestibule, which is really a part of each of the canals since all open into it at each end, there are entangled in the ends of the hairs little particles of mineral matter called *otoliths,* the purpose of which seems to be that of weighting the hairs so that their bending will stimulate the sensory nerve-endings more strongly.

Back of the semicircular canals the vestibule rolls up into a spiral, shaped much like a snail shell and named from the Latin word *cochlea,* meaning "snail." Within the cochlea is a narrow membrane extending throughout its length, the *basilar membrane.* The membrane contains many thousands of fibers running across it. At one end the membrane is comparatively narrow and the fibers are short and very tightly stretched; at the other end, where the membrane widens out, they are longer and less taut, thus making a structure something like a harp. On the basilar membrane the receptors for hearing are located. These receptors consist of hair cells with the sensory nerve-endings twined about their bases.

Although both the physical properties of sound and the general structure of the inner ear which is the receiving instrument for the sound waves have long been known, the exact manner in which the auditory mechanism works is still uncertain. We know that the actual receptor for sounds is the basilar membrane in the cochlea. It is reasonably certain that what we perceive as *loudness* depends upon the number of sense cells and their associated nerve fibers stimulated at one time. It is less certain just how the differences in the frequency of sound waves produce the differences in *pitch* that we hear. With the development of new techniques of electrical recording of nerve potentials, new and more complex theories as to just what happens in the cochlea are gradually replacing the controversy between opposed theories around which this field of knowledge has been organized.

THE NERVOUS SYSTEM

The great communication system of the body that makes all complex behavior and experience possible is the nervous system. As has been indicated in the previous chapter, it begins to develop very early, and all of its principal structures are available for use at the time of birth, though growth of fibers continues indefinitely.

The first distinction that can be made is between *central* and *peripheral* sections. The central nervous system is made up of the brain and spinal cord and serves to co-ordinate impulses coming in from all parts of the body and to connect them with outgoing impulses. The peripheral part of the nervous system consists of nerves or long bundles of fibers along which impulses coming from and going to various parts of the body travel. *Afferent* nerves (from Latin *ad ferre,* meaning "carry to") are those that carry impulses from the sense organs to the centers in the spinal cord or brain. *Efferent* nerves (from Latin *ex ferre,* meaning "to carry away from") are those that connect with muscles and thus activate movements. Figures 24 and 25 give some idea of what the nervous system is like.

The places where incoming and outgoing nerve impulses are brought together are known as *centers*. Most of them are within the brain and spinal cord, but there are some, called *ganglia*, outside of the cord itself.

These centers that co-ordinate the activity of receptors, nerves, and muscles are of different degrees of complexity. In general, the higher up one goes, the more complex they get. In the spinal cord there are centers for connecting sensory impulses from specific parts

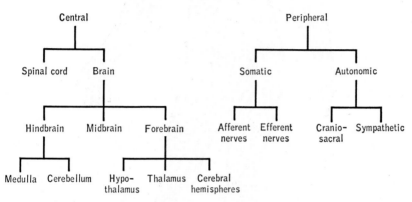

FIGURE 24.   Diagram showing the main divisions of the nervous system.

of the body with motor impulses to those parts, so that what we know as a reflex can occur. For instance, a tap on a certain spot below a person's knee will produce immediately a quick jerk of the leg. Usually even these simple reflexes involve more than the spinal centers. Sensory impulses are passed along up the spinal cord to the centers in the brain stem and brain, and there they can be combined in more complex ways with one another and with electrical activity already in progress in these centers. The *hindbrain* consists of the medulla, with its centers that control breathing, swallowing, heartbeat, and other essential bodily processes and the *cerebellum*, at the back of the head, with centers for body balance and the co-ordination of skilled movements. Deep inside the head, surrounded by other brain structures, is what is called the *midbrain*, made up of what might be thought of as relay stations for the assembling and sorting of all sorts of incoming and outgoing impulses. What is known as the *forebrain* is made up of the *thalamus*, the *hypothalamus*, and the *cerebral hemispheres*. It is in

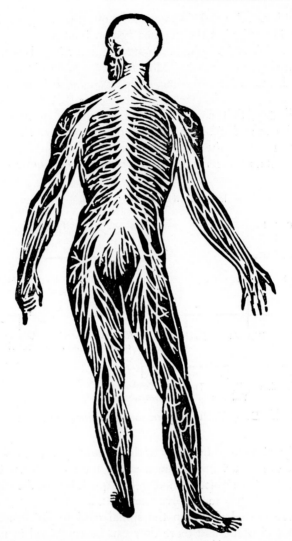

FIGURE 25.   Diagram illustrating the general arrangement of the nervous system. (From Martin's *Human body*. Courtesy Henry Holt and Co.)

this region that the most complex combinations of nervous activity occur, the combinations that make possible learning, remembering, thinking, and emotional experience.

When we analyze in more detail what goes on in the nerves and centers themselves, we find that they are made up of large numbers of individual cells called *neurons*. Each contains a cell body with a nucleus and one or more fibers growing out from it. Some have many such fibers, others only one or two. Some are of microscopic length; others, like those from the spinal cord to the limbs, may be several feet long. Figure 26 shows various types of neurons.

The fibers branching out from the cell bodies can be classified into two types. The *dendrites* are the ones that pick up or receive the nerve impulse from another neuron. The *axons* are the ones that pass on an impulse from one neuron to another or to a muscle cell. The point at which the dendrite of one neuron comes into a functional

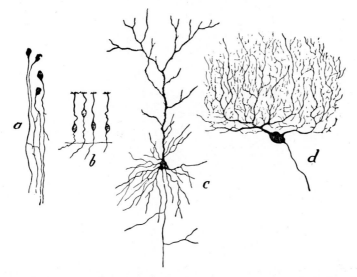

FIGURE 26. Different forms of neurons: *a*, unipolar cell; *b*, bipolar cell; *c*, pyramidal cell; *d*, Purkinje cell. (From Emil Villiger. *Brain and spinal cord.* Courtesy J. B. Lippincott Co.)

contact with the axon or cell body of another is called a *synapse.* (See Figure 27.) The neurons do not fuse with one another. They simply meet in such a way that the electrical current can pass from one to the other. A synapse is like a one-way turnstile; the nerve impulse can pass through it in only one direction. The impulse comes to the synapse over the axon of one neuron and, as a rule, is taken up on the other side by the dendrites of another. In some cases the synapse is made directly on the cell body of the second neuron. A given mental act may involve few or many neurons, but there is reason to think that the number involved is far greater, as a rule, than was formerly supposed.

Let us see how this arrangement works out. One of your sense

organs, let us say an end-organ of touch, is stimulated by some object
touching the skin. The fine endings of the sensory neurons that lie
within it are aroused to action, and the energy thus generated is transmitted along the external branch of the sensory neuron inward
through the cell body and thence, by means of the spinal branch of
the neuron, to the spinal cord. There the neuron endings form synapses
with the dendrites of other neurons. Some of these have axons that run
out to the muscle cells; others are association neurons whose axons

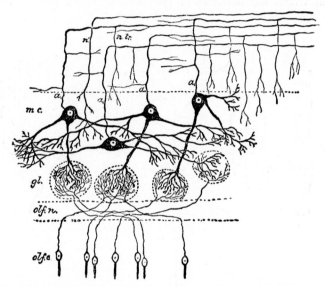

FIGURE 27. Diagram showing synapses between the olfactory nerve
cells located in the nasal mucosa and nerve cells in the olfactory bulb
(an enlargement of the olfactory nerve at the point where it enters the
brain). (From H. E. Jordan. *A textbook of histology.* D. Appleton-Century Co.)

run upward toward the brain. Thus almost simultaneously a number of
things can happen. Sensory areas in the cerebrum are aroused, and as
a result you "know" that you have been touched. Various association
neurons within the cerebral cortex (outer gray portion of the cerebrum) are also aroused, the impulse flashes on to the neurons controlling the muscles that move the eye, and you look to see what it was
that touched you. Now the sensory end-organs within the eye are set
in action, and the impulse is flashed back by way of the optic nerve to
the optical centers in the brain stem. But in order not merely to see
but to understand what you see, associations of many kinds must be
made; and in order that these may be made, neurons in the cerebrum

are again aroused to action. As a result of their action you "recognize" that you have been nudged by a friend, and at the same time realize that he has probably done so for a reason. A fresh set of neurons is now brought into action and by means of a complicated interplay of motor, sensory, and association centers you are enabled to ask him, "What do you want?" Even before this, and probably before you had time to realize that anything had happened, a synaptic connection was made with the motor neurons in direct communication with the part of the body that was originally touched. These neurons at once leaped into action, and as a result the body or some part of it was jerked back automatically without waiting to see whether or not there was need,

All this, just because your friend nudged you with his elbow as a preliminary to borrowing a pencil. Complicated as it sounds, the account given here is unquestionably much simpler than what actually takes place.

We have been using the term *nerve impulse* as though it were comparable to an electrical current flowing along a wire. This is no more than a rough analogy. What happens when a nerve impulse is propagated is a complex change in the nerve fiber with both electrical and chemical aspects. Furthermore, since methods of amplifying and recording faint potentials from different parts of the nervous system have become available, the methods we call *electroencephalography* (EEG), it has become apparent that electric activity in nerve fibers is not a matter of stimulation alone. Complex rhythmic electro-chemical activity is in progress all the time, and new activity arising out of stimulation is assimilated to it. Instead of the analogy of a telephone system that used to be used to explain the working of the nervous system, modern theorists are more likely to refer to the complex electronic computers that have come into use in recent years. Thinking about such computers has led to new ideas about brain processes.

We have been talking largely about the central nervous system. It is important to keep in mind that the peripheral nervous system has two main sections. (See Figure 24.) The *somatic* system (Greek *soma*, meaning "body"), connects with the sense organs and muscles. The *antonomic* system ("self-governing" or "independent") controls the actions of the internal organs over which we have but little voluntary control. Its nerves run to the stomach, the intestines, the heart, the lungs, the walls of the blood-vessels, the ciliary muscles that dilate or contract the pupils of the eyes, the sweat-glands, the liver and other viscera, and the ductless glands. It maintains its connection with the central nervous system by means of a series of neurons with cell bodies in the cord and in the brain stem, neurons that send their axons out to the autonomic ganglia and make synaptic connection with them.

Thus, although it is able to carry on its everyday functions of regulating the vital processes of the body without the direction of the brain, the autonomic system is nevertheless capable of being influenced by brain action, by thoughts, ideas, associations. The student at the start of an important examination may turn pale and perspire; his breath may come quickly and his heart beat faster. All these physical symptoms are the direct result of the action of the autonomic nervous system which comprises the channel through which events in the brain arouse activity in the smooth muscles and glands. So the autonomic nervous system is connected at all points with the central nervous system and works along with it.

The fibers that connect the autonomic ganglia with the central nervous system do not leave the cord in a regular unbroken series, but are divided into three distinct groups: (1) an upper group that has its origin in the brain stem and is known as the *cranial division*, (2) a middle group that runs out from the upper regions of the cord and is known as the *sympathetic division*, and (3) a lower group that emerges from the lower part of the cord and is called the *sacral division*. (See Figure 28.)

The cranial division of the autonomic system is particularly concerned with the process of digestion, the movements of the stomach, the secretion of saliva and of gastric juice. By its action, too, the pupil of the eye contracts and the heart rate is slowed. All this goes along with a calm, relaxed, organic state. The baby who has just been fed drops peacefully off to sleep. When the child who is "hungry and cross" is given food, the crossness usually disappears along with the hunger. It is a stupid wife who has not learned to take advantage of her husband's after-dinner mood.

The fibers of the sacral division run out to the organs that have to do with the removal of waste material from the body. Like the cranial division, they are concerned with processes that make for greater comfort. They also innervate the contractile tissues of the external genitals and thus are actively concerned in sex emotion.

Unlike the fibers of the two foregoing divisions, which run to only a small group of specific organs and in general make for organic states of calmness, peace, relaxation, and pleasure, the nerves from the sympathetic division are widely distributed over the entire body. Wherever they are found, their relationship to the action of the cranial and sacral divisions is antagonistic. The cranial supply to the eye contracts the pupil, the sympathetic dilates it; the cranial slows the heart, the sympathetic accelerates it; the sacral contracts the large intestine and relaxes the exit from the bladder, the sympathetic relaxes

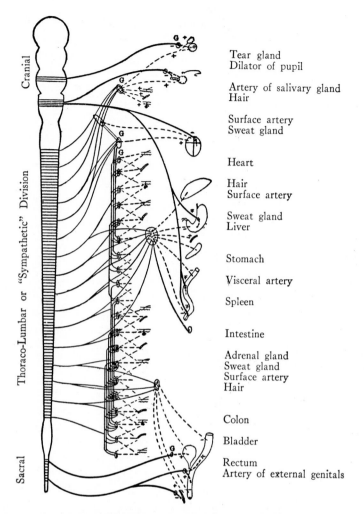

Cranial

Thoraco-Lumbar or "Sympathetic" Division

Sacral

Tear gland
Dilator of pupil

Artery of salivary gland
Hair

Surface artery
Sweat gland

Heart

Hair
Surface artery

Sweat gland
Liver

Stomach

Visceral artery

Spleen

Intestine

Adrenal gland
Sweat gland
Surface artery
Hair

Colon

Bladder

Rectum
Artery of external genitals

FIGURE 28. **Diagram of the more important distributions of the autonomic nervous system.** The brain and spinal cord are represented at the left.
The nerves to skeletal muscles are not represented. The preganglionic fibers
of the autonomic system are in solid lines, the postganglionic in dash lines.
The nerves of the cranial and sacral divisions are distinguished from those
of the thoracolumbar or "sympathetic" division by broader lines. A + mark
indicates an augmenting effect on the activity of the organ; a − mark, a
depressive or inhibitory effect. (From W. B. Cannon. *Bodily changes in pain,
hunger, fear, and rage.* D. Appleton-Century Co.)

the intestine and contracts the exit from the bladder. [1] And the organic states that accompany the action of the sympathetic division are, as might be expected, the opposite of those that go with the activities of the cranial and sacral divisions. Instead of peacefulness, calm, contentment, relaxation, we have excitement, anxiety, restlessness. Moreover the entire sympathetic system is connected up by fibers that run from one ganglion to another (see Figure 28) in such a way that when the system goes into action not one but all the organs which it innervates are affected. Under strong emotion this is very apparent to every one. In extreme excitement the pupils of the eyes dilate, the heart beats fast, the breath comes quickly, the muscles at the base of the fine hairs on the skin contract and the hairs stand erect (this is more easily seen in animals than in human beings), the mouth becomes dry, and perspiration pours out on the skin. The sympathetic discharge is thus seen to be diffuse rather than specific, while the sacral and cranial discharges may affect single organs without inducing any change in others. The process of digestion does not necessarily affect the flow of saliva once the food has been swallowed; the bladder may be emptied without intestinal action. In this connection, Cannon aptly compares the sympathetic system to the loud and soft pedals of a piano which modulate all the notes together, while the sacral and cranial divisions are like the keys, acting either separately or in combination.

We shall have more to say about the functions of the autonomic nervous system in later chapters when we are considering emotions.

It has been possible in this chapter to give only an over-all summary of the structure of the human nervous system as a whole. Because of its complexity, perhaps the schematic diagram shown in Figure 24 will help to keep the details in the right relationship to one another. It includes only the most important of the structures. The total picture is enormously more complicated than this diagram.

SUMMARY

The newborn infant begins his career in the world with a set of structures capable of carrying out all of the complicated activities that life will require of him. They are not yet ready to function in a completely efficient fashion. Growth and learning will modify their functioning and increase their usefulness as he matures. What we can expect of a human being is always conditioned and limited by the nature of these structures that constitute his basic equipment.

---

[1] In co-operation with the action of the central nervous system. Elimination is partially automatic, partially voluntary.

They can be divided first of all into *effectors* (muscles and glands), *receptors* (sense organs), and *connectors* (nervous system). Each of these main types of structure can in turn be broken down into its principal subtypes. Under effectors we have striped muscles and smooth muscles, duct glands and endocrine glands. Under receptors we have the skin senses, smell, taste, vision, hearing, and the organic and muscle senses. Under connectors we have the central and peripheral parts of the nervous system, each with its own important subdivisions.

A BOOK YOU WILL ENJOY

WALTER, W. Grey. *The living brain.* New York: Norton, 1953.

One of the most fascinating new lines of research on the nervous system that has come into prominence in the last two or three decades is electroencephalography, the measurement of electrical activity in the living brain. In this nontechnical book written for the general reader, Dr. Walter tells about these methods and explores some of the theoretical ideas and the practical applications to which they lead.

CHAPTER 6

What is meant by homeostasis, and why has it proved to be such an important idea in psychology?

What happens when a part of the body is injured or exposed to a sudden stress?

What is it about the functioning of the person that gives rise to motives? to emotions?

Is it possible for a person to free himself from emotions entirely?

What are the essential features of the learning process?

Equipment for Living:
Basic Processes

LIFE AS PROCESS

AN EXAMINATION of the structures a human being possesses gives an incomplete picture of his total assets. It is as though we were to attempt to evaluate the skill of a garage mechanic by taking an inventory of the equipment and tools in his shop. It is obvious without demonstration that the skill that enters into the process of repairing an automobile motor is something different from these tools, something that must be described in different terms.

Often the analogies that are used to help students understand what the *structures* of the body are like make it more difficult for them to grasp the meaning of the complex *processes* that occur. The eye is like a camera, we say, and so it is. But the act of perceiving the visual world is quite different from anything that the most complex and elaborate camera does. We say that the nervous system resembles a telephone exchange with its linking of incoming and outgoing messages. But such an analogy is of no use in comprehending what the complex adaptational process of a living organism is like.

Therefore, in this chapter we shall discuss some of the most important processes in which the organism as a whole is involved. They can best be viewed not as the sum of a number of activities going on in separate structures such as the muscles, nerves, and glands, but as things that occur as natural aspects of *life*. Philosophers have argued for centuries about whether living beings differ in kind or only in degree from nonliving organizations of matter. But whatever the ultimate philosophical explanation may be, there is definite scientific evidence that principles in addition to those carried over from physics and chemistry are needed to describe what happens as a living creature carries out its life activities. It is these principles, as applied to the living creature we call man, that we shall attempt to clarify.

Some of the most fundamental of these principles have already been taken up in Chapter 1 and in Chapter 4. Unlike the mechanic's tools or the telephone company's wires and switchboards, the structures of the body *develop* as they function. At different stages they grow larger, differentiate into separate parts, and activate themselves. The capacity for patterned change is a fundamental characteristic of living matter.

HOMEOSTASIS AND RESPONSE TO STRESS

Though it may at first glance look like a contradiction to the previous statement, it can also be said that a capacity for stability, constancy, or *sameness,* is characteristic of living things. It was the brilliant work of the physiologist Cannon (1929) that first called our attention to the process called *homeostasis,* the maintenance of a constant internal state under changing external circumstances.

The nature of the process is perhaps most apparent in the way in which a person adapts to extreme changes in temperature. It is a striking fact, when one begins to consider it, that whether a human being goes to the Arctic regions where the external temperature is 60° or more below zero or to the desert where it may be 120° above, his own body temperature remains very close to the normal 98.6°. How does this come about?

It has become apparent that the maintenance of this steady temperature in the face of environmental changes requires a number of complex, co-ordinated physiological processes. When external cold threatens, the thyroid gland automatically increases its secretion rate. This increases the heart rate and the general level of muscular activity and raises the general metabolic rate so that more energy is obtained from the food that has been eaten. Another group of changes serves to reduce the rate of heat loss from the body. The blood vessels on the external surfaces become smaller so as not to circulate so much blood to the cold regions. The hair on the body erects. (In man this does not help much, but in furry animals it may produce a good insulating coat.) There is a tendency to take a position that will expose a minimum of body surface. (Like the animals to whom he is related, a person who becomes chilled will roll up into a ball if he is in bed, or will fold his arms if he is standing or sitting.)

One of the interesting things about homeostatic mechanisms is that they include *behavior* as part of the same pattern that involves the physiological changes. Shivering and rolling up into a ball are automatic, reflex-like activities that contribute to the general reaction-to-low-temperature pattern. But there are others much more complicated and more directly in the special province of the psychologist. An animal may move to a warmer corner, build a nest, hoard food, increase its food intake, or change its diet. A man may do any of these things and, in addition, may build a fire, turn up the thermostat, or put on a sweater. The behavior is part of the whole process. It is hard to separate the psychological from the physiological.

A number of the homeostatic systems have been intensively studied. There are complicated regulatory mechanisms for keeping the acidity of the blood constant and for maintaining the same blood sugar level. Many organs participate in these organized processes—the pituitary, thyroid, and adrenal glands, the pancreas, the liver, the whole digestive system, the lungs, the heart and circulatory system, and the nervous system. Such processes are among the "givens" of life. A person does not have to will them or to learn them. Cannon, who did the basic research on these processes, called his book about them *The Wisdom of the Body*. [1]

More recently Selye (1956) has demonstrated that there are even more complex, co-ordinated changes that occur when the body is exposed to danger or unnatural conditions—what he calls *stress*—for long periods of time. The same *general adaptation syndrome* occurs whether the stress comes from infection, injury, excessive heat or cold, or nervous strain. There is a temporal pattern to this response, as shown in Figure 29. The first stage is an alarm-reaction, the condition of reduced activity called "shock." The second stage is *resistance*, in which the body mobilizes all its resources to deal with the danger. The third stage is *exhaustion* in which the body gives up and the complete adaptation is lost. It is important to realize, Selye believes, that the organism cannot put up an organized resistance to stress indefinitely.

Selye has also investigated the relationships between the response to a *localized* injury and the general adaptation syndrome of the previous paragraph. There is an intricate series of events involving the pituitary and adrenal glands by means of which *inflammation* at the site of the injury serves to limit it, wall it off from the rest of the body, and get rid of the specific danger, while *anti-inflammatory*

[1] W. B. Cannon. *The wisdom of the body.* New York: Norton, 1939.

hormones that are a part of the general adaptation syndrome keep the inflammation itself from becoming too severe. The best known of these anti-inflammatory hormones is one produced by the adrenal cortex, cortisone, which came to public notice because of its effects on the inflammation of the joints known as arthritis.

The direction research has taken on these hormones represents a profound change in our thinking about bodily processes, a change that should be thoroughly assimilated by all students of human development. It is still natural for us to assume that each organ of the body has its specific purpose, and that they do their separate jobs more or

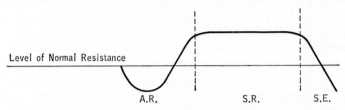

Level of Normal Resistance

A.R.   S.R.   S.E.

FIGURE 29.   Temporal course of general adaption syndrome. (From H. Selye. *The stress of life.* New York, 1956, p. 87. Courtesy of Mc-Graw-Hill Book Company, Inc.) In the acute phase of the alarm reaction (A.R.), the reaction to the stress situation falls below normal. Then adaption begins to occur, and during the stage of resistance (S.R.), the capacity to resist is intensified. If stress continues, the third stage, the stage of exhaustion (S.E.), sets in and resistance drops below normal or ceases altogether.

less independently of one another. It seems sensible to consider each one as a unit, find out what it can do, and treat it by itself if it is not functioning properly. The work on stress has shown that such ideas must be replaced by others that take the *interrelationships* into account. The shift is well illustrated in the case of *cortisone.* When it was first discovered, it was used rather widely as a treatment for arthritis. It soon became apparent that one could not markedly change the concentration of this one adrenal hormone in the body without disorganizing the whole delicate balance between the pituitary and the adrenal glands on which so much adaptational activity depends. Thus many patients after an initial improvement were thrown back into an illness more serious than the one they had at the beginning. For *diseases of adaptation* (the term Selye uses for arthritis, allergies, and a number of other conditions that are essentially complex reactions to stress) the whole adaptational syndrome must be considered when treatment is planned.

We should miss some of the significance of the kinds of processes we have been considering, however, if we thought entirely in terms of *extreme* dangers to the organism. The homeostatic mechanisms are in constant operation, adjusting internal conditions to slight changes in temperature, oxygen, or food composition. Stress can be minor as well as major. To some degree it characterizes all of life. What this means for the psychologist is that he can assume that the person's basic equipment for living is *designed* to meet stress. A living being is in constant interaction with its environment, equipped from the beginning to make highly adaptive organized responses to environmental change.

In fact, some experiments have shown that to be deprived of a large part of the environmental stimulation that is normal for a human being can be a very disturbing experience. College students who were paid to stay in bed for two or three days in isolated cubicles containing almost no sources of stimulation showed decreases on intelligence tests and abnormalities of perception, in some cases even hallucinations. Much as we may sometimes think that we would enjoy being absolutely free from all the stresses of life, such experiments show that we probably would not enjoy it at all. Responding to what goes on around us is as natural and fundamental as breathing.

MOTIVATION

Probably the most interesting of all questions in psychology to most people who study it is the question of motivation. Why do people act as they do? We try constantly to develop a better understanding of the motives of our friends, relatives, and associates. In some professions, such as teaching and social work, some understanding of motivation is essential to the carrying out of the tasks.

Psychologists have often defined motivation as the process by means of which activity is aroused and directed or regulated. If we keep in mind the basic processes of homeostasis and bodily response to stress imposed by an ever-changing external environment, we do not need any special principle to explain how activity is *aroused.* It is inherent in the very conditions of life itself. What psychologists must try to explain is the directedness and specificity of such activity. How does the adult pattern of wishing and striving develop out of the diffuse activity of the newborn infant? Why do different persons wish and strive for different things? Are there some motives universal enough so that it can be assumed that wherever we go anyone we meet will be activated by them?

The words *need, drive, motive, incentive,* and *goal* all are used in discussing motivation, and different authors distinguish them in different ways. Whatever the specific terms are taken to mean, there are three aspects of the whole motivational process that can be differentiated. One aspect is the general state of the organism, always not quite in balance, not quite satisfied. It is this state we were discussing in the previous section. Another aspect is the external substance, object, or environmental change that would serve to satisfy or correct a particular need-state at any given time. The third aspect is the psychological movement that connects the first with the second—the *wish* for some one kind of change in one's surroundings. In talking about the whole motivational process, we will call these three aspects of it *needs, goals,* and *motives.* While it does not constitute a very precise definition, a motive can be thought of as a *wish* for some change in one's surroundings that will satisfy an inner need of some kind.

Naturalists who have observed birds, insects, fish, and other complex nonhuman forms of life have been much impressed with the motivational processes they called instincts. In these species, a complicated pattern of what looks like skillful, purposeful activity arises spontaneously the first time a particular need-state occurs.

For many years most psychologists argued against instinct theories of human motivation on the grounds that there is no one pattern of behavior in any situation that is *fixed* for a human individual. His manner of satisfying his needs for food, for shelter, and for a mate are *learned.* Thus psychologists and biologists have often contrasted instinct with intelligence or learning ability.

More recent research on both the animal instincts and the human learned behavior patterns has led to a reformulation of these ideas. The contrast is not as great as we once thought that it was. What we seem to have are patterns of behavior of different degrees of fixity and susceptibility to change. The basic motivational process is common to all living things. Goal-directed activity in response to internal need-states is another of the "givens" of life. We shall be concerned in all subsequent chapters of this book with tracing the outlines of such activity as it occurs in the successive stages.

If we adopt this basic assumption, that motivation is a part of a person's equipment for living, arising inevitably out of the interchange between organism and environment, it enables us to understand the meaning of *emotions* also. Here, too, there have been many theories and controversies down through the centuries, and sharp contrasts have often been drawn between emotion, on the one hand, and reason, on the other. Better understanding of the underlying physiological conditions has enabled us to realize that a living organism is always in some sort of a "stirred-up" state and thus can be said to have always some sort of emotion. Sometimes the stirring-up is minor enough so that is does not come to conscious awareness and we do not sense any emotion at all. Sometimes, under great stress, we are aware of what we have learned to call a highly emotional state, and we are able to give the experience a name such as excitement, anger, or fear. But emotion as such is not a distinct category of behavior or experience. It is really part of the same ongoing process we have called motivation. When we consider the wishing, striving aspect of this process, we speak of motives and goals. When we consider the feeling aspects of it we call it emotion. Emotion too will be discussed again and again in subsequent chapters.

In our century, Freud and the other psychoanalysts have stressed the fact that all of these basic processes may be going on without conscious awareness. They are more fundamental than consciousness. A person may be striving for goals of which he is unaware and in the grip of powerful emotions which he does not recognize. Thus it is imperative, if we expect to understand ourselves and others, that we realize that psychological processes of the kind we have been outlining do occur, whether or not we sense them in ourselves. The report of conscious experience is a very incomplete indicator of what they are. The lazy schoolboy and the neurasthenic housewife are not *un*motivated. They too are wishing, striving, experiencing emotion. But it may be a complicated and difficult problem to identify the real goal of the striving, the precise quality of the emotion.

LEARNING

There is one other fundamental process that occurs constantly in living organisms and especially in the human being. As has been explained in Chapter 1, the person's basic equipment for living *changes* in accordance with the way it is used. This constitutes another way in which the mechanical analogies to explain anatomical structures are inadequate. Neurophysiologists are convinced that the complex nervous structures are constantly modified as a result of what the organism does in response to stimulating conditions. While it has been difficult to identify just what these modifications are, so that the structural changes are still more a matter of hypothesis than of proof, the changes in *behavior* that come about as a result of learning are everywhere apparent. The experimental investigation of the learning process has been a high-priority activity for psychologists.

Learning is one of those terms the meaning of which everybody understands in a general way but nobody defines very satisfactorily. It refers to changes in behavior that occur over a period of time, but not *all* changes are included. There are developmental or *maturational* changes that come about regardless of what the person's situation has been, or how he has responded to it. An Indian baby who is bound to a cradle board during all the early months of life will walk when he reaches the normal age for walking. Apparently learning is not the decisive factor making for change in this case. There are changes in a person's behavior over a period of time that are due to fatigue, to

FIGURE 30. Ivan Petrovitch Pavlov. (Reproduced from I. Pavlov, *Lectures on conditioned reflexes*, by courtesy of International Publishers, New York City.)

progressive illness, or to drugs. Such changes also do not come under the heading of learning. The gradual wearing out of tissues that occurs in old age does not constitute learning either. Learning is the kind of behavioral change over a long or short period of time that we have left after we have allowed for these other change-producing influences. It is important, too, that many processes of change are *partly* a matter of learning even when maturation, illness, or aging can be shown to be the major factor producing them.

In later chapters, some of the specific kinds of learning will be examined in more detail, as they come into prominence at different stages of development. Here we shall only sketch in broad outline some of the main kinds of behavioral change that are involved. There is, first of all, a constant process of *shifting* of responses already in the person's repertory (either innate reflexes or previously learned responses) to new stimuli and situations. It was this sort of process that the famous Russian physiologist Pavlov brought to our attention as the *conditioned response.* It is natural for a flow of saliva to begin when food enters

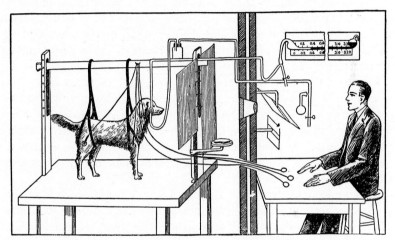

FIGURE 31. Pavlov's arrangement for studying the process of salivary conditioning in the dog. (Reproduced from I. Pavlov, *Lectures on conditioned reflexes,* by courtesy of International Publishers, New York City.)

the mouth. Pavlov found, using dogs as his subjects, that if some other quite irrelevant stimulus, such as a bell or a light, was presented just before the food came, the flow of saliva would soon occur regularly as a response to this stimulus. Figure 31 shows the sort of arrangements Pavlov worked out for investigating this phenomenon. While not many of us are vitally interested in what goes on inside a dog's mouth, we are interested in a large number of learning situations for which this turned out to be a prototype, and thus the conditioning experiment is considered to be a landmark in the history of psychology.

Another main variety of change occurring with learning is a progressive *discrimination* between stimuli and progressive *differentiation* of motor responses. This process has been studied through conditioned response experiments, but there are other ways, as well, of getting at it. We learn not to react in the same way to all loud sounds, but only to certain ones. We learn that only a bell of a certain loudness and pitch means telephone, that another one much like it means a visitor at the door, and that still another one means a child going by on a bicycle. We come to discriminate many thousands of different colors, pitches, and odors. At the same time, the responses our muscles make also become more precise and adaptive.

Still a third main variety of change that occurs through learning can be described most simply as *organization*. The whole process of concept formation involves classifying large amounts of material in a limited number of categories. It is because the human being is equipped to carry on this process so efficiently that he can code and store away such large amounts of information and then produce it when he needs it. But the whole process of organizing experience is much broader than the memorizing of facts. It plays an important part in perceptual learning by means of which we become able to get the meaning of a situation as soon as we see it, as for example, when a highway policeman almost instantaneously grasps the main features of an accident that has just occurred. It also makes for the building up of increasingly complex motor skills, such as typing or ballet dancing. Probably the most basic and important task each human being faces is to organize his own particular psychological world.

When we have analyzed the aspects of learning that result in changing stimulus-response associations, increasing discrimination and differentiation, and organizing one's experience and activity efficiently, there is one other aspect of the learning process that we must still make room for in our outline. Learning produces *new* solutions to problems, *original* inventions, and *creative* achievements. It may be that such novelty or originality is really only a matter of a superior sort of organization. A person's reasoning or problem-solving activity may serve to bring different combinations of things into alignment with one another and thus produce concepts or skills that did not exist before. But whether or not originality and creativity represent a separate kind of learning process, they are an important part of what we must keep in mind when we try to understand learning and the part it plays in the devolpment of a human being.

SUMMARY

Each person comes into the world with some complex basic processes that have already begun to function or will soon be activated. From earliest childhood on they all operate all the time. There are homeostatic systems for maintaining constant internal conditions and automatic reactions of the whole body to stress. The processes of growth and development produce gradual changes in size and shape, in feelings and behavior. The polarization toward and away from various goals—the sum total of which we call motivation—inevitably comes about. In combination with all these other factors, learning immediately begins to produce the habits, concepts, and skills that will enter into everything the person thinks or does.

As we proceed with our psychological study of the successive periods of life we shall often be looking at one of these processes in isolation from the others. But it is important to remember that it never *occurs* in isolation. These things all go on at once. At any one moment what a person does is related to all of them. Keeping this in mind can serve to counteract oversimplification and to prevent error and misunderstanding. Man is a complex creature and we must have complex concepts to enable us to understand him.

A BOOK YOU WILL ENJOY

Selye, Hans. *The stress of life.* New York: McGraw-Hill, 1956.

Dr. Selye not only describes his experiments and outlines the general theory that seems to account for all the findings, he also introduces the reader to himself. He tells us how he came to be interested in this problem and how the ideas developed as the work progressed. At the end he discusses what his work has taught him about the general conduct of life. The style of writing is clear and simple.

PART III

The Principal Life Stages

CHAPTER 7

What distinguishes the period of infancy from all later states of life?

Why do some babies show many more kinds of specific responses immediately after birth than others do?

What is meant by "spontaneous activity" and why is it important?

Is there any relationship between a baby's physical characteristics—his size, his growth rate, etc.—and the psychological characteristics he will develop as he gets older?

What kind of body structures grow most rapidly in the first few months?

How does a six-months-old baby differ from a three-months-old baby in his way of grasping a toy that is held out to him?

What seems to be the motivation for the baby's practice of motor skills like reaching, creeping, and walking?

The First Two Years: Physical and Motor Development

THE PROBLEM OF DEFINING STAGES

ANYONE WHO DISCUSSES development must divide it up in some way in order to talk about it. However this is done, there is an element of arbitrariness about it. In the process itself there are no marked divisions, no signposts that define boundaries between one stage and another or between one kind of psychological process and another. Infancy merges into childhood, childhood into adolescence, adolescence into maturity. Physical development cannot be separated from the growth in motor skills that accompanies it; emotional and intellectual development are interwoven with one another.

Realizing that there are no breaks in development itself, we have placed the arbitrary divisions at points that correspond to differences in the major tasks or challenges faced by the person. As indicated in Chapter 1, there are critical phases for certain processes. They are not so well-marked or perhaps so irrevocable in postnatal psychological development as they are in prenatal physiological development, but they are apparent enough so that they can serve as guides to our thinking.

Viewed in this manner, the first stage is the period during which the human individual progresses from almost complete helplessness to relative autonomy and self-determination. Many writers have called attention to the absolute dependence of the newborn human being on those who care for him. In many other species, the young are able to get about and to meet most of their own needs almost from the start. The human child must go through a developmental process lasting many months before he can do this. It is this fundamental and complex set of changes we shall consider in the next five chapters.

It is obvious that it is only *relative* autonomy that is achieved during this initial period. No human being *ever* becomes completely free from dependence on others; interdependence is characteristic of our species. And certainly during childhood's long years, the care and guidance given a child by his family continue to be tremendously important in his development. But when we compare the condition of the newborn with that of the two-year-old, we can see that the major tasks have been accomplished when the person has become able to eat solid food, to walk, to make co-ordinated movements of all sorts, to speak and understand, and to exercise some control over bodily processes of elimination. Compared with the accomplishments of this two-year period, what is achieved during any later period of life is less impressive. Thus we shall pay particular attention to this early period, important as it is for all the others.

BIRTH—ADAPTING TO THE EXTRA-UTERINE WORLD

The first two weeks after birth are best considered somewhat apart from the general course of development because of the unusual difficulties which must be met at that time. Not only must the child adjust to a change of environment greater than he will ever again meet, but he also has to recover from one of the most difficult and dangerous events of life. Although being born is not only a natural but a necessary part of every child's experience, it is not an easy one. For hours he is subjected to dragging and pushing, to strong compression—particularly of the head, which at this age is the widest and most resistant part of the body.

Because of the hazards of the birth process, a small minority of infants begin life handicapped, unable to meet all its demands. As medical progress has reduced infant mortality, the number of these unfortunate children whose injuries lead to paralysis or mental defect, or both, has increased. Interest in helping such persons (usually classified under the diagnosis of "cerebral palsy") has also been increasing, and the prospects for a satisfying, useful life for such individuals are much brighter than they once were.

However, the vast majority of infants come through the birth experience without permanent ill effects. Temporary effects are probably greater than most psychologists realize. It is likely that for some hours at least, the general mental and physical condition of the newborn child is analogous to that of an older person who has just undergone a major operation, and when labor is unduly difficult or prolonged, or when forceps have been used, several days may elapse before recovery is complete. However normal may be the fact of birth, the newborn child is nevertheless not in a normal condition for some time thereafter.

For this reason it is unsafe to judge the abilities of an infant on the basis of his behavior immediately after birth. The length of time that must elapse before complete recovery from the minor injuries of a so-called normal birth will vary from child to child, but it is safe to say that for the first two or three days at least, and for a longer period when delivery has been unusually difficult, the fact that a child fails to show a given form of behavior must not be taken to mean that he would not be able to show it if his physical condition were normal. Accordingly, the fact that some babies, shortly after birth, are able to yawn, sneeze, bring their hands to their mouths and suck their fingers, raise their heads, and so on, is probably more significant than the fact that not all do so. Success means that the ability has been established; failure may be due to any one of a number of causes. It may be due to more than usually severe birth injury, to premature birth, [1] or to genuine backwardness. It is probable that the hope expressed by some psychologists that the time may come when the intelligence of the newborn may be tested as accurately as we are now able to test the ability of older children will not be realized for many years to come, if at all. Certainly until more accurate methods for determining the real age [2] of the newborn child and for measuring the extent of birth injury have been worked out, it is very unsafe to attempt to predict from his behavior during the first few days of life how a given child is likely to develop later on.

The physiological adjustment that the infant has to make during the first few days of extra-uterine life is very complicated. Evaporation of water from the tissues, together with imperfect nutrition while the new process of digestion is being established, results in a loss of weight

---

[1] Gesell, who has followed the early development of a number of premature infants, has been able to show that in most respects at least the behavior of the child who is prematurely born is retarded during infancy by about the extent of his prematurity. For example, the baby born two months ahead of schedule shows about the same level of mental and physical development at four months after birth as he would have reached at two months had he been born at the usual time. In reality, the child born two months early is a seven-months fetus and should be looked upon as a fetus rather than as a full-grown baby. Cf. Gesell's *Infancy and human growth*. New York: Macmillan, 1928. Ch. XV.

[2] By present methods, age at birth can be determined only within rough limits. The error of estimate may be two weeks or even more unless the date of conception is known. See Chapter 4.

during the first few days after birth. This loss usually amounts to several ounces, and it may be ten days or two weeks before the birth weight is regained. With the taking-on of such new functions as breathing, eating, digesting, and assimilating, numerous changes occur in the internal organs and glands. Still other adjustments are required by the sudden change from a constant temperature of approximately 100° F. to one that is not only much lower on the average but varies within comparatively wide limits, and from uniform protection of all parts of the body to exposure of certain parts while the remainder is kept covered. There are also the new postures and the comparatively rigid means of support in place of resting in a fluid medium and shifting position only at the dictates of its own needs. All this has its psychological as well as its purely physiological aspect, and the adjustments required are not the less important because as yet their exact nature is uncertain.

For all these reasons, much caution must be observed in interpreting the results of experiments carried out with very young infants. Nevertheless, if the points that have been mentioned in the foregoing paragraphs are kept in mind, much that is of great importance may be learned from the study of the abilities shown by the infant as soon as the grosser effects of birth have worn off. Although growth and development have their beginning long before birth, most of the infant's learning may fairly be said to start at birth, since, no matter what his abilities may be, his opportunities for learning before birth are very limited. If we are to understand his later development, we must therefore try to get as clear an idea as possible of the initial equipment with which the newborn baby sets out to discover and explore the world about him.

ACTIVITY IN INFANCY

As quiet as a newborn baby may seem to us to be when we look at him in his crib, there is a great deal of active movement going on even during the earliest days of life. Psychologists in the 1920's developed a kind of experimental device called the stabilimeter. All the movements a baby makes when lying on it are automatically recorded on a moving tape which can be analyzed. Irwin,[3] working with this apparatus, was able to demonstrate a surprising amount of general activity in the newborn. One child, for example, made more than 2,000 movements on the first day after birth. The average for four infants was more than 1,700.

[3] O. C. Irwin. The amount and nature of activities of newborn infants under constant external conditions during the first ten days of life. *Genet. Psychol. Monogr.*, 1930, 8, 1-92.

Much of this is mass activity—by which we mean diffuse, undifferentiated movements of the whole body. As has been noted in our discussion of Coghill's work on embryology, one very influential theory of development has held that all specific responses differentiate out of this general activity of the total organism. The details of the controversy over this theory need not concern the general reader. There seems

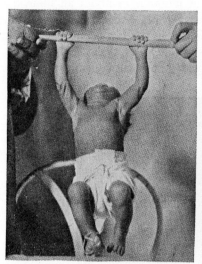

FIGURE 32.   The grasping reflex. *A.* Month-old baby supporting weight by both hands. Many babies are able to do this at birth, and frequently by the use of only one hand, but as a rule the weight cannot be sustained in this way for more than a minute or two. The reflex reaches its maximum strength about the fourth month, then wanes and later reappears as a voluntary act. The voluntary grasp is, however, different from the reflex grasp of the newborn. In the voluntary grasp the thumb plays an important part, while the reflex grasp is performed entirely by the fingers (see Figure 33). (Courtesy *Journal of Heredity.*)

B. Newborn monkey supporting weight by one arm. This position was maintained for thirty-three minutes. (From C. P. Richter. The grasping reflex in the newborn monkey. *Arch. Neurol. and Psychiat.*, 1931, 26, 784-790. Courtesy of the publishers.)

to be evidence for some differentiated activity of parts of the body and some specific responses to particular kinds of stimulation from the very beginning, in addition to the mass activity. But it is this diffuse kind of movement that predominates at the start, and in general the direction of development is toward a gradual replacement of movement of this sort by more limited but more effective activity.

Psychologists are particularly concerned with responsiveness to stimulation of various sorts. The stimuli that set off the general mass activity are mainly internal. It seems probable that they come from the alimentary tract, since the level of activity depends to a considerable extent on the time that has elapsed since feeding. The contractions in the stomach that occur when it is empty are probably not the only stimuli for this activity, however. Aserinsky and Kleitman [4] demonstrated that there are motility cycles even during sleep, waves of activity that arise and then subside at intervals of about an hour. The sleeping infant will stir, thrash about a bit, and then become quiet again. There appear to be nerve centers in the central nervous system that control such rhythms. Changes in some part of the body's complex chemical system may also be involved. About all we can say with cer-

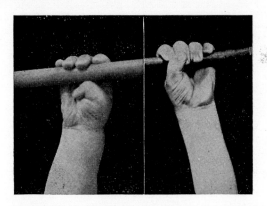

FIGURE 33. Difference between the reflex grasp of the newborn and the voluntary grasp of the older infant. (From Myrtle B. McGraw. *Growth: a study of Johnny and Jimmy.* D. Appleton-Century Co.)

tainty is that activity which is spontaneous—that is, stimulated from within rather than from without—occurs universally.

Even before investigators become interested in measuring the total amount of general activity in the newborn and charting its rhythms, other psychologists had been attempting to make a sort of inventory of all of the kinds of responses that could be elicited at the beginning of life. Pratt [5] has summarized a large amount of such research. It constitutes a truly impressive list of items one might call the "raw material" of behavior. It has been shown that the newborn infant reacts to visual stimuli, sounds, odors, tastes, pressures, and changes in temperature or position of his body. His response repertory includes sucking, grasping, sneezing, crying, frowning, smiling, and dozen of other actions. We

[4] E. Aserinsky and N. Kleitman. A motility cycle in sleeping infants as manifested by ocular and gross motor activity. *J. Appl. Physiol.*, 1955, 8, 11-18.

[5] K. C. Pratt. The neonate. In L. Carmichael (Ed.), *Manual of child psychology.* (2nd Ed.) New York: Wiley, 1954. Ch. 4.

shall note in detail only a few of these, but it is important for the student of human development to remember how rich and complex human behavior possibilities are before any kind of learning process begins.

The general term for these unlearned varieties of response to stimulation is *reflex*. In many cases, such acts are similar to those we encounter in the nonhuman species nearest to man in the evolutionary scale. Figure 32 illustrates this point with the grasping reflex, which appears to be very similar in the newborn child and newborn monkey. Figure 33 shows that this grasping reflex is quite different from the voluntary grasp that develops later.

PHYSICAL GROWTH DURING INFANCY

The changes in a child during the first two years that are most obvious to everyone are the changes in size and shape. Although these are outside the territory psychologists ordinarily consider their own, they are of considerable interest to them.

One of the reasons is that there is a widely held theory, going back at least as far as Aristotle's period four centuries before Christ, and perhaps a good deal farther, that certain kinds of temperament or personality go with certain kinds of physique. Plump people are expected to be more jovial and placid than thin people. Thin people are expected to be brighter and more high-strung than their stout or muscular companions. Statistical studies have shown that such relationships are by no means as universal or as clear-cut as they are assumed to be. When large numbers of people are examined, one finds only a slight degree of relationship between *any* physical trait and *any* mental trait. There are almost as many exceptions as there are people who follow what is thought to be the rule. Furthermore, what relationship there is does not necessarily demonstrate any *genetic* linkage. It is just as possible, for example, that children with good muscular development tend to develop the traits making for leadership, because their appearance and their athletic skill give them *social* advantages in our kind of culture, and at the same time make it easy for them to develop self-concepts of a dominant self-confident sort.

Thus, while psychologists have been becoming more and more skeptical about the idea that there is an inevitable biological relationship between physique and either intellect or temperament, they have become more and more interested in the relationship arising from social roles and self-attitudes. The idea of biological differences in temperament has not been abandoned. Sheldon [6] and his co-workers have been doing active research showing that such differences exist. But whether

[6] W. H. Sheldon. *The varieties of human physique.* New York: Harper, 1940.

we attach a great deal of importance to them or not, we are interested in physical growth for its own sake because it is an important element in the intricate pattern of developmental processes that combine to make the individual person what he is. The special kind of body one develops is a highly essential part of one's basic equipment for life, and in each individual case we can see that in one way or another it plays an important role in the total complex of factors that form the personality. The relationships that matter may not show up in group statistics because they work out in different ways under different conditions. Consider, for example, the boy who is so much smaller than his schoolmates that he cannot compete with them successfully in games or sports where size and strength are important. This fact will almost inevitably influence his behavior, but not all children will respond in the same way. Some find companionship among children younger than themselves, among whom, because of their greater experience, they frequently assume the role of leaders and sometimes of dictators. Others turn to solitary activities such as reading or various intellectual hobbies. Still others develop some form of compensatory behavior which they sometimes carry to such an extreme degree that we speak of it as "overcompensation." They attempt to make up for their short stature by carrying themselves very erect, usually with the chin held as high as possible. They adopt an attitude of cocksureness, are frequently very talkative and fond of argument. Thereby they demonstrate to themselves if not to others that their gifts more than make up for their physical inferiority. Still others show behavior that is quite the opposite. They become fearful, timid, and if they are unable to find satisfaction in pursuits of their own, they cling to their earlier relations with adults, maintaining a position of childlike dependence until long past the usual age.

Another reason for the interest of psychologists in the laws of physical growth arises from the fact that these laws often suggest new problems or ways of attacking them that may apply to behavior as well as to structure. The principle of development by differentiation, first noted in the study of physical growth, has been found to apply to most aspects of mental growth as well. The rules of cephalocaudal (from head downward) and proximo-distal (from trunk outward) progression that seem to characterize physical growth hold, within limits, for motor skills as well as body structure (see Figure 34). Other examples of general laws that apply to psychological as well as physical development will be cited in later sections.

When we analyze the growth data that are now available from many excellent studies, we are impressed with two facts. First, like the prenatal period that preceded it, the period of infancy is characterized by extraordinarily rapid growth. For most of the individual cases whose detailed measurements are presented in the monograph by Tudden- ham and Snyder, [7] the weight at six months is more than double the birth weight. The tempo slows down somewhat after this, but is still rapid. At the age of two years, most children in this group weigh from three to four times what they did at birth.

The brain participates in this general growth. It more than doubles in size during the first two years. The gain in the first year is about 130 per cent, as compared with a gain of 25 per cent the second year and about 10 per cent the third year. Growth, however, is not equally divided among the parts of the brain. The cerebrum, which was so precocious in growth during the prenatal period, is already beginning to slow down. Its gain in the first year is only about 115 per cent, while the cerebellum shows the enormous increase of 300 per cent. Since, as we pointed out before, the cerebellum is par-

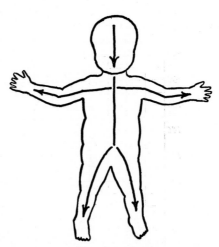

FIGURE 34. Diagrammatic repre- sentation of the directional tendency in physical and motor development.

ticularly concerned with the control of posture, its rapid growth at the time when the child is first gaining the ability to sit and stand is significant.

At about the time of normal birth a marked change in the growth patterns of the different bodily tissues can be noted. If their prenatal growth is measured in terms of the percentage of their birth weight that has been attained at each prenatal age and the results are plotted to form a growth curve, it is found that each of the different bodily tissues grows at a uniform rate throughout the prenatal period. But if a similar procedure is followed for postnatal growth and the results are ex- pressed in terms of the percentage of the total amount gained between birth and maturity that has been attained at each succeeding year of postnatal age, it is found that the rate of growth is no longer uniform and that the forms of the growth curves for the different bodily tissues after birth differ greatly from each other. (See Figure 35.) The nervous

[7] R. D. Tuddenham and M. M. Snyder. Physical growth of California boys and girls from birth to eighteen years. *Univ. of Calif. Pub. in Child Devel.*, 1954, 1, 183-364.

system grows very rapidly at first and more slowly thereafter; it has attained 90 per cent of its adult size by the age of six years. The lymphoid tissues (tonsils, lymph glands, and the like) increase in size up to about the time of puberty and decrease thereafter. The genitals grow very slowly until shortly before the time of puberty and then with extreme rapidity. The postnatal growth curve of the general body tissues, including bones and muscles, blood, and most of the internal organs, shows a double flexure, with rapid growth at first, then a period

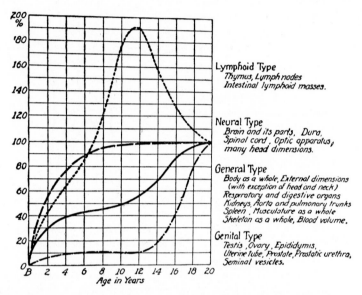

FIGURE 35. Four main types of postnatal growth. (From R. E. Scammon. The growth of the body in childhood. *The measurement of man.* Courtesy Univ. of Minnesota Press.)

of slow growth that lasts until about two years before the onset of puberty, when a second period of rapid growth known as the "preadolescent spurt" takes place, after which the growth rate again becomes slower and continues to slow down until adult size has been attained.

One thing that growth studies have repeatedly shown is that there are large individual differences in the growth patterns of children. Periods of slower than average growth may be followed by temporary spurts. One child may start out with a rapid growth period and then slow down. Another may show the opposite trend. Figure 36 shows the change in weight recorded during the first two years for two girls in the Berkeley Survey. They began with exactly the same weight. Case 351 grew much more rapidly at first and then slowed down. Case 354 continued to gain. One of the interesting things about these two

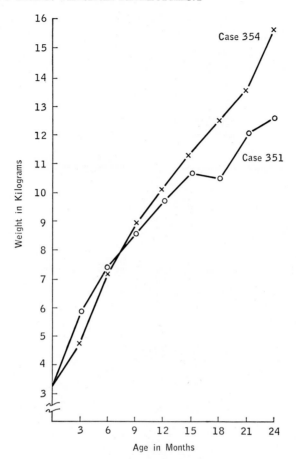

FIGURE 36. Growth curves for two female infants. (Data from R. D. Tuddenham and M. M. Snyder. *Physical growth of California boys and girls from birth to eighteen years.* Berkeley: Univ. of California Press, 1954.)

cases is that if one examines the rest of the weight figures given by Tuddenham and Snyder, one notes that at the age of thirteen, Case 351 overtook 354 and from then on averaged consistently heavier once more. At eighteen, the last age at which measurements were made, Case 351 weighed 64.5 kg. and Case 354, 56.8. While this is a more striking contrast in growth patterns than many of the others, it is by no means exceptional.

What adults dealing with children and what children themselves should realize is that many different patterns of growth are *normal.* Much unnecessary anxiety and many personality difficulties centering

FIGURE 37. The motor sequence. (From Mary Shirley. *The first two years: a study of twenty-five babies.* Courtesy University of Minnesota Press.)

around "body image" or self-concept could be avoided if people in general had grasped this idea.

MOTOR DEVELOPMENT IN INFANCY

At birth, as we have seen, the child's activity consists chiefly of mass movements, with a few specialized responses that are fairly well co-ordinated. Show the month-old baby a toy, say a rattle, shake it about, and what are the results? He may not respond at all; if he does, the most we can expect is some increase in general activity, perhaps momentary fixation of the eyes on the object, a little harder kicking, a few extra waves of the arms, or mouth movements as in sucking.

Return six months later. The baby who formerly lay helpless on his back is now sitting in his high-chair with only such support as it affords; perhaps he may even be able to sit alone on the floor for a minute or two without toppling over. Show him the rattle. The baby watches with interest as you take it from your bag; his gaze, formerly so uncertain and wavering, now follows your every movement. As you extend the toy toward him he reaches for it without hesitation. The forward thrust of the hand may not be perfectly aimed, but any error in direction is promptly corrected and the extended fingers close about the toy as soon as it is touched. Once in his hand the rattle is manipulated in a dozen different ways. It is waved about, hammered, chewed, sucked, rubbed against his face, passed from one hand to the other, laid down and picked up again, scratched and patted, all with an intentness of expression which rivals that of the scientist engaged in investigating the possibilities of a new laboratory instrument. The remarkable advance in motor abilities that has taken place in the short space of six months is seen in every movement; in his posture with erect neck and shoulders and well-co-ordinated head movements, in the dexterity of his hand movements and his ability to direct the movements of his hands by the use of sight, in the readiness with which he is able to follow a moving object with his eyes, and most of all in the decrease in nonspecific mass activity and its replacement by adaptive movements of local parts. Although he is still inclined to "wriggle all over" when he tries to do something, particularly if it is something new, his wriggling is more likely to produce the desired result, even though a good many unnecessary movements are involved.

Try the same experiment six months later. We now find the year-old baby creeping about with considerable agility, sitting alone with perfect balance, and changing from the sitting position to the creeping position without hesitation or difficulty. He pulls himself to a stand by the help of a piece of furniture, walks with the aid of a supporting hand

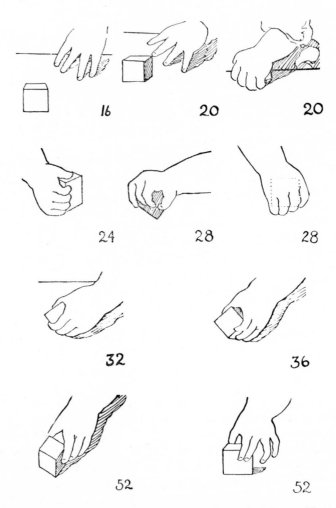

FIGURE 38. Development of manual prehension in infancy. The ten stages in the development of the ability to seize and hold a one-inch cube have been named by Halverson as follows: (1) reach but no contact, (2) contact but no grasp, (3) the primitive squeeze, (4) the squeeze grasp, (5) the hand grasp, (6) the palm grasp, (7) the superior palm grasp, (8) the inferior forefinger grasp, (9) the forefinger grasp, and (10) the superior forefinger grasp. The numbers below the drawings show the ages at which each of the above stages is likely to appear. (Reproduced by permission of the author and the publisher from H. M. Halverson. An experimental study of prehension in infants by means of systematic cinema records. *Genet. Psychol. Monog.*, 1931, 10, 107-286.)

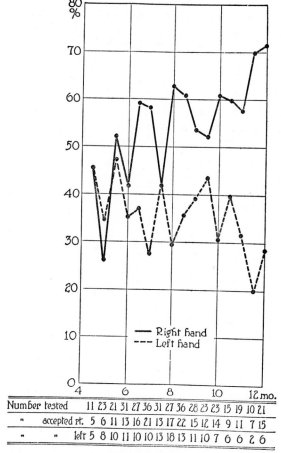

Number tested	11 23 21 31 27 36 31 27 36 28 23 23 15 19 10 21
" accepted rt.	5 6 11 13 16 21 13 17 22 15 12 14 9 11 7 15
" " left	5 8 10 11 10 10 13 18 13 11 10 7 6 6 2 6

FIGURE 39.   Development of right-handedness in infants. (From H.
S. Lippman. Certain behavior responses in early infancy. *J. Genet.
Psychol.*, 1927, 34, 424-440. Courtesy Clark Univ. Press.)

or the rails of his crib. At six months he could manipulate fairly good-
sized objects, using his entire hands without very much independent
finger movement; by nine or ten months, finger movements have advanced to the stage at which he can pick up tiny objects between his
thumb and finger. (See Figure 37 and 38.) Before the end of the first
year the index finger is used alone for pointing, touching, and exploring
objects in many ways.

By this time, too, most children show some tendency to use one hand
in preference to the other, though the difference is not very marked.
Hand preference at this stage is, in fact, so slight that nearly all babies
will be likely to grasp an object with the hand nearest it whenever there

is a definite advantage of position; but if care is taken to offer an object exactly in the median line of the child's body so that neither hand is given any advantage over the other, it is found that as age advances more and more children come to reach with the right hand rather than with the left. (See Figure 39.) We have no way of knowing, at present, whether this general preference for the right hand is determined by some native process of maturation or whether it is the result of training. Undoubtedly most mothers tend to encourage children to use the right hand whether or not they are aware of doing so. Objects are put into the right hand more often than into the left; the right hand is more likely to be picked up and patted or stroked (as a result of the hand-shaking habits formed in ordinary adult intercourse). Some mothers from the beginning make a definite effort to train the child to be right-handed. They feel that since this is a right-handed world, with its machinery and its social customs adapted to right-handed people, the child who is right-handed has a distinct advantage over the one who is left-handed. It is possible, therefore, that hand preference is entirely a matter of early training, but the fact that right-handedness is the rule among practically all races of mankind makes it seem probable that some neurological factor is involved as well. However, whatever native features are involved cannot do more than establish a tendency, for children who appear to be "naturally" left-handed can, as we all know, be trained to use the right hand, though the process of training may be difficult. Whether or not it is desirable to do this is another matter, which we shall consider in a following chapter.

The average child learns to walk alone by the age of fourteen or fifteen months. Nearly all can do so by eighteen months. After the child has learned to walk, motor development is seen less in the appearance of "new" abilities than in the extension and improvement of earlier accomplishments. The major organizations of motor acts have been laid down, the basic motor patterns have been designed. From now on, although the baby's motor development will include the acquisition of many new skills, these skills will differ from those acquired earlier in several respects. They will vary more from child to child and will be more closely related to his individual experience; that is, the element of learning will be more conspicuous. They will be more narrowly related to particular situations and particular purposes. For example, some children learn to write, while others do not, and whether or not writing is learned will depend not only upon ability but upon opportunity and experience. And writing is used in fewer situations than the basic skills of reaching, grasping, holding, and the co-ordination of eye and hand by which the movements of the pen are directed. The same thing is apparent in other motor skills gained after the period of infancy.

Walking and running are basic skills acquired by all normal persons. They are used in an extremely wide variety of circumstances. But such specialized adaptations of these acts as dancing, walking a tightrope, and skating are not universally learned and have a much narrower range of usefulness.

On the basis of all the research, we must conclude that the acquisition of motor skill by the infant is not, as some have thought it to be, merely the result of "accidental" conditioning through experiences gained in "random" activity. In the first place the child's activities are not "random" at all. They seem to be the direct result of an organic craving for sensory stimulation—a craving that is secondary only to the primary organic drives of hunger and thirst. This craving alone, in the normal child, is sufficiently pronounced to insure that in any ordinary type of environment that the child is free to exploit, enough self-initiated practice will take place to give reasonable proficiency in such basic motor skills as sitting, standing, walking, running, and handling objects. Few people realize the enormous amount of practice in these arts that every child gains in the course of his everyday activities. From morning to night he is busily exploring the world about him. Every new object he sees is exploited in a dozen different ways and by the aid of as many senses as he can bring to bear on it. It is felt, tasted, hammered, pushed about, dropped and picked up again, turned over and over, looked at from every angle, listened to, dragged about, and stuck into every available crevice, and its possibilities as a noisemaker, a scratching or engraving tool, a lever, and a poker are tried out on as many different objects as possible, not forgetting the parlor furniture. Not only does this incessant practice bring about rapid improvement in motor skills, but it also provides the personal experience that gives form and meaning to the sensory impressions that accompany all the child's activities. Objects lose their impersonal character, if, indeed, they existed as objects for the child before experience had brought them into some kind of personal relationship to him, which seems rather doubtful. The cup from which he drinks his morning milk is no longer merely a visual pattern of lights and shades or something that stimulates his organs of touch but is also a *desired object*, a giver of pleasure, a satisfier of his bodily needs. It is not a thing completely external to himself but something that has a very intimate relationship to himself.

Thus we see once more how the intimate connection between the varying aspects of the developing personality makes it impossible to consider one of these aspects without reference to all the rest. The infant acquires control of his motor processes through the modification of his movements in such a way as to gain greater satisfaction of his need for sensory experiences. And all the time that he is acquiring

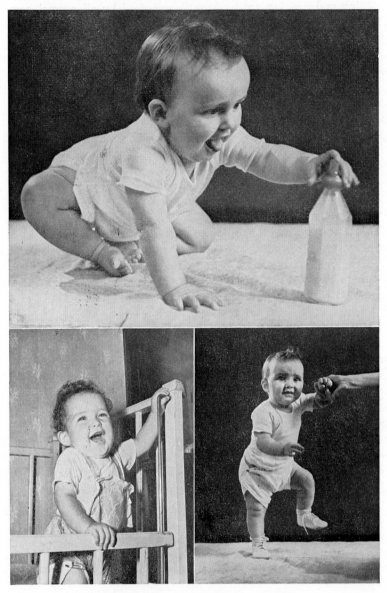

FIGURE 40.   Some early motor skills.
(Photographs by Harold M. Lambert.)

these experiences and gaining these skills he is learning many other things. He is beginning to grasp some of the properties of things, the everyday laws of the physical world, so that he knows more exactly what to expect from his actions. When an object with which he has been playing slips from his grasp, he no longer gazes helplessly in all directions but he leans from his high-chair to look and gesture toward the floor. Moreover he demonstrates that he has acquired some knowledge of human psychology as well, for if help is not immediately forthcoming, the chances are that he will scream until he gets it. He is becoming more discriminating in his reactions both to persons and objects. He has learned that this thing hurts, that this person will always yield to his demands if he is sufficiently insistent, while that one is likely to remain obdurate. He learns that certain objects are adapted to particular uses, while others will not serve. Thus his behavior becomes better suited to the gratification of his needs and desires.

Learning how to control his own body is of the utmost importance to the infant for its own sake. But the child does not acquire his motor skill just for the sake of becoming skillful. That which he aims at is the mastery of his world, to which end the mastery of his body is merely a necessary means. In the course of his incessant practice and experimentation he gains quite as much in the way of intellectual experience as in motor skill, and his patterns of personality and social reactions undergo quite as marked changes as does his motor ability. We shall turn to some of these matters in the next chapter.

SUMMARY

The first two years, the period often labeled *infancy*, constitute the developmental stage during which the individual emerges from complete dependence on others. He acquires the strength, skill, and basic habits that make possible some control over his own behavior. At birth the predominant kind of activity to be observed is of the mass or random variety, but many specific reflexes, such as sucking, yawning, grasping, and the like can be elicited by appropriate stimuli.

Physical growth during the first two years is more rapid than at any subsequent period of life. While there are general trends shown by all children, there is considerable individuality in growth curves as well. It is not certain whether there is any *necessary* relationship between varieties of physique and varieties of personality, but the fact that a person's size, skill, and appearance influence both the attitudes others show toward him and his own self-concept makes it important for the psychologist to understand physical growth. Furthermore, developmental principles characterizing this growth process have proved serviceable in analyzing other less tangible aspects of development.

During the period of infancy there is a continuous increase in motor skill. By the age of six months the average baby can sit alone, follow moving objects with his eyes, and use his hands without separating the fingers. By the end of the first year he can creep, raise himself to a standing position, and manipulate objects fairly skillfully by using thumb and index finger. There is a distinction between the universal skills of walking, grasping, holding, and so forth, that all physically sound children develop regardless of their particular circumstances and the more specialized skills, such as writing, skating, and playing the piano, that develop only as a result of particular learning experiences. Learning is a factor even in the early or universal skills, however. There seems to be a need for sensory stimulation to serve as motivation for the practice of these skills.

THE BIOGRAPHY OF A BABY

FENTON, Jessie Chase. *A practical psychology of baby-hood.* Boston: Houghton, 1925.

In this chapter and in the ones immediately preceding and following it you have been told something about the typical course of development during the period of infancy. But no two babies are alike, and in order to see how all these manifold aspects of ability and experience work together in producing the highly individual personality of a living child we must deal not merely with averages but with individuals.

Many accounts of the growth and development of individual children have appeared since Tiedemann, in 1787, published a report of the early responses of his little son. The book by Mrs. Fenton is not new, but it is one of the best of its kind that has appeared. It has the merit of being written by a psychologist who was at the same time alert to the fact that many of her readers were likely to be interested in practical questions of child care and training as well as in the more strictly scientific questions of the manner and order in which new forms of behavior emerge. Based as it is upon painstaking records of the development of the author's little son, it is replete with interesting and illuminative anecdotal accounts of actual episodes that lend vividness and meaning to the factual material.

Young people sometimes think that books of this kind are suitable only for those who are already parents. This is not true. Parenthood, like other major concerns of life, demands preparation in advance if its responsibilities are to be adequately met and its joys fully realized. Young men as well as young women will profit by gaining a more concrete acquaintance with babies and their development. To many young fathers as well as young mothers their first child with his constant exhibition of "ways that are dark and tricks that are vain" is indeed an alien creature. Reading about the growth and behavior of a baby is by no means equivalent to raising one, but it may be the best available substitute.

CHAPTER 8

What characteristic of behavior do we mean when we call it "adaptive"?

How do Bühler's three types of social behavior as seen in the infant compare with your observations of older children and adults?

What kinds of infant behavior are essential to the later development of intelligence?

How much can you tell about a baby from an infant intelligence test?

The First Two Years:
Development of Adaptive Behavior

THE NATURE OF ADAPTIVE BEHAVIOR

As has been brought out in Chapter 6, the human organism is designed for adaptation. Its organ systems respond in complex, co-ordinated ways to all sorts of changes in external circumstances. What we call behavior is a part of this general pattern. Almost from the beginning it serves the purposes of adaptation.

The distinction between "motor behavior," which was considered in the last chapter, and "adaptive behavior," which is our present concern, is largely arbitrary, determined for the most part by the interest of the observer. Adaptive behavior itself is not necessarily different from that previously discussed. Behavior as such cannot be divided into classes, for no form of behavior ever stands alone. But the interest and attention of the observer may so shift from time to time that for the moment he is willing to ignore all aspects of a given bit of behavior except the one that temporarily interests him. So whereas we were formerly concerned with the increasing complexity of the child's movements with advancing age and with the accuracy of his bodily co-ordinations, we shall now turn our attention from the form of the movements to their success or failure in attaining the goals at which they appear to be directed and to the changes in the stimulus-value of these goals with changes in maturity and experience. In so doing we shall often find ourselves impelled to depart from pure description and pass over into the more debatable area of interpretation and inference. The hazards are obvious; yet they must sometimes be risked if we are to avoid the sterility of mere enumeration of observed fact. But if we are careful to note the points at which observation leaves off and interpretation begins, many of the most serious pitfalls can be avoided.

Responses are termed *adaptive* when they are not merely repetitive activities but when their patterns change with each new performance, in a more or less systematic fashion and with relation to a goal. The idiot who sits on the floor and rocks himself forward and backward all day long is not exhibiting adaptive behavior. Neither is the child who sits aimlessly at his desk covering sheet after sheet of paper with meaningless scribbles. (Even in these cases small adjustive movements or almost imperceptible changes in the pattern may be taking place, but for practical purposes they can be ignored.) If the idiot begins to vary his rocking by additional movements of his body so as to intensify the bodily sensations, or if he shifts his position away from the wall or furniture so as to gain greater freedom, we can recognize adaptive characteristics in what he is doing. If the child begins to draw a picture or write a story, his activity can then be seen to be adaptive.

Adaptive behavior is behavior directed toward a goal, toward the satisfaction of a need or desire. It is characterized by attentiveness or bodily set and by changes that show a systematic trend, though this trend may be broken by interruptions and retrogressions. In order to adapt, the individual must be able to utilize the experiences of the past as directional cues by which to steer his behavioral course toward its goal. At least in a rudimentary way he must make discriminations, classifications, judgments. He must remember and he must also be able to forget.

The child's early adaptive responses are directed toward the outside world and initiated almost entirely through stimulation of the exteroceptors rather than the interoceptors. Internal sensations can be intensified or abolished, but they do not change greatly in quality. A stomach-ache may indirectly give rise to adaptive behavior when it changes a child's mood or affects the behavior of adults toward him. But the infant himself cannot change its form or intensity through any kind of behavioral adaptation of his own. In contrast, external stimulus objects and conditions can give rise to a wide variety of sensations and changing activities. An article of food can be seen, smelled, and in the mouth of an unskilled eater, even heard! It stimulates organs of touch in fingers, mouth, lips, and throat, and it stimulates temperature senses. And all these experiences can be varied within rather wide limits by changing the relationship of the body to the source of the stimulation.

Increasingly psychologists are becoming aware of the fact that human beings *need* sensory stimulation. Experiments (see Chapter 6) have shown that a situation in which there is nothing to see, hear, or feel rapidly becomes intolerable for the normal adult. His intellectual performances deteriorate and he develops abnormal symptoms of various sorts. Less well-controlled experiments [1] have suggested that rather extreme abnormalities in infant development may arise from the lack of sensory stimulation. To feed a child and keep him warm and dry is not enough. For the development of this very important adaptive aspect of behavior he needs to be provided with a variety of things that he can see, hear, taste, smell, and handle. Adaptive behavior begins early in life, long before speech.

ADAPTIVE RESPONSES TO OTHER PEOPLE

In all forms of conditioned behavior, the process of learning is *circular*. What this means is that the stimulus that arouses the organism is followed by a response that induces return sensations which in turn act as new stimuli. Behavior is not a succession of isolated acts but a continuous series in which each element is at once a response to the preceding event and a stimulus for that which is to follow. It is therefore not surprising to find that those responses which induce intense and widespread stimulation of the organism bring about more rapid and clearly patterned modification of the child's responses than those that are faint and poorly localized.

For the young infant, nothing else in his environment fulfills these conditions so uniformly and completely as the human beings who minister to his daily needs. Spatially they are large objects upon which his uncertain gaze can focus without undue strain. They move about, intercepting the light and providing points of fixation for the eyes to follow. They make sounds of varying pitch and intensity. And most important of all, their presence is associated with most of the child's sensations of comfort and relief. They provide food when he is hungry, give warmth when he is cold. They ease his tired muscles, soothe his chafed skin, and quiet his wailing by tender caresses. Small wonder that his earliest adaptive responses are usually directed toward people rather than inanimate objects; that his earliest indications of "memory" have to do with people, that his eyes follow their movements so insistently that in experiments carried out with infants between the ages

[1] See R. A. Spitz. The role of ecological factors in emotional development in infancy. *Child Develpm.*, 1949, 21, 145-156.

of two and six months [2] it is often found necessary to screen the experimenter from the infant's sight before any other stimulus can be made effective.

The baby's first reactions to human beings are positive. (See Figure 41.) He watches them, smiles when they speak to him. It makes no difference, in the beginning, whether the voice is kindly or threatening, whether the face smiles or frowns. All his associations with human beings are pleasant; he expects, we may say, nothing but kindness from them. But at about the age of five or six months his re-

FIGURE 41. A four-months-old baby greets his father.

sponse to frowns and a threatening voice or gesture begins to be somewhat different from that shown to a smiling face and a friendly voice.[3] To the latter he continues to respond by smiling and approaching movements; but the threat or the frown is likely to cause withdrawal and in many cases crying. A little later, many children begin to reinterpret the threat as a form of play, and after a moment's hesitation respond once more by smiling and laughing.

Awareness of strangers appears at about the same time that the differentiated response to friendly and unfriendly voices can be observed. The baby is less responsive when a stranger appears; he sits quietly and stares without smiling. If the stranger approaches too near him or tries to take him in his arms, the baby draws back and perhaps begins to cry. In all this there are great differences between children, differences that it is often hard to account for purely on the basis of experience. It is very probable

[2] These ages are approximate. However very young infants have not yet had time to build up very distinct social reactions, and at a later age their developing ability to manipulate objects and consequent interest in them brings about a partial displacement of the early and all-consuming interest in persons.

[3] Cf. C. H. Bühler and H. Hetzer. Das Verständnis von Ausdruck im ersten Lebensjahr. *Zeitschr. f. Psychol.*, 1928, 107, 50-61; and R. A. Spitz and K. M. Wolf. The smiling response: a contribution to the ontogenesis of social relations. *Genet. Psychol. Monogr.*, 1946, 34, 57-125.

that hereditary tendencies are involved as well; tendencies that do not fix the behavior irrevocably, but that predispose some children to be unduly disturbed by unfamiliar and perhaps unskilled methods of handling and hence, all other things being equal, to be more easily "conditioned" against unfamiliar social contacts thereafter.

The very young infant is less likely to respond to other children than to adults, but this is probably because adults are larger and more active, because they are likely to make stronger attempts to attract his attention, and—perhaps most of all—because adults rather than children have ministered to his daily wants and have therefore become objects that have special and personal meaning for him. Bühler [4] in a study of the social reactions of infants, reports that when two babies less than six months old are placed in the same crib face to face they are likely to pay little attention to each other. If an infant happens to meet another's look, he may smile as he would at an adult, but at this age babies do not make active advances toward each other. In the second half-year, however, the baby begins to make definite attempts to attract the other child's attention. He touches him, makes cooing sounds, and interferes with his activities. If the other baby does not respond he may go further. He squeals, pulls the other child's feet or clothing, snatches at his toys. Before the end of the first year, practically all the forms of social behavior seen in later life can be observed in embryonic form. There is domination of one child by another, leadership, rivalry, bullying, and submission. There is imitation, co-operation, generosity, and selfishness. There is the dog-in-the-manger child, who snatches all the other babys' toys but makes little attempt to play with them. There is the overgenerous child who proffers all that he has to the other.

Elsewhere Bühler describes three general types of social behavior that can be observed in children between the ages of six and eighteen months, as follows: [5]

(a) The *socially blind* infant behaves in the presence of another child as if nobody were present; he looks at the other without any emotion, he takes toys, plays and moves without any regard for the other child; he does not pay any attention to the other's movements; he is neither impressed nor interested in the other's presence or activities. (b) The *socially dependent*, on the contrary, is deeply impressed by the other's presence and activities; he can either be inhibited or else be stimulated by the other's presence. In the first case he will not move, will watch the other or copy him, will obey him, and sometimes even give signs of fear in front of him;

[4] C. Bühler. Die ersten sozialen Verhaltungsweisen des Kindes. in *Soziologische und psychologische Studien über die erste Lebensjahr.* Jena: Gustav Fischer, 1925.
[5] C Bühler. The social behavior of the child. In C. Murchison (Ed.), *Handbook of child psychology.* Worcester, Mass.: Clark Univ. Press, 1931.

in the second case, he will display in front of the other, will demonstrate objects and gestures, will try to rouse the other, and sometimes will even get enthusiastic and excited. In both cases all his movements are dependent on the presence of the other child; he observes the effect of his behavior on the other and carefully watches the other's reactions. (c) The _socially independent_ child is still different. He is one who—though aware of the other's presence and responsive to his behavior—yet does not seem dependent on him. He is neither intimidated nor inspired. He reacts to the other, wards him off when necessary, yet never becomes aggressive himself. He may or may not join the other in play, is not inconsiderate, but sometimes even consoles the other, encourages him, takes part in his activities; yet, with all that, he remains independent in his movements; for instance, he may suddenly turn away and do something for himself.

Maudry and Nekula [6] have reported their observations on the social behavior of 92 children, ranging in age from six to twenty-five months. Two children would be placed in a play pen with certain standard toys, and the observer would see what they did. Infants in the six to eight month group typically pay no special attention to their partners. The partner is not treated very differently from the play material. At the nine to thirteen month level there is more interest in the other person, and attempts to get the play material away from him may lead to fights. At the fourteen to eighteen month level there are fewer fights and many more positive social reactions. At the oldest age level covered in this study, nineteen to twenty-five months, positive reactions predominate and real co-operative play is in evidence. There is a steady progression from indifference to social interest.

Social training, then, does not begin when a child enters dancing-school or when he goes to kindergarten, or even when he begins to speak and is taught to say "thank you" and "if you please." Social habits have their starting point much further back. Their basic patterns are laid down in early infancy, before formal training begins, in the unremembered period before speech when impulses and attitudes are translated directly into action. The social behavior of the infant differs from that of the adult in many of its details, but its broad outlines foreshadow the form that it may later assume.

ADAPTION TO THE PHYSICAL WORLD— ORIGINS OF INTELLIGENCE

The child's preoccupation with sensory stimulation leads him to constant exploration of objects and their properties. Although the normal baby repeats the same sensori-motor activity over and over

---

[6] M. Maudry and M. Nekula. Social relations between children of the same age during the first two years of life. _J. genet. Psychol._, 1939, 54, 193-215.

again, he soon begins to introduce variations into his play. He scratches the surface of objects with his nails and then shifts to patting them with his open hand or trying to get them into his mouth. He manipulates his own toes, hands, and ears, pulls at his clothing, drags himself to a stand by the aid of the bars of his crib. From the results of these manifold operations he soon begins to learn the laws by which his physical world as well as his social world is governed. The infant of six months at first reacts to practically every new object in much the same way. He reaches for it and if he succeeds in getting hold of it he manipulates it in various ways, fingering it, scratching it, hammering it, waving it in the air, dropping it, and picking it up again. The mouth as well as the fingers participate in this activity, regardless of whether or not the object actually goes into the mouth, for the lips and tongue are in almost constant movement and the increased flow of saliva often dribbles from the lips. The seemingly undiscriminating character of this behavior in which a shoe, rattle, a wooden block, and an apple are received with equal apparent enthusiasm and are handled in as nearly identical fashion as the structure of the objects permits might lead one to wonder whether the infant, at this age, responds to the external characteristics of objects enough to make it possible for him to classify or assort them at all.

The psychologist who has done more than anyone else to systematize observations of adaptive behavior in infancy and build them into a coherent theory about the development of intelligence is Piaget. [7] His basic concept is that of the *schema* (plural, *schemata*). By this he means an organized pattern of action or perception or both. For example, the sucking reflex is a schema. Turning toward the source of a sound is another. The thing that stands out about this theoretical system is its contention that behavior is *organized* at all stages. Later behavior develops from the differentiation and combination of already existing schemata into others more complex.

The processes by which such development occurs have been labeled *assimilation* and *accommodation*. Piaget considers them the most basic of all life processes. *Assimilation* is his term for the tendency to *take in* material from the surroundings and make it part of oneself. On the physiological side eating and digestion are its clearest exemplification. Behavior shows this same tendency to reach out and grasp whatever is usable in one's environment. What one experiences is incorporated into some schema one already possesses. The other key concept, *accommodation*, refers to the fact that the living creature is always *changed* in some way by his encounters with the world outside himself. For

---

[7] J. Piaget. *The origins of intelligence in children.* New York: International Univ. Press, 1952.

the psychologist this means that the use of any schema a person may have will transform the schema itself into something different from what it previously was.

Using these ideas, Piaget distinguishes six separate stages in the development of adaptive behavior during the first two years. They are not completely separate. Each merges into the next, and a child may still be using some schemata from an early period after he has acquired others typical of a later stage. But their main features can be distinguished.

The first stage is simply the use of reflexes present at birth. Sucking is the most salient of these and the one in which it is easiest to see the processes of assimilation and accommodation at work, gradually transforming the pattern of behavior as it existed at the beginning, making it more adaptive. Sucking is the infant's primary means of assimilation and he uses it in all sorts of situations. Almost immediately, however, it begins to show accommodative changes. The baby becomes able to find the breast with a minimum of groping. When a finger is placed against his cheek, he turns his head so as to bring his mouth into contact with it. He makes movements suggesting a directed search for something to be sucked.

The second stage is what Piaget calls *primary circular reaction.* The term *circular,* as explained in a previous section, means that the activity is self-stimulating. What the person does acts as a stimulus that makes him do it again. Thumb-sucking represents such a reaction. The thumb that is sucked stimulates the roof of the mouth and thus leads to more sucking. The new thing at this stage is that the child's own action produces the stimulus to which he responds. Grasping an object put in his hand and looking at an object in his field of vision are the other important self-stimulating patterns of action that characterize this stage. Its culmination is the integration of these three separate schemata into one that includes seeing, grasping, and putting-in-the-mouth. The co-ordination of these separate patterns is no slight achievement, though it often passes unnoticed in our observation of infant development.

The third stage, which Piaget calls *secondary circular reaction,* is the earliest one at which something that might be called *intention* can be distinguished. At this stage the child is able to *re-*discover gestures or actions that previously had a favorable effect on things, and, in Piaget's words, to use "procedures to make interesting spectacles last." For example, when toys have been fastened to his crib so that his movements make them shake, he will start kicking after being quiet for a time, looking expectantly at the toys. It is to be noted that the end product of this stage is not one of the reflexes present at birth, but some new activity that has been learned.

At the fourth stage, usually not reached until the eighth or ninth month, schemata previously developed are co-ordinated and *applied to new situations*. It becomes possible for the child to use one object to exert influence on another and to remove an obstacle with one hand while he grasps a toy with another. At this stage there is some exploratory activity, trying out new objects in the various schemata he has acquired.

The distinguishing feature of the fifth stage is the *tertiary circular reaction*. Like the previous circular reactions, the child's own action constitutes the stimulus to the next response, thus keeping an activity going. But now he engages in active experimentation rather than simply to continue any activity that happens to occur. Dropping different objects to watch them fall, pulling toys in by means of strings, and using sticks to push things around are typical behavior patterns of this period.

The sixth stage is marked by the *invention* of new means through *mental* combinations. The child may, for example, pick up a stick and use it as a tool for drawing a piece of bread toward him even though he has never used such a tool for such a purpose before. The thing that sets this stage off from those preceding it is that it requires some sort of *representational* process, an image or an idea. What is done is not completely determined by present circumstances. Memory, imagination, and planning ahead are now possible. In most children this stage will have been reached by the end of the second year.

In another book, Piaget [8] has traced the changes in the child's construction of the outer world as he moves through these stages. To begin with, there are no *objects* for him. Sights, sounds, tastes, and feelings are parts of the all-encompassing pattern of his own activity. Gradually, through his experience with stimuli that appear, disappear, and reappear, and through the differentiation of separate schemata and their recombination in many ways, he constructs a stable, dependable world of objects related to one another, objects of which one's own body is one, the kind of world in which most adults live. Until one realizes this, it is a puzzling thing to watch a baby searching for a toy that has been covered by a cloth or paper. Until he reaches a fairly advanced stage in his development (stage five in Piaget's system) he acts as though he is not sure the object is still there when it is no longer visible.

We have come to realize that the ability to perceive the world around oneself, its myriad details and the relationships between its parts, is not something that any human being is born with or acquires instantaneously. It seems quite certain that the infant does not at

[8] J. Piaget. *The child's construction of reality.* London: Routledge and Kegan Paul, 1955.

first see the world as adults do, but that during the first two years some very important changes in perception occur. Furthermore, Piaget's observations indicate that becoming able to perceive a stable orderly world of objects and spatial relationships is not a *passive* process but an integral part of the elaboration of schemata by means of which a person's *activity* in relation to his surroundings is organized.

THE MEASUREMENT OF INTELLIGENCE IN INFANCY

Piaget's theory is based on a very intensive observation of a small number of infants. Similar kinds of behavior at the successive age levels have, however, been recorded for considerable numbers of children, by psychologists who were interested in establishing age norms and thus making possible the standardization of infant intelligence tests. On the basis of careful observational study, Gesell and his associates at Yale have presented developmental norms for many kinds of behavior at ages from one month on up. [9] A number of scales for the measurement of infant intelligence are now available. They have been widely used in adoption and child care agencies. Figure 42 illustrates one of the items from one of the best-known of these scales.

A series of items from the Bühler tests, [10] showing the kind of items of which such tests consist, is as follows:

Age in Months	Test Item
1	Turns head when touched (feeding reaction)
2	Turns head and eyes to look around when being carried
6	Distinguishes between bottle and rubber doll
9	Uncovers a hidden toy
12	Pulls self to a standing position with support
15	Obeys simple commands
18	Inhibits action in response to "No, no."

Much time and thought have been spent in these attempts to develop a useful measuring instrument that would enable us to go beyond the level of description in our attempts to study mental progress during the period of infancy. Such a measuring device (if we had it) would be of great practical service as well as an important tool for scientific research. Even as matters now stand, the time spent in developing tests has by no means been wasted, for they have provided us with a far more exact account of the course of behavioral development in

[9] A. Gesell and C. S. Amatruda. *Developmental diagnosis: normal and abnormal child development*. New York: Hoeber, 1947.

[10] C. Bühler. *Testing children's development from birth to school age*. Tr. by Henry Beaumont. New York: Farrar and Rinehart, 1935, p. 191.

infancy than it is likely we should otherwise have secured. And by the application of these tests we can make much more precise statements about the present developmental level of an individual baby than would be possible by any other means. But the infant tests have thus far failed to justify one important assumption that we commonly associate with intelligence tests as they are used with older children. *We cannot predict a child's later intellectual standing on the basis of tests given in infancy.* The relationship between the mental test scores earned before the beginning of speech and those earned by the same children during the nursery-school and elementary-school periods have been studied by a number of investigators, all of whom have obtained

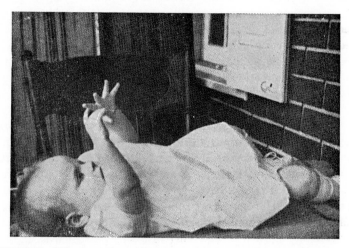

FIGURE 42.   **An infant of three months discovers his fingers.** This is one of the items in the Cattell series of infant intelligence tests. (Reproduced by courtesy of Dr. Psyche Cattell.)

closely similar results. The "bright" infant who does exceptionally well on these tests is no more likely to do well on the tests given later than is the one whose performance when a baby is average or below, nor is he any more likely to be thought to be exceptionally bright by his teachers. Tests for infants tell us a good deal about what an individual child is like now; but very little about what he may become.

The effort to construct infant intelligence tests that will be predictive of intellectual development at later stages has not been abandoned, and a few studies suggest that there may be some kinds of behavior during the first two years that are more predictive than others. Gesell has insisted that an intensive over-all diagnosis of developmental trends, including test data but not depending exclusively on it, can

forecast later developmental trends with considerable success. Both
Macrae [11] and Simon and Bass [12] have presented some evidence that
supports this idea that the general judgment as to whether a child
is retarded, average, or superior is more predictive of later status than
the test score is. But the fact remains that for the vast majority of
human infants, the IQ's they will obtain at the grade school or high
school levels cannot be predicted from the IQ's they obtain in infancy
on any of the standardized intelligence scales now available.

Why is this? No completely conclusive reason can be given. There
are probably a number of difficulties that enter in. For one thing,
intelligence tests above the infant level contain primarily material of a
symbolic nature, such as words, concepts, geometrical shapes, and the
like. As we have seen in the previous section, even the simplest representational processes do not occur until Piaget's Stage 6, so that there
may actually be very little overlap between what is measured at the
later ages and what is measured in infancy. It may be, too, that there
is more actual fluctuation in the rate of mental development during
infancy than there is later on. If this were true, an index of the level
reached at any one time would necessarily be an undependable indicator of the level even a few months in the future. Furthermore, it
may well be that it is only the *origins* of intelligence we are able to
observe during the first year and not intelligence itself, as the title of
Piaget's book signifies. Perhaps it makes little difference whether a
child is able to distinguish between a bottle and a rubber ball at five
months or at six. The important thing is the total ongoing *process* of
development of adaptive behavior and none of the test items we have
used may really show how far along in it the individual is. It is only
after a number of partial schemata have been welded together into
complex acts that we can determine how successful the process has
been.

SUMMARY

By adaptive behavior we mean activity that is directed toward
some goal and that accomplishes its purpose increasingly well as the
person engages in it. The first adaptive behavior involves responses
to other people. These become increasingly differentiated during the
first few months of life. Response to adults precedes response to other
children, but several different kinds of social behavior are in evidence
by the time the first two years are over.

[11] J. M. Macrae. Retests of children given mental tests as infants. *J. genet.
Psychol.*, 1955, 87, 111-119.
[12] A. J. Simon and L. J. Bass. Toward a validation of infant testing. *Amer. J.
Orthopsychiat.*, 1956, 26, 340-350.

A number of stages in the development of adaptive sensori-motor behavior can be distinguished, starting with the progressive modification of reflexes present at birth. Circular reactions, in which the child's own activity serves as a stimulus for the next response, are particularly important. The name Piaget gives these organized patterns of activity is *schema,* and he shows how they enlarge and develop through processes of *assimilation* and *accommodation.*

The same kinds of infant behavior that Piaget has considered have been observed by psychologists attempting to standardize intelligence test items for the first two years of life. Correlations between IQ's derived from infant tests and IQ's obtained during the school years and at maturity have been very low. It may be that it is impossible really to measure what we are accustomed to call intelligence until language has developed.

A STUDY OF EARLY ADAPTIVE
BEHAVIOR IN A CHIMPANZEE

HAYES, Cathy. *The ape in our house.* New York: Harper, 1951.

This book is a very entertaining and enlightening account of a project in which a husband and wife team of psychologists undertook to bring up a baby chimpanzee, Viki, in exactly the same way that a child is ordinarily brought up. The reader is likely to be surprised at the amount of childlike behavior that occurs under such circumstances. Viki's crowning achievement was to learn to talk. Her vocabulary was very limited. (At the time the book was written she could say "mama," "papa," and "cup.") But the fact that even the rudiments of language can be mastered by a chimpanzee is of considerable interest. The main value of experiments of this sort, however, is that they enable us to understand better the developmental processes that go on in children during their first two years.

CHAPTER 9

What is the difference between vocal sound and speech? What organs are chiefly concerned in the production of vocal sound? What additional organs are brought into play in the production of speech?

Does a child when first learning to talk make use of the same mental processes employed by an older person in learning a foreign language? If not, in what respects do their learning processes differ?

What is meant by the "period of the single-word sentence" and why is it so called? What is meant by the term "trick vocabulary"?

What part does the jargon of infancy play in facilitating the development of true speech?

What are some of the theories proposed to account for the acquisition of speech by primitive man?

How does the study of the language of twins help us to understand the social factors in language development?

What are some of the factors likely to cause retardation in language development?

If you wished to stimulate a child's progress in language as much as possible, at what age would you begin and what methods would you employ?

》》》》》》》》》》》》

The First Two Years: The Beginnings of Speech

THE IMPORTANCE OF LANGUAGE IN HUMAN LIFE

OF ALL THE DEVELOPMENTAL tasks of infancy, the acquisition of language is perhaps the most important. Whether or not it is the use of language that most clearly gives man an advantage over other animals, as many philosophers have contended, there is no question as to its indispensability in human affairs as they are now organized. Because of language complex social structures can function smoothly, complex co-operative tasks can be carried out, and the knowledge accumulated in one generation can be passed on for the use of the next.

The foundation of all of this superstructure is the process by means of which babies learn to talk. Certainly we do not understand it completely. Many ideas about how it occurs are unsupported by any sort of scientific evidence. But through the work of physiologists, psychologists, and speech pathologists, a considerable amount of knowledge about speech and language has accumulated. It can give us a better understanding of what is going on as a fifteen-month-old child attempts to make himself understood, and it can help us facilitate his language development and prevent some of the difficulties that commonly occur.

THE SPEECH MECHANISMS

Among the parts of the body chiefly involved in the production of vocal sounds we refer first to the diaphragm, the lungs, and the

165

muscles of the thorax that co-operate in the act of breathing, whereby air is forced up the windpipe and over the vocal cords in the *larynx* or "Adam's apple." The larynx is the prominent movable lump which can easily be seen about the middle of the front part of the neck in men and in boys who have attained maturity. In women and children the larynx is less prominent but can still be felt by passing the fingers over the corresponding part of the neck. The vocal cords are two membranes stretched across the inside of the larynx in such a manner that air must pass between them in the process of breathing. They are separated by an opening called the *glottis*. The membrane of which the vocal cords are composed is highly resilient. Their state of contraction or expansion is controlled by means of a complex series of muscles which likewise regulate the size of the glottis. When the muscles are relaxed and the glottis is consequently wide open, air passes through the glottis without producing sound. When the muscles are contracted, the vocal cords more tightly stretched, the glottis is reduced to a narrower slit, and the passage of air forces the cords to vibrate, giving rise to waves or vibrations in the air as it passes out of the mouth. Thus vocal sounds are produced. The quality, intensity, and pitch of the tones vary with a number of factors such as the degree of tension of the vocal cords, the size of the opening between them, the length of the cords, and the condition of the resonators provided by the cavities in the chest, throat, nose, mouth, and the bones of the head. Because the larynx is relatively small and the vocal cords short in women and children, their voices are typically high in pitch. The change of voice so noticeable in boys after they have arrived at puberty results from the rapid increase in the size of the larynx and the consequent lengthening of the vocal cords that occurs at that time.

Speech consists of interrupting and otherwise modifying the sound waves as they pass through the nose and mouth by making intricate movements of the tongue, lips, teeth, and soft palate. The movements necessary for the production of comprehensible speech involve such extraordinarily fine co-ordination of these muscles, such precise timing [1] and delicate adaptation of the extent and force of the muscular

---

[1] A fluent speaker will utter, on the average, from 300 to 350 words per minute; an exceptionally rapid speaker may run as high as 500 words per minute. The number of movements involved in the production of these sounds cannot easily be calculated, but a conservative estimate would put the figure at not fewer than 1,000 per minute. Let the reader repeat to himself the time-honored sentence, "The big black fox jumped over the lazy dog," observing the number and kind of motor co-ordinations that must be made both successively and in combination with each other and how careful the timing must be if the sentence is to run off smoothly and easily, and he will gain a limited appreciation of the complexity of the speech process. There is also the adjustment of the voice-producing mechanism to be considered, the changes in pitch, intensity, resonance, and rhythm that lend expressive quality to what is said.

movements, that the wonder is not that disturbances of speech sometimes occur but rather that they are not more frequent. Nor is it remarkable that the infant must spend a year or more of intensive practice in gaining enough control of the speech mechanisms to permit the utterance of even a few imperfectly articulated words. The marvel is that he begins so soon.

THE VOCALIZATION OF INFANCY

The first vocal reaction of the newborn infant is the "birth cry" which accompanies the passage of air over the vocal cords in the larynx as the lungs are expanded for the first time. Crying, as a spontaneous response to physical discomfort of any kind, occurs from birth onward. Even during the first week of life, individual differences can be observed among babies both in respect to the amount of time spent in crying and in the volume and timbre of their cries.

The cries of the very young infant are almost wholly laryngeal, slightly if at all modified by the organs of speech. During the first few days of life vocalization other than crying is rare, but by the age of two weeks or even earlier, occasional low grunts and cooing sounds are uttered. These increase very rapidly in number and variety. The first sounds have been described by Shirley [2] as "vocal grunts" frequently with some nasal involvement, resulting in sounds that may be indicated phonetically as *ug, ng,* or *ungh*. Soon afterward, vowel sounds appear, at first as single syllables often long drawn out, such as *ah-h-h, oo-o-o,* and later as reduplicated syllables, *ah-ah-ah*. Consonants are soon added to the child's repertory. Careful observation by Irwin [3] has shown that there is a definite sequence in the development of the consonant sounds. Those formed at the back of the mouth come first. The *h* sound seems to be earliest. These back consonants or "glottals" decrease in frequency as the sounds shaped by teeth and lips become more common. The young child is polyglot. The French nasals, the German gutturals, the Hottentot "click"—linguistic peculiarities of primitive and civilized nations alike can be distinguished in the untutored babblings of the growing infant.

Although there is not complete agreement as to the details, certain broad features in the developmental sequence of infant vocalization have been fairly well delimited. The single syllables of the young infant are followed at first by reduplication of the same syllable. The syllables uttered rapidly take on variety, both by the addition of a

[2] M. Shirley. *The first two years: a study of twenty-five babies.* Vol. II. *Intellectual development.* Univ. of Minn. Inst. Child Welf. Monogr. Series, No. 7. Minneapolis: Univ. of Minnesota Press, 1933.

[3] O. C. Irwin. Infant speech. *Sci. Amer.* 1949, 18, 22-24.

greater number of consonantal and vowel sounds and by uniting these sounds into new combinations. This ushers in a period during which the normal child spends a large share of his waking hours in a kind of vocal play that the Germans call "Lallung." Lying in his crib, the infant repeats over and over again, "da-da-da-da" or "ngee-ngee-ngee," occasionally varying his performance by changes in tonal inflection or volumes of sounds, or by suddenly shifting to some other type of oral activity such as forcible expulsion of frothy saliva from his lips— "blowing bubbles"—or shifting to a new sound-pattern. At first the child seems to carry on these vocal experiments purely for his own amusement, and if we can imagine the case of a child brought up by some kind of totally unresponsive machine, it is unlikely that they would ever serve any other purpose. But children are not reared by machines but by human beings who respond to their activities in ways that are highly satisfying to the infant. Before long, therefore, the child's vocalizations are no longer wholly self-centered. They become socialized. Shirley has designated this as the third stage in the infant's progress toward speech. The infant now begins to squeal or shout at the approach of a familiar person and to utter responsive gurglings and coos when played with or talked to by some one accustomed to doing so. (See Figure 41.)

The fourth stage begins when the simple reduplication of the same syllable is elaborated by the combination of two or more different syllables to form a more highly organized "word." From his simple "da-da-da," the child progresses to "daddle-daddle-daddle" and to "daddle-ee-oog-ee-ug-ug-uggle," with increasingly varied syllabification and such "expressive" tonal inflection that it often sounds amusingly like true speech. This "expressive jargon," as Gesell, who has given the most complete account of its development, has christened it, usually begins during the second half of the first year and reaches its height early in the second year, when it overlaps with and is gradually replaced by actual speech. Children differ greatly both in the length of time for which this jargon-period persists and in the extent to which the sounds and their inflection are elaborated. A little girl of my acquaintance chattered away so incessantly with so natural an inflection and such a wide variety of different sounds that her hearers almost invariably remarked, "She sounds exactly as if she were speaking a foreign language." In her "conversations" some syllables were stressed, others slurred over; there were rising inflections as in questioning, and falling inflections that sounded like a response. There were pauses as if concluding a sentence, staccato phrases like commands, and short, strongly emphasized sounds indicative of emotional stress that her father insisted were "swear words."

THE ORIGIN OF SPEECH IN THE INDIVIDUAL

The question arises, by what process does this jargon of sounds develop into comprehensible and meaningful speech? Up to this point, progress seems to have been largely due to the increased neuro-muscular motility that goes along with the maturation of the organism, and the consequent increasing variety of sounds brought about more or less fortuitously as vocalization happens to coincide with differing positions of the lips, tongue, and soft palate. Add to this the fact that the child hears and is apparently interested in the sounds that he makes, and learns to reproduce them and to vary them by a gradual association of kinesthetic sensations in the vocal organs with the sounds heard, and we have one side of the mechanism by which progress from the babblings of the infant to fully developed speech may be accomplished. It shows, that is, how the child's repertory of speech sounds becomes elaborated, but it does not show how these sounds are brought into conformity with the language patterns of other people. It shows how the child learns to "jabber," but it does not show how he learns to speak.

People formerly thought that formal speech is acquired by a more or less conscious process of imitation. It was taken for granted that children learn to talk in much the same manner as older persons learn a new language, by listening to the sounds made by others and trying to imitate them. But few psychologists now believe that imitation, in this sense, plays a very important role in the early stages of speech. According to modern theory, the elements of speech, the vowels and consonants and short syllables, are not learned by imitation at all. They develop spontaneously in the course of the child's vocal play. What is learned by imitation is not the mechanical formation of sounds but the *selection* of certain sound-combinations from the rich variety of elementary sound-forms that the child has "taught himself" to pronounce and the *application* of these sound-combinations to the particular situations in which he has heard them used by others. So the incomprehensible babbling of the younger child passes over into true speech, not so much by a process of extension as by one of limitation.

Formerly the sight of his well-loved kitty called forth an unassorted jumble of vowels and consonants in all sorts of combinations. One day, perhaps quite by chance, the *k* sound is made. His mother hears it and explains in delight. "Just hear him! He's trying to call his kitty!" She repeats the word, "Kitty, kitty!" perhaps picking up the kitten and carrying it to the child as she does so. Now the child does not have to *learn* how to pronounce the sound *k*. He knows that already; he has been doing it in play for some time. What he has to learn is to use the *k* sound in connection with the "kitty" situation and refrain from using the *g*'s and *s*'s and *m*'s and *p*'s that were a part of his former response. So when the mother selects this sound out of all the rest and holds it up, as it were, for admiration, repeats it, and praises and caresses him for having said it, perhaps crowns the occasion by capturing and presenting him with the elusive kitten that he has been vainly pursuing for some time, all these pleasant experiences operate to bring about a closer connection between the sight of the flesh-and-blood kitty and the utterance of the *k* or, as it soon becomes, the *kee-ee* sound. [4] This may have to be repeated many times, but sooner or later, as a result of repeated experience in this and similar situations, the great idea dawns. *There is some kind of sound that is the key to every situation. When one utters the right sound, other people obey one's will.* We cannot suppose that the child of sixteen or eighteen months formulates the idea as clearly as this, yet that some sort of generalizing process has taken place in his mind and that this idea has come to him rather suddenly seems evident from the marked change in his behavior that takes place within the short space of a few days.

This association of word with object which marks the beginning of true language is a very different matter from the mere repetition of words to win social approval—an art that most babies acquire to some extent at an earlier stage of development. As was pointed out in an earlier chapter, infants begin to respond to social stimuli, on the average, by the time they are a few weeks old, and it is not long before they begin to make definite attempts to secure the attention of others for the sake of social satisfaction alone, even when there is no bodily need that requires attention. Before the end of the first half-year, the normal baby has become a definitely socialized creature. Most babies, by that time, have learned the important lesson that by the exercise of various little tricks and wiles they can often gain adult attention and fondling that is not to be had so readily by any other means. So when by chance in the course of his babbling, the reduplicated syllable *ma-ma* happens to be made, and the mother responds by praising and fondling the child and by repeatedly urging him on this and other occasions to "say ma-ma" the child eventually connects the request with the motor performance and becomes able to repeat the sound on demand. The process of acquiring new words in this way is a slow one because the discrimination demanded is fine and the child's learning is still at an early stage. The stimuli to which he must respond are simply vocal

[4] In the beginning the child commonly uses initial consonants only. Later on final consonants are added, and still later consonants in the middle of words appear. The first words are usually monosyllables, reduplicated monosyllables such as "pa-pa" or "bow-wow," or monosyllables with a single vowel syllable appended, such as "dog-ee," "ta-ah" (tail), "tab-oo" (table).

sounds—"ma-ma," "daddy," "bow-wow"—and the response serves no other purpose than that of winning social approval which can often be gained by other and less arduous means. This stage in the development of speech overlaps with the later stages of the "jargon period." Early in the second year, most children learn to say a few words of this kind, which, because they serve no purpose beyond that of a social trick which the child uses to win the approval of adults, are often referred to as the child's "trick vocabulary." A period of at least two or three months commonly elapses between the acquisition of the first "word-trick" and the beginning of active speech. During this time new words are acquired slowly and the child's attitude toward their acquisition is one of distinct indifference. Since the pronunciation of any word in his small repertory is received with acclaim, why should he go to the bother of learning new ones?

But with the discovery that speech is not merely a parlor trick but can be used to control the world in hitherto unsuspected ways, the picture changes. Now he has become the active seeker after words. He learns that everything has a name. "What's that?" "Who's that?" is his constant demand. No longer need he be urged to show off his verbal accomplishments. He practices them on all occasions. "Baby!" "Doggie!" "Car" he calls out in delighted recognition when he is taken out for a walk or as he turns the pages of his picture book.

Now his vocabulary grows apace, and as it grows his sentences expand in length and complexity. In his first use of language the single word is made to serve the purpose of an entire sentence; it is at once subject, predicate, and object—a question, a command, or a statement. "Milk!" calls the baby as he hammers the table with his cup. This is the infantile equivalent of "I want some milk" or "Give me some milk." "Milk," he announces with satisfaction as he sees the arrival of the milkman. This time he is giving information. "Milk?" he inquires with rising inflection as he points to the picture of a bottle in the morning paper. So characteristic is this stage in the development of language that many writers have referred to it as the "period of the single-word sentence."

LINGUISTIC PROGRESS IN EARLY CHILDHOOD

Figure 43 shows the average number of words in fifty consecutive remarks recorded by McCarthy[5] for twenty children at each of the following ages: eighteen, twenty-four, thirty, thirty-six, forty-two, forty-eight, and fifty-four months. Table I shows the average size of vocabu-

[5] D. McCarthy. *The language development of the preschool child.* Minneapolis: Univ. of Minnesota Press, 1930.

lary at successive ages from eight months (at which age few children can say any words) up to six years as reported by Smith.[6] The sudden and marked change in the average number of new words added to the vocabulary in the course of a single month that occurs at about the age of eighteen months is striking illustration of the effect of the shift from the passive attitude toward words that is characteristic of babies who are still in the period of the "trick vocabulary" to the active interest in word-learning that suddenly appears when language becomes a tool. (Like all the other developmental changes we have considered, this one does not occur at exactly the same age in all children. There are marked individual differences in size of vocabulary from the earliest age at which it is possible to evaluate this characteristic.)

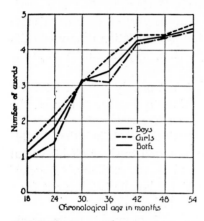

FIGURE 43. Changes in average length of sentence with age. (From Dorothea McCarthy. *Language development of the preschool child.* Courtesy Univ. of Minnesota Press.)

As children grow older their language changes in other ways. Nouns and interjections form a smaller proportion of the total. Pronouns, verbs, adjectives, conjunctions, and prepositions increase in frequency. Table II shows the proportion of the different parts of speech at three different ages as found by McCarthy.[7] However, the conventional classification of words into parts of speech which is based upon the language usage of adults is not entirely appropriate to the speech of children who have as yet not developed far beyond the stage of the single-word sentence. Moreover, the relative frequency with which certain parts of speech are used by children at play with other children differs markedly from that observed in conversation with an adult. McCarthy has shown that many more interjections are used in the former situation than in the latter, while Goodenough[8] finds that the proportionate use of pronouns of the first person singular during play with other children is almost twice as great as it is when engaged in conversation with an adult. This is understandable enough when one

[6] M. Smith. An investigation of the development of the sentence and the extent of vocabulary in young children. *Univ. of Iowa Stud. in Child Welf.*, 1926, Vol. 3, No. 5.

[7] *Op. cit.*

[8] F. L. Goodenough. The use of pronouns by young children: a note on the development of self-awareness. *J. genet. Psychol.*, 1938, 52, 333-346.

stops to think that it is in the former rather than the latter situation
that the child finds the greater need to assert himself as an individual.

THEORIES ABOUT THE ORIGIN OF LANGUAGE IN THE RACE

The question of how man first acquired a language has awakened
the curiosity of scientists for generations. In no other aspect of his be-

TABLE I

AVERAGE SIZE OF VOCABULARIES OF 273 CHILDREN FROM
EIGHT MONTHS TO SIX YEARS OF AGE

Age in Years and Months	Number of Children	Average Vocabulary Number of Words	Average Gain per Month
0-8	13	0	—
0-10.	17	1	0.5
1-0	52	3	1.0
1-3	19	19	5.3
1-6	14	22	1.0
1-9	14	118	32.0
2-0	25	272	51.3
2-6	14	446	29.0
3-0	20	896	75.0
3-6	26	1,222	54.3
4-0	26	1,540	53.0
4-6	32	1,870	55.0
5-0	20	2,072	33.7
5-6	27	2,289	36.2
6-0	9	2,562	45.5

Adapted from Smith

TABLE II

PERCENTAGES OF THE DIFFERENT PARTS OF SPEECH
USED BY YOUNG CHILDREN

Age in Months	Nouns	Verbs	Adjectives	Adverbs	Pronouns	Conjunctions	Prepositions	Interjections	Unclassified
18	50.0	13.9	9.6	7.9	10.3	0.5	0.0	7.6	0.0
36	23.4	23.0	16.1	7.0	19.2	2.4	6.9	1.5	0.5
54	19.3	25.1	15.2	7.0	20.5	3.8	7.1	1.2	0.8

havior is the difference between man and animal so apparent, for while it is true that animals have certain crude methods of communicating with each other,[9] even the most primitive of the races of man known to us today have advanced far beyond the most highly developed animal in command of speech. It almost seems as if something analogous to the "discovery" of the function of speech by the infant occurred at some undetermined point in the evolution of man, a discovery that set him apart from the rest of the animal world for all time to come. Of course this cannot have been literally true. The child finds a language ready fashioned to his tongue; man had to build up his system of symbols by slow and laborious stages. Nevertheless, if we make allowance for the inevitable difference in the time factor, the analogy may not be as far-fetched as it seems, for there must have been a time, far back in the history of mankind, when, as generation succeeded generation, the advantages of a system of verbal symbols whereby ideas about objects and events could be communicated in the absence of the material facts to which they applied became slowly but surely apparent.

Many theories have been advanced to account for the origin of language in the human race. Because among the lower animals the chief purpose of vocalization seems to be the expression and communication of emotional states, as well as because interjections constitute a much greater percentage of the total number of words used by young children than of the number used by older children or adults, some anthropologists have taken the interjections to be the most primitive type of word form and have ascribed the origin of language to a gradual differentiation among vocal symbols in order to convey more exact shades of meaning in the expression of emotion. This is known as the "interjectional theory" of the origin of language.

Another theory known as the "onomatopoeic theory" is concerned particularly with the question of how words acquired their particular forms. Those who advocate this theory point to the fact that even in the languages of groups of widely separated geographic and ethnic background, there is greater than chance resemblance in the form of certain words, particularly those having to do with natural phenomena. "Thunder," "tonnerre," and "Donner" are all quite similar in sound, and all carry a certain quality of resonance that by the exercise of a moderate degree of imagination may be thought to suggest the sound of thunder. The fact that what seems like the same idea is in other

---

[9] In his *Pilgrim's Progress,* Bunyan gives the following quaint description of the "language" of the hen:
"So they gave heed and perceived that the Hen did walk in a fourfold Method toward her Chickens. 1. She had a *common call* and that she hath all day long. 2. She had a *special call* and that she had but sometimes. 3. She had a *brooding note* and 4. She had an *outcry.*"

instances expressed by very dissimilar words in different languages is explained by saying that few of the facts of nature are simple and that the particular words selected to convey a particular meaning may owe their origin to quite different aspects of the thing each has been chosen to symbolize. Moreover, inasmuch as languages have changed so greatly, even within the brief period over which our written history extends, it is not to be expected that its present form should show more than occasional faint traces of the seeds from which it grew. The onomatopoeic theory thus assumes that language arose through the playful attempts of primitive man to imitate the sounds of natural phenomena as children often do today. As one member of the tribe began to imitate a particular sound, others joined in and in so doing were influenced, not only by the sound originally heard, but also by the attempts at reproducing it made by each other. Thus the sounds made would, in the course of time, crystallize into a comparatively uniform pattern that by common consent would be accepted as the "right" way to make the sound of thunder, of running water, of wind in the trees, of the hum of bees, or the cry of a particular animal. From this simple beginning, two things would almost inevitably follow. First, people would begin to make these sounds on occasions when the thing imitated was not actually present and when this occurred, others who had learned to make the same kind of reproduction would know what the sound made by his neighbor represented. Thus a new kind of communication would be established between them. Various uses for this verbal relationship would soon become apparent. It could convey a warning or serve as a reminder. The cave woman could make the "bear sound" when her husband started out for his daily hunt to remind him of what he was expected to bring home for dinner; the "thunder sound" would convey warning of an approaching storm. Secondly, the word forms thus established would be passed on to succeeding generations as children learned to copy the "speech" of their elders. Each new generation would add new forms to the list. Once the process of symbolization has begun, its continuance is well-nigh assured. The weak point in the onomatopoeic theory is its basic premise. We have no evidence that before his development of speech, primitive man felt any more urge to imitate the sounds of nature than is now evinced by the most intelligent of our domestic animals or by the anthropoid apes.

Whatever may have been the mode by which speech first came into being, every situation carries within itself the soil from which the growth of language is nourished. Each new situation demands a new word or phrase by which it may be fixed in memory; and the more apt the phraseology, the more completely the experience can be exploited to the advantage of the individual and of society. If two persons with equally acute hearing attempt to describe a tone that both have heard, the one who has had musical training can do so better than the other who has no knowledge of musical terms. The physician can give a better description of the symptoms shown by a sick person than can the layman, not only because he knows what to look for but also because he has acquired a vocabulary that enables him to express the results of his observations in precise rather than general terms. So the child, as he grows older and is subjected to an ever-widening range of experiences, is continually forced to revise and improve the symbols of these experiences that he carries with him as guides for the future. At one time the dominant psychological theory about thinking was that thought is nothing but subvocal speech. There is some sound evidence that such a process does occur—that a person who is thinking may actually be "talking to himself." It seems now, however, that the mental processes that involve the use of symbols are not limited to speech, and that there are other ways in which thinking can occur. Gestures, for example, can carry symbolic meaning. But even if it does not account for everything we classify as thinking, language is certainly a highly important factor making for increased precision and clarity. It is no accident that vocabulary tests have turned out to be our best single indicator of intelligence.

FACTORS INFLUENCING THE DEVELOPMENT OF LANGUAGE IN CHILDREN

The talkativeness of the female sex has formed one of the chief stand-bys of the comic papers for generations. Like many other stock jokes, it has some foundation in fact. Nearly all investigators have found that on the average girl babies begin to talk a little earlier than do boys, that their vocabularies at any age are a little larger, and that they use longer sentences. McCarthy found that at the age of eighteen months 14 per cent of the boys' remarks and 38 per cent of those made by the girls were comprehensible to a stranger. At twenty-four months the proportions of comprehensible responses were 49 per cent for the boys and 78 per cent for the girls. In various aspects of language development, girls seem on the average to be a little more precocious than boys. (See Figure 43.)

In a more recent study by Templin,[10] girls are less superior to boys than they had appeared to be in former studies. Templin chose her sample with particular care so that it would be really representative of the urban population. Thus the failure to get sex differences in any

[10] M. C. Templin. *Certain language skills in children: their development and interrelationships.* Minneapolis: Univ. of Minnesota Press, 1957.

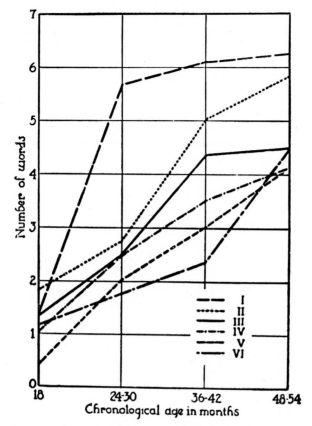

FIGURE 44. Relationship between paternal occupation and average length of sentence used by children of preschool age. (From Dorothea McCarthy. *Language development in the preschool child.* Courtesy University of Minnesota Press.)

aspect of speech except articulation of sounds suggests that there may actually be less difference between boys and girls than there was twenty years ago with regard to discrimination of sounds, vocabulary, and sentence length. Perhaps changes in child rearing methods are having some unexpected effects. In this connection it is also interesting to note that the average scores for the children studied by Templin are significantly higher than those of a generation ago.

Language development is closely related to general intelligence or "brightness." Studies of bright, average, and dull children have universally shown that the brighter children begin to talk at an earlier age than those who are backward; their vocabularies increase faster; as a rule their articulation is better; and they use longer and more correct sentences. Indeed, the quality of a child's speech is one of the chief things by which we are guided in judging his intelligence.

Social class is also related to language development. Not only do children from cultured homes speak more correctly than those from the lower social classes but their speech is more advanced in other ways. As will be shown later, they also rank higher on intelligence tests, but the intelligence difference between social classes is smaller than the difference in language development. Environment as well as intelligence probably has something to do with it. Figure 44 shows the extent to which children from different social classes differ in respect to average length of sentence. In this figure, Group I represents children whose fathers belong to the professional classes—doctors, lawyers, college professors, and so on. Group II is made up of the children of business men. Group III is composed of the children of clerical workers and skilled tradesmen, and Group IV of the children of semiskilled workers, chiefly factory hands. Group V includes children whose fathers are icemen, drivers of milk-wagons, junkmen, and men following other trades which require little skill. Group VI is made up of the children of day-laborers. At the age of three, the children of Group I use, on the average, more than twice as many words to the sentence as the children in Groups V and VI. The more recent Templin study still finds these socio-economic differences.

Another example of the way social stimulation affects language development is seen in the development of language in twins. Most children learn their language from persons older than themselves. If there are younger children in the family, the difference in age is great enough for the older to feel his own linguistic superiority to the baby so that he is unlikely to copy the latter's mode of speech. But twins are in a different category. Because of their similarity of age and interests they spend much more of their time together than brothers and sisters of different ages are likely to do, and for the same reason they are less dependent upon adults for companionship. Twins play together; they talk together; and they imitate each other's speech. There are a number of instances on record in which a pair of twins have developed a language of their own, comprehensible to each other but to no one else. Sometimes this secret language is continued into adult life, but as a rule it is discarded as soon as normal speech is learned. The learning of normal speech, however, is likely to be considerably delayed in these cases. In one such case a pair of twin girls four and one-half years old used no words at all that could be understood by others. They were unquestionably of normal intelligence. In some ways they were distinctly in advance of their age. To each other they chattered continually, and their behavior gave clear evidence that they understood each other.

Yet their language was entirely incomprehensible, even to their parents.

Although the development of an independent language is unusual, Day [11] has shown that twins, on the average, make slower progress in speech than single children. This retardation is shown in practically all aspects of speech development—in vocabulary, in average length of sentence, and in articulation. Figure 45 shows the extent of this retardation in respect to average length of sentence.

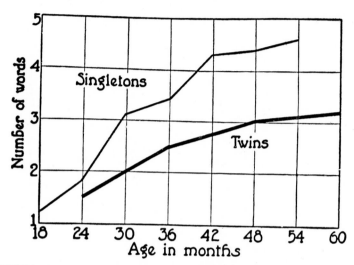

FIGURE 45. Language retardation in twins. (From Ella J. Day. Development of language in twins. *Child develpm.*, 1932, 3, 179-199. Courtesy Dr. Buford Johnson.)

That the language retardation of twins is a social rather than a biological phenomenon is neatly shown in a follow-up of Day's study by Davis,[12] who compared the language development of twins with that of single children after they had been subjected to the wider social experience of school life. Davis used as subjects children of five and one-half to nine and one-half years of age and followed the procedure used by McCarthy and by Day exactly except for the substitution of different toys and picture books more suited to the interests of older children. Her findings indicate that even a half-year of kindergarten is sufficient to erase most, if not all, of the difference between the groups as far as average length of sentence is concerned. Apparently the wider

[11] E. J. Day. The development of language in twins: I. a comparison of twins and single children. *Child Develpm.*, 1932, 3, 179-199.

[12] E. A. Davis. *The development of linguistic skill in twins, singletons with siblings, and only children from age five to ten years.* Univ. of Minn. Inst. Child Welf. Monogr. Series, No. 14. Minneapolis: Univ. of Minnesota Press, 1937.

social contact with children of normal speech development was having its effect. The greatest residual effect of the early handicap was noted in respect to articulation. Even at the age of nine and one-half, the number of twins with faulty articulation was distinctly greater than the number of single children with such defects.

Davis also compared the speech development of "only" children with that of twins and of singly born children from families of more than one child. Her assumption was that if the imperfect language of twins is the result of hearing and imitating each other's faulty speech,

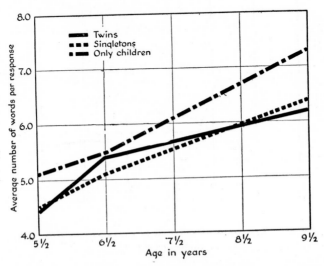

FIGURE 46.   Language development of only children compared with that of singly-born children in families of more than one child and of twins. (After Davis.)

then "only" children, whose early association is almost exclusively with adults should, on the average, be more advanced in speech than the general run of children from larger families. That this hypothesis was amply substantiated by her results [13] is shown by Figure 46.

This brings us back to a further consideration of the role of imitation in the acquisition of language. Evidently we cannot discard the concept entirely. Common sense alone would show the fallacy in doing so. Imitation of the speech of others sets the pattern for speech and provides

[13] It may be well to note that Davis, Day, McCarthy, and Templin were all careful to guard against errors resulting from unequal sampling of cases from the various socio-economic levels by matching each of the groups which they studied to the occupational distribution of employed males for the cities of Minneapolis and St. Paul as reported in the U. S. Census.

the necessary basis for acquiring new words, once the linguistic process is under way. Thus the progress in speech made by any child is determined to a great extent by the kind and quality of the language that he hears. Not only does a child learn to speak a particular language —English, German, French, or Chinese—according to the language of the home in which he is reared, but an English-speaking child who hears only good English will himself speak better English than another whose early training has been less fortunate. Children imitate the speech of those about them, whether this speech be good or poor. It is important, therefore, that they be given as good models for imitation as possible. Adults should not use "baby-talk" in speaking to children if they wish the children to learn correct articulation. And when children are unavoidably exposed to imperfect speech, as in the case of twins where each hears the undeveloped language of the other, special care should be taken to see that they also get their full share of conversation with older persons and that any specific speech defects which arise be corrected as promptly as possible in order that mutual imitation may not cause these defects to persist to an age at which they would become a serious handicap. Not all twins are backward in language development. Whether or not they shall be so depends upon the kind of attention and training that is given them in the home.

LANGUAGE AS AN INDEX TO OTHER MENTAL TRAITS

Before the beginning of speech we are very often at a loss to interpret the baby's behavior. "If he could only *tell* me what ails him," laments the mother as she tries to quiet her baby's wails, and again, "I simply cannot understand what he wants," as he squeals and tugs at her skirts. But once speech has developed, the relationship of the child to others changes in many ways. It becomes more intimate; its outlines are more clear-cut. Now the child can do more than show that he wants something. He can make requests, ask questions, give commands. He can understand and respond to the requests of others. With the beginning of speech the entire pattern of social intercourse clarifies. Its details as well as its broad outlines can now be seen.

We therefore study and record what the child says in various situations not only as an index to his language development but in order that we may better understand the child himself. When we do this, we find that children differ quite as greatly in the uses to which they put their new accomplishment as in respect to the accomplishment itself. Johnny is continually asking questions. Mary's speech is a succession of commands. Polly uses six *I*'s to every *you*. Billy has little say about himself but much about the other children.

All these differences have a meaning. When properly understood they throw much light on the total personality of the child. More than anything else in his behavior, the child's language provides us with a key to his character. Through his answers to our questions and his own spontaneous remarks and questions we are also able to find out something of his thought processes, how he reasons, what he believes. We cannot see the world through the child's eyes without danger of distortion, but after he is able to talk he can give us some idea, imperfect though it may be, of how the world appears to him.

DISCUSSION

Putting together the material presented in this and preceding chapters, we note first of all that like all other forms of behavior, the ability to communicate with others by means of language does not come into being all at once but has a history of its own. Its development conforms to the same general principles that hold for other learned skills. It is motivated by organic drives and acquires its special form by a process of associative learning. It is subject to loss through disuse [14] but can be re-established more easily than if it had never been acquired, and it is probably the most effective of all learned reactions for facilitating further learning. Its usefulness as a mechanism for short-cutting, for substituting symbols that can be quickly and easily handled for time-consuming and laborious muscular acts can hardly be overestimated. As facility with the speech mechanisms and their uses is gained, finer distinctions appear. To the very little child, all feathered bipeds are "chickies" or "birdies"; to the nonmechanically minded adult, almost any complex arrangement of metal parts is a "machine" or a "gadget." To be sure, the application of special names to particular classes of objects involves much more than the mere development of a new verbal response. But the distinctions noted are not easy to hold in mind without the integrative aid of particularized verbal symbols.

In this chapter, only one aspect of the development of the art of communicating with others has been considered. It is necessary to

[14] Helen Keller, who lost both sight and hearing at about the age of nineteen months, had begun to learn to speak before the illness that destroyed her sensory apparatus. Except for the retention of a single word, "water," the language ability previously gained gradually disappeared. Even so, it is probable that, as she herself points out, the retraining which was begun shortly before the age of seven was facilitated to some extent by the skill acquired earlier of which practically all observable traces had disappeared. Many studies have shown that deaf-mutes who lost their hearing after some facility in speech had been gained are usually easier to train than those whose loss goes back to early infancy and that the difference is more apparent in respect to the acquisition of oral speech than in learning the manual alphabet.

remember, however, that communication is carried on by other devices as well. Even before speech is established, the use of gesture by the infant is well under way. Indeed, if "gesture-language" is so thoroughly established that the child finds it sufficient for most if not all of his needs, he may be slow in acquiring speech. But gesture is too crude and too much an affair of the moment to be effective for all purposes. Sooner or later, even the child who has been able to get what he wants by the primitive methods of crying, pointing, and snatching will feel the need of other devices for controlling his expanding universe.

SUMMARY

The speech mechanism is a complex combination of respiratory system, larynx, nose, and mouth. A great many accurate and well-co-ordinated muscle movements are involved in the utterance of even a single sentence.

During the first few months there is a steady increase in the number of different sounds the infant produces. "Circular" vocal responses—repeating the same syllable over and over again—constitute the second stage. Gradually this vocalization becomes socialized, and the child begins to make new combinations of the sounds he is able to produce.

The crucial step in the development of true language is the realization that certain sound patterns have meaning or can be used to represent desired objects. This seems to occur through the differential reinforcement of sound combinations that occur at first spontaneously. "Trick" words, spoken just to obtain approval, often precede by several months the association of word with object that constitutes true language.

Word learning is slow at first but proceeds with great rapidity from about the age of eighteen months on. Changes in the proportions of various parts of speech that are used also occur and sentences become longer and more complicated.

There have been a number of theories with regard to the origin of language in the human race, none of them altogether satisfactory. Theorists are agreed that language plays a very significant part in thinking as well as speaking and writing.

A variety of factors influence language development in individual children. Girls, on the average, are ahead of boys. Children from upper socio-economic levels are ahead of those from poorer homes. Only children make faster progress than children with brothers and sisters, and twins make slower progress than siblings in general. Factors of this sort point to the importance of social influences on language development.

HOW A BLIND AND DEAF CHILD
ACQUIRED A LANGUAGE

Keller, Helen. *The story of my life.* New York: Doubleday, Page and Co., 1905.

In this book, written in her early twenties, Helen Keller tells of her childhood and youth. The difference in age and experience as well as the fact of
her remarkable intellectual brilliance necessarily make her story of the way
she first acquired the ability to communicate with others somewhat different
from the process by which the normal child gains this accomplishment. The
difference is further accentuated by her sensory limitations which for many
years reduced her associations with the language of others to that maintained with her teacher. Despite these differences, the points of similarity
between her experience and reactions and those of the normal infant are
both striking and informative. Her discovery, so vividly described, that
everything has a name, and the almost phenomenal advance in her vocabulary that immediately followed this discovery provides one of the most
dramatic descriptions in biographical literature. Even the account of her
temper tantrums that resulted from her inability to make herself understood
find their parallels in miniature in the history of most normal babies.

Miss Keller tells her story so skillfully as to hold the reader fascinated to
the very end. The appended letters by her famous teacher, Miss Elizabeth
Sullivan, which tell the story of the same events as they were observed by
her at the time, make a valuable and instructive supplement to Miss Keller's
own account of the experience through which she lived and the responses
they aroused in her.

CHAPTER 10

Why do we think that there is a relationship between the experiences and characteristics of a person during infancy and the kind of personality he shows when he grows up?

What kinds of emotions does the newborn child show? How do they change as he grows?

How well can adults identify emotional states in an infant?

What aspects of the parents' treatment of the baby have the most important effects on his emotional development?

How do motives change as an infant grows older? Why do they differ in different children?

What do follow-up studies show about the relationship between individual differences in personality during infancy and differences at maturity?

The First Two Years: Foundations of Personality

INFANCY AND ADULT PERSONALITY

How OFTEN do we hear someone say as he watches a tiny baby, "I wonder what he will be like when he grows up?" The steady, mysterious transformation of infant personality into adult personality is a phenomenon at which we cannot cease to wonder, no matter how often we see it repeated. Again and again the question comes up, "Why should this kind of baby grow into this particular kind of man?" Does a person have traits from the beginning that predispose him to a certain kind of personality? Are there things about the ways babies are treated and handled that have lifelong effects? Or doesn't it really matter much what happens to them while they are too young to think or remember, so long as they are fed and kept warm and given a chance to grow?

It has been assumed for centuries that childhood is a formative period. "The child is father of the man." "As the twig is bent, the tree inclines." "Bring up a child in the way he should go, and when he is old he will not depart from it." There are many such quotations and proverbs expressing common beliefs about the effect of childhood experience on adult personality. But it is easier to see how they apply to the child who is old enough to talk, act, and be deliberately trained in some of the accepted adult ways than to the newborn infant. Consequently the importance of the first two years in personality formation was not recognized as clearly nor as soon as were the more directly observable effects of the later periods of childhood.

The present interest in tracing origins of personality in infancy rests to a large extent on psychoanalytic observations and theory, as formulated by Freud and a number of other writers. At first it was based primarily upon things patients on the analytic couch remembered about their early experiences and relationships with their parents. Obviously this is not a very sound basis for generalizations about human nature in general, and critics were quick to point out the inadequate nature of the evidence, and to question the solidity of any structure of theory that was based exclusively on it. But as time passed, more and more observations were made of infants themselves, and more and more studies were planned specifically to test out the psychoanalytic hypotheses. Most psychologists would not consider that the results so far substantiate *all* of the psychoanalytic ideas about early personality development, but there is enough evidence to suggest that the first two years are extremely important, perhaps the most important of all, in their effects on the individual's subsequent life.

While therapists were developing theoretical hypotheses out of their activities, scientific workers in child development centers throughout the country were gathering facts about the ways young children actually behave, and how their behavior changes as they grow. Dependable information about emotions and their expression, behavioral effects of different kinds of training methods, and the relationship between individual traits manifested at earlier and later stages was made available. We can now say with some certainty that personality has its origins in infancy, but we are still a long way from complete knowledge of what all the complex developmental sequences are.

People differ, of course, in the ways they define personality. Some think of it primarily in external terms—the impression a person makes on those who know him—whereas others think of it as an internal affair —the way the person feels. Some define it very broadly, so that it covers *all* of a person's abilities, knowledge, and habits, as well as his temperamental and motivational characteristics. Others restrict the term to the less tangible aspects of total functioning.

For convenience, we are using the term *personality* to apply to the still quite broad group of characteristics that we have *left* after taking out physical characteristics, abilities, and developed skills, the things we have considered in some detail in previous chapters. In general, this complex of traits is concerned more with how the person feels about things than with how much he knows about them. Two boys who are the same age and the same size, with identical IQ's, may still differ a great deal in their emotional responses to situations, their attitudes toward people, their interests, their goals, and their ideas about themselves. It is such differences we must try to understand.

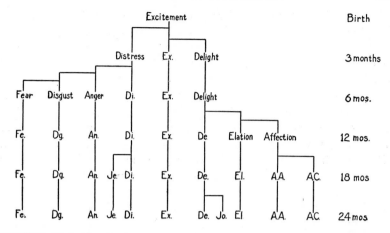

FIGURE 47. Bridges' scheme of emotional development during infancy. By the age of three months, the primitive excitement which is observable at birth has differentiated into the two contrasted states of distress and delight. The distress pattern later differentiates further into fear, disgust, and anger, along with the more primitive pattern of simple distress. By the age of twelve months, elation and affection as well as simple delight can be distinguished on the positive side of the emotional picture, and in another half year a distinction can be observed between affection for adults (A.A.) and affection for children (A.C.). At the same time a further division of the distress pattern can be seen with jealousy (Je.) coming in as something distinct from ordinary distress. By the age of twenty-four months, a distinction can be made between the high-pitched emotional fervor of delight and the more stable emotion known as joy. (Reproduced by permission of the author and the publishers from K. M. B. Bridges, Emotional development in early infancy. *Child Develpm.*, 1932, 3, 324-341.)

Such distinctions—between ability or skill, on the one hand, personality or motivation, on the other—must *not* be considered to correspond to any actual division within the person. Personality is an organized whole. Increasing skill leads to changes in ways of expressing emotion; differences in abilities make for differences in social roles and thus for differences in attitudes and goals. As has been said before, in studying development we may consider various processes one at a time, but in understanding any particular person we must think of all aspects and be aware of their interrelationships.

THE EARLY DEVELOPMENT OF EMOTION

As has been explained in a previous chapter, one of the most general principles that characterize all of development is the tendency toward increasing differentiation. The development of emotions is no exception to this trend. At first, any stimulus or situation we would think of as likely to lead to an emotional response serves mainly to increase the general activity level of the infant. He gives no sign that he can make any distinction between states we would call anger, fear, or sadness. The word that would seem best to describe the general undifferentiated state that is all he knows of emotion is *excitement*.

As the months pass, evidence of different kinds of response to different emotion-producing situations appears. Bridges, [1] on the basis of very intensive observations of about sixty infants over a period of several months, was able to draw up the general chart or schema shown in Figure 47 indicating the ages at which the successive differentiations are made. By three months the infant's behavior makes it clear whether he is experiencing distress or delight. By six months distress comes in three different varieties. By twelve months different kinds of delight can be distinguished. (As in all such developmental studies, ages are only approximate and children differ from one another in their individual developmental patterns.)

Another sequence that proceeds from general to more differentiated is the development of emotional relationships with people. The first stage consists of a powerful attachment to one person—the mother or the mother-person who cares for the baby. This is something that takes a few months to develop. At the beginning the infant gives no sign that he can differentiate between his mother and other human beings, and he shows no special attachment to anyone. But once this strong dependent attachment has formed, it is several years before the differentiation of this one love into many different kinds of emotional ties to different persons is accomplished. It is important that the child go through this stage of loving dependency. It is equally important that it be transformed into more differentiated feelings. But this particular shift is more a challenge of the preschool period from two to five than of the years of infancy.

Considerable research attention has been given to the question of whether there are uniform recognizable patterns of emotional *expression*. When a certain variety of emotion has been differentiated out of the original matrix, does it produce facial expressions, gestures, or other behavior that are similar enough from person to person so that it would be clear even to a stranger what the emotion is?

Many of the experiments were generated by a theory proposed by Darwin [2] and by Spencer [3] in 1872. They held that emotional behavior

---

[1] K. M. B. Bridges. Emotional development in early infancy. *Child Develpm.*, 1932, 3, 324-341.

[2] C. Darwin. *The expression of the emotions in man and animals.* London: John Murray, 1872.

[3] H. Spencer, *Principles of psychology.* (2nd Ed.) Vol. II. New York: D. Appleton, 1872.

of human beings has an evolutionary origin, and that many of the apparently unserviceable acts shown under strong emotion are merely survivals of actions that had a useful function in a more primitive state of existence. For example, the uncovering of the canine teeth so often seen in anger or sneering was said to be a survival from the time when our prehuman ancestors did much of their fighting with their teeth. Frowning is explained as a residual effect of an action originally useful in shielding the eyes from the direct rays of the sun during fighting when clear vision is most essential. Certain other forms of emotional expression Darwin was inclined to trace back to the infancy of the individual rather than the infancy of the race. Shaking the head as a sign of denial or unwillingness is an act that appears early in most children and is continued throughout life. Darwin ascribed this to the survival of a habit formed during the nursing period when turning the head to the side was the natural way of rejecting unwanted food.

Another influential theoretical formulation was that of J. B. Watson. His basic hypothesis was that three primary emotions, fear, rage, and love, can be identified even in very young infants. The natural stimulus for fear is a loud sound or loss of support, for rage, interference with movement, and for love, stroking of sensitive areas of the skin.

The conclusion one can draw from all of the experiments centering around these issues is that observers cannot agree very well about what specific emotion is being expressed unless they are in a position to see what the stimulating situation was. Just the expression or behavior alone is hard to identify. This is especially true when the subjects are newborn infants. A careful study by Sherman [4] using motion pictures of babies who had been stimulated in various ways showed rather conclusively that neither trained nor untrained observers could agree whether the behavior should be labeled fear, rage, or love unless they saw the stimulus that had led to it.

In older children and adults, in spite of marked individual differences based on learning, there seems to be some standardization of facial expression, so that emotions can be distinguished, though not with any great accuracy. A study by Goodenough [5] of a child who had been blind and deaf from birth on and thus had never had an opportunity to see how others expressed fear, anger, or pleasure showed that there was enough resemblance between her patterns of expression and those we are accustomed to so that her feelings could be recognized. Ordinarily, of course, when we try to understand what kind of an emotion either a child or an adult is experiencing, we see the situation

[4] M. Sherman. The differentiation of emotional responses in infants. I. *J. comp. Psychol.*, 1927, 7, 265-284. II. *Ibid.*, 7, 335-351. III. *Ibid.*, 8, 385-394.
[5] F. L. Goodenough. Expression of the emotions in a deaf-blind child. *J. abnorm. soc. Psychol.*, 1932, 27, 328-333

along with the expression, so that we do not have to judge from expression alone.

There are two kinds of unlearned responses or reflexes which are easily recognizable even in infancy and may be said to have some connection with emotions. The first of these is the "startle pattern." By means of slow motion photography it has been possible to observe a uniform standard pattern of response to sudden stimulation that occurs regularly from about the fourth month on. Before that it is masked by another response, the Moro reflex, a pattern of behavior that is characteristic of the immature nervous system but has no connection with emotion, so far as we know. The Moro reflex typically disappears when a certain level of brain development has been reached but the startle pattern persists throughout life. While it now seems to have less to do with subsequent emotional development than its discoverers thought it had, it is of some interest as an example of a fairly complex unlearned reaction that is independent of sex, age, race, and home background. Figure 48 shows what it looks like.

Another unlearned response that may have a much more important connection with emotional development is the smile. We have noted in a previous chapter its significance for social development. It seems to be a specific response to one particular kind of stimulus—the human face. Spitz and Wolf [6] have shown that between the second and the sixth month the infant will smile when confronted with any sort of face-like object. Whether it is a mask or a real person, whether the expression is a laugh or a frown makes no difference at first. During the last half of the first year the child begins to distinguish between faces, smiling at some and not at others.

The fact that only two "instinctive" or unlearned patterns of emotional response have stood up under continuing investigation fits in with the idea of development as increasing differentiation. We are tempted to connect the startle pattern and the smile with the distress and delight Bridges found to be in evidence early. But there is no real evidence for this. It may be that these reflexes are not really emotional at all at the beginning but become connected with stimulating situations and differentiated feeling states as development proceeds. Certain it is that learning plays a considerable part in the varieties of emotional expression individuals come to show. There is indeed a "language of the emotions" but it is not so easy to read it as we once thought it was going to be.

There is one more aspect of emotional development to which the principle of increasing differentiation with age applies. Stimulating

[6] R. A. Spitz and K. M. Wolf. The smiling response: a contribution to the ontogenesis of social relations. *Genet. Psychol. Monogr.*, 1946, 34, 57-125.

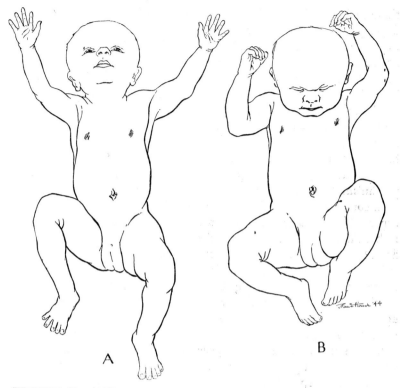

FIGURE 48. Difference between the Moro reflex (A) and the startle pattern (B) in infancy.

situations are increasingly distinguished from one another. Many more different kinds of things become stimuli for fear responses. Unfamiliar persons and "uncanny" things like a doll's body without a head begin to act as fear-producers. A little later, fear of animals often shows up. Similarly, smiling occurs now in some situations, not in others. Such changes seem to occur naturally as the child's perceptions of the world around him improve. They seem not to be based on particular frightening or pleasure-giving experiences. Emotional development is partly a matter of perceptual development.

SOCIALIZATION AND PERSONALITY DEVELOPMENT

It has been noted in Chapter 8 that one of the earliest kinds of adaptive behavior a child shows consists of responses to the people around him. There has been an increasing awareness among psychiatrists, psychologists, and other students of personality that the nature of these early social interactions may play a very large part in personality development. Through these relationships the basic emotional attitudes that characterize the cultural subgroup into which a person has been born are mediated to him. To some extent these relationships to persons in his immediate family set the pattern for all his later relationships. Years later, for example, the way he feels about his wife will depend partly upon what his relationship with his mother was like. It is believed that his deepest feelings about himself—whether or not he feels that he is strong, competent, and worthy of love and respect— have roots in these early social interactions. And, finally, his expectations of life and of other people—such things as basic optimism or pessimism, trust or suspicion—are thought to rest on these experiences.

In considering such ideas, it is necessary to say that these important aspects of personality "are thought to" depend upon infantile experience rather than to say definitely that they do. It has been extrordinarily difficult to get unambiguous evidence with regard to this problem, though it has been a meeting ground for the efforts of psychiatrists, psychologists, and social anthropolgists. Because the child before he learns to speak cannot tell us directly what his experience is, we must depend upon observations which turn out to be interpretable in more than one way, and upon reconstructions of early family relationships from what patients and experimental subjects say in interviews years after the period we are trying to understand is over. There has been much theorizing and speculation that rests on very little real fact. Gradually, however, some evidence has accumulated that enables us to say some things with reasonable certainty.

A great deal of the discussion has centered around the importance of emotional closeness to the mother during infancy. Ribble (p. 535) has reported observations leading to the conclusion that infants need the kind of stimulation that comes with the fondling, petting, and caressing a loving mother naturally gives, and that without such physical stimulation neither physiological nor psychological development can proceed normally. The nature of the evidence for this idea is the finding that children reared in an institution where nutrition and medical care are entirely adequate may still be weak, emaciated, and retarded unless they get this kind of attention from some mother-person. Spitz [7] has described in words and pictures some alarming examples of this kind of neglect. Examination of all of the evidence, however, by skeptical reviewers [8] has cast a good deal of doubt on the idea that such outcomes

[7] R. A. Spitz. The role of ecological factors in emotional development in infancy. *Child Develpm.*, 1949, 21, 145-156.

[8] See H. Orlansky. Infant care and personality. *Psychol. Bull.*, 1949, 46, 1-48. Also S. R. Pinneau. The infantile disorders of hospitalism and anaclitic depression. *Psychol. Bull.*, 1955, 52, 429-462.

are universal or inevitable results of the lack of physical "mothering" in infancy. Outstanding personalities as well as stunted ones have been known to come out of orphanages. We shall consider this problem at more length in a later chapter.

Another principal idea around which research and discussion have centered has to do with effects of the way the child's feeding and elimination behavior is brought into line with the customs of the society in which he lives. According to Freud's famous doctrine of infantile sexuality, erotic satisfaction comes to the infant first in connection with oral sensations and responses and, at the next stage, through anal activity. Unless a person can be helped during his first two years to negotiate these stages successfully, he may be "fixated" at one of these early levels so far as personality traits are concerned and may carry on into adulthood some troublesome infantile characteristics. The demanding, over-dependent person can be seen as someone who never outgrew an early oral stage. The stingy, stubborn adult can be thought of as an "anal" character behaving in essentially the same way as the two-year-old who refuses to let his feces go.

Psychoanalysts have thus placed special stress on the training methods used in connection with oral and anal behavior. "Self-demand" feeding schedules to insure that the baby will be fed when he is hungry, gradual and unhurried weaning, tolerance for thumb-sucking and other kinds of sucking behavior are recommended. Postponement of toilet training until the infant is old enough to understand what is expected of him and exercise a good deal of control over his own muscles is considered advisable.

With regard to the effects of methods of habit training, as with the general "mothering" idea, the evidence is not at all conclusive. The methods recommended by psychoanalysts can be endorsed, whether or not one is committed to the theoretical viewpoint. What should be kept in mind, however, is that we certainly do not *know* that dire consequences always follow when other methods of habit training are followed. One unfortunate effect of the wide circulation of these ideas has been that individuals who know that their treatment during infancy has been unsatisfactory often get a feeling that their lives have been blighted and that there is nothing they can do to improve their situation. It is well to remember that personality is extremely complex and influenced by a great many factors, not the least of which is the person's own attitude toward his resources and limitations. Stress or frustration during infancy may mean that a person will be somewhat different throughout his life than he would have been had it not occurred, but it does not sentence him to failure or despair.

Most of the evidence we do have about the effects of infantile experience on personality can be interpreted to mean that it is _general attitudes_ and the _total situation_ rather than the specific child-rearing practices that matter most. For example, this total situation is quite different for an infant whose mother fondles him and plays with him because she loves him and enjoys doing these things than it is for the infant whose mother religiously takes him out of the crib and pets him for a half hour each morning and afternoon because she has read Ribble's book and is convinced that this is her duty. Similarly, the mother who resentfully washes her baby's diapers long after it seems to her that he could be clean if he wanted to, because she has heard that premature toilet training is a bad thing, is really not creating the same kind of emotional situation for the child as is the mother who takes this task as a matter of course and watches with loving interest the progress he is making toward maturity. The general attitudes will make themselves felt in a thousand minor ways, and a baby quickly becomes sensitive to these clues.

This broadened view of what the psychoanalytic work on the crises of infancy really means is well expressed in the discussion by Erikson [9] of the first two "stages of man." What the child needs to learn during the first stage is a basic trust in existence itself. What he needs to learn during the second stage is to come to terms with his own autonomy, his own freedom to choose between "holding on" and "letting go." What Erikson says about the maternal relationship with the child during the first stage sums up very well this view of what the really important things are. "The amount of trust derived from the earliest infantile experience does not seem to depend on absolute quantities of food or demonstrations of love, but rather on the quality of the maternal relationship. Mothers, I think, create a sense of trust in their children by that kind of administration which in its quality combines sensitive care of the baby's individual needs and a firm sense of personal trustworthiness within the trusted framework of their culture's life style." [10]

THE EMERGENCE OF MOTIVES

It is generally agreed that one of the most important aspects of personality is the individual's unique pattern of motivation. When we know what a person really wants, what he wishes and strives for, we feel as though we understand him in a way we can never do if we know only his actions. As we have explained in Chapter 6, this motivational aspect of human life is not sharply separated from emotion or adaptive behavior. When a stirred-up state is supplemented by or contains within

[9] E. H. Erikson. _Childhood and Society._ New York: Norton, 1950, p. 221.
[10] _Ibid._, p. 221.

seemed to correlate most highly with similar scores for later ages. Talkativeness and linguistic skill, when they became measurable, were also fairly constant from age to age. Traits showing least constancy were irritability and sociability. Other workers have shown that differences in the amount of smiling and of crying characteristic of different babies persist through the first two years.

In one study [12] careful ratings of fifteen behavior traits of five infants made from moving picture records were compared with ratings of the same children on the same traits *five* years later. There was much similarity. Of the seventy-five judgments, forty-eight agreed exactly, and another twenty-one were only one step apart on a five-step rating scale.

The most important question of how much relationship there is between infant personality characteristics and the personality traits an individual shows at *maturity* has not been answered very satisfactorily as yet. As we have seen, so-called infant intelligence tests do not predict mature intelligence with any more than chance accuracy, but that may be because the abilities it is possible to measure before speech develops are not really comparable with what we measure as intelligence later in life. In one very interesting attempt to bridge the gap between infancy and maturity, Neilon [13] made a thorough study of the personalities of fifteen of the persons who had been in Shirley's group of twenty-five infants. At the time of Neilon's study they were seventeen years old. She wrote personality sketches describing them at this age and asked judges to match them with the sketches Shirley had written of their personalities when they were two years old. The matching was done with considerably more than chance accuracy, though it was by no means perfect. Both the Gesell and the Neilon studies suggest that there may be some general core of individual personality that persists over the years. We need more such evidence.

The soundest conclusion would seem to be that infancy plays an especially important part in shaping personality, but it is not *all-*important. Because these are the *first* needs, the *first* skills, the *first* people one encounters, they stand out as no later ones can. But later experience will modify and refine the attitudes, expectations, and motives developed in infancy. If we are to understand ourselves and others we must neither ignore nor overrate the effects of early experience on personality.

[12] A. Gesell and L. B. Ames. Early evidence of individuality in the human infant. *J. genet. Psychol.*, 1937, 47, 339-361.

[13] P. Neilon. Shirley's babies after fifteen years: a personality study. *J. genet. Psychol.*, 1948, 73, 175-186.

SUMMARY

Personality theory elaborated by Freud and other psychologists has placed a great deal of emphasis on the origins of personality in infancy.

Research on infant emotions has shown that development consists of the differentiation of a general emotional state that might be called excitement into more and more diverse and specific emotions. Experiments have shown that observers cannot identify separate emotions in young infants unless they can see the stimulating situation. Only two genuine reflexes that seem related to the emotional life have been observed—the startle pattern and the smile. There probably are some "natural" ways of expressing the other basic human emotions as they develop, but they are influenced considerably by learning that may differ from one person to another.

Psychoanalysts have stimulated discussion and research on socialization, the means by which the ways of his culture are impressed upon the young child. There is some evidence, not convincing to all psychologists, that close contact with a mother or mother substitute during the early months is essential for both physical and psychological health. The child-rearing methods by means of which feeding and elimination behavior is brought into line with social customs have come in for special study because of their possible relationship to "oral" and "anal" personality characteristics in adult personality. The safest conclusion to be drawn from information now available is that general attitudes are more important than specific procedures.

Motives develop out of original "needs" by a kind of learning process. The needs themselves become differentiated from one another, and the ways in which they are met lead to individual patterns of expectation and striving for satisfaction. The child's own activities and his relationships with adults generate other positive and negative kinds of motivation.

There is some stability about the individual characteristics that distinguish one infant from another, but evidence as to just how these early differences are related to personality differences at maturity is lacking.

A BOOK ABOUT WHAT MOTHERS DO

SEARS, R. R., MACCOBY, E. E., and LEVIN, H. *Patterns of child rearing*. Evanston, Ill.: Row, Peterson, 1957.

This is an account of a careful study done at Harvard in which the mothers of 379 five-year-olds were interviewed about their children and the ways they handled them. In a simple, readable way the authors report what these mothers said about feeding and weaning, toilet training, bedwetting, and the handling of dependency and aggression. Since they also described how their children behaved, and the problems they had encountered in trying to train them, the authors are able to point out relationships between some kinds of training and behavior. Attractive drawings add to the reader's pleasure in the book.

CHAPTER 11

Why should psychologists have been interested in trying to distinguish the changes that occur as a result of maturation from those that occur as a result of learning? What differences in child-rearing does emphasis on one rather than the other factor imply?

How would you go about it to try to prove that a certain kind of change reflects maturation rather than learning?

What is meant by the method of "co-twin control?"

Does a baby have to be taught to walk? Explain.

In what ways is the learning that occurs during infancy like that which goes on later, during the school years? How is it different?

The First Two Years: Maturation and Learning

GENERAL PRINCIPLES OF DEVELOPMENT

THROUGHOUT THIS BOOK, from the first chapter on, we have tried to emphasize broad general principles that can serve as guides to those who are trying to promote optimal development in themselves and others— their children, their students, their employees, or their counseling clients. We saw in Chapter 1 that development at each stage is a complex outgrowth of the stage that precedes it, and that it depends upon structures and processes brought into existence by heredity, previous maturation, learning, and the particular situation in which the person finds himself. We saw too that it always involves some spontaneous activity, and that the person's choices or decisions influence the course that it takes.

The studies of prenatal development discussed in Chapter 4 have called our attention to the fact that development brings about the actualization of some potentialities at the expense of others. From the beginning it proceeds by separating out differentiated parts from a more or less homogeneous whole and then organizing those differentiated parts into a more complex kind of pattern. We pointed out the crucial importance of timing. A given kind of external influence coming late in fetal development will have an effect quite different from the effect it would have had in the early weeks after conception. We noted also the tendency for structures to be ready for use considerably earlier than the time they are ordinarily needed—what is often called the "law of anticipatory function."

The problem of deciding what the basic developmental principles are becomes far more complicated in postnatal than in prenatal stages, because of the increasing importance of learning. What the person will do comes to depend not just on the sense organs and muscles, the nerve cells and glandular system, that have become differentiated out of the original fertilized ovum and linked together in natural patterns of relationship, but also on the *particular* kind of experiences he has undergone, the *particular* skills he has practiced. During infancy *both* kinds of factors, the inevitable maturation sequences and the controllable learning processes, are intertwined with one another in a complex way. We shall see in this chapter what can be done to disentangle them.

SCIENTIFIC STUDY OF MATURATION AND LEARNING

The student's first reaction to a discussion of the maturation vs. learning problem may be a puzzled "What difference does it make?" A little more thought will show why the problem is one that psychologists have considered to be very important. Different conclusions with regard to it imply quite different attitudes about child-rearing. Those who are impressed with the significance of learning tend to emphasize active training in skills that are socially desirable. Those who are more impressed with the effects of maturation tend to leave everything to nature. There have been some periods of history and some societies in which one type of approach dominated people's thinking, some periods and societies in which the other was in the ascendant. It is only fairly recently that we are in a position to organize a combination of both that can serve as a sound scientific basis for child-rearing practice.

Most of the experimental work has been focused on the development of motor skills of one kind or another—walking, grasping, and the like. Such behavior is of course easier to observe than are changes in perception or "thinking." It seems likely, however, that the conclusions about motor skills apply to these other less visible kinds of development as well. Some of Piaget's penetrating observations, discussed in Chapter 9, permit us to make inferences about these intellectual or pre-intellectual processes in which both maturation and learning are involved.

If one simply watches what a baby does over a period of time under natural conditions, he will never be able to separate the effects of maturation from those of learning. Everything the infant does reflects *both.* What the experimenter tries to do when he wishes to assess the influence of maturation alone is to create a situation in which *no practice can occur.* After such a "no-practice" interval any change in behavior that shows up must be based on maturation rather than learning.

As in many other experimental areas it is easier to set up such conditions for animal than for human subjects. One of the earliest reactions to be studied in this manner was that of pecking in baby chicks. Under normal circumstances, newly hatched chicks begin to peck at grain immediately, and the accuracy of their performance increases constantly during the first few days. What Bird [1] did was to feed chicks forcibly by hand for several days after hatching so that they would get no pecking practice at all. He then tried them out to see whether the pecking performance had been perfected through maturation alone.

The chicks' first attempts after this treatment were not very skillful. Their aim was so inaccurate that they would often miss the grain completely. If one succeeded in picking it up, he might drop it again before he had succeeded in shifting it to the back of his mouth in order to swallow it. In the beginning, only about 15 per cent of the pecks were completely successful, but they improved rapidly with practice.

So far, it appeared that practice or learning is the important factor in the development of a skill such as pecking. Other aspects of the experiment, however, showed that practice is not the only factor determining success. The older chicks, even those who had not been allowed to practice, were *somewhat* more accurate than the newly-hatched; and when normal feeding was permitted they *improved more rapidly* than the younger chicks did. Within a few days those for whom pecking had been experimentally delayed reached the same level of efficiency as the ones who had been fed naturally from the start. The most reasonable conclusion is that the maturation process brings the behavior pattern up to a minimum level of efficiency necessary to sustain life, but that after this point (which is normally reached before the time of hatching), practice is needed to bring about a high degree of skilled co-ordination in aiming, striking, seizing, and swallowing the grain.

Other animal studies have also demonstrated the importance of maturation. Avery, [2] for example, was able, by means of X-ray photographs, to show that unborn guinea-pigs shortly before the time of

[1] C. Bird. The relative importance of maturation and habit in the development of an instinct. *J. genet. Psychol.*, 1925, 32, 68-91.

[2] G. T. Avery. Responses of fetal guinea pigs prematurely delivered. *Genet. Psychol. Monogr.*, 1928, 3, 245-331.

normal delivery make no attempt to right themselves when the body of the mother is placed in such a position that the fetuses are upside down, but that they do so immediately and without difficulty if placed on their backs after artificial delivery a few hours later. Even more convincing are the experiments of Carmichael [3] who divided a mass of frog's eggs into two parts, one of which was kept in plain water and the other in water containing chloretone, a drug which anesthetizes the developing animals so that they do not move within the egg, but which has no effect upon their physical growth. After a time the eggs in both groups hatched as usual into tadpoles. Those in the plain water shortly began to swim, but the anesthetized group remained motionless. After the normal animals were swimming well, the others were removed to fresh water that did not contain any drug. Within a short time all began to swim, and in a few minutes they were swimming just as well as those that had been practicing the art for some time. As soon as the effect of the anesthetic had worn off, the behavior appeared; it did not have to be learned. Salamander's eggs, treated in the same way, gave the same results.

While it is obviously impossible to keep babies anesthetized throughout the early stages of their development in order to see whether or not similar results would be obtained, a few experiments have been performed that throw some light on the question. All of you have seen pictures of Indian babies bound to a kind of wicker framework known as a "cradle board." In the tribes among which the cradle board is used, the infant is bound to it shortly after birth and is kept upon it almost continuously, being removed only for the brief periods necessary for his physical care. Obviously this practice provides us with an excellent opportunity for studying the effects of restricted practice upon the development of such motor skills as sitting and walking, even though the position on the cradle board does not completely abolish all activity.

Dennis and Dennis [4] undertook to investigate the maturation question, using as subjects the infants of Hopi Indian tribes that had been sufficiently under the influence of white civilization to induce some of the Hopi mothers to discontinue the use of the cradle board, while others still kept their infants bound as their ancestors had done. This situation was most fortunate in preventing the occurrence of a scientific error that might easily have arisen if all members of the tribe had

[3] L. Carmichael. The development of behavior in vertebrates experimentally removed from the influence of external stimulation. *Psychol. Rev.*, 1926, 33, 51-58. Also, a further experimental study of the development of behavior. *Psychol. Rev.*, 1928, 35, 253-260.

[4] W. Dennis and M. G. Dennis. The effect of cradling practices upon the onset of walking in Hopi children. *J. genet. Psychol.*, 1940, 56, 77-86.

been using the board, for it was found that the Indian children were, on the average, about one or two months later in learning to walk than American white children. But that this is a racial characteristic and not the result of the cradling practice was apparent when it was found that the children who had spent the greater part of their first year bound to the cradle board learned to walk just as early, on the average, as those who had been allowed to move freely from the time of birth. [5] Another study by Dennis [6] (1935) provides further evidence on this question. A pair of twin babies were kept in a special observation room from the end of their first month until the age of nine months. During this time each child was kept on his back in his own crib from which he was removed only for necessary physical care. Even then they were kept in the horizontal position as much as possible. While in their cribs they were prevented from using their hands to reach for objects by keeping the bedclothes drawn around their hands and bodies so tightly that the hands could not be withdrawn. [7] In feeding, the hands were so restrained that they could not touch the bottle or spoon. They had no opportunity to practice sitting or standing or many of the other common activities of infancy until the experiment was discontinued.

The most striking result of this experiment is the exceedingly small effect of the restriction upon activities that, in the normal child, usually appear before the age of nine months, and that were not rendered impossible for these children by very reason of the restriction. Even the latter, however, in a number of instances appeared spontaneously during the brief periods of freedom necessitated by bathing, dressing, and so on. Although lack of opportunity for practice brought about some degree of retardation in such skills as sitting and walking, the retardation was not great. One of the twins was able to sit unsupported for a full minute by the 298th day; the other not until the 326th day. The first twin was able to walk alone at seventeen months which, while later than the average, is still within the range shown by perfectly normal children. The second twin did not walk until after the age of two years but this cannot fairly be attributed to the restriction of

[5] When bound to the board the infant can move only the head. There is wide variation in the age at which the board is completely discarded, but after the age of three months most infants are given short daily periods of freedom. Typically, however, the child is kept bound to the board for the greater part of the day until toward the end of the first year.

[6] W. Dennis. The effect of restricted practice upon the reaching, sitting, and standing of two infants. *J. genet. Psychol.*, 1935, 47, 17-32.

[7] Of course the restriction of activity was not so great as to run any risk of injury to the child's health or general bodily development. The children were able to turn and wriggle around under the bedclothes, but they were unable to withdraw their hands or to sit or stand. Throughout the experiment they remained in good health and maintained a normal rate of physical growth.

practice but rather to the fact, later discovered, that a mild injury at the time of birth had produced a slight paralysis of the left arm and leg. [8]

As a result of his experiments Dennis came to the conclusion that, once a given level of maturation has been reached, children will develop most of the basic skills in a relatively short time and with only such stimulation as is given by their own organic needs and by the stimulation of their sense organs through the sights and sounds, the odors and tactile contacts of an ordinary environment. Except for a few reflexes, specific forms of motor reaction are not acquired without practice, but if the child is normal and is given freedom to initiate such practice he will do so himself as soon as he is sufficiently mature to learn the act. The little child does not need to be taught his motor skills, nor does he have to be urged or reminded to practice them. Only give him a chance; he will take care of all the rest by himself.

Just as is true with older persons, the amount of practice needed to perfect a given skill differs from child to child. A number of carefully controlled experiments have demonstrated that at least during the early years a child who is physiologically more mature will usually be able to learn many of the ordinary motor acts with a smaller amount of practice than a younger child. The favorite method for studying questions of this kind has been the procedure known as *co-twin control,* first used by Gesell and later adopted by a number of other investigators. The procedure is a neat one because it makes it possible to vary experimental procedures while keeping the subjects in the experiments essentially the same; a thing that is impossible by any other known method. The secret lies in the use of identical twins as subjects. One of the twins is put on a particular kind of training regimen, the other on a different kind or simply in an ordinary environment. Because identical twins can for practical purposes be regarded as almost exact duplicates of each other, any differences in their behavior that appear at the end of the period of special training can be ascribed to the training with more assurance than is warranted when the possibility of differences in the ability of the children themselves is not ruled out.

Gesell and his co-workers have employed this method in studying the acquisition of a number of motor skills and other developmental traits such as block-building, stair-climbing, and the acquisition of language. Their results have been fairly uniform in showing that when one twin is given a specified amount of daily practice in these skills while the other is prevented from practicing them at all, the trained

[8] See note on pp. 196-197 of Norman L. Munn. *Psychological development.* Boston: Houghton, 1955, in which a personal communication from Dennis is cited.

twin will acquire some proficiency while the other will fail to make noticeable headway. But if, at the end of the period, the untrained twin who now has the advantage of some additional weeks of age is subjected to the same kind of training as was given to the other, he will acquire a comparable amount of skill in a shorter length of time. This is, of course, about what one would expect because of the extraordinarily rapid rate at which development proceeds during the period of infancy. Since ability as well as practice affects the rate of learning among people of all ages the twin who is older when training is started should, of course, learn more easily. McGraw, [9] in her widely known study of Jimmy and Johnny, obtained results that do not differ essentially from those just described.

How can we summarize in some general form what these studies of animals and of young children have taught us? One of the most usable theoretical concepts is Piaget's notion of the *schema* that is modified as it accommodates itself to new situations and uses. (See Chapter 8.) It would appear that a considerable number of basic schemata or patterns of behavior are developed as maturation proceeds. Practice or training modifies and perfects them but does not *create* them. The timing or readiness principle discussed earlier is very important in this connection. In general, the experiments cited have shown that improvement in any skill occurs more rapidly than usual if practice is deferred until a later date than is customary for the behavior. Thus a child retarded for a time by external circumstances soon *catches up* with the one for whom the situation was all along more stimulating. This must undoubtedly be true only up to a point, however. Too long a period of forced inactivity might well be much more detrimental than the relatively short periods that have been used in experimental work. About all we can safely say about timing of practice is that it should not be given *before* the child has reached the maturational level at which he is ready for it. But this generalization in itself is of considerable practical importance.

KINDS OF LEARNING—THE CONDITIONED RESPONSE

Keeping in mind, then, that learning cannot occur until maturation has brought the person to the point where he is ready for it, let us turn to a survey of some of the kinds of learning that occur during the first few months of life. Some psychologists would object to the phrasing "kinds of learning." Much theoretical thinking, much experimental ingenuity, has gone into a search for general principles under-

[9] M. B. McGraw. *Growth: a study of Johnny and Jimmy.* New York: D. Appleton-Century, 1935.

lying all of learning. The fact that there is still a considerable amount of disagreement as to what these principles are and as to whether such a general formulation is possible means that it is more useful for the practical student of human behavior to know what kinds of changes occur under what circumstances than to understand the theoretical controversies. So we shall look at some of the main kinds of modification of behavior as a result of practice for which there is experimental evidence.

We have spoken earlier of the highly significant work on conditioned responses. Its main feature is the linking of a naturally occurring response to a new stimulus. (See Figure 49.) Through this kind of

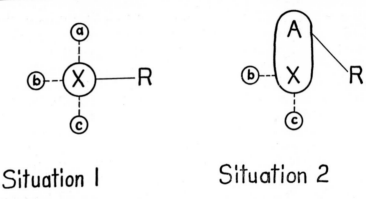

Situation 1   Situation 2

FIGURE 49.   Diagram illustrating the formation of a conditioned response.

associative process it becomes possible to get many sorts of new combinations of stimulus and response. For example, after a child has learned to wink when a bell rings, because the bell has for several trials been rung just before a bright light flashes, the combination of the saying of the word *wink* with the bell may lead to the response of winking long before the age when the child knows the word's meaning. This is called a "second-order" conditioned response. It is easy to see that through this kind of shifting of responses to new stimuli, highly adaptive behavior may be produced. It makes it possible for a person to respond to a *cue* or *signal* that something is about to happen.

Psychologists know a great deal about this sort of learning from animal experiments. There are certain key concepts. *Reinforcement* refers to the presentation of the natural stimulus for the behavior along with the stimulus to which the new association is to be formed. With Pavlov's dogs, reinforcement consisted of actual food in the mouth. The formation of a conditioned response requires reinforcement, but it is not necessary that it occur on every trial. In extending learning theory to wider and wider areas, psychologists have broadened the meaning of the term *reinforcement* so that it has become almost synonymous with *reward.* Any consequence of an act that alleviates an uncomfortable state or reduces drive or tension is considered to be a reinforcer in this broadened sense. It is often useful when one is analyzing a child's behavior with the aim of improving it to consider the question of what reinforcers are operating, and what actions are being reinforced.

The second key concept is *extinction.* This refers to the disappearance of the conditioned response when reinforcement is no longer given. Like the original conditioning, this is a gradual process. It takes a considerable number of nonreinforced trials to eliminate a response completely. At first glance, extinction seems to be just another name for forgetting. But there are important differences. A response that has been extinguished is not really *gone* from an animal's repertory. It may take only one reinforced trial to bring it back in full force and it will sometimes occur spontaneously. An extinguished response is somehow "there" even when it is not in evidence. Much experimental work seems to show that forgetting is not so complete or absolute as we think it to be either. Perhaps we should modify our ideas about what forgetting is to bring them more in line with what we know about extinction.

One of the most beautifully controlled examples of the facilitating effect of previous experience upon the later acquisition of an act is to be found in an experiment carried out by Burtt [10] with his little son. Beginning when the child was fifteen months old, Burtt read aloud to him daily a twenty-line selection of Greek drama. The child had no knowledge of Greek and therefore, of course, could not understand the meaning of the poem at all. But even as early as fifteen months, most bright babies respond to the rhythm of poetry, a fact that has led many of the makers of nursery-rhymes to embellish them with meaningless lines and nonsense-syllables that are nevertheless highly attractive to children. The same selection was read every day for a period of three months, and then a new one of the same length was begun which also was read daily for a three-month period. The procedure was continued until the child was three years old, a new selection being used every three months. No further practice was given until the age of eight and one-half years. Then the child was taught to repeat from memory the selections that had been read to him in early childhood as well as an equal number of other selections of the

[10] H. E. Burtt. An experimental study of early childhood memory. *J. genet. Psychol.*, 1932, 40, 287-295.

same length not previously heard. The new selections required an average of 435 repetitions per selection before they could be repeated without error, whereas those heard in early childhood required, on the average, only 317 repetitions. The effect of maturation and of elaboration of response patterns that goes along with it is shown by the fact that the selections read later in childhood, that is, shortly before the age of three years, were learned more readily than those originally heard before the age of two, but even the latter were learned more easily than the new ones that had never before been heard.

Not all of the selections heard in childhood were memorized at the age of eight and one-half. Some were reserved for a later experiment which was carried out when the boy had reached the age of fourteen. [11] Again the comparison was made between the number of repetitions necessary for the learning of completely new selections with that needed for material heard during very early childhood. Some advantage of the latter over the former was still apparent except for the very earliest read of the selections, but the effect of the early childhood experience had become much less apparent as a result of the longer interval.

Two features of conditioned responses that have received a great deal of study are *generalization* and *discrimination*. At the outset, a conditioned response that has been established to one particular stimulus will occur as a response to other similar stimuli as well. The dog salivates to a tone pitched at *B, C,* or *D, G, F,* or *E,* as well as to the standard *A* that has been used in the experiment. But as repeated trials are given, if *A* is the only tone ever reinforced, responses to the others are extinguished and only the one narrowly-defined stimulus remains effective. These characteristics of conditioned responses are very important in the learning of adaptive behavior patterns. The initial generalization gives a person a means of coping with new situations. The increasing discrimination makes for more accurate and precise fitting of behavior to specific situations.

One other concept, one that is required to explain how discrimination occurs, is *inhibition*. The animal or person develops a tendency *not to respond* to some kinds of stimuli which are initially effective. It is plain that this learning not to do what comes naturally is a very important part of a child's progress toward maturity.

There have been a number of experimental attempts to show that conditioned responses can be formed by newborn (or even unborn) infants. While it is of considerable theoretical importance to find out how early some kind of learning begins, experiments with buzzers and

[11] H. E. Burtt. A further study of early childhood memory. *J. genet. Psychol.,* 1937, 50, 187-192.

bells have few practical implications. The experiment of Marquis, [12] however, is interesting from both the practical and the theoretical standpoints. The amount of bodily activity of two groups of healthy newborn infants was measured by means of stabilimeters, [13] attached to their cribs. One group of infants was fed at three-hour intervals for the first eight days of life; the other group was fed at four-hour intervals. Throughout this time, the average amount of activity was greater

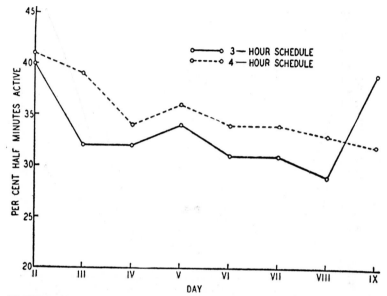

FIGURE 50.   Relative activity of infants fed at longer and shorter intervals. Comparison of three- and four-hour groups in total amount of activity per day. Average of all subjects. (From Dorothy P. Marquis, Learning in the neonate: the modification of behavior under three feeding schedules. *J. exper. Psychol.*, 1941, 29, 263-282. Courtesy of author and publisher.)

for the group less frequently fed than for those whose hunger was satisfied at more frequent intervals. But on the ninth day, the three-hour group was changed to a four-hour schedule. After their usual feeding hour had passed, these babies showed a much greater increase

[12] D. P. Marquis. Learning in the neonate: the modification of behavior under three feeding schedules. *J. exper. Psychol.*, 1941, 29, 263-282.

[13] A stabilimeter consists of a spring balance on which the support (bed, bassinet, chair, etc.) in which the individual rests is attached. The balance is made sufficiently delicate so that each movement of the subject is conveyed to a writing attachment which traces a record on a kymograph. A simultaneous time record is made by a separate instrument. By this means the amount of activity occurring within any specified period of time can be measured very exactly.

in activity than did the group who had been accustomed to wait an additional hour. Before the four hours were up, this activity had reached a point at which it actually surpassed that of the other group who had previously been the more active of the two. Figure 50 shows the differences between the two groups in total amount of active time per day over the period from the second to the ninth day, while Figure 51 shows the data for the ninth day in terms of each successive

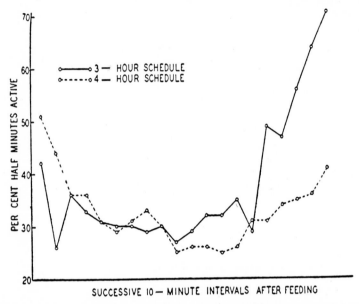

FIGURE 51. Effeffct of a change from a three-hour to a four-hour interval between feedings upon the activity of infants. Comparison of three- and four-hour groups on Day IX when the three-hour group changed to a four-hour schedule. Average of morning and afternoon periods for all subjects. (From Dorothy P. Marquis, Learning in the neonate: the modification of behavior under three feeding schedules. *J. exper. Psychol.*, 1941, 29, 263-282. Courtesy of author and publisher.)

ten-minute interval after the last feeding. Note that practically all of the change in activity of the three-hour group took place during the last hour. The group previously accustomed to the longer interval also showed some increased activity during the final hour, presumably as a result of the onset of hunger, but the change is small in comparison with that of the group previously conditioned to the shorter interval.

Marquis thinks that this adaptation to temporal intervals is a rudimentary kind of conditioned response. Just what the stimuli or signals are that the infant becomes able to respond to cannot be determined.

But the differences between the three-hour and four-hour group on the ninth day show definitely that there is *some* difference in the stimuli to which the activity is connected. Something has been learned.

The fact that newborn infants can learn responses to different feeding schedules does not, of course, mean that one schedule is as good as another. As indicated in a previous chapter, most authorities on child-rearing now advocate a self-demand schedule rather than one fixed in advance. But the fact that learning can occur from the very beginning may help to explain why some children seem to thrive under conditions that authorities would consider unfavorable to good personality development. The basis for adaptation to a wide variety of circumstances certainly exists in the human individual. But it would seem desirable not to put too great a strain on these capacities.

Another reason for the interest psychologists have shown in conditioned responses during infancy is that it appears likely that many persistent fears are established in this manner. The classical experiment on this problem was done by Watson and Watson, [14] who experimentally produced a conditional fear response in a healthy child less than one year of age. First the child was shown a white rat. He reached for it repeatedly, showing no sign of fear. It was plain that the animal itself, in the absence of any unpleasant associations with it, was not a fear-provoking object. Now the rat was shown again, but this time, just as the baby reached for it, an iron bar just behind him was struck, and there was a loud bang. This is a stimulus to which a child of this age naturally responds with evidences of fear. He starts violently, draws back, perhaps tries to escape or cling to someone for protection, and his crying takes on a sharper and shriller note. In this instance, the child who was reaching for the rat jerked back his hand, started violently, screamed, and tried to crawl away. A week later when the rat was shown again, mild evidence of fear, or at least of avoidance, appeared, and after two or three reinforcements (repetitions of the combination of rat and loud sound) the mere sight of the rat was enough to provoke very marked evidences of fear.

The importance of this kind of conditioned response in emotional development is increased because of the phenomenon of *generalization* described earlier. In the Watson experiment it was found that the child's fear response to the rat had generalized to all sorts of furry or fuzzy objects—a piece of cotton wool, a fur coat, a Santa Claus mask. In a conditioning experiment, a child can learn to differentiate by being exposed to a series of trials, in which response to only one particular stimulus is reinforced. But in real life it seems quite possible

[14] J. B. Watson and R. R. Watson. Studies in infant psychology. *Sci. Month.*, 1921, 13, 493-515.

that a person might never get beyond this initial generalization stage in the acquisition of a fear response, and that he might thus carry with him into maturity fears that appear irrational but are actually based on an understandable learning situation. Such fears would be unlikely to undergo extinction, since a person does not repeatedly expose himself to the fear producing situation, as he would need to for extinction to occur.

The hypothesis that fears for nondangerous objects or situations are conditioned responses of some sort has led to the formulation of methods for treating such fears. M. C. Jones, [15] by presenting a feared rabbit to a child while he was reacting positively to food, succeeded in establishing a positive reaction to the animal in place of the fear. (It was important not to bring the rabbit too close the first day or the conditioning process might have worked the wrong way and the negative response to the animal attached itself to the food stimulus as well.) A more recent application of this method in the case of an adult with a severe fear of going out by herself is described by Meyer. [16] First a strong positive feeling about the experimenter himself was established. Then, little by little, this feeling was conditioned to the outside world that the woman feared. First she walked for a little while with the experimenter in the hospital roof garden. Next she went with him into the hospital grounds. From there they progressed to back streets, then main streets, then bus trips. As the positive feeling became attached to all these formerly feared situations, she became more and more confident and less and less dependent on the experimenter's presence.

When the work on conditioned emotional reactions first appeared, it was hoped that it would constitute a sort of universal explanation and a scientific basis for treatment of undesirable emotional characteristics. Time and the progress of research have shown that it is not as all-inclusive a principle as it was thought to be. Fears (and other kinds of emotional reaction) may arise as conditioned responses. But there are other ways also in which they may originate. The process of maturation and the improvement it brings in the accuracy of perceptual discrimination causes a child to fear at one stage objects that at a previous stage left him quite unmoved. Some things are feared because they are symbols of an unknown evil. Psychiatric reports of such cases are very common. Treatment based on conditioned response principles works in some cases, not in others. In the Meyer report cited above, another patient with similar symptoms did not improve in the same kind of treatment situation. There is still much

[15] M. C. Jones. A study of the emotions of preschool children. *Sch. and Soc.,* 1925, 21, 755-758.
[16] V. Meyer. The treatment of phobic patients on the basis of learning principles. *J. abnorm. soc. Psychol.,* 1957, 55, 261-266.

that we do not know about the development of individual patterns of emotion. But the work on conditioned responses has done psychology a great service by clarifying one kind of process that contributes to it.

PERCEPTUAL LEARNING AND PROBLEM-SOLVING

One of the most important kinds of learning about which as yet we know very little is the process by means of which a person becomes able to *perceive* an orderly organized world of recognizable people and things. When the baby first opens his eyes he does not see what we see. William James' famous phrase, "a blooming, buzzing confusion," suggests what the world must be to him. Before he can become aware of the differentiated environment in which he lives, a great deal of both maturation and learning must occur.

Hebb [17] has stressed the point that this early perceptual learning may be a different sort of process from the perception that has been studied experimentally in older children and adults. Since babies cannot tell us what they see or do not see, it has been necessary to depend upon other kinds of research for clues as to what this process may be like. Riesen, [18] for example, reared two chimpanzees in darkness to the age of sixteen months. He then tested them out to see what kinds of visual perception had developed in the absence of all opportunity to practice. While their pupils contracted under bright light like those of ordinary animals, they did not blink when an object approached their eyes, and it was several days before they became able to recognize by sight things like their feeding bottles with which their sensations of touch and kinesthesis had made them very familiar.

Similar difficulties in learning to recognize forms with which they were very familiar through senses other than vision have been described by persons who were born blind and later recovered their sight. Senden [19] collected and analyzed published reports of such cases. There is some indication (though because of the nature of the evidence it is not very clear) that even to recognize the shape of a triangle involves a long and laborious learning process.

Infants usually seem to have accomplished this task of learning to see shapes by the end of the first six months. From then on they make rapid progress in learning to pay attention to form differences and to use these discriminations in adaptive activity. An experiment by Ling [20]

[17] D. O. Hebb. *The organization of behavior.* New York: Wiley, 1949.
[18] A. H. Riesen. The development of visual perception in man and chimpanzee. *Science,* 1947, 106, 107-108.
[19] M. V. Senden. *Raum und Gestalt-auffassung bei opierten Blindgeboren vor und nach der operation.* Leipzig: Barth, 1932.
[20] Bing Chung Ling. Form discrimination as a learning cue in infants. *Comp. Psychol. Monogr.,* 1941, 17, Serial No. 86.

tells us something about this learning process. Babies between the ages of six and twelve months were seated before a table on which were two (or more) bright yellow wooden blocks of different shape and size. The apparatus was constructed in such a way that either of the blocks, regardless of its position, could be fastened to the table, thus making it impossible for the child to secure it. The other block could readily be picked up and handled. To make the stimulus of the "correct" block even stronger, before each trial it was first carefully sterilized and then dipped into a saccharine solution that made it taste sweet if put into the mouth. The purpose of the experiment was to find out whether infants as young as six months of age could learn to discriminate between two blocks of different shape, say a cross and a triangle or a circle and a square. After he had had time to find out that one of these blocks could not be budged from its place no matter how much tugging was applied, while the other could be easily secured and was pleasantly flavored as well, would a time come when the child would reach directly for the correct block and pay no attention to the wrong one, no matter what the relative position of the two might be?

This proved to be the case. The number of trials needed to establish the association varied greatly from child to child, as might be expected in view of what we know about individual differences. When the forms used were very different from each other, as a circle and a cross, fewer trials were required for the infants to make the discrimination; when they were more nearly similar, as a circle and an ellipse, more time was needed. Shape seemed to be the basic discriminatory cue.

There was evidence that the process of learning involved something more than just making the discrimination required at the moment. The *first* discrimination was always harder to learn than those that came later in the series, a fact which suggests that the babies were not merely learning particular discriminations but were learning *to discriminate*. Moreover, there were several children who showed evidence of a still higher type of generalizing process. These infants were first trained to select a circle and ignore a square. After this reaction had been thoroughly built up, the principle was suddenly reversed. Now it was the circle that would not be dislodged and the square that had become the motivating stimulus. For the greater number of the children, this was indeed bewildering. They continued to tug at the circle and frequently cried or became angry. Even after lucky accident had demonstrated that the despised square now had acquired all the virtues formerly possessed by the circle, they were slow to respond to the cue and would revert to the circle at frequent intervals long after the shift had been made. But there were four of the eighteen infants with whom this experiment was tried who behaved very differently from the others. After a few preliminary assaults on the circle, the discovery would be made that the square could be easily dislodged. Unlike the other members of the group, these babies showed signs of surprise and interest in this fact. Whereas the other babies had handled the square only briefly and then renewed their attacks upon the circle, these children immediately shifted their attention to the square. They examined it at length, turning it over and over, occasionally bringing it to their mouths as if to verify the flavor. "From that time on," so says the author, "the facial expression relaxed, the fretful bewildered vocalization was promptly replaced by a cheerful and contented one and the infant seldom or never returned to the once highly motivated circle." The author regards this as affording some indication of the early stages of what the Gestalt psychologists call "insight," which means that the subject reacts to a new situation on the basis of some general principle (as "squareness" or "roundness") that enables him to make the correct response almost immediately without going through the slow and laborious process of learning by conditioning or by "trial and error."

Since this time there has been a great deal of research on such processes as Ling's general "learning to discriminate." Harlow [21] has made such phenomena, to which he has given the name *learning sets,* fundamental to his whole theory of learning. It would seem that the acquisition of some of these basic learning sets may be one of the major achievements of infancy, though we have so far given it little attention.

The most thoroughgoing theoretical description of the stages through which a child passes in learning to perceive the world of reality has been presented by Piaget, [22] whose ideas have been discussed in Chapter 8. The development of object perception goes through several successive stages and depends upon the child's own responses to the situations he encounters as well as upon the maturation of the necessary anatomical structures. Concepts of space, time, and causality all develop together as the infant interacts with his world.

There are other kinds of learning process that occur along with maturation so that it is difficult if not impossible to separate one from the other. A rudimentary kind of problem-solving makes its appearance during the first year, and there is evidence here also for what in older subjects we would call insight. Richardson [23] observed what

[21] H. F. Harlow. The formation of learning sets. *Psychol. Rev.,* 1949, 56, 51-65.

[22] J. Piaget. *The child's construction of reality.* London: Routledge and Kegan Paul, 1955.

[23] H. M. Richardson. The growth of adaptive behavior in infants. *Genet. Pyschol. Monogr.,* 1932, 12, 195-359.

happened when a group of sixteen children, ranging in age from twenty-eight to fifty-two weeks, were confronted with situations in which a string was to be pulled or a lever turned in order to bring a toy within reach. The typical behavior in the first trial was what is usually called "trial and error"—miscellaneous activity more or less directed toward the desired object but showing no understanding of what had to be done to obtain it. After an apparently accidental success, however, the time required to obtain the toy would decrease markedly in subsequent trials until something like insight was in evidence. The older infants were much more likely to solve the problems and to proceed in a manner that showed insight than were the younger ones. This age difference represents an unanalyzed mixture of changes due to various kinds of maturation and learning. It is interesting to note that a *demonstration* of the nature of the problem did *not* seem to improve the child's understanding of it, though for the older ones in the group it appeared to increase their motivation to solve it. It is the *child's own activity* that constitutes a learning situation for him.

THE FACILITATION OF DEVELOPMENT IN INFANCY

While there are many items of detailed knowledge still missing from our over-all theories of infant development, the main outlines are clear enough to constitute a very useful guide to parents and others who carry responsibility for young lives. The most important concepts are maturation, learning through motivated activity, and individual differences.

To promote optimal development we must first of all provide an environment that meets the infant's basic needs—for nourishment, for closeness to other human beings, for stimulation of his senses. This enables the maturation process to occur without hindrance. We must avoid working at cross purposes with this process, either by trying to train the child in particular habits of behavior too soon, or by preventing him from practicing skills he is ready to try. At the stage when he is ready to learn some new kind of behavior—stair-climbing, talking, discriminating between colors or shapes, for example—we can help by seeing that he has a chance to practice, by furnishing suitable toys and play materials, and by reinforcing the right responses. Finally, we must remember always that there are marked individual differences in developmental patterns. It is wise to let each person follow his own. Trying to force him to conform to norms or averages does not really accelerate his progress, and it may leave emotional scars. The fact that the work with infant intelligence tests has shown that maturation rates during infancy are not correlated to any great extent with ultimate intellectual levels should make it easier to accept these individual differences without undue concern.

SUMMARY

To separate the effects of maturation from those of learning it is necessary to set up an experimental situation in which no practice of some particular skill can occur. Experiments with both animal and human subjects have shown that the capacity to perform acts characteristic of the species—such as pecking for chicks, swimming for frogs, and walking for human beings—develops without practice. Practice improves the quality of the performance, however.

Among the kinds of learning that occur during infancy the conditioned response stands out. Through this process the responses the child is able to make at any stage in his development can be shifted to new stimulating situations. Many emotional attitudes are probably learned in this way.

While there has not been as much experimental research in these areas, it seems likely that a great deal of perceptual learning occurs in infancy and that the acquisition of learning sets and problem-solving skills may be an important outcome of the child's interaction with the world around him.

FOR FURTHER READING

GESELL, A., and ILG, F. L. *Infant and child in the culture of today.* New York: Harper, 1943.

Many books by Gesell and his co-workers have been published during the long years that the Yale Clinic of Child Development has been studying children. This is one of the most useful for parents and others who are responsible for the care and guidance of infants and preschool children. The authors discuss in brief, simple fashion the general developmental principles upon which they place most emphasis. Then they describe in graphic, concrete terms what a child is like at each successive stage, what he needs and prefers with regard to feeding and sleeping, activity and social stimulation.

Students who make the acquaintance of this book now will probably turn to it again and again after they have children of their own.

CHAPTER 12

What developmental features set off the period of early childhood from those that precede and follow it?

What are the most conspicuous changes in motor abilities that take place during early childhood? What are some of the changes that occur toward the end of this period in respect to the child's utilization of his motor skill?

Which plays the greater part in the perfection of a skilled motor act— addition of new movements, or the loss of some movements formerly present? Explain.

How does the efficiency of each of the two hands become modified in the establishment of hand preference?

Is there a relationship between handedness and stuttering?

Early Childhood: Physical Growth and Motor Development

DISTINGUISHING CHARACTERISTICS OF THE PERIOD

THERE IS NO REAL BREAK between infancy and early childhood. Growth continues. Movements become more skillful. Speech improves, and words are constantly added to the vocabulary. Yet, out of a large number of such gradual quantitative changes there arises a *qualitative change* that is quite apparent to observers. How often has it happened, for example, that some member of the family who has been away for several months exclaims when he sees his two-year-old brother, "He's not a baby any longer!"

One way of describing this rather elusive change is to say that once the groundwork for basic skills, such as walking and talking, self-feeding and control of elimination, has been laid, the person is ready to launch out into the wider world outside the four walls of his home. Playing with other children, in neighborhood or nursery school, increases enormously the complexity of his life. He is a person in his own right. If the essential change during the first two years is from dependence to autonomy, the progress during this early childhood period can be characterized as the transformation of autonomy into *initiative*. By the end of this period the child is ready to take a good deal of responsibility for his own actions.

Another way often used in marking off this period from those that precede and follow it is to call it the preschool period. With the kind

of social and educational system we have, children usually enter public
school at the age of five (or six if the community does not have kinder-
gartens). At this time they *must* take responsibility for themselves,
adjust to the regulations of a large, impersonal institution, and enter
into social relationships with considerable numbers of other children.
The task of the developing individual during the years from two to
five is to get ready for this major step by perfecting his basic skills,
enlarging his social experience, and becoming aware of himself as
one person among others. Much is accomplished during this three-year
period. We will consider these accomplishments in this and the following three chapters.

MAJOR FEATURES OF GROWTH DURING
EARLY CHILDHOOD

The rapid physical and mental growth that was characteristic of the
period of infancy described in the last chapters is continued with
only a small decrease in rate throughout early childhood. By the
age of five, most of the basic motor skills have been well perfected.
The child walks, runs, handles objects, jumps, and climbs almost as
well as he will ever be able to. As his legs grow longer he will be able
to run faster, and there will be further gain in speed of movement
and in motor control, particularly of the fine muscles of the hand and
fingers, but the motor development that takes place after the age of
five is very small when compared to that occurring earlier.

Even more sharply than by the changes in motor development, this
period is set off from those that precede and follow it by the mastery
of speech. Before the age of fifteen to eighteen months the average
child makes small use of speech. By the age of five he has commonly
acquired all the basic speech forms used among adults. He asks questions, makes long and involved statements, uses phrases, clauses,
adjectives and adverbs, pronouns, and interjections. His grammatical
construction is well-nigh as good as that of the adults with whom he
associates and from whom his language has been learned. As he grows
older his vocabulary will become larger and his sentences show some
further increase in average length, but the basic language forms are
all acquired during the preschool period. Articulation, too, is well
perfected during this time. In the average child "baby-talk" has become
pretty much a thing of the past by the age of five years.

Physical growth is likewise rapid. Up to the age of five years children gain rapidly in height and weight. Their bodily proportions are
changing; the arms and legs are lengthening out, the lower part of the
face is growing rapidly, while the forehead and cranium are making
but small gain (see Figure 52), and the features are taking on clearer

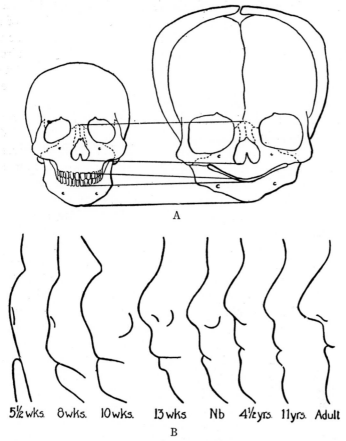

5½wks.   8wks.   10wks.   13wks   Nb   4½yrs. 11yrs. Adult

B

FIGURE 52.   Changes in facial proportions with age. *A.* Skulls of the adult
and the newborn drawn to the same face height to illustrate changes in the
relative proportions of the neural and facial portions at birth and in maturity.
   B. Changes in facial profile from the middle of the embryonic period to
maturity.
   (After Holl, from chapter on Developmental anatomy by R. E. Scammon in
Morris's *Human anatomy.* Courtesy P. Blakiston's Son and Co.)

outlines. After the age of five, growth is less rapid, and it continues
at a comparatively slow pace until the prepubertal spurt begins
at eleven or twelve years.

MOTOR DEVELOPMENT

Although walking is begun by most children toward the end of the
prelinguistic period, few children become really skillful walkers before
the latter part of the second year. The child's first steps are likely

to be unsteady, performed with the feet widely separated in an apparent attempt to secure better balance by widening the base of support. Even so it does not take much to upset him, and for some time after walking begins he is likely to revert to the role of quadruped whenever the surface of the ground is irregular. However, his interest in walking is so great and he practices it so incessantly that the period of early childhood is often referred to as the "run-about age."

A conspicuous result of the child's rapid gain in motor control is seen in his growing ability and desire to do things for himself. Over and over again comes the insistent demand "Let me do it. *I* want to do that! Let me carry it! I can open it myself! No, don't help me! Let me wash my own face!" At this age the normal child's interest in *doing* is almost unbelievable. Again and again he repeats the same simple action, apparently for the sheer pleasure of producing a result that he can see. Scupin reports that his young son once opened and closed the hinged cover of a box seventy-nine times in immediate succession, and it is probable that careful observation of any normal baby would reveal many similar instances. It is a pity that instead of cultivating and encouraging this worthwhile tendency in young children, many parents are led by thoughtlessness and hurry or by overconcern about the material result to curb the child's attempts to do for himself at the very age when this natural tendency is at its height. Because Johnny's attempts at face-washing stop short some inches in front of his ears and are likely to be interrupted by investigations on the best manner of causing soapsuds to pile up in the basin; because Mary once dropped the cup she had begged to carry; because Peter fails to adjust his cap at the angle his mother thinks most becoming—these are by many parents deemed sufficient reasons for insisting that such things shall be done for their children "until they are old enough to do them the right way." Unfortunately, by that time the urge to do them has too often waned or entirely disappeared.

The most conspicuous changes in motor abilities that occur during early childhood have to do with co-ordination and balance and with the uses of the finer muscles of the hand and fingers. The child of two can stand and run, but he cannot balance himself on one foot even for a few seconds. The three-year-old can stand momentarily on one foot, but he cannot hop on one foot or skip. In watching the behavior of groups of children of different ages in a nursery school, one is immediately struck by the differences in their gross bodily control. The two-year-old moves more slowly, and he is more clumsy in seating himself in a chair or in rising from it than the child of three or four. Frequently one sees the child of two or younger back up to a chair and, bending over, carefully inspect it between his legs before venturing to sit down. Apparently he is uncertain how to get himself into the chair unless he is able to see its position. The importance of the eyes in guiding the movements of the body is never so great as when a new act of skill is being learned.

T. D. Jones [1] has described a number of developmental stages in the use of wheeled toys—wagon, kiddie kar, tricycle, and the like—by children between the ages of twenty-one and forty-eight months. He found that the children under two years spent most of the time in simple manipulative activities involving pushing and pulling, with very few attempts at propelling themselves about. Beginning at or about the age of two, attempts at riding the kiddie kar and, later on, the tricycle became more frequent. Once this had begun, the amount of time spent in practice rapidly increased. At first the child's movements had the appearance of a series of separate activities. They were jerky, uncertain, and so poorly co-ordinated that progression would often be momentarily halted or even reversed in direction. However, as soon as learning had reached a stage at which the child's whole attention no longer had to be fixed on the motor performance itself, a merging of the separate parts of the activity began to take place and continued until the whole thing eventually ran off as a unitary pattern. By the age of forty-eight months most children had succeeded in perfecting these skills to a point where they were no longer the child's primary concern, but had become adjuncts to a more complex form of imaginative and dramatic activity. The child became a cowboy or a mounted policeman, the tricycle his horse. The wagon became a fire-engine or an automobile or a "choo-choo-train." Among the younger children there was little evidence of deliberation or, as Jones phrases it, of "thought before action." They plunged ahead. If things went right, well and good; if wrong, they depended upon muscular struggle or upon adult aid to extricate themselves from their difficulty. But the older children gave evidence both by behavior and conversation that they were beginning to substitute thought for action. After the age of three years, such remarks as "I better not ride my kiddie kar over here, I might get hurt," or "If I make my feet go like this I go that way; when I make them go like *this*, I go the other way" became increasingly frequent.

Dexterity of hand improves rapidly. Before the age of five the average child has learned to feed himself, using spoon and fork, to put on his own shoes, stockings, and other clothing that is not too complicated, to fasten buttons and snaps that he can see. Shoelaces

[1] T. D. Jones. *The development of certain motor skills and play activities in young children.* Child Develpm. Monogr., No. 26. New York: Teachers College, Columbia Univ. Bur. of Pub., 1939.

are likely to baffle him for another year or two, especially when it comes to tying them, and the simultaneous use of knife and fork in cutting meat, or the nice adjustment of movement and pressure involved in spreading butter on bread continue to present difficulties.

This improvement in the use of the hands is shown in another way, which illustrates the fact that differentiation of local movements from movements of the body as a whole is not yet completed. As age advances and manual dexterity improves, the child becomes less likely to engage in general bodily contortions along with his hand movements. The little child who is just beginning to draw or write usually goes through all sorts of unrelated movements along with it. He hangs out his tongue and twists it up and down with each movement of his pencil. He moves his body from side to side, contorts his neck, twists his feet around the legs of his chair, breathes hard. As he grows older these accessory movements drop out one by one, and the movements of the hands become more nearly independent of the rest of the body. Age, however, is not the only factor. Practice has something to do with it. Even you and I, when we try to learn a new motor skill, will find some difficulty at first in refraining from useless accompanying activities of other parts of the body. One of the most conspicuous features of the acquisition of skill consists in the dropping out of necessary acts that interfere with the speed and smoothness of the motor performance. Motor learning consists quite as much in learning what not to do as of learning what to do.

THE ESTABLISHMENT OF LATERAL DOMINANCE

Hand preference, which began to be apparent during infancy, is well established before the age of five. There is, however, a distinct relationship between the complexity of the task and the extent to which the hand preference is shown. The right-handed child or adult will commonly use the right hand in preference to the left in reaching and grasping if the object is equally convenient to both hands, but a slight advantage of position will cause him to change to the left. However, if the task is one requiring considerable dexterity, say the manipulation of a difficult fastening, he will use the right hand even at the cost of considerable awkwardness and inconvenience. The development of handedness is most clearly shown in tasks involving complex movements rather than in the simpler ones. It is more apparent on trained tasks, such as eating with a spoon, than it is on untrained, such as eating with the fingers. [2]

[2] G. Hildreth. Manual dominance in nursery school children. *J. genet. Psychol.*, 1948, 72, 29-45; The development and training of hand dominance. *Ibid.*, 1949, 75, 197-275; The development and training of hand dominance. *Ibid.*, 1950, 76, 39-144.

The difference between the performance of the two hands is brought about by a steady improvement in the skill of the right hand, while the left shows little change. This is strikingly shown in Figure 53, which is based upon Wellman's [3] study of the ability of young children to trace a path through an alley decreasing in width from 5 mm. at the start to 1 mm. at the end without coming into contact with the sides. At the age of three years, the difference in skill shown by the two hands is slight. As age advances, however, the improvement in the

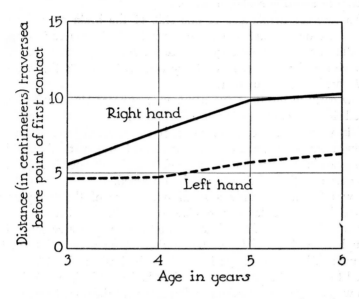

FIGURE 53. Comparative improvement in control of the right and left hands from the third to the sixth year. (Adapted from Beth Wellman. The development of motor co-ordination in young children. *Univ. of Iowa Stud. in Child Welf.,* 1926, Vol. 3, No. 4, p. 93.)

performance of the right hand is rapid, in that of the left hand, slow. The right hand gains more in the fourth year of life alone than the left hand gains in the entire three years covered by the study.

The problem of the origin or cause of right or left handedness in the individual is a very complex one. Explanations have ranged all the way from completely biological theories emphasizing hereditarily determined dominance of one cerebral hemisphere over the other to completely cultural theories emphasizing the spontaneous learning and the systematic training that occur as the growing child practices new skills. Hildreth, [4] in a series of papers, has discussed many aspects of

[3] B. L. Wellman. The development of motor co-ordination in young children: an experimental study of arm and hand movement. *Univ. of Iowa Stud. in Child Welf.,* 1926, Vol. 3, No. 4.

[4] *Op. cit.*

this question, bringing together the available research evidence. The bulk of this evidence seems to indicate that a great deal of the typical progress children make toward right-handedness comes as a result of training in the customary ways of our society. At the age of two no child is *consistently* left-handed. Whether left-handedness develops as a permanent habit may depend on the attitude the parents take and the way in which they express it. It may also depend upon how self-assertive the child is, as well. Insistence on using his left hand may be his way of resisting social pressure.

The case for dominance of one side of the brain over the other rests partly on the fact that there are natural differences in eyedness as well as handedness, and this function would not seem to be subject to much social pressure. In ordinary near vision we "sight" with one eye in preference to another.

How early in life does eye dominance appear? Updegraff [5] has reported the results of a study of 190 children between the ages of two and six years. These children were given repeated tests at intervals varying from two months to two years. In this way, not only could eye dominance at a given time be studied, but also the persistence of the trait over a period of time could be observed.

It was found that only a small percentage of the two-year-olds showed definite eye dominance. However, by the age of three, not only did over 75 per cent of the children use the same eye very consistently throughout a single series of ten trials, but on a second test given two months later no change in eyedness had taken place. They continued to sight with the same eye they had used before. Of the children who showed no definite eye dominance at the age of three, about 75 per cent had become definitely right-eyed or left-eyed by the age of five or six. Studies of older persons have shown that a small percentage of cases (most investigators have found fewer than 5 per cent) remain "indefinite-eyed" throughout life, that is, they sight sometimes with the right eye and sometimes with the left.

Eye dominance then seems to be established in most children somewhere between the age of two and three years. In some cases it occurs earlier and in some not until several years later, while a few people remain indefinite-eyed throughout life. Updegraff found not only that the percentage of indefinite-eyedness decreases with age but that changes in eye dominance occur somewhat more frequently in young children than in older ones or in adults.

Right-eyedness, like right-handedness, is more common than left-eyedness, but the difference is less marked than in the case of the

[5] R. Updegraff. Ocular dominance in young children. *J. exper. Psychol.*, 1932, 15, 758-766.

hands. At all ages after three years, from 60 to 70 per cent of all people are right-eyed, but more than 90 per cent are right-handed.

Unfortunately for our attempts to formulate theoretical explanations, there is no clear relationship between eyedness and handedness so far as individuals are concerned. All possible combinations of right and left handedness with right and left eyedness occur in normal people. Hildreth states that about half of the left-handed are right-eyed.

The problem of the meaning of the dominance of one side of the body over the other would not have generated so much interest had it not been for the possibility of a relationship between dominance and speech. Stuttering, in particular, has been observed in a considerable number of cases to accompany the lack of hand dominance or difficulty in establishing it. The tie-in is by no means perfect and it is far from clear just how it comes about. Among speech experts there has been a shift away from biological explanations of stuttering as produced by abnormal brain conditions preventing clear cerebral dominance toward explanations centering around emotional factors affecting the development of both speech and handedness. There is much still to be learned in this area.

INCREASING IMPORTANCE OF LEARNING IN SKILL DEVELOPMENT

It has been shown in the previous chapter that much of the increase in motor skill that occurs during infancy can be attributed to maturation. During the preschool period learning becomes a much more important determiner. How important it is, however, depends upon the *complexity* of the skill. Several studies have shown that climbing, cutting, throwing at targets, and finding one's way through a simple maze improve about as much without specific practice as with it. Mattson,[6] however, was able to demonstrate that for more complex maze problems, trained five- and six-year-olds performed very much better than untrained.

All of these studies indicate also that the amount of improvement that practice brings is not related to age within the preschool range. The five-year-old may start out at a higher level than the three-year-old does, when he begins the learning of a new skill, because of his greater all-round maturity. But for both of them the learning process takes the same course. Figure 54, based on results from a maze-learning study

[6] M. L. Mattson. The relation between the complexity of the habit to be acquired and the form of the learning curve in young children. *Genet. Psychol. Monogr.*, 1933, 13, 299-398.

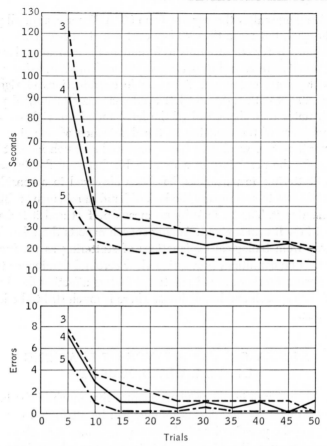

FIGURE 54. Learning curves for time and errors for
three age groups. (From E. McGinnis. The acquisition and
interference of motor habits in young children. *Genet.
Psychol. Monogr.*, 1929, 6, 203-311.)

by McGinnis, [7] illustrates this finding. The similarity of the learning
curves for three-, four-, and five-year-olds is apparent.

SUMMARY

The developmental stage between the ages of two and five can be
defined psychologically or socially. Viewed from the individual's standpoint it is the period in which the baby becomes a person—capable
of doing many things and entering into complex social reationships
with a variety of people outside his family. From the social standpoint

[7] E. McGinnis. The acquisition and interference of motor habits in young
children. *Genet. Psychol. Monogr.*, 1929, 6, 209-311.

it is the preschool period, the stage during which the individual develops the characteristics he must have before he is ready for formal education.

All kinds of physical and mental growth proceed very rapidly during the period. There is a striking improvement in motor skill accompanied by motivational changes—interest in trying all sorts of things and in doing things for oneself. Increases in dexterity involve the differentiation of finer from larger muscle movements and the dropping out of unnecessary movements.

Consistent patterns of hand dominance—right-handedness in most cases—are developed during this period. To a considerable extent this is the result of training the child is given, but biological factors related to the dominance of one side of the brain may also play a part. The origins of left-handedness in some individuals and the relationships between hand dominance and speech difficulties are still obscure.

Maturation and learning both influence skill development. The more complex skills are never brought into existence through maturation alone but must be practiced. The course of the learning process, as shown by learning curves, does not change with increasing age during this period. The younger children improve as much with practice as the older ones do.

A BOOK OF PHOTOGRAPHS

> Association for Childhood Education (International), 1951. Bulletin No. 59. *Pictures of children living and learning.*

Next to actually watching preschool children for considerable periods of time, the best way to come to know what they can do is to study pictures of their activities.

This is an outstanding collection of photographs illustrating good experiences for children in the two to seven age group. Outdoor activities, indoor play activities, social activities, and school activities are all represented. The pictures were originally selected at the request of the U. S. State Department to be sent to education centers in West Germany.

CHAPTER 13

In what ways do the development of walking and speech affect the child's social relationships?

Does the saying, "Opposites attract," apparently hold for children's friendships? Illustrate.

Are quarrels among children usually a sign of maladjustment?

In what ways are the emotional responses of early childhood different from those of infancy?

What is meant by the Oedipus complex? Why do psychoanalytically oriented psychologists attach a great deal of importance to this idea?

Why do psychologists not recommend that young children be removed from unsatisfactory homes and placed in orphanages?

»»»»»»»»»»»»

Early Childhood: Social and Emotional Behavior

THE TOOLS OF SOCIAL INTERCOURSE

Before the child is able to walk, his avenues for communication with others are limited. He cannot approach the people of his choice or join effectively in their activities. But once he becomes able to move about at will, his social horizon as well as his physical horizon is greatly broadened. As his motor skill increases with age, we find him making increased use of his newly acquired abilities in furthering his social relationships. He runs, climbs, jumps, and dances with other children. He co-operates in the building of block houses, and he uses his fists to enforce his authority. In almost every area of social behavior, the motor skills that children have developed play an important role in determining the reactions they show.

Equally important or perhaps even more important as a tool of social intercourse for the child is his newly developed speech. By the use of speech he is able to influence the behavior of others in a host of direct ways, in comparison with which his earlier language of gesture and facial expression seems pitifully inadequate and clumsy. He does not learn the possibilities of his new tool all at once, but as he grows older we find that an increasingly greater proportion of his conversations with children of his own age is directed toward modifying their behavior in some way. He gives more commands, offers more suggestions, makes very many more criticisms, asks more questions.

Physical strength, motor skill, intelligence, range of information, linguistic ability—every asset that the child possesses is enlisted in the service of his social desires.

OBSERVATIONAL STUDIES OF SOCIAL BEHAVIOR

One of the ways of studying social behavior in young children is to find a place where a good view of a play area can be obtained and then carefully note all the kinds of interaction that take place. This can be done informally for any neighborhood play group. But the fact that many children in the two to five age group go to nursery schools has made it possible for students and research workers to do this systematically and make detailed notes of their observations.

Classification of the different incidents that occur in such situations is not easy or obvious. Parten [1] used a scale that was based on the *amount* of participation without reference to its desirability or undesirability. Her six categories were as follows: (1) solitary without apparent occupation, (2) solitary but occupied, (3) physically solitary but engaged in watching the activity of other children with apparent interest, (4) "parallel" activity in which a child plays *beside* other children but not with them, [2] (5) associative group play in which children work at the same kind of project jointly but without differential assignment of roles, or join in play of a kind where all do the same thing either simultaneously or in succession, and (6) co-operative group play in which there is not only association but each makes his own specialized contribution to the success of the enterprise as a whole, as in "playing house."

This outline has been used to investigate age trends and individual differences in general social development. The categories form a rough hierarchy from least advanced to most advanced social activities. As children grow, the kinds of participation that are higher in the scale become more and more frequent.

In addition to such general observations, however, psychologists have studied many specific aspects of the social behavior of children. One of these is ascendance vs. submission. This in turn has many

[1] M. B. Parten. Social participation among preschool children. *J. abnorm. soc. Psychol.*, 1932, 27, 243-269.

[2] This is a form of social relation that is particularly characteristic of two-year-olds. It is seen at the sand table in a nursery school where half a dozen young children may work together with little or no indication of social interaction. There is little conversation and no attempt at co-operative play. Each child has his own sand toys which he uses by himself and keeps for himself. Yet all are aware of each other in a gregarious sort of way. When one child leaves the group, others are likely to follow; if one child pours sand from cup to pail, an epidemic of sand-pouring may start. But each child pours for himself and not for his neighbor.

aspects. There is, for example, a difference between leading a group and dominating over an individual. There is a difference between compliance and submission. There is a difference between commanding and requesting. Our interest in each of these may center around the manner by which social ascendance is attained or in the characteristics of the child who attains it; or, on the other hand, it may shift to the conditions that contribute to the display of ascendant behavior on a given occasion or that induce a particular child to maintain a dominant or a submissive role in most of his social relationships.

Parten [3] made a special study of leadership as it appeared in the behavior of preschool children. Even at this early age it was apparent that some children were exerting a much greater influence than others upon the behavior of the entire group, and that in the relationships of individual children with each other, one child commonly assumed the dominant role. Moreover, two definite classes of ascendant children could be distinguished, the "diplomat" and the "bully." The former worked by indirect suggestion and by so doing maintained control over large groups; the latter depended upon brute force in bossing the small number of children in his own "gang." The first type is admirably illustrated by the following episode.

A group of four-year-olds were playing house in a large packing-box. They had built a number of crude pieces of furniture out of their blocks, but as space within the box was limited, it was necessary to move about with extreme caution in order to avoid knocking things over. Clumsy and excitable Jimmy found this well-nigh impossible. After half a dozen accidents, the "father" of the family announced in the tones of one who had just made a thrilling discovery, "We gotta have a dog, too! Jimmy, you be the dog! You have to stay outside and bark whenever anybody comes by the house. Bark *loud!*" A place had been found for Jimmy, and he entered into his new role with energy and enthusiasm.

In this little incident is exemplified what is perhaps the most important attribute of the successful leader of any age or level of development; ability to recognize the special abilities and limitations of others, together with versatility in devising roles into which these characteristics will fit. Too, the able leader usually shows a knack for depicting these roles in such glowing colors that the person for whom they are designed will not merely agree but will actively desire to accept them. The "Bark loud!" in this case was a stroke of genius. It provided Jimmy with just the outlet for his overflowing energy that he needed. So in

[3] M. B. Parten. Leadership among preschool children. *J. abnorm. soc. Psychol.*, 1933, 27, 430-440.

later years the person who is full of ideas that meet the needs of his associates and who can present his ideas in attractive terms is more likely to be sought for and to have his plans accepted than is another whose ideas, though equally good in the abstract, are not so well suited to the individual interests of the members of his group, or a third whose ideas may be both good and suitable but who is unable to present them in vivid and forceful terms. The successful leader is able to forestall dissension among the members of his group without losing anyone from the ranks.

The question of whether leaders are born or made by their experience is still unanswered, but it is probable that here as elsewhere the truth lies somewhere between the two extremes. Investigations of leadership in adult groups has shown that the whole question is very complex. The nature of leadership activity varies from group to group so that there are many individuals who are leaders in some situations, followers in others. What these preschool studies have shown is that some sort of differentiation on the basis of ascendance and submission begins very early in life.

Can anything be done for the child who is so lacking in self-assertiveness that he almost always assumes the nonascendant role, allowing himself to be bullied or imposed upon by almost any one so inclined? According to Jack [4] and Page [5] this is quite possible if the usual principles of learning that have been found to apply in other fields are kept in mind. That is to say, the child must have an incentive to learn, he must be given opportunity for practice under such conditions that success is not beyond his power to achieve, and as his skill increases the difficulty of the task must be proportionately advanced. So the nonascendant children in the groups they studied were placed in experimental situations where some degree of competition existed, with children so much smaller and weaker than themselves that domination was both natural and easy. As their self-confidence increased they were given opponents who were not so easy to control. At least in the experimental situations and in the nursery school where the experiment was conducted, the behavior of these nonascendant children is said to have changed rather markedly in the direction of greater self-assertiveness.

Rather less attention has been paid to the question of too great assertiveness in the child's relation to other children than to that of too little. However, a number of studies have been made of factors influencing the child's readiness to comply with the rules and requests of adults.

[4] L. M. Jack. An experimental study of ascendant behavior in preschool children. *Univ. of Iowa Stud. in Child Welf.*, 1934, Vol. 9, No. 3.
[5] M. L. Page. The modification of ascendant behavior in preschool children. *Univ. of Iowa Stud. in Child Welf.*, 1936, Vol. 12, No. 3.

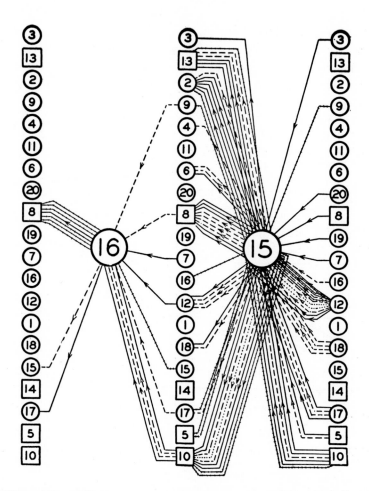

FIGURE 55. **Differences in the number of sympathetic social contacts made and received by two nursery-school children: diagram of individual roles in the group.** The columns of squares and circles at right, center, and left represent the different members of a nursery-school group. Circles indicate boys; squares, girls. The lines running from the two central characters of this study show the number of times each of these children approached, or was approached by, each of the other children with apparent intent to give help or comfort (sympathetic behavior) or the reverse (unsympathetic behavior). The direction of the arrow heads indicates the direction of the contact. The solid lines indicate some form of active attempts to help or comfort; the dash lines represent verbal sympathy or desire to help; the cross-hatched lines represent instances of unsympathetic behavior or attempts to increase another child's distress, while the dotted lines represent other responses to the unhappiness of a playmate, not clearly belonging under any of the three heads just mentioned. (Reproduced from Murphy, *Social behavior and child personality* by permission of the author and of Columbia University Press.)

These will be considered elsewhere but we may note in passing that the judgment that is made of the desirability or nondesirability of ascendant behavior appears to vary according to the position of the judge.[6] There has also been some research on *aggression* in young children which we will consider later in this chapter.

As early as the age of two years, children begin to show distinct preferences for the society of certain playmates. That elusive but highly important characteristic which we call "popularity" can be

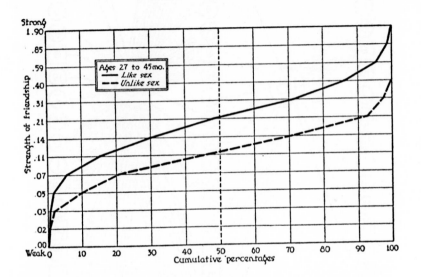

FIGURE 56. Showing the proportionate number of times nursery-school children were found playing with members of their own and of the opposite sex. (Reproduced by permission of the author and the publisher from Robert C. Challman. Factors influencing friendships among preschool children. *Child. Dev.*, 1932, 3, 146-158.)

observed even among the youngest children in a nursery-school group. (See Figure 55.) But apart from this matter of general personality, individual friendships also show up. The bases that determine these friendships are exceedingly complex, but just as with adults they are more often based upon similarities between the friends than upon the possession of opposite characteristics, which the popular saying about

[6] Even the language used in the two situations is different. In the child-adult situation we hear of "resistance," "compliance," "obedience," "negativism." Rarely if ever are such terms as "leadership" or even "ascendance" heard in this connection. But it is almost, if not equally, uncommon for adults to make such statements as "he is a good follower" with unqualified approval in speaking of a child's social relations with his companions.

the "attraction of opposites" would lead us to expect. For example, in a very carefully conducted study of the number of times any two members of a nursery school group were found playing together, Challman [7] found no clear-cut indication of the "attraction of opposites" but clear evidence of the "attraction of likes." Girls form friendships with girls, boys with boys. (See Figure 56.) Similarity in age, in physical activity, and in play interests are also important. But little children apparently hold different standards of personality values from those of adults. Little relationship was found between the popularity of a given child with his playmates and his average rating by adults on a scale for judging "attractiveness of personality."

Friendship is not simply the opposite of enmity. It is a positive matter where agreement or disagreement between the friends is of relatively little consequence. A number of carefully conducted studies have shown that, at least in early childhood, quarrels between friends are much more common than they are between those members of a nursery-school group who rarely seek each other's society. [8] In like manner, Murphy [9] reports that children who were most aggressive were also the most sympathetic members of the groups she studied. The same child who at one moment pulled a playmate off his kiddie kar in order that he might ride it himself would run to comfort another in distress. As a matter of fact, it not infrequently happened that the aggressor himself would be the first to attempt to console his victim. Do we not see the same thing happening at a later age?

All this seems to point to one conclusion. The particular pattern of social relationship is less important than the fact that social relations exist. The primary cleavage is between those who do and those who do not seek the companionship of others or those who seek it less urgently and less frequently. The amenities of social behavior must be learned, just as is true of other skills, and the process of learning them is not basically different from that seen in other areas of acquired behavior. Here, as elsewhere, practice is necessary. Quarrels and disagreements are normal features of the pattern of social life among children, and unless they become excessive they need cause no concern. Learning rarely if ever proceeds without error, and the learning of social relations is so complex that few adults completely perfect their social skills.

[7] R. C. Challman. Factors influencing friendships among preschool children. *Child Develpm.*, 1932, 3, 146-158.
[8] E. H. Green. Friendships and quarrels among preschool children. *Child Develpm.*, 1933, 4, 237-252.
[9] L. B. Murphy. *Social behavior and child personality: an exploratory study of the roots of sympathy.* New York: Columbia Univ. Press, 1937.

EMOTIONAL CHANGES IN EARLY CHILDHOOD

We have seen in Chapter 10 how the initial "stirred up" state that constitutes emotion in the newborn becomes differentiated into separate emotions differing from one another with regard to the stimulating situations in which they occur, in the expressive behavior they produce, and presumably in the feelings the child experiences. During the preschool period the child continues to differentiate more separate kinds of emotion and connect those he has already experienced with a wider variety of stimuli and situations. Language provides a new and very important basis for emotional reactions. During infancy his emotions could be aroused only by means of things done to him or in his presence. Now he can be made angry or afraid or sympathetic or jealous through things that are said.

Even during infancy, development of perceptual discrimination brings with it new fears of what can now be distinguished as strange. Similarly, the increasing mastery of symbolic processes may change the pattern of things that bring fear, anger, or pleasure.

A little boy, not quite three, was very fond of being taken to a nearby lake to bathe. He showed not the slightest fear of the water and delighted in being taken far out from shore by his father, who was an expert swimmer. One day he was taken fishing in the same lake and this too he appeared to enjoy greatly. He sat in the boat, "fished" with a light rod, and shrieked with glee when he succeeded in catching a small fish. A few days later he was again taken swimming. To the amazement of every one he refused, with every sign of fear, to go near the water. His father finally undressed him by force and attempted to carry him in, but no sooner had his feet touched the water than he began screaming in such extreme terror that it was thought best not to force or urge him further. He could give no explanation of his fear at the time, but a few days later he confided, "Mummy, do you know why I couldn't go in ze water one day? I was apraid ze pish would bite my peet [afraid the fish would bite my feet]."

His reasoning was simple enough. On the fishing trip there had been much talk of the way the fish were "biting." At the time this did not trouble him, for he was safe in the boat and the fish were in the water. But the next time he was called upon to go into the water with nothing to protect his "peet" from the biting fish, the situation was entirely different. Fear appeared, and not, it should be noted, through the mechanism of simple "conditioning" but through a more complicated intellectual process. So, as understanding grows, emotional reactions also grow and change. New information may give an entirely new meaning to any object or situation, making fearful that which was formerly enjoyed, turning annoyance into pleasure, likes into dislikes, admiration into disgust.

One of the most striking features of the emotional changes that occur during the period is the increasing relationship of emotions to social stimuli and situations. Somewhere around the age of two, a child begins to show a distinct difference between his emotional responses to people and to things. Both in his anger and in his fear one can note an element of expectancy when people are concerned that is less apparent in their absence. His screams will be momentarily interrupted as he assumes a "listening" attitude to see if they are taking effect. Social stimuli either directly or indirectly become the chief sources of the child's emotional reactions as he grows older, and his responses to these stimuli are likewise directed toward human beings in increasing degree.

The increasing importance of both symbolic processes and social stimulation is shown in the study of children's fears by Jersild and Holmes. [10] (See Figure 57.) This figure is based upon observations made by parents of children between the ages of two and five years who reported every instance of fear shown by their children during a period of three weeks. There was a steady decrease with age in the proportionate number of fears caused by immediate concrete factors and a corresponding increase in those having to do with imaginary terrors or the anticipation of future events. Jersild suggests that the marked increase in fear of the dark during the years from three to six may be related to social development, in that darkness separates the child from others by making them invisible to one another. Thus darkness may mean aloneness. It may also mean helplessness in the face of unknown dangers.

These aspects of emotional development illustrate the principle that every developmental change that occurs influences many aspects of a child's behavior. Each new skill, each new bit of information, each new kind of social experience, may modify his behavior in ways that at first appear only remotely related to the area immediately involved. It is the *child* that changes, not just the trait or habit.

As explained in Chapters 5 and 6, emotion has its physiological as well as its psychological aspect. The autonomic nervous system and the adrenal glands are involved in complex ways in emotional states. There have been some attempts to study emotional development by observing indicators of these physiological activities. Because of increased secretion from the sweat glands during emotion, it is possible

[10] A. T. Jersild and F. B. Holmes. *Children's fears.* Child Develpm. Monogr., No. 20. New York: Teacher's College, Columbia Univ. Bur. of Pub., 1935.

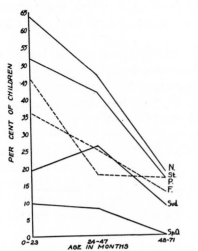
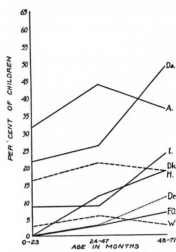

FIGURE 57. Age changes in the stimuli inducing fear. The left-hand chart shows the proportionate number of children who, in the course of a twenty-one day period of observation, showed fear at least once in response to certain stimuli that in general are less likely to arouse fear as age advances. The right-hand chart shows the corresponding data for stimuli that become increasingly likely to cause fear (at least in childhood) as children grow older. The interpretation of the symbols is given below:

N—Noise

St—Strange events, objects or persons

P—Pain

F—Falling

Sud—Sudden or unexpected events, shadows or flashes of light

Sp. O.—Special objects or things, also fears of which the cause could not be determined

Da—Being alone in the dark

A—Animals

I—Imaginary creatures or objects

Dk—Darkness

H—Real or imagined bodily harm

Dr—Fears experienced when dreaming: night terrors

F. O.—Signs of fear in other persons

W—Fears aroused by warnings of adults

(Adapted from A. T. Jersild and Frances B. Holmes. *Children's fears.* Bureau of Publications, Teachers College, Columbia University.)

to place the electrodes of a sensitive galvanometer (an instrument for measuring the strength of an electric current) at two different places on the skin and record the changes in electrical conductivity accompanying emotion. This is called the galvanic skin response, and has had some practical applications in lie detection work. Figure 58 shows what such a record is like.

H. E. Jones [11] made simultaneous records of the galvanic skin reflex

[11] H. E. Jones. The galvanic skin reflex as related to overt emotional expression. *Amer. J. Psychol.*, 1935, 47, 241-251.

and of behavior as directly noted by a concealed observer in preschool children who were subjected to a number of stimuli that might be expected to arouse fear, such as a loud sound, a white rat suddenly released in their presence, and so on. He found that there was not much relation between the two forms of response. This, he thought, suggested that even in childhood some individuals express their emotions by outward signs that any one can see, while in others the bodily response is largely covert, a matter of the internal organs and glands. In later

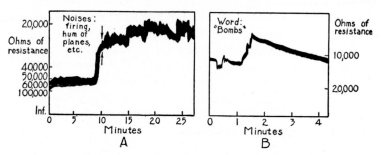

FIGURE 58.   Changes in the electrical responses of the skin during emotional stimuli. The left-hand chart (A) shows the changes recorded for a woman subject during an air raid over London in World War I. At about the beginning of the tenth minute she heard the sirens indicating the approach of enemy planes, then the humming of the planes and the sound of anti-aircraft fire, which continued for some time. The right-hand chart shows the response of the same subject on another occasion to the mere pronouncement of the word "bombs" when no air raid was in progress. It shows how effectively a word can function for the thing which it symbolizes. (These charts are based upon a study by A. D. Waller published in *Nature*, 1921, 107, p. 185 and in the *Proceedings of the Royal Society of London, B,* 1917, 90, 217, and have been reproduced here from *Fundamentals of general psychology,* by J. F. Dashiell. Houghton Mifflin Co.)

studies, Jones [12] showed that differences between "externalizers" and "internalizers" are apparent in adolescents as well as younger children. There can be no doubt that both children and adults differ greatly in their bodily responses to emotional stimuli. A very extreme fright may cause one child to scream and another to vomit. In anger some people flush, and others grow pale; still others flush and pale alternately. Social training leads to the suppression of certain forms of emotional responses, and even at the nursery-school ages the effect of such training has begun to appear.

Many other forms of bodily change have been and still are used as indicators of emotional responses. Changes in the systolic blood pres-

[12] H. E. Jones. The study of patterns of emotional expression. In M. L. Reymert (Ed.), *Feelings and emotions.* New York: McGraw-Hill, 1950. Pp. 161-168.

sure rank as a close second to the galvanic reflex in popularity, while other devices that may be mentioned are the *plethysmograph* for measuring changes in the distribution of blood to different parts of the body, as well as various devices for measuring changes in heart rate or in the rate of breathing. All of these have been used much more extensively with adults than with children.

The possibility that there may be individual differences in the *patterns* of autonomic reactivity during emotion opens up new vistas for research. Wenger [13] has demonstrated that both school-age children and adults show reliable individual differences in *autonomic balance,* which is a score that reflects the predominance of sympathetic or parasympathetic activity in the person's physiological responses (see Chapter 5). Lacey [14] has shown for adults that there are individual differences in the extent to which the different organ systems react to stress. Each person has his own characteristic patterns. As yet we know little about the origin of these differences and can only speculate about their existence in preschool children.

PSYCHOANALYSIS AND THE STUDY OF CHILDREN'S EMOTIONS

Increasingly, during the middle years of our century, research on children's social and emotional development has been influenced by the psychoanalytic theory of personality. Involved and intricate as this system is, a complete account of it is outside the scope of this book. But we can examine some of the concepts that have been most influential in our thinking about child development.

To Freud and his followers life from the very beginning was a *dynamic* process. We have already discussed the implications of this idea in Chapter 6. It means that there is energy being expended—that the organism is constantly wishing, seeking, and striving. The effect on general psychological thinking has been to place increasing emphasis on motivation as a key concept.

Freud in his earlier writings contended that all of motivation was basically sexual—that the fundamental motive was the search for pleasure. In order to make such a theory plausible it is, of course, necessary to define sexuality as something broader in its scope than the reproductive behavior of the adult organism. We have seen how for Freud the sex "instinct" was related to all the sensitive areas of the body, so that sucking, for example, could be considered a kind of sexual

[13] M. A. Wenger. The measurement of individual differences in autonomic balance. *Psychosom. Med.*, 1941, 3, 427-434.

[14] J. I. Lacey. Individual differences in somatic response patterns. *J. comp. physiol. Psychol.*, 1950, 43, 338-350.

response. The idea that the sex motive is not something that comes into existence suddenly at puberty, but is a natural part of all the pleasure seeking of the individual from birth on has had many kinds of effect on our thinking and attitudes. For example, it has enabled parents to be less concerned and punitive about masturbation and sex play in young children. It has made it seem natural to satisfy their curiosity about sexual matters whenever they begin to ask questions.

In his later years Freud became convinced that in addition to this universal striving for pleasure there was another darker side of human nature. He called this other fundamental motive the death instinct. In his view, it led not only to a deep-lying wish for one's own return to the peace of the nonliving state, but the urge to destroy others as well. From it arises the aggression that constitutes civilized man's most serious problem.

While this concept of the death instinct has been less widely accepted than most of Freud's other ideas, it has led to a large amount of research on aggression and its possible sources, research that has been very important at the preschool level we are considering. One of the first alternative theoretical formulations was that of Dollard and his colleagues [15] who held that aggression is the natural response to frustration. [16] We shall turn shortly to a consideration of the most definitive work on aggression in young children.

Another extremely influential aspect of Freud's theory was his insistence that much motivation is *unconscious*. A person himself may not be aware of the needs he is trying to meet and his typical ways of meeting them. In psychotherapy with adults, where the idea originated, it led to an emphasis on free association and dream analysis as ways of getting beneath the visible conscious surface of things. In research with children it led to increased interest in play observation and free expression, such as drawing and finger painting.

In connection with this interest in unconscious motivation there has come a focusing of attention on anxiety as a source of many diverse kinds of behavior. Anxiety differs from fear in its lack of connection with any particular kind of stimulus. It is vague, diffuse, intangible. To analyze Freudian thinking about its original sources would take us into areas were there is still much uncertainty and controversy. What most personality theorists have come to agree on, however, is that each

---

[15] J. Dollard, L. W. Doob, N. E. Miller, O. H. Mowrer, and R. R. Sears. *Frustration and aggression.* New Haven: Yale Univ. Press, 1939.

[16] These psychological terms perhaps need to be defined for students encountering them for the first time. *Aggression* means any sort of hostile attack on others, verbal as well as physical. *Frustration* means the thwarting of some wish or motive that has been aroused.

person develops a complicated system of *defenses* against anxiety. [17]
Behavior that at first glance appears useless or harmful to the person
often becomes intelligible when viewed in this way. Anxiety and defenses against it have been observed even in very young children.

In his later formulations, Freud conceptualized these and other
principles into a view that personality is basically a three-part structure.
Underlying all is the *id*, the unconscious reservoir of instinctual energies
pressing for release. The *ego* is the conscious agent mediating between
the id and the external world, striving to get all the satisfaction possible
within the limits set by circumstances. Defense systems to protect the
person against anxiety are ego structures. The *superego* is the individual's conscience, the voice of society within him. Like the id from
below, it from above, so to speak, puts pressure on the ego and may
generate guilt feelings, against which defenses must be kept up. The
preschool period we are considering is especially important in that it is
the stage during which the ego becomes firmly structured and the
superego comes into existence.

We have discussed in a previous chapter the Freudian concepts of
psychosexual developmental stages, and we have considered the earliest
oral and *anal* periods. During the period we are now considering,
usually in his fourth or fifth year, the child enters what is known as the
phallic [18] phase during which the central source of pleasure is the
genital organs themselves. Masturbation, sex play, and exhibitionism
may become much more prominent features of behavior than they were
before. But the overwhelmingly important event of the period, according to Freudian theory, is the growth and resolution of the *Oedipus
complex*. The name is derived from the old Greek legend of Oedipus,
who unknowingly killed his father and married his mother. Analysts
hold that all boys fall in love with their mothers and develop hatred
and jealousy toward their fathers, whom they see as rivals. (There may
of course be many other feelings mixed with these. Each case is different.) Along with these feelings the child develops a terrific fear of
castration [19] as a punishment for such unlawful emotions. Energized
by this powerful motive, his growing ego by a mighty effort represses
the guilty desires, the forbidden aggression, and by a process of *identification* with the father starts his life out upon a new path. It is through
this identification, this taking into himself of the standards and attitudes
of the adult, that the superego originates. From now on the person is

[17] The whole subject of anxiety and psychological defenses against it will be
considered in more detail in Chapter 24.
[18] The word *phallic* is derived from *phallus*, which is a name for the male sex
organ.
[19] *Castration* means forcible removal of the male sex organs. It is often used by
psychoanalysts in a figurative sense to refer to punishment of other sorts.

not dependent upon punishment by others for the inhibition of prohibited actions. He can punish himself and thus keep his own impulses and behavior under control.

For the girl, the situation is somewhat different, but she too must learn to repress sexual wishes directed toward her father and identify herself with her mother. Omitting the details and controversial aspects of the Freudian formulations, we can say that a major developmental task that should be accomplished by the end of the preschool period is to learn to love the male and female parents in different ways and to identify with one of them or the other. Superego development and the increase in awareness of differences in sex roles will of course continue through all the rest of the childhood years. But the initial step occurs early.

The psychoanalysts who broke away from Freud's leadership somewhere along the way—Adler, Jung, Rank, and the so-called neo-Freudians, such as Sullivan, Horney, and Fromm—do not formulate their theories of development in just this way. They are in agreement, however, that the most important stages in *ego* development occur in early childhood. All of these writers tend to put more emphasis than Freud did on the constructive, creative work of the ego and to argue that socialization is not fundamentally a thwarting of the person's natural instincts but a means for their fulfillment. Adler, in particular, attaches a great deal of importance to a child's relationships with his brothers and sisters as well as with his parents.

At first these concepts about the emotional struggles of infancy and early childhood were based entirely on memories uncovered in neurotic adults during the course of psychoanalytic therapy. But as new techniques have been developed for examining the motivation of young children themselves, better evidence for at least some of these hypotheses has accumulated. The most valuable of these methods have been the observations of spontaneous play activities.

Psychologists have always been interested in children's play, and many theories have been formulated with regard to its meaning. Spencer thought that it was simply an outlet for superfluous energy—a letting off of steam. Groos, in his book *The Play of Man*, emphasized the utility of the child's play as a preparation for life. G. Stanley Hall put forward the recapitulation theory—that the child, in his development, repeats the history of the race.

The theory of the child analysts and research workers is that the child in his play is expressing his own motives, motives that he is not able to put into words. Fears and hatreds, wishes and longings may show up in what he does with toys, finger paints, or building blocks.

In one type of play interview the child is provided with dolls named for the members of his family. Their sizes and clothing are roughly appropriate to the ages and sex of the persons they are to represent, and as they are handed to the child, one by one, the experimenter in a playful manner names them for him. "You have a daddy at home, haven't you? Then we'll play this doll is Daddy. See, he has a coat and trousers and a shirt, just like Daddy. And this one we'll call Mother, and this is sister Mary, and this is baby Dick. And *this* one," with smiling emphasis as he points from doll to child, "is Caroline" (or whatever the child's name may be). "And here are some things to put in their house," giving the child some pieces of toy furniture. "Now I have some writing to do so you may take all these things to play with for a while. You may do whatever you like with them. You needn't worry about hurting them." And later on, if the child does not appear to be playing freely, the experimenter repeats, "You may play with the things just as you wish. I don't care what you do to them."

As the child plays, notes are made of his behavior with each of the dolls. The number of times he caresses or spanks each one, his remarks to and about each, the special favors he bestows upon them together with many other aspects of his behavior in the play situation are looked upon as diagnostic signs of the child's attitude toward the real members of his family. Such interviews serve a therapeutic as well as a diagnostic purpose. They have come to be a standard part of the work child guidance clinics do in helping children learn to handle their own emotional problems better.

Sears and his associates [20] have used these methods very effectively to test hypotheses about aggression they had formulated on the basis of both psychoanalysis and learning theory. What comes to light in the standardized doll play situation is somewhat different from the behavior many children typically show in the usual social situation of the nursery school. Sears and his co-workers divided the children into three groups according to the severity of the punishment they were accustomed to receive from their mothers. Results of the experiments showed that the ones with the nonpunitive mothers showed the least aggression in both types of situation (play interview and nursery school). Those with the severely punitive mothers made few aggressive responses in school but more than any of the other groups in the freer situation of the experimental play room. The results showed clearly that even in young children, motives and emotions that do not ordinarily show up in behavior do exist and will seek expression when circumstances permit.

[20] R. R. Sears, J. W. M. Whiting, V. Nowlis, and P. S. Sears. Some child rearing antecedents of aggression and dependency in young children. *Genet. Psychol. Monogr.*, 1953, 47, 135-234.

Another study by Sears and associates [21] furnishes some of the clearest evidence we have that a process of identification actually occurs. As is usually the case in such studies, there was a marked sex difference in the amount of aggression expressed by these three-, four-, and five-year-old children. But this work was being done at a time when many of the fathers were away from home in one of the military services, and it seemed useful to compare the children from "father-absent" with those from "father-present" homes. For the girls, the absence of the father made no difference, so far as aggressive behavior was concerned. But the boys from "father-present" homes were significantly more aggressive than those who did not know their fathers. Differences were most pronounced at the three-year level. It is as though boys who have fathers at home develop even by the age of three a concept of masculinity that includes aggressiveness. Other boys develop the concept also, but more slowly. (This study of course does not prove that identification occurs as a solution for Oedipal problems. In fact, it suggests that the process begins some time before the period at which the Oedipus complex is said to reach its crisis. There is, however, some miscellaneous evidence that castration anxiety does occur in young children. Friedman, [22] for example, found such evidence in analyzing projective stories told by five- and six-year-old subjects.)

Stolz and her co-workers [23] made a very thorough study of the relationships of war-born children to their fathers. It seemed clear that in families where fathers had been absent during the first year or more of the oldest child's life, the impairment of the father-child relationship had some unfavorable effects. War-separated children had less adequate ways of getting along with their companions and with adults. The effects of the experience were somewhat different for boys and for girls, as would be expected.

Many psychologists, in and out of the psychoanalytic camp, are interested in the process of identification, by means of which children take on many characteristics of their adult models all at once. It is easiest to see the process occurring in the development of sex-appropriate behavior. Children differentiate sex roles long before the preschool years are over. D. G. Brown [24] found in analyzing the results obtained with a new type of picture test that these concepts as to what the sex roles are appear to be more definite and uniform for boys

[21] R. R. Sears, M. H. Pintler, and P. S. Sears. Effect of father separation on preschool children's doll play aggression. *Child Develpm.*, 1946, 17, 219-243.

[22] S. Friedman. An empirical study of the castration and Oedipus complexes. *Genet. Psychol. Monogr.*, 1952, 46, 61-130.

[23] L. M. Stolz *et al. Father relations of war-born children.* Stanford: Stanford Univ. Press, 1954.

[24] D. G. Brown. Sex-role preference in young children. *Psychol. Monogr.*, 1956, Vol. 70, No. 14.

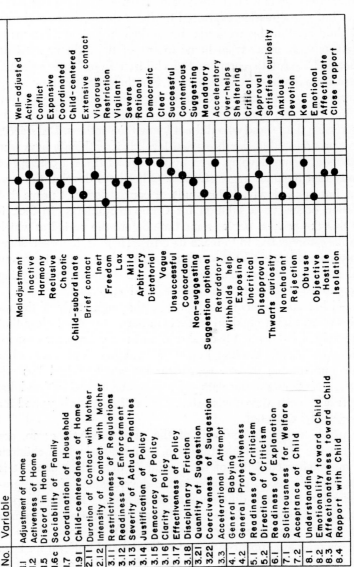

FIGURE 59. Ratings given to an intellectual democratic home on the Fels Parent Behavior Scales. (From A. L. Baldwin, J. Kallhorn, and F. H. Breese. Patterns of parent behavior. *Psychol. Monogr.*, 1945, Vol. 58, No. 3, p. 45.

than for girls. E. W. Goodenough [25] shows that preschool girls, like older members of their sex, are more interested in persons than in things and that they seem to have learned this through identification with their mothers and through attempts to live up to the expectations of their fathers. She too finds that the roles are less sharply defined for girls than they are for boys. It is more acceptable for a little girl to be something of a tomboy than for a little boy to be a sissy.

As has been noted in an earlier chapter, Freudian theories have stimulated a great deal of research on parent-child relationships and the effect of various child training methods on personality. While the expected relationships between personality traits and such variables as age of weaning and age at which toilet training is begun have not turned out to be of much importance, studies in which the general *attitudes* of the parents and the whole emotional climate of the home are assessed have produced significant findings. The most extensive of these studies is one conducted by Baldwin and his co-workers [26] at the Fels Institute of Human Development. They worked out rating scales for thirty home characteristics grouped into nine clusters. (See Figure 59.) An experienced home visitor made the ratings, which were then correlated with evalutions that had been made of the children's behavior in nursery school. As had been anticipated, warm democratic homes produced active, assertive, socially outgoing children. Homes characterized by a high degree of control with low democracy produced well-behaved children somewhat lacking in aggressiveness and originality. Many other detailed relationships have been explored.

From the mental health standpoint the most harmful attitude a child can encounter in his home is active rejection. This may take many forms—neglect, hostility, criticism. If the parent has heard or read that love is essential, he or she may feel guilty about feelings of rejection and attempt to compensate by overindulgence or sporadic demonstrations of affection. Whatever the form it takes, rejection is especially hard for a young child to cope with and many personality problems can arise as a result of it.

Particularly since the mass evacuations in England during World War II, psychologists have been concerned about the effects of *separation* of the young child from his mother. It has taken on the status of a major mental health concept. The most inclusive summary of a large number of separate studies is the one made by Bowlby [27] for the World

[25] E. W. Goodenough. Interest in persons as an aspect of sex difference in the early years. *Genet. Psychol. Monogr.*, 1957, 55, 287-323.

[26] A. L. Baldwin, J. Kalhorn, and F. H. Breese. The appraisal of parent behavior. *Psychol. Monogr.*, 1945, Vol. 58, No. 3.

[27] J. Bowlby. *Maternal care and mental health.* Geneva World Health Organization. Monograph Series, No. 2, 1951.

Health Organization. Two main kinds of evidence have been collected. One consists of the examination of family backgrounds of psychopathic individuals who seem incapable of forming close emotional relationships to anyone. In the large majority of such cases it is found that there has been no early close relationship to some one mother-person. An institution or a succession of foster homes made such a relationship impossible. The limitation of this kind of research evidence is that it cannot tell us whether or not other children suffering similar hardships grow up to be normal, law-abiding citizens.

The second main source of evidence consists of studies made in institutions such as orphanages and hospitals. In one such series of studies, Goldfarb [28] compared children from similar heredity (as well as this could be judged from background information) who spent their first three years in institutions with those who went directly to foster homes in which they remained. When they were studied at the age of ten to fourteen years, the foster-home group had the advantage over the institutional group in many aspects of intellectual, social, and emotional development. Here again, the results do not tell us why *some* of the institutionalized children turn out satisfactorily.

The fact that in many cases the lack of a close relationship with some one adult, or separation from this important mother-figure during the first few years, often has unfavorable effects on development has been demonstrated. What is needed now is a more discriminating analysis of just what the processes are and how they occur. It may be, for example, that failure to form any close emotional tie during the first year leads to the shallowness and indifference of the psychopathic personality, whereas long or sudden separations *after* the tie has been formed make for excessive craving for affection and uncontrollable hostility. We need much more evidence before we can formulate solid conclusions. Above all, we need to know the circumstances under which individuals can counteract such influences and learn to cope with the emotional stresses involved. The study by Lewis [29] of 500 children who had been in the care of a reception center near London for considerable periods of time shows that the relationship between separation and emotional disturbance, while positive, is far from perfect. Some children under such circumstances remain normal. Dennis and Najarian [30] showed that children less than a year old in an institution for Lebanese children were severely retarded on infant tests. Children of four and one-half to six years who had spent all their lives in

[28] W. Goldfarb. The effects of early institutional care on adolescent personality. *J. exp. Educ.*, 1943, 12, 107-129.

[29] H. Lewis. *Deprived children.* London: Oxford Univ. Press, 1954.

[30] W. Dennis and P. Najarian. Infant development under environmental handicap. *Psychol. Monogr.*, 1957, Vol. 71, No. 7.

the same institution, however, scored little below American norms on the kind of nonverbal tests for which comparisions could be made. Dennis concludes that a developmental deficit at one period can be made up when opportunities for learning become more favorable. This study, however, has nothing to say about the emotional effects that writers like Bowlby consider to be the most serious.

Clearly there is much we do not yet know about the effects of institutionalization, separation, and other kinds of severe emotional stress on young children. We can safely say that such stresses are not *good* for children, and should be avoided and prevented to the limit of our ability. But we must not make dogmatic statements about the extent and permanence of the damage that has been done in any individual case. Children are resilient creatures and at least some of them appear to be able to cope with severe circumstances. Some day perhaps we shall know more about the nature of such coping activity. Current emphasis in psychoanalytic research on the ego and its functions is attempting to deal with this problem.

SUMMARY

Observational studies of children in nursery schools have shown that their behavior becomes increasingly social as they grow older. "Parallel" play gradually gives way to co-operative activities, although there are individual differences and variations from time to time at all ages. Children differ in the extent to which they show such traits as ascendance and sympathy, as well as in over-all sociability. Learning can modify ascendant or submissive behavior. Children's friendships are based more on similarities than on differences.

Emotional responses during the preschool period are increasingly attached to social situations and abstract or symbolic kinds of stimuli. They can be measured physiologically as well as through behavior. The galvanic skin response is one method of measuring autonomic reactivity. There are individual differences in the amount and pattern of physiological reactions to emotional situations.

According to Freudian theory, the preschool period is the stage during which the Oedipus complex reaches its crisis and is resolved. Freudian thinking has led to emphasis on the nature and sources of sexuality and aggression in young children, and on unconscious motives and emotions. Methods of assessing them through the observation of play situations have been worked out. Increasing attention is being given to the process of identification through which a child internalizes adult values and standards. Sex roles are apparently learned in this way during the preschool years.

Studies of family relationships and the effects of different home characteristics on the personalities of children are in progress. While certain broad trends have emerged, the complexity of the whole area and the many individual exceptions to reported trends make most generalizations premature.

A considerable body of evidence of varying degrees of dependability tends to highlight the importance of the close dependent emotional tie a young child forms with his mother. Both institutionalization that prevents the formation of such a tie and various kinds of separation that may occur during the first three of four years have unfavorable effects on both intellectual and emotional development.

A BOOK TO ENJOY

MURPHY, Lois B., and associates. *Colin—a normal child.*
Vol. 2. *Personality in Young Children.* New York: Harper,
1956.

Focusing all sorts of observational and projective methods on the understanding of each child, Mrs. Murphy and her co-workers have been able to give us an idea of what life is really like for a preschool-age child. Colin "comes alive" as an interesting, lovable person with considerable creativeness.

The emphasis on the ways children cope with their experiences rather than on so-called problems, symptoms, and maladjustments is one of the things that makes this book valuable to all those whose work requires an understanding of people.

CHAPTER 14

When a two-year-old looks around him, does he "see" the room and the
things in it in the same way that an adult sees them?

How can we find out what a young child's perceptions are like?

How does the study of perceptual illusions contribute to our knowledge of
the development of perception in the child and the factors influencing
perception in the adult?

Do we perceive in wholes or in parts that are later pieced together to form
wholes? Cite evidence in support of your answer and if possible give an
illustration from your own experience.

What are some of the external factors affecting attention? The internal factors? What is the relative importance of external and internal factors in
determining the attention-getting value of an object or situation at the
age of three months? At the age of twenty?

What are some of the factors affecting the length of time that can be interposed beween stimulus and response in childhood?

What appear to be some of the main characteristics of child logic? Do
adults ever reason in a similar manner?

What kinds of distinctions between people do preschool children make?

>>>>>>>>>>>>

Early Childhood: The Growth of Perception and Understanding

THE CHILD'S PERCEPTUAL WORLD

As far as we can judge from his behavior, before the end of the first year the child's sense organs are functioning as well as they ever will. As a result of his growing experience he soon learns to interpret most of the simple impressions he receives through his senses with a high degree of accuracy. Careful experiments have shown that by the age of four or five years, children will react to distance by reaching to the correct point, will match lines of different length, and will choose the heavier of two weights almost if not quite as exactly as adults.

But we must not fall into the error of supposing that, because simple perceptual skills such as these have approached the adult level of development, the world as a whole looks to the child the same as it does to the adult. A simple experiment will illustrate. When children of different ages are shown, one at a time, a series of colored geometrical forms—stars, circles, squares, and the like—and are asked in each case to choose between matching the figure with another similar in form and size but differing in color, or with one of the same color but differing in form, it has been found that children under two and one-half years usually match on the basis of form. [1] At about the age of two and one-half or three years a swing toward color appears. Thereafter an increasingly greater percentage of the matchings are made in terms of color, ignoring differences in form, until a maximum preference for

[1] C. R. Brian and F. L. Goodenough. The relative potency of color and form perception at different ages. *J. exper. Psychol.*, 1929, 12, 197-213.

color is reached at about the age of four and one-half. Then the tide of interest again turns. Form and not color decides the issue in more and more of the choices until the adult level is reached, at which time about 90 per cent of the matchings are made in terms of form and only 10 per cent in terms of color. (See Figure 60.)

Just how the elementary attributes of perception that enable us to respond correctly to differences in distance, depth, form, and so on are built up is not completely known for any of the senses. We do know something about the cues by which such qualities may be judged, and we do know, furthermore, that a change in the usual cues may at first be so deceptive that very erroneous responses may occur. Persons reared on the eastern seaboard who are accustomed to estimate distance in terms of the atmospheric conditions of that climate find it almost impossible to believe that a peak in the Rockies seen for the first time can be as much as fifty miles away. "I'm sure I could walk to it in less than an hour," says the tenderfoot. More than one life has been lost as a result of just such perceptual errors. Some of the early painters took great pains to make use of false cues in producing deceptive effects in their painting. In the refectory of an old Spanish monastery, the guides find never-ending amusement in calling the attention of tourists to a picture apparently suspended from the wall by a large nail. "That," they tell you solemnly "is a very remarkable picture. And the nail from which it hangs is equally remarkable, for it is the very same nail by which it was first hung, more than five hundred years ago." You are urged to examine both picture and nail very carefully. "Don't you see anything strange about them?" the guide asks. You look again but see nothing unusual. Then you are told to walk to the end of the room, stand directly beneath the picture and look upward at it. You do so and to your amazement the illusion of depth disappears. Both picture and nail are painted on the wall! By a clever arrangement of lights and shadows the medieval artist was able to produce so perfect an illusion of depth that it does not disappear even after the trick is discovered. On walking away from the wall and viewing the picture once more from the usual angle, the nail again emerges, almost as if it were on a pivot, while at the same time the upper edge of the picture "swings out" from the wall.

Figure 61 is a good example of an illusion of this kind. If you lay a ruler along the edges of the letters, you can demonstrate for yourself that they run horizontally and vertically. But they continue to "look" tilted, even though you know this is not the case. Here the effect is due to much the same principle as that of the Müller-Lyer illusion shown in Chapter 2. The eye tends to follow the oblique pattern of the background figures.

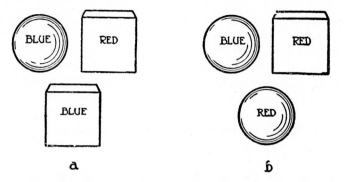

ILLUSTRATING PLACEMENT OF FORMS BEFORE CHILD

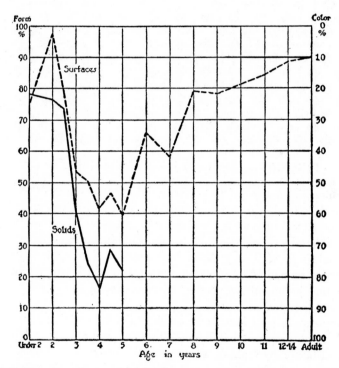

FIGURE 60. Age changes in color-form perception. (From C. R. Brian and F. L. Goodenough. The relative potency of color and form perception at different ages. *J. exper. Psychol.*, 1929, 12, 197-213. Courtesy Psychological Review Co.)

Illusions such as these have provided us with valuable confirmatory evidence about the manner in which the infant and young child learn to interpret their sensory experiences. The process is not essentially different from that of other acts of learning. In the course of the child's incessant preoccupation with his own sensory and motor processes, in his looking, reaching, grasping, touching, and handling, a host of associations are formed between visual, auditory and motor performances at a very early age. Most of these associations remain unverbalized throughout life unless some special exeprience (such as taking a course in elementary psychology) calls attention to them. Even then, you

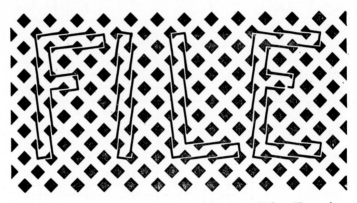

FIGURE 61.   The twisted cord illusion. (After Fraser.)

determine the nature of the cues by which you are able to say that this book is further away than that one, or that a given sound comes from the right, not from the left, more by a process of reasoning and inference than by direct attention to your own perceptual processes. And your only way of finding out whether your inference is sound is by alerting or removing, one by one, the cues to which you attributed the perceptual judgment and noting whether or not the perception itself is altered thereby.

Many experiments have been conducted with a view to ascertaining whether the perceptual judgments that we make quite automatically and constantly throughout all our waking hours were learned by experience or whether they result from neurological organizations inherent in the growth of the organism. For instance, it is known that the rays of light reflected from seen objects are inverted as they pass through the optic lens and thus fall upon the retina "upside down." The question is, How does it come about that we see them right side up? In an attempt to answer this question, Stratton [2] had a system of

[2] G. M. Stratton. Some preliminary experiments without inversion of the retinal image. *Psychol. Rev.*, 1896, 3, 611-617.

lenses made that artificially reversed and inverted the images of all objects seen through them. These lenses were fastened over his eyes in such a way that no light could enter except through the lenses, which he wore for twenty-four hours distributed over three days in his first experiment, and for eighty-seven hours distributed over eight days in a second experiment. He reported that at first he felt very helpless and confused, and had great difficulty in locating objects by the use of sight. But experience helped. In the course of a few hours localization of objects had become easier, and by the fourth day that process was on the way to becoming so automatic that he frequently reached directly for an object with no feeling of confusion. Stratton [3] also reported that by the end of the experiment, his visual world no longer seemed grossly out of harmony with the impressions gained through other senses. He *felt* that his legs were where they looked to be, and that the sound of a bird's song came from the direction where the bird was seen. Other experimenters, however, have not completely verified Stratton's reported experience. Like him, they found that learning to make the proper motor adjustments to the changed visual cues took place rapidly, but they failed to confirm Stratton's claimed "feeling of normalcy" in their subjective visual experience. The world still "looked" upside down.

Inasmuch as none of the later persons who repeated Stratton's experiment (and there have been several who wore the lenses continuously for two weeks or longer) succeeded in relearning their visual cues well enough to make the world seen through the reversing lenses appear to them as it had under normal vision, some people have taken the position that for the most part, at least, perception is as much a matter of the child's native equipment as sight or hearing. According to this point of view, the ability to perceive form, size, depth, distance, position, and so on is chiefly a matter of innate neurological organization. They believe that we do not learn to *perceive* these qualities but merely learn to react correctly to them. But when it is recalled that the adults who carried out these experiments had been practicing their perceptual skills for many years, the two or three weeks over which their experimental period lasted seems too short to provide crucial evidence. Moreover, if we remember what we have already learned about the principles of conditioning, the reason why the new motor adjustments took place more rapidly than the perceptual adjustments becomes readily apparent. For we know that learning proceeds most rapidly if every trial brings an unequivocal result. A conditioned salivary response in the dog will be established slowly and with great diffi-

---

[3] G. M. Stratton. Vision without inversion of the retinal image. *Psychol. Rev.,* 1897, 4, 341-360; 463-481.

culty if food is sometimes given when the bell is sounded but more often not given. [4] Now when the wearer of reversing lenses *reaches* for an object where his vision erroneously indicates that it is located, his mistake is immediately apparent. But when he merely *looks about him*—as he inevitably will be doing much of the time—there is no necessary correction of the perceptual relationships. Thus while his motor errors are invariably made known to him, the greater number of his perceptual errors remain unobserved and uncorrected. Accordingly the perceptual habits perviously established are less readily changed.

All in all it seems probable that we learn to perceive in much the same manner as we learn to walk. In both cases the physical and neurological mechanisms that make the learning possible are inherent in the organism; in both cases the basic drive, the urge to put these mechanisms to work, is equally a part of the basic equipment with which nature has endowed us. Our tools are the combined experiences derived from the simultaneous operation of many sense organs in a world where the physical laws are stable. Light rays do not pass through opaque solids; hence when we see all of one member of a pair of juxtaposed objects and only part of the other, we have a cue that in connection with many others enables us to learn to "see" that the second object is more distant than the first. Of course this is only part of the story. Sensations of eye convergence play a part. The fact that since the eyes are differently situated in the head the two images come in at different angles and are therefore not identical with each other aids in giving an impression of depth. Atmospheric effects, lights and shadows, and the integration of all these with the simultaneously experienced proprioceptive and tactile sensations associated with the movements involved in reaching, grasping, and manipulating objects, in approaching, passing and going away from them, all serve as cues by which perception is learned. When the cues are changed, perception changes accordingly. And the change is a total change, for perception is unitary. We do not merely see, but we see something; we not only hear, but we hear something. We may not know what the "something" is. Its form and structure may be so weak that it changes continually (see Figure 62), but it always maintains some kind of internal unity and coherence.

We have mentioned in a previous chapter that the most significant phases of the development of perception may be those that take place in early infancy. It seems probable that the newborn baby "perceives" nothing at all until integration of his sensory experiences has begun to give form and structure to the amorphous raw material provided by

[4] Learning experiments using a somewhat different type of response (to be discussed in Chapter 18) have shown that such intermittent reinforcement produces responses that are unusually resistant to extinction, once they are formed, however.

his sensory and motor activities. As has been noted in a previous chapter, the little evidence that is available from observations of blind persons who began this process of perceptual learning at a late enough age so that they could describe it suggests that one must undergo a difficult and protracted learning process before he can see even common shapes like squares and triangles clearly.

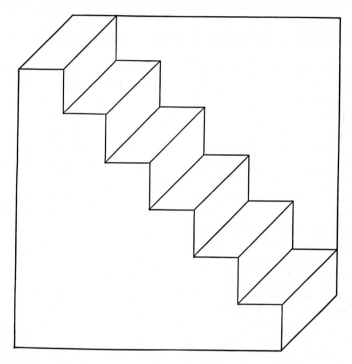

FIGURE 62. The alternating figure illusion. If you look intently at this figure for some minutes you will find that the aparent perspective shifts from time to time so that the staircase is seen sometimes from the front, sometimes from the rear. (From H. E. Garrett. *Great experiments in psychology.* D. Appleton-Century Co.)

Previous knowledge about a thing has a great deal to do with perception. We perceive things as we know they are or as we think they should be, and we overlook much that is there but that does not fit into our preconceived pattern. Persons inexperienced in proofreading find it difficult to see typographical errors unless they are very glaring. Careful experiments have shown that even persons with excellent hearing actually *hear* only about 75 per cent of the sounds in an ordinary conversation. The gaps are filled in by means of the context, and the listener is so unaware of the process that he cannot tell which parts he actually hears and which he supplies. He thinks he hears it all. This tendency to fill in gaps, to complete every experience and make it into a perceptual whole, shows itself in many ways. Little children just learning the alphabet frequently confuse the letter C with the letter O. The C to them is broken O; they fill in the gap without knowing it, and the C becomes an O. But once they learn to identify the C as a C, the broken circumference becomes an integral part of the thing perceived. It is no longer an accident to be overlooked but an important part of the new picture. When this stage is reached, the letters are no longer confused.

Whatever else perception may be, it is always an act of integration, of the construction of meaningful wholes. When elements that seem necessary to complete a perceptual unit are lacking, they will be supplied if the gap is not too great; when discordant elements are present, they will be overlooked or pushed out of the picture into the background or the whole scheme may be remodeled to fit them into it.

Perception varies with the phenomenon known as attention. Probably all of you, when sitting in a train and looking more or less idly at another train on an adjacent track, have suddenly "felt" your own train begin to move backward. The illusion is complete; you even make postural adjustment to it. You receive an actual physical jolt when the last coach of the other train passes out of your view, and your eyes and body readjust to the fact that you have remained in the same place all the time. But if, instead of keeping your attention fixed on the other train, your gaze had shifted back and forth from the train to the people on the platform or to the other objects unconnected with the moving train, no such illusion would have occurred. Perception is so largely governed by attention that at times the two seem merely different aspects of the same thing. Yet attention is not its sole determinant, for two people may pay equally close heed to the same object, and yet their perception of it may differ greatly. Perception varies, not only according to set or attention, but also according to one's subjective and objective points of regard. A cup viewed from above does not look the same as when viewed from the side, nor, in effect, does the cup look the same to any two people, regardless of the angle from which it is seen. To the child or the savage, a gaudily painted cup from a cheap variety store may be far more beautiful than one of fine old Sèvres china.

One of the striking things about perception is the fact that the subjective point of regard so soon gains ascendancy over the objective impressions brought in by the senses that the latter seems to be almost, though not completely, disregarded. Actually, of course, they are not disregarded at all but are reorganized in conformity with the subjective features of the perceptual experience. Seated at the dinner table, you do not "see" the plate belonging to your friend at the other end of the table as something very much smaller than your own. You may even look enviously at his piece of apple pie and think that the waitress has treated him more generously than you. Yet the visual angle subtended by your own plate may be several times as great as that of your friend's plate. A camera which has an "eye" but no central nervous system, records the light rays as they actually strike the lens with no subsequent reorganization. Figure 63 illustrates the difference between what the eye sees and what the total organism perceives.

FIGURE 63.   The camera records the actual projection of the image. Note the comparative size of head and feet as "seen" by the camera.

Not only size but practically all other aspects of our perceptual experience exhibit this characteristic feature of experiential constancy to a greater or less extent. A piece of anthracite coal viewed in bright sunlight reflects far more into the eyes than does a dull white object seen in shadow. Again the camera would reveal this fact, but to the eye the coal is still black and the white object remains white. A melody transposed to a different key is still the same melody. However, we do not completely lose sight of the objective factors in perception. We say, "Bring that nearer, so I can see it better," or "Take those two colors into a better light; I can't tell which is darker." At times we may be caught unaware, and then the facts given by sensation are reorganized into a very deceptive but equally clear perception. An irregularly shaped spot on the windshield of your car may be momentarily seen as a far-off airplane, or conversely, the faint scream of a distant siren on a hot night may be "heard" as a mosquito close to your ear.

As with other perceptual phenomena, there is not complete agreement among authorities as to the relative importance of neural pre-organization and subsequent life experience in the establishment of attribute constancy. Particularly the more elementary aspects, such as size constancy, have been shown to exist in well-developed form at a fairly early age. By the time a child's vocabulary has advanced to a stage at which he knows the meaning of "bigger" or "smaller," he has no difficulty in selecting the larger of two blocks so placed that the visual angle subtended by the smaller block is greater than that of the larger block. Nevertheless when we recall his enormous amount of previous experience in the manipulating of objects seen at varying distances, it is evident that there is plenty of time for such perceptual learning to occur long before the beginning of speech. Attempts have been made to conduct similar experiments with infants, using reaching as a criterion, but these have not been very successful because of the difficulty of knowing whether the infant who reaches for the small object nearer at hand really "sees" it as larger or merely grasps it because it is more conveniently placed. Cruikshank [5] noted some evidence in the way a baby closed his fingers as he reached for the nearer rattle, suggesting that size constancy occurs in the infant of six months.

ATTENTION AND MOTIVATION

We have seen that perception, the way objects and events are apprehended, varies with many factors, one of which is the behavioral "set" of the individual at the moment. We may ask, then, what factors affect attention. As with perception itself, these may be divided into two classes: the external features of the object or situation and the internal predispositions and activities of the subject. Among the former are such attributes as size, intensity, duration, [6] movements, and so on.

[5] R. M. Cruikshank. The development of visual size constancy in early infancy. *J. genet. Psychol.*, 1941, 58, 327-351.
[6] The effect of the duration of a stimulus upon attention varies in an exceedingly complex way. Under certain conditions, longer duration makes for attention, as when the automobile driver engaged in lively conversation gradually becomes aware of a slight "knocking" in his engine and turns his attention to it. Under other conditions it may make for negative adaptation— you become "used" to a sound that originally annoyed you and no longer notice it. The effect of duration or repetition of a stimulus appears to be

Internal predispositions vary both in intensity and in duration. On the one hand we have the shifting and more or less recurrent physiological drives. Every restaurant window catches the attention of the hungry man, but after lunch he passes them without a look. Circumstantial factors of many kinds temporarily induce shifts in attitudinal set. You inspect the windows of the clothing stores more closely than usual when you are in need of a new suit, and you scan the headlines of the morning paper with more eagerness at times of an international crisis. But more important than all of these are the comparatively habitual "sets" or attitudinal predispositions that each of us builds up in the course of his everyday living.

Nowhere in the study of human behavior is the circular effect of action and reaction more clearly shown than in the matter of attention. All sorts of factors, both external and internal, affect the child's momentary reactions to passing events. But through these reactions attitudes are built up that later on will determine much of his perceptual experience. Two children walking along the same street see and hear very different things. To the one, the trip is an exciting adventure. He reaches home eager to tell of what he saw and heard. His parents discuss it with him and provide information that directs and intensifies his original predisposition to give heed to the world about him. The second child takes little note of his surroundings. He is preoccupied with thoughts of the report card in his pocket and of the scolding he is almost certain to get when his father sees it. Because his attention is differently directed, he fails to gain a number of things that his companion obtained from that half hour of life. Not only did he miss the particular bits of information acquired by the other lad, but he lost what is of infinitely more importance from the standpoint of his developmental progress. He failed to gain the disposition, the attitudinal set that would lead to further observation and the acquisition of further information. With repeated experiences of this kind we get the man who travels around the world and at the end of his trip can tell you little beyond the cost of his ticket and the fact that he encountered bedbugs in Naples. Paraphrasing Anita Loos's epitomized account of her party, "So one thing led to another and then the police came," we may say, "So one thing leads to another and thence attention grows."

One of the predominant research interests during the 1950's has been the relationship between what an individual perceives and his stable, relatively *permanent* motives and personality characteristics. Tests like the Rorschach ink blots are based on the hypothesis that there is such

---

chiefly a matter of the predisposition of the subject. This shows that the internal and external factors that affect attention are not truly distinct, though for practical convenience they may be so regarded.

a relationship. Experimental situations in which inventories of values are followed by very brief presentations of words to be recognized have shown that what a person believes to be true or feels to be good helps to determine what he actually sees. Each person develops a somewhat individual "style" of perceiving. We do not live in the same "life space."

FACTORS AFFECTING MEMORY IN YOUNG CHILDREN

Psychologists are accustomed to classify acts of memory under three heads: *recognition, recall,* and *reproduction.* Each of these presupposes two things, that the fact or skill has been *acquired* at some time in the past and that it has been *retained* up to the time of the test. Although in an academic sense we speak of the act of acquisition as "learning" and that of retention as "memory," we have no means of knowing whether or not either has taken place except by noting whether or not it can be recalled, reproduced, or recognized. It is customary, however, to classify investigations that analyze the effects of changing the conditions under which the facts or skill is acquired as studies in *learning*. Experiments in which a comparison is made between different methods of demonstrating retention or of different conditions during the period of retention are considered studies of *memory*. Thus a study of the relative effectiveness of longer or shorter periods of study would be classed as an investigation of learning, while one dealing with the comparative amounts retained after a specified number of hours spent in sleep or in ordinary daytime activity would be called a study of memory. The term *memory* is also used to denote studies of the ability to reproduce material seen or heard but a single time.

It is evident that infants remember, for we know that they learn, but because they do not co-operate actively in the testing situation (that is, they do not respond to verbal instructions), it is not always easy to study the matter directly. Many of the tests for infants described in an early chapter have to do with indications that they recognize something previously shown or that they are surprised at some experimentally introduced change in it, but the scoring of these responses is for the most part based upon the child's vocalization, facial expression, or similar matters that are often hard to interpret. For example, in one of the Bühler-Hetzer baby tests, the child of twelve to fifteen months is given a small rubber ball. When the ball is squeezed a chicken or rabbit comes out. The child is allowed to play with the ball for a minute, making the animal come in and out with the examiner's help. Then the ball is taken away and the child is given other toys for a period of three minutes, after which he is given another ball, like the first except that the chicken has been removed. The test is passed if the child shows indications of surprise or distress at its absence.

The most satisfactory method so far devised for studying the retention of previous experience in children whose speech is not yet well advanced is the "delayed reaction technique." In experiments of this type the aim is to find out how long a time can be allowed to intervene between the presentation of a stimulus and the making of a correct response.

The subject is first taught to respond to a signal. He is placed before a box that has two or more doors, exactly alike except for the one thing that is to serve as the signal. Perhaps one of the doors has a lighted electric bulb behind it. This light is changed irregularly from one door to the other but always marks the one behind which food or some other lure is to be found. Both animals and children will soon learn to respond to such a signal. When it is given, they will run promptly to the correct door and pay no attention to the other. The question then arises, Suppose the light is shown only for a moment and then turned off? If the subject is restrained from responding at the time, how long a delay can be interposed without interfering with his ability to choose the correct door? How long, that is, can he "remember" the position of the signal, and what factors other than time affect his ability to do so?

Hunter, who conducted the pioneer experiment in this field, [7] found that most animals that are able to learn to respond to a signal will continue to respond correctly after a brief delay. With rats the maximum is about five seconds. Unless the act can be carried out within that time it cannot be done at all. Cats can wait a little longer, perhaps a quarter of a minute, and raccoons and dogs still longer. Children can delay longer still, the exact time depending on the age of the child. Hunter's figures for children are not very reliable because of his few cases, but Skalet, [8] who conducted a similar experiment with larger groups, found that even after several days had passed, children of two to four years could select the one of three plates under which they had previously seen the experimenter put an animal cracker. She also found that the length of delay after which a correct response could be made varied with the kind of stimulus used. The more concrete and meaningful the situation, the longer was the possible delay. Children would respond to the animal cracker situation after a longer delay than was possible when the task was to select the right one of three pictures of common objects; and the picture situation, in its turn, permitted a longer delay than was possible when meaningless geometrical figures were used. Tinkle-

[7] W. S. Hunter. The delayed reaction in animals and children. *Behavior Monogr.*, 1913, 2, 1-86.

[8] M. Skalet. The significance of delayed reactions in young children. *Comp. Psychol. Monogr.*, 1931, 7, 82 pp.

paugh, [9] with monkeys as subjects, used a plan similar to Skalet's first experiment. He would put lettuce or banana under one or the other of two inverted cups while the monkey looked on. The monkeys, like the children, were able to respond correctly after a considerable delay, in some cases after several hours. This is not equal to the performance of the children, but it is far better than any of the other animals that have been studied were able to do.

In addition to the time over which the reaction could be delayed without interfering with the response, Hunter noticed another point. The less intelligent animals usually have to keep their eyes, heads, and bodies turned in the right direction all through the period of the delay. If the bodily orientation is lost, the response cannot take place.[10] But with the children, the monkeys, and some of the dogs and raccoons, a change of position during the period of delay makes little or no difference. The children and the monkeys can even leave the room, go on with their regular occupations, and still respond correctly on their return, provided the interval is not too long.

Although a change in bodily orientation does not make it impossible for a child or adult to respond correctly after a delay, it does increase the likelihood of error, and there is evidence that some persons are more disturbed by such a change than others are. Many of you have probably noticed this in yourselves. You enter a large building by one door and after wandering about for some time you leave by a different door. You may then find that you have become "turned around" so you can no longer find your way without reorientation, or you may even walk off confidently in the wrong direction.

By way of testing Hunter's observation more carefully, Emerson [11] studied the ability of children between the ages of two and five years to reproduce the position of a large wooden ring on the second of two easels fitted with a number of wooden pegs on which the ring could be hung. In successive trials the easels were so placed in reference to each other and to the child as to provide a graded series of tasks ranging all the way from that in which the child was merely required to replace the ring on the same peg after it had been momentarily removed, through varying levels of reorientation up to one in which the two easels were placed back to back, thus forcing the child to walk all the way around and face in the opposite direction in order to place

[9] O. L. Tinklepaugh. An experimental study of representative factors in monkeys. *J. comp. Psychol.*, 1928, 8, 197-236.

[10] More recent experiments suggest that bodily orientation toward the goal is not an absolute requirement for success, even in the case of rats, but if bodily orientation is lost the reaction cannot be delayed for as long a time.

[11] L. L. Emerson. The effect of bodily orientation upon the young child's memory for the position of objects. *Child Develpm.*, 1931, 2, 125-142.

his ring. It was found that even among children of similar age and mentality, there were marked individual differences in the extent to which success was affected by the change in orientation, though all children made more errors when the amount of such change was increased.

For the group as a whole, the average number of successful placements for each of nine positions arranged in order of the amount of ocular and bodily reorientation demanded were as follows: 17.8, 6.5, 6.8, 5.5, 5.0, 5.4, 4.6, 3.7, and 1.8. It will be noted that the largest change in the number of successes occurs between the first and second positions. In the first position no change in orientation at all was involved. Only one easel was used. The child was merely required to replace the ring on the same peg from which the examiner had just removed it. In the second position the child had to make a complete shift in ocular orientation but only a slight shift in muscular adjustment. Here the two easels were placed side by side within the child's easy reach, and the child was required to place his ring on the second easel in a position corresponding to that selected by the examiner on the first easel. The next largest difference is found at the end of the series, where actual rotation of the child's body is involved. The two easels were placed back to back, so that the child had to walk around and face in the opposite direction in order to place his ring. Although on the average the older children were more successful than the younger ones, there were great differences between children at all ages. We see the same thing among older persons. Some find their way about a strange city with little difficulty, while others become "lost" after the first few turnings.

Many experiments, both with children and adults, have shown that the ability to apprehend and remember the individual items of a series varies according to the extent to which they can be grouped into meaningful wholes. A child of three has less difficulty in reproducing such a sentence as "I have a little dog" than in repeating three digits like 5-2-8 after a single hearing. The older person who has learned to read will be able to reproduce about as many short words as single letters after a brief exposure, and many more if the words are arranged to form a sentence. We shall have more to say about these matters in a later chapter.

THE FORMATION OF CONCEPTS

It has been shown that simple processes of generalization and comparison are present even among animals. For example, cats, raccoons, and apes can be trained to discriminate among simple forms (as a triangle, a circle, and a square), and they will continue to make the correct choice even when the size of the figures is changed or the shape of the triangle is altered. Infants as young as six months have been similarly trained. But until speech has appeared, only very simple generalizations seem possible. Language appears to lie very close to the base of truly symbolic processes. Without its aid the child particularizes, but as far as we are able to discover, his generalizations are few and simple, not permitting much change from the particular object or situation in connection with which his reactions have been built up. Even among children of nursery-school age, only relatively simple concepts of a generalized nature have been established. And when a young child has learned to respond correctly to some general principle, he often has difficulty in stating the principle by which he is reacting. He cannot easily put ideas of relationship into words.

This is well shown in an experiment reported by Heidbreder. [12] In this experiment it was found that children of three and four years had little difficulty in learning to react correctly to a general feature in a simple situation but that they could not, as a rule, describe the principle to which they were reacting. When the problem consisted of choosing the one of two boxes which contained a small doll and the solution lay in always taking the nearer box, regardless of its markings or of whether it was placed on the right or left of the subject, children who had learned to choose the correct box without hesitation could not formulate the reason for their choice. When urged to tell why they chose that particular box, they could not, as a rule, get beyond such vague statements as "Because I took it," or "I just knew it." Often the time sequence of ideas was reversed, that is, the reasons given were in terms of events occurring after the choice had been made, such as "Because I opened it and saw her."

In a previous chapter we have discussed the analysis Piaget has made of the development of children's thinking. After the six stages in the growth of what he calls sensori-motor intelligence in infancy comes a stage that covers approximately the age range from eighteen months to four years. He calls this the period of *pre-conceptual* thought. The child during this period uses symbols to which he gives some meaning, but these meanings are not of the same character as the ones more mature people use. Adults distinguish clearly between a particular object and a general class of objects. To the two- or three-year-old this distinction is not yet clear. As Piaget puts it, [13] "The child aged two to three years will be just as likely to say 'slug' as 'slugs' and 'the moon' as 'the moons' without deciding whether the slugs encountered in the course of a single walk or the discs seen at different times in the sky are one in-

[12] E. F. Heidbreder. Reasons used in solving problems. *J. exper. Psychol.*, 1927, 10, 397-414.

[13] J. Piaget. *The psychology of intelligence.* London: Routledge and Kegan Paul, 1950.

dividual, a single slug or moon, or a class of distinct individuals. On the one hand, he cannot yet cope with general classes, being unable to distinguish between 'all' and 'some.' On the other hand, although the idea of the permanent individual object has been formed in the field of immediate action, such is by no means the case where distant space and reappearances at intervals are concerned; a mountain is still deemed to change its shape in the course of a journey . . . and 'the slug' reappears in different places."

Social psychologists searching for the origins of prejudice have shown that children begin very young to sort *people* into categories and thus form concepts upon which later attitudes are based. Three- and four-year-olds are aware of different ethnic groups, and by the time they enter school they usually know the one to which they and their parents belong. Even before this, children show by their play that they are aware of sex differences. While the evidence showing that concepts based on group differences have their origin very early in life has been somewhat disturbing to those who are trying to overcome prejudices of all sorts, it is of considerable interest to those who wish to understand the process of intellectual development itself. It is probably inevitable and very necessary that the young child organize in some way the highly complex social world that confronts him. This organizing activity and the factors on which it depends are matters well worth further study. The fact that some of the child's earliest concepts (or *pre-concepts,* if we wish to use Piaget's term) are classifications of *people,* is something we should always keep in mind.

Along with this organization of the world of *other* people comes the development of the self-concept. It too is at this stage more of a pre-concept than a clear delineation of who one is and what his characteristics are, but it is the foundation upon which later elaboration will be made.

A major element in the skill some adults manifest in dealing with preschool children is their ability to grasp what an individual child's concepts are like. It is through such understanding that we are able to communicate meaningfully with children. By answering a child's questions and pointing out likenesses and differences in the many objects, events, and people he encounters, we can help him bring order and intelligibility into his personal world.

SUMMARY

The fact that a child's sense organs are functioning as well as those of a mature person does not mean that he sees and hears things in the same way as an adult does. It takes a long period of learning to respond to the right cues before one can perceive distance, depth, form, and color differences in a mature way. Perceptions are determind to some extent by previous knowledge. We see thing as objects with the shape and size we know them to be, rather than exactly as they are pictured on the sensitive surface of our eyes.

There is a circular relationship between perception and attention. One observes best what he is attending to; the observations then help to determine what one attends to later. A person's temporary motivational states and lasting personality traits also have an effect on what he attends to and what he perceives.

Delayed reaction experiments have shown that very young children can remember where something has been placed, but, as in the case of animals, this is easier if they are allowed to maintain their bodily orientation toward the object to be remembered. There are marked individual differences in this ability.

Concepts of young preschool children are simpler and less abstract than those of adults. Children cannot yet distinguish clearly between a single object and a class of objects. Piaget has labeled this kind of mental activity pre-conceptual thought. Even during this period, however, children become aware of differences between some *kinds* of people, male and female, for example, or Negro and white, and acquire rudimentary self-concepts.

HOW IDEAS ARE BUILT UP

PIAGET, Jean. *Children's philosophies.* In Carl Murchison (Ed.), *A handbook of child psychology* (2nd Ed.) Worcester, Mass.: Clark Univ. Press, 1933. Pp. 534-550.

In this short chapter, Piaget describes some of his studies dealing with children's ideas of natural phenomena. He reports the answers of children to such questions as "With what do we think?" or "Where do dreams come from? With what do you dream?" and notes the changes in their ideas with advancing age. For example he asked "What makes the sun move?" or "How can you tell whether something is alive?" After the child had given his ideas on the nature of life, he was questioned further, "Is the sun alive?" "Is an automobile alive?" "How do you know?"

Piaget cites many examples of children's answers to these questions. These answers are both amusing and illuminating because they show the type of logic characteristic of the untutored mind. Although later investigation has indicated that many of the explanations that Piaget ascribed to the immaturity of the child's ways of thinking are in all probability the result of lack of information rather than of a fundamental difference in mode of thought, it is unquestionably true that in childhood the two are associated. Knowledge provides the tools of thought. In its absence no one can think efficiently.

CHAPTER 15

How well can we judge from a child's everyday behavior whether he is bright or dull?

Why is casual observation not always a safe guide in estimating the intelligence of others?

What do we mean by an intelligent action? By an intelligent person?

What are some of the advantages of an "intelligence test" as compared to casual observation? Who devised the first useful intelligence test?

What is the meaning of the term mental age? *Intelligence quotient? Percentile rank?*

What, approximately speaking, is the highest IQ known to have been earned on the best of the individual intelligence tests in present use?

Does the IQ always remain the same for a given individual? What are some of the chief factors making for large changes upon retest?

What are some of the practical uses of intelligence testing in early childhood?

Are there sex differences in intelligence? What factors other than sex show a relationship to intelligence?

Should intelligence be thought of as a general quality characterizing all of the individual's actions, or are there different kinds of intelligence?

Is it ever possible to place a young child in surroundings that will stimulate faster mental growth than has occurred before?

Early Childhood: General Intelligence and Its Measurement

WHAT IS MEANT BY "GENERAL INTELLIGENCE"?

"My, isn't he smart!" exclaims the cordial visitor, as she watches the antics of her friend's baby. "You would think he was a year old instead of six months!"

"Helen is the brightest child I ever saw," says a teacher. "She learns a thing almost before you have told it to her and never forgets it afterward."

"I never saw anything like the way George will figure things out," says another. "He found an old alarm clock that his father had thrown away, took it all apart, and fixed it so that is runs as well as ever again."

We hear judgments such as these almost daily. Brightness, smartness, cleverness, brains—whatever this quality may be called, it is universally recognized as one of the most important attributes of any individual at any age. Probably as far back as the times of our cave-dwelling ancestors, intelligence, particularly that aspect of intelligence which we call "mental alertness," was recognized as important, and those who were most alert mentally had some advantage in the struggle for existence over those who were more dull and sluggish.

But although we may talk about it glibly enough, when it comes to stating clearly just what we mean by *intelligence* we find ourselves in some difficulty. What causes us to classify this child as bright, that one as stupid?

Before we can answer this question, we must first of all rid ourselves of the idea that intelligence is any kind of quality or substance that exists in man apart from his action. Just as we may say that John runs or dances gracefully or speaks eloquently or writes fluently, so we may say that he acts intelligently or unintelligently. Too, just as we may on occasion use any of the foregoing terms to describe a single action, an individual bit of behavior, so we may also use them in a more general sense to characterize the most usual or typical quality of the actions of any person. We may say, "How fast John is running!" Here we refer only to the action of the moment. There is nothing in the statement that indicates John's usual speed. But if we say, "John is a swift runner," then we have reference not to a single performance but to the average of many. *Intelligence,* like *speed, grace, eloquence,* is nothing more than a term used to characterize certain qualities of human action. Like them it is manifested in varying degrees by different persons or by the same person on different occasions.

What qualities of action are included under the term *intelligence?* To answer this question we shall do best to think first of a single act. Instead of trying to say what a person must be like in order to be intelligent, we shall first ask, What is an intelligent action?

Most of us will agree that an act which is well adapted to achieving its object, a plan that works quickly and easily, should be classed as more "intelligent" than one that fails to work at all or that accomplishes its results only at the expense of much waste motion and after many false starts. Now if we go a bit further and ask what it is that makes for a well-adapted action, for "intelligent" action as opposed to stupid bungling, we are likely to come to the conclusion that we act most intelligently when we respond to relationships between things, to abstract ideas and general principles, and not when we respond only to single items that are only a part of the situation. Terman, who is the author of our most widely used "intelligence test," is of the opinion that *we are able to act intelligently in proportion as we are able to think in abstract terms.*

Consider a few examples. If you put a hungry hen on one side of a fifteen-foot length of wire fence and scatter corn on the other side, the hen will dash at the fence, beat her wings against it, rush back and forth for short distances, but it will be a long time before she finds her way around it. If you continue to do this every day, using the same fence in the same place, after a time the hen will learn to run around the fence very quickly when she sees the corn. But now if you take her to a new place and substitute a wooden picket fence for the wire fence, her previous experience will not help her much. She will go through the same old round of fluttering her wings against the fence, dashing against it, running back and forth along it until finally she happens to find her way around. Each new fence in a new place is a completely new experience to her because she is responding only to the individual items—the particular fence, the particular place. But to a human being, even to a child, the two situations would have so much in common with each other and with other previous experiences of a like nature that they would present but few difficulties. A child of three years or an ape will pile boxes one on another in order to secure an object that is beyond his reach, but a goat sees no relationship between a box that he could easily push into position and food that is too high for him to secure.

Responding to relationships, to abstract ideas rather than to single concrete facts, has another consequence which we also associate with intelligent action. This is *adaptability*. An abstraction embraces many facts to all of which the same rules will apply. The baby whose cart is caught by the rocker of a chair pulls and jerks at it and perhaps screams for help, but he does not look to see what is holding the wheel or how it may be loosened. The child of five looks for the cause of the difficulty and tries out one plan after another until he succeeds in freeing it. Each of these plans is based on some idea of relationship, not clearly thought out, perhaps, but nevertheless distinctly more than just random fumbling.

As a first step toward our definition we may then say that intelligent action is action that is governed by broad rather than narrow meanings. It is response to relationships, to likenesses and differences, to principles rather than to isolated facts. If the principle is right, then the action will meet our first practical criterion of effectiveness. It will "work." But even when the principle selected is wrong, the action that is based upon a general idea differs from that determined by single isolated facts that have not been brought into relationship to each other. The former action is organized. Its parts follow each other in a patterned order. The latter has no very clear-cut pattern, or at most its pattern consists of the repetition of a single act that may or may not be appropriate to the situation.

A child is playing on the floor with his blocks. At first he piles the blocks aimlessly, putting two or three together, then knocking them down, stopping now and then to hammer one against another or to toss them about the room. Suddenly he stops, pushes all the blocks to one side so as to leave a clear space, then selects certain ones and begins to arrange them in a definite order. You say, "He has an idea." You do not see the idea. You may not even be able to guess what it is. But the change in his behavior is so marked that you cannot help but notice it. Now his plan may not work. Judged from an adult standpoint it may even seem foolish, unintelligent. But here is the important thing. By making a plan, even a bad plan, and actually putting it to the test, he has given himself a kind of experience that is highly charged with meaning. And the next time he tries, he will be far more likely to devise a plan that does work than he would be if he had spent the same amount of time in the random activity with which he began.

We often hear it said that the intelligent person is the one who profits most by his experience. It would be more correct to say that the experiences of the intelligent person are more likely to be of a kind that facilitate learning. Experiences with carrying out a plan, with testing an idea, with seeing a relationship, carry more meaning and so leave a more lasting impression than experiences that deal only with isolated concrete facts.

In summary, then, it may be said that intelligent action is planned action, action that is determined by the organization of many simple meanings into a complex and relatively complete whole. A practical test of intelligent action is the extent to which it "works," how effectively it achieves the desired result. For we all know that when our plans fail to work it is usually because they are incomplete, because we have failed to take account of something that has an important bearing on the result. Now the only practical way of handling many facts at once is to pack them up into a series of mental bundles, being careful to put into the same bundle only those things that have a like relationship to our problem. Instead of having to handle each little fact separately, we can then deal with a multitude of facts at once because we can think in terms of the various bundles, that is in terms of rules, relationships, principles, instead of the isolated concrete facts on which they are based.

Still greater efficiency is gained when we cease to work even with these more conveniently handled bundles of facts, and substitute for each a symbol that is to the bundle what a luggage check is to the heavy and clumsy trunk that it represents. The modern engineer would be hard put to it if he had to plan his bridges, his tunnels, his skyscrapers in terms only of such miscellaneous unmeasured blocks of stone as might be available, hunks of metal, spadefuls of cement, as does the African native in building his hut of mud and reeds. Even weights and measures, strains and stresses, velocities and forces are clumsy material for thought in comparison with the compact mathematical signs that stand for them.

Mental activity is classed as intelligent activity in proportion as it substitutes broad abstract meanings that can be efficiently manipulated in many situations for the narrow concrete meanings that are applicable to but few situations. But to meet our additional criterion that intelligent action is action that "works," that brings results, these abstractions must be built up on a sound basis of facts as they exist in nature. The visionary whose head is always in the clouds is not necessarily a man of high intelligence. Abstraction is not an end in itself. It is a tool which, if properly forged and efficiently manipulated, enormously extends man's control over his concrete environment.

JUDGING INTELLIGENCE FROM BEHAVIOR

Observation of the everyday behavior of children or older people gives us some basis for judging how intelligently they usually act. This one shows planfulness, resourcefulness, judgment. He can do many things. He has a large fund of information on many subjects. He talks well, and this is a fact that it is important to note, for words are symbols, and facility in their use is good evidence of the ability to think in abstract terms. Another has a small vocabulary which he uses inexactly; he is inept, attacks problems in a random, fumbling manner, and rarely succeeds in solving them. Even the most casual observation leaves little doubt that a real difference in ability is to be seen here. But how great is this difference? Observation alone does not tell us.

Observation, moreover, is not always a safe guide. Everyday behavior tells us something, but chance circumstances rarely provide the best possible conditions for judging ability of any kind. Not all of the child's conduct provides a fair picture of his intelligence any more than his everyday play always gives evidence of his physical strength. The child who is sitting quietly on the floor looking at a picture book is not using enough of his physical strength and energy at the moment to give us much idea of what he could do in a pinch; nor is the one who is sitting at the window aimlessly looking out into the street using enough of his mental ability, just then, to provide much basis for judging his real intelligence. Of course if we watch children or older persons for a long period of time, enough situations will naturally arise that challenge either their physical strength or their mental powers to tell us something about their ability along those lines. But these situations vary so greatly from one person to another that even long acquaintance will not provide more than a rough basis for judgment.

If you take a group of children of the same age and ask two persons, both of whom have known them intimately, to arrange them in order of intelligence, complete agreement between the judges will rarely be found. Here, for example, is the way two nursery-school teachers working with the same group of fifteen children estimated their relative intellectual abilities. All the children were between the ages of three and four years.

Teacher A	Teacher B
1. Polly	1. Polly
2. James	2. Peter
3. William	3. Mary
4. Mary	4. Emily
5. Harry	5. James
6. Stanley	6. Catherine
7. Peter	7. William
8. Thomas	8. Harry
9. Betty	9. Frank
10. Frank	10. Stanley
11. Emily	11. Thomas
12. Joan	12. Joan
13. Catherine	13. Betty
14. George	14. Sidney
15. Sidney	15. George

Both teachers agree in placing Polly at the head of the list and in regarding George and Sidney as the most backward. But Peter, whom Teacher B ranks next to the top, is placed near the middle of the group by Teacher A. William, Emily, and Catherine are also judged very differently. Of the fifteen children, only Polly and Joan are given exactly the same rank by both teachers. Yet there is some tendency to agreement. Children placed near the top of one list are not found at the bottom of the other, though they may have moved downward a few places. The agreement is better than chance, though it is by no means perfect.

People disagree when they attempt to rate the intelligence of others on the basis of casual observation, not only because so many of the situations they have observed offer no effective challenge to ability but also because, often without being aware of it, they are influenced in their judgments by many things that are not intelligence at all. Rare indeed is the person who can successfully disentangle a child's everyday manifestations of intelligence from his dirt, dimples, curls, and cuddliness. Mary is regarded as bright because she has big dark eyes and pretty manners; Tommy is looked upon as stupid because he is physically clumsy and is subject to colds in the head that force him to breathe through his mouth. Peter is so large for his age that every one judges him by the standards of children two years older than he is. Because he does not always meet these standards, he is thought to be mentally backward. Really he is of average mental ability for his age though not for his size. Doris is so shy that few people ever get a glimpse of her real ability, while Edward displays himself and his ideas without stint before anyone who will pay him a moment's attention.

EARLY ATTEMPTS AT "MEASURING" INTELLIGENCE

Early in the present century, Alfred Binet, a French psychologist who for many years had been studying differences in ability as shown by school children, was entrusted by the school authorities of Paris with a difficult and important task. "How," said the school people, "are we to know what causes children to fail in school? Some children fail because they are lazy and mischievous. Others fail because they cannot learn as easily as the average even when they try. Is there no way of telling which children cannot profit by the ordinary kind of teaching so that we can pick them out and put them in special schools where they will no longer hamper the progress of the others but can be given work that they can learn to do?"

Binet undertook to answer this question. First he tried to see how well teachers could judge the ability of children. He found, just as we saw in the last section, that there was a good deal of disagreement among them even when the children were well known to them. When he asked the teachers what they took into account in making their judgments they gave various answers. Some relied mainly on the child's appearance—the shape of his head, the "glance of the eye." Others mentioned such things as his powers of observation, his memory for things seen and heard, his range of information. But none of them had more than a vague and general idea about what store of information it is fair to expect of a child at any age, how good his memory or his ability to observe should be.

This was in 1904-1905. The idea of devising tests of mental ability was not a new one at that time; for more than a decade psychologists in England and America had been experimenting with simple tasks that they called "mental tests." But to Binet belongs the credit of first devising tests that really worked, that did to a fair extent serve to differentiate the dull from the bright. Binet succeeded where others failed because of two important differences between his method and those of his predecessors. Earlier workers had thought it not feasible to try to test anything but the "simpler" abilities. They had hoped to find out how fast a person could think by seeing how rapidly he could move his fingers in a tapping test; how soundly he could reason and draw conclusions by finding out how well he could judge the length of lines or distinguish small differences in weight. Furthermore, they had hoped that a person's "general" ability could be determined by means of only a small variety of tests.

Binet's plan was very different. In his tests he emphasized difficulty rather than speed, complexity of performance rather than simplicity. He aimed to set for his subjects tasks that would really serve as a

challenge to their mental powers. So he tried to test their ability to
solve difficult and complex problems by setting them problems of increasingly greater complexity until a level of difficulty was reached
at which they could no longer succeed. Binet, moreover, did not confine himself to a few kinds of test. Children, in his opinion, differ so
greatly in special aptitudes, in individual experiences, and in home
training, that to rely exclusively upon a small number of measures is
likely to mean that some children who have had unusual advantages
along these particular lines will be unduly favored, while others with a
different background of experience will be handicapped. His selection
was therefore made with the idea of including as great a variety of
performances as possible. Although to an inexperienced person his
tests seem rather like a hotchpotch, actually no test was included in
the series that had not been shown by actual trial to differentiate between children whom their teachers thought to be dull and those who
were adjudged bright.

Binet's first series, known as the "1905 scale," included thirty tests
arranged in order of difficulty. In giving it, the easier tests were first
tried, then the harder ones, until it became evident that the child could
go no further. The number of tests he could pass was then taken as an
index of his level of ability. The method was crude, but it worked
better than any that had been tried before.

Still Binet was not satisfied. He had devised a method of testing, to
be sure, but there was no very meaningful way of expressing the results.
He could say that Mary had passed seventeen of his tests while Johnny
could only pass twelve, but what of it? Did that mean that both were
backward, but Johnny more so than Mary; or that both were bright, but
Mary was the brighter? And what about ages? If Mary were older than
Johnny, we should expect her to do better. Prehaps in proportion to age
the two were equally bright.

Then Binet had a happy thought. Since ability increased with age
throughout the period of childhood, why not make use of this fact in
interpreting test performance? Why not find out just what children of
different ages can do on tests of this kind and make up a series of tests
for each age? Then when other children are to be tested, we can first
try them with the tests at their own age level. If they cannot do these,
the tests for the age next lower can be tried and so on until a level is
reached at which the child can just barely succeed. In this way his performance takes on a more definite meaning, for if he is ten years old
and yet can only do the tests that the average five-year-old can pass,
we have gained a much clearer picture of his ability than is given by
finding out that he can only pass nine out of a series of thirty tests. It
is like saying that at ten years a child is so small than he only takes a five-

year size in suits. We not only know that he is retarded in growth, but we have a fair idea of the amount of his retardation.

In 1908, Binet published his first "year scale" in which the tests were arranged in groups according to the age at which they could ordinarily be passed. There were four or five tests for each age. Scores earned on this scale were no longer to be expressed simply in terms of the number of test items passed but as "mental ages," a new expression destined to become very popular. A child who can pass the six-year-old tests but not those designed for seven-year-olds is said to have a mental age of six, no matter what his actual chronological age may be. If he is only four but can nevertheless pass the six-year-old tests, then he is much brighter than the average. If he is nine years old but has still not advanced beyond the six-year test level, he is backward; perhaps he should be classed as feeble-minded.

Binet died in 1911, just after revising his scale of tests a second time. But although his methods were then far from having been perfected, their possibilities had been glimpsed by many persons. In America both the 1908 scale and the 1911 revision had been translated into English by Goddard and were already gaining extensive use. Later on, Terman, Kuhlmann, and others worked out further modifications in the scale as it was left by Binet and succeeded in correcting a number of its weak points. They also extended it at each end. As left by Binet, the scale included tests for the ages from three to thirteen years. Terman extended it upward to the adult level; Kuhlmann added tests for very young children and infants down to the age of three months.

A further step of great importance in interpreting the results of tests was taken when, in 1912, William Stern of the University of Hamburg proposed the use of the intelligence quotient, now generally known as the IQ, to show the relationship between a child's mental age and his chronological age. It obviously is much more significant for a child of four years to be mentally two years in advance of his age than it is for a child of twelve to be accelerated two years, for the former has had only four years in which to gain his advanced standing while the latter has taken twelve years to do so. The intelligence quotient, which is obtained by dividing the child's mental age by his chronological age (omitting the decimal point) is designed to reduce the amount of acceleration or retardation to a uniform standard for all ages by expressing the one as a percentage of the other. A child of six with a mental age of eight would thus be said to have an IQ of $\frac{8}{6}$ or 133. One whose chronological age is six and whose mental age is only four would have an IQ of $\frac{4}{6}$ or 67.

The IQ was first made popular by Terman and is now the most widely used method of expressing the results of intelligence tests when

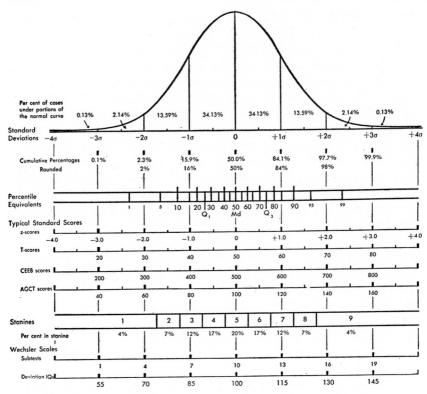

FIGURE 64.   Relationships between various types of derived scores.
H. G. Seashore. Methods of expressing test scores. Psychol. Corp.
Test Service. Bulletin, No. 48, 1955.

given to children. For older persons other methods of specifying test
results are preferable, because after mental maturity has been reached,
the age comparison ceases to have meaning, just as it would be foolish
to say that a man of thirty years is only as tall as the average man of
twenty-five.

THE DISTRIBUTION OF INTELLIGENCE

Common observation shows that not all people are equally gifted in
mentality. The differences among them range all the way from the level
of the vegetative idiot who can neither walk nor talk to the genius of
an Aristotle, a Liebnitz, a Goethe, or an Einstein. The number of cases
at either of these extremes is, however, small in comparison to the great
mass of ordinary people who are neither geniuses nor idiots but range
about midway between the two.

If you were to select a thousand people by some method that would give you a random sample of the population (a difficult task, by the way) and appraise their general intelligence by the best methods now available, you would find that a graphic representation of the numbers of persons scoring at the different intelligence levels would look something like Figure 64. It is the *normal curve,* upon which much of statistical reasoning is based. As used by specialists in mental measurement, distances along the horizontal base line represent *scores.* The midpoint of this line represents the mean or average. Areas between this base line and the curve above represent *proportions* of the people tested who scored at the various levels. It is clear that the largest proportions of the total area are those near the average. The area included under the curve is exceedingly small for both the very low and the very high

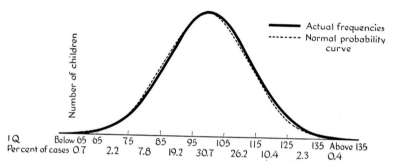

	Actual frequencies
	Normal probability curve

IQ   Below 65 65   75   85   95   105   115   125   135 Above 135
Per cent of cases 0.7   2.2   7.8   19.2   30.7   26.2   10.4   2.3   0.4

FIGURE 65.   Distribution of IQ's of 14,463 Kansas City first-grade children tested by the 1916 Revision of the Stanford-Binet Scale. (The data for this graph were taken from Lexie Strachan. Distribution of intelligence quotients of twenty-two thousand primary-school children. *J. educ. Res.,* 1926, 16, 169-177.)

scores. This is because the proportion of the population getting extremely high and extremely low scores is very small.

Figures 65 and 66, which are based upon the actual testing of fairly representative groups of children, show how closely the distribution of measured intelligence conforms to the theoretical curve that has been imposed upon it for comparison. This is not a thing that just happens by itself. A part of the skill that is needed in constructing tests for general use is to select combinations of items that will result in normal distributions of scores for specified populations.

The reason psychologists seek this statistical characteristic in mental tests is that by means of normal curve theory it is possible to render scores on different tests statistically comparable. If two distributions are both normal, distances along the horizontal base line can be directly compared. It is customary to use a unit called the *standard deviation* to measure such distances. Even without understanding how it is computed (any good statistics text will give you this information if you wish to obtain it) you can get some idea from Figure 64 as to how it is used. The various horizontal lines under the curve show different ranges of scores that are obtained from tests in common use. Scores under one another are equivalent because they represent equal distances from the mean of the normal distribution that all these tests have in common. A score of 120, for example, on the Army General Classification Test, represents the same level of intelligence as an IQ of 115 on the Wechsler-Bellevue.

Another device for indicating the part of a distribution in which any particular person's score falls is to express the score as a *percentile*.

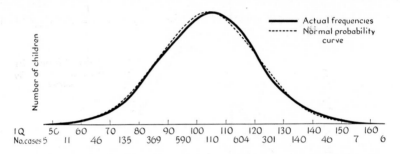

FIGURE 66. Distribution of IQ's of 2,970 children tested by the 1937 Revision of the Stanford-Binet Scale (original standardization group). It will be noted that this curve is decidedly flatter than that shown in Figure 65, with more cases having very high and very low IQ's and fewer in the middle ranges. A part of this difference may be due to a difference in the populations tested, but in the main it may be accounted for by a difference in the tests used. The significance of an IQ varies to some extent with the test from which it is derived.

Such scores are based on the *area* under the curve rather than on horizontal distances from the average. A percentile of 85 means that 85 per cent of the persons in the norm group obtained scores lower than the one under consideration. If the distribution is normal, percentile scores have a fixed relationship to those based on standard deviation units. By referring to the two lines for percentiles and for Binet IQ's in Figure 64, for example, we can convert an IQ into a percentile, or vice versa.

THE INTERPRETATION OF MENTAL TESTS

An important application of the statistics of probability to the study of intellectual differences consists in making more exact estimates than would be possible without their use of the amount of confidence that can be placed in the results of a single test. All persons having anything to do with tests or with the results of testing—and that, nowadays, means practically everybody—should realize that no test is infallible. If the same child is tested on two consecutive days under the best possible conditions and by the most competent examiners, the chances are that the results will not be precisely identical, though it is unlikely that they will differ enough to affect any practical recommendations that might be made. Momentary fluctuations of the child's attention, small differences in the precise wording of a response, slight changes in the inflection of the examiner's voice when asking a question, and a host of other small matters that are difficult to bring under close control may be enough to shift the balance of success or failure on a particular item for which the chances of success or failure were almost equal at the start. The number of such shifts will be small in most cases, and their effect upon the total score will for practical purposes be negligible; yet the fact that small changes in standing upon retest are the rule rather than the exception is sufficient evidence of the fallacy of the saying, as people often do say, "John has an IQ of 125." A correct statement would be, "On such-and-such an occasion John earned an IQ of 125 on the ——— test."

In order to make such a statement really meaningful, two things must be known. First, we may ask what proportion of children in the population at large do as well as this. In the second place, we wish to know the likelihood that John's standing will be maintained. In more precise language we may say, What are the chances that if retested tomorrow or after some other stated interval, the IQ obtained would be as low as 100 or, on the other hand, as high as 150?

This is not the place to explain the procedures by which answers to questions such as this can be obtained. For this, the interested reader should consult any of the standard texts on mental measurement. The important thing is for all to realize that information of this kind is not only essential but is also available, and that any person who gives a mental test should be able to provide it. Inability to do so should be looked upon as *prima facie* evidence that the examiner is incompetent. [1]

It is impossible to make any statement whatever about the probable variation of IQ's upon retest unless these things are known: (1) the particular test used on each occasion, (2) the age of the child at the time of first testing, and (3) the length of the interval between the testings. A few general principles can be laid down as follows:

1. As a rule, when the same test is used on both occasions, the variation in the child's standing will be smaller than will be the case when

---

[1] Assuming, of course, that the test was given for the practical purpose of comparing the child's standing with that of others and that a standardized measuring instrument was therefore used.

the test used on the second occasion is a different one. This results from the fact that no test can include more than a small sample of the tasks that a child is able to perform, and there is greater chance of a shift in the character of the sample when changing to a different test, even though the child has developed so much in the interval between testings that his ability is measured by a quite different level on the scale. The differences in content of two different scales is usually greater than the difference between two different levels of the same scale.

2. The younger the child at the time of first testing or the longer the interval between tests, the greater is the change in standing likely to be.

3. Test results may be and frequently are unfavorably affected by lack of interest, shyness, or similar nonintellectual factors that affect a child's effort and co-operation. This is particularly likely to occur if the child is young and unaccustomed to strange places and strange people.

4. No test worth giving has ever been devised that is not susceptible to the influence of direct or indirect coaching on the particular items of which it is made up. This point must always be kept in mind in trying to evaluate the statements frequently put forth about the effects of some special system of teaching that is said to improve the intelligence of children. One must always ask, Has the *general* intelligence of the children been improved, or have they merely received a kind of indirect coaching that enables them to make a better showing on the particular items included in the test?

5. Mere experience in taking a test introduces a certain opportunity to learn the art of test-taking. While this "practice effect," as it is called, is usually greatest when the same test is repeated after a short interval and the subject therefore is given the same tasks to perform on both occasions, it is to be seen even when the two tests used include no duplicate items. It is usually most apparent when the subjects are young children who had no experience in taking tests previous to the first occasion. Better adjustment to the whole situation undoubtedly accounts for some of the apparent gain that commonly appears when the results of a second examination are compared with those of a first. But even at the college level, experience still counts. Students who have become well accustomed to taking the modern "objective" types of examination have a measurable advantage over those of equal competence whose previous acquaintance was limited to tests of the "essay" or "question and answer" variety. Something is gained by merely "learning the trick."

6. Because of a statistical principle known as "regression toward the mean" children initially testing high are more likely to lose in standing on later tests than they are to gain. Conversely, those initially testing low are more likely to gain than they are to lose. Neither loss nor gain in these cases necessarily represents a real change in the child's ability.

It means only that because every test involves some degree of error in measurement, when the IQ obtained is high, there is greater probability that the error of measurement has been added to the child's true score than it has been subtracted from it. In like manner, when the IQ is low, there is greater probability that it has been spuriously reduced below its true magnitude by subtracting the error of measurement from the true score than the opposite has occurred. In both cases it must be remembered that we are dealing with *probabilities* and not with facts that invariably occur. A child initially testing high may gain in standing upon retest; one initially testing low may rank still lower.

7. Every test is to some extent "unreliable." This means that the score a person makes is partially determined by chance factors having nothing to do with the characteristic the test is designed to measure. Reputable test makers specify the "standard error of measurement" that goes with scores obtained on the test. Since this figure differs from one test to another, it is always necessary that we specify what test was used as well as the child's standing on the test if the results are to be interpreted meaningfully.

8. The method of deriving the IQ carries with it the statistical necessity that, other factors remaining equal, high IQ's will vary more from test to test than low ones do. The reason for this, while perfectly straightforward to the mathematician, is rather too complicated to be explained here.[2] The reader is therefore asked to take the statement "on faith" and in doing so to remember that this, as well as the principle of "regression toward the mean" which was discussed in a preceding paragraph, is a mathematical and not a psychological phenomenon. Bright children do not actually vary more in ability from one occasion to another than backward ones do, but the way the IQ is derived makes it appear as if this were the case.

Keeping all of these qualifications in mind, we may now consider a few cautious figures with regard to the range and stability of IQ's.

The distribution of IQ's for the two Stanford Revisions of the Binet Scale, which have been the most widely used tests for children, covers a range of approximately 200 IQ points, from very close to zero in the case of the hopeless idiot to the 200 which a very small proportion of brilliant children obtain. The available evidence would seem to indicate that the range of ability does not change with age, although the test

[2] Those interested will find a clear exposition of the principle together with the necessary formulas for determining the relationship involved in an article by Quinn McNemar. The expected average difference between individuals paired at random. *J. Genet. Psychol.*, 1933, 43, 438-439. A further discussion of this principle together with a table showing its application to the 1937 Revision of the Standard Binet test is to be found in L. M. Terman and M. Merrill. *Measuring intelligence.* Boston: Houghton, 1937. Pp. 44-47.

itself is inadequate for measuring the highest levels of ability among subjects over the age of fifteen or the lowest levels among the younger subjects.

Analysis of the distribution of IQ's for the 1937 Revision of the Stanford-Binet [3] shows that only about one child in 10,000 gets an IQ higher than 160. One in a hundred scores 136 or higher. About the same proportion scores 64 or lower. Almost half (46 per cent) of the children tested are between 90 and 110. (These rough norms are for children of school age for whom this test is most suitable. Preschool children, older adolescents, and adults do not always conform to these proportions because of deficiencies in test standardization for such groups. Many college students, for example, obtain IQ's in the 140's on the Stanford-Binet. This does not mean that they have rare gifts.)

There has been a great deal of attention devoted to the problem of the constancy of the IQ. Growth studies, in which the same children are tested at different stages in their development, have shown that there is more shifting up and down than the early mental testers expected there to be. Changes of 15 or 20 IQ points are by no means uncommon. In rare cases shifts of 40 or 50 points occur. [4]

Such studies have made it clear that we cannot judge a child's intelligence level by *one* test. Schools must provide for *periodic* testing if they hope to assess the capacity of each child accurately. However, some publicists who have made much of the fact that an IQ can change have enormously exaggerated the research findings about IQ shifts. The general rule is that bright children remain bright throughout their growing years. Dull children in most cases remain dull.

Much of the confusion that often exists with regard to the use of intelligence tests in the guidance of children could be avoided if educators would remember that the *mental age* and the *IQ* reflect different aspects of intelligence. For most educational decisions it is the mental age rather than the IQ that must be considered, because it indicates the difficulty or complexity of the material a child is ready to learn. For example, a child is ready for the kind of activities most good nursery schools provide when his mental age is approximately three. A two-year-old with an IQ of 150 or a four-year-old with an IQ of 75 may be equally ready for this experience. The mental age is emphatically *not* constant during childhood. A child who is quite unable to cope with arithmetic this year may grasp its fundamental principles fairly easily next year. He is *growing*, mentally as well as physically. Too much emphasis on the IQ and its constancy has sometimes blinded us to this important fact.

[3] Terman and Merrill, *op. cit.*

[4] M. P. Honzik, J. W. MacFarlane, and L. Allen. The stability of mental test performance between two and eighteen years. *J. exper. Educ.*, 1948, 17, 309-324.

The mental age concept is useful because it gives us an inkling of the level of development to which a child's ability most nearly corresponds, but we must not take the picture too literally. The bright child differs from the backward child of the same mental age in the *quality* of his intelligence. He is more alert, he has greater zest in doing and in learning new things. The backward child is inclined to wait for experiences to come to him; he is the tool of circumstance. The bright child does not wait for events. He goes in search of them. He creates them and bends them to his will. So as age advances the bright child continues his rapid mental growth, while the dull child also gains but at such a slow pace that the mental distance between the two steadily increases.

MODERN INTELLIGENCE TESTS FOR YOUNG CHILDREN

Early intelligence tests were designed primarily for children of regular school age, six and above, although they often included easier material so that backward or dull children could be assessed. With the rise of child study centers and nursery schools in the 1920's and 1930's there was a considerable demand for tests that would be of the right level of difficulty for preschool children and would be interesting enough to them so that their best efforts could be enlisted. A number of good preschool tests were standardized during this period.

The Merrill-Palmer Tests, devised by Rachel Stutsman [5] and her assistants at the Merrill-Palmer nursery school in Detroit, are intended for use with children between the ages of eighteen months and five years. They make only a small demand upon language, since they include chiefly tests of fitting blocks of different geometrical forms into their corresponding recesses in a board known as a "form board," tests of ability to button and unbutton, tests of the ability to put cut-up pictures together, to copy simple designs, and so on. Figure 67 shows a child of four years working at a block-building test.

The Minnesota Preschool Tests are divided into a verbal scale, a nonverbal scale, and a combined scale which makes use of both verbal and nonverbal responses. The materials for these tests are shown in Figure 68.

Current revisions of standard individual intelligence tests for children of all ages include items suitable for preschool testing. Two tests now lead the field. One is the Stanford-Binet 1937 Revision [6] that has already been mentioned. This follows the practice begun by Binet himself of

[5] R. Stutsman. *Mental measurement of preschool children.* Yonkers, N. Y.: World Book Co., 1931.

[6] A new revision is being prepared for publication.

FIGURE 67. Success with the block-building test. (From Florence L. Goodenough and Katherine M. Maurer. *The mental growth of children from two to fourteen years.* Courtesy of the Univ. of Minnesota Press.)

FIGURE 68. Some of the materials used in the Minnesota Preschool Test. (Courtesy Educational Test Bureau, Minneapolis.)

arranging the tests in groups according to the ages at which they are commonly passed. A few of the tasks used with children of preschool age are listed below:

Two years	Naming a series of well-known objects, such as a cup.
	Building a tower of four or more blocks.
Three years	Copying a circle.
	Repeating three digits after a single hearing.
Four years	Matching simple geometrical forms.
	Making a string of at least seven wooden beads.

The other leading individual intelligence test is the WISC (Wechsler Intelligence Scale for Children). Its organization is different, in that it groups all the tasks of the same sort together and provides that the child be tested on increasingly difficult items of each type until he reaches a level where he can no longer answer correctly. The examiner then turns to easier items of a different type. The advantage of this way of standardizing a test is that separate scores can be given for the different kinds of task. A child may be comparatively high on vocabulary, for example, and comparatively low on digit span. Separate verbal and performance IQ's, as well as the IQ on the total test, are obtained.

The exact manner of presenting the material, including the wording of the instructions to the child, is carefully specified in the case of each test. The quality of the responses required for passing the test is also indicated in each manual, as well as the exact objects to be named (which are supplied as a part of the standardized material), the forms to be matched, the digits or sentences to be repeated, and so on. Small changes in matters of this kind may alter the difficulty of a test item far more than the inexperienced person is likely to realize. One of the first things that has to be impressed upon students who are learning to give tests is the necessity for adhering strictly to the standard procedure. Many find it hard to understand why small changes that enable a child to pass a test which he would otherwise have failed are not permissible. Such a procedure is comparable to shortening the length of the inches on a scale used for measuring height in order to make a subject seem taller. His real height is not increased, but the measurement is ruined.

FACTORS RELATED TO MENTAL DEVELOPMENT

Over the half century in which intelligence tests have been used, the relationship of the trait measured by such tests to a variety of other traits and social characteristics has been thoroughly explored. Some of the findings of these studies should be kept in mind by those who must interpret test scores.

First of all, differences in intelligence, like the differences in language development we have discussed in Chapter 11, are associated with differences in socio-economic status. Table III brings together the results of five large-scale studies that show this tendency in an unmistakable way. Two are on children, three on adults. Three are in the United States, two in Great Britain. They all show an average gap of 20 IQ points or more between day laborers (or their children) and professional people (or their children). It must be remembered that these are *average scores*. Within each occupational group there are *individuals* who score at all the intelligence levels.

TABLE III

ESTIMATED AVERAGE IQ's FOR DIFFERENT OCCUPATIONAL LEVELS

Study	Children			Adults	
	Terman Merrill	Duff and Thompson	Army Alpha	Cattell	AGCT
Class					
I. Professional	116	115	123	132	120
II. Semi-professional Managerial	112	113	119	117	113
III. Clerical, Skilled Trades, Retail	107	106	108	109	108
IV. Rural Owner Farmers	95	97	97	—	94
V. Semi-skilled, Minor Clerical	105	102	101	105	104
VI. Slightly skilled	98	97	98	—	96
VII. Day Laborers	96	95	96	—	95

The question of whether these differences are caused by heredity or environment cannot be answered in any absolute fashion. As indicated in Chapter 3, both factors operate together. Undoubtedly persons get into the more favored positions in our society at least partly as a result of good mental equipment inherited from their parents and ancestors. In these positions they are able to place their children in stimulating educational environments, so that good genes and good training work together. We can perhaps account for some of the below average scores made by underprivileged children on the basis of the unfavorable influences they have encountered in their homes and neighborhoods. But it is difficult to account in this way for the *high* scores encountered quite frequently in poor children and adults.

Do boys and girls do equally well on intelligence tests? The answer here is that it depends on the make-up of the particular test used. Early studies usually showed small differences in favor of girls on tests of the Binet type—at least for groups under high school age. This arose from the verbal nature of many test items. As we have seen, females show a slight but consistent superiority in verbal development. As tests drawing upon a larger variety of tasks were made available, the sex difference disappeared. The practice now is for test makers to exclude items that would give a considerable advantage to either sex, or to include equal numbers of those at which girls and boys excel. Having done this, they obviously can make no general statement as to which sex is the more intelligent. All we can conclude is that males tend to be better at some things, females at others. These differences in patterns of ability may arise from either biological differences between the sexes or from differences in what is learned. We have noted in a previous chapter that even during the preschool years children become aware of differences in sex roles.

Whether or not there are any bodily characteristics by which mental differences may be recognized is a question that has been hotly debated for decades. Many people think that the shape of the head, the features, or the facial expression provide a sound basis for distinguishing the bright from the stupid. But when people have actually been set the task of making these distinctions among children who are unknown to them, so that they have nothing but physical traits to go by, they do not as a rule have much success. Except in the case of certain types of mental deficiency which can be recognized by physical signs, neither the features, the shape of the head, nor the bodily form tell us much about the mental capacities either of children or of older persons. Not even the "bumps" or protrusions of the skull beloved of the phrenologists can give us any useful information about the mental traits of their possessor. Indeed it would be very surprising if they did, for mental traits are not correlated with the development of particular small areas in the brain. In most forms of mental activity the entire cortex is likely to be involved. Moreover, such tendencies to localization of function as exist do not follow the plan of the phrenologists' "skull maps" at all. And finally, the contour of the skull gives but slight indication of the contour of the brain within it. Unless the size or shape of the head falls completely without the limits of normal variability—and these limits are larger than most people think—we shall not find these characteristics of much help in diagnosing mental traits.

What about bodily size and form? Are tall children likely to be brighter than short ones? Is there any relationship between intelligence and weight?

Apparently there is, at least during childhood. But the relationship is very small both as regards height and weight, and there are so many individual cases that do not obey the rule that measurements of height and weight are of little help in diagnosing mental ability. If used, they would lead us astray almost (though not quite) as often as they would help us to a correct decision. Much the same thing appears to be true of most of the specific physical conditions related to health. Children of low intelligence more often than those of high intelligence are found to be suffering from diseased tonsils and adenoids, decayed teeth, rickets, and so on, but this may be only because stupid parents are more likely to have stupid children and also to give them poor physical care. The relationship of intelligence and health is a matter that opens up a number of interesting and important scientific problems, but practically speaking the question is of less significance. Good health is important enough to be sought for its own sake, no matter what relationship it may bear to the IQ.

THE NATURE OF MENTAL ORGANIZATION

It is characteristic of human nature to hope that our inferiorities in one line may be counterbalanced by superiorities in other lines. Dozens of popular phrases attest to this: "clever but dishonest," "slow but accurate," "brilliant but emotionally unbalanced." In individual cases these combinations may be found, as we all know. But are they the rule or the exception? Is correlation or compensation more often found when the various characteristics of the same individual are compared with each other?

The fact is that it is very hard to find any two desirable traits that are not a little more likely to occur together than to run contrary to each other. Not all clever men are honest. Not all rapid workers excel in accuracy. Not all brilliant people are emotionally stable. But on the average, honesty and cleverness, speed and accuracy, intelligence and emotional stability are more likely to be found in combination with each other than with the opposites of these traits. This is true at all ages. Some traits are very closely bound together so that only occasionally will exceptions be found to the rule that a person who stands high in one will also be above average in the other. Some are more loosely connected, so that individual cases frequently break away from the rule. Sometimes the association is so slight that conformity with the rule is just barely more common than are exceptions to it and the rule itself can be discovered only by careful and unprejudiced examination of the facts for large numbers of cases.

The tendency for general superiority or inferiority to show itself in many if not most kinds of mental activity and conduct has been of great interest to psychologists concerned with the questions of the organization of our mental traits. The problem, briefly stated, is, Have we *intelligence* or *intelligences*? Spearman, one of the most eminent British psychologists, accounted for all the relationships between scores on diverse types of tests on the basis of a single factor or kind of ability he called *g*. Some people have more of this ability than others do; some tests draw on it more heavily than others do.

While this theory explained many of the kinds of correlation between tests, it became apparent as it was applied that it did not account for all of them. Thurstone, an outstanding American psychologist, pioneered the idea that there were several primary abilities. Various tests measure one or more of them. He utilized a mathematical technique called *factor analysis* to discover what some of these primary abilities are, and presented evidence for six of them: V (verbal meaning), W (word fluency), N (numerical aptitude), S (spatial aptitude), P (perceptual speed), R (reasoning). Separate studies based on groups of different ages and educational levels led to some additions and modifications, but this general structure appeared in the analyses of many groups and tests.

It appears now, however, that the principle of positive correlation between desirable traits applies even to these primary abilities themselves. When tests for measuring them separately were devised, tables of scores showed that there was some tendency for people who scored high on one to be higher than average on at least some of the others. It is now agreed that both Spearman and Thurstone were right. There is a general characteristic common to all tests of mental ability, and some people have more of this than others. But there are also more limited kinds of mental ability making for skill with such tasks as computations, verbal expression, or mechanical problems, and people differ from one another in the pattern as well as the general level of their ability. It has become common practice for a psychologist who tests a child or an adult to include in his report a description of the *kind* of intelligence the person shows as well as an IQ or over-all figure of some sort reflecting the *amount* or *level*.

CAN WE STIMULATE THE COURSE OF MENTAL GROWTH?

Few questions in the entire field of psychology have been debated so hotly as this one, and few have stimulated so many investigations in the attempt to secure an incontrovertible answer. Yet in spite of all this, no answer that satisfies everybody has so far been obtained. But the situation may perhaps be clarified if the nature of the question and the limitations of the possible answers to it are clearly understood.

One of the basic principles of logic may be stated as follows: *It is impossible to prove a universal negative.* One can *disprove* such a statement, for the clear demonstration of a single positive instance is enough to show that the negative claim is not truly universal. An English statistician, R. A. Fisher, has called attention to the importance of this principle in designing problems for experimental study. The *null hypothesis,* as Fisher called it, states that because of the impossibility of proving that a given principle is universally untrue, we shall avoid confusion in our thinking if we begin by positing such a general statement and then setting up our experiment to see whether any consistent exceptions to the rule can be found. That is to say, we test the invulnerability of our target by seeing whether we can demolish it. If we do not succeed, we have by no means proved that it cannot be done, but only that our own attempts have failed to do so. A clear understanding of this principle and its application to scientific investigation would do away with a good many controversies at the start, and would likewise show the underlying fallacies in some of the broad generalizations that have been too hastily drawn from insufficient data.

What of the application of the null hypothesis to the modifiability of mental growth? Evidently the question posited at the beginning of this section can never be answered in the negative, for no one can say what changes might conceivably result from methods that have not yet been tried. Moreover, it is not a very useful way of putting the question. What we want to know is not simply *whether* or not the course of mental growth can be experimentally accelerated. We want to know *how* to do it.

From time to time, rather startling claims are made about the discovery of some special method for improving the intelligence of children. These methods range all the way from some new kind of glandular treatment to a particular kind of educational regime. Much as we all wish that a method for accomplishing so important a result might truly be discovered, we should be wary of accepting these claims at their face value unless they can meet this simple test: Have the methods used been described so clearly that others can duplicate them and secure similar results? Thus far, no method that has been reported has been universally successful.

Under some circumstances, when extremely unfavorable influences of some sort have prevented normal mental growth for some time, the removal of these limitations produces marked changes in children. We have spoken earlier of the good effects of providing thyroid medication at the proper time for children whose own thyroid glands are deficient. Some educational "prescriptions" work in similar ways. A nursery school in a drab, unstimulating orphanage produced significant increases in the children's IQ's. [7] But to recognize that a nursery school can stimulate the mental growth of underprivileged children does not justify a conclusion that the rate of development can be stepped up for children who are already surrounded by the best environment a good home in a good neighborhood can provide. There has been much confusion centering on this issue.

From our earlier discussion of the factors that must be considered in interpreting mental test results, it should be obvious that a change in test score does not of necessity mean that intelligence itself has been altered. It is always possible to change the sign without modifying the thing signified. A child's IQ is not identical with his intelligence. His IQ is merely a rough index by which we are enabled to make a more adequate appraisal of his present ability than would be otherwise possible and from which we can, within limits, draw some conclusions with respect to his potentialities for future growth. But testing is a tricky business, and the statistical treatment of test results is even more tricky. It is easy to be deceived by one's own figures.

PRACTICAL APPLICATIONS OF INTELLIGENCE TESTING IN EARLY CHILDHOOD

People sometimes say, "But after all, why do we need to worry about the intelligence of children before they are old enough to go to school? Provided they are not feeble-minded, what real difference does it make whether they are bright or stupid? And, in any case, why do we need to know any more about their ability than we can find out by watching them?"

Long before they enter school, children form habits and attitudes that affect their later progress in many ways. Important among these are attitudes toward success and failure. The child from whom more is expected than he is able to give is likely to develop a feeling of inadequacy and insecurity that he carries with him into the schoolroom, making it unlikely that he will accomplish as much there as he could if he were unhampered by expectation of failure. On the other hand, the exceptionally bright child whose ability has gone unrecognized may become an active problem to parents and teachers because his alert mind is not given enough useful employment, and he is thus forced to seek it for himself. In the search he gets continually into mischief.

[7] Cf. B. L. Wellman and E. L. Pegram. Binet IQ changes of orphanage preschool children. *J. genet. Psychol.*, 1944, 65, 239-263; Q. McNemar. Note on Wellman's reanalysis of IQ changes of orphanage preschool children. *J. genet. Psychol.*, 1945, 67, 215-219.

It is true that wrong diagnoses of ultimate capacity are sometimes made by the use of intelligence tests, particularly with very young children. But unaided human judgment is even more prone to error. Since we cannot put children into cold storage and leave them there until we have worked out infallible methods of dealing with them but must instead make decisions of both major and minor importance for their future welfare as the occasions arise, we shall do well to make use of all the evidence we can secure that will help us in making such decisions as wisely as possible. In spite of their imperfections, intelligence tests for children who are old enough to talk are nevertheless sufficiently accurate to aid materially in forecasting what a child's future development is likely to be.

SUMMARY

It is difficult to define intelligence precisely. It involves thinking in abstract terms and thus facilitating adaptation to complex situations. Observation of the actions and verbal behavior of children is a practical but not very accurate way of evaluating their intelligence. The scale of graded questions and problems devised by Binet was the first of a long line of such standardized situations designed to supplement such informal observations. These tests are scored in terms of mental age, which shows the growth stage the child has reached, and IQ, which indicates how rapid his growth has been in comparison with that of other children.

When a large group of persons is tested, the scores usually fall into a normal distribution. This is a mathematical curve, bell-shaped in appearance, indicating that the largest proportions of the cases score near the average, with smaller and smaller proportions scoring at greater distances in either direction from the average. The known mathematical characteristics of this distribution make it possible for us to render scores on different tests comparable to one another.

Mental testing, especially of young children, is not an exact, objective science. Many factors must be taken into consideration in interpreting test scores. An IQ cannot simply be accepted at face value.

While there is a strong tendency for bright children to remain bright and dull children to remain dull, individual growth curves differ, and considerable shifts in IQ level do occur in some cases. For this reason schools should provide for retest at intervals.

The two leading individual intelligence tests for children are the Stanford-Binet and the WISC. Items included in the two scales are similar, but they differ in arrangement and provisions for scoring. There are several special preschool tests that have also been widely used.

Intelligence is related to socio-economic level but not to sex. Body size and general health are positively but only slightly correlated with intelligence.

Studies of mental organization have shown that both concepts of general ability and concepts of primary abilities are meaningful. A person can be evaluated for both level and pattern of intellectual functioning.

The search for general ways of increasing the rate of mental growth in children has been unsuccessful. Under special circumstances of deprivation, providing the needed medication or stimulation has produced beneficial effects. But under normal favorable circumstances, an individual's mental development proceeds at its own natural pace, and is not much affected by experimental attempts to speed it up.

A SHORT BOOK ON INTELLIGENCE

BISCHOFF, L. J. *Intelligence: statistical concepts of its nature.* Garden City: Doubleday, 1954.

In the brief space of thirty-three pages, the author gives an account of various theories of the nature of intelligence and explains in some detail what the primary mental abilities discovered by Thurstone are like. The reader is invited to take some short sample tests himself in order to become acquainted with the kinds of questions and problems of which they are made up.

CHAPTER 16

What challenges or tasks distinguish the period of middle childhood from the earlier and later stages of development? How are these related to biological growth characteristics and to social influences?

What are the main differences between the motor accomplishments of school children and those of preschool children?

What new method of measuring intelligence not suitable for little children is widely used in the elementary school?

Do boys or girls usually have a wider range of general information? What are some of the possible reasons for this difference?

In what ways do children's drawings throw light on their intellectual processes? How do drawings made by feeble-minded children commonly differ from those made by younger normal children?

What qualitative changes in ways of perceiving and thinking occur during this period?

》》》》》》》》》》》

Middle Childhood: Abilities and Skills

DIFFERENTIATING CHARACTERISTICS OF THE PERIOD

As WE HAVE EXPLAINED before, the marking off of one developmental period from another must necessarily be somewhat arbitrary. It can be done on the basis of changes in physical growth rates or differences in the provisions society makes for the treatment of different age groups. We have chosen to place the emphasis on the special tasks and challenges characterizing each period. What do we expect the person to accomplish during the years from five or six to eleven or twelve?

When we define the period in this way, we can classify the many kinds of changes that go on under three main headings. For one thing, the person is expected to acquire during this period most of the information and skills that his particular society considers it necessary for all its members to have. For most individuals, much formal education will occur at later periods and learning, of course, will continue throughout life, but what will be learned from early adolescence on varies much more from one person to another than it does in these middle years. The elementary school curriculum is much more uniform than that of higher schools. The kinds of behavior and attitude demanded of a child by his particular subculture, as represented in his home and his neighborhood, can be thought of as another such standard "curriculum."

For another thing, it is expected that during this period he will move out of the home, figuratively speaking, and learn to relate himself to

a much wider variety of people than his family represents. Such re-
latedness is more than a simple increase in sociability. He must develop
ways of "getting along" with the larger group and being accepted by
them, making such modifications in his own habits and emotional reactions as are necessary; and he must also get some comprehension of
the complex *structure* of this society, so that he can see what special
roles he is expected to play and choose those that suit him. The peer
group supplants the family as the central social reality. In one way
or another each child must come to terms with this change.

The middle childhood years also give each person an opportunity to
develop many kinds of *competence,* for his own sake rather than
society's. For the child himself they are long years, and the time
stretches out indefinitely before him. He puts a kind of undivided
effort into the practice of skills of different sorts that it is difficult if not
impossible for him to mobilize at later periods. Athletics, music, dancing, sewing, painting—one or more of many special kinds of skill may
be built into the permanent structure of the person's life during this
period. A person who knows how to handle himself well in many kinds
of situations and who has experienced the delight of participation in
what human beings have found rewarding is less vulnerable to strain
and misfortune than he would otherwise be. He has ways of coping
with the unpredictable stresses life brings. His realization that this
is so constitutes a basic kind of self-confidence that is, in itself, a source
of strength.

Both physical growth trends and our society's arrangements for children in this age group facilitate development along these lines. In a
previous chapter we have noted that there are two periods of especially
rapid physical growth—from birth to five years and from just before
puberty until the pubertal changes have been completed. In the period
between the two, the one we are now considering, physical size increases at a much slower rate and other bodily changes are less marked.
It is difficult to give exact ages for the beginning and ending of the
period, since individual growth curves differ from one another, and girls
tend to go through it somewhat earlier than boys do. The fact that
physical development is slowed down gives opportunity for perfecting
skills and for gaining control over motor, mental, and emotional processes that up to now have been growing and changing so rapidly that it
has been hard to keep pace with them.

Modern educational practice sets off this period in its elementary
schools. The child enters kindergarten at five, or, in communities where
no kindergarten exists, first grade at six. He remains in this school, with
its emphasis on common knowledge and its opportunity for participa-

tion in a fairly small group, for six or eight years. Junior and senior high schools, with their greater emphasis on individual initiative and personal responsibility and their more highly differentiated curricula and activity programs, are different in many ways from the schools of the middle period. Like the period of maturity that is to come later on, the period of middle childhood is more clearly marked by the stabilization and perfection of characteristics and skills already present than by the emergence of new traits.

THE KINDERGARTEN CHILD

The year that the child spends in kindergarten is in many respects a transitional period for him. Physically he is changing from an organism that is growing and changing very rapidly to one whose rate of growth is much slower. Mentally he is changing from the unforeseeing little child whose conduct is determined almost wholly by the needs and interests of the moment to the older child who works for more remote goals. Socially his interests are reaching out to include more persons. Formerly his preference for certain persons was determined chiefly by the extent to which they ministered to his bodily needs. Even in his play, his interests centered largely about himself. Although, as we saw in an earlier chapter, children of three and four show the beginnings of truly socialized play, nevertheless their ideas of what play is are still, for the most part, very egocentric. The four-year-old still says, "I want some one to play *with me.*" But a year or so later comes the dawn of a new social concept. Now we more often hear "I want to go and play *with the other children.*" The child no longer sees himself purely as an individual but is beginning to identify himself with the group.

The kindergarten period is then primarily a time when the child's newly acquired abilities and skills lose something of their purely individualistic goals and begin to take on a more socialized character. Running and jumping are still fun in themselves, but they are more lively fun if done in company and as part of a game. Conversation more often takes on the character of a discussion, of an exchange of ideas and information. Emotional behavior is modified in various ways in order to conform to the ideas and customs of the group. In all his actions and attitudes the child of kindergarten age gives evidence of the dawning of a group consciousness, of a reaching out after companionship not simply for amusement but as a means of extending the range of his own personality. Vaguely but surely he is coming to see that "we" is an expression that carries more weight in the world of affairs than "I" can ever hope for.

MOTOR ACTIVITIES DURING MIDDLE CHILDHOOD

The delight in motor activity so characteristic of early childhood shows little sign of abating during the early part of this period. As age advances, however, differences between children become increasingly apparent. These differences are shown in many ways. Some children retain the clumsiness of very early childhood. They balance badly, and when they attempt to emulate the achievements of others in such matters as climbing, jumping, or doing "stunts," they are particularly prone to accident. As a result they may lose interest in motor skills and turn to more sedentary or less hazardous enterprises. Children also differ greatly in dexterity of hand. Even at an early age, some little girls learn to perform remarkable feats of needlework, and boys at the same age gain considerable skill with their jackknives. But these cases are exceptional. [1] Upon the whole, manual dexterity of a kind that demands close co-ordination of hand and eye remains at a rather immature level until middle childhood is drawing to a close.

This is pre-eminently a period of large-muscle activities. Skating, swimming, diving, climbing trees, walking fences, rowing, jumping rope, spinning tops, flying kites, and a host of other active games and sports occupy every free hour. Although many of these new skills are learned and enjoyed for their own sake, as a rule the skill itself is secondary to some game of which it is a part. Baseball, marbles, jackstone, and hopscotch are examples of the many games of motor skill that first become highly popular at these ages.

INTELLECTUAL DEVELOPMENT

Unlike the curve of growth in general bodily size, Figure 35 (Chapter 7) shows that the growth curve of the brain does not change in form with relation to puberty. As far as we are able to determine, the same thing is true of mental growth. [2] Although the extremely rapid

[1] That is, exceptional under modern methods of child rearing. That they can be acquired is shown by the remarkable examples of needlework found in some of the "samplers" that every little girl was once required to make as a part of her early education. But that this skill was not acquired with ease is attested by practically all of the very old women whom I have questioned about the matter. Although most of them report that they accepted their daily "stints" of sewing and knitting as a matter of course because all their companions had similar tasks, they did not find them pleasant, and they report many tearful hours spent in taking out irregular seams or "picking up" dropped stitches.

[2] The lack of relationship between the pubertal changes and intellectual development is clearly demonstrated in cases of precocious puberty. A fairly large number of children in whom physiological maturity of the sex organs was attained in early childhood have been studied. These children show marked acceleration in respect to growth in height and weight, but their intellectual development does not appear to be affected.

mental development that was characteristic of infancy and early childhood is already a thing of the past, intellectual growth continues at a rate that is still rapid enough for the annual gains to be easily perceptible throughout middle childhood.

As before, language provides one of the surest indications of the growing intelligence of the individual child as well as of intellectual differences between children. The relationship between the size of a child's vocabulary and his mental age is so high that with children from English-speaking homes who are not suffering from any marked defect of speech or of the senses, a good vocabulary test alone can serve as a rough measure of intelligence. As command of language is gained, the content of the child's speech provides many further cues by which we are able to judge the level of his conceptual thinking, and his range of comprehension and information, as well as the character of his interests and many of his personality traits. From now on, more and more of our understanding of and knowledge about children will be based upon information obtained from their speech.

Before the age of five, the average child is rarely able to *define* words. He cannot distinguish the attributes of an object from the object itself, or at least he cannot do so spontaneously. He can only say, "A chair is a chair," or, if pressed, he may point to one and say, "That's a chair." But children of five or six, after a few preliminary trials in order to give them the idea, can respond to a number of the simpler abstract relationships between words. Given an action they can name the agent. That is, if asked, "What runs?" "What burns?" "What flies?" they will give appropriate answers. They can also name easy word opposites such as "yes-no"; "little-big"; "hot-cold." Giving definitions, giving word opposites, naming the agent of an action, and similar tasks all throw much light on the development of abstract thinking and so are often used as parts of intelligence tests.

The amount and kind of information possessed by children at the time of entering school is far less extensive and exact than most people suppose. Children chatter away so glibly on many topics that it is only when their actual knowledge is probed by means of careful questioning that the gaps in their information are revealed. One of the first persons to make an inquiry of this kind was G. Stanley Hall.[3] In an article published in 1891 he presented the results of a study in which five-year-old children were asked a number of specific questions such as the origin of various articles of food and clothing, the use of certain household articles, and simple facts of local geography. His results showed that children on entering school are likely to be woefully ignorant of many things that their teachers frequently take it

[3] G. S. Hall. The contents of children's minds on entering school. *Ped. Sem.*, 1891, 1, 139-173.

for granted that they know. More recently, Probst,[4] working on the same problem with Minneapolis kindergarten children, found much the same thing to be true. In order to make sure that the hundred kindergarten children whom she studied constituted a fair sample of the Minneapolis population, she consulted the census figures to find what percentage of the adult males in the city belonged to each occupational class. Then the occupations of the children's fathers were ascertained, and enough children from each group were selected to match these percentages exactly. In each group the number of boys and girls was also kept equal. All the children were between five and a half and six years old.

TABLE IV

SAMPLE ITEMS FROM THE PROBST TEST OF GENERAL INFORMATION AND PERCENTAGE OF CORRECT RESPONSES MADE BY CHILDREN OF DIFFERENT SOCIO-ECONOMIC STATUS AND BY THE TWO SEXES

	Per Cent Correct				
Question	U	L	B	G	Total
How many eggs in a dozen?	18	6	16	8	12
Who was the first president?	68	42	56	54	55
Of what is snow made?	80	70	78	72	75
What did Cinderella lose at the ball?	50	26	40	36	38
On what part of the violin do you play?	52	40	54	38	46
From what are little chickens hatched?	74	52	66	60	63
How many horns has a cow?	84	90	86	88	87
What is paper made from?	32	18	28	22	25
What makes a sailboat go?	60	30	58	32	45
For what is baking-powder used?	92	76	86	82	84

Table IV shows samples of the questions asked by Probst and the percentages of children who were able to answer them correctly. In this table the column headed *U* shows the percentage of correct replies given by children whose fathers belonged to the three upper groups of the occupational classification; *L* shows the corresponding percentage for the three lower groups; *B* gives the figures for the boys and *G* for the girls of all groups. The total percentage of correct answers is shown in the last column.

The superiority of the more favored social classes in general information is shown very clearly, not only in these samples but in almost all of the 132 items making up the list. (See Figure 69.) Also there is a tendency, not quite so marked but still very consistent, for

[4] C. A. Probst. A general information test for kindergarten children. *Child Develpm.*, 1931, 2, 81-101.

the boys to do better than the girls. The social difference is easily understood, but the sex difference is harder to explain. It is not a matter of "general intelligence" of the kind measured by the ordinary "intelligence tests," for such a test was tried and it was found that the girls actually did a little better than the boys.

It is interesting to know that wherever tests of general knowledge or information have been tried, all the way from kindergarten to

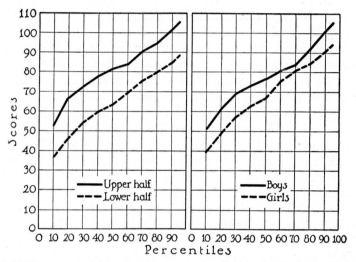

FIGURE 69. Relationship of the scores earned by 100 Minneapolis kindergarten children on the Probst Test of General Information to the occupational level of their fathers and to sex. The curve should be read as follows: Ten per cent of the children whose fathers belonged to the lower half of the occupational classification made scores below 37; 20 per cent made scores below 46; 30 per cent below 54, etc. At every level of ability the children from the upper socio-economic levels do better than those from the lower half and the boys do better than the girls. (Drawn from data presented in Catheryn A. Probst. A general information test for kindergarten children. *Child Develpm.*, 1931, 2, 81-101)

college, it has been almost the universal finding that boys and men rank superior to girls and women. We can only speculate as to the reasons for this difference. Perhaps boys have more curiosity than girls. Perhaps, even at the age of five, they are allowed to run about and investigate things for themselves more freely than girls are permitted to do. Perhaps parents, without being clearly aware of their attitude, nevertheless feel that Johnny should be taught facts, since he will some day grow into a man whose success or failure in life will be affected by the amount of knowledge he acquires, but that a knowledge of facts will be of little service to Mary in her future job of catching a husband. And it is of course possible that the explanation is to be found in heredity; that is, there may be sex-linked genes which, while not actually giving knowledge, may nevertheless predispose one sex more than the other to go in search of it. Which of these explanations is right or whether the true reason must be further sought for, no one can say at present. But the difference exists wherever the experiment has been tried. They are as well marked among children and adults who, by other criteria, are ranked as intellectually brilliant as among those who are backward or of average intelligence. They appeared in Hall's study made more than half a century ago, and there is no clear evidence that the picture is changing with the passage of time. Moreover, it appears from Terman's study of mental masculinity and femininity that persons whose mental characteristics resemble those of the opposite sex show, on the average, a corresponding variation in both the amount and kind of general information they have at their command. "Masculine" women on the whole are better informed than their more "feminine" sisters; "feminine" men have a narrower range as well as a different kind of knowledge than those more like the generality of their sex.

Before leaving the subject of the amount of information possessed by children, it may be well to point out that many of the unexpected and "ridiculous" things that children [5] do and say arise from incomplete knowledge or understanding due to confusion of a part of the stimulus with the whole. For example in Probst's study such responses as the following were common:

Butter is made by butterflies.
Baking-powder is what ladies put on their faces.
At the Ford plant they make potatoes and corn.

The sources of confusion here are obvious, but in actual life they are not always so clear. Here is a story of an actual episode that illustrates how lack of understanding of the basic principles involved sometimes leads to behavior that to the adult may seem incomprehensible or even very "naughty" when, as a matter of fact, the child was doing his best to conform.

Two small boys, aged respectively five and six years, had been brought up in a rather secluded rural district with relatively few social contacts outside their immediate family. One summer an aunt visited the farm for a few days and on a hot afternoon offered to take the boys for a swim. The children were highly delighted at the prospect,

[5] Adults do the same things under similar circumstances. Social blunders, such as drinking from a finger-bowl are often responses to a familiar aspect of a complex situation.

but their mother, a woman with strict Puritanical ideas, demurred on the ground that the boys had no bathing suits. The aunt pointed out that it would make no particular difference, since the lake to which they planned to go was not visible from any house or highway. Nevertheless the mother still hesitated. Finally she turned to the boys and said, "I'm sorry but I don't think it would do. I think you boys are getting too big to dress and undress before Aunt G." At this point the aunt once more intervened, this time with a compromise proposal. Some old overalls or a couple of worn suits of underwear would do exactly as well as formal bathing suits. To this the mother agreed, and in a few minutes the expedition set off, each lad carrying a small bundle. [6] On arriving at the lake shore the boys made a great ceremony about their preparations. Bush after bush was examined until at last one sufficiently dense to meet their requirements as a dressing-room was selected. Repeatedly the aunt was warned not to look or approach the bush. Her surprise and bewilderment were accordingly great when, after a few minutes, both boys dashed from their shelter and made for the lake in a state of complete and unembarrassed nudity. However, she was wise enough to ask no questions. After the swim the boys once more retreated to their bush, repeating their injunctions that the aunt must keep at a distance. The mystery was explained on the way home when the older of the two, with obvious pride in his handling of the situation remarked, "There, that was all right wasn't it? You didn't see us dress or undress at all, did you?"

The person who lacks all information on a subject usually betrays his ignorance at the outset and so is less likely to be misjudged. The one with just a little information, particularly if he does not know his own limitations, is likely to act on that information with as much apparent assurance, as much evidence of intent, as the one who is fully informed. Because the period of middle childhood is a time when really adequate information about the social and ethical concomitants of many of the affairs of everyday life is likely to be lacking, while partial associations, incomplete meanings, have been built up in large numbers, misunderstanding of child behavior is very common, especially among parents and teachers. Had the mother of the two boys learned of their solution of the problem of the bathing suits, she would almost certainly have felt that they had been highly disobedient. Their failure to adhere to the spirit as well as to the letter of her instructions would, to her, have been the important thing, and it is not unlikely that she would have imputed some degree of sexual wrongdoing to their behavior. Instead she should have regarded it merely as a not unintelligent attempt to conform to their

[6] Later found to contain a supply of apples and doughnuts!

limited understanding of the peculiar social demands necessitated by their "getting big" in a way that to them seemed just as good or even better than that laid down by the mother.

THE INTELLECTUAL FACTOR IN
CHILDREN'S DRAWINGS

Primitive man used picture-writing as a means of expressing his thoughts. Modern children draw for much the same reason. They do not, to be sure, make much use of drawing in order to communicate with each other as certain primitive tribes are said to have done, but this is easily understood, since long before a child is able to write for himself he knows what writing is and understands its purpose. To the young child, drawing is more nearly akin to talking to himself than to talking to others. It is a way of dramatizing his ideas through making them visible. In this sense it is a language.

Children draw what they know rather than what they see. The truth of this oft-quoted statement has been recognized for decades. The little child does not care whether or not his pictures are beautiful, but he wants them to tell what he has in mind. Details do not trouble him; he goes straight for what is to him the main fact. So if he wants to draw a man with trousers on, he draws the man first and adds the trousers afterward. The fact that the legs show through the trousers does not trouble him a bit. The man is there, so are his trousers, and who could ask for anything more complete? If he wants to draw a little girl picking flowers in a field he first draws the girl, then the flowers, then, in order to connect the two, he extends one of her arms down to the flowers at her feet in happy disregard of the laws of anatomy. Armholes may seem to be the most important parts of a coat when one is just learning to find his way into them without help, so it is not uncommon to find the armholes drawn with care on a figure that is otherwise completely nude except perhaps for a hat, which as every one should know is a far more important part of the drawing than is the hair, for hair stays on with no trouble whereas a hat must be looked after. At the age of five, approximately 35 per cent of children's drawings of the human figure include the hat, but only 13 per cent show the hair. At the age of eight the percentages have increased to 72 and 45, but baldness is still more common that hatlessness.

The changes in children's drawings that take place from age to age as well as many of the differences between the drawings of children of the same age have been shown to be far more closely related to general intelligence than to special artistic talent in children under the age of ten or eleven years. Older and brighter children less often omit essential parts of a drawing; they show a better sense of proportion; their ideas of the relationship of different parts of a drawing to each other are more definite. Children of four or five in attempting to draw the human figure make all sorts of amusing errors in assembling the different parts. Arms are frequently attached to the head or to the legs, even when the trunk is shown. Legs also are often attached to the head. This is the most logical place to put them if the trunk is omitted, but even when the trunk is added, backward children often continue to attach the legs to the head on either side of the trunk, which is then suspended between them. Sometimes the legs are attached to the arms or even to the brim of the hat.

FIGURE 70. Drawings of a man by bright, average, and dull kindergarten children. (From Florence L. Goodenough. *Measurement of intelligence by drawings.* Courtesy of World Book Co.)

Figure 70 shows drawings by bright, average, and dull kindergarten children. For comparison, Figure 71 shows drawings of bright, average, and dull children of eight years. Although the drawings by five-year-olds are on the average inferior to those of the eight-year-olds, this is not true in every case. In the present case, the bright five-year-old does distinctly better than the backward child of eight and almost as well as the average child of that age. [7]

The drawings of bright children are not always or necessarily more artistic than those of backward children, but they excel in such matters as the number of items shown, the correctness with which the parts have been assembled, the relative proportions of the different parts, and in the control of eye and hand movements as shown by the regularity of the lines and the smoothness of their joinings.

Examples of the queer errors often made in children's drawings of the human figure are shown in Figure 72. The fact that bizarre character-

[7] F. L. Goodenough. *The measurement of intelligence by drawing.* Yonkers, N. Y.: World Book Co., 1926.

istics of this kind are so much more frequent in the drawings of the mentally retarded than in those made by normal children leads us to examine their nature and origin more closely. When this is done we note that in the great majority of cases the peculiarities can be traced to a kind of mental nonadaptability, to residual features carried over from earlier drawing schemes without adjustment to the new patterns. For example, before the age of eight or nine years, most children draw the human figure in full face, after which the majority shift to a profile view as their preferred style. In three of the four drawings shown in Figure 72, some of the parts of the full-face draw-

FIGURE 71.   Drawings by bright, average, and dull eight-year-olds. (From Florence L. Goodenough. *Measurement of intelligence by drawings.* Courtesy of World Book Co.)

ing have been continued, along with those appropriate to the profile position. Although normal children as well as backward ones sometimes make errors of this kind, they are usually corrected after a few trials. Feeble-minded children often carry along such peculiarities for years with no apparent awareness of the discrepancies. This fact is of some importance in relation to Lewin's theory, described in Chapter 23, of the "mental rigidity" of the feeble-minded.

GROUP TESTS OF INTELLIGENCE

The methods employed for measuring the intelligence of elementary school children are much the same as those for younger children that were described in the last chapter. The chief difference consists in the supplementation of the individual tests by group tests that can be administered to an entire class of children at one time. Group tests

FIGURE 72. Some oddities in children's drawings. Errors of this kind are especially frequent in the drawings of backward and feebleminded children. (From Florence L. Goodenough. *Measurement of intelligence by drawings.* Courtesy World Book Co.)

have the further advantage that because the instructions for giving and scoring the tests are simple and highly formalized, the ordinary classroom teacher is able to handle them. They are less dependable than individual tests but serve well enough for purposes of general classification. They should always be verified by individual testing when important decisions are involved or when there is marked discrepancy between the results of the group test and other indications of a child's ability.

The following are illustrations of the kind of items used in many of the standardized group tests. [8]

WORD OPPOSITES

Instructions: If the two words given below mean the same or nearly the same, draw a circle around the letter S. If they are opposite or nearly opposite in meaning, draw a circle around the letter O.

Examples: Slow—fast S (O)
Large—big (S) O

Now try these. Work as fast as you can.

1. Little—small S 0   20. Tidy—neat S 0
2. Open—shut S 0   21. Damp—moist S 0

GENERAL INFORMATION

Instructions: Draw a line under the one word that makes each statement true, as in the following examples.
The number of cents in a dime is—5, 10, 15, 25.
The color of a ripe lemon is—blue, red, yellow, pink.
1. The number of eggs in a half dozen is—6, 10, 12, 20.
2. A bird with a reddish breast is the—sparrow, crow, wren, robin.

For children in the primary grades whose reading ability is limited, for deaf children, and for use in schools where many of the children come from homes where a foreign language is spoken, tests like those shown in Figure 73 which make little demand upon verbal ability are often preferred. Instructions can be given by pantomime.

Although the number of separate items in a group test may be considerably greater than is usually found in an individual test of the Binet type, the variation in kind of task is commonly much smaller. A typical group test for elementary school children may include from four to eight "subtests." Each subtest is made up of ten to forty items of the same general kind, such as word-opposites, vocabulary, information, analogies, arithmetic reasoning, and so on. This plan has the

[8] The first extensive use of group tests dates back to the World War of 1914-1918. After America entered the war, more than a million soldiers were given tests especially developed for that purpose by a group of psychologists under the chairmanship of R. M. Yerkes.

merit of making for quick and easy administration because a smaller proportion of the testing time is required for giving instructions, but there is greater danger that the tasks used may be nonrepresentative of the total pattern of abilities of a particular child. Either his talents or his defects may be disproportionately emphasized, with correspondingly distorted results. It is also obvious that an examiner giving an individual test knows more about the motivation of each child he tests than he can ever know in group testing situations. It is part of his job to make sure that the person being tested is really trying to do the best he can.

Because different group and individual tests are not made up of exactly the same sorts of questions and tasks, are not given under precisely similar conditions, and are not standardized on identical samples from the population, it can be expected that IQ's obtained by any one child may vary somewhat from test to test. There is no one IQ we can use as a definitive measure for an individual. In reporting a child's intelligence rating it should always be specified what test was used.

QUALITATIVE CHANGES IN THINKING

The marked mental growth that occurs during the middle childhood years is not simply a *quantitative* increase. It is not just that the person thinks better or more efficiently at twelve than he does at five. He thinks differently; there is a *qualitative* change.

Piaget, who has devoted special attention to this process whereby childish reasoning is transformed into adult logic, calls the period from four to seven (approximately) the stage of *intuitive thought,* and the period from seven to eleven the stage of *concrete operations.* What he means by these terms can best be explained by some examples. In one of the experiments he cites, [9] two small glasses and a number of beads are used. The child sees the beads being poured from the shorter, wider glass into the taller, thinner one. The whole situation makes it perfectly clear that no beads have been added or removed. But a child in the intuitive stage, when asked whether there are now more or fewer beads than there were before will usually answer that there are more (because the level is higher) or fewer (because the glass is narrower). The reason for this kind of error is that the young child's thought and attention is "centered" on his perceptions. He cannot quite take the perception apart, as it were, and consider the relations and facts about it separately.

[9] J. Piaget. *The psychology of intelligence.* London: Routledge and Kegan Paul, 1950.

In each line cross out the picture that does not belong there as in the two examples shown.

The large figure at the left in each line can be built up from the four small figures to the right of it. In the first two examples, lines have been drawn to show how this is done. Complete the others in the same way.

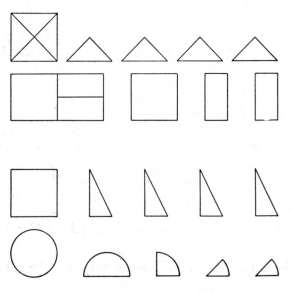

FIGURE 73.   Examples of nonverbal group tests.

As time passes, through repeated experiences in which he centers first on one part of a total perception and then on another, thus bringing the perceptual schemata he has built up all during infancy and early childhood into contact with one another (see Chapter 8), he becomes aware of discrepancies and ambiguities. His thinking can then be done by means of concepts that maintain their identity no matter what the perceptual situation in which they are embedded. Piaget calls these concepts "operations" because they are actually internalized *responses*. Thinking is an *active* process, although the activity may not show on the surface. By means of such operations the child can manipulate classifications, relationships, and numbers. But he is still limited to thinking about practical problems and concrete situations until he reaches the stage of *formal operations*. This does not usually come until the adolescent years. The distinction between concrete and formal operations can be understood if we think of the difference between arithmetic and algebra. Operations to be carried out with abstract symbols rather than definite specific numbers are usually too difficult for elementary school children.

The curious and amusing answers obtained in the Probst study quoted earlier in this chapter can be interpreted in terms of Piaget's descriptions of intuitive thought. In each case a kind of concrete perceptual centering has occurred. When the child says "Baking-powder is what ladies put on their faces," he is centering his attention on the "powder" part of the question and not considering the rest of it. Many other remarks, questions, and conversations overheard in young children become intelligible in these terms.

In his earlier books, Piaget described the intuitive thinking of young children as characterized by *egocentricity* and *syncretism*. These descriptive terms have stimulated a great deal of discussion and research. By *egocentricity* Piaget means that the young child rarely questions whether his ideas about objects are understood by others (unless, of course, their failure to understand interferes with the gratification of his wishes). The child's language and his thought are self-centered; he does not attempt to place himself in another's position, and he does not trouble about the latter's point of view.

When Piaget says that a child thinks *syncretically* he means that the child's ideas of objects and events are not based on an analysis of their qualities. As explained in previous pages, he thinks of concrete objects, persons, and events, rather than of the characteristics that they have in common or by which they are differentiated from one another. He thinks of individuals rather than of classes.

Observation of many groups of children in European countries and America has made it clear that the Piaget stages in the development of thinking cannot be thought of as fixed or universal characteristics of particular ages. Children vary widely in the rate at which they progress toward mature logical reasoning. The form of the question and the circumstances under which it is asked have some influence on the nature of the answers children are likely to give. Much egocentricity and syncretism persist into adult life, and certainly there are many adults who never make much use of what Piaget calls formal operations. But as labels for different kinds of thinking that can be arranged in a rough developmental hierarchy, these Piaget ideas are proving very useful. We shall understand children and adults (and ourselves) better if we recognize that there is more than one way in which thinking processes occur.

SUMMARY

During the middle childhood years the child learns most of the basic things his society expects him to know, expands his social world to include considerable numbers of children and adults outside his family, and develops competence and skill that enable him to cope with life's problems.

Much progress is made in the development of motor skills, especially those involving large muscle activity. Intellectual capacity increases steadily. General information, very inadequate during the preschool years, is rapidly expanded. Comparisons have shown that boys at all ages tend to be better informed than girls, and children from the upper socio-economic groups tend to be better informed than those from the lower groups.

Children's drawings of the human figure reflect the intellectual changes that are taking place. As development proceeds, they show more specific details, such as eyes, fingers, and hair, and the proportions and relationship of parts to one another are more correctly represented.

Group tests are widely used for measuring intelligence during this period. The kinds of questions asked are similar to those in individual tests, but there are fewer varieties, and the instructions for administering the test are simpler. IQ's based on different tests are not precisely equivalent to one another.

Piaget has shown that there are qualitative changes in children's thinking as they emerge from the intuitive thought most characteristic of four-to seven-year-olds into the stage of concrete operations. Much of what seems like peculiar logic in young children can be explained in terms of perceptual centering. It takes time and repeated experiences, before concepts become independent of the contexts in which they occur.

SUPPLEMENTARY READING

BIBER, B., MURPHY, L. B., WOODCOCK, L. P., and BLACK, I. S. Language and thinking in their social context. In *Child life in school*. New York: Dutton, 1942. Ch. 3.

This book gives a fascinating picture of ten seven-year-old children in a private school in New York. They are brighter than the average group of seven-year-olds would be. Their IQ's on the Stanford-Binet test ranged from 104 to 161. Each is an individual. The account in this chapter of what they talk about at the lunch table, and what they do in the various school situations really gives the reader a feeling for this period of life.

CHAPTER 17

About how many different "episodes" or separate units of activity would a child be involved in during a typical day? What does this suggest about personality development?

What is meant by "level of aspiration" and why is it important?

Are praise and reproof equally effective in securing maximal effort from children? Do all children react to incentives in the same way?

With what broad factors are children's interests associated? How lasting are they?

At what age do prejudices toward special groups of people first appear and what produces them?

What is the difference between a "personality trait" and a "personality type"?

Are such traits as cheating, lying, or stealing likely to be shown to about the same degree on all occasions? Is there any such thing as a consistently honest person?

How can a child be helped to improve his personality?

»»»»»»»»»»»»

Middle Childhood: Personality and Social Characteristics

THE CHILD IN HIS SOCIAL ENVIRONMENT

THE SECOND of the broadly-defined developmental tasks a child faces during the elementary school years is to bring himself into some kind of relationship with a world much wider than his home. While it is apparent to everyone that this development does take place, until recently there has been very little detailed knowledge of just what this total world of the child is like. Barker and a group of research associates decided to make a thorough study of what they call the "psychological ecology" of a small community they named "Midwest" for the purposes of the study. [1] The little town, with a total population of 707, had 119 children under twelve years of age. The task the investigators set for themselves was to analyze and describe this environment and the nature of children's interactions with it.

The method was to identify the different behavior settings, behavior objects, behavior-situation episodes, and the varieties of social interaction that occurred, so that they could all be accurately categorized by observers. Working in half-hour shifts these observers would accompany a single child through a whole day, noting down just what occurred.

Even in so small a town, the environment to which a child is respond-

[1] R. G. Barker and H. F. Wright. *Midwest and its children*. Evanston, Ill.: Row, Peterson, 1954.

327

ing turns out to be very complex. The catalogue of community behavior settings (such places as Pooles' Grocery, County School Music Office, Old Settlers' Reunion, Amateur Show, and Pearson Dairy Barn) lists 585 items, and a large proportion of these were entered by children over a period of time. On a single typical day, a Midwest school child would enter about 8 per cent of these places. Behavior objects (social ones such as mother, father, playmates, and the like; and nonsocial ones such as books, hats and coats, toys and tools) are even more numerous. Raymond, one of the children who was observed throughout a whole day, used 671 different objects in 2,282 separate behavior transactions! The number of behavior episodes (differentiable things a child does during the day such as Moving Crate across Pit, Teasing Charlotte, Trying to Get Kitten from Sister) ranged from 500 to 1,300 per day. The richness of the child's world and the innumerable opportunities it brings has been clearly demonstrated in this thorough study of one small Kansas town and the people who live there.

CHANGES IN MOTIVATION

In this complex social environment, taking in school and community as well as home, children become aware of the many ways human beings relate to one another. Tendencies to react in certain ways are picked up without any explicit teaching. Social incentives and rewards motivate behavior as strongly as material ones do.

Children of preschool age are not highly competitive. Not until around the age of five does the average child show much interest in comparing his own performance with that of other members of his group or strive to outdo his fellows for more than brief and spasmodic periods. Little children run in company with each other, but they do not run races; they contend with each other for the possession of a toy but rarely for the sake of mastery. The four-year-old who, aping his elders, shouts joyfully, "I beat him!" frequently shows by his behavior that he has no real comprehension of the meaning of the term. Even the child leader described in an earlier chapter does not, at first, appear to be aware of or to derive special pleasure from his ascendant position. He manipulates his social world in order to effect his designs. Usually he is quite ready to yield his position temporarily to some one else whose plans chance to appeal to him. For the child of preschool age, social dominance is not an end in itself but only a means toward an end.

But at about the time of school entrance the picture changes. Now the five-year-old begins to compare his possessions with those of his mates. At first the comparisons are direct and concrete. "My dress is the nicest in the whole room," said one of the kindergarten children studied by Wolf. [2] And this was satisfaction enough for her; she showed little desire to excel in other respects. Later on, children become able to differentiate between persons or objects and their attributes. They can tell what characteristics they value in others, what things they like and what they dislike. They can make comparisons that have more than immediate reference. They can set goals for themselves and recognize when and by how much they fall short of achieving them. They are beginning to develop scales of values that include more than two categories. They recognize the ameliorating factors of circumstances and motives. An unintentional offense is judged less harshly. "Did he *mean* to do it?" is heard with increasing frequency as we pass up the age-scale, and the answer to this question determines to an ever-increasing extent the appraisal of the action in question. Motives, goals, intentions—all the hidden forces that lie back of behavior—become real facts to the child long before he has reached the age of twelve.

Even before entering school, children respond to praise or reproof. But at the early ages the social incentive alone is less dependable. As a rule it must be reinforced at frequent intervals by reward or punishment of a more concrete nature. The reward may be nothing more than a caress; the punishment may be equally slight, but with the majority of very young children the purely verbal type of motivation soon loses its effectiveness.

During the school years, the influence of the group upon child behavior becomes far more apparent. From this time on one can note a clear distinction between the child's behavior toward his mates and his attitude toward adults. He senses more clearly the distinction between the generations. These are his kind. With them he must compete. By them he will be judged. So as he grows older the influence of adults becomes relatively weaker.

Figure 74 shows the relative effect of two kinds of social incentive upon the length of time five-year-old children would voluntarily continue to persist in a given activity. [3] In the first situation, the only incentive was the interest afforded by the activity itself. In the second a familiar adult was present who praised his performance at frequent intervals. In the third situation each child worked in competition with three of his classmates. In order to make sure that the differences obtained were not due to the particular kind of task set rather than to the incentive used, the experiment was repeated four times with each child, using a different kind of task or "game," as the children called it,

[2] T. H. Wolf. *The effect of praise and competition on the persisting behavior of kindergarten children.* Univ. of Minn. Inst. Child Welf. Monogr. Series, No. 15. Minneapolis: Univ. of Minnesota Press, 1938.

[3] *Ibid.*

on each occasion. The tasks included inserting small pins with colored beads into a peg-board, crossing out all the pictures of dolls on a series of mimeographed sheets, dropping marbles into a slot, and throwing colored rubber rings over posts attached to the backs of animals on a moving "merry-go-round." Every child performed every task three times, once under each of the three kinds of incentive previously described. In each case so much material was provided that even the most persistent worker never exhausted his supply. Although it is evident that competition was on the average by far the most effective of the incentives used, examination of the records of individual children showed that this was not true of all. Several children (generally speak-

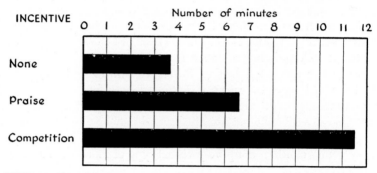

FIGURE 74. Median time in minutes for four tasks under each of three kinds of incentive. (After Wolf.)

ing, these were the younger and less mature members of the group) gave little indication of a competitive attitude in any of the activities that were tried. The following brief summaries of two of the case reports presented by Wolf will illustrate.

G. D. was one of these children who showed little or no competitive spirit. Of this child, a little girl four years and ten months of age, with an IQ of 100, Wolf says: [4]

G. D. is a very pretty child, very proud of her appearance and apparently overpetted and spoiled by her parents and other adults who have lived in her home from time to time. . . . Neither at home nor at school will she work hard at any difficult task. At home, at any rate, she can get praise and attention without doing this. The only evidence of a competitive attitude that G. D. showed during the entire experiment was when she once asked, "Who's got the prettiest dress on?" looking very pleased as she smoothed out her own dainty little dress. . . . It is significant to note that although in the experimental situation, praise was the most effective

[4] *Ibid.*, p. 81.

of the motivating conditions used, in no instance did it bring about a large gain over the "no-incentive" performance. . . . We may conclude either that G. D. did not understand competition or that she received so much praise at home that she was not constrained by a "need" to stay at a task that was not agreeable to her.

A different sort of individual reaction to the standard test situation was shown by B. E., a boy of five years, ten months, with an IQ of 117.

For this child praise, at least from the particular adult who conducted the experiment, [5] had relatively little effect upon his performance, but he displayed a highly competitive attitude when working with other children. Perhaps the most interesting feature of B. E.'s performance, however, is the marked contrast in his performance on the "merry-go-round" with that on the peg-board, which, in his case, was given about a month later. In spite of obvious fatigue he stuck to the "merry-go-round" for a full hour, outstaying his nearest competitor by two minutes. Toward the end of the hour, when all the others except one child had given up, in an apparent attempt to bolster up his own resolution B. E. remarked to the experimenter, "I am staying because it is fun. Other children might not stay so long." It is noteworthy that the satisfaction derived from this one complete victory apparently carried over to subsequent occasions. Although he usually stuck to the task longer when motivated by competition than under either of the other two conditions, never again did B. E. hold out until all the other children had given up. A month later, when competing with the peg-boards, he was the second child to leave, and as he did so he remarked to one of the other boys, "I don't care if you do get your name at the top. I got mine at the top before." Here we see the working of a principle not unlike that noted in the case of G. D. Just as the latter's drive to excel was so thoroughly satiated by the attention paid her at home and elsewhere [6] that she did not feel the need to demonstrate her superiority in ways that might involve special effort, so B. E.'s one heroic effort with its resultant success brought enough satisfaction to suffice him for at least a month. Like the rat who has just eaten to satisfaction, he no

---

[5] Wolf pointed out that praise from some other person, possibly his kindergarten teacher, of whom he was very fond, might have produced different results and presents some evidence in support of this suggestion. Again the extremely specific nature of social interaction appears. Praise from A is not the same thing as praise from B; competition gains or loses in strength according to the interpersonal relationships among the competing individuals.

[6] Visitors to the kindergarten were likely to pay special attention to G. D. because of her personal beauty and attractive clothing. Even though the regulations for visitors did not permit speaking to or about the children while in the room, it was obvious from G. D.'s behavior that she was well aware that she was receiving the lion's share of their glances and smiles.

longer felt the need to strive mightily against fatigue and boredom to reach a goal that from his point of view was already won. The verbal reminder, "I got mine at the top before" was quite sufficient.

Thus both general tendencies to respond in certain ways to standard social situations and the individual differences that make up each person's unique personality develop in the complex social matrix with which school and community surround children.

Another aspect of motivation growing out of social interaction is the person's *level of aspiration,* or the nature of the goals he sets for himself.

These goals vary both qualitatively and quantitatively according to the units of measurement by which the individual judges his own achievement. One person merely aspires to beat some particular competitor; he is satisfied with having accomplished this end no matter how many others may outdistance him. Another sets out to reach a certain point at a given time. He measures his progress in terms of what he does himself; his aspiration has no special reference to other persons. For another, the goal is marked neither by direct comparison with the accomplishments of other people nor by his own progress as such. It is a matter of reputation. For him the thing that chiefly matters is the opinion of other people, their praise or their blame, their admiration or scorn. Both children and adults differ greatly in respect to the units by which they gauge their own achievement and with the degree of accomplishment to which they aspire. Some "hitch their wagons to the stars"; others are satisfied with a very low level.

Consider the academic aspirations of the college students whom you know. Some measure their achievement by that of other students, either particular individuals or groups. They are satisfied if their grade is as high or higher than Bill Smith's or if it exceeds the class average. Others use a different system of measurement. They aspire to "pass the course" or, at a higher level, to get an "A," or perhaps a "B." Others—unfortunately too few—are activated chiefly by a desire for knowledge. They measure their achievement in terms of its contribution to their intellectual and cultural development or perhaps in terms of the particularized skills and knowledge required for their chosen profession.

Probably no one's aspirations are measured in the same terms or maintain the same level in all areas of activity. Peter works hard to keep at the head of his class in arithmetic but is little disturbed by the fact that his handwriting is poor. Mr. Brown has held the same position in the office for twenty years and is content in the knowledge that his work is satisfactory and his salary sufficient to maintain his family and himself. What he wants is to improve his golf score. His wife's great ambition is to be elected president of the local women's club. That her family frequently has to get along with make-shift dinners and unmade beds seems to her of as little consequence as the fact that she herself must spend long hours cultivating the friendship of influential women whom she dislikes. Mrs. Peters, who lives across the street, cannot understand this. It is her boast that her house is always in order to receive guests. Woe to the luckless child who forgets to wipe his feet before venturing upon her spotless floors or to her husband if he carelessly drops his newspaper where he happens to be sitting instead of folding it neatly and putting it in the rack!

Just as with all other attributes of behavior, the development of aspiration levels is a circular process. That is, each response is both an effect of those that have preceded it and a cause of those that follow. Laboratory experiments set up to study goal-setting behavior in children and adults usually follow a pattern in which the subject is given a trial at some kind of task or game (it may be anything from target shooting to working arithmetic problems) and then asked what score he expects to get in the next trial. If this procedure is repeated several times, the experimenter can observe not only the level of aspiration, defined as the difference between the person's performance and his expectations, but the shifts in this aspiration level as he encounters success and failure. Individuals differ from one another in their characteristic ways of adapting to failure. Some work harder and state more ambitious expectations than before. Some give up and cease to try altogether. Some lower their sights in a realistic sort of way. Some shift to an entirely different field of endeavor.

These differences are shown in an interesting way in the fifth situation Wolf

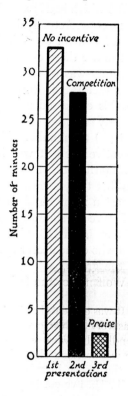

FIGURE 75. Performance of B.A. with Tinker Toy in three test situations. (Reproduced by permission of the author and the publisher from Theta Holmes Wolf. *The effect of praise and competition on the persisting behavior of kindergarten children.* Univ. of Minnesota Press.)

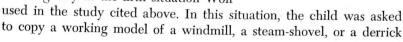

used in the study cited above. In this situation, the child was asked to copy a working model of a windmill, a steam-shovel, or a derrick from "Tinker Toys."[7] The models were purposely selected to appear easy. As a matter of fact, many of their elements could be constructed with tantalizingly little effort by all the children.

At the initial presentation the Tinker Toy models aroused by far the greatest interest of all the tasks used. Practically all of the children were at first very confident of their ability to reproduce the examiner's model which had been set up beforehand and left where they could use it as a copy. Actually, however, the models had been intentionally made too difficult for even the most skillful child to complete. It was found that under these circumstances the external incentive—praise or competition—was of relatively little significance in comparison with two other factors, (a) the strength of the child's apparent interest in the task and his expressed confidence in his ability to succeed with it which we may regard as the best available evidence of his "level of aspiration" and (b) the number of his previous failures. Regardless of the type of incentive used, it was found that the length of time a child would voluntarily persist in his attempts to build the model was greatest on the first trial, decreasing materially on the second, while on the third occasion many children gave up after relatively little effort.

Figure 75 shows the results obtained for B. A., a boy of six years with an IQ of 116, whose initial interest in the task was unusually great and who came nearer to attaining complete success than any other child in the group.

Wolf makes the following comment on this child's reactions:

It was evident that B. A.'s level of aspiration for the first two performances was very high. He was "set" to make a complete copy of the model. He handled his work with considerable ability and in the first model, when he was working alone, he completed everything except the proper placing of the pulley belts. Once he called to the experimenter in a high voice, "Miss H., I've got into quite a problem," but he kept at the task assiduously when told that he must work by himself. . . . In the next, the competitive situation, he worked fifteen minutes longer than his nearest competitor [8] but left the task before he had worked as long as before. On the third

[7] A type of building material consisting largely of wooden pins and spools with holes drilled in them from which models of various objects can be assembled. To make the models used in this experiment, a system of belts and pulleys was included so that the completed models could be "worked" by hand. A different model was used in each of the three situations.

[8] Apparently the chief motivating factor here was not competition but the child's own aspiration to complete the task. Had competition been the goal, it seems unlikely that he would have remained so much longer than was necessary, inasmuch as it was carefully explained at the beginning of each competitive situation that the child who worked for the longest time would be the one to get his name and photograph at the top of the list. Note here the comments of B. F., previously reported.

occasion he stayed just long enough to put six pieces together, although praise had been an effective incentive in the case of the other four tasks.

The case of B. A. raises an interesting question of widespread import in human behavior. What constitutes failure? Looked at from the standpoint of objective accomplishment, B. A.'s performance on both the first and the second trials were the best in the entire group. But the loss in both accomplishment and effort from the first to the third performance was also greater than for any other child in the group. Although the majority of the children showed a tendency similar to that of B. A., the average difference in "persisting time" from initial to final performance was much smaller, and there were a few cases in which no relation whatever to order of presentation appeared. G. D., the little girl previously described, is an example. The "persistence times" for G. D. are as follows: first presentation, no incentive, 1.2 minutes; second presentation, competition, 3.2 minutes; third presentation, praise, 5.5 minutes. It is clear that there is no cumulative effect of "failure" in this case. In no situation, Wolf states, did G. D. try hard and in no situation did she give any evidence of intending to finish the model.

Psychologically speaking, then, failure cannot be measured in terms of overt performance. G. D. did not really fail, although her actual accomplishment was negligible in quality and quantity. Her only effort was directed toward securing praise from the experimenter and even that aspiration was not sufficiently strong to induce her to go to much trouble to secure it. B. A. did fail, in spite of his superior performance. As a matter of fact, his psychological failure was the greater because he came so near to reaching his goal. Do we not all of us regret more keenly the prize that we barely fail to win? Success or failure can be defined only in relation to one's own aspiration. The emotional significance of either success or failure for the individual is likely to bear a direct relationship to the amount of effort voluntarily expended toward achieving it. A success too easily won is not likely to bring the same degree of satisfaction or to have as much effect upon later accomplishments as one achieved after long struggle. The "wounding" effect of failure is greatest when supreme effort has been put forth to no avail.

Inasmuch as social approval is a goal to which most of us aspire, though in varying degrees, and since disapproval is something that most of us seek to avoid, it is not surprising to find that both praise and reproof have generally been found to lead to increased effort on the part of children. In the greater number of the experiments on this topic, verbal incentives have been used but once. Children are first tested as to their performance of a task with no special incentive, after which one-half of the group is praised, the other half reproved for the quality of their work. On the following day the task is repeated. The second performance of the praised group is then compared with that of the reproved group and with that of other children who have merely been given a second test with no further incentive used. As a rule the results have indicated that either praise or reproof is followed by a somewhat better performance than that when there is neither, but the difference between the results under the two kinds of incentives is negligible and varies from child to child. Hurlock, [9] however, has called attention to an important factor which most of the studies have failed to reveal because they were not carried far enough. Although a *single* instance of praise or reproof does not clearly differentiate the relative value of the two incentives, since the average improvement has usually proved to be about equally great in both instances, *continued* administration of either produces very different results. In Hurlock's experiment, a group of elementary school children were given arithmetic tests for five successive days. On each of the last four days they were praised for their work on the preceding day. These children continued to gain in score throughout the course of the experiment. A second group who were reproved according to the same plan, gained about as much as the praised group on the first occasion after the reproof had been administered but lost steadily thereafter. A third group who were given the tests for five days with no comment at all gained little (but not much) on the first day of retest and thereafter lost.

This experiment may throw some further light upon the fact that the relative effect of negative and positive incentives appears to vary with the individual, for the life experience of any child extends back far beyond the classroom experiment. The child who has been continually reproved is more easily discouraged. He no longer sets as high a goal for himself because he despairs of being able to reach it. Strong effort no longer seems worthwhile.

One further point. Since this is a social world, the direction and intensity of the aspirations of one person have a strong effect upon those of his associates. People may be stimulated to greater accomplishment, either through the desire to surpass another's achievement (for competition is actually a state in which the level of aspiration is fixed by the accomplishment of other persons) or merely by the power of social suggestion and the influence of prestige. If the accomplishments of another are obviously beyond their own powers, some persons drop out before beginning the race. Sometimes people become so irritated

[9] E. B. Hurlock. An evaluation of certain incentives used in school work. *J. Educ. Psychol.*, 1925, 16, 145-159.

when another's ambitions infringe upon their own desires or personal comfort that their emotional response spreads over to the goal toward which their neighbor is striving. We not infrequently hear remarks like the following: "I vowed long ago that I'd never make my children take piano lessons because I used to get so annoyed by hearing the woman who lived across the hall perpetually nagging at her children about their practicing," or "When I was a child my mother fussed so about my always keeping my room in order that, now I have a house of my own, I get a lot of satisfaction out of just leaving things around. My rooms are always in a mess but I don't care." And in both these remarks, the effect of the social interaction between individuals is again apparent. For if the woman across the hall had been some one who was both liked and admired, the effect upon her neighbor would probably have been quite different. Instead of a negative reaction to piano practice the latter might have developed a strong aspiration to give her children as much musical training as did the woman she admired. In like manner, the orderly habits of the mother might have set a similar pattern for the aspirations of the daughter had their personal relations been different.

Many aspects of the problem of achievement motivation have been studied in a systematic way by McClelland and others. [10] The method these workers have used is to analyze the stories their subjects tell about pictures that have been specially selected to suggest some kind of striving (see Figure 76). The study that Winterbottom [11] made of children as part of this program of research indicates that the influence most likely to stimulate strong drives toward achievement in boys is the mother's encouragement of *independent* activities as early as possible. Mothers whose sons are high in achievement motivation think it important even for a child of seven to know his way around the city, to try new things for himself, to do well in competition, and to make his own friends. They place fewer restrictions on their children's activity. It is interesting to note that girls react differently. Independence training seems not to produce achievement motivation in girls.

Nothing is more important for the child's future than the level and type of the goals he sets for himself. And because these goals are not clearly realized until after the crystallizing effect of verbal formulation has taken place and the distinction between the self and the not-self has become sufficiently advanced to give form and pattern to the child's social attitudes, the period of middle childhood takes on special importance, for it is then that the child for the first time faces his future.

[10] D. C. McClelland, J. W. Atkinson, R. A. Clark, and E. L. Lowell. *The achievement motive.* New York: Appleton-Century-Crofts, 1953.
[11] *Ibid.*, pp. 297-304.

INTERESTS AND ATTITUDES

For a boy or girl of elementary school age the world can be a rich and wonderful place in which each day brings new discoveries. Spontaneous interest in all sorts of things is much in evidence. One has only to watch the enthusiasm with which games are played, the absorption in a book or television program, the effort that is put into the learning of a new skill, to sense this quality in children's experience.

Because there are so many possibilities, so many interesting things to be done, choices must be made. Some kinds of activities must be

FIGURE 76.   Picture used in testing achievement motivation. (From D. C. McClelland, J. W. Atkinson, R. A. Clark, and E. L. Lowell. *The achievement motive.* Courtesy of Appleton-Century-Crofts.)

given up or ruled out in order to make others possible. How does a child make this selection, in the years before he has any clear life plans to guide him?

There have been many surveys in which large numbers of children were asked what they liked to do, how they spent their leisure time, what books, radio programs, and movies they liked best. These studies show that there are two factors that operate very early as organizing principles for children's likes and dislikes. One is the factor of age. Preferences for some activities consistently decline as children grow older. The six-year-old rejects things that appear babyish to him; the ten-year-old plays games he sees as appropriate to his advanced status. Part of this age change is related to general mental development. Games with complicated rules, requiring highly developed motor skills, such as baseball, are beyond the competence of first-graders but become quite possible for fifth-graders. However, there are also group expectations, "unwritten laws," which help to shape the interest of a child into a pattern his peer group considers to be appropriate. It is because of the universality of this age typing of children's interests that a toy manufacturer can indicate on the label of a game, tool, or model the group for which it is designed, and that a salesperson in a book store can give Aunt Ellen good advice about what book to choose as a Christmas present for her seven-year-old nephew, Billy, whom she has never seen.

The other organizing principle that has shown up in all the studies of children's interests is the factor of sex. Even during the early preschool years, boys and girls begin to choose different kinds of activities and experiences. As development proceeds, the dividing line between the sexes becomes increasingly apparent. Boys are attracted to vigorous games and sports, guns and shooting, fast-moving vehicles, tales of adventure in far places. Girls tend to prefer less vigorous games, such as hopscotch and jumping rope, the enactment of ordinary scenes at home or school, and stories about people like themselves. There is at least scattered evidence that the sex differences are much more striking than the differences between one country and another. Tyler, [12] for example, found that American boys were much more like English boys in the order of preference they gave to activities than they were like girls in their own country. American girls resembled English girls more than they did boys in their own country. Similarly, Terman, [13] in his study of gifted children, found that in their interests, high ability girls were more like average girls and high ability boys more like average boys than the gifted boys and girls were like each other.

This sex differentiation of interests seems to rest on developing concepts about the role one is expected to play in life more than it does on physical differences. We have seen how such concepts originate in the preschool years through an identification with the parent of the same sex. During the school years, the peer group adds its influence. Children are somewhat more tolerant of a girl who is a tomboy than of a boy who is a sissy, but in both cases the child who is a member of a group is made aware of what the group expects.

Besides these broad interest patterns related to age and sex differences, other more limited and specialized individual patterns of interest emerge during middle childhood. Interests in specific activities and occupations, however, are not as likely to be lasting as parents and

[12] L. E. Tyler. A comparison of the interests of English and American school children. *J. genet. Psychol.*, 1956, 88, 175-181.

[13] L. M. Terman and M. Oden. *The gifted child grows up.* Stanford: Stanford Univ. Press, 1947.

teachers often think they are. A boy who collects butterflies and polly-wogs may become a biologist in later life, but he is about as likely to go into law or business or engineering. It is the general attitudes about one's own sex role, about school, and about work and other matters, upon which later interest development rests. Middle childhood is typi-cally a period for trying out many kinds of interesting activity rather than for lasting devotion to any one of them. There are, of course, ex-ceptions to this generalization. A girl begins taking lessons in ballet dancing and concentrates the major part of her energy for the rest of her life on this activity. A boy may start taking old cars apart when he is ten and never waver in his interest in mechanical activities from then on. But such cases are not typical.

While some psychologists have been scrutinizing the development of children's attitudes toward self, activities, and work, others have been particularly interested in their attitudes toward *groups* of people, attitudes that in adults we label prejudice. As the famous lines from *South Pacific* put it: You have to be taught to hate and fear. . . .[14]

Just how does such teaching occur? At what age and in what manner do children become anti-Negro, anti-Jewish, anti-foreigner?

In one of the most extensive studies of this problem, Trager and Radke-Yarrow, [15] with the co-operation of teachers in Philadelphia, worked out some ingenious tests to be given to children in kindergarten, first, and second grade. The tests consisted of pictures showing persons of different races interacting in different ways and a set of white and colored dolls, good and poor clothes and houses, that could be com-bined in different ways. The children were asked simple questions about these pictures and toys. One of the pictures, for example, showed a scene in which several white children were playing and a colored child was standing by himself in the foreground. The child being in-terviewed would first be asked simply to tell about the picture and then to answer more specific questions such as "Why don't they ask him to play?" "Is this little boy glad he is colored? Why?" "Will they ask him to play? Why?" In the test with the toys, the child being inter-viewed was asked to pick out some clothes and dress each of the dolls and then to put them in the houses. The examiner observed whether or not he gave the Negro doll the working clothes, the poorer house.

The results showed that even among these five- to eight-year-olds there was a considerable amount of discrimination on the basis of race. Furthermore, the rate of rejection increased sharply from age to age within this group among the white children. Thirty-four per cent

[14] From Act II, Scene IV of *South Pacific* by Richard Rogers, Oscar Hammer-stein, 2nd, and Joshua Logan.

[15] H. G. Trager and M. Radke-Yarrow. *They learn what they live.* New York: Harper, 1952.

of the white kindergartners excluded the boy in the picture from playing because he was a Negro. Forty-eight per cent of the first graders and 61 per cent of the second graders gave this kind of an answer. It is interesting to note that the majority of both Negro and white children assigned the poorer clothes and the poorer house to the Negro doll, although the proportion who did this was lower for the Negroes than for the whites. Furthermore, 54 per cent of the Negro children (as against 90 per cent of the whites) actually said they *preferred* the white doll. Anti-Catholic, anti-Protestant, and anti-Jewish attitudes were less apparent in this age group, but did show up in some cases.

This and other studies have shown that children acquire their prejudices not from experience with the minority group itself but by a sort of contagion from their families and friends. Like the interests we have been discussing, these attitudes seem to arise partly through identification with adults, partly through sensitivity to the expectations of the peer group. Thus the combatting of prejudice is no easy matter. Information alone does not touch its source. The Philadelphia investigators experimented with things teachers could do to create group situations that would generate accepting rather than rejecting attitudes. This appears to be a promising approach to a serious social problem.

One other aspect of the research on children's prejudices is worth noting. It is that the whole process of identification with adults that we have stressed because of its general significance for personality development is far more difficult and complicated for a child who is a member of a minority group. A Negro child in a predominantly white school must face the fact that the more he follows in the footsteps of his well-loved father the less will be his acceptance in the group to which he would like to belong. Minority group children must face at an early age *conflicts* of values and loyalties that are very unsettling even to mature personalities. Those who learn to cope in a constructive way with such conflicts acquire an asset that will help them meet all the later stresses of life. But unless they are given some help and understanding in facing this challenge, there is a real probability that the confusion and bitterness they experience during the early school years will leave serious scars.

PERSONALITY TYPES AND TRAITS

Pigeonholes are convenient. Classifications reduce multiplicity and thereby lessen confusion. Arrangement, to be useful, must start with a system of ordering the things to be arranged according to one or more of their attributes such as size, color, the purpose for which they are to be used, or the order in which they are to be selected.

All of us, whether we stop to think about it or not, are forced to do a certain amount of human classification. The very adjectives that we use in describing the people that we know show that this is the case. We say, "William is stubborn, Peter is friendly, Amos is reserved, John is good-natured." But some people have gone much further than this. They believe that certain kinds of personality traits are linked together into such definite patterns that by identifying the pattern or "type" to which a person belongs it then becomes possible to describe most of the significant features of his personality. It is a matter of considerable practical importance in bringing up children to know whether basic

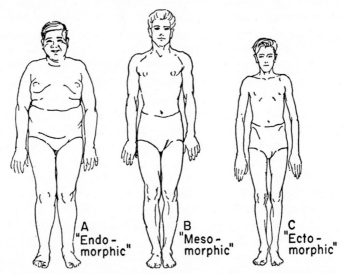

FIGURE 77. Examples of different body builds. (From N. Bayley and R. D. Tuddenham. Adolescent changes in body build. *Adolescence*, Forty-third Yearbook, National Society for the Study of Education, 1944. Courtesy of Univ. of Chicago Press.)

temperaments are different enough so that individuals require different kinds of treatment.

The idea itself is as old as science. It is found in the writings of Aristotle and in the philosophic discussions of the seventeenth century. In modern times, hardly a decade passes without the presentation of a new system for classifying human "types." Some of these systems have been based entirely upon the individual's behavior; others have included physique as well. The most influential present system linking temperament to physique is that of Sheldon. [16] There are three main types with many variations and intermediate types. (See Figure 77.)

[16] W. H. Sheldon. *The varieties of human physique.* New York: Harper, 1940.

The *endomorph* is wide for his height, soft and plump. The temperament that goes with the type is *viscerotonia*, which stands for placidity, sociability, and a liking for food and other material satisfactions. The *mesomorph* is muscular, well-built, and well-co-ordinated. The temperament characteristic of this type is *somatotonia*, a term covering energy, aggressiveness, and an interest in vigorous physical activity. The *ectomorph* is thin, fragile, and fine-grained, with more surface area than bulk. The temperament characteristic of this physical type is called *cerebrotonia* and covers sensitiveness, nervousness, and fondness for intellectual activities.

Of the more purely behavioristic classifications, that of the Swiss psychiatrist Jung, a pupil of Freud who later rejected much of Freud's teaching, is best known. Jung's attempt to divide mankind into two general groups, the *extroverts* and the *introverts*, has attracted enough popular as well as scientific attention to make the terms a part of the vocabulary of most educated persons. According to Jung's descriptions, the extrovert is seen in the man of affairs, rushing from one conference to another, prominent in local politics, a member of clubs and lodges, a committee man, a high-power salesman of ideas or of goods, better at getting things started than at seeing them through under difficulties. Then there is the introvert. The introvert is the man whose attention is more inwardly directed. He is interested in ideas, theories, philosophies. He is not gregarious, though he may have a few close friends whom he finds intellectually stimulating. He would rather see things work than make them sell. But he is likely to brood over matters that the extrovert would soon forget in the press of new interests. He is sensitive to rebuff and because of his self-consciousness may imagine slights where none were intended.

Because people, whether they be children or adults, unquestionably differ in characteristics of this kind and because the traits said to be characteristic of each type do "hang together" rather better than those of many typologies that have been proposed, a number of devices for classifying individuals according to this scheme have been worked out. There is one main conclusion we can draw from all the work with these tests. People do not fall into two or more fairly well-separated groups as the typologists would lead us to expect. Instead, the form of the "extroversion-introversion" curve appears to be much like that of the distribution of general intelligence shown in Chapter 15. Although some fairly pronounced examples corresponding to the "types" are found, the great majority of people are neither introverts nor extroverts but fall midway between the two. Some of their characteristics resemble those of one type, some the other. Moreover it appears that most people behave in an introverted manner at some times and under some conditions; at other times or under different conditions they behave like extroverts. Jung seems to have been right to this extent. He has described certain patterns of behavior that have sufficient cohesion to warrant our speaking of introversion-extroversion as a continuous *trait* that is displayed by all persons in varying degrees. A trait may be defined as a continuous personality variable with respect to which individuals can be measured with greater or less precision.

Present-day students of personality think more in terms of traits than of types. Sheldon's system provides for all *degrees* of ectomorphy, mesomorphy, and endomorphy and their accompanying temperaments. Research such as that of Eysenck [17] on the introversion-extroversion dimension uses the idea of type only as a more general term for the predominance of one kind of approach or the other. In individual cases we no longer expect the kind of consistency a type label suggests. No one expects an endomorph to be unfailingly good humored under all circumstances. No one expects an introverted child to be always thinking and dreaming. The classifications serve as guides showing us what to look for in individual cases, not as complete descriptions.

Turning to more specific traits rather than general types, we find that there are many kinds of characteristics to be assessed. An area in which parents and teachers have a special interest is the one that includes the *character* traits. For a long time it was rather generally supposed that such characteristics as honesty, co-operativeness, perseverance, and so on were rather stable qualities of the individual; that, for example, an honest person is honest in nearly all situations, that a resourceful person will show his resourcefulness under almost any circumstances, that a persistent person can be depended upon to stick to almost any kind of task, and that an optimist goes about whistling in all weathers. But careful investigation does not bear out this idea. It is true that both grown people and children show a good deal of consistency in their conduct from one time to another, if the situation remains about the same. Because we so often observe persons repeatedly under similar conditions we become impressed with this consistency and assume that they will behave in just the same way under all circumstances. The teacher who sees Jimmie and Johnnie only in the classroom and finds that Jimmie seizes every opportunity to copy his lessons from his neighbor while Johnnie's eyes never wander from his own paper no matter how many chances for cheating are given him concludes, not unnaturally, that Jimmie is a wretched little cheat and Johnnie is the soul of honesty. If questioned about their "personality traits," she will almost surely rate Johnnie high and Jimmie low on all aspects of

[17] H. J. Eysenck. *The scientific study of personality*. London: Routledge and Kegan Paul, 1952.

honesty and trustworthiness. But she fails to take account of the fact that Johnnie has little need to cheat, for he is at the head of his class anyway and doesn't have to worry about promotion. Moreover it would be silly for him to copy from his neighbor when the chances are that his own answer is the right one. The situation for Jimmie is very different. He is on the verge of failure, and his father has promised him a "good licking" if he doesn't bring home a better report card next time. The two boys differ in classroom conduct, to be sure, for Jimmie cheats and Johnnie doesn't. And there is a real difference in "personality" besides, for Jimmie feels the need to cheat and Johnnie doesn't. But are we safe in assuming that Johnnie is consistently honest and Jimmie dishonest?

Let us follow them out to the playground. Now Jimmie, who is shaky on the multiplication table, who mixes up all the dates in his history lesson, and who spells sugar with an *h*, is a "crackerjack" when it comes to marbles, but Johnnie is all thumbs. If an opportunity for cheating comes will it be Jimmie or Johnnie who yields to the temptation?

Some years ago Hartshorne and May [18] undertook to find out what the chances are that a child who is dishonest in one situation will also be dishonest in others, or in other words, how consistently the same kind of character or personality traits will show up in all kinds of surroundings and conditions. So they invented a large number of "tests" of deceit. In all there were thirty-two different kinds. The tests were given to more than 8,000 children from all ranks of society. Some of the tests were given to children as homework, some in their school classrooms, some at parties. Some of them were made to seem like school lessons; others took the form of games. But the tests were all alike in that an opportunity for cheating or dishonesty of some kind was always given, and, although care was taken to keep the children from finding it out, some special device was always provided for finding out which children cheated and how much they cheated.

For example, the children were given an arithmetic test similar to those they were used to having in school but too long and hard for any of them to finish within the time allowed. When the time was up, the papers were collected and taken away and a duplicate of each was prepared by a clerk. At a later time the papers were given back together with an answer sheet, and each child was told to score his own. Plenty of opportunity was allowed for changing the answers or adding to the amount done. Afterward by comparing the corrected papers with the copies of the originals the amount of cheating done by each child could be determined.

In other tests, athletic stunts such as measuring the strength of grip on a dynamometer or chinning a bar were used, and opportunity was

[18] H. Hartshorne and M. A. May. *Studies in deceit.* New York: Macmillan, 1928.

given for faking a record. Others consisted of games that could easily
be won by cheating, such as pinning the tail on a donkey or seeing who
could carry the most beans from one box to another in a given length
of time by taking only one bean at a time. Cheating in this case consisted of taking more than one bean. Tests that provided opportunity
for stealing small sums of money with which the children were provided
for use in working out problems in making change and which was
supposed to be returned at the end of the lesson were also tried out.
So also were tests of lying either to avoid disapproval or to secure approval.

When the same tests were tried twice on different occasions, but with
other conditions remaining the same, it was found that the children
behaved very similarly from one trial to another. Children who cheated
at lessons the first time were likely to do it the second time; those who
were honest the first time were honest the second time. There were
some exceptions, of course, but the general tendency toward consistency was fairly marked. Likewise those who cheated on athletic
contests or who lied to secure approval behaved about the same way on
repeated trials. But when the performances of the same children in different situations were compared, the results were very different. There
was little, if any, greater likelihood that the child who consistently
cheated in the classroom type of situation would fake an athletic record,
cheat in games, or steal money than that the one who was honest in
classroom work would do so. Children who cheated on their homework
did not necessarily cheat at school. Lying and stealing showed only a
small tendency to go together. All in all, the results of these experiments
seem to show that conduct is decidedly specific, depending in each
case upon the particular child and the particular situation.

The same specificity of behavior was found when other so-called
traits were studied in a variety of situations. Generosity was found to
vary with the things about which one is called upon to be generous.
Some people are generous with their time, others with their money.
Most of us find it quite easy to share the things we care little about.
Hartshorne, May, and Maller [19] found that the children whom they
studied were no more consistent in the kind of things they were willing
to do for others than in the kind of situations under which they would
be dishonest. This is not strange. Consider the following situation:

Each child was given a pencil box containing ten articles: a drinking
cup, a pencil sharpener, a ruler, an eraser, a pen, a penholder, a double
pencil, and three ordinary pencils. Then it was suggested that each one
might give away a part of his kit to help make up kits for poor children

[19] H. Hartshorne, M. A. May, and J. B. Maller. *Studies in service and self-
control.* New York: Macmillan, 1929.

who had none. They were scored according to the number and kind of articles they were willing to give away.

Suppose, however, that Peter's father had been out of work for two years and no one in the family had a cent to spend for anything beyond the barest necessities. For months Peter had longed for one of these pencil kits, but there seemed to be no chance of his getting one. Across the aisle from Peter sat Billy, who was an only child of parents in comfortable financial circumstances, and who had a number of devoted aunts and uncles besides. The day before the kits were given out, Billy had had a birthday and received no less than four kits of this kind, most of them of better quality than the one he had just been given. If Billy gave away all the articles in the new kit and Peter refused to part with any, can we be sure that Billy is the more generous of the two?

But the rule that behavior depends on the circumstance rather than on the child is not an absolute one. In practically all their experiments, Hartshorne and May found that although for the children who sometimes cheated there was little consistency in behavior from one situation to another, there were some who were consistently *honest,* who never cheated no matter what the temptation nor how obvious the opportunity. This is a highly significant fact, for it indicates that socially desirable traits, once they have been established, may become relatively stable. So we may justifiably say of an individual that he is honest or co-operative or generous or truthful with some feeling of assurance that his subsequent behavior will bear out our statements. But this is not true at the other end of the scale. It would appear as though the comment made by Hartshorne and May that "there are no such things as honest or dishonest children but only honest or dishonest acts; no such traits as co-operativeness, service, self-control, and so on, but only people who at times act co-operatively, at times perform services for others, and at times exhibit self-control," might perhaps be qualified. Concretely, of course, what they say is entirely correct; the same statement might be made with respect to all the other abstract nouns by which we describe the attributes of an individual. But it would appear that some people do set goals for themselves that make for a very high degree of stability of behavior in certain areas. In this sense we may speak of honesty, truthfulness, and so on as "character traits," because some people display them consistently. But dishonesty, untruthfulness, and similar forms of behavior are not "traits" because they are circumstantial rather than personalized forms of response. They are negative reactions, showing that the individual has *failed to develop* the positive side of his character. Resistance to temptation is a positive characteristic, depending on the establishment of definite attitudes toward the world and the self. Not-cheating is a more mature form of behavior than cheating because it is a response to a more highly organized incentive. It is a more stable, dependable form of reaction because it is a response to an attitude that has become relatively detached from the outside world and referred back to the self. I do not cheat because *I* do not cheat. The reasons for not cheating have become organized within the self; they no longer have much reference to the outside world. But for the person in whom such organization has not taken place the conditions are very different. For him, cheating or not cheating depends upon circumstances. He cheats when he feels the need to cheat if he thinks he can get away with it; he refrains from cheating when nothing is apparently to be gained by it or if he thinks the risk of being caught is too great. Cheating is unpredictable because it depends upon circumstances that cannot be predicted in advance. But honesty can be predicted because it depends upon the individual. In this sense we may say that honesty is a character trait but dishonesty is not, at least in a culture like ours where honesty is a goal toward which people consciously strive.

Closely related to this finding are the results of a study by Rundquist and Sletto. [20] They were concerned with certain technical problems involved in the construction of attitude scales. One of these questions is this: When a statement can be expressed either in a form that conforms with or runs contrary to that generally regarded as "socially acceptable" is there any technical advantage in using one type of phraseology in preference to the other?

Consider the following examples. (In each case the subject is asked to mark the statement *A* if he agrees with it, *D* if he disagrees with it.)

_____ It is all right to evade the law if you do not actually break it.
_____ It is wrong to evade the law even though you do not actually break it.
_____ Most people are honest.
_____ Most people are dishonest.

Inasmuch as one is free either to disagree or to agree with the ideas expressed, at first thought it would seem as though it makes no particular difference which one of the paired statements is used. On the basis of logic, one would expect that everybody who "agrees" with the statement that more people are honest would "disagree" when the same idea is expressed in the opposite form. But this has been found not to be the case. Just as not-cheating seems to be a more highly organized and therefore more dependable form of response than cheating, so disagreement with a statement that is disapproved by most

[20] E. A. Rundquist and R. F. Sletto. *Personality in the Depression: a study in the measurement of attitudes.* Minneapolis: Univ. of Minn. Press, 1936.

people has been shown to be a more revealing and more dependable type of response than agreement with it. Many people who will not take the trouble to deny the statement that "most people are dishonest" will also agree with the statement that "most people are honest." [21] Apparently agreement with either statement sometimes means no more than that the subject has no pronounced feelings about it one way or the other. But disagreement means that he has previously done some thinking about the matter and as a result has formed a really positive attitude on the subject. Disagreement, in such instances, indicates a more highly organized and therefore more revealing attitudinal state than agreement, which may arise from mere passivity. This is perhaps related to the importance of *dislike* responses on interest inventories as indicators of individual interest patterns.

WHAT THE SCHOOL CHILD'S PERSONALITY SIGNIFIES

Even if we could measure the personality of school children with absolute precision, it is unlikely that we could tell from such measurements into what kind of an adult each individual child is going to develop. To do that we should have to know not only what a child is like now but what influences are going to come into his life from now on. But there is no doubt that we could make a guess which would be much more likely to be right than wrong. Even with the imperfect methods of studying and describing personality that have been worked out so far, we can detect in the school children of today many of the traits that will characterize them when they grow up. The solitary child with few friends may grow to be a man with marked social interests, but the chances are against it. The child who rebels against all authority may, as he grows older, become a docile follower of the crowd, but he is more likely to develop into an aggressive, truculent type of person who goes around with a chip on his shoulder and takes offense at the least excuse. Habits and attitudes that are so greatly "overlearned" in childhood as these are likely to be, in time become as automatic as reciting the alphabet or swimming. The same laws of learning that apply to typewriting, memorizing nonsense syllables, learning to run a maze, or becoming "conditioned" to expect food when the dinner bell rings, hold good also for learning to run away from school or home, taking other people's possessions or refraining from doing so, lying to

---

[21] Of course both statements are not used in the same questionnaire, since too many people would notice that they carry the same idea and so would see to it that their answers agreed with each other. The finding mentioned here is based upon the use of different questionnaires administered to the same subjects on different occasions separated by so short a period of time that one would not expect many real changes in attitude.

get out of trouble or telling the truth, preferring to play alone or with other children, or preferring "boys' games" to "girls' games."

Of course these alternatives are not equally balanced in regard to ease of learning. The little child does not have to be taught to take what he wants if he can get it; it is refraining from taking what is not his own that has to be learned. Probably it is easier to teach children to lie as a way of getting out of trouble than it is to teach them to tell the truth and face the consequences. Probably, too, there are inherited differences among children of a kind that make it easier to teach some to inhibit their natural tendencies to grab whatever they want, or to train them to stick to a thing until it is accomplished, or to develop in them the kind of behavior that makes them popular with other children. The evidence for the inheritance of such behavior tendencies is not so clear as is the evidence in regard to the inheritance of either general ability or certain special talents such as musical ability. It seems fairly certain that at most what is inherited in these cases is not an absolute determining factor but only a tendency, a predisposition, that may make it more difficult to develop the right kind of social and emotional habits in some children than it is in others but does not render it impossible to do so. Some psychologists refuse to concede heredity even as minor a role as this in the determination of behavior, but put their whole faith in the side of learning. That learning plays a tremendous part there can be no doubt.

Parents and teachers are particularly likely to overlook the personality defects that are of chief concern to the child himself. They worry about the child who disobeys or fights or steals or gets into sex difficulties because such behavior is both conspicuous and disturbing to other people, especially to those in charge of him. But the child who has troubles of his own and keeps them to himself, worrying and brooding over them in secret; or the one who finds real life so hard and unpleasant that he slips away into a dream world, shunning companionship and withdrawing further and further into his unhappy self, is not likely to impress many people as being a problem because he does not bother anybody except himself. But in reality such children are quite as much in need of help as the one who makes himself actively troublesome. Often their need is greater, for if matters are not corrected and such a child continues to spend a large part of his time and emotional energy in brooding over his troubles when he should be doing something worthwhile, if he stays off by himself instead of learning how to get along with other people through the give and take of healthy play, if he forms the habit of retreating from difficulties instead of meeting them squarely, he will be poorly equipped for holding his own in the active competition of adult life. Behavior such as this is always a sign of mental ill-health. The child may get over it, to be sure, just as he may recover from physical illnesses that are allowed to run their course without proper attention. But it is foolish to trust to luck when a child's future success and happiness are at stake.

What can be done? The rule is easy to state, but to carry it out often means long and painstaking effort.

Find out the cause of the trouble.

Remove the source of difficulty if possible. If not, help the child to take an unemotional attitude toward it. This can best be done by so arranging his life that the troubling factor, whatever it may be, will interfere with it as little as possible.

Help him to form a new set of behavior patterns. Even if the actual difficulty is removed, his old habits which have been practiced so long will continue to assert themselves unless new ones are acquired. Keep the principles of learning in mind. Make sure that desirable behavior brings satisfaction. See that he has plenty of opportunity for practicing his new social skills, but don't overdo it. Avoid forcing him into too many new and untried situations at once.

Most important of all, find out the level and type of his aspirations. What goals has he set for himself? How valiantly is he striving to reach them? Are they realistic and practical or only daydreams to be carried out in some improbable future?

The same principles hold good with the delinquent child who is a more active source of difficulty. Here, too, there is a reason or perhaps a whole series of reasons back of the antisocial behavior. But even after the reason has been discovered and the original difficulty corrected, the problem of retraining remains. Habits practiced for years will not disappear by magic. Definite effort is necessary to get rid of them. And here, too, the child's aspirations for himself, the goals for which he strives and his confidence in his own ability to reach these goals, are of paramount importance. We have seen that much delinquent behavior arises from a low level of character organization. The child cheats or steals or commits other offenses because he has never built up a clear concept of an ideal self to which his behavior must conform. He is swayed by each passing impulse because he lacks the ballast that is provided by a major aspiration that can be openly fostered by his own efforts and strengthened by a sense of social approval.

Training should be positive. Just harping on what not to do will not take one very far, for character is positive, not negative. The thing that the child needs is to learn what to do and to derive satisfaction from doing it.

SUMMARY

Studies by Barker and associates have shown that even in a small rural community the environment of the school child is very complex. He learns how to act in hundreds of different situations and how to deal with all sorts of different people and things.

Important changes in motivation occur during middle childhood. The influence of the child's peer group supplements that of his family. He learns to compete with others and to work for social as well as material rewards. He develops his own goals toward which he strives. Marked individual differences in level of aspiration can be observed.

Individual patterns of interests develop as children rule out whole sets of activities they once liked but gradually come to see as inappropriate for their age and sex. Prejudices toward various minority groups also take shape under the influence of family and peer groups.

Efforts to classify people into a few main personality types have not proved very fruitful, but they have led to the measurement of important traits of personality and a study of the ways in which they are related. Character traits, such as honesty and co-operativeness, are often specific to the situation in which they are measured. A child who cheats in the schoolroom will not necessarily do so on the playground. There is some evidence, however, that socially desirable traits can become fairly stable. Some children develop general concepts of honesty and self-control that they apply in all situations.

Learning is very important in the development of personality and character. Adults can help children by understanding them and getting them into learning situations that are likely to produce favorable changes.

FOR FURTHER READING

BARKER, Roger G., and WRIGHT, Herbert F. *One boy's day.* New York: Harper, 1951.

This book records what the observers saw when they followed seven-year-old Raymond Birch around for a whole day from the time he got up to the time he went to bed. It is the clearest, most complete picture we have of what life is like for a normal child in a normal little town.

Trager, Helen G., and Radke-Yarrow, Marian. *They learn what they live.* New York: Harper, 1952.

This is the story of the study made in Philadelphia of the prejudices of young children and the possible ways of checking their spread. It is written in a simple and interesting way. The reader is told how the teachers felt about the research project, and the part they played in it, what the children and parents said, and how the experiment turned out.

CHAPTER 18

What kinds of changes in the way children learn occur as they grow toward maturity?

What are the most efficient ways of learning verbal material such as one is expected to master in school?

What are the most efficient ways of learning motor skills?

Does learning one thing make it easier to learn other things?

What have the experiments designed in the service of modern learning theories taught us about reward and punishment?

Middle Childhood: Some Additional Principles of Learning and Retention

INCIDENTAL VS. INTENTIONAL LEARNING

WE HAVE SAID that the period from five or six to twelve is above all a period of learning. It would be more accurate to call it a period of planned, *intentional* learning. Most societies provide that during this period *teaching* will occur so that the child's learning process will not be dependent on chance circumstances. A tremendous amount of learning occurs during infancy and the preschool years. But mainly it is incidental to the person's efforts to do the things he wants to do. He does not think of it as learning. After he starts to school he knows what it means to *try* to *learn*.

What difference does it make whether one learns a thing intentionally or by accident? We can say at once that it makes no difference at all provided that it is actually learned and learned with equal thoroughness. But there's the rub. What kind of things do we learn by accident, and how thoroughly do we learn them?

Many years ago, Myers[1] undertook to find out something about the precision of incidental observation when there was no particular intent to learn. He asked several hundred people, including business men, college students, high school students, and grade school children, to

[1] G. C. Myers. A study in incidental memory. *Arch. Psychol.*, 1913, No. 26.

draw a rectangle of the same size as a dollar bill and another of the same size as the colored portion of a two-cent stamp. They were also asked to select from a number of circles those of the same size as a cent, a dime, a nickel, a quarter, and a half-dollar. Even bankers and merchants who handle money all day long were decidedly inaccurate in their guesses, though they did somewhat better than those who had had less experience with money.

The subjects were then told that they would be given a spelling test. Six very easy words were dictated as fast as they were able to write them down, but they were not told to try to remember what the words were. As soon as the list had been dictated the subjects were told to turn the papers over and write the words from memory in the order in which they had been given. Not one out of twenty was able to do this without error. On this test the grade-school children did about as well as the adults. Failure to learn was not due to the difficulty of the task but to the fact that the subjects had given their attention to spelling the words as separate units. They had not tried to memorize the list as a whole.

In another experiment, Myers asked his subjects to count the O's in a group of eighteen letters arranged in three rows of six letters each. There were twelve O's, with the following additional letters interspersed at irregular intervals: X, A, P, I, E, and K. Myers points out that in order to count the O's it must have been necessary for them to see the other letters at least clearly enough to recognize that they were not O's. Nevertheless, when immediately after the O's had been counted, the card was withdrawn and the subjects were asked what other letters they had seen, not one of 390 persons tested was able to recall all six letters correctly. The average number remembered was one. When they were asked how the letters had been arranged, more than half thought there had been four lines of five letters each. Many had failed to notice the color of the letters (bright red) or the color of the background (bright yellow), and few had formed more than a hazy idea of the border by which the letters were surrounded.

Many other experiments have been made with similar results. One of the most common is the "testimony" experiment. Sometimes this experiment is given the form of a mock crime. Before an unsuspecting group of students in a lecture room two or more of their associates suddenly appear and go through the form of a robbery, an assault, perhaps a murder. Immediately afterward or perhaps a day or so later the students are questioned about what took place. Sometimes in addition to answering the questions they are asked to state the degree of assurance they feel in replying, which facts they are uncertain about, and to which ones they would be willing to swear. Practically always it is found that many students report that they saw all kinds of things which did not happen at all. Often they feel so sure of these false observations that they would be willing to swear to them, while many of the actions that really did take place will be found to have escaped notice entirely.

The psychological laboratory provides other evidence as to how little is learned with precision when there is no particular intention to learn. The color-naming experiment is an example. Subjects are shown a series of small disks of different colors, arranged in successive rows like a page of print. They are asked to name the colors as fast as they can, beginning at the upper left corner and proceeding from left to right and downward as in ordinary reading. The time required to name all the colors is taken at each trial so as to keep the emphasis upon speed. Nothing is said about learning the order of the colors. One would think, however, that after two or three hundred repetitions, always in the same manner, the order would be learned anyway, whether the subjects tried to do so or not. Not at all. Without the intent to memorize, most students will have made hardly any progress at all toward memorizing. Their attention has been centered on naming each color as a separate unit. They have not thought of the colors as forming a connected series.

All this seems to show that we learn very little about the events taking place around us unless something about them attracts our attention. Even then, what we learn is limited almost entirely to the particular thing that we chance to notice, while other and perhaps more important features may be overlooked entirely. The trouble with incidental experience is not that it doesn't teach us anything, for it usually does, but we can't be sure just what it is going to teach.

SELECTING THE THING TO BE LEARNED

I know a woman who had great difficulty in recognizing people even after she had met them a number of times. Often she was embarrassed by her failure to recognize persons whom she should have known at once. Finally she decided to try to look into her difficulty. She found that much of her trouble was due to her habit of noticing people's clothes rather than their faces. If they happened to be dressed differently, when she met them a second time, there was nothing by which she could recognize them. After she found out what was wrong and made a definite effort to see the persons themselves rather than their clothing, there was much improvement.

Children and older people as well often fail to learn because they do not center their attention on the right things. A child of ten has to learn how to spell the word *niece*. He repeats the letters over and over to himself, but he gives no more attention to one letter than to another. As a matter of fact, while his lips and tongue are moving silently and he therefore takes it for granted that he is "studying," his fingers are busy with the marbles in his pocket and his mind is rehearsing the particular kind of "shot" by which he plans to defeat all his rivals as soon as school is over. One hundred repetitions! But when he is called upon to write the word he spells it *neise.*

Now in reality, no study at all was needed for him to know that the first letter of the word in question is *n.* He could tell that by the sound. What he chiefly needed to notice was the *ie* following the *n,* and the fact that the sibilant sound is given by a *c* instead of an *s.* The final *e* would require only a moment's notice, since it follows the general rule that monosyllables containing a long vowel sound end in *e.* One minute of attentive study devoted to the parts of the word on which study was needed would have been worth far more than the hundred or more monotonous repetitions with the mind elsewhere.

In all learning, intelligent selection of the things to be learned is of utmost importance. It does not pay to spend one's time and effort in learning trivial details while the main issues are overlooked, or to give as much attention to the familiar and obvious parts of a task as to those which are new or difficult. The school child who is only just beginning to learn how to study a lesson or to play a musical instrument or to perform some complicated act of skill cannot be expected to know how to direct his efforts most effectively without help. But it is easy to find grown men and women whose methods of learning are as childish and inefficient as those of the average six-year-old. Sometimes this is because they are really stupid; often it is just because they have failed to acquire good habits of learning. They read a book with the intention of remembering it, but they grasp blindly at every detail, and in their attempt to retain everything they come out with only a confused impression that has little meaning at the time and is soon lost. Or they read through it mechanically with their thoughts somewhere else and then wonder why they remember so little. Although it is never too late to correct bad habits of this kind, it is better to form good habits from the start. In the education of the school child nothing is more important than this. He should learn how to learn.

The experiments by Harlow [2] mentioned in Chapter 11 have focused attention on the importance of this principle even in animal learning. After a monkey has learned in a series of trials that a prize is to be found in a square box, but not in a round box, if conditions are suddenly reversed so that it is the round box that now contains the reward, one trial is enough to enable him to respond perfectly to the new situation. The important thing he acquired from the experience with the boxes

[2] H. F. Harlow. The formation of learning sets. *Psychol. Rev.,* 1949, 56, 51-65.

was a *learning set*. Once he has it, any new discrimination problem can be solved with ease.

WHAT KIND OF MATERIAL IS EASIEST
TO LEARN AND REMEMBER

Here is a list of twelve nonsense syllables. Try to learn them in order. Keep count to see how many times you have to read them before you can recite them all without a mistake:

Mup, sil, fut, wal, lub, seg, yin, taz, bip, ron, pij.

Now try this sentence, which contains twelve one-syllable words:

The boy tore a great big hole in his new red coat.

How many readings were required to learn the list of nonsense syllables? How many for the sentence?

Tomorrow see how many of the nonsense syllables you can recall. And see if you can still remember the sentence.

Material that has meaning, that is knit together to form a connected whole, is easier to learn and is remembered much longer than the same amount of material made up of disconnected bits that have to be memorized separately. Children often have difficulty in learning because they do not comprehend the material that is given them to learn. One way of making learning easier is to try to get as much meaning into the thing to be learned as possible. Modern educators realize this principle and so try to have a large share of the child's schoolwork revolve about actual, meaningful experience. Children learn to make change by playing at storekeeping; they learn geography by making maps for themselves which they ornament with actual samples of the products of the different regions. Mississippi gets a tuft of cotton, Pennsylvania a lump of coal and a bit of iron, Minnesota some grains of wheat. The child who has once helped to construct a map of this kind is far less likely to forget the facts he has learned in making it than the one who has spent his time studying the same facts from a printed book.

When material that has few logical connections within itself has to be learned—for example, dates, lists of persons or places, and the like —it is often helpful to build up artificial associations at the start in order to get the facts firmly anchored in the mind. Rhymes and jingles may be invented. When some of us were children, much of the content of our geography lessons in the primary grades consisted in the memorizing of states with their capitals, principal rivers, and so on. Since at that tender age few of us had any clear idea of what was meant by a "state," and a "capital," if it meant anything at all, was the kind

of letter that must be put at the beginning of a sentence on penalty
of being "kept in" at recess time to correct one's errors and repent, the
whole performance was pretty much on the level of memorizing a list
of nonsense syllables. But one enterprising teacher found a way to
lighten the task. She set the whole thing to the tune of "Yankee Doodle,"
and to this day fragments of the ditty remain in my mind.

> Pennsylvania—Harrisburg
> Upon the Susquehanna;
> Oh, Pennsylvania—Harrisburg
> Upon the Susquehanna.
>
> State of Maine—Augusta
> Upon the Kennebec River

. . . .

Many a person has mastered the date of the discovery of America by
means of the well-known rhyme

> In fourteen hundred and ninety-two
> Columbus sailed the ocean blue.

Calendar reform might have been forced from sheer desperation long
ago had not the present system been made endurable by the help of
"Thirty days hath September."

IS IT EASIER TO LEARN IN WHOLES OR IN PARTS?

A common way of having children memorize poetry is to teach them
a line or a short stanza at a time and then try to have them put the bits
together into a whole. But experiments have shown that this is usually
not the best method. One learns most easily when meaning is most vivid,
and to break up meaningful material into parts almost always results
in a loss of associations that would be helpful in learning, even though
not all the thought is lost by the division. Sometimes, however, if the
selection to be learned is so long that the task of learning it all at once
seems overwhelming and the apparent lack of progress when the
attempt is made leads to discouragement and loss of interest, better
results are obtained by dividing it into sections, taking care to make
the division at points where there is some break in the thought so that
as little of the meaning will be lost as possible.

A common example of the wastefulness of learning in parts what
should be grasped as a whole is seen in those persons who fail to make
preparation for a task in advance and so have to be continually stopping
their work to hunt up needed tools.

Observe two students preparing a lesson. One gets his materials ready before he starts and puts them where he can lay his hands on them as needed. The other begins to read his assignment, then decides he had better take notes and goes for his notebook. Then he must make a search for his fountain pen. A little later he finds that the pen is going dry and what can have become of the ink bottle? Found at last, but when the pen is filled he has nothing to wipe it on and in consequence his hands become so daubed with ink that he has to stop once more in order to wash them. Ten minutes later he realizes that he is still wearing the heavy shoes he put on for hiking in the afternoon, and so another halt ensues while he changes to his slippers. Then when at last his reading is done he complains that he doesn't have any idea what the darned stuff is all about!

Of course he hasn't! The continued breaks in thought resulting from all these interruptions have so destroyed continuity that the task becomes about as difficult as learning a list of nonsense syllables. The importance of advance preparation in enabling one to carry through an entire task without interruption to the train of thought is something that the school child can hardly learn too early or too thoroughly.

THE VALUE OF RECITING TO ONESELF

After one has determined or has been shown just what it is that he needs to learn, what is the best way to set about it? Suppose that it is a passage or a poem to be learned by heart. One way to learn it is to read it over and over again, but this is not the quickest method nor the one that makes for best retention over a period of time. It is better to spend part of the time in trying to recite it to oneself. If, instead of learning by rote, the task is that of learning the general content of a history lesson or a geography lesson, the same principles hold good. First the assignment should be read through one or more times in order to get an idea of the general drift and to decide what are the important things to be remembered. Children should be taught to do this as soon as they begin to read for information. Afterward, reciting the main facts to oneself and checking up to see what has been omitted will result in much better mastery of the material than will be had from spending the same amount of time in merely reading the assignment over again and again. Not only will the lesson be learned more quickly by this method, but it will not be so soon forgotten.

Tables V and VI give you an idea of how much time and effort can be saved by following this plan. They are taken from a study by Gates. [3]

In the experiment employing nonsense syllables it was found that

[3] A. I. Gates. Recitation as a factor in memorizing. *Arch. Psychol.*, 1917, No. 40.

TABLE V

Scores Earned in an Experiment on Memorizing Nonsense Syllables When Different Percentages of the Total Time Were Devoted to Self-Recitation

School Grade	Percentages of Time Spent in Self-Recitation				
	0%	20%	40%	60%	80%
4	9.5	12.0	16.1	17.0	20.0
6	13.2	20.2	22.6	25.2	30.5
8	16.9	23.9	25.8	27.3	35.5

Adapted from Gates.

TABLE VI

Scores Earned in an Experiment on Learning Biographical Data When Different Percentages of Learning Time Were Devoted to Self-Recitation

School Grade	Percentages of Time Spent in Self-Recitation					
	0%	20%	40%	60%	80%	90%
4*	14.6	16.9	16.4	18.8	17.6	17.2
6	15.1	16.6	18.0	17.7	17.8	16.6
8	20.8	22.4	24.8	25.0	25.3	23.8

Adapted from Gates.
* The fourth-grade children were given easier material than those in the upper grades. This accounts for the small apparent change in performance from the fourth- to the sixth-grade level.

in every grade more than twice as many syllables were learned in a given length of time when the children spent 80 per cent of their time in reciting the list to themselves as when they merely read the syllables over and over without testing out their progress. Fourth-grade children who spent 60 per cent or more of their time in reciting to themselves learned as rapidly as eighth-grade children who merely read without reciting. When meaningful material in the form of short biographies of famous men was used instead of the nonsense material, it was found better to spend a little greater proportion of the time in reading and a little less in reciting, but here, too, learning was improved by spending a part of the time in self-recitation. For the biographies, the best division of time seemed to be about 40 per cent reading and 60 per cent reciting; for the nonsense syllables, at least 80 per cent of the time might profitably be spent in reciting.

Later studies using many kinds of materials besides nonsense syllables and many types of activity besides straight recitation have made it possible to express this principle in more general terms. What really seems to be important is that the learner take some *action* with regard to the material to be learned and not let himself be just a passive recipient. Students who make it a practice to try to summarize the content of a chapter they have read in a textbook, and then check their own summaries for important points they may have omitted generally do better on examinations than those who simply read the book, even those who read it several times. A student learns more from making his own outlines of reading assignments and lectures and then comparing them with those produced by someone else than he does by purchasing or borrowing the best outlines available. Active participation is fundamental to intentional learning.

THE DISTRIBUTION OF PRACTICE

Are one or two long practice periods or several short ones with time in between more effective for learning? Many experiments have been carried out in an attempt to answer this question. The results have usually been in favor of a number of short periods spaced some time apart rather than longer periods occurring close together. The rule is usually stated as follows: Distributed practice is better than massed practice. But of course such a statement needs to be qualified, for it would be absurd to suppose that the shorter or the further apart the practice periods, the better will be the learning. Really what it means is that a proper distribution of work periods and rest periods (or periods involving a change of occupation) makes it easier to learn, and that people in general are more likely to err on the side of making their study periods too long and too close together than the reverse. This is especially likely to be the case when the learning is to be done by children and the length of the practice periods is determined by teachers or parents, for it is less bother to keep children plugging away at a single task than to be always finding a change of occupation for them.

It is impossible to lay down any single fixed rule as to the best length of the practice periods or how long a time should elapse between them, for it will vary according to the kind of thing that is being learned and the age and mental characteristics of the subjects. In general we may say that in tasks made up of many short independent units, such as learning to throw at a target or learning a spelling lesson, greater efficiency is gained by distributing the practice over a large number of very short periods than by massing it all into a few longer ones. Kirkwood,[4] in a study in which children under seven years learned

---

[4] J. A. Kirkwood. The learning process in young children. Univ. of Iowa Stud. in Child Welf. 1926, Vol. 3, No. 6.

to associate pictures of common objects with geometrical forms roughly resembling them (such as a diamond-shaped block to be matched with a picture of a kite), found that children who practiced on alternate days required fewer trials to learn the series than those who practiced daily. (See Figure 78.) The length of the practice periods was the same for both groups.

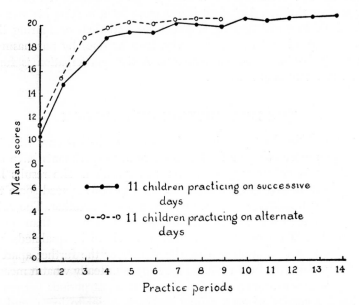

FIGURE 78. Learning curve of children practising on alternate days compared with that of children practising on successive days. (After Kirkwood from Learning in children, by Joseph Peterson. In Carl Murchison (Ed.) *A handbook of child psychology*. Courtesy Clark Univ. Press.)

Starch [5] had four groups of subjects learn to substitute letters for numbers according to a key like the following in which each digit has its corresponding letter:

O 1 2 3 4 5 6 7 8 9
R M Q H E B S V A L

The results, in terms of the number of correct transpositions for each five-minute period, are shown in Figure 79.

Other experiments on the learning of the so-called drill subjects in school have given similar results. It has been found, for example, that in teaching primary number work, practice periods as short as two minutes are desirable for the youngest groups, although the time may

[5] D. Starch. Periods of work in learning. *J. educ. Psychol.*, 1912, 2, 209-213

be increased somewhat for the older ones. But when the material to be learned involves the setting-up of a train of ideas, as in literature, history, or science, it is wasteful to make the practice periods so brief that meaningful associations are cut short before they are fully developed. Interest also plays an important part. If the task to be learned is monotonous and uninteresting, the practice periods should be shorter and further apart than is necessary when enthusiasm runs high. As a matter of fact, it is very possible that most if not all of the advantages

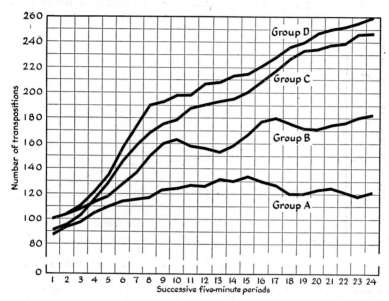

FIGURE 79. Relation of the distribution of practice to rate of learning to substitute numerals for letters. All groups had 120 minutes of practice. Group A worked 120 minutes at a single sitting. Group B worked 40 minutes at a time on alternate days. Group C worked 20 minutes at a sitting on consecutive days. Group D worked 10 minutes twice a day on consecutive days. (After Starch.)

coming from distributed practice are due to the greater zest with which even a task that is intrinsically uninteresting will be attacked if practice is never carried to the point of fatigue and boredom. Learning is an active process. Just going through the motions doesn't help much.

CONTINUED PRACTICE OR "OVERLEARNING"

A list of nonsense syllables learned to the point of one correct repetition with no further practice will soon be forgotten. Ebbinghaus [6] who

[6] H. Ebbinghaus. *Memory* (1885). Trans. by H. A. Ruger and C. E. Bussenius. New York: Teachers College, Columbia Univ. Press, 1913.

conducted the first extensive study on memorizing and to whom we are indebted for the first experimentally determined "curve of forgetting" (see Figure 80), found that more than half of a list so learned would be forgotten within an hour and that by the end of a few months practically no memory of it would remain.

The twenty-six letters making up the English alphabet bear a fairly close correspondence to a list of nonsense syllables, since there is no logical connection from letter to letter. But all of us go not merely for hours but for days, weeks, perhaps even months at times when

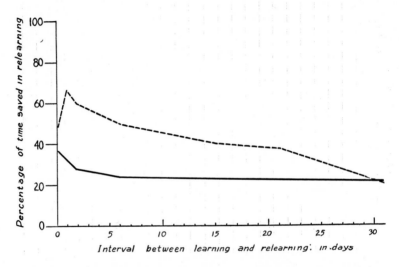

FIGURE 80.   Relation of overlearning to retention. The solid line shows the percentage of time saved in relearning nonsense syllables originally learned to the point of one correct repetition. The broken line shows the amount of saving when the list is learned to the point of two correct repetitions. (Adapted from E. L. Thorndike. *Educational psychology*, Vol. II. Data from Ebbinghaus and from Radossawljewitsch. Courtesy of the Bureau of Publication, Teachers College, Columbia University.)

we chance to have little use for a dictionary, without reciting the alphabet or thinking anything about the order of the letters. Nevertheless we do not forget it, and when the need arises we run through the letters as smoothly and with as little hesitation as if it had been recited half a dozen times daily.

The amount of practice after the original learning is what makes the difference. Anything that is just barely learned and never used again will soon be forgotten, particularly if it has no logical connections or personal associations to make it stick in the mind. But even a little additional practice aids retention, and material that is greatly "overlearned" or skills that are practiced over and over again are retained so well that the ordinary lifetime is not long enough for them to be completely forgotten. It is said that a skilled swimmer never entirely forgets the art even though he may go for many years without practice. A student who had practiced typewriting for 200 hours dropped it entirely for a year, but an hour's practice was sufficient to make up all the ground that he had lost. Four people practiced ten minutes daily for seventeen weeks in reading ordinary prose in a mirror. After two years without further practice all regained their previous levels in less than a week's time by practicing the same amount daily as before.

Figure 80 illustrates how much retention can be improved by even a small amount of overlearning. Here the solid line shows the rate of forgetting nonsense syllables practiced to the point of one correct repetition only. The dotted line shows the rate when two correct repetitions are required before practice is discontinued.

The way to remember is to review, and to review early, for the time immediately after learning is the time when forgetting is most rapid, as you can easily see by looking at the curves. The best kind of reviewing is that which comes with putting the material that has been learned to some actual use, for use gives it more vivid and personal meaning, which, as we have seen, is one of the chief factors that make for retention. One reason why we remember the order of the letters in the alphabet so well is because we have so often made use of that order in consulting dictionaries, encyclopedias, and indexes. With plenty of additional practice to fix the newly learned accomplishment in mind and occasional reviews thereafter to renew efficiency when it has lapsed through disuse it seems safe to say that anything that has been once learned can be retained as long as it seems worthwhile to make the necessary effort to do so.

It would be a mistake, however, to say that overlearning is beneficial in *all* learning situations. If a person is likely to be facing *new* problems rather than requirements identical with those previously made upon him, it may be a disadvantage for him to have acquired fixed habits of procedure. Experiments on memorizing and retention do not tell us what we need to know about *problem-solving*. Teachers need to keep this distinction in mind as they plan learning experiences for their classes. For example, anything that can be done to induce boys and girls to overlearn the multiplication tables is all to the good. This knowledge must be delivered promptly, dependably, and efficiently in its original form throughout the rest of the learner's life. But a child who overlearns one standard method of solving "story problems" in arithmetic is taking on a handicap that will stand in his way as he faces later problems differing from these in unpredictable ways.

THE TRANSFER OF TRAINING

Does learning one thing make it easier to learn something else? Can the ability to learn be improved by practice?

A generation or two ago it was believed by many people that all formal studying, that is, studying with the intent to learn, had a disciplinary effect upon the mind of the student, which made learning easier for him thereafter. The study of abstract subjects such as mathematics or Latin was assumed to have a marked effect upon the student's ability to learn other things, while studying the more concrete subjects such as drawing or cooking had less effect upon general learning ability.

While the belief is still common that the studying of "hard" subjects trains the mind in some general way, psychological experiments have tended to disprove it. There is some transfer from one learning task to another, but the basis for it seems to be some kind of similarity between the fields in question. This is often a matter of identical elements in the two complex situations. In some cases transfer seems to be based on similar structure or organization. The student who already knows French can learn Italian more easily than another of equal ability who knows only English, because French and Italian are so much alike. A knowledge of French will be less helpful in learning Chinese, but some transfer is to be expected even here, for there are a number of special habits or devices that are useful in learning languages in general which will be carried over from the learning of one language to the learning of another, even though the languages themselves may be of very different origin. But learning French will not have much effect upon one's ability to learn to drive an automobile. At the present stage of research, we know that transfer of training depends upon similarity of the new learning situation to a previous one, but we cannot give a very precise definition of "similarity." There are probably many ways in which a new situation can be similar to an old one. The learning sets and attitudes of which we have spoken earlier may transfer over a wide range of behaviors and skills which in themselves possess few elements in common. One may build up (that is, learn) an attitude of pride in one's ability to achieve, and this attitude may affect one's persistence and effort in such widely diverse skills as playing golf or learning calculus. One may form habits of giving up when a task becomes hard or of sticking it out to the end in spite of difficulty. While there is little or no reason to believe that study will improve one's *ability* to learn, there is good evidence that *attitudes* can be learned which will make for greater or less efficiency in learning.

Here too there are clues as to what good teaching should accomplish. If the teacher wishes to produce as much transfer as possible, he will do well to emphasize general principles rather than disconnected details in the subject matter with which he is concerned. It is these principles that are most likely to be similar to those in other fields of knowledge. A child who learns to play the piano will not be able to transfer habits of striking the right notes on the keyboard if he later undertakes the study of the violin. But he will be able to use everything he knows about note reading and musical theory.

We must remember also that *negative* transfer can occur. As we noted above in connection with overlearning, this can be circumvented to some extent by avoiding too much drill on habits one is not going to need in a fixed, unchanging form. It cannot be avoided altogether. The man who keeps reaching for the gear shift lever in his new car with an automatic shift is experiencing negative transfer from one learning situation to another. Fortunately, when the source of the negative transfer effect is apparent, as in this case, it is not too difficult to overcome it. Students and teachers would do well to be on the lookout for impediments to learning that arise in this way. Once the interfering factor is recognized, some extra practice on this one specific part of the new skill or idea will serve to remove the block.

THE OVERLAPPING OF ELEMENTS
IN SERIAL LEARNING

A favorite method of studying the learning of a connected series of activities is by the use of mazes. A maze, you know, consists of a series of alleyways opening one out of another in such a way that a subject who is put into the maze at the starting point can, by taking the right turnings, find his way out at the other end. But all along the way there are blind alleys (*cul-de-sacs*) that he must learn to avoid. At the beginning the learner has no way of distinguishing between the true path and the blind alleys. Only by actual trial can he find out which is which. But by repeated trials he eventually masters the pattern. Purely empirical learning of this kind in which logic or reasoning can play no part is usually called learning by *trial and error*.

Mazes used in the psychological laboratory are of many kinds and have a wide range of complexity. With animals of very low neural

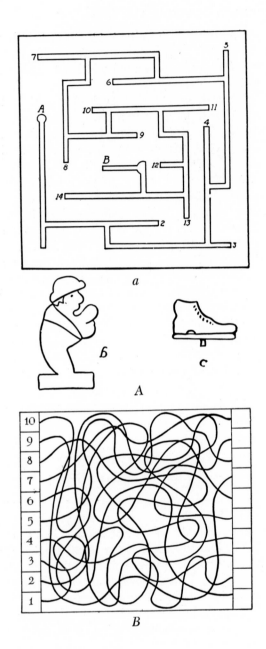

a

Б

с

А

В

organization such as the earthworm, only an exceedingly simple maze can be used; for the higher animals, including man, they may be very complicated indeed. In some of the more recent and elaborate models, an electrical recording system is used that does away with all chance of errors of observation on the part of the experimenter, but for most studies direct observation is relied upon. Those intended for use with animals are usually made large enough for the animal to run

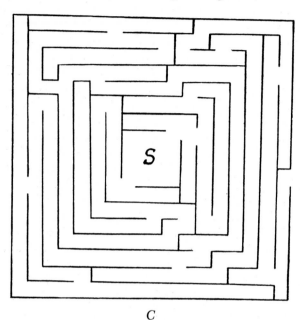

C

FIGURE 81. Different types of mazes. A. The Young Slot Maze (*opposite page*). The toy clown is set into the groove at B; the shoe is placed at A. The child is told to take the shoe to the man. (From Esther McGinnis. The asquisition and interference of motor habits in young children. *Genet. Psychol. Monog.*, 1929, 6, 234. Courtesy Clark Univ. Press.)

B. An eye maze (*opposite page*). The lines must be followed with the eye only. The ending of each line is to be indicated by placing its number in the appropriate space in the column at the right.

C. One of the mazes in the series designed by Porteus. (Courtesy of the C. H. Stoelting Co.)

through them; with human beings smaller models to be traced by hand are often substituted. Sometimes the subject is allowed to do this with his eyes open, but more often he is blindfolded or the maze is placed under a screen where he cannot see it. Tracing is done with the tip of the finger, sometimes even with the great toe, or with the point of a stylus. Sometimes the eye alone is used. Examples are seen in Figure 81.

When a hungry white rat is put into a maze leading to a food box at the other end, he has at first no idea that food is to be found there. But his hunger makes him restless and so he explores the maze. At first he is as likely to enter the blind alleys as to follow the true path, but after repeated trials he learns the right way to go. Eventually he becomes so expert that he starts running as soon as he is put into the maze, dashes through at top speed without even pausing at the blind alleys, and reaches the food box in a short fraction of the time it took him at the beginning. He has learned just which turns to take and where they are located so well that he even makes anticipatory adjustments to them in advance. While he is dashing around one corner he is getting set to run just so far and no further before he swerves again. This has been shown by experiments in which the length of an alley has been shortened after the rats had learned to run the maze without errors. It is found that the rats in such an experiment will run full tilt up against the wall at the point where the runway has been cut off. You and I do the same thing at times and for the same reason. Have you never misjudged the height of a chair on which you were about to sit down and fallen with an embarrassing thud the last few inches after your muscles had relaxed in anticipation of a support that failed to appear? And on negotiating a moderately familiar stairway in the dark, have you never experienced the shock of having the floor seem to rise to meet you when the bottom is reached a step sooner than you expected?

This anticipation of the next thing to be done in the course of running off a learned reaction is often spoken of as the "overlapping" of elements in a pattern reaction, and it is one of the chief reasons why a well-learned action seems to be done so smoothly and evenly as contrasted with the uneven, jerky, disconnected movements that are characteristic of the beginning stages of learning. At first the learner has to give his entire attention to the thing he is doing at the moment. He cannot spare any thought to the question of what is coming next. The present task requires his entire effort. But as the separate parts are gradually mastered, he begins to look ahead and prepare himself for the next stage while he is actually carrying out the last. Then, and not until then, does he become able to pass from one part of his performance to the next with no apparent breaks or irregularities.

The importance of this overlapping of elements in learning a serial reaction is nowhere better shown than in reading. The child just beginning to read, the older person of little education, or you, when you are beginning a foreign language, must give so much attention to each separate word that the reading of a paragraph is likely to be slow, halting, jerky, and disconnected. With gain in skill, however, certain familiar or striking phrases begin to link themselves together, and when you come to these passages your reading, for the moment, runs along smoothly. Your eyes look ahead for the next words while your lips are pronouncing those seen an instant before. One of the chief things that distinguishes the good oral reader from the poor one is the extent to which his eyes and his understanding are able to keep ahead of his voice. This makes it possible for him to vary his tonal inflection as he goes along instead of having to wait until the thought of the passage is completed, when it will be too late.

In all aspects of everyday life, the factor of overlapping elements or anticipation of the second and third steps while taking the first marks off the efficient worker from the inefficient one. Watch two housewives in their kitchens. One steps briskly about her tasks without hesitation, planning for one thing while doing another, taking advantage of the moment while the dishpan is filling to get the tea towels ready, reaching for the flavoring extract with her left hand while stirring her cake with the right. The other "putters" about, perhaps moving just as fast or faster, but everything she does requires a separate effort of mind and body. She carried in the broom, then goes back for the dustpan; later still another trip must be made for dust cloths.

The secret of a smooth and well-organized motor performance lies in the ability to keep the attention centered on what is coming rather than on what is being done at the moment. The tennis player judges the angle at which the ball is coming and adjusts his stroke accordingly. If he waits for it to arrive before making his preparations to receive it, he will be too late. If he stops in the middle of his stroke to think how he is holding his racket, whether or not his feet are at the right angle, the ball will escape him before he gets around to striking at it. But in order to free his attention from the activity of the moment and center it on preparing for the act that is to come, he must have learned by experience to *interpret* the sensations coming in from his muscles and joints in such a way that he gets a continual check-up as to whether he is right or wrong. The skilled tennis player does not have to look where the ball has gone to know, within rough limits, whether his play has been good or bad. He knows by the "feel" of it. Learning the theoretical principles of correct playing will prevent the development of many bad motor habits that might otherwise be set up, but only actual practice and plenty of it will serve to transfer this knowledge into the world of kinesthetic meanings where it will be of real service.

But if one had to give separate attention to each tiniest part of an act, if one had to think separately about holding the racket, moving the feet, raising the arm, bringing it forward with just so much force and no more, and then keep track of each of the kinesthetic sensations resulting from these acts in order to know whether or not the play was right, the situation would be quite as bad as that described in the well-known rhyme:

> The centipede did very well
> Until the ant in fun
>   Asked, "Pray, which leg goes after which?"
>   Then left him helpless in the ditch
> Considering how to run.

Evidently too much attention to the separate parts of an act can impede learning. Before a high level of efficiency can be gained, the simple and elementary units of which an act is comprised must be bound together into larger patterns that are performed as wholes. In many of the ordinary acts of life so much of this organizing process takes place at a very early age that long before the child enters school we find the patterns already laid down and operating so smoothly and efficiently that only by a careful process of analysis can we break up the act into its original units. The psychological laboratory, however, has thrown some light on how the original process of consolidation takes place.

In this connection an experiment on the learning of telegraphy, carried out many years ago by Bryan and Harter [7] has been much quoted. They studied the progress of a number of students who were learning to send and receive messages by telegraph. Learning curves were plotted for each student, showing the weekly gains in the number of letters he was able to send or receive per minute. They found that the practice curves for sending were not unlike those characteristic of maze learning. There was rapid gain at the beginning with slowing off later on, making the kind of curve that we describe as *negatively accelerated* because gains become less per unit of time as practice increases. The curves for receiving, however, were found to have a peculiar steplike form in which an initial period of gain was followed by a period when little or no advancement seemed to occur.

To such a period Bryan and Harter gave the name *plateau*. Their explanation for the plateau is this: In the beginning the student who is receiving listens to the clicks of the instrument and spells them out letter by letter. All his attention goes to the letters. He does not attempt to group them into words until after he has taken them down

---

[7] W. L. Bryan and N. Harter. Studies in the physiology and psychology of the telegraphic language. *Psychol. Rev.*, 1897, 4, 27-53.

on paper. At first he does this very slowly, but as he becomes accustomed to the sounds his speed improves. Presently he is taking down the letters about as fast as he can hear them separately. Now it seems as though he could make no further gain, and as a matter of fact he does not gain much for a while. But sooner or later a new factor comes in. He hears the letter *t* but instead of writing it down at once he waits to see what else is coming. Yes, it is *h, e,* and the word is *the.* Now he begins to listen to the clicks in a new way. Instead of hearing each short letter-group separately, he learns to recognize the longer patterns that go to make up entire words. Now his speed begins to improve again and he gains rapidly for a time as more and more "word habits" take the place of the slow and laborious "letter habits" that he used before. After he has learned to recognize most familiar words with ease, the gain in speed begins to slow off once more, but it may pick up again if, as the best operators do, he begins to form "phrase habits" or "short sentence habits" which enable him to work in still larger units.

The ability to recognize words as wholes without giving separate attention to the letters has two advantages. The telegrapher who has learned to do this hears and recognizes a whole word almost as easily as he can hear and recognize a single letter, just as you do when reading from a book. Think how slowly you would read if you had to pause and look at each of the separate letters of each word before you could tell what it is. In addition to the enormous gain in speed made possible in this way, there is a further gain due to the fact that, when large rather than small units are employed, the overlapping of the two acts involved in the perceptual process of hearing and understanding the clicks and in the motor performance of taking down the message as it is heard is facilitated. There is time to write the last word or phrase while listening to the next. The individual letters come so close together that one cannot keep far ahead of them, but if words or phrases are heard as wholes there is ample time, while each is being completed, to write down what was heard before.

The appearance of a plateau in a learning curve, that is of a fairly long period during which little or no improvement takes place, followed by a sudden shift for the better, usually means that the subject has substituted a more efficient for a less efficient method of work. One way of doing this is by organizing small units into larger ones, as Bryan and Harter have shown. But any other fundamental improvement in method, coming after the limits of improvement by the old method have been reached, will bring about a similar change in the curve. A sudden increase in interest and effort, following a long period of discouragement or boredom, may also bring a plateau to

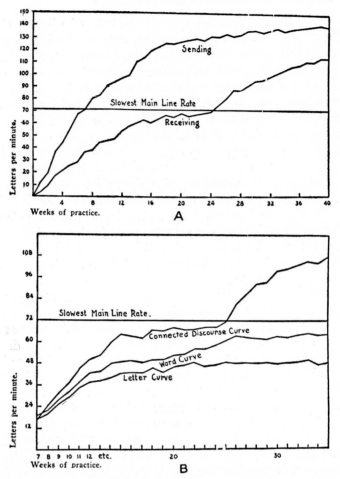

FIGURE 82. **The integration of simple skills into higher units as illustrated by the learning of telegraphy.** *A.* Learning curves for sending and receiving of one subject during forty weeks of practice.

B. Analysis of plateaus as shown by learning curves for receiving unconnected letters, unconnected words, and connected discourse. The letter curve reaches its upper limit by about the twentieth week and shows no further improvement thereafter. The word curve, however, makes a decided gain after letter skill has been perfected, and the curve for connected discourse rises very sharply after the ability to receive unconnected words has reached its limit. (From W. L. Bryan and N. Harter. Studies in the physiology and psychology of the telegraphic language. *Psychol. Rev.*, 1897, 4, 27-53. Courtesy Psychological Review Co.)

an end and speed the learning curve upward once more. Children who seem to have made little or no progress in their school work for some time often get a fresh start and learn with fair rapidity after a change to a more sympathetic teacher or one who makes use of methods that arouse their interest. Factory workers whose output, when they were paid by the day, remained at a dead level for months or years have been known to show a surprising spurt in production after a change to the piece-work system.

THE EFFECT OF PRACTICE UPON INDIVIDUAL DIFFERENCES

When a number of different persons take part in a learning experiment, they do not all show equal ability at the start. A part of this difference in initial ability may be due to differences in the amount of practice on similar performances before the formal experiment was begun, for it is very hard to select any kind of task that has nothing in common with the activities of everyday life. Differences in performance that are entirely due to unequal amounts of previous practice will tend to disappear in the course of time when all subjects are given the same amount and kind of training.

Even when equal opportunity for learning is given, some subjects learn more easily than others. However, if the task to be learned is so simple that even the poorest learners are able to master it when they are given sufficient time, differences in the performance of good, average, and poor learners tend to disappear as all the subjects approach the *physiological limit,* that is, as all learn to perform the act as rapidly as their bodily mechanism will permit. But if the task is very difficult, and particularly if it is one that makes a great demand upon abstract intelligence, the poorest learners will soon reach a point at which very little further improvement is possible for them, while the best learners will continue to gain. In this case, differences in the performance of the subjects will become greater with increased practice. The effect of increased practice upon the differences in the performance of individuals will therefore depend upon the difficulty of the task to be learned and the amount and kind of previous experience of the subjects. If the initial differences are chiefly due to unequal amounts of incidental practice on similar activities before the experiment was begun, these differences will become smaller when all are given equal amounts of practice in a learning experiment. If the amount of previous incidental practice has been approximately equal for all and the initial differences between the subjects are due to the fact that some have profited by this experience more than others because they learn more easily, the effect of further practice will vary according to the complexity of the task to be learned. In general, when previous experience has been equal for all subjects, with further practice the differences between individuals will be lessened if the thing to be learned is comparatively simple and concrete. In learning difficult or abstract tasks the initial differences between the subjects are likely to increase rather than decrease with practice.

PROBLEM-SOLVING AND REASONING

Psychologists who have focused their attention on the adaptive behavior of animals and children in new situations have often concluded that this type of learning involves something different from the processes that seem to be involved in the learning of nonsense syllables or the running of mazes. That something is *insight,* a sudden grasp of relationships between parts of a total situation that makes it possible for the learner to deal with it in a new way.

The question toward which many of the experiments have been directed is the relationship between the occurrence of insight and what is usually called *trial and error* behavior. This is much in evidence in animals, young children, and adults. The person faced with a problem tries a number of things in what appears to be a random fashion. Most of us have experienced this kind of behavior in searching for a lost object. We pull out drawers, go through pockets, look on the floor and shelves, trying every possibility that comes to mind.

Actually, there has turned out to be no clear boundary line between what we label *trial and error* and what is clearly *insight.* A person will usually make some unsuccessful attempts to solve a problem before insight occurs. These "trials," however, are not a chance assortment of activities. Past experience with similar problems and abstract concepts about the qualities of things serve to limit the things that are tried in a new situation. By making the relationships between parts of a complex problem situation clearer or more obvious, solutions based on insight rather than pure trial and error activity can often be facilitated.

The degree of insight shown by any person depends both upon his level of intelligence and upon the amount and kind of experience he has had in similar situations. Animals below the level of monkeys show little insight because they react to objects and situations as wholes rather than to their separate qualities. But human beings of equal intelligence show varying degrees of insight according to their experience. A skilled mechanic faced with a strange piece of machinery is likely to show much more insight in dealing with it than a lawyer of equal or greater general intelligence who has had little experience with machinery will display. Although the machine as a whole is unfamiliar to both, the mechanic will see in it many familiar principles, the workings of which he understands. But the lawyer is bungling and slow because he has not built up a system of "higher units" that apply to the machine situation. Nevertheless, in dealing with legal quirks and tangles that the mechanic would find hopelessly puzzling, he may display a promptness and efficiency that would be amazing to any one who had previously watched him poking stupidly at the various parts of the machine. Insight is not independent of earlier trial and error behavior but results from it, though in varying degrees according to the intellectual level of the individual concerned.

REINFORCEMENT AND THE FACILITATION OF LEARNING

Psychologists perform learning experiments not primarily for the purpose of helping parents, teachers, and animal trainers do their jobs more skillfully, but rather to bring to light basic processes of great scientific importance. The search for a general learning theory that will cover all sorts of learning of all kinds of living organisms goes on, and many experiments are designed specifically to test predictions made from one or another of these theories. Often, however, findings of considerable practical utility result from such experiments.

We have seen in earlier sections of this book (Chapters 6 and 11) how learning theorists attempted to use Pavlov's conditioned response experiments and the many others modeled upon them as prototypes of the learning process as we encounter it in much more complex situations. Through the concepts such experiments produced, we are able to understand how a response that naturally tends to follow a certain stimulus can be associated with many new kinds of stimulus. It was Skinner [8] who first made learning theorists aware of another kind of elementary learning situation which resembled the Pavlovian conditioned response in many ways but differed from it in others.

He called this bit of behavior an *operant*. The standard experiment that defined it was one in which a rat is placed in a box, empty except for a bar on the wall that can be pressed, and a food tray, usually near the bar. Things are so arranged that when the rat presses the bar a pellet of food drops into the tray. The thing that distinguishes this simple learning situation is that there is to start with no one

[8] B. F. Skinner. *The behavior of organisms: an experimental analysis.* New York: Appleton-Century-Crofts, 1938.

response naturally linked to the sight of a bar on the wall in the way salivation is linked to the presence of food in the mouth. To start with, there is no special reason for a rat to press the bar at all. When placed in the box he engages in a good deal of general, apparently random, activity. Bar-pressing is likely to occur as part of this complex. It is the reinforcement following this particular act that establishes it as a differentiated response. As we explained in an earlier chapter, the word *reinforcement*, largely as a result of experimental work with *operants* of this type, has come to be roughly synonymous with reward.

The principal theoretical controversies have centered around the question of whether or not some kind of reinforcement is essential if learning is to occur. The details of the controversy need not concern us here. Even if it be true that some learning occurs without reinforcement of any sort, there is no doubt that the presence of reinforcement increases its efficiency. Two aspects of the experimental work on the role reinforcement plays in learning are of special importance for those who are interested in the learning that occurs in practical situations.

One of these findings is that behavior that is reinforced only part of the time is more resistant to extinction than behavior rewarded at every trial. If we wish a child to develop really strong habits of hanging up his coat when he enters the house, one effective way would be to surprise him every now and then with a nickel immediately after he has hung the coat up. If we give him a nickel every time for a period of a week or so, he is much more likely to discontinue the good work when the reward is no longer forthcoming. Probably the tenacity of many of our hard-to-break habits arises from the fact that over a long period of time they were *occasionally* reinforced.

The other useful conclusion that has come from these studies of reinforcement is that reward is far more effective than punishment. This conclusion, of course, has been put forward by many persons besides learning theorists on the basis of a good deal of practical evidence. Animal experiments of the "Skinner-box" type have suggested that reward is really the *only* reinforcement. Responses that have been rewarded will be repeated again and again after reward is no longer given. But responses that are punished will only be held in check during the time the punishment is in effect. They are likely to reappear immediately when punishment for them is discontinued. In their effects on learning, reward and punishment are *not* opposites.

Other kinds of learning experiments have called attention to the fact that reward ordinarily gives the learner a great deal more *information* than punishment does. A child who is punished for doing something wrong may try twenty other wrong ways before he hits upon the right one. When he is rewarded for doing something right, he knows immediately, "This is it."

We would not suggest that punishment serves no purpose in the home, the school, or the larger society. Punishment does serve as a way of keeping under control behavior that has already been learned. For this purpose, in some instances it is indispensable. For safety's sake, Billy may have to be deterred from climbing on the fence around the bear's cage or from throwing rocks at his sister Susy. But learning how to handle his relationships with both bears and sisters will come not from punishment but from other kinds of experience.

Being able to analyze the actual reinforcement situation for a child, from the child's point of view, is one of the most useful skills a parent or a teacher can have. By planning carefully the rewards a child can obtain for his behavior, the nonmaterial as well as the material ones, we can facilitate his learning of all the things he will need to know as a mature adult in our society.

SUMMARY

Intentional learning is far more efficient than incidental learning. The school child becomes able to master large amounts of useful knowledge when he finds out what it means to try to learn.

Learning is an active process. The person who selects what needs to be practiced, organizes materials into a meaningful whole, and recites to himself as he goes along learns much more than the one who waits passively for something to "soak in."

In general, learning is more efficient when there is an alternation of work and rest periods. Cramming does not pay.

Overlearning, or continuing to practice after correct responses are consistently being made, is important for the retention of things that have been memorized, but may be a handicap in meeting novel situations or solving new problems.

We can expect positive transfer of training from one field of study to another if the two fields are similar to one another or if an attitude or learning set developed in one can be used to advantage in the other. We can also expect negative transfer in some situations where an old, well-practiced response must give way to a new one.

In complex skills where one part after another must occur in the right order, improvement comes with increasing organization of overlapping elements into larger wholes. Organization is important in problem-solving and reasoning also where seeing the relationships between parts of the total situation leads to insight.

Current learning theories devote much attention to reinforcement or reward as a facilitator of learning. Among the interesting experimental findings are the facts that irregular rewards produce firmer habits than consistent rewards, and that punishment serves chiefly to prevent the occurrence of some sort of behavior rather than to promote learning.

A PRACTICAL BOOK ON LEARNING

DUDYCHA, George J. *Learn more with less effort.* New York: Harper, 1957.

This attractive little book brings together all the knowledge psychologists have accumulated about the kinds of learning students are expected to accomplish in school. It is directed especially to the college student who finds it difficult to study efficiently. The author explains how to improve one's own motivation, how to organize one's study situation, how to master various kinds of assignments, and how to prepare for examinations. Clever, cartoon-type illustrations enliven the text.

CHAPTER 19

What are the principal developmental tasks that society expects a person to accomplish during the adolescent period?

At about what age is puberty reached in girls? In boys? How much normal variation from these averages occurs in individual cases?

What other kinds of physical changes occur during the period from eleven or twelve to twenty?

What aspects of these physical changes give rise to adjustment difficulties in individual cases?

What aspects of the social situation in which an adolescent finds himself may lead to conflict and strain?

What purposes does the peer group serve?

Through what means does the individual achieve a clear sense of his own identity?

Adolescence

DEFINING CHARACTERISTICS OF THE PERIOD

A COMPLEX PERSON in the complicated society human beings have
built up for themselves cannot grow up overnight. The attainment of
sexual maturity does not automatically lead to maturity in the other
aspects of life. Much must be experienced, much must be learned,
before the individual can take his place as an adult in the grownup
world. Adolescence can be defined simply as the period in which the
transition from childhood to adulthood occurs.

This general statement about the meaning of adolescence can be
analyzed into a number of separate parts. Havighurst[1] outlines the
developmental tasks that must be accomplished as:

1. Achieving new and more mature relationships with age mates of
   both sexes.
2. Achieving a masculine or feminine social role.
3. Accepting one's physique and using the body effectively.
4. Achieving emotional independence of parents and other adults.
5. Achieving assurance of economic independence.
6. Selecting and preparing for an occupation.
7. Preparing for marriage and family life.
8. Developing intellectual skills and concepts necessary for civic competence.
9. Desiring and achieving socially responsible behavior.
10. Acquiring a set of values and an ethical system as a guide to behavior.

[1] R. J. Havighurst. *Human development and education.* New York: Longmans,
Green, 1953.

When we look at the tasks of adolescence in this way, one by one, the list assumes formidable proportions. We begin to wonder how so many individuals manage to negotiate the difficult crossing from childhood to adulthood as successfully as they do! But for the child himself the whole process is a more natural one of meeting each new challenge as it arises, making use of whatever help he can get from his family, his friends, and his school. For him it is all one process of growing up. One of the best analyses of what the person is striving for, seen from his own point of view rather than from that of society, has been offered by Erikson.[2] He sees the basic goal of development during this stage as a sense of *identity*, the knowledge of who one is, what one is, where one belongs. We shall have more to say of this later.

GROWTH CHANGES AND THE PERSON'S ADJUSTMENT TO THEM

The most striking physical change in this growth period is of course the sexual maturation that marks the attainment of *puberty*. In girls, the *menarche*, or first menstruation, shows that puberty has been reached. In boys there is no one conspicuous observable event that marks the change, but ejaculation, voice changes, the growth of beard, and changes in the amount and character of pubic hair can all be used as evidence that puberty has been attained.

In both sexes, age at puberty is subject to great individual variation. Although well over half of American girls first menstruate between the twelfth and fourteenth birthdays, a few reach menarche as early as the age of nine or ten years, and in exceptional cases menstruation may be delayed until nineteen or twenty. In boys much the same range of individual differences is found, but the average age at puberty is from one to two years later than it is in girls.[3]

Carefully conducted growth studies in a number of places have made it clear that adolescence really begins before puberty is reached. One of the first and most dependable signs of its beginning is a sudden and very marked spurt in physical growth, especially growth in height. For girls, the average age for the beginning of this growth spurt is

[2] E. H. Erikson. *Childhood and society.* New York: Norton, 1950.
[3] An increasing body of evidence is accumulating which indicates that in the present generation, the average age at puberty is somewhat earlier than was true of preceding generations. That the average height of college students is greater than that of their parents of the same sex has been demonstrated for both men and women in a number of universities. The reason is not entirely clear, although differences in dietary habits appears to be the most plausible explanation for both changes.

about twelve; for boys it is about fourteen. But here too there are marked individual variations. For some children the period of accelerated growth comes earlier than this and for others it comes much later. During this stage the long bones of the arms and legs stretch out with such amazing rapidity that gains in height of as much as six inches in a single year have been known to occur. Trousers, skirts, and sleeves have to be continually lengthened, only to be outgrown again almost before the remodeling is completed. Gain in weight also occurs, but as a rule it fails to keep pace with gain in height, and so for a time we have the gangling long-legged boys and girls who seem to be chiefly made up of knees and elbows. After puberty is attained, bodily growth begins to slow down, and the gain becomes less and less each year until it finally ceases completely.

The facial proportions change. The lower jaw has been growing much faster than the upper portions of the skull since birth, and it now participates in the general growth spurt with the result that in a few months much of its former childish contour is lost and the face begins to take on a definitely grown-up appearance. (See Figure 52, Chapter 12.) This is accompanied in boys by a decrease and in girls by an increase in the layer of fat just underneath the skin. This causes the girls' faces to become softer and more rounded in outline, while the boys' faces grow more angular and their flesh feels harder.

The fine hairs on the surface of the body become somewhat coarser and longer and more strongly pigmented. This is true in both sexes but especially in the male. In the male, too, the beard begins to grow at about the time of puberty, and within a year or so shaving becomes necessary. In both sexes the voice also changes at adolescence, becoming lower in pitch and more resonant. In girls, however, the change in voice is much less pronounced than it is in boys. In boys the larynx or "Adam's apple" becomes noticeably enlarged, and the vocal chords within it increase greatly in length. It takes a year or more for this change to be completed. During this time the voice may be noticeably harsh and discordant, often getting out of control. Sometimes there are queer and unexpected shifts in pitch, when the voice without warning jumps from a deep bass to a husky squeak.

Physical characteristics of this kind, which do not involve the primary sex organs but which nevertheless differ for the two sexes, are known as *secondary sex characteristics.* For the most part, secondary sex characteristics are small and inconspicuous during childhood, but they begin to show up clearly at puberty, and in the adult they are very marked. Nevertheless in most cases the differences between the sexes in regard to these matters are differences of degree rather than of kind. Most men have beards and mustaches and most women do not, although in many women there is a visible heavier growth of the surface hairs on the upper lip than on other parts of the face. In most men, the shoulders are wider than the hips, while in women the reverse is true; but the rule does not always hold good. On the average, men's voices are deeper and more resonant than women's, but this is not invariably the case. So with the other secondary sex characteristics. On the average they differ for the sexes after the age of puberty, but there are individual exceptions.

There is a popular notion that the adolescent is always awkward and clumsy. Stories of adolescents usually picture them as perpetually knocking things over, stumbling over their feet, breaking everything that they touch. The reason commonly given is that the arms and legs have grown so fast and take up so much more space than they ever did before that their owner no longer knows how to handle them. This idea is of course sheer nonsense. Even the most rapidly growing child does not increase in size so rapidly that he cannot adjust his kinesthetic perceptions to the changes as they take place. [4] Nevertheless it is easy to see why some children do show an increased motor awkwardness at this time. Changes in their appearance are so marked that people are always commenting on it, often in rather tactless fashion.

"Gracious, how John is stretching out. And look at the size of his feet!"

"My goodness, don't tell me this is little Mary! Why, she used to be such a dainty little girl. I never in the world would have known her."

Daily exposure to remarks of this kind can hardly help but embarrass and annoy a sensitive child, even though no unkindness is intended. Often the adolescent member of a large family is made the butt of a great deal of chaffing about his appearance. His clothes that are perpetually too short, his hands and feet which are doubly conspicuous by protruding so far out of his outgrown garments, his voice with its unexpected growls and squeaks, all come in for their share of banter. Even though he takes it good-naturedly, some degree of self-consciousness is almost certain to be the result, and as most of us know from experience there is nothing like self-consciousness for disturbing one's motor control. It is an exceptional golfer whose drive cannot be interfered with by remarks about his personal appearance, particularly if he knows them to be true. The adolescent who is so clumsy and awkward that disaster seems to follow wherever he goes may show surprising dexterity of hand in his workshop when no one is watching him

---

[4] Note the experiences of Stratton and others, described in Chapter 14, on the length of time required to adjust the motor behavior to a complete reversal of the visual field. Compared to this, the motor adaptations demanded by the bodily changes of the growing child are trivial indeed.

and splendid bodily control on the athletic field. His awkwardness in public is not due to lack of motor skill but is the result of embarrassment and self-consciousness.

Fortunately, there has been a considerable amount of research on motor skills in the adolescent period. At several child study centers, results have been reported based on longitudinal studies, in which the same children were tested, measured, and observed year after year. This type of investigation has many advantages over the more common *cross-sectional* investigation, in which different age groups are tested at the same time. We can be more confident that the differences we find are really growth changes rather than accidental or chance variations in the samples we happen to get at the different ages. [5]

Espenschade [6] reports the scores made on a series of tests of motor abilities at successive half-year intervals by about seventy-five children of each sex during the period extending from the thirteenth birthday to the age of sixteen and one-half years. Figures 83 to 86 show the results obtained in each of four common athletic performances. Figure 87 shows the findings on a composite test of motor ability devised by Brace. [7] These graphs show that boys continue to improve in athletic skill throughout the adolescent years covered by the study. Girls, however, show little if any improvement.

The situation is somewhat different with regard to fine motor skills such as reaction-time, eye-hand co-ordination, and steadiness. Figures 88 and 89 show in graphic form results obtained by H. E. Jones. [8] There is a steady improvement for both boys and girls in skills of this type, and in some of them girls show a slight superiority. These sex differences will be discussed in more detail in a later section.

The fine motor skills tend to be specific and independent of one another. A person may be very quick in his reaction time but only mediocre on co-ordination or steadiness tests. For the large muscle

[5] In actual practice, this statement does not always hold good. Because of the long period of time over which such studies must extend, some cases are almost inevitably lost from the original group as a result of moving from the community, death, loss of interest in the project, and so on. If, as sometimes happens, the cases that drop out differ in some systematic fashion from those that remain, and if all available cases are used at each age, the sampling error of a longitudinal study may even be greater than is likely to occur in a well-conducted cross-sectional study. If, on the other hand, only those cases retained to the end of the study are used in the age comparisons, the process of elimination may have left only a highly select group, no longer representative of the general population from which it was originally drawn.

[6] A. Espenschade. Motor performance in adolescence. *Monogr. Soc. Res. Child Develpm.*, 1940, No. 5.

[7] D. K. Brace. *Measuring motor ability.* New York: Barnes, 1927.

[8] H. E. Jones. *Motor performance and growth.* Berkeley: Univ. of California Press, 1949.

50-YARD DASH

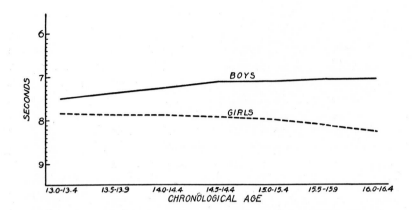

FIGURE 83. Age and sex differences in speed on the 50-yard dash. (Reproduced with slight modification from Anna Espenschade. *Motor performance in adolescence.* Courtesy of the author and the Society for Research in Child Development.)

BROAD JUMP

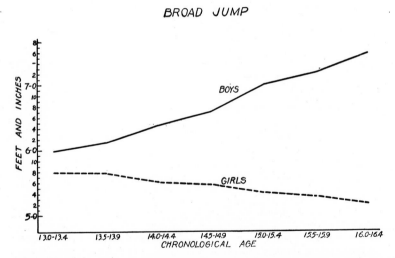

FIGURE 84. Age and sex differences in performance on the broad jump. (Reproduced with slight modification from Anna Espenschade. *Motor performance in adolescence.* Courtesy of the author and the Society for Research in Child Development.)

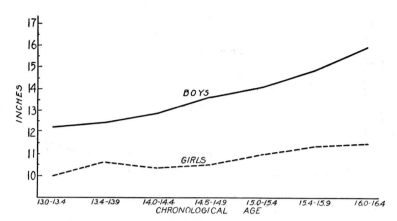

JUMP AND REACH

FIGURE 85. Age and sex differences in performance on the "jump and reach" test. (Reproduced with slight modification from Anna Espenschade. *Motor performance in adolescence.* Courtesy of the author and the Society for Research in Child Development.)

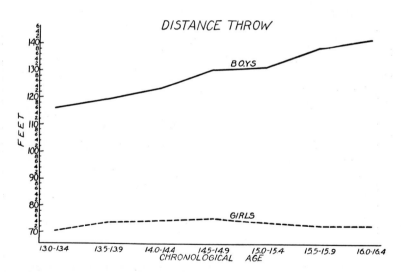

DISTANCE THROW

FIGURE 86. Age and sex differences in performance on the distance throw. (Reproduced with slight modification from Anna Espenschade. *Motor performance in adolescence.* Courtesy of the author and the Society for Research in Child Development.)

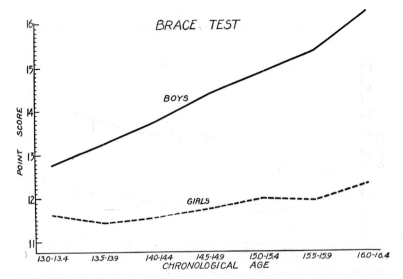

FIGURE 87. Age and sex differences in scores on the brace test of motor abilities. (Reproduced with slight modification from Anna Espenschade. *Motor performance in adolescence.* Courtesy of the author and the Society for Research in Child Development.)

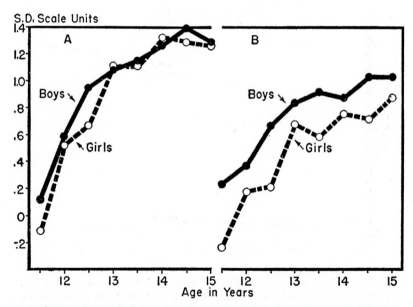

FIGURE 88. Growth curves for (A) reaction time to sound and (B) spatial eye-hand co-ordination. (From H. E. Jones and R. H. Seashore. The development of fine motor and mechanical abilities. *Adolescence,* Forty-third Yearbook, National Society for the Study of Education, 1944. Courtesy of Univ. of Chicago Press.)

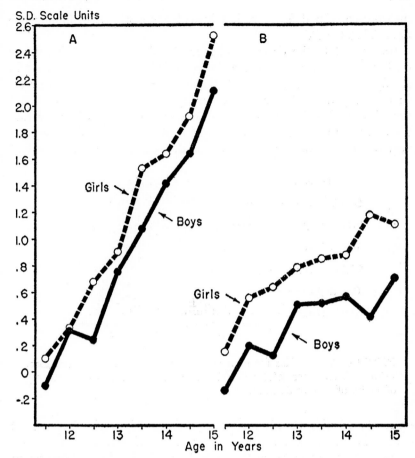

FIGURE 89. Growth curves for (A) serial discrimination and (B) manual steadiness. (From H. E. Jones and R. H. Seashore. The development of fine motor and mechanical abilities. *Adolescence*, Forty-third Yearbook, National Society for the Study of Education, 1944. Courtesy of Univ. of Chicago Press.)

activities, however, Jones has shown that a common factor of strength is important in all of them. He selected from his experimental group in one of the California longitudinal studies two subgroups representing contrasting extremes of strength. The strong boys were considerably above average for all the kinds of athletic skills measured. The weak boys were consistently below average. (See Figure 90.)

This fact is important to us in understanding adolescents because of the relationship of strength and athletic skill to popularity and success among adolescent boys. The California studies show that a strength measure correlated far more highly with popularity than intelligence or social status did.

In contrast to the dramatic changes in physical status that occur during adolescence, mental development follows a course of smooth, steady improvement, becoming less and less marked from year to year. In the early days of intelligence testing it was thought that mental growth ceased at fifteen or sixteen. More recent studies indicate that there are continued increases up to at least twenty, but that they are very slight in the latter part of the period. They depend to some extent

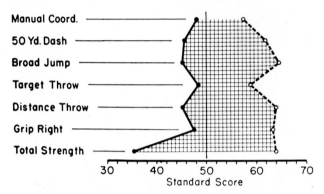

FIGURE 90.   Profiles for contrasting groups in motor performance. (From H. E. Jones. *Motor performance and growth.* 1949. Courtesy of Univ. of California Press.)

on continued education. Lorge [9] showed that children who dropped out of school in the early high school years were inferior when tested several years later to classmates of the same initial level who had continued their schooling.

The mental development that occurs during adolescence may not show up as large increments on intelligence test scores, but, as Piaget [10] has pointed out, it does produce the stage at which real abstract thinking is possible, thinking that involves the manipulation of higher-order abstract concepts in logic, mathematics, or philosophy. This kind of thinking does not come as a completely new phenomenon. In unusually bright children it may appear at the age of eight, nine, or ten, as followers of the Quiz Kids or $64,000 question program are well aware. In those of below average intelligence it may never occur at all. But the fact that this is the period in which real abstract thinking first becomes possible for the majority of boys and girls has important im-

[9] I. Lorge. Schooling makes a difference. *Teach. Coll. Rec.,* 1945, 46, 483-492.
[10] J. Piaget. *The psychology of intelligence.* London: Routledge and Kegan Paul, 1950.

plications for education. Secondary education is different from primary education in quality as well as in difficulty.

Along with the increases in size, skill, and intellectual capacity, rapid and complex changes in the physiological systems of the body (the person's "internal environment") lead to emotional states that show up in various ways in behavior. Shock [11] has commented that adolescence may be regarded as a period of "physiological learning." The person must not only learn to cope with the increased sexual drive that comes with the glandular changes accompanying sexual maturation but must also adapt himself to sudden changes in metabolism and circulation that occur without his knowledge. Is it any wonder that an individual may show more moodiness and emotional flareups during the adolescent period than he does in earlier and later stages of his development?

INDIVIDUAL DIFFERENCES IN GROWTH

The aspect of adolescent development that produces more adjustment problems than any other is its variability from person to person. Because of the enormous variation in the ages at which the biological growth changes begin and end and in the rates at which they occur, children of very different levels of development are thrown together for school and leisure time activities. Plans made for one will not suit another, and to work out some master plan that would meet the needs of all the individuals in this age group would be a really formidable undertaking.

There are, first of all, the sex differences. As has been mentioned earlier, girls experience the pre-adolescent period of accelerated growth and reach maturity about two years sooner, on the average, than boys do. This means that in every junior high school there are many girls who are ready for grown-up kinds of social activity and who look with disfavor on the majority of the "little boys" who are their age mates. At first glance it might appear that this problem could be solved by allowing girls to advance more rapidly in school and reach the senior high school at an earlier age than boys do. This idea would not work, however, because of the lack of relationship between mental and physical growth rates. Mentally the average twelve-year-old girl is no more advanced than the average twelve-year-old boy. However grown-up she may look, she does not belong in a ninth grade curriculum.

Furthermore, within each sex there is tremendous variation. As has been mentioned earlier, there is a range of several years in the in-

[11] N. W. Shock. Physiological changes in adolescence. In *Adolescence: 43rd Yearbook N.S.S.E.* Chicago: Univ. of Chicago Press, 1944.

dividual ages at which puberty is reached. Figure 91 illustrates the magnitude of the difference between two fourteen-year-old boys who might be sitting side by side in any eighth- or ninth-grade classroom, both perfectly normal in their development.

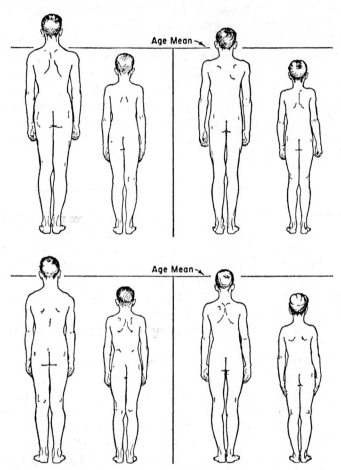

FIGURE 91.   Comparison of four pairs of boys at age 14. (From H. E. Jones. *Motor performance and growth.* 1949. Courtesy of Univ. of California Press.)

In one of the California growth studies, M. C. Jones and Bayley [12] have made a special study of psychological differences between the early and late maturing adolescents. The most interesting finding is that the effects are different for the two sexes. Boys who mature early, ad-

[12] M. C. Jones and N. Bayley. Physical maturing among boys as related to behavior. *J. educ. Psychol.*, 1950, 41, 129-148.

vanced as they are in the strength and skill that make for athletic prowess, tend to be popular and successful leaders in school activities. Boys who mature late, even if they have been well regarded by their classmates in elementary school, often have adjustment difficulties in high school. For girls the effect is in the opposite direction. It is the early maturers who fall behind in popularity and prestige. The late maturers experience more acceptance and recognition.

In addition to these differences between groups of adolescents, there are innumerable individual differences in growth pattern, idiosyncracies that may be very disturbing to the persons themselves. Thrown together as they are with their age mates for large portions of each day, children become acutely aware of individual characteristics that set them off from the others. In one California study, Stolz and Stolz [13] found that at least 31 per cent of the boys and 41 per cent of the girls had suffered some anxiety about their physical characteristics. For a boy, the source of the discomfort might be small size, fatness, lack of strength, or acne. For a girl it might be large size, heaviness, facial features, or small breasts. Many other things that bothered one or more persons are listed by these authors.

While individual differences are a universal phenomenon it seems likely that at adolescence they constitute a more important source of unfortunate by-products, such as social maladjustments and inferiority feelings, than they do at other ages. Perhaps more awareness among children themselves of the wide range that normality covers would help them to accept with less anxiety their own unique patterns of progress toward maturity.

THE SOCIAL SITUATION OF THE ADOLESCENT

The special psychological characteristics that accompany adolescence are only partly accounted for by the biological changes occurring during the period. The child in this intermediate age group finds himself in a social situation that is in many ways difficult to cope with. We can describe his progress toward maturity in terms of the adjustment he makes to this situation as well as to his own maturing body.

Barker and associates [14] have described the life space of the adolescent in terms of *overlapping situations*. At some times and in some settings he must play the role of an adult. At other times and in other settings he is expected to act like a child. He feels pressure upon him

[13] H. R. Stolz and L. M. Stolz. Adolescent problems related to somatic variations. In *Adolescence: 43rd Yearbook N. S. S. E.* Chicago: Univ. of Chicago Press, 1944.
[14] R. G. Barker, B. A. Wright, L. Meyerson, M. R. Gonick. *Adjustment to physical handicap and illness.* (2nd Ed.) New York: Social Science Research Council, 1953.

to be independent, but when he tries to act in an independent manner, the behavior may lead him into difficulties. It is no wonder that adolescent behavior sometimes appears changeable and inappropriate. It takes time to come to terms with overlapping situations and one can expect many false moves and emotional upsets while the process is going on.

The child's relationship with his parents is complicated by this factor. The boy who has suddenly shot up in height until he is almost as tall as his father looks in the glass and says to himself, "Now I am a man." And he expects people to treat him as a man. But his childish habits still have him in their grip. He borrows his father's neckties and fusses about the crease in his trousers, but he neglects to wash his ears. He wants to drive the family car, but he cannot remember to keep the garage door locked. He spends his allowance for ice-cream and candy and has nothing left for more important needs. He wants to be independent, to look after himself and manage his own affairs, but his old childish habits of expecting somebody else to take the real responsibility continually get him into trouble. Like Alice in Wonderland, he is grown up one minute, and the next minute he is a child again.

The adolescent is not the only one who has to form new habits as a result of his growing up. His parents are faced with the same problem. All his life they have been used to watching over him, making decisions for him, demanding obedience from him in little matters as well as in greater ones. Now the time is coming when they must relax their hold in preparation for the time when it must be relinquished completely. This is not easy. It is made more difficult by the fact that there is no hard and fast rule concerning the time when parental control shall come to an end. Although legally a parent's control ceases when the boy or girl comes of age, which in most states is at twenty-one years, many young people are still in college and financially dependent upon their parents at that time, and it is perhaps not unnatural for parents to feel that personal and financial dependence should go together. Even after the child is earning his own living, the old habits of parental dominance may still hold sway. Particularly for the mother whose whole life has been given up to her children is it difficult to let them go and live lives of their own in which she will play a much smaller part.

The conflict between old habits and new requirements—represented on the part of the adolescent by his feeling that he is grown up, that he wants to be treated like a grownup, while he still has habits of acting like a child, and on the parents' side by their recognition that the child is growing up, their feeling that he ought to act more like a grownup, although from force of habit they continue to treat him as if he were still a child—often makes for a good deal of friction. This friction can be greatly lessened if both parties realize that they have a definite kind of adjustment to make in which old habits have to be broken up and replaced by new ones. The adolescent has to stop acting like a child and behave like a grownup. The parent has to stop treating him as a child and permit him adult freedom, responsibilities, and privileges. If each will bear in mind that no habit is overcome all at once and that occasional lapses into the old ways must be expected, much of the irritation that is otherwise likely to result from the fact that the old ways of doing things still crop out now and then will disappear. A good deal of tolerance is needed on both sides.

Another aspect of the adolescent's social situation that may make life particularly difficult for him at this time is that when he enters a large high school he comes into contact with a wide range of attitudes, customs, and value systems all at once. There has, of course, been a sudden expansion of the individual's social world at the time he entered grade school. But often a grade school, located in the part of town where he lives, represents families fairly similar to his own. A large metropolitan high school draws students from both "sides of the tracks," from city, suburb, and farm, and from all ethnic and religious groups in the area. The young person may suddenly be made painfully aware that there are many kinds of people with attitudes and standards greatly different from those his family has held up to him. And he is expected to come to terms with this diversity somehow.

The special problem that has been most thoroughly studied is that of social status. In spite of our American ideals of equality and democracy, many (if not all) communities are organized along social class lines. Cliques form within this framework. Upper-class girls do not date lower-class boys. Representatives of the upper middle class tend to capture the principal leadership positions in school organizations. A book by Hollingshead [15] gives a detailed account of the way these class distinctions work in one Midwestern town.

It is the representatives of the lower socio-economic classes who are most likely to be made acutely unhappy by this situation. A child belonging to a minority race, ethnic, or religious group may have even more serious problems to contend with. In earlier times, the most common solution for persons in this position was to drop out of school. With changes in compulsory school laws this has become increasingly difficult in many states.

Increasing awareness of this problem is leading to better ways of dealing with it. Social barriers are man-made and not inevitable. It seems likely that they are much more formidable in some communities

[15] A. Hollingshead. *Elmtown's youth.* New York: Wiley, 1949.

than in others. Sargent, [16] for example, describes a California community where class-consciousness does not appear to be very strong. There is evidence that in this town athletic prowess, intelligence, or good looks often count for more than social position in high school leadership. The person from a lower class background starts with a handicap in many areas of American society, but it is one that can be overcome.

The bad effects of restrictive cliques on excluded individuals should not lead us to condemn all informal adolescent social groups. They seem to constitute a very valuable part of the life experience of the participants. For one thing, they serve as protection for a time from the confusing pressures of the larger society in which the young person is not yet ready to take his place. Each member of the group draws strength and courage from his like-minded companions. When this strength and courage is directed into a conflict with society and its laws, as in delinquent gangs, the results are obviously unhappy, but when it goes into constructive activities it is extremely useful.

Another purpose served by adolescent peer groups is to make possible a great deal of learning of social skills. Belonging to a group makes it easier for each member to put up with the awkwardness that marks initial efforts in dating, carrying on conversations with strangers, or applying cosmetics, just as it does one's initial stages in the learning of any skill. Much of the apparent "silliness" in the behavior of adolescents, a quality especially likely to exasperate adults, can be viewed as a part of this social learning.

Peer groups also provide an intermediate stage in the attainment of independence from one's family. It may seem for a time as though such independence as is achieved is a small gain if the person shifts into slavish submission to peculiar and irrational customs, such as ducktail haircuts and "rock and roll" dances. But conformity to these standards and requirements is in most cases only a transitional stage. In entering it the person leaves behind many of the dependent attitudes of his childhood. He emerges from it into a state far closer to real maturity.

Unquestionably the influence of his associates upon the way the adolescent thinks and acts is very great; greater, probably than at any previous stage of his life. For the adolescent there can be no stronger argument for behaving or doing a thing than the fact that "all the others are doing it." Nothing is likely to awaken so great an emotional disturbance or cause so much worry as the feeling that he is in some way different from the others. "Others" in this case, means

[16] S. S. Sargent. Class and class-consciousness in a California town. *Social Problems*, 1953, 1, 23-27.

the other members of his own particular group; he is not especially concerned about resembling those belonging to some other clan. A fashion started by the leaders of a group, even though it may happen to be uncomfortable or inconvenient, is faithfully copied by all the lesser members. Opinions, prejudices, beliefs, likes, and dislikes are likewise determined by the group, and the boy or girl who differs is made to feel the force of group ostracism unless he has sufficient force of personality to bring the others around to his point of view. Mastery, conformity, or exclusion—these are the social alternatives with which the adolescent is faced, and no half-way measures are possible. Organizations such as the Scouts, the Campfire Girls, the junior Y.M.C.A. and Y.W.C.A. are doing a good deal to capitalize the group interests of the adolescent and to mold the attitudes of the individual by tactful modifications of the standards of the group. Those who teach or direct adolescents are convinced that it is better to work with their peer groups than to condemn them.

THE SEARCH FOR PERSONAL IDENTITY

To think of adolescence purely in terms of *adjustment* to pressures from within and without would be to miss an important part of its significance. In the important book to which we have referred several times, *Childhood and Society*, Erikson [17] described the basic challenge the adolescent faces as a demand that he develop an identity of his own. This means that he must find out who he is and where he belongs. Several of the more limited developmental tasks outlined by Havighurst and other students of adolescence can best be understood as aspects of this more basic identity-seeking process.

Success with such a search seems to depend on several things. For one thing, the individual must *accept willingly*, even proudly, the limiting factors that surround one's own life. The most fundamental of these is one's own sex.

It has been recognized for a long time that sexual development is an important feature of adolescence. For some time, the emphasis was on the biological drive itself, its imperious demands, and the problems that may arise because of the necessity of deferring or limiting sex satisfaction until maturity. This is a problem with which all adolescents must contend, and they handle it in ways that vary from one cultural group to another, from one period to another, and from one person to another. Individual differences both with regard to the strength of the drive and the methods for controlling it complicate the picture.

During the 1930's, the attention of research workers was focused

[17] E. H. Erikson. *Op. cit.* New York: Norton, 1950.

on masculinity-femininity as a pervasive over-all trait that showed up in many kinds of attitude and behavior. The most inclusive study was the one by Terman and Miles. [18] They tabulated the responses many groups of males and females of different ages and educational levels made to various kinds of items commonly found on personality tests, items having to do with interests, general information, associations to words and to ink blots, and emotional attitudes. By putting together into one inventory the items for which there were clear-cut sex differences, they constructed an M-F test. The new test was given to many boys and girls, men and women, and attempts were made to find out what kinds of things this personality trait was related to. As might be expected, masculinity scores for boys and femininity scores for girls reach their peak during adolescence. As groups, boys and girls get markedly different total scores, but individuals in each sex group also differ quite widely from one another. The attempts to define clearly what these differences mean have not been altogether successful. Scores are not very closely related to masculinity or femininity in either appearance or behavior. They show some relationship to occupational interests and choice, to age, education, and cultural level, but the correlations are not very high.

During the 1950's, the research emphasis shifted to the problem of sex *roles* and the means by which individuals come to accept or reject them. It is this emphasis that is closely tied in with the more general problem of ego [19] identity. What is perhaps more significant than any general *trait* of masculinity-femininity is the set of roles an individual sees as appropriate for males or for females, and the extent to which he or she accepts one of these roles as an organizing factor in his or her own life. The M-F scores obtained from the Terman-Miles test or from the other personality tests for which special M-F keys have been constructed may tell us something about a person's concepts of sex roles and the way he relates himself to them.

The fact that in our complex and rapidly changing society there is a good deal of confusion about what the sex roles are makes things more difficult for adolescents. Can Bill put his energy into writing music rather than playing basketball without branding himself as a sissy? Is it unfeminine for Lucille to major in mathematics, a subject for which she shows marked aptitude? Questions like this must be faced again and again as an individual considers his or her identity.

---

[18] L. M. Terman and C. C. Miles. *Sex and personality.* New York: McGraw-Hill, 1936.

[19] The term *ego* is used in the psychoanalytic sense to refer to the part or aspect of the personality that meets and copes with the realities of the person's internal and external world. It is roughly synonymous with the term *self*.

It is easy to say that acceptance of one's own sex is a requirement. It is far from easy to put such acceptance into practice.

Other limiting realities present some of the same problems. A Negro must accept his race. A crippled child must accept his disability. Each person has a unique set of realities he must accept if his sense of selfhood is to rest on a solid foundation.

The second means by which a person attains a clear identity of his own is *identification*. We have seen in an earlier chapter how this begins at the preschool level when the little girl identifies with her mother and the boy with his father. The earliest concepts of sex roles have their origin here, as well as the internalization of standards of conduct that will become conscience. As the child moves out into the neighborhood, school, and community, he encounters other persons with whom he finds it easy to identify. Favorite teachers, aunts and uncles, scoutmasters and camp counselors, older boys and girls—the possibilities for identification are numerous and varied. After a child learns to read and to follow movies and television shows, he may identify with heroes and heroines he encounters in these imaginary realms. Of all the human beings he encounters, the ones a child chooses to identify with have an influence on his development that is far greater than the influence the others exert. Identification is more than piecemeal imitation. It is a sort of total attempt to act, feel, and be like the other person in every way.

People identify with groups too. The word probably carries a somewhat different meaning here, but about the process itself there is little doubt. A boy or girl's major identification may be with Scouts or 4-H Club.

The problem an adolescent faces is to merge these identification experiences through which he has come into one unified self. In some ways it is like the making of a composite portrait out of many negatives superimposed upon one another. But it is in essence a more active process than this. The mature person is not just a replica of the persons with whom he has identified. He is a genuine new model.

The third process leading to the attainment of one's own identity is the making of life decisions and commitments. Adolescence is the period when many of the most important choices of one's life must be made. Whether or not to continue in school, which college to attend, what career to embark upon, whether to marry now or wait until later—all these major issues confront the teen-ager. The *way* in which the decisions are made may be as important for identity formation as just what they are. Some adolescents act as though they had unconsciously chosen *not to choose*. They drift through high school and college doing the things that seem easiest at the time or the things others are doing. But even these persons who do not see themselves as decision makers are unconsciously moulding their own lives into the shapes they will take in the years to come. Identity rests on choices, conscious or unconscious.

The fourth kind of process that leads to a mature sense of identity is the putting together of a coherent philosophy of life. For some boys and girls this involves a religious experience and a commitment to the way of life represented by a church. For others it is a more individual matter, as the person sorts out from all the values and beliefs to which he has been exposed the ones that really matter to him. The long and involved "bull sessions" that occur among college students seem to facilitate this sorting process in many cases. In this area as in the one that involves practical decisions, it would appear that many individuals do not make their choices consciously. They find themselves going to their parents' church or acting in accordance with a set of principles without knowing just where or when the guiding pattern took shape. The amount of inner struggle and soul-searching that precedes the formation of a mature value system varies enormously from person to person. But the system itself is basic to ego identity, however it came into being.

In listing these four processes separately—acceptance of limiting factors, identification, decision making, and value formation—we do not mean to suggest that they are independent of one another or that they go on separately. Each is tied in with the others. Values help to determine career decisions, and vice versa. Both values and decisions arise out of identifications. Acceptance of one's own limiting characteristics is a part of decision making and is both a cause and an effect of the development of values. It is probably true that a change in any one of these four factors affects all the others.

The development of ego identity does not end with adolescence. It may well continue throughout all the rest of life. But the surer the foundation that is laid during this period, the more likely it is that the individual will be able to withstand unsettling experiences, to choose wisely among courses of action available to him, and to elaborate and enrich his own philosophy. In a very real sense, identity is the *crucial problem* of adolescence.

SUMMARY

Adolescence is defined as the period of transition from childhood to adulthood. It is characterized by a number of distinct developmental tasks. The person is faced, first of all, with the necessity of coming to terms with a rapidly changing, often unstable body. Typically there is a preadolescent growth spurt which brings marked changes in height and weight. Large motor skills improve in boys but not very much in girls. Fine motor skills show improvement in both sexes. There are marked individual differences in age of puberty and the accompanying physical changes. On the average, girls mature about two years younger than boys. Early maturing boys are more likely to be popular and successful than are the late maturing, but the reverse is true for girls.

The adolescent must also learn to find his way around in a social situation much more complex than any he has heretofore known. His marginal status as part child, part adult leads to difficulties in his relationships with parents and other grownups. The contacts with classmates from many subcultures are often unsettling. Social status differences become very apparent to a person of this age. Informal peer groups seem to ease some social tensions for the individual and enable him to learn new social skills and attitudes.

The pre-eminent challenge to the adolescent is to develop a clear sense of his own identity. Acceptance of limiting factors, especially one's sex, identification with individuals and groups, the making of important life decisions, and the construction of a personal philosophy all contribute to this process.

THE STORY OF AN ADOLESCENT BOY

JONES, Harold E. *Development in adolescence*. New York: Appleton-Century-Crofts, 1943.

This is the story of John Sanders, a boy of about average ability, who grew up in an ordinary type of home in a middle-class neighborhood. Perhaps John had greater difficulty than most boys in meeting the new social requirements that come with adolescence, but certainly his problems were of a kind that many boys and girls experience. The report shows in detail the methods used by the author and his colleagues at the University of California for studying growth and behavior during the adolescent period. It is illustrated by a large number of graphs that demonstrate the many changes in skills, interests, and personality characteristics that took place in John between the ages of eleven and eighteen years. After reading it you should have a much clearer idea than you are now likely to have of the methods used by psychologists for studying children, and you will also gain a keener appreciation and understanding of the difficulties with which many adolescents have to cope.

CHAPTER 20

What developmental task is most characteristic of early adulthood?

What justification is there for considering college students to be adults rather than adolescents?

In what ways do college students as a group differ from noncollege people of the same age?

What are some of the most important causes of failure in college?

What can a slow reader do to increase his rate of reading?

How can one improve his comprehension of what he reads?

What is the relationship between needs and motives?

In what way does Maslow's theory of motivation differ from previous "need" theories?

How do self-concepts affect motivation?

What do scores on vocational interest tests show about a person?

Do personality changes occur during the college years? If so, what kind?

>> >> >> >> >> >> >> >> >> >>

Early Adulthood: College Years

CHARACTERISTICS OF THE PERIOD

LIKE THE LIFE STAGES that have preceded it, the beginning of adult life brings its special tasks, its special challenges. The person is for the first time "on his own." He must find a place where he can work, take on responsibilities, such as the support of a family, begin to play an active part in community and civic affairs. This does not, of course, happen all at once. It is convenient to distinguish between an exploratory and an establishment stage, but no definite line can be drawn between them.

Until recently this period has not received very much study from psychologists or sociologists. A few specialists in manpower problems were always interested in the means by which a person finds his place in the occupational structure. A few specialists in marriage and the family tried to find out how families get started. The persons who are unsuccessful in carrying through the developmental tasks of this period, the dependent and the maladjusted, have always demanded society's attention. During the 1940's and 1950's, however, considerable research effort has been focused on the adult years. Follow-up studies of groups first studied in childhood, such as Terman's group of gifted children, career pattern studies in occupational sociology, intensive research on the family, and detailed accounts of individual lives as they reveal themselves in therapeutic interviews—these and many other sources of evidence have helped to give us a more comprehensive picture of the early adult period—its goals, its rewards, and its hazards.

Many would question whether the college years ought to be included in this period. Are they not, rather, the last phase of adolescence? Certainly panty raids and water fights do not suggest adulthood. Certainly there is much in college life that marks it as a transition period in the passage from childhood to maturity. As we have said before, development is not characterized by hard and fast lines. Stages merge into one another.

College as an institution, however, is basically designed for adults, and students who enter without realizing this fact often find themselves in difficulties. Furthermore, an increasing proportion of college students, in this second half of the twentieth century, are young men and women who are already carrying adult responsibilities. Many of them are married; many are entirely self-supporting; many have behind them a period of military service. For these people, college is not just preparation for life. It *is* life.

To make the most of college requires that one possess an awareness of his own identity as discussed in our last chapter—that he know what his basic choices are, and that he accept the realistic limits within which he must operate. Clear purposes and mature motivation are needed in college perhaps more than anywhere else. What the college years offer, however, is a little more time to develop these qualities. College life can be considered as *both* an extension of adolescence and the beginning of adulthood. The emphasis is on the adult side.

WHO GOES TO COLLEGE?

College plays a part in the lives of only a minority of the population, but in the United States this is a rapidly growing minority. In 1900 the number of college graduates amounted to only 1.7 per cent of all persons reaching the age of twenty-two in that year. By 1953 the comparable figure was 12 per cent, even when the veterans (who do not represent the same population trends since they are making up for lost time) are excluded. There is every indication that this increase will continue. Many educational experts anticipate that the fraction of the population obtaining some college training may soon be as high as one-third.

Most of the educators who have considered this matter (and it has been considered at length because of America's need for specialized professional men and women) do not anticipate that the proportion of our young people who go to college will ever approximate 100 per cent. For there is one way in which college students as a group differ from their noncollege age-mates. They are more intelligent.

Figure 92, taken from a thorough analysis of these issues by Wolfle, [1] shows graphically how at each successive educational level the total number of students (represented by the area under the curve) decreases, and the average intelligence level (represented by the figure on the horizontal base line over which the peak falls) increases. In Figure 93 we see that the same trend continues in college. Those who complete two years are a little brighter than the total group of those who enter. Those who graduate are a little brighter than those who

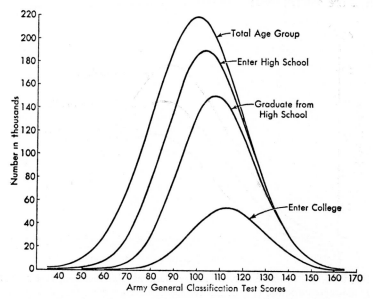

FIGURE 92. Distribution of Army General Classification Test scores of all members of an age group and of those reaching several educational levels. (From D. Wolfle. *America's resources of specialized talent.* New York, 1954, p. 144. Courtesy of Harper and Brothers.)

complete only two years. Wolfle uses Army General Classification Test scores as his units for comparison purposes, expressing other kinds of scores in terms of this well-known scale. To get the full meaning of the graphs we should keep in mind that 100 is the score that represents the population average. All but a small proportion (about 10 per cent) of college graduates are above this. Their average AGCT score is 121.

The Wolfle figures show plainly that there is a considerable range of intellectual ability in college students, even though the average of the group is high. One reason for this is that colleges differ in the

[1] D. Wolfle. *America's resources of specialized talent.* New York: Harper, 1954.

ways they have of selecting students. Some depend chiefly upon difficult entrance examinations; others place more emphasis on outstanding
grades in high school; many use combinations of examination and high
school record. But some colleges prefer not to set the standards so
high as to exclude any students who really wish to try. Thus a student
of only average talents can usually find some school that will admit
him. And in many individual cases, as the graphs show, such students
succeed in completing their college work, although the general probabilities are against them.

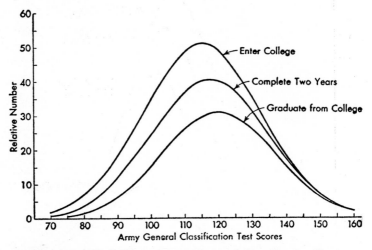

FIGURE 93. Distribution of Army General Classification Test scores
of college students. (From D. Wolfle. *America's resources of specialized talent.* New York, 1954, p. 145. Courtesy of Harper and Brothers.)

By no means all of the persons with college-level intelligence go to
college. In some cases their high school grades are low even though
their ability is high, and they find it difficult to gain admittance. College
admissions officers have found that high school grades are a better
predictor of college success than any kind of test scores. In many cases,
family financial limitations make college plans impossible. In many
cases the desire for college training is missing. A boy may decide to
enter an apprenticeship, a girl may decide to get married, rather than
to seek further academic education. There are consistently more men
than women in college. The proportions run about 60 per cent men,
40 per cent women in the college enrollment.

With the post-Sputnik emphasis on developing the human resources
of our country as fully as possible, there has been increasing concern
about the fact that young people from the lower social levels and

from some minority groups are not likely to reach college even if their abilities are high. There is, of course, a relationship between socio-economic status and intelligence, so that a larger proportion of the children of professional men than of laborers' children have the intellectual qualifications college requires. But if a college professor or a doctor has a son with an IQ of 140, the probability that this boy will go on to college is far greater than that the equally brilliant son of a day laborer will go. Wolfle's figures show that 67 per cent of the children from professional families enter college as compared with 26 per cent of those from laborers' homes. Once they enter, however, students from the less favored cultural backgrounds do at least as well as those from the higher levels of society. Real efforts have been made to reduce inequalities of opportunity by making scholarships available. There are probably differences between the socio-economic groups in attitudes with regard to education also, differences that it may be important for us to understand if we are to make our educational system serve all the people.

FACTORS CONTRIBUTING TO SUCCESS OR FAILURE

Many studies have shown that students vary greatly in the extent to which they succeed in their college work. Some fail miserably and sooner or later drop out; some succeed by taking more than the allotted time; others make brilliant records and graduate with high honors.

In trying to account for these differences we naturally think first of the question of intelligence which we found so important in determining school success among younger children. In college, too, differences in the intelligence of the students account in part for the differences in their academic accomplishment, but nonintellectual factors likewise have a good deal to do with it.

Differences in early preparation play a part. Particularly when they first enter college, students whose high school preparation has been poor are at a disadvantage as compared to their classmates. But if they are intelligent and industrious, this can usually be overcome. However, neither intelligence nor the kind of high school attended can entirely account for all the differences found in the quality of the work done by college students.

Poor health accounts for some failures and for a good many cases of delayed progress. Defective sight or hearing, sometimes unrecognized by the student himself, may cause difficulty. Financial conditions that make it necessary for some students to earn all or part of their expenses impose further strain, particularly with overambitious students who insist upon carrying too heavy a load of class work along with their outside jobs, and who pay the penalty in broken health or low marks.

But although all these things are significant, the fact remains that there are many students of good intelligence and excellent health, not handicapped by lack of funds, who nevertheless fail in their courses, while there are others of less ability who do good work in spite of adverse conditions. Although many factors contribute to these differences in achievement, two are of outstanding importance: differences in study habits and differences in motivation.

Many different kinds of habits and skills can be classified under the study habits category. To a considerable extent good study habits are simply the consistent application of the general principles of learning we have discussed in Chapter 18. There is one special skill, however, that takes on particular importance during the college years. This is *reading*. When great quantities of material from books must be mastered, the rapid reader has a distinct advantage over the slow reader. Differences in reading comprehension enter into achievement differences in practically all the fields of college work.

Great strides were made in our understanding of what goes on when a person reads after E. Javal pointed out in 1878 that the eye does not follow a line of print with a steady sweep but moves in a series of rapid jumps interrupted by pauses during which a fixation occurs. Perception of words and phrases occurs during the fixation pauses, not during the movements. Many studies using a special kind of camera for photographing eye movements showed that rapid readers differed from slow ones in having: (1) a smaller number of fixation pauses per line; (2) a shorter time for each fixation pause; and (3) fewer regressive or backward movements.

It seemed for a time as though these discoveries had opened the way to a simple technique for improving reading speed by training people in correct eye movements. Reading clinics still make use of mechanical devices for forcing subjects to take in a larger number of words at a glance and to avoid backward movements. But the general conclusion that has emerged from research on reading is that faulty eye movements are more the *result* of poor reading than its *cause*. Thus the kind of special practice that is usually recommended now to a person who wishes to step up his reading rate is simply to practice rapid reading directly. He should train his brain to grasp meanings quickly rather than try to train his eyes to move in the proper way. He needs to read *more* so that he gets a larger total amount of practice and he needs to make a definite *effort* to read rapidly. A few minutes spent each day in testing to see how much of the contents of a page of easy fiction can be grasped within a space of time that is considerably shorter than is usually taken for reading a similar amount is a device that many people have found helpful.

Reading speed is perhaps a less important characteristic than the attention it has received would suggest. Some persons who read slowly get great enjoyment from the activity and are very capable students. Some kinds of reading material, such as poems full of symbolic meanings and technical scientific discussions, are meant to be read slowly. The good reader is one who can adapt his approach to the material with which he is dealing and the purpose he has in mind.

Reading *comprehension* is more essential for success in college than a high degree of speed. Training oneself to understand better what one reads is primarily a matter of replacing an attitude of passive receptivity with one of active searching. This means looking for the larger units, the basic structure around which a chapter or an article is organized. It means making outlines that embody this structure, and then checking them against what the author actually said. It means asking oneself questions, and then referring to the printed pages in an effort to judge whether one's answers were correct. (The reason for the questions at the beginning of each chapter in this book is that we wish to encourage this active searching attitude.)

Needless to say, large numbers of students do not proceed in this fashion. They do not *feel* like putting this much active energy into the task of studying. We blame their scholastic difficulties on *lack of motivation*. But just what does this mean? Is it really *lack* of motivation or is it that the *kind* of motivation under which they are operating is not of a sort that leads to school success? Let us take a closer look at this whole complex area of motivation as it shows itself in the young adult.

THE NATURE OF VARIETIES OF MOTIVES

In Chapter 6 we expalined that activity and the striving to which it gives rise are fundamental to life. The psychologist's task is to explain the directions this striving takes in each individual case. We distinguished there between needs, goals, and motives, and defined motive as a wish for some change in one's surroundings that will satisfy an inner need of some kind.

How each person's distinctive pattern of inner needs begins to take shape was explained in Chapter 10. The needs arise not only out of the universal biological drives but also out of the person's exploration of his world and the social interchange with members of his family. Individual differences in the strength of specific motives and the ways in which they are organized into a total pattern are clearly in evidence in earliest childhood. Experience during the school years modifies these patterns and makes them more complex. It must be remembered that a large part of a person's motivational system is unconscious. It operates without his awareness.

It has seemed to many psychologists that in order to understand another person (or ourselves) we must find out what needs are most salient in his life and what their relative strengths are. This approach to the study of personality leads to some sort of catalogue of human needs that can be used to enable us to take an inventory of how much of each one a person possesses. Murray,[2] after an intensive study of a group of college men, presented such a catalogue. Since that time it has been used in hundreds of research projects and clinical studies. Some examples of the needs Murray lists are:

n *Order.* To arrange, organize, put away objects. To be tidy and clean. To be scrupulously precise.

n *Dominance.* To influence or control others. To persuade, prohibit, dictate. To lead and direct. To restrain. To organize the behavior of a group.

n *Deference.* To admire and willingly follow a superior allied person. To co-operate with a leader. To serve gladly.

n *Affiliation.* To form friendships and associations. To greet, join, and live with others. To co-operate and converse socially with others. To love. To join groups.

n *Nurturance.* To nourish, aid, or protect a helpless person. To express sympathy. To "mother" a child.

n *Abasement.* To surrender. To comply and accept punishment. To apologize, confess, atone. Self-depreciation. Masochism.

Even if we were able to measure the strength of all the fundamental needs in a personality, we would still have an imperfect understanding of motivation as it shows itself in behavior. Which needs will come into play in any given situation depends on the circumstances. Furthermore, people learn different ways of satisfying the same need, so that two persons with equally strong n *Affiliation,* for example, may not show it in the same manner. And perhaps most important of all, the different needs on any list we may construct of them are not really parallel to one another. Some must be satisfied *first,* before the others can appear at all. The clearest example of this principle is a need so self-evident that we did not include it in the sample list from Murray's catalogue, the need for food. If it really becomes acute, it is the only motivation the person experiences until he succeeds in satisfying it.

Maslow[3] has stressed the fact that needs differ in what he calls

---

[2] H. Murray. *Explorations in personality.* New York: Oxford Univ. Press, 1938.
[3] A. H. Maslow. *Motivation and personality.* New York: Harper, 1954.

prepotency. The most prepotent ones must be satisfied before those at the next level are felt at all. When they are satisfied, however, they cease for the time being to generate motives, and it is needs at the next level of prepotency that clamor for satisfaction. A fugitive from justice who has not eaten for twenty-four hours or more may be motivated almost entirely by a search for food. But if he finds a dollar bill and buys himself a meal at a restaurant he probably will start being concerned about his position and prospects. Anxiety about being caught, hardly felt at all while the hunger lasted, now becomes acute. If then he happens to read in a newspaper that the police are no longer looking for him because the real culprit has confessed, the need to be with people who love and accept him takes the place of his previous fear.

Maslow's arrangement of the basic needs in the order in which they must be satisfied is as follows:

1. The physiological needs
2. The safety needs
3. The need for belongingness and love
4. The need for importance, respect, self-esteem, independence
5. The need for information
6. The need for understanding
7. The need for beauty
8. The need for self-actualization

Interesting confirmation of this theory about how man is motivated comes from a study by Centers [4] in which 1,100 male adults, a good cross-section of the population, were interviewed. They were questioned about the satisfactions and frustrations they found in their jobs. There were significant differences between white-collar workers and blue-collar workers in the factors they stressed. The manual workers placed more emphasis on security, the professional men on self-expression. A person who knows that he can be laid off tomorrow and realizes the hardships this would entail is strongly motivated to obtain a job he can be absolutely sure of keeping. But the white-collar worker who already has a secure job does not experience the need for security as a motive but feels a need for something more like Maslow's self-actualization.

Whether Maslow's formulation is exactly right or not, this way of thinking about motives often proves practically useful. The action to which it leads is to recognize and satisfy whatever "lower" needs are preventing the appearance of the "higher" ones. In college classrooms, for example, we expect students to be motivated by the needs at

[4] R. Centers. Motivational aspects of occupational stratification. *J. soc. Psychol.*, 1948, 28, 187-217.

Maslow's levels four through eight—information, understanding, beauty, self-actualization. If Henry Burke is not doing at all well, the reason may lie in the fact that his dominant motivation is at one of the lower levels. If Henry is starving or ill, so that it is clear that he is functioning at level one, it is likely that any of his classmates or teachers who finds out about his plight will recognize what his trouble is, help him to get food or medical treatment, and not hold his poor academic record against him. But if his motivation is at level two or three the situation may not be so clear. Neither he nor the persons with whom he is associated in the classroom may realize that he *must* find some way to protect himself against overwhelming anxiety (level two) or find some person or group who will like and accept him (level three) before he can put his effort into anything except a search for these necessities. It is here that psychotherapy of some kind can often help.

The analysis of needs and the means by which people satisfy them has been one way of studying motivation. There is another approach to this complex subject which has proved extremely useful. Instead of examining the separate needs and motives, we can look instead at the person's *self-concept*, the complex picture he has built up of the person he is and is becoming. We have spoken of such concepts in the previous chapter when we discussed the pre-eminent developmental task of adolescence—the attainment of a sense of ego identity. There is increasing evidence that once such a clear self-image has taken shape, it exercises an important motivating influence on all of behavior, taking precedence in many instances over even the most imperious biological needs. To be complete, our theories of motivation must account for *martyrs* as well as workers and customers. It seems possible that what Maslow calls self-actualization is not just another level of need but another kind of influence entirely, affecting behavior in a different way.

We have said that one's identity arises from his acceptance of limitations, the aspects of himself and his circumstances that cannot be changed, from his identifications with persons in and out of his family, and from the choices he makes. As he comes up through childhood and adolescence he tries out many *roles*, some overtly, some only in his imagination. Some of these he rejects as he goes along. Others are incorporated into his constantly developing picture of himself. Jerry comes to see himself primarily as an athlete, with the strength, courage, and healthy competitiveness that seem to him to go with the role. In order to act in accordance with this guiding self-concept he turns down cigarettes and cocktails, and leaves parties early to go home to bed, even though he has a strong need to belong to the group and to be liked. Susan thinks of herself as an artist—sensitive, serious, original. Against the advice of her family and friends, she marries a man with great talent but no financial assets or social position, even though this action goes against her basic needs for safety and belongingness.

At least some of these central identity concepts can be brought to light by means of vocational interest tests. In our kind of society a person's self-concept is quite likely to be expressed in occupational form. When a father in querying his daughter about a man she is going to marry asks, "What does he do?" it is not just the young man's income and schedule of daily activities that are in question. We assume that a business man differs from a college professor, a reporter from an engineer, in many ways, and they see *themselves* as different kinds of people.

Evidence has been accumulating over a considerable period of time that the Strong Vocational Interest Blank is a dependable indicator of motivation. The test consists of a large number of items, to most of which the respondent simply answers *L* (like), *I* (indifferent), or *D* (dislike). The many occupational scoring keys that have been constructed are based on item-by-item tabulations of the responses successful people in the various occupations typically give to these items. The responses given by a group of successful engineers, for example, were tabulated and compared with the responses of a mixed group of men in general. Every item for which there was a signficant difference in the proportions of the two groups marking it *L, I,* or *D* became a part of the Engineer key. When a young man's paper is scored by this key, a high score shows that he has much in common with engineers. His self-concept is in many ways like the one that is typical for this profession. (See Figure 94.)

Such scores have turned out to have a high degree of permanence. Strong [5] found when he readministered the test to men who had first taken it in college as much as twenty years before, that the scores obtained on the second test were in almost all cases very similar to those obtained on the first. Long before a college student actually becomes a member of the medical profession his likes and dislikes have taken on the pattern they will show throughout his long career as a physician. Before a girl knows whom she is going to marry—or indeed, whether she is going to be married at all—her interests will have taken on the characteristic "Housewife" pattern.

Strong has also presented the clearest evidence we have that such attitudes about oneself are important motivating factors in human life.

[5] E. K. Strong, Jr. *Vocational interests eighteen years after college.* Minneapolis: Univ. of Minnesota Press, 1955.

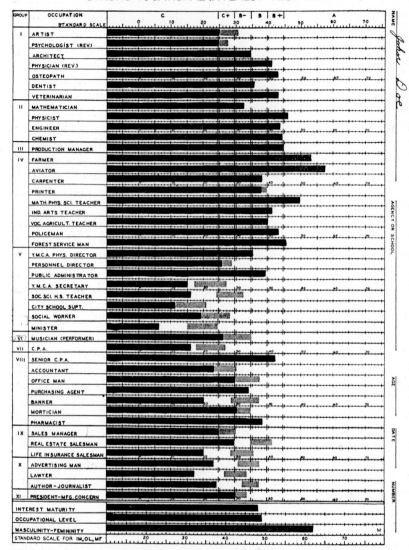

FIGURE 94. An interest profile on the Strong Vocational Interest Blank—engineering interests.

A score obtained on the interest blank in college predicts with considerable accuracy later developments in a person's occupational career. The twenty-year check-up on Stanford University men showed that those who had entered occupations compatible with their scores on the interest blank had in the large majority of cases remained in the original occupation they had chosen. Those who had entered occupations of a different sort from those the interest scores suggested were likely to have shifted to other fields. In many instances the shifts had been in the direction of the interest scores. The follow-up study of a group of gifted children reported by Terman and Oden [6] also produced evidence about these interest patterns. When they compared the least successful with the most successful of these men and women, all of whom had had IQ's of 140 or more in childhood, they found that the unsuccessful had chosen occupations out of line with their Strong scores in a disproportionate number of cases.

Tests like the Strong Vocational Interest Blank and the other interest tests now being widely used in guidance programs do not clarify all the varieties of self-concepts that may be acting as motivating factors in individual lives. There are many types of identity that have little or nothing to do with any occupation and thus do not show up in scores of this kind. Furthermore, there are all degrees of clarity in self-concepts. Many college students, in fact, many persons of all ages, are still confused and uncertain about who they are and the shapes they really wish their lives to take. To examine one's self-picture and organize one's choices and rejections is one way of improving motivation, making it steadier, more dependable, stronger. For any individual it is often more important to decide what in his life is really worth striving for than simply to attempt to put more effort into the thing he happens to be doing, or to meet the separate needs of which he happens to be aware.

This whole discussion of motivation may seem like a long detour branching off from the statement that lack of motivation is one of the most common causes of failure in college. If any justification is needed, it may be found in the fact that most people, students and teachers alike, are unaware of the complexity of motivational states. A rather pathetic student who had been doing very poorly in a general psychology course sought his instructor out during office hours to say "I know I deserve the grades I've been getting. I just don't study. But here I am. Can you motivate me?"

When there is a more general understanding that motivation involves an intricate system of interrelated needs and a complex self-concept

---

[6] L. M. Terman and M. Oden. *The gifted child grows up.* Stanford: Stanford Univ. Press, 1947.

built upon years of choosing, rejecting, and role playing, perhaps our approach to problems of scholastic failure and many other things will be sounder and more likely to bring about constructive change. As things are now, many human beings go through life confused, unsatisfied, and unable to mobilize their energy in the pursuit of meaningful goals. The field of motivation is one of the most challenging of all areas for psychological research.

PERSONALITY DEVELOPMENT DURING COLLEGE YEARS

The parents who send their sons and daughters to college, the professors who plan curricula and courses, and students themselves all assume that college will stimulate intellectual development. That after all is its major purpose. A person who spends four years pursuing knowledge must obviously be better equipped to carry on some kind of intellectual work.

There would be less agreement among educated adults about what colleges can expect to accomplish in the area of personality development. Many psychologists have assumed that the really important personality patterns were shaped in infancy and early childhood; others have considered adolescence to be a critical period but assumed that it was practically over by the time of high school graduation. Many educators who are not psychologists take the position that personality development is not the responsibility of the college. Still others believe that colleges should promote personality growth in students but do not agree about the directions such growth should take.

Because of the scarcity of dependable knowledge as to the kinds of changes in people that are brought about by higher education, the reports from a large scale study initiated in 1952 at Vassar College are of particular interest. [7] Several consecutive entering freshman classes have now been tested, each consisting of more than 400 girls. For comparison purposes, the senior classes are being given the same test battery. As the freshmen in the first group approached graduation, they were tested as seniors, so that changes that had occurred in individuals could be assessed with considerable accuracy. The personality test used consisted of about 1,100 items taken from many kinds of personality measures. Along with the consideration of quantitative differences, the plans call for interview studies to supplement the testing, and clarifying the nature of the changes that are found.

The results show that significant changes do occur in the four-year period. Sanford has grouped them under three main headings. The

[7] N. Sanford. Personality development during the college years. *Personnel Guid. J.,* 1956, 35, 74-80.

first he calls *stabilization of ego identity.* The identity development is not a continuous process proceeding smoothly in one direction. In many ways the seniors are more disturbed, less certain of their direction in life, than the freshmen are. Sanford attributes this to the kind of reorganization that must occur when a person strives to "include more in"—to become a more complex and subtle individual. Seniors are faced with important choices, too, and their attempts to meet these challenges may temporarily disorganize their previous identities.

The second main line of change noted by Sanford is a general *humanizing of values.* Seniors are more flexible, tolerant, rebellious, and unorthodox. They are as a group less willing to accept authority as a basis for beliefs, more independent in their attitudes about many things.

The third and most inclusive kind of change he calls *general ego growth.* The term *ego* is used here as it is in *ego identity* to mean the part of the personality that faces reality and copes with problems without and anxieties within. Seniors show more "neurotic" symptoms than freshmen do. The broadening of interests and liberalization of values may lead to an increase in anxiety. But this is not a handicap if the ego strength needed to cope with it is increasing too.

In another publication, Webster [8] describes some of the changes in measured masculinity-femininity. Three aspects of femininity were considered separately: (1) conventionality, (2) passivity, and (3) feminine sensitivity. On the first two of these seniors score lower than freshmen, thus making them appear more "masculine." But on the third, what slight difference there is suggests an increase in "femininity." What seems to occur is an increase in feminine sensitivity accompanied by an increase in what these investigators have come to call *impulse expression.*

These trends we have been summarizing can certainly not be generalized to all kinds of students in all kinds of colleges. Even among the Vassar girls there are many individual variations; several quite different "subtypes" have already been identified. In a men's college, a coeducational university, or a school with a different kind of intellectual atmosphere or social program, the range of variation would undoubtedly be much wider, and the general trends might be different. The important thing about this study is its demonstration that personality growth occurs during the college years and that it is not simply an improvement in general "adjustment" or the consolidation of patterns and trends laid down in earlier years. It opens the way to similar studies of other institutions, other situations, out of which a better

[8] H. Webster. Some quantitative results. *J. soc. Issues,* 1956, 12, 29-43.

understanding of the processes of personality change in adults may arise.

MAKING THE MOST OF COLLEGE

A student who really wants to use the opportunity college offers him to achieve significant personal growth can think of his task as having two parts or aspects. In the first place he needs to improve his own efficiency so that he can learn as much as possible. This applies to the social and cultural sides of college life as well as to course work. Social skills—dancing, conversation, what to do, say, and wear on various occasions—can be learned through directed practice as study skills are. The person who hears nothing but a confused mass of sound when he listens to a Bach fugue or a Bartok concerto can learn to perceive the structure of the music. College presents a person with time and opportunity to learn the things that will broaden his horizons and enrich the substance of his life.

The other thing a student can do if he wishes to maximize the contribution college can make to his life is consciously to make choices and thus contribute to the shaping of his own identity. As we have said, much of motivation is unconscious, and a person must always be activated to a considerable extent by needs that cannot be ignored. There are always limits to the amount of choice that is possible. One cannot choose to deny the existence of the sex drive or the hunger for human companionship without creating repressions that shackle personality. One cannot choose to be a member of a sex or a racial group to which he does not belong. The short man, the plain girl must come to terms with their physical limitations (although there are many things they can do to make them less apparent). But within such limits, there is always an area where choice is possible. The person who can take the helm of his own life and steer it in the direction he wishes to go will *get* more from his college experience. He will also *make* more out of life.

SUMMARY

Early adulthood is the period in which a person is faced with the task of establishing himself. College students are in a marginal group, in some ways still adolescents, in many ways adults. The emphasis is on maturity.

College students as a group are definitely above average in general intelligence. They have in the past come predominantly from middle and upper socio-economic levels, but there is an increasing emphasis on encouraging capable young people from all social classes to attend.

Failure in college is most commonly caused by inadequate intellectual ability, but it may arise from a variety of other causes, many of them remediable. Slow readers can increase their speed by timing and testing themselves. Comprehension can be improved by the application of general learning principles to the study situation. An active, searching attitude makes for success. What is often described as "lack of motivation" usually means a pattern of motivation unsuitable for college tasks.

Motives can be thought of as learned ways of satisfying basic needs or as expressions of individual self-concepts. Maslow has classified needs in terms of their prepotency. Those at lower levels must usually be satisfied before those at higher levels can have any influence. At least some aspects of the self-concepts that motivate behavior can be identified by means of vocational interest tests. Scores on one of these tests have been shown to predict whether or not a person will stay in the occupation he chose during his college years.

A large-scale study at Vassar College has shown that personality changes do occur between the freshman and senior years. Girls develop richer, more complex patterns of ego identity, more humanistic and liberal values. Greater sensitivity along with greater freedom to express impulses distinguishes seniors from freshmen.

There is much that a college student himself can do to enrich his college years.

CHANGES IN ADULTHOOD—A BIOGRAPHICAL APPROACH

WHITE, R. W. *Lives in progress.* New York: Dryden, 1952.

While novelists and playwrights have given us many impressive portraits of all kinds of people, most case studies made by psychologists have been of individuals abnormal enough in some way to require psychiatric treatment. White's book is a refreshing change. He gives a careful, sympathetic, complete account of the lives of some normal people, showing how they reacted to circumstances and how they changed as time passed. It makes interesting reading and throws new light on the question of how personality develops during the early adult years.

CHAPTER 21

What distinction can be made between adulthood and maturity?

What kinds of characteristics distinguish the truly mature person?

What factors help to determine a person's choice of a particular occupation?

What differences are there in "career patterns" for persons at different occupational levels?

What psychological principles are important in maintaining efficiency?

What are the most important factors upon which marital happiness depends?

Do people who are opposites usually attract each other?

How do adult friendships and social activities differ from those of adolescents?

Adulthood: The Twenties and Thirties

THE MEANING OF MATURITY

IT IS NOT DIFFICULT to specify what we mean by adulthood. By the time a person is twenty, physical growth has practically ended. Intellectual growth may still be occurring, but at a very much slower rate than it did in his earlier years. In many cases formal education has been completed; in others it has taken on an adult pattern, different from the schooling of children. At twenty-one the status of adulthood is legally conferred upon a person when he is allowed to vote for the first time.

Maturity is a much more elusive concept and it is not easy to specify precisely what we mean by it. It means more than physical, intellectual, and legal "growing-up," and it often takes many years to attain. Psychological maturity, in the broad sense, involves the total personality, as indicated in the familiar words of St. Paul to the Corinthians: "When I was a child I spake as a child, I understood as a child, I thought as a child, but when I became a man I put away childish things."

It is this "putting away of childish things," of *feeling* oneself to be an adult, ready to assume adult responsibilities and take one's place in the world of men and women, that marks the boundary between the youth and the man, between the girl and the woman. Some reach this point early, some not until much later. Some never really attain it. But maturity, like every other stage in the growth process, is essential

425

for a healthy life. Without experiencing it to the full, in all its phases and aspects, one misses many of life's chief satisfactions. The period reaching from the twenties to the forties is a time of exploration and establishment. For many individuals it is the richest, most rewarding period of life.

Psychologists have tried, with only partial success, to put into some concrete terms the meaning of a term they use a great deal, *emotional maturity*. Willoughby [1] collected a considerable number of statements having to do with this characteristic and then asked clinical psychologists, social workers, and psychiatrists to rate them for the degree of maturity they expressed. From these ratings scale values were derived. The following examples show the kinds of things these experienced workers thought to be indicators of maturity and immaturity.

Items with high scale values:

S (the subject) chooses a course of action with reference to maximum long-time satisfaction of the entire group of persons involved. (Score 8)

S welcomes opportunity for exercise of precise or realistic thinking. (Score 7)

S welcomes legitimate association with members of the opposite sex and is not ashamed, fearful, or unduly preoccupied with the topic of sex. (Score 9)

S is clear-cut in his decisions; when it is necessary to relinquish an objective he relinquishes or postpones it entirely; when retaining it he retains all of it and without regret. (Score 7)

Items with low scale values:

S chooses his courses of action with reference to his own immediate satisfaction. (Score 1)

S characteristically appeals for help in the solution of his problems. (Score 1)

S's daydreams usually represent the reversal of situations that are humiliating in the real world. (Score 2)

S passes rapidly from one interest or attachment to another. (Score 2)

S is jealous of his spouse; feels insecure when any other interest claims spouse's attention. (Score 1)

When the Willoughby scale was tried out on a group of subjects who were rated by persons who knew them and who also rated themselves on these items, the relationship between the assessment made by the outside judges and the one made by the person himself was not very high. This situation has characterized many different kinds of research on personality. The person viewed "from the inside" does not look exactly like the person viewed "from the outside." Which of the two

---

[1] R. R. Willoughby. A scale of emotional maturity. *J. soc. Psychol.*, 1932, 3, 3-36.

types of information is the more dependable is a debatable question. Certainly the only person with whom one is constantly associated is oneself. No one else has direct access to his thoughts and feelings, his dreams and aspirations. But, on the other hand, it may be that by no one else is he so likely to be deluded. Many people refuse to look their own faults or weaknesses squarely in the face; some, through mistaken ideas of modesty or as a means of gaining attention, may magnify them unduly.

But whether the precise degree of emotional maturity can be judged either by oneself or by outside observers, there is considerable agreement as to the qualities of which it consists. Looking toward the future, abiding by realistic choices and decisions one has made, involving oneself in deep and permanent relationships with people, acting on plans rather than impulse—all these are aspects of what we mean when we say "a mature personality."

Erikson [2] defines the essential qualities of maturity under the two broad labels of *intimacy* and *generativity*. Once the person's identity struggles are over (or at least past their crisis) he is able as he never was before to put himself into close personal relationships. Because he no longer needs to fear becoming too dependent on others and thus losing himself in a love affair or a friendship, he is now free to give himself to others far more freely and deeply than he could before or during adolescence. True intimacy becomes possible. What Erikson means by *generativity* is the kind of long range concern for the young that is involved in motherhood and fatherhood at its best. But the concept is broader than parenthood alone. Teachers, ministers, social workers, scout masters, Sunday school teachers—all those who willingly and with satisfaction to themselves help to further the development of the new generation—show this kind of maturity.

Perhaps the most vivid statement of what maturity means is one which Erikson [3] quotes Freud as having made when he was asked what he thought a normal person should be able to do. Instead of the complicated answer the questioner expected, what Freud said was simply "Lieben und arbeiten," *love* and *work*.

Let us now turn to a more detailed consideration of the shape these qualities take in early adult life.

FINDING ONE'S PLACE IN THE WORLD OF WORK

We mentioned in the chapter on adolescence that the choice of an occupation is one of the major decisions upon which a person's identity

[2] E. H. Erikson. *Childhood and society.* New York: Norton, 1950.
[3] *Ibid.,* p. 229.

rests. It has become increasingly clear, however, as information about people and occupations has accumulated, that the choice of an occupation is not something that occurs all at once and forever. Those who have given most thought to this question are more likely to use the phrase *vocational development* and to think in terms of a succession of choices rather than a single decision.[4] This must necessarily be true because the actual entry into an occupation depends upon *both* the person and the occupational world to which he must adapt himself. The young person must *synthesize* (to use Super's word) his increasingly specific awareness of what his *preferences* are for different kinds of work and his increasingly clear *expectations* of what the prospects are in different broad occupations and specific jobs. It is a far more complex proposition than it was once thought to be. Perhaps the majority of adults never achieve a completely satisfactory synthesis. Circumstances force them to act on their expectations with regard to security or financial success even though their preferences are violated. And even when it is successful, the act of synthesis takes time.

What comes first after a boy or girl leaves school is a period that some sociologists have called *floundering*. The person works at a succession of short-term jobs. One study [5] showed that young people just out of school average eight job changes per year. John may start work at a paper mill, be laid off there when business becomes a little slack, sell shoes for three months at a shoe store, drive a delivery truck for a short time, and then settle down to a long career with the telephone company. Rosemary may go to New York to try to get work as a model, work as a salesgirl in a department store, come back home and run a bookkeeping machine at the bank for six months, apply for training as an airline stewardess, work at this for a year or two, and then marry a pilot. This sort of multi-job experience is the rule, not the exception, in the years before twenty-five. It is true for white collar as well as industrial workers, for college graduates as well as high school graduates. College students, however, are somewhat more likely to obtain at least some of this varied experience in part-time and summer work while they are still in school.

Through this trial-and-error process the young person brings his self-concept into alignment with the complex occupational world. He finds out which roles suit him and which he cannot play. He discovers what qualities in himself he can change under the pressure of occupational demands, which are too firmly fixed to be modified without

---

[4] D. E. Super. *The psychology of careers.* New York: Harper, 1957.
[5] *Ibid.*, p. 125.

great effort, which are part of his value system so that he would not wish to change them if he could. Thus he finds his place.

Sociological studies of *career patterns* have shown that not all lives follow this most typical sequence from floundering to stability. Many professional people begin the stable phase of their careers as soon as they leave college. Many semi-skilled and unskilled workers never really settle down to one job at all, but continue to do a good deal of shifting throughout their working lives. Girls may marry as soon as they leave school (or even before) and have no work experience in the world outside the home. But even though there are these different sorts of career patterns, it is useful to know what the most typical sequence is. Young people themselves can cut down on the amount of floundering that occurs by thinking things through and making some of their basic choices while they are still in school. The counseling that many high schools and colleges makes available to their students can help them in this thinking and choosing.

When we remember that the *Dictionary of Occupational Titles* lists more than 22,000 separate jobs, we can see why this task of finding one's place in the world of work is so complicated. There have been many systems of classifying occupations, designed to produce some workable systems that would facilitate thinking about the occupational problems of the individual and society. Most of these involve two kinds of distinction that can be made, distinctions of *field* and of *level*. Occupations differ qualitatively in the kind of activity they require. They also differ quantitatively in income, prestige, and the education they require. Recently Super[6] has added to these two kinds of classification a third, a classification by *enterprise*. This third concept refers to the nature of the industry in which the work is done. Under it come such headings as Construction, Wholesale and Retail Trade, Transportation, and Communication. Using these three bases of classification simultaneously Super[7] has worked out the over-all classification system shown in Figure 95. The "X" with dotted lines extending from it in two directions represents a specific occupation, that of an engineer employed in conservation work by the National Park Service. He is in Field V, at Level 2, in Enterprise A.

Using such a system, theoretically a person who knew his own interests well enough to locate the field in which he would like to work, who knew his own abilities, educational opportunities, and aspirations well enough to locate the appropriate level, and who knew census figures and his local situation with regard to different kinds of enterprise, could locate quite precisely an occupation that would

[6] *Ibid.*
[7] *Ibid.*, p. 48.

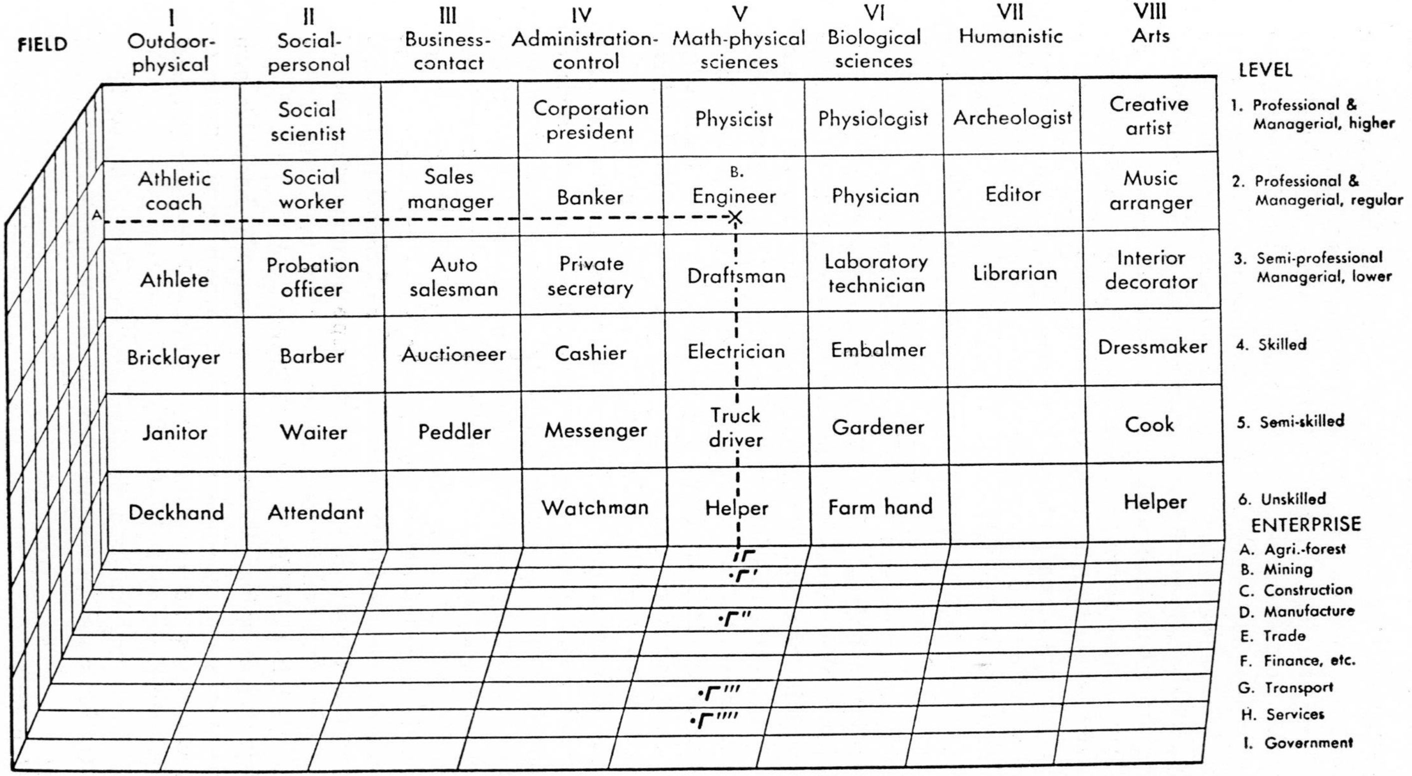

FIGURE 95

FIELD	I Outdoor-physical	II Social-personal	III Business-contact	IV Administration-control	V Math-physical sciences	VI Biological sciences	VII Humanistic	VIII Arts	LEVEL
1	Athletic coach	Social scientist		Corporation president	Physicist	Physiologist	Archeologist	Creative artist	1. Professional & Managerial, higher
2		Social worker	Sales manager	Banker	B. Engineer	Physician	Editor	Music arranger	2. Professional & Managerial, regular
3	Athlete	Probation officer	Auto salesman	Private secretary	Draftsman	Laboratory technician	Librarian	Interior decorator	3. Semi-professional Managerial, lower
4	Bricklayer	Barber	Auctioneer	Cashier	Electrician	Embalmer		Dressmaker	4. Skilled
5	Janitor	Waiter	Peddler	Messenger	Truck driver	Gardener		Cook	5. Semi-skilled
6	Deckhand	Attendant		Watchman	Helper	Farm hand		Helper	6. Unskilled

ENTERPRISE

A. Agri.-forest
B. Mining
C. Construction
D. Manufacture
E. Trade
F. Finance, etc.
G. Transport
H. Services
I. Government

FIGURE 95. A scheme for classifying occupations by level, field, and enterprise. (From D. E. Super. *The psychology of careers.* New York, 1957. Courtesy of Harper and Brothers.)

suit him. Needless to say, real decisions can never be made in this completely rational manner. All sorts of attitudes and family expectations complicate the picture. But it is often a help to a person who is striving to synthesize many kinds of factors into a clear personal identity if one whole set of them can be simplified for him in this manner.

As we have said, the exploratory period for most people gives way to the establishment stage. With a definite commitment made, the young man or woman can now direct his or her efforts toward the attainment of success and satisfaction in the chosen field of work. What do we know about the factors upon which such success and satisfaction rest?

EFFICIENCY AND PRODUCTIVITY

Even in primitive societies, the difference between savagery and social organization of at least a simple kind is determined largely by the margin between productivity that is just barely sufficient to support life and that in which some individuals at times amass enough of a surplus to permit leisure for thinking and planning. Increased productivity of the individual per unit of time makes for increased leisure, for a higher standard of living with more material comforts and luxuries, or for both. Increased leisure can be employed in the advancement of the arts and sciences, for enlarging the mental and cultural horizon of the individual and providing him with the means for deeper and more lasting pleasure in living. The material comforts and conveniences of modern civilization are also worth having, and as yet the production of material goods is far below the level that it must attain if all are to have as much as they can profitably use and enjoy. Society needs increased productivity as well as a more equitable distribution of the products of industry among the producers.

Even under existing conditions, when the rewards of industry are not always justly apportioned, efficient work is an advantage to the individual as well as to society as a whole. In times of unemployment, on the average, the inefficient worker loses his job first, and this in spite of some instances of retention because of political or personal preferment. There is still room for individual merit to win out. The poor boy *may* become president, in spite of his unfavorable start. The pages of *Who's Who in America* are by no means filled with the names of rich men's sons.

Just as the more able and efficient worker is more likely to win advancement than the one who is inefficient and lazy, so the manager who provides his men with proper conditions of work, both physical and psychological, is likely to find their efficiency increased. A large share of our present industrial unrest can be traced directly to failure on the part of both employers and employed to realize fully the close interaction within all parts of our social and industrial machine. Lowered efficiency, no matter where it is manifested nor from what bases it arises, has a repercussive effect upon all members of society. In the long run, efficiency means social progress; inefficiency makes for social decadence.

Psychologists studying work and efficiency have given a good deal of attention to the problem of *fatigue*. Workers get tired and their efficiency falls off. Why? One of the outcomes of this research has been the realization that fatigue is a complex matter involving a variety of different conditions within the individual and many diverse external conditions. It may be the result of long-continued or intensive muscular effort or mental work. It may come from monotony or boredom or even, paradoxically enough, from long-continued inactivity of mind or body. It may be induced by physiological conditions that have little reference to work or effort. There are drugs that make for earlier appearance of fatigue and others that temporarily delay its onset. It affects and is affected by the mental states and attitudes of the individual, and yet a change in mental state is not always evidenced by a change in individual output. Increased effort may offset any differences that would otherwise appear. Indeed there are persons who characteristically speed up work when they first begin to feel tired, either because the fatigue acts as an increased incentive to complete their task or because they dislike to admit weakness.

Thus it has become common practice in industrial research to measure separate outcomes of different experimental conditions rather than to talk about their effects on general fatigue. One can make physiological tests showing the state of the worker's muscles. One can keep careful records of his output. One can obtain information about his feelings of tiredness. The three kinds of data often tell different stories. A person's output may be falling off while he continues to report freedom from tiredness. A person may say that he is exhausted while his physiological tests show that he is in first class condition. Furthermore, people differ in the relation they show between feelings and output. Some are able to continue much longer than others after tiredness and boredom set in. There is no simple way of avoiding all sorts of fatigue in everybody.

There are some findings with regard to output in industrial situations, however, that are general enough to be useful to everybody. One is the matter of rest pauses. Proper spacing of work and rest improves productivity just as we have noted in a previous chapter that it improves learning. People tend to make their individual working periods too long, their rest periods too infrequent. In most industries ten and twelve hour working days have passed out of the picture, except under exceptional circumstances, and periodic rest pauses have been incorporated in each person's daily schedule. Research from the World War I years on to the present has demonstrated conclusively that the shorter day with frequent breaks results in greater production and fewer errors.

Just as was found true in respect to the distribution of practice in learning, no universal rule can be laid down about either the optimal length of the working period or the most favorable distribution of rest pauses. As with learning, it is safe to state that the tendency in most cases is to make the working day too long and the rest pauses too few. It is also true that routine activities, as a rule, show greater improvement from the interposition of rest pauses than do more complex activities or those demanding the working out of a train of ideas. That writers and scientists often keep hours that to the more practical mind may seem little short of "scandalous" is well known. Flushed with a new and exciting idea, it is said that Edison frequently remained at work in the laboratory for twenty hours or more without food or rest. According to his wife, he never kept to regular hours of work, sleep, or eating. When he was seized with an idea he commonly carried it through to the crucial test without pause; after which his debauch of work would be followed by a profound sleep "as peaceful as that of a child" which would last for many hours. In spite of all this, Edison lived to the advanced age of eighty-five without marked diminution of his scientific activities. During his lifetime, 1,098 patents were issued in his name. The patent right for his final invention did not appear until after his death.

One's subjective feeling of fatigue is not always a valid indicator of the actual amount of his work decrement. However, a good many of the laboratory studies that have been conducted on this topic may be somewhat misleading because of their relatively short duration. Increased effort may make up for loss through nervous and physical fatigue over a period of hours or even for several days, but that does not necessarily mean that the same rule will hold good over a period of weeks or months. No one's reserves are inexhaustible. For shorter periods, however, the determination to keep going will carry one along without marked loss of efficiency far beyond the time when the feeling of fatigue becomes manifest. This is true of both mental and physical work.

Since the period of World War I, industrial psychologists have carried out a great many experiments designed to show what effects temperature, lighting, humidity, noise, and other aspects of the physical environment have on productivity. In general it can be said that these effects are measurable but not very large. Improvements in such external factors cannot be expected to produce striking changes in output rates. But it was in connection with a large-scale investigation of these matters that Roethlisberger and Dickson [8] happened upon a finding of the greatest importance. They discovered that a group of workers placed in an experimental room in the Hawthorne plant of the Western Electric Company continued to show increases in productivity regardless of what particular changes were made in schedule and external conditions. This led to a redirection of the whole field of industrial psychology.

Since 1939, when this work was reported, there has been increasing emphasis on the importance of *attitudes* and *social* factors in productivity. The advantage the girls in the Hawthorne experimental room had over their fellow-workers seemed to consist of a greater feeling of security and importance, and a greater opportunity for the growth of a friendly group spirit. It has come to seem like good business to try to maintain high morale among workers and to allow informal work groups to function in a natural way. Much attention is being devoted to all aspects of human relations—labor-management co-operation, training of supervisors, and the like.

For the individual, this emphasis in the newer research on work and efficiency brings the whole problem closer to the problem of vocational *choice*, that we have already discussed. One will function best if his work is meaningful to him as an individual, and his work will be most rewarding to himself and to society if he succeeds in finding a situation where his fellow-workers are congenial. There are, of course, definite limits to a person's freedom of choice in this area. But within whatever limits his own characteristics and the community and economic situation impose, he still can seek for a place that minimizes frustration and maximizes satisfaction. To a considerable extent, his accomplishment depends upon how well he succeeds in finding such a place.

There is one other set of factors related to efficiency that has been studied very extensively by psychologists. It is possible to analyze the performance of any complex skilled operation into its component parts. By scrutinizing the actual movements that are made it is possible to draw conclusions about the way in which superior performers differ from the mediocre, about optimum arrangements of tools and work space, and about improvements that could be made in the

[8] F. J. Roethlisberger and W. J. Dickson. *Management and the worker.* Cambridge, Mass.: Harvard Univ. Press, 1939.

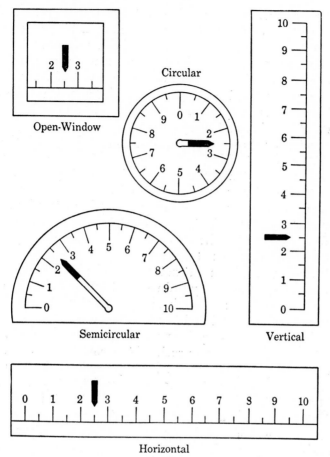

FIGURE 96. Examples of common types of dials. (From R. B. Sleight. The effect of instrument dial shape upon legibility. *J. appl. Psychol.*, 1948, 32, 170-188. Courtesy of American Psychological Association.)

design of machines and equipment. Since World War II there has been a flourishing research specialty usually called *human engineering* concerned with the design of equipment that fits the characteristics of its human operators. Figure 96 is an example of the sort of question such psychologists ask. Which of the dials pictured there would be read most easily with a minimum of error? A study by Sleight [9] shows that when only brief exposures are allowed, the Open-Window type shown at the upper left has a considerable advantage over the others.

[9] R. B. Sleight. The effect of instrument dial shape upon legibility. *J. appl. Psychol.*, 1948, 32, 170-188.

The information coming out of such studies is too specific and concrete to help an individual with the problem of making his own work more efficient. We know from such reports, however, that it is possible to redesign almost any work situation in a manner that enables the workers to accomplish more with the same amount of effort. Each of us can carry on a small scale experiment of this sort for himself. A little time taken to analyze where tools should be placed, how high the table should be, and whether the light should be moved, for example, might well save appreciable amounts of anyone's time and add to his enjoyment of his work. Here too there are often limits to the amount of control a person has over his working conditions, but some modification is almost always possible.

It goes without saying that efficiency in work, as in all aspects of life, depends upon good physical and mental hygiene. A discussion of all the factors upon which health depends is outside the scope of this book. It is enough at this point to say that some attention must be given to nutrition, rest, exercise, emotional strain, and a host of other miscellaneous influences, if efficiency and productivity are to be maximized.

The relationship between health and productivity works both ways. A person who is successful and happy in his work is less susceptible to neurotic symptoms and psychosomatic ailments than the person who is not. The genuine self-esteem such achievement brings protects him against disabling anxieties and inferiority feelings. An occupation serves as a solid core for his sense of personal identity. In our kind of society, work is not just a way to make a living, it is a dominant motif in the pattern of life itself. Thus the importance of careful planning and wise choices during adolescence and early adulthood cannot be overemphasized.

PSYCHOLOGICAL FACTORS IN MARITAL HAPPINESS

Early adulthood is the period when marriages are usually made— and, unfortunately, often unmade. That an appallingly large number of marriages end in divorce or separation is attested by court records. In 1950 there were 24 divorces for every 100 marriages. Thus, according to the last census, something like one in every four marriages ends in the divorce court. Why should this be so? Why should so many young people who, only a few short years or even months before, had believed themselves to be passionately in love with each other become so disillusioned that they see no way out except running away? Surely no young person anticipates such a disappointing outcome of the marriage upon which he embarks so joyfully and with such high faith in the rightness of his choice. Where, then, lies the fault?

Obviously the answer to this question is not a simple one. In most cases of marital unhappiness not one but many factors are involved, and the most important factor in the unhappiness of one couple is not necessarily significant for all. In spite of this difficulty, a number of people have hoped that by careful study of the characteristics of happily married couples in contrast with those who, by their own admission, are unhappy in their marriages and who state that if they had it to do over again they would not remarry the same person, some facts that might be practically helpful to young adults in the selection of their future mates could be obtained. Skeptics, to be sure, have questioned whether such a guide, even if it existed, would be consulted by young people who are, or believe themselves to be, in love, inasmuch as in our culture mutual attraction—"falling in love"—has long been emphasized as the primary requisite for marriage. Romantic literature, the stage and the screen, the poet and the artist have stressed the love interest, often to the exclusion of all other factors. And there can be no doubt that love is important. But what many people fail to realize is that the correlation between falling in love and staying in love is far from perfect. And it is a measure of the likelihood that two people will *stay* in love, rather than a measure of their present attraction for each other that is needed. Probably most, if not all, of the divorced couples as well as those who, although unhappily married, have not sought relief in divorce, were once in love with each other. How, then, is the young person to distinguish between evanescent attraction and the love that will endure for a lifetime?

Let the cynics say what they will, the healthy-minded young man or woman of today is interested in this question. "Marriage courses" in our colleges and universities almost invariably draw a large enrollment, and the popularity of such courses, if the subject matter is well selected, is increasing as inhibitions and embarrassment which at first tended to prevent some students from registering have gradually disappeared.

The complexity of the marriage relationship is so great that it is not surprising that no simple or sure guide to the choice of a mate has been found. Yet some progress has been made, at least in the direction of noting factors that lessen or increase the probabilities of happiness in marriage even though they do not insure it. That mutual attraction before marriage is of first importance need not be stressed, for without such attraction the likelihood that marriage will be entered upon is small. What young people are less likely to remember is that mutual attraction alone is not enough, since it so often fails to survive the first few months of marriage.

Of the many studies on marital happiness and unhappiness that have

appeared, two only will be considered here. [10] They have been selected
because they are based upon careful study of large groups of married
couples who were at least reasonably representative of the upper
middle-class population of today. These subjects were not "abnormal."
They were like the people you meet every day, and, like them, some
were more happy in their marriage than others. Their degree of
happiness was judged by their scores on a questionnaire [11] which was
filled out separately by each person concerned. Much care was taken
to insure that individual privacy was respected. Questionnaires were
not signed, and husbands and wives worked independently of each
other. Thus the chief barriers to frankness were removed, and the
internal evidence of the reports suggested that most, at least, responded
as honestly as they were able. The amount of difference in reported
happiness is indicated by the fact that in Terman's study, on a scale
allowing a possible "happiness" score of 87, the actual range of scores
made by the 792 couples (1,584 persons) whom he studied was from
2 to 87.

In both studies it was found that the couples who reported happiness
in marriage differed significantly from the unhappily married in a
number of respects. Looking first into the early histories of these
persons, it was found that many more of the unhappily married reported unhappy marriages on the part of their parents and stated
that their own childhood had been unhappy. There is evidence that
in part, at least, this may be not so much an indication of real differences in family background and early experience as a difference in
outlook, reflecting a kind of embittered attitude toward life which
caused these persons to magnify their small troubles into major misfortunes. Like Mrs. Grummidge in *David Copperfield,* they "felt
smoky chimneys more than other people." In line with this is the
finding in both studies that the unhappily married reported many
more grievances of almost all kinds than did the happily married. This
does not necessarily mean that the factors about which complaint was
made were never present among the happily married, but the latter
were less likely to be disturbed by them. In Terman's study this
factor was checked by asking first whether or not the condition in
question existed and secondly whether, if present, it had been a source
of unhappiness or worry to the person reporting. There was much less
difference in the frequency with which the two groups reported
various adverse conditions as existing than in the frequency with

---

[10] Cf. L. M. Terman. *Psychological factors in marital happiness.* New York:
McGraw-Hill, 1938; E. W. Burgess and L. S. Cottrell. *Predicting success or failure
in marriage.* New York: Prentice-Hall, 1939.

[11] The questionnaires used in the two studies were not identical but were very
similar.

which they were complained about. For example, only 3 per cent of the happy wives who reported that their husbands were addicted to swearing found this a source of unhappiness to themselves, but of the unhappily married, 62 per cent of those who stated that their husbands swore were emotionally upset by it. Although both the husbands and wives of the unhappily married group cited "insufficient income" as one of the major factors in their marital difficulties, when actual incomes were compared it was found that there was no difference between the happily and the unhappily married in average size of income. Not the lack of money but the attitude toward the lack was the disturbing factor.

All in all, there seems to be a sound basis for the conclusion reached by Terman, who after reviewing all the evidence says: [12]

Our theory is that what comes out of a marriage depends upon what goes into it and that among the most important things going into it are the attitudes, preferences, aversions, habit-patterns and emotional-response patterns which give or deny to one the aptitude for compatibility. In other words, we believe that a large proportion of incompatible marriages are so because of a predisposition to unhappiness in one or both of the spouses.

This, of course, does not mean that some people are born to be unhappy. It does mean that habits of unhappiness can be so firmly established early in life that when the time for marriage comes they are likely to persist. It means, too, that troubles do not, as many people think, lie outside the individual. There are many people who can remain serene in the face of great disaster; there are others who find disaster in a broken teacup.

Practically all investigators have found that *similarity* rather than dissimilarity of interests and attitudes is favorable to happy marriage. To achieve the most from marriage, husband and wife should be comrades as well as lovers. Questions that young people contemplating marriage may well ask themselves are these: Is our pleasure in each other's company chiefly dependent upon "necking," or can we be good companions without physical contact? Is our conversation mostly about ourselves, or do we find plenty of other subjects to talk about? Do we respect each other's opinions and enjoy an exchange of opinion whether or not we agree? Is either one of us jealous of the other's friendships, feeling hurt and neglected if he seems to enjoy the companionship of any one beside oneself?

While it is clearly advantageous for a married couple to have similar interests and attitudes, there is some evidence [13] that it is better that

[12] *Op. cit.*, p. 110.

[13] R. F. Winch, T. Ktanes, and V. Ktanes. The theory of complementary needs in mate selection: an analytic and descriptive study. *Amer. sociol. Rev.*, 1954, 19, 241-249.

their underlying needs be complementary rather than similar. A man with strong dependence needs, for example, may be very happy with a wife who is somewhat high on the dominance side. Marriage counselors have discovered that there are many kinds of combinations that seem to work fairly successfully even when both marriage partners are a little neurotic. In such cases changing the emotional need pattern of either the husband or the wife can lead to a worsening rather than an improvement of their relationship. As one song that attained a fair degree of popularity in the late 1950's puts it, "I can't get adjusted to the you that got adjusted to me!" Thus young people contemplating marriage need to ask themselves (though perhaps the asking must be done in some unconscious intuitive way rather than explicitly): Do I feel satisfied or frustrated by this relationship? Does my fiancé expect from me a kind of feeling it is natural for me to experience?

Questions such as these cannot be answered on the basis of a brief acquaintance. Both Terman and Burgess and Cottrell found that their unhappily married groups included many more than a chance proportion of couples who had known each other only a short time before their marriage, who had rushed to the altar upon the urge of immediate desire without serious thought to the life that was to follow. This, as we have repeatedly pointed out, is a childish rather than a mature kind of behavior. The old saying, "Look before you leap," is nowhere more appropriate than in its application to marriage. The fully adult personality does not stand timidly on the bank afraid to try the crossing at all, but he scans the opposite shore with care until he can make the leap gladly, and with confidence that he will find sure footing on the opposite side.

OTHER SATISFACTIONS OF MATURITY

Early adulthood is for many persons the happiest period of life. In Table VII we see that almost half of a group of old people who were asked how they felt about different periods designated twenty-five to forty-five as the happiest years. In another study [14] where adult subjects were asked to chart their degree of happiness on an age line, the peak turned out to be in the five-year period from twenty-five through twenty-nine. It seems that after the challenges of adolescence and the uncertainties of the exploratory stage that follows, many people enter a rich and fruitful era. What are some of the things that make it so?

Foremost in the minds of many would be the birth of their children

[14] R. G. Kuhlen. Age trends in adult adjustment as reflected in happiness ratings. Unpublished paper presented at meeting of Amer. Psychol. Assn., Boston, 1948,

TABLE VII

PERCENTAGES OF PERSONS OVER 65 WHO DESIGNATED
VARIOUS PERIODS AS HAPPIEST

(N=370)

Period	Per Cent
Childhood (5-15 years)	14.5
Youth (15-25 years)	18.9
Young Adulthood (25-45 years)	49.1
Middle Age (45-60 years)	12.4
Later Life (60 and up)	5.1

From C. M. Morgan. The attitudes and adjustments of recipients of old age assistance in upstate and Metropolitan New York. *Arch. Psychol.,* 1937, Vol. 30, No. 214, p. 131.

and the many kinds of satisfactions that come from taking care of them and guiding their development. Important as this experience is, psychologists have as yet devoted very little study to it. Hundreds of papers have been written about *rejected* children and unhealthy parent-child relationships, but there is little concrete psychological knowledge of the emotional satisfactions coming to parents who are on good terms with their children. Erikson's concept of *generativity* discussed at the beginning of the chapter refers to a very significant life experience.

For many, adulthood brings a kind of social life more rewarding than previous social experiences have been. Adolescents form closely-knit groups and cling to their special friends because such associations afford them a certain amount of protection against the many pressures of the outside world and an opportunity to express their common feelings. But once an individual's identity has been clearly shaped he is freer to appreciate other individuals—to like them for themselves rather than for what they can do for him. Adult friendships can be stable and permanent. Year after year, even when circumstances place thousands of miles between them, friends maintain a kind of intimacy that contributes much to the meaningfulness of life.

Needless to say, not all adult social activity is of this nature. Much of it is based on propinquity and geographic location. In their study of a housing project for married students, Festinger, Schachter, and Back[15] showed that the couples who lived in units in the middle of the project participated more in informal social activities than did those who were out on the edges. Entertaining of business associates is common practice. Many kinds of social affairs—receptions, teas, cocktail parties, and the like—are designed to enlarge one's circle of

[15] L. Festinger, S. Schachter, and K. Back. *Social pressures in informal groups.* New York: Harper, 1950.

superficial acquaintances rather than to promote close friendships. All of these kinds of informal and formal social activities undoubtedly contribute to adult development. Like parenthood, they have as yet been little studied by psychologists.

For many persons one major source of mature satisfaction is the participation in groups devoted to community service. There are so many of these organized groups that an individual has no difficulty in finding one that fits his own kind of identity. Often it becomes an important bulwark of this identity as the years pass. Church groups, Girl Scouts, League of Women Voters, Rotary Club, Welfare League, United Nations Association, Symphony Orchestra Board, Foreign Policy Association—there is no limit to the length of the list that could be made. Efforts expended on the activities of these organizations add meaning to many adult lives.

Another kind of satisfaction is that obtained from hobbies and avocations. The diversity in these is at least as great as that of the organizations discussed in the previous paragraph. (In fact, many of these groups are made up of like-minded enthusiasts.) Collecting stamps or china, building models of planes or railroads, playing in amateur orchestras or chamber music groups, taking pictures, painting, weaving, pottery-making, dahlia growing, dog breeding—these and hundreds of others are available to any who are interested.

The very richness of the possibilities open to adults can easily make for confusion, frustration, and dissipation of energy. It is for this reason that ego identity is so important a basis for everything else in adult life. A person who has developed an inner picture of himself, who knows who he is and the direction he wishes to go, can choose from among these varied offerings the ones that are right for him. With the constant decrease in working hours and the accompanying increase in leisure, and with constantly rising income levels that open up more kinds of possibilities to people at all occupational levels, having a basis for choice is more necessary than it has ever been before. It is only those with clearly-delineated self-concepts who can really say:

> The world is so full of a number of things
> I'm sure we should all be as happy as kings.

SUMMARY

Simply becoming an adult is no guarantee of maturity. To be truly mature one must be able to make plans and carry them out, establish deep and permanent relationships with other persons, and accept one's share of the world's responsibilities. One must have the capacity to love and to work.

Finding one's occupation requires a developmental period in which preferences and expectations can be synthesized. Typically a person goes through a period of floundering after he leaves school, trying out a number of jobs. Career patterns differ, however, and some stabilize sooner than others.

Occupations can be classified by field, level, and enterprise. A good choice of an occupation requires that the person locate something that is right for him in these three respects.

Once an occupation is chosen, productivity depends upon several factors: the optimum distribution of effort in work and rest periods, maintaining favorable attitudes toward one's work, constructive social relationships in the working group, and good organization of the whole working situation including materials, equipment, and similar factors. Good mental and physical health makes for working efficiency, but success at work also promotes good health.

Studies of marital happiness have demonstrated the importance of personality factors, often directly related to the person's experience in his own childhood home. Husbands and wives tend to have similar interests and attitudes but there is some evidence that it is an advantage to them to have complementary rather than similar needs.

Other potential satisfactions during the adult years are parenthood, friendship, participation in community activities, and hobbies and avocations. To make best use of all these possibilities, one needs a firm sense of personal identity to enable him to choose the ones that will be self-fulfilling for him.

FOR FURTHER READING

Super, Donald E. *The psychology of careers.* New York: Harper, 1957.

The book was written by a man who stands out as the person having done most to bring order and clarity into the complex field of vocational development. He and his colleagues are engaged in a long-range study of the boys in one high school class, designed to show just what happens during the transition period from adolescence to adulthood.

Super discusses the nature of work and the purposes it serves in life, the course and cycle of the working life—exploration, floundering, establishment, maintenance, and decline—and the separate factors upon which vocational development rests—aptitudes, interests, personality, family, economic factors.

The book can be very useful to those who are concerned with their own vocational development as well as to counselors who are attempting to help others.

CHAPTER 22

Why do psychologists think that middle age and old age should receive some special study as developmental stages?

What special situations and tasks does the aging person face?

Why is it harder to measure mental abilities in adults than in children?

Do mental abilities begin to decline as soon as their maximum level has been reached or do they maintain this level until old age?

What kinds of ability decline most rapidly with aging? Which show least change?

Do all people grow old at the same rate?

Is the saying that "you cannot teach an old dog new tricks" partially or wholly true for human beings? What are some of the chief reasons why older people seldom acquire new skills? What kinds of things are hardest for older people to learn?

What can a person do to improve his chances for a useful and happy old age?

The Second Half of Life

CHARACTERISTICS OF MIDDLE AGE

MORE AND MORE we have been coming to realize that development includes much more than growth. Change is an inexorable aspect of the life process. The man of forty differs from the youth of twenty in ways that are not wholly dependent upon his greater experience. The man of sixty is a still different person, facing different problems from the forty-year-old.

With the changes in physical appearance we are all familiar; so much so that although now and then we meet someone whose appearance greatly belies his age, as a rule we estimate the ages of strangers with a fair degree of accuracy. We all know, too, the gradual loss of the overflowing physical energy that sets young men to wrestling and tussling with each other even when the thermometer stands at 100°. Although at forty the man who has always done heavy manual labor may carry on his work about as efficiently as before, he does not put so much snap into it. His muscles may still be strong, but they are less resilient. The person of forty moves more slowly than the twenty-year-old, and the person of sixty has slowed up still more.

The physical changes that occur as life progresses are many and complex. But as has been pointed out in previous chapters, it is more meaningful to characterize developmental stages in terms of the tasks or challenges they bring than in purely biological terms. An individual during middle age must come to terms with the physical changes that are occurring, but his reactions are also determined by social expecta-

445

tions and psychological needs. It is this total situation, internal and external, that we shall try to clarify.

Essentially what makes the latter half of life different from the periods that preceded it is the likelihood that *expansion* or *forward movement* will cease, and that the person will have to reorganize his pattern of life first around *maintenance,* and later around *decline.* For some persons this is a task fraught with difficulties. Let us then consider in more detail what these concepts of expansion, maintenance, and decline mean.

The most obvious kind of expansion, physical growth, is complete by the early twenties. Mental growth, the actual increase in mental *capacity,* as distinct from knowledge or skill, probably ends at about the same period. (It is not possible to give a precise figure for this, because in practice capacity cannot be separated from knowledge and skill.) But all during early adulthood other kinds of expansion are occurring. Some people invest enormous amounts of energy in their work, striving for promotions and raises, a higher standard of living, and social position. Others take great satisfaction in their growing families. Year by year the changes in the children give them a sense of forward movement. A writer tries to broaden the world's horizons by expressing what has not been expressed before. A scientist struggles to unlock closed doors. For all these kinds of young adults, the road stretches ahead into the indefinite future, clear and promising.

In each of these lives there comes a time when the expansion stage is over. There is a great deal of variation in timing and circumstances from one person to another. A business man of fifty may suddenly realize that he has achieved everything he has been working for and that he is now caught up in a round of activities that lead nowhere. A woman may come to this turning point when her youngest child leaves home and she no longer has anyone to care for. Everyone must face the inexorable fact that life is finite, and that each person can accomplish and experience only a limited amount.

In many instances, misfortunes or frustrations intensify people's problems or bring them to the turning point prematurely. A debilitating illness or a serious accident may bring the expansive phase of life to a sudden halt. For a woman the menopause serves as a reminder that her biological usefulness is over, and her sexual attractiveness on the wane. To these physical threats must be added the purely psychological stresses that result from such causes as the facts that many firms do not hire men over forty, many adolescents are contemptuous of their parents, and most of the spokesmen of our culture, such as magazine writers and radio advertisers, place a high value on youth.

The transition from an outlook based on expansion to one centering around maintenance of what one has need not be an unhappy change. How a person reacts to it seems to depend a great deal on the kinds of choices he has made at previous periods of his life. If Lorraine has built her identity around physical beauty and attractiveness to men, she will probably suffer more when this wanes than will Henrietta, who is the responsible clubwoman type. Mr. Clyde, who loves the outdoors and whose job has always been of less importance to him than his week ends beside trout streams, will not mind the fact that he was passed over for promotion in favor of a younger man, whereas Mr. Esmond, whose heart and soul were devoted to the business, will be crushed by such a blow. In fact, there is such a large variation from person to person in the timing of these changes and the particular shape they take that there is considerable doubt as to whether it is really meaningful to talk about this stage in a general way.

Eventually, in lives that are not prematurely terminated as a result of illness or injury, the maintenance stage gives way to a period of general *decline*. Physical health and strength decrease markedly. All of the senses become less and less keen. Mental abilities are impaired, and special defects in memory make their appearance. Along with these changes, social participation declines also, and the aging person often gets out of touch with the lives of other people and the ongoing march of events.

To many people, perhaps the majority in our society, the shift from expansion to maintenance and then to decline constitutes a grim picture. Concern about it has become widespread since medical advances have lengthened the average life span so that most men and women now can expect to live to old age. What has become apparent as a result of the research that has grown out of this concern, however, is that the prospect need not be an unhappy one. These stages of life, like those that precede them, have advantages and rewards that can outweigh the disadvantages if we know how to capitalize upon them. An understanding of developmental psychology, viewed as a lifelong process, should help us in this task of planning wisely for all of life and not just for the first forty years.

What are some of these positive aspects of the stages of maintenance and decline? We can see what they are by studying the lives of individuals who live these periods most richly. For many men and women, the years of middle life bring an opportunity to broaden horizons that have necessarily narrowed during the years of youth and early adulthood. Mrs. Carey at forty-five suddenly finds herself with time on her hands. Her youngest son has gone away to college. Her husband has been financially successful enough so that she has been able to acquire all the labor-saving equipment it is possible for a modern home to have.

Now that she and Mr. Carey are alone, the work of running the house and preparing the meals requires only two or three hours of each day. What shall she do with the others?

There are many possibilities. Perhaps she can resume a career that was interrupted twenty years earlier. Perhaps she can put ideas and efforts into one or more of the community organizations in which she has been an interested but not very active member. She can begin to develop talents that have lain dormant for some time—to work at violin playing, weaving, or pottery-making. The middle years can be a period of self-fulfillment.

Mr. Carey may see the period not so much in terms of more free time (he probably must work as many hours a week as he ever did), but in terms of release from the necessity of constant, competitive striving. Once he has reached the highest rung of his individual ladder of success, he can relax somewhat and enjoy some of the benefits it brings. He can feel free to spend his evenings and weekends doing what he likes to do and to cultivate as friends the people he himself finds interesting rather than those who are important to his career.

Middle life is a time in which men and women can think through their value systems and attain really satisfying philosophies of life. After the kinds of experience of all sorts that forty years of living have brought, a person can sort out what really matters to him from the trivial and the insubstantial. While the attainment of ego identity is a developmental task of adolescence, awareness of one's own selfhood continues to grow and to bear rich fruit during the latter half of life. Individuals who have met the challenges of middle life successfully need not fear the impairments of old age. Knowing what matters most to you makes it possible to keep the central satisfactions even when life becomes more limited.

Research on aging is an interdisciplinary endeavor. Physiologists and medical men, sociologists, labor economists, and housing experts—these and many other kinds of specialists—are devoting their attention to the problem of making the whole life span happy and productive. The principal contributions psychologists have made to this co-operative task are of two kinds. First, they have charted "mental growth curves" for the later periods of life showing how much and what kinds of mental ability adults of different ages can bring to bear on their problems. Second, they have taken at least the initial steps in studying the personality changes that often occur in old age and unraveling their complex and varied sources.

Individual differences are of crucial importance in both these areas of psychological study. It is the success with which some persons manage these developmental stages of maintenance and decline that point the way to a more satisfying life for all.

ADULT MENTAL ABILITIES

Obtaining mental test data for adults is not nearly so easy as getting similar data for children. For one thing, it is far more difficult to get a good representative sample of the population. Practically all the ten-year-olds in a community are to be found in the elementary school, most of them in the fifth grade. There is no comparable group that includes all of the fifty-year-olds in the community. Church groups, luncheon clubs, and labor unions all represent samples *selected* in some special way and thus not typical. In some of the earlier studies on the abilities of very old persons, the subjects were taken almost wholly from charitable institutions, poorhouses, and homes for the aged. The very fact that these persons had failed to make provision for their old age when they were younger suggests that they were not highly competent at any age.

Another special problem is to find tests that are really suitable for persons of all ages. As people grow older, they are likely to become less interested in merely trying their skill; they want to see reasons for their work. Tasks that merely test what they can do are therefore less certain to draw forth their best efforts. Differences in recent experience also play a part. Many of the older subjects will have lost interest in activities that have no relationship to their life work and so make a poor showing on certain tasks, not so much through genuine loss of ability to acquire these skills as through being out of practice in performing them. With increasing age, interests and activities become more highly specialized. Perhaps the fairest way to test the ability of an adult would be to see how well he can do his chosen kind of work. But if we did this, scores for different occupational groups would not be comparable.

There is a third source of error in conclusions that may be drawn from adult test data in the fact that the mental abilities we test are affected to some extent by education. In a country like ours where the level of such schooling has been going up decade by decade, we would expect the older age groups to score somewhat lower than the younger simply because they had been exposed to less of this educational influence during their formative years. Thus lower average scores in older men and women might not really represent a *decline,* though at first glance they would appear to do so. For this reason, comparisons of cross-sections of the population at different ages can never be con-clusive with regard to the question of mental growth or decline in the same individuals.

During the 1950's the results of several *longitudinal* studies were reported. The findings differed considerably from those that the earlier cross-sectional studies had produced. While they are limited as yet to a few groups of adults under somewhat special circumstances, still they have made necessary a modification of some of the former conclusions with regard to age changes. Let us turn first to what these conclusions were and the kind of evidence upon which they were based.

With regard to general intelligence, there have been a great many studies apparently showing a decline in capacity setting in almost immediately after full capacity has been reached, and proceeding with greater rapidity as the years pass. Figure 97, based on the study by H. E. Jones and H. S. Conrad,[1] shows a curve similar in its shape to that reported by several other investigators. Jones and Conrad obtained an exceptionally complete sample, testing practically the entire population of nineteen New England villages with Army Alpha, the group intelligence test that had been widely used in World War I. It is clear that the peak age is twenty. Each later age group averaged appreciably lower than the one that preceded it.

Jones and Conrad were also interested in the question of whether different special kinds of mental abilities tend to decline at the same rate. The Alpha test is divided into eight subtests, each comprising a different kind of task. Jones was interested in seeing whether the age decrement is equally great along all the lines tested. He found that it is not. Test 4, which is an "opposites" or vocabulary test, and Test 8, which is a test of general information, show no indication of a decline with age up to age sixty. The curves remain stationary. Arithmetical reasoning and the ability to rearrange the words in "dissected" sentences show only a small loss. The ability to follow oral directions shows a fairly sharp loss from the early twenties up to about thirty-five, after which no further change takes place before the age of sixty. The greatest age decrement is seen in the tests of mathematical completion and giving analogies, and in a so-called test of "common sense," in which the subject is required to select the best one out of a list of answers to each of a number of everyday questions. These differences between rates of decline for different abilities have also been corroborated in a number of other studies. Vocabulary and information scores show the least age decrement. Nonverbal tests and those requiring quick adaptation to new situations show the most.

There was another large-scale study in the 1930's focused especially on the question of what the age trends were for different kinds of abilities. It included a much broader range of things than just the types of task one usually finds in intelligence tests. Miles[2] enlisted the

[1] H. E. Jones and H. S. Conrad. The growth and decline of intelligence; a study of a homogeneous group between the ages of ten and sixty years. *Genet. Psychol. Monogr.*, 1933, 13, 223-298.

[2] W. R. Miles. Age and human ability. *Psychol. Rev.*, 1933, 40, 99-123.

interest of clubs and social organizations of various kinds by offering
to pay the organization for the time spent by its members and their
relatives in taking a series of tests. A special bonus was offered for bringing in old people. By this means he was able to be reasonably sure that
his subjects were of about the same social class and presumably of about
the same native intelligence, regardless of their ages. The fact that
they, or rather the organization, was receiving pay for the work un-

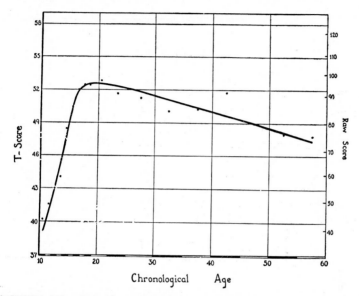

FIGURE 97. Growth and decline of intelligence as measured by
the Army Alpha Test. (From H. E. Jones and H. S. Conrad. The
growth and decline of intelligence: a study of a homogeneous group
between the ages of ten and sixty. *Genet. Psychol. Monog.*, 1933, 13,
223-298. Courtesy Clark Univ. Press.)

doubtedly lent it additional importance in the eyes of the subjects,
and so made it less likely that they would fail to put forth their best
efforts.

The tests used were of many kinds. In addition to formal intelligence
tests there were a number of tests of motor ability, of perceptive ability,
of learning and memory, of speed of reaction. Self-estimates and questionnaires, calling for opinions and points of view on many subjects
and for expressions of interest in various activities, were also employed.
Table VIII shows the general trend of the results. In this table the
scores for the different age groups have been expressed as percentages
of the average score made at the age when the particular ability was at
its peak. The peak is always counted as 100 per cent. Thus, in speed

of reaching and grasping the highest average score was made by the subjects who were between eighteen and twenty-nine years, and this score is therefore counted as 100. Subjects between the ages of ten and seventeen years attained, on the average, 92 per cent of this high mark; those between the ages of thirty and forty-nine, 98 per cent; those from fifty to sixty-nine, 88 per cent; and the old people between the ages of seventy and eighty-nine averaged 70 per cent of the maximum.

In the Otis intelligence test it was found that the peak came at about eighteen years of age. Since we do not know where the zero point of

TABLE VIII

RELATIONSHIP OF CERTAIN ABILITIES TO AGE

Ability	Age Groups				
	10-17	18-29	30-49	50-69	70-89
1. Reaching and grasping..	92%	100%	98%	88%	70%
2. Speed of rotary movement (turning a crank)	90	100	97	89	72
3. Speed of finger reaction ..	87	100	98	99	71
4. Learning a maze	95	100	92	83	55
5. Comparison and judgment	72	100	100	87	69
6. Visual acuity (with glasses if worn)	100	95	93	76	46

Adapted from Miles.

this test lies, it is not easy to express the results as percentages of the maximum as has been done in Table VIII. Miles uses a number of devices to show the relationship of scores to age, but, since most of them involve the use of somewhat complicated mathematical procedures, we shall present only the simplest and most easily understood figures here.

Table IX shows the average IQ's computed on the basis of the Otis norms [3] for each successive decade from the twenties to the nineties. The subjects have been divided into three groups according to education.

From Table VIII it appears that older people suffer a greater handi-

[3] Although the use of the intelligence quotient with adults is open to question, we have presented the results in this form because it is one with which students are familiar. It should be noted, however, that whereas Otis, following the example of Terman, assumed that the ability measured by this test reaches its maximum at sixteen years, these results as well as those secured by a number of other workers show that some further growth occurs after the age of sixteen. This accounts for the fact that the average IQ of all three groups during the decade of the twenties is somewhat above 100.

cap in the more purely physiological functions, such as visual acuity, than they do in the kind of activities we term *intellectual*. There is some evidence, too, that the loss in those functions that are most often practiced comes about a little more slowly than it does in those that are rarely used. The ability to learn to trace a maze, for example, shows a much more rapid decrease than reaching and grasping. Although we think of the former as a more intellectual function, it is one that is little practiced outside the psychological laboratory. On the

TABLE IX

RELATIONSHIP OF INTELLIGENCE QUOTIENTS TO AGE AND SCHOOLING

Age	Eighth Grade or Less	One to Four Years High School	One or More Years in College
20-29	101	107	118
30-39	94	106	116
40-49	93	105	117
50-59	89	100	111
60-69	85	95	106
70-79	82	95	100
80-89	75	85	91
90-99	—	79	—

Adapted from Miles.

Otis tests, which make use chiefly of verbal tasks, the ability of the subjects who never attended high school and who probably were for the most part engaged in manual labor shows a somewhat earlier decrement than that of other groups who were, we may assume, getting more practice in work of this kind.

Miles also points out that in general the decrement in performance with age appears most strongly in tasks in which speed is a factor. Older people do best in tasks "where diligence is more important than speed." Older people also have much difficulty in learning new material that conflicts with well-established habits, such as a series of wrong products like $4 \times 5 = 28$. It may be noted here that some workers in the animal field have found that old rats have more difficulty than young ones in learning new mazes so planned that the habits formed earlier in learning other mazes conflict with those required by the new maze.

Most significant of all, perhaps, is the fact that even in those tasks where, on the average, the decrement with age is large, some of the older people continue to do better than the average of the younger ones. In this connection, Miles makes the following comment:

Although younger adults tend regularly to score higher in most of the measurements made and older adults to score lower, it is by no means true that all of the high scores belong to the young, the low ones to the old. . . . The measurements of dispersion are consistently large from decade to decade. In reaction time, 25 per cent of the people over seventy years of age were as quick as the average for the total group. In intelligence also, even when speed is a factor, approximately a quarter of the oldest subjects equaled or exceeded the general adult average.

On the basis of results like these, the general consensus until the early 1950's was that, if we consider the average of many different kinds of intellectual performance, a small but steady decline in ability must be expected from the early twenties on. The first of the longitudinal studies that has led to a questioning of this conclusion is that of Owens. [4] During 1949 and 1950 he tested 127 men who had taken Army Alpha thirty years before at the time they were entering college. They were now nearing the age of fifty. But instead of scoring lower on the test taken in their youth, they averaged significantly *higher*. The upward trend was in evidence for all the subtests as well as for the total score. Bayley [5] has reported similar increases for Terman's group of "gifted children" who are being tested periodically as adults.

Thus, at least for well-educated adults, we now have good evidence for a maintenance period extending throughout middle life. One need not anticipate an inevitable loss of mental capacity during the thirties, forties, and fifties. Longitudinal studies of the aged have not as yet been reported. It seems likely, however, that some decline in mental status does occur during life's final stage, since cross-sectional studies have produced evidence for it among groups representing all educational levels. And at all ages, individual differences are very marked. Some remain intellectually "young" until they are far advanced in years. In general, the outlook appears more promising than it once did on the basis of evidence psychologists were presenting.

There are two supplementary research questions that are of some interest to those who wish to understand age trends in the later years. One is: How well do adults of different ages *learn*? The other is: How *productive* are they? It should be apparent when one gives the matter a little thought that neither the rate at which a person learns new things or the amount of work that he accomplishes is closely related to intel-

[4] W. A. Owens. Age and mental abilities: a longitudinal study. *Genet. Psychol. Monogr.*, 1953, 48, 3-54.
[5] N. Bayley. The maintenance of intellectual ability in gifted adults. *J. Geront.*, 1955, 10, 91-107.

ligence. A student may lack the intellectual capacity to master abstruse philosophical concepts or higher mathematics and yet *learn* typing skills or baseball statistics very readily. A man may have a brilliant mind and an outstanding talent for writing and yet cease to turn out anything for publication.

The first comprehensive study of the learning capacity of adults of different ages ranging from twenty to fifty-seven was that made by E. L. Thorndike. [6] The general conclusion from this study is expressed graphically in Figure 98 and summed up in the statement that adults twenty-five to forty-five learn at nearly the same rate and in nearly the same manner as they would have learned the same thing at fifteen to twenty. In these days of widespread adult education, this is hardly a startling conclusion.

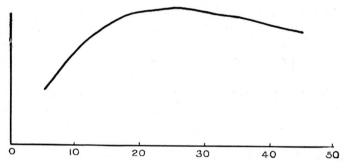

FIGURE 98.   The general form of the curve of learning ability with age. (From E. L. Thorndike. *Adult learning.* Courtesy The Macmillan Co.)

The Thorndike studies suffered from some inadequacies in sampling and experimental technique, and they did not cover the later years when we would expect decline in learning ability to become most apparent. There have been a number of other investigations of this problem in which subjects past fifty have been included, and in which the focus was on the special *kinds* of learning deficit that appear. In general, they have shown that the decline is most marked in learning situations where the new habit or skill interferes with an old one, least marked in situations where the established habits can be used. Thus it is difficult for an older subject in such an experiment [7] to learn to follow with a stylus a moving object seen in a mirror, although he learns readily enough to follow one that can be seen directly.

[6] E. L. Thorndike and associates. *Adult learning.* New York: Macmillan, 1928.
[7] F. L. Ruch. The differentiative effects of age upon human learning. *J. gen. Psychol.,* 1934, 11, 261-286.

The most interesting experiments centering around the learning of motor skills were carried on at Cambridge University and reported by Welford. [8] The experiments showed that the *methods* by means of which older persons accomplish a skilled act differ from those of younger persons more than their *scores* on the performance do. Usually without awareness of what he is doing, the older person compensates for his decline in speed and keenness of perception by greater carefulness. This tendency may account for the well-known fact that while younger automobile drivers are unquestionably higher in perceptual and motor skills, middle-aged drivers have fewer accidents.

The most important practical conclusion that has come from the experiments on age differences in learning is that learning is possible at any age. It may be somewhat slower at sixty than it was at twenty, certain kinds of things may be harder to learn than others, and the method it is natural for an older person to use in approaching the learning task may not be exactly like those a younger person prefers. But learning can continue throughout life. In our rapidly changing society it is important for people of all ages to understand this and to make the effort necessary to keep their "learning machinery" functioning smoothly. Like other kinds of machinery it becomes rusty with disuse.

Productivity at different ages has been studied largely through the analysis of biographical information to find out the ages at which important work has been done. In some of these studies, the criterion used has been maximum productivity, as indicated by the number of books and scientific articles, works of art or mechanical inventions produced in a single year. In others, the age at which the single work that competent authorities regard as the person's masterpiece has been the index used. Still others have employed a financial yardstick, regarding the age at which the highest salary was earned as the best indication of the time when his ability was at its peak. But regardless of the basis of judgment, the general results are much the same. The diversity from person to person is so great that a citation of averages misleads almost as much as it informs.

Lehman [9] has assembled a large amount of information that appears to show that the peak age for important achievement in science, art, or literature comes fairly early in life, although masterpieces have been produced by persons of all ages, even into the eighties. More recently, however, Dennis [10] has shown that if we consider not all scientists but

---

[8] A. T. Welford. *Skill and age.* London: Cambridge Univ. Press, 1951.

[9] H. C. Lehman. *Age and achievement.* Princeton: Princeton Univ. Press, 1953.

[10] W. Dennis. Predicting scientific productivity in later maturity from records of earlier decades. *J. Geront.*, 1954, 9, 465-467.

only those who live to be seventy or over, their achievements do not show a peak in the thirties, as Lehman's figures suggest, but continue to increase throughout the forties and fifties. Even during the sixties and seventies these men continue to produce.

The age of greatest earning capacity will obviously vary considerably with the type of work in which the person engages. For workers in occupations where muscular strength is the chief requirement and for which little or no time is spent in training, the peak comes early; for those in the learned professions it is much later. Thorndike made a study of the salaries received by Methodist clergymen at different ages. For his group of 143 cases there was a steady increase up to about age forty, followed by a plateau which lasted until about fifty-six, and a fall thereafter. High-salaried men and low-salaried men showed about the same tendency to vary with age, except that the age changes were most pronounced for those earning the highest salaries.

The outstanding result of all these studies is to show that although we may compute averages, the variations from these averages in individual cases is so great that, if we except the years of early childhood and the late nineties, there is no age within the life span of man at which great accomplishment has not been recorded. Some of our great musicians published work of considerable merit as early as the age of five or six years. Sophocles wrote his *Oedipus* at ninety. Folwell, former president of the University of Minnesota, wrote his monumental *History of Minnesota* during the last years of his life, finishing it just before his death at the age of ninety-six. In his *Senescence*, Hall [11] cited many other instances of outstanding accomplishment performed long after the traditional age of "three score and ten years."

While there is no question but that the years from twenty to fifty are the ones when many people do their best work, fifty is by no means a universal dividing line between excellence and mediocrity. Look at Edison! Indeed the more one studies the lives and characters of those who have continued to do creative work up to a late age or of their humbler fellows who, although they never achieve fame, nevertheless continue to fill useful positions in the world for many years after the majority have dropped out of the race, the more strongly one comes to feel that the vast majority of individuals grow old long before there is need for them to do so. It would be foolish to claim that age is just a notion. It is a fact to which all must adjust as it comes to them. But it is equally foolish to anticipate its ravages before it has actually arrived or to use age as an excuse for failure to accomplish what a little greater effort would have enabled one to perform.

[11] G. S. Hall. *Senescence: the last half of life.* New York: D. Appleton, 1922.

MENTAL HEALTH IN OLD AGE

When one examines census figures it is easy to see why concern for the aged is increasing. In 1930, the proportion of the population that had reached the customary retirement age, sixty-five or over, was 5.4 per cent. By 1950 it had jumped to 8.2 per cent. In actual numbers of people affected, the increase is even more striking. In 1930 there were a little over six and one-half million persons in the United States who had reached the age of sixty-five; in 1950 there were more than 12 million.

As the proportion of "senior citizens" in the population has increased, it has become increasingly important for society to find out why some are able to live out their allotted span in peace and contentment while others become increasingly insecure and unhappy. Many psychologists, along with medical men, sociologists, and others, have been studying this problem.

It is clear that the number of potential frustrations is somewhat greater in old age than in previous periods. One important source is the inevitable deteriorative changes in the body itself. The wrinkles, the graying hair, the stooping shoulders are familiar to all of us. There is a general loss of resilience in all the bodily tissues. The bones become more brittle; the amount of connective tissue in the muscles increases at the expense of muscle fibers, giving to the limbs the knotted and stringy appearance that is characteristic of old age. The brain slowly decreases in weight. In the brain as well as in the muscles, the supporting tissues increase in amount, while the functional cells, particularly among the very old, are likely to degenerate. Increase in connective tissue and often of fat in and about the heart makes it necessary for the organ to enlarge its size in order to do its work. The gradual stiffening of the arteries adds to the cardiac strain. Many changes also take place in the ductless glands. At about the age of forty-five in women and several years later in men the reproductive capacity ceases.

Automatic regulation of bodily functions no longer takes place so promptly. The old "feel the cold more" because heat losses are not so quickly made good. If, through unexpected exertion, they become out of breath, it takes a longer time for the breathing and heart rate to get back to normal. Other regulatory responses show a similar drag.

All the senses usually show a loss of acuity. We are familiar with the fact that the old usually suffer some impairment of sight and hearing. The visual deficiency is commonly greatest for near objects through loss of elasticity in the lens, which can no longer become sufficiently convex for adequate near vision. This causes the "far-sightedness" of old age.

Loss of hearing in the old is usually greatest for the higher pitches. Drying and hardening of the skin results in loss of sensitivity to touch. Changes in the sense of taste also occur. The taste buds on the top of the tongue gradually atrophy. Beginning at the tip of the tongue the insensitive area extends farther and farther toward the back as age advances. Taste buds on the inner surface of the cheeks also become fewer. The old often complain that "nothing tastes as it used to." Since the olfactory senses, too, usually become less acute in old age, and since, as we have seen, foods owe much of their flavor to the sense of smell, dullness of the olfactory organs is a contributing factor here.

The breaking down of motor skills proceeds in inverse order from that in which the skills were developed. The fine co-ordinations which were the last to appear are the first to be lost. The same rule is very noticeable in the field of memory. Old associations persist; new ones disappear. The very old often remember the events of their childhood, while they forget those of yesterday. Undoubtedly the principle of overlearning plays a part in this selective forgetting, but it is possible that the unknown physiological changes that form the basis of learning may become less stable as age progresses, thus making for quicker forgetting of material learned during the later years.

Changes in the mental abilities of the aged were described in the previous section and need not be repeated here. We shall only note, by way of summary, that if we make a rough division of activities into three classes—perceptual, motor, and intellectual—investigation seems to show that the perceptual skills which are most directly dependent on the functioning of the sense organs are the ones that show the earliest and most rapid decline. Motor skills come next, while the intellectual functions are the last to show marked decrement.

We must remember too that these hazards of old age affect each individual through their impact on other people as well as on himself. A woman may be healthy and full of energy, but if her husband is a chronic cardiac patient her opportunity for travel and new experience must necessarily be limited. And if he dies before she does (as statistics show is probable) she must adjust herself to widowhood with its new problems and frustrations.

The changes in actual capacity to do the things that have brought satisfaction in previous periods of life are very real, and one of the major developmental tasks of old age is to come to terms with them. But there is another set of frustrating conditions that are not perhaps so inevitable. This is the common loss of status that occurs in the declining years. Sometimes this is a matter of money, and the drastically reduced standard of living a retirement income forces upon the individual. Sometimes it is a matter of work, and the feeling of uselessness and loss of identity that overtakes a person when he can no longer organize his self-concept around his occupation. Sometimes it is a matter of the social isolation that can occur as one's friends and associates die or move away. All of these and many other potential sources of frustration could be decreased by planning for the whole life span rather than ignoring the last period until its problems are thrust before us. Society as a whole must make some of these plans —for adequate retirement incomes, for suitable housing, and the like— but individuals can do much for themselves.

So far as the physical changes are concerned, in the vast majority of cases they need not become disabling. Everyone, as he grows older, owes it not only to himself but even more to those with whom he is associated to subject himself to periodic physical examinations in order that the early symptoms of the diseases or degenerative conditions to which persons of his age are especially prone may be detected in their initial stages while it is still possible, in most cases, to do something about them.

Accidents can be avoided if the aging person compensates for his losses in sensory acuity and motor speed and co-ordination by exercising cautious judgment. The important thing is for the aging individual to recognize his limitations as facts to be compensated for by bringing other assets into play, instead of denying the existence of these handicaps and thereby bringing unnecessary danger to himself and others.

Loss of contact with the world around one, and the self-centeredness that comes with such isolation, can be avoided. It often happens that as the old person's senses grow duller he is more and more cut off from other people. Particularly is this true if he suffers a complete or nearly complete loss of hearing. One of the most important aspects of the mental hygiene of old age is therefore to use every possible artificial aid to compensate for the increasing sensory weakness. Properly designed hearing aids, perfectly fitting glasses, are necessities, not luxuries, for a happy old age.

Financial planning for the post-retirement years is being emphasized a great deal in our society—and rightly so. But there is another form of "old age insurance," just as important, about which less is said. Every young person should see to it that he acquires a store of interests, skills, friendships, and life objectives that will outlast his youth. Some people, no matter what their years, never seem to grow old in spirit. These are the ones who have laid up for themselves a store of all-engrossing occupations with which to fill the gaps that inevitably occur with the passage of time. Just as in youth we prepare for the work of maturity, so in maturity some thought should be given to the activities of old age. Most fortunate are they whose life occupations are of a kind that can be continued into old age, for they are the ones from whom the years exact least in the way of adjustment. Edison, Luther Burbank, Justice Holmes, and others who continued to do productive work for years after most people find it necessary to stop, escaped many of the most trying situations of old age. The years bear heaviest upon those to whom they bring an enforced leisure with nothing to fill it that seems worth the doing.

Many of the personality changes that so often come with age—the increased irritability, the self-centeredness, the tendency to magnify bodily ills which sometimes amounts to genuine hypochondria [12]— are less the direct result of age than of the sense of discouragement and frustration that comes from a realization of increasing inability to do the things that were formerly done. We shall see in a later chapter how conflicting impulses or continued frustration may find an abnormal outlet in behavior that in extreme cases leads to complete disintegration of the personality. But old age does not always bring frustration. To some it means increased leisure for the development of long-treasured hobbies and interests, and this is as it ideally should be. Not all forms of ability decline at an equal rate, and most abilities decline slowly enough to enable the old to participate in many activities with enjoyment and profit, if they care to do so. But although the old may continue to carry on the activities of their youth with but slightly abated ardor as long as their physical and mental condition permits, they are not facile in developing new interests. They may renew old hobbies or take advantage of increasing leisure to do some of the many things for which a busy maturity left too little time. But these interests and hobbies must in the main be drawn from the reserves that were accumulated earlier. Too many old people, when confronted with the new leisure that is thrust upon them with the years, find that they have no psychological reserves from which to fill it. Morgan,[13] for example, in his study of recipients of old-age assistance in the State of New York, found that a small number of factors could account for most of the differences between those who seemed happy and well adjusted and those who were continually bewailing their lot. The former had kept up many more pleasant associations with friends and relatives than the latter; they had more outside interests and hobbies; and they habitually sought and found opportunity to perform some kind of useful work. They were also in better health, a fact that may perhaps be as much a result of their more wholesome way of living and behaving as a cause of it.

---

[12] The term *hypochondria* refers to an obsessive interest in one's bodily health, a tendency to magnify bodily ills out of all proportion to their true significance.

[13] C. M. Morgan. The attitudes and adjustments of recipients of old age assistance in upstate and metropolitan New York. *Arch Psychol.*, 1937, Vol. 30, No. 214.

Senescence, which Hall so aptly calls "the youth of old age," is a time when a new kind of psychological weaning must take place if the years that follow are to be satisfying. The adolescent must free himself from emotional dependence upon his parents; the senescent in like manner must free himself from emotional dependence upon his own youth. Each age has its own satisfactions for the person who will take them. Growing old is as normal a part of life as growing up. In age, as well as in youth, the well-integrated personality lives in the present and plans for the future.

SUMMARY

The major developmental task of middle age is to shift from *expansion* to *maintenance*. There is a great deal of variation from person to person with regard to the timing and circumstances of this shift. Old age brings the necessity for adapting oneself to a decline in strength, ability, and status.

Psychological studies of mental development during the adult years have shown that the peak is reached in the twenties. The earlier cross-sectional studies suggested that decline sets in immediately but does not become marked until the sixties. More recent longitudinal studies suggest that abilities are maintained throughout middle age. Verbal skills hold up best. Tested abilities in which speed is an important factor decline most. There is good evidence that learning and productivity can continue throughout life.

Maintaining mental health in old age involves using the resources one still has to make up for the loss of others. Planning for the whole life span enables individuals to fill their declining years with satisfying thoughts and activities.

SUPPLEMENTARY READING

ANDERSON, John E. [Ed.] *Psychological aspects of aging.* Washington, D. C.: Amer. Psychol. Assn., 1956.

This book is the report of a conference that was held in 1955, at which psychologists and representatives of other professions concerned with problems of aging met for four days to discuss what we now know and what kinds of research are most needed. Most students will not wish to read the whole volume, but the separate papers on such topics as adjustment, perceptive and intellective abilities, learning, motivation, efficiency, and skill are interestingly written and constitute a valuable summary of the *information* that has been collected in these areas. Besides this, the *ideas* the authors express about these problems and the discussions of these ideas by all the participants make us aware of the complexity of the problems and of the ingenuity some research workers are showing in solving them.

PART IV

Developmental Deviations

Is it possible to set a definite level, in terms of IQ, below which all persons should be classed as feeble-minded?

What advantage has the use of the term "intellectually-inadequate" over such expressions as "mentally-defective" or "feeble-minded"?

What facts other than the intellectual level of the individual must be considered in deciding whether or not he is to be looked upon as "intellectually-inadequate"?

What are some of the main deviations from the usual or normal pattern of early development shown by most feeble-minded children? Do normal children ever show similar deviations?

What two important differences in the mental organization of normal and feeble-minded individuals have been pointed out by Lewin? What are the practical implications of these differences for the care and training of the feeble-minded?

On the basis of the degree of defect, into what three main classes is it customary to divide the feeble-minded? Is it always possible to say to which of these classes a given individual belongs?

Why is institutional care usually better than home care for children of the lowest intellectual levels, even when the family is financially able to support the child at home?

What are the most important principles to be observed in the training of feeble-minded children?

Mental Deficiency or Intellectual Inadequacy

DEVELOPMENTAL DEVIATIONS

IN THIS CHAPTER and the two that are to follow we shall take up three main ways in which the developmental process may deviate from what we consider to be normal. This whole concept of a "normal" developmental process to which the lives of some persons constitute exceptions does not give a very accurate picture of the true state of affairs. As we have tried to emphasize in previous chapters, *individual* patterns of development are the rule, not the exception. Each person has his own characteristic rate of maturing with regard to each separate psychological function. Johnny is slow about walking but ahead of the norms in learning to talk. Phyllis shows very rapid social development but lags behind her classmates in reading and arithmetic.

Furthermore, there are qualitative differences in the ways individuals carry out the developmental tasks each new period brings. Billy handles the new demands made upon him when he enters school by proceeding very cautiously, doing what the teacher expects him to, getting acquainted with his classmates one at a time. Tommy, in the same situation, seems to be trying to make himself as conspicuous as possible, talking in the classroom, shouting and fighting on the playground.

As adults look back over their own development they can see that there are lapses or weaknesses at different stages. Seldom does a person succeed in coming through all the successive challenges with flying colors. As psychoanalysts have pointed out, unhappy emotional attitudes arising from weaning or toilet training may leave traces on adult personality. One person may have avoided coping with school-room demands during his elementary school years; another may never have really solved the social problems of adolescence. Probably none of us comes through the developmental process unscarred and adequate in all respects.

The reason for giving special consideration to these three kinds of developmental deviation is that they constitute recognized social problems. The classification is basically sociological, not psychological. Society has made special arrangements for the feeble-minded, the mentally ill, and the criminal. In order to utilize wisely the available social assets for treatment or for prevention of these undesirable developmental outcomes, we need to understand them psychologically. And in asking ourselves the question about these particular kinds of cases, "How did development go wrong here?" we can perhaps at the same time increase our understanding of the many other individuals we are classifying together under the ambiguous heading, "Normal."

WHO ARE THE MENTALLY DEFICIENT?

The fact that people differ in mental ability is well known to every one. That general intelligence is distributed within the population in a form that conforms fairly closely to the bell-shaped "normal prob-ability curve" has also been demonstrated, at least for the populations of most American communities. The question then arises, Can we mark off any definite area of the curve (as shown in Figure 99-A) and say that all who fall below this point on some specified test are feeble-minded; all above it, normal?

All who have read this book as far as the beginning of the present chapter should see at once why no such simple rule can be applied. In the first place, standing on mental tests, as was pointed out in Chapter 15, is not an absolutely fixed matter but one that varies within limits that can only be described in terms of probability. The chances that on retesting after a stated interval, John Doe's IQ will not vary from that obtained on the first test by more than five, ten, or twenty points can be stated with reasonable assurance. But those are merely the "betting odds." If there is only one chance in a hundred that his IQ will vary by more than twenty points, there is still a possibility—though less than one chance—that the change may be as great as thirty points, and an even more remote likelihood that the difference may exceed thirty points. However, it is of the upmost importance to remember that the *rare event sometimes occurs*. The bridge player's chances of being dealt thirteen cards of the same suit are exceedingly small, yet such hands occasionally result even from unbiased dealing. If we had a complete record of all the bridge hands dealt in this country over a period of time, we should in all probability find that among those properly shuffled and dealt, the frequency of one-suit hands would correspond very closely to chance expectancy.

The fact that mental test scores may change when children are retested is not, however, the only objection to the use of the IQ as the sole basis for a diagnosis of mental deficiency. As the term is used in practical life, social and economic factors enter in, as well as those that we are accustomed to regard as "intellectual." The child of a day-laborer may be able to substitute brawn for brain and thus win for himself a useful place in the economic world, even though ten years in the schoolroom proved insufficient to take him beyond the educational requirements of the third grade. Furthermore, if he has been trained to conform to the ordinary laws of society, if he is sober, honest, and industrious, can we fairly label him as "mentally deficient," no matter what his IQ may have found to be?

The variation in the intellectual demands of different social and vocational spheres has always been a major stumbling-block in the way of those who would like to find a single objective basis for the "all-or-none" division of society into sharply distinguished classes. Nevertheless this variation is a fact that must be admitted and one to which our practical criteria of mental deficiency must conform. Because it is true, practically speaking, a person may be "feeble-minded" in one kind of social or vocational setting and "normal" in another, it has been suggested that in place of such terms as *mental deficiency* or *feeble-mindedness* we substitute the term *intellectual inadequacy*. The advantage of the latter expression lies in the fact that it does not imply a universal condition that is wholly a matter of the individual himself. Rather, it raises the question, *Inadequate for what?*

Many years ago Tredgold, an English psychologist who was particularly interested in questions of mental retardation and the social care of the intellectually inadequate, formulated a definition that is often quoted. "The feeble-minded," [1] said Tredgold, "are those who, by reason of imperfect or incomplete mental development, existing from birth or from an early age, are . . . unable to conduct themselves and their affairs with ordinary prudence or to compete on equal terms

[1] Tredgold, in common with other English writers, used the term *feeble-minded* in the same sense that we in America use the word *moron* to signify persons belonging to the highest, that is, most nearly normal ranks of the mentally defective group.

with their normal fellows in the struggle for existence within the ranks of society to which they were born." Although American people in general have been loath to accept the final clause of this definition, the fact remains that it cannot be completely ignored. For the chances that the backward child of a successful lawyer or an important business man will form the kind of attitudes and learn the simple but necessary muscular skills needed for him to adjust successfully and happily to the life of a laborer with pick and shovel do not equal the likelihood that the child whose own father earns his living in that way will do so, even though the intellectual capacities of the two children are identical. A level of ability that is "adequate" for certain intellectual demands may be quite "inadequate" if the demands upon intelligence are increased.

Actually, then, when we speak of a given child or adult as "feeble-minded" or "mentally defective" we mean that his intellectual ability is so limited that it will in all probability be found inadequate to meet, by his own unaided efforts, the demands of any kind of environment *in which he is likely to be placed.* The profound idiot at the lowest extreme of the intellectual scale, who can neither walk nor talk, who has never learned to distinguish between food and filth but swallows indiscriminately everything on which he can lay his hands, who has never learned to control his bodily functions or to dress himself, is clearly "inadequate" for the intellectual demands of even the simplest environment. It is necessary to move a considerable distance up the intellectual scale before a level is reached at which the possibility of finding a niche which the intellectually backward person can fill without supervision becomes worthy of serious consideration. Other things remaining equal, however, the likelihood of successful adjustment increases as we move from the lower to the upper ranges of the intellectual distribution. Eventually, a point is reached at which we are reasonably safe in saying that intellectual inadequacy can no longer be invoked as an important determinant of an individual's ability to "get along" in the world, inasmuch as there are a sufficient number of avenues open to him which he is competent to pursue if he will. True, such a person may still select an avenue for which his intellectual powers are inadequate. But in such cases we ascribe his failure to a wrong choice, rather than to intellectual inadequacy in the broad sense of the term.

The division between feeble-mindedness and normality thus corresponds more nearly to the diagram shown in Figure 99-*B* than to that of Figure 99-*A*. It is not a sharp line but a zone in which the probability that an individual will be able to "conduct himself and his own affairs with ordinary prudence" or to "compete on reasonably equal terms with his normal fellows" is limited to a smaller and smaller extent by the purely intellectual aspects of his personality make-up as we advance from the lower to the higher levels of intellectual ability. We may thus regard the proportionate number of dots at each level of intelligence shown in Figure 99-B as roughly analogous to the proportionate number of individuals at each level who, because of intellectual inadequacy, will be unable to meet Tredgold's criterion.

It follows that there must be some determinable point in the distribution of scores earned on a well-standardized intelligence test at which the probabilities of social adequacy and those of social inadequacy are evenly balanced. Below that level the odds are against the successful economic and social adjustments of the person so rated unless he is given some external supervision or other assistance. Above

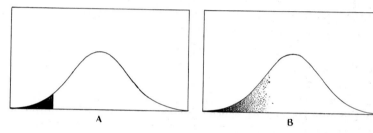

FIGURE 99. Correct and incorrect representation of the distribution of the intellectually inadequate in relation to mental test scores.

it the chances are in his favor. In either case, the prediction takes on increased certainty as we move further away from the point where the odds are even.

The exact point of evenly balanced probabilities has never been determined with certainty for any test, and authorities differ somewhat in their estimates of its location. Probably an approximation is all that can ever be established. For, as we have seen, social conditions as well as the characteristics of the individual cause it to vary. It will be higher in times when there is much unemployment than when there is plenty of work for all who can perform it; higher in communities where the demand is chiefly for highly skilled labor than in regions where there is more need for unskilled workers. However, with conditions as they now exist in the average American city, it appears that a Stanford-Binet IQ of somewhere in the neighborhood of 70 is at least not far removed from the point in question. It should go without saying that this is by no means equivalent to saying that all children whose IQs fall below 70 on this test should be classed as feeble-minded or all above that level as normal. We are not dealing with certainties but with probabilities. Moreover, when we are faced with the need for making practical decisions about the treatment of any individual child, other facts in addition to his purely intellectual ability must be taken into account. Of two children with the same level of intelligence, one may be removed from the regular classroom and placed in a special class because he is not only learning little or nothing from the ordinary type of instruction but is such a disturbing influence that he interferes with the progress of the other children. The other, who is industrious and hard-working, sensitive about his backwardness and eager to do his best on all occasions, may be left where he is, inasmuch as his behavior does not handicap the other children but may even stimulate them to greater effort, while a transfer might prove definitely harmful to the child himself if it made him feel that his best efforts had resulted in failure. The nature of the special class would also have to be considered in deciding whether or not a transfer should be made in an individual case. If a useful and realistic [2] kind of program has been worked out, or if successful methods for improving the personal-social adjustments of the backward child have been devised, the recommendations would differ from those made in cases where the chief purpose of the special class is to relieve the drag upon the regular classes caused by the presence of children who cannot keep up. The child's intelligence is only a part of his equipment for meeting the demands of life. Other assets and liabilities both in the child and in his environment must also be considered.

In the past, too much emphasis has undoubtedly been placed upon the classification of individuals as an end in itself. Only recently have we begun to realize that the mere labeling of a child as "feeble-minded" is of little practical aid in guiding his future development. Better that we should ask, For what is he mentally *adequate*? The answer may be, For nothing except permanent custodial care. Or it may be, Inadequate for an unsupervised existence outside an institution but capable of at least partial self-support, as he grows older, by work within the institution. Or at a still higher level the prediction may be, Inadequate for undertaking the care and rearing of a family but capable of self-support in the outside world if he is given some supervision and if reproduction is prevented by sterilization.

Within the mentally deficient group, three levels are usually distinguished. Following Tredgold, most authorities define the *idiot* as the person whose intelligence is at so low a level that he cannot be taught to look after his own bodily needs, such as eating, dressing,

---

[2] Although training in manual arts is usually emphasized in these classes, this training may be of a kind so far removed from anything required in the actual world of industry that it can hardly be classed beyond the level of "busy-work."

and elimination, or to protect himself against ordinary danger. Left unguarded he is likely to wander into the path of an approaching automobile, to fall from his bed or chair, or to swallow any substance left within his reach. In terms of his performance on mental tests, such an individual does not, as a rule, exceed the level of 20 IQ. Most idiots do a little better on nonlinguistic than on linguistic items.

The *imbecile* is one whose defect is not so grave as to make him incapable of protecting himself against ordinary physical danger or of caring for his everyday bodily needs, but who cannot be taught the elementary skills that, under favorable conditions, might enable him to maintain an independent economic existence. The imbecile cannot, as a rule, learn to count beyond ten or to make change even for small amounts. He cannot learn to read or to write his name. His practical judgment is so poor that he cannot be trusted to perform even very simple operations without constant supervision. On standard intelligence tests his IQ usually falls within the range of 20 to 50.

The *moron*, with IQ of about 50 to 70, is the most nearly normal of the defective group. As can be seen from a brief glance at the curve of distribution of intelligence, morons are by far the most numerous of the three classes. Because, especially at the higher levels, their behavior differs so little from that of children with better mental endowment, their handicaps frequently remain unrecognized. Because teachers and parents do not understand them, they are punished and scolded for their poor grades at school; they are held up to ridicule for blunders that could have been avoided by the exercise of better judgment than that with which nature has endowed them. Often they become the dupes of the unscrupulous and so get into trouble with the law. The moron falls between two stools, for were he a little more stupid than he is, his condition would be recognized and allowances made for his defect; if he were a little brighter he would stand in no need of such allowances but could hold his own without help.

Above the moron level there is another even larger group of *dull* children, not classified as feeble-minded, but meeting many of the same problems the moron encounters. A child with an IQ in the 70-90 range usually has trouble in school, where the level of assigned work is designed for the student with average or better intelligence. Now that compulsory education laws are requiring school attendance through all or most of the adolescent years, such borderline children often have increasing difficulty when they get into high school. It is important that schools and communities recognize the existence of this group as well as of those carrying the definite label of mental deficiency.

It would be beyond the scope of this book even to try to summarize the many and varied causes of mental deficiency. Some cases result from structural damage to the brain at the time of birth. Some arise from diseases that affect the brain. Other organic conditions associated [3] with mental defect include the cases with abnormally small heads known as microcephalic idiots or imbeciles and the hydrocephalic cases whose huge bulging skulls result from a pathological accumulation of fluid within and around the brain. Still other cases include the *cretins* described in Chapter 5, whose condition is the result of insufficient functioning of the thyroid gland in the neck, and the *mongolians,* so called because of the fold in the inner corner of the eyelid which gives to their eyes the appearance of a downward slant like that seen in the Japanese or Chinese. [4]

But by far the largest number of mentally deficient persons, almost all of the morons and some of the imbeciles and idiots, owe their condition to whatever hereditary determiners are responsible for intelligence differences in the whole human family. They represent simply the low end of the intelligence distribution for people as a whole. This is not a matter of a single defective gene, as some early workers thought it would turn out to be, but of the combined effects of many genetic determiners. Because this is true, the concept of *cure* for such cases is inappropriate. The treatment should be directed toward the goal of enabling each individual to make the best possible use of all of the assets he does have.

THE DEVELOPMENT AND BEHAVIOR OF THE INTELLECTUALLY INADEQUATE

Because the feeble-minded differ among themselves in traits other than intelligence almost as much as do normal people, it is impossible to give more than a very sketchy account of some of the ways in which the majority of the former differ from the majority of the latter. There is overlapping of the groups in practically all of the characteristics described.

1. *Developing of early motor skills such as sitting, standing, walking, grasping and handling objects, especially with thumb opposition.* In practically all of these, the typical feeble-minded child shows some degree of developmental retardation. The idiot is likely never to

[3] The term *associated with* is used here in preference to *caused by* because in many of these conditions we do not know which is cause and which is effect. For example, it was formerly believed that microcephalic idiocy was caused by failure of the skull to grow and provide adequate space for the growth of the brain. Now most authorities believe that it is the other way around. The skull remained small because the tiny brain provided no impetus for it to increase in size.

[4] There is, of course, no racial connection here; it is just a matter of superficial resemblance.

acquire more than imperfect command over his gross bodily responses. Walking, if learned at all, may be delayed until the age of four or five years, and the gait remains shambling and awkward. Even the mental defectives of higher grade usually (though not invariably) are from one to three or four months later than the average in learning to sit and walk alone. Many never develop the "light-footedness" of normal childhood. By comparison their step is heavy and "flat-footed"; they frequently make more than normal use of the arms in maintaining balance and may always show a tendency to shuffle. Opposition of the thumb in grasping is typically slow to appear, and even after childhood is well advanced, many backward children continue to approach an object to be grasped in such a manner that the first contact is with the palm of the hand, after which the fingers close around it in a manner not unlike that of the infant.

2. *Development of language.* Because language is a symbolic process, its development in the feeble-minded child is almost invariably slow. The idiot never acquires a vocabulary of more than a few simple words. Few of the feeble-minded begin to talk before the age of two. In many cases speech is delayed until much later. At all ages the vocabulary remains small in comparison with that of normal persons, and the articulation is likely to be imperfect and slovenly. Speech defects of all kinds are more common among the feeble-minded than among persons of normal intelligence.

3. *Emotional development and emotional control.* The chief difference in the emotional life of normal and feeble-minded persons can be roughly summarized under two heads. Emotional reactions among the feeble-minded are chiefly aroused by concrete stimuli immediately present. Except in a limited way, they take little thought for the future and soon forget the joys and sorrows of the past. Secondly, their emotional reactions are expressed more openly than those of normal people are likely to be. They are slower to learn ways either of covering up their real attitudes or of assuming the outward signs of emotions not actually experienced. In both respects their emotional behavior resembles that of children considerably younger than themselves.

4. *Learning.* It is usually agreed that the feeble-minded learn more slowly than average children and do not adapt themselves readily to new conditions. This deficiency, however, is more apparent than real. When such children are compared with others of the same *mental* age rather than of the same *chronological* age, they do not appear to be so deficient in their ability to learn. The trouble has often been that the feeble-minded are confronted at each stage of their lives with learning situations that are too difficult, too abstract, too complex.

Often they become discouraged and give up any attempt to learn. There is much encouraging evidence that at least imbeciles and morons can learn a great deal in an educational program geared to their level of ability.

5. *Rigidity.* Some of the most interesting studies of differences between the mentality of feeble-minded and normal individuals grew out of the theoretical formulations of Lewin. [5] He hypothesized that the main differences between the normal and the feeble-minded can be defined in terms of *tension-systems* and the *rigidity of the boundaries* by which these systems are separated from each other. Both these concepts require explanation.

According to Lewin, a *tension system* is merely an organized system of responses all of which lead, or are designed to lead, toward some particular goal. A given tension system may be trival and of short duration, as when a child climbs over a fence to secure a ball on the other side of it, or significant and enduring, like the continued efforts of an ambitious man to attain success in his profession. The *strength* or *rigidity* of the *boundaries between systems* is manifested in the readiness with which the activities belonging to one can be made to overflow into another. We all know how easily, as a rule, the desires of the young child can be satisfied by the substitution of some other objective for the one initially sought. The baby who cries for the moon is quickly diverted by a shiny rattle; the older child who hoped for a clear Saturday in order that he might play baseball consoles himself by spending the rainy day in his workshop. With the adult these transfers of interest are less readily made. If necessity demands that a projected activity or one already started be discontinued for a time, there is less likelihood that the temporary substitution of some other activity will serve as a lasting distraction. The chances are that it will be only an interruption, with resumption of the unfinished act as soon as the interruption is over. There is little or no breaking down of the boundaries between the two tension-systems. Each maintains its own integrity. But in the case of the infant, and to a lesser degree in the older child, there is more likelihood that the new activity or interest will displace the old either wholly or in part. The baby forgets the moon in his delight in the rattle; the boy, as a result of the day in his workshop, may transfer a part of his interest in baseball to carpentry or electricity, with the result that some of the time previously spent in the former activity is thereafter given over to the latter. As age advances, therefore, there is a gradual tendency for the boundaries between tension systems to become stronger, more clearly defined, with less tendency for energy to overflow from one system to another.

[5] K. Lewin. *A dynamic theory of personality.* New York: McGraw-Hill, 1935.

The older person thus tends to become more persistent in his efforts toward a particular goal and less adaptable in the sense of being able to shift easily from one goal to another. The old saying that "you cannot teach an old dog new tricks" is evidence that this observation is neither new nor confined to the professional psychologist.

Adults differ from children in the number of their tension-systems as well as in the rigidity of the boundaries between these systems. As age advances, interests and goals become more numerous and more diversified. This point has been discussed in a number of previous chapters and requires no further consideration.

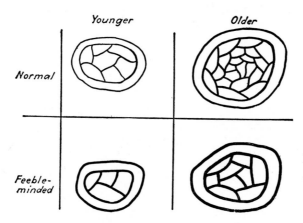

FIGURE 100. Diagrammatic representation of Lewin's theory of feeble-mindedness. (Reproduced by permission of the author and publishers from Kurt Lewin. *A dynamic theory of personality.* McGraw-Hill Book Co.)

In some ingenious experiments, Kounin [6] showed that feeble-minded persons do tend to react as the Lewin theory would predict. (See Figure 100.) Because of their poor potentiality for development they do not attain a very complex or differentiated structure. As rigidity increases with age, they show an increasingly stereotyped kind of behavior.

Rigidity is still a somewhat controversial concept in psychology. Different workers define the term in different ways. But whether we call it rigidity or not, there is a good deal of evidence that the feeble-minded often do have a greater than average tolerance for monotonous, repetitive activity. There is an old story of a feeble-minded woman who was an inmate of a county poorhouse. Usually she worked in the

[6] J. S. Kounin. Intellectual development and rigidity. In R. G. Barker, J. S. Kounin, and H. F. Wright [Eds.], *Child behavior and development.* New York: McGraw-Hill, 1943. Ch. 11.

laundry, but one day when they chanced to be short of help in the nursery, she was given a baby to wash. She did so in boiling water with disastrous consequences.

This "rigidity" of the feeble-minded is shown in another way. They have little capacity for devising artificial means of maintaining interest in a task beyond the point at which psychological "satiation" sets in, that is, beyond the point where they began to feel "fed up" with it. But the normal person can resort to various devices to whip up his flagging interest. An experiment by Lewin [7] illustrates this. Two groups of children, one of normal intelligence and the other made up of feeble-minded children were urged to draw "moon faces" such as

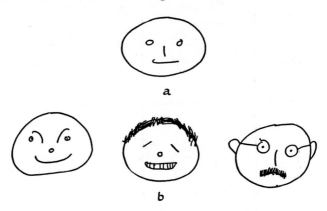

FIGURE 101.   Bright children maintain their interest in a monotonous task by varying their manner of performing it.

those shown in Figure 101-*a*. They were urged to keep on making these faces as long as they would. It was fun at first, but eventually all tired of it. However, the normal children found means to relieve their boredom by varying the task, after the fashion shown in Figure 101-*b*. Few of the feeble-minded did this. They continued drawing faces in much the same way until their patience became exhausted. Then they stopped.

Wolf [8] reports various similar devices by which the five-year-olds in her study were able to increase their "persistence time." For example, one child contrived to renew his interest in the rather monotonous task of canceling out dolls by devising a route whereby all those on a sheet could be crossed out by a single continuous line, or by effacing the figure completely by vigorous scribbling, or by adding various

[7] Lewin, *op. cit.*, p. 198.
[8] T. H. Wolf. *The effect of praise and competition on the persisting behavior of kindergarten children.* Univ. of Minn. Inst. Child Welf. Monogr. Series, No. 15. Minneapolis: Univ. of Minnesota Press, 1938.

appurtenances or embellishments, such as drawing houses around them or adding special decorations to their clothing.

6. *Personality problems.* As psychologists have worked with mentally inadequate boys and girls in schools and community agencies they have become increasingly aware that a large part of the problem such children present comes from personality difficulties that would not need to arise if circumstances were more favorable for their development. The myth of the "happy little moron," immune to the sufferings that brighter people must endure, has been exploded. Actually, just the opposite situation holds in the majority of cases.

In the previous section we mentioned that the mentally inadequate tend to be more impulsive than average in expressing emotion. This is not because the emotions themselves are any different from those of the rest of us, but because their slow rate of development prevents them from learning emotional controls of various kinds at the ages when children usually acquire them. In psychoanalytic terms, *ego* development is retarded, and thus they are more at the mercy of basic *id* impulses. If parents, teachers, and others understand and face this problem, they can help retarded children to learn emotional control by extending the learning process to a later age than is customary.

Another source of personality difficulties is the *rejection* such children often encounter in their homes, schools, and neighborhoods, and the attitudes they develop as a consequence. When he begins to realize that he is different from other children, the retarded child may develop painful inferiority feelings. The awareness that his parents are more ashamed than proud of him may lead to a great deal of anxiety against which various defenses are raised. One person may become isolated and withdrawn, another hostile and aggressive, in his attempt to handle such unconscious feelings. Here too more under-standing attitudes and better educational programs can head off such problems. The personality difficulties are in most instances *by-products* of the mental deficiency rather than essential components of it.

THE EDUCATION OF THE INTELLECTUALLY INADEQUATE

It should be evident from what has been said that boys and girls at the low end of the intelligence distribution require a somewhat different kind of treatment from that given the average child, if they are to make the most of the assets they have. Work with the feeble-minded, like that with the aged referred to in the previous chapter, is an interdisciplinary undertaking. The psychologist is only one member of the team. With the extremely retarded, the idiots and many of the imbeciles, the problem is essentially a medical one. Physicians, and other medical workers such as nurses and physical therapists, must play the major roles in any treatment that is given. With persons at the higher levels, the morons and trainable imbeciles, a teacher becomes the key member of the team.

The first decision that parents of a retarded child must make is whether to keep him at home or place him in a special residential institution. Many factors enter into such a decision. The seriousness of the defect is perhaps the most crucial. There is usually no place for an idiot or low-grade imbecile in the ordinary home. Sometimes parents through a misguided sense of personal responsibility or because of parental love and pity for the child's helpless condition, insist upon keeping such a child in the household, even though his presence may impose such a burden upon those who must care for him and causes such acute embarrassment to the other children that family life becomes completely disrupted. Because most of the conditions that produce these *severely* handicapped cases have nothing to do with heredity, they are as likely to occur in families of the middle and upper social levels as in the lower classes. It is often especially hard for well-educated, intelligent parents to accept a feeble-minded child, yet they feel guilty about putting him in an institution. The problem is complicated by the fact that in many states the available institutions for the feeble-minded have long waiting lists, and it may be months or years before a child can be admitted.

For "high-grade" mental defectives, the necessary training can be given in the home and in special classes of the public schools, although there are many communities in which such programs are still not available. For such cases, whether the education is carried on primarily in the home, in special classes, or in residential schools or colonies, the characteristics it should have are the same. For one thing, a different curriculum is necessary. It is not satisfactory just to present at a slower rate the material usually presented to children of the same chronological age. When we remember what the IQ means, we can see why this is true. A six-year-old moron with an IQ of 60 has a mental age of just a little over three and one half. He is obviously not ready for reading. Normal three-year-olds do not learn to read except under exceptional circumstances. This moron child will not reach the mental level at which reading can easily be mastered until his chronological age is *ten*. If we expose him to four years of discouragement and frustration before he reaches this level, he may never learn at all, and his personality may carry for the rest of his life the scars of this bitter experience. In a special class with a curriculum of its own, backward children can enjoy learning a great many useful things before they tackle reading and arithmetic.

The emphasis in the special training programs for the mentally inadequate falls more on the concrete and practical than on the abstract and highly verbal. Looking at the IQ again, and remembering that on tests like the Binet, fifteen is the age level that represents maturity, we can calculate that our moron with an IQ of 60 will end up with a mental age of nine. [9] Nine-year-olds do not learn algebra or even the more complicated parts of arithmetic. Their vocabularies and their powers of abstract reasoning are limited.

But too much emphasis on the limits of what mentally inadequate children are able to learn should not keep us from realizing how much knowledge *is* open to them. Well-planned special classes devote attention to the skills of everyday life, such as grooming, manners, and finding one's way about in the city. They include all kinds of opportunities for self-expression in the arts and crafts. They teach the most essential parts of reading, writing, and arithmetic when the pupil is ready to learn them. They seek out the special talents and aptitudes each person shows and encourage him to develop them. They prepare him to do some kind of self-supporting work in the community, so that he can live a useful, independent life. And they give him the help he needs in finding a job and getting started on it.

THE OUTLOOK FOR THE MENTALLY DEFICIENT

During the years that such special classes have been in operation, an impressive body of evidence has accumulated that low-IQ children can grow up to be useful, productive citizens. One of the best of such studies was the one reported by Baller [10] in 1936, in which 95 per cent of a group of former "opportunity-room" students in Nebraska were located several years after they left school. All of them had tested below 70 IQ during their school years. Their general adjustment and success was compared with that of a high normal group whose IQ's had ranged from 100 to 120. The feeble-minded had encountered more difficulties. A larger proportion of them had come to the attention of courts and social agencies, and they had been unemployed more often. But their over-all record was surprisingly good. The great majority of them had kept out of trouble and remained self-supporting. Eighty-three per cent of them had been self-supporting at least part of the time.

[9] These are of course just estimates and would not be expected to hold exactly in any individual case. Results from some studies have shown that mental growth continues after fifteen, although at a very slow rate. Other studies have shown that individual growth curves are not all alike.

[10] W. R. Baller. A study of the present social status of a group of adults who, when they were in the elementary schools, were classified mentally deficient. *Genet. Psychol. Monogr.*, 1936, 18, 165-244.

What makes this study especially interesting is that Charles [11] made a second follow-up many years later when the subjects had reached an average age of forty-two. The results still showed that most of them had been self-supporting and kept out of serious difficulties. The jobs they had been doing covered quite a wide range of unskilled, semi-skilled, and skilled activities. It seems clear on the basis of this and a number of other similar studies that children classified as feeble-minded during their childhood years can grow up to be useful citizens.

Some psychologists have been interested in the question as to whether there may be an increase in the IQ's of people like this who have the benefit of a stimulating and encouraging educational situation. Some studies have suggested that this may in fact occur. In the Charles study mentioned above, for example, individual mental tests were administered to twenty-four of the middle-aged subjects. The average IQ for this group on the verbal section of the test was 72. On the performance section it was 88, and on the test as a whole 81. Since these were all persons who had scored below 70 when they were in school, the figures point to a moderate increase. Charles himself is cautious in his conclusions about this, however, as it is always possible that the original scores were in error. At any rate, whatever increase has been indicated in this and other studies is not very great when we compare it with the full IQ range. Individuals who are originally classified as morons seldom rise above the dull normal level.

Most workers in this field would prefer to emphasize the real probability that retarded children can grow up to lead useful, happy, independent lives rather than the slight possibility that time may bring an increase in the intellectual level itself. Too many heartaches have resulted from fruitless attempts to make such children "normal." Too many children's personalities have been warped by the attitudes of parents who refuse to accept them as they are and constantly push them beyond their abilities. The feeble-minded child needs to experience the joy of success. Our responsibility is to see that he learns as much as he can and uses his own assets to their fullest extent.

SUMMARY

It is not really as easy as it might seem to decide just who should be classified as mentally deficient. Social and economic factors vary so much from place to place and from time to time that persons who are not intelligent enough to make their own way in one society may

[11] D. C. Charles. Ability and accomplishment of persons earlier judged mentally deficient. *Genet. Psychol. Monogr.*, 1953, 47, 3-71.

get along fairly well in another. An IQ of 70 is usually taken as a rough dividing line. Within this low-intelligence group three levels are usually distinguished, idiots, imbeciles, and morons.

The causes of mental deficiency are many and varied. It may come from illness or injury to the brain, glandular abnormalities or defective genes. By far the largest number of cases do not seem to have any cause. They simply constitute the low end of the intelligence distribution in the population.

The mentally deficient are slow developers in most respects. It takes them longer to acquire the basic skills like walking and talking. Language development is especially inadequate. Emotional controls are acquired later and with more difficulty. At all ages, however, they can learn things suited to their *mental* age level. Behavior tends to be more rigid and stereotyped than that of the average child. Personality problems are common, but they seem to be indirect effects of the way the children are treated rather than inevitable products of the deficiency itself.

The treatment of the intellectually inadequate varies with the seriousness of the deficiency. For the lowest cases, good custodial care is important. In certain cases, medical treatment is of some value. For the high grade feeble-minded a good educational program makes a great deal of difference in the way they cope with life. Special schools or classes are needed to give this kind of training.

Follow-up studies have shown that it is possible for the majority of morons who have been educated in this way to become self-supporting members of the community.

A MOTHER'S BOOK ABOUT HER CHILD

Buck, Pearl S. *The child who never grew.* New York: John Day, 1950.

In this small volume, Pearl Buck, the famous novelist, tells what it is like to have a feeble-minded child. The story is told with great simplicity and sincerity. The reader gets a better realization of what the behavior of such a child is like than he can ever derive from general discussions. He also realizes how the mother feels and how difficult some of the decisions are for her.

CHAPTER 24

What specific kinds of things do we mean when we say that a person is "emotionally immature"?

Why is "anxiety" such an important concept in the thinking psychologists do about personality?

To what extent are mental abnormalities determined by heredity?

What is the difference between neurosis and psychosis?

What is schizophrenia?

Do normal people always perceive things as they are? What is the difference between an illusion and a hallucination? Are there any conditions that will produce hallucinations in people who are not insane?

Do you think that the different mental disorders are separate diseases or merely different methods or devices by which persons attempt to deal with their problems and their anxieties?

Maladjustment and Mental Illness

COMMON HANDICAPS OF NORMAL PEOPLE

IN ONE SENSE, mental abnormalities are the most "normal" things in the world. This often comes as a shock to the student beginning his study of abnormal psychology. Many of the symptoms he reads about even in descriptions of serious cases are quite familiar to him. He has encountered them frequently in himself and in his friends. It is no wonder that psychology students sometimes make themselves anxious by doubting their own sanity, or unpopular by doubting the sanity of their associates. All of us, faced with the complexities of our life situations and the realities of our developmental handicaps from previous periods, show some behavior that is strange, some that is childish and immature. Consider the following not uncommon cases:

John C. is a hard-working, serious young man who could not afford to go to college but went to work in a bank as soon as he graduated from high school. He was thorough, conscientious, and accurate, and after three years was promoted to a supervisory position with four girls working under him. He has always been shy and uncomfortable with women, and he is reluctant to do the "bossing" that the new job requires. He finds himself feeling increasingly tense and anxious, irritable at home and at work. His stomach is upset much of the time, and he begins to fear that he has an ulcer, or perhaps something worse. He feels that the girls in his department are ridiculing him behind his back. This makes him furious, but there is nothing he can do about it. Sometimes he is afraid he is "cracking up."

Evelyn B. is a senior in high school. She is an only child, and her mother boasts that Evelyn is not silly like other girls, that she spends all her spare time at home and does not go out to dances and parties with the other young people of her age. Actually Evelyn is so shy and self-conscious that she cannot feel at ease with the other boys and girls. She has never learned to dance and is afraid to try for fear that she will be laughed at. Secretly she longs for "dates" and tries to make up for their lack by reading cheap fiction and by daydreaming about all sorts of emotional scenes in which she is the heroine.

Unlike Evelyn, George S. is out for a good time, regardless of the cost. He is impatient of all restrictions, and in constant trouble with parents and teachers. After failing in his high school work he was sent to boarding school but ran away because the rules were too strict. Now he refuses either to enter school or to get a job. He loafs around town and is beginning to associate with undesirable companions picked up around pool halls.

Alfred M. is a college student. His two older brothers made brilliant academic records, and Alfred feels that he is expected to equal their achievement. This he finds very difficult, if not impossible, and so he tries to account for his lower level of achievement in various ways that protect his self-esteem. He feigns ill health and claims that his vision is so poor that he cannot study without difficulty. He complains that his instructors do not make things clear and that they do not always grade fairly. Once, through stenographic error, his real grade of B was recorded as a D. Although the error was promptly corrected, he has never forgotten it but takes every opportunity to tell his friends that "the marks you get here don't mean anything. They make so many mistakes over at the registrar's office that you can't tell a thing from the grades they send out." He insists that other students obtain their high standing by cheating or through favoritism, and he greatly enjoys repeating cynical stories about members of Phi Beta Kappa and other honorary societies.

Caroline S., also a college student, is brilliant but unpopular. As a child she attracted a great deal of attention because of her precocity. Several newspaper articles were published about her achievements, and when she was ten years old a small book of her poems was printed. Now, in a college of high standards where she is for the first time meeting real intellectual competition, she cannot bear to have any one share the spotlight with her. She has developed a number of personal mannerisms to attract attention to herself, spreads ill-natured rumors about other students, and seizes every chance to tell of her own accomplishments. Her book of childish poems occupies the most prominent position on her study table.

Mrs. Gray, married ten years and childless, assumes the role of child in her associations with her husband. She demands constant petting and indulgence, cries when she cannot get her own way, uses baby talk, and dresses in juvenile styles that are no longer becoming. She complains bitterly because her husband spends so many of his evenings at his office or at his club. She has few friends because people in general find her boring and are annoyed by her affectations. She has few resources for amusing herself and is usually very lonely and unhappy.

You have all met people like these. None of them would be classed as definitely abnormal, but all display personality traits that interfere with their happiness and handicap them in their chances for success in life. Although their problems seem very diverse both in form and origin, one thing can be said about all of them. These persons have not grown up. Somewhere along the line their personalities have suffered from arrested development.

In John and in Evelyn we see adults who have never really come to grips with the developmental tasks of adolescence. George is still the spoiled baby to whom his rattle and his bottle of milk are all-important. He is deliberately shutting his eyes to the world where men work and achieve and reap the benefits of their labor. Instead he tries to cling to the privileges and immunities of babyhood.

Alfred and Caroline have advanced to a somewhat higher level, but both have stopped short of complete maturity. They have failed to develop the broader sense of social values that would enable them to view themselves and their own achievements with some detachment, to appreciate what others do and to take a sportsmanlike attitude toward honest defeat. Egocentricity is a normal attribute of early childhood, but long before a boy or girl has reached the age of entering college, this narrow preoccupation with self should have expanded into a wider conception of social aims and an appreciation of what others are doing toward fulfilling those aims. To the truly socialized person the natural disappointment over his own failure is tempered by the knowledge of another's success, but to the immature adult who has never outgrown the egocentricity of childhood, seeing another person succeed merely adds gall to the bitterness of his own defeat. We may note, too, that Alfred appears to have moved a little further along the road from egocentricity to socialization than Caroline has, for in his concern with covering up his own failures there is tacit recognition of and a covert admiration for the accomplishments of others. Caroline, on the contrary, sees only herself.

Little need be said of the case of Mrs. Gray. Like George she clings to the things of childhood, but, perhaps because of the license accorded to her sex, her behavior is more open and unabashed. George covers up his real desire to remain a child with a blustering kind of aggression that nevertheless is closely allied to the temper tantrums of infancy.

Fortunately, many such manifestations of immaturity are only temporary. Evelyn may turn over a new leaf when she leaves home to go to college. Encouraged by the girls in her dormitory, she may take some dancing lessons and begin to go to college parties. Little by little she may succeed in overcoming her shyness. John C. may encounter a wise physician who realizes that his continuing digestive disturbances reflect some emotional difficulty and who can help him learn to handle executive responsibility without suffering. George S. may go into one of the Armed Services and do some serious thinking about himself and his future when he comes out. He may then complete his high school work through correspondence courses and examinations, and make a creditable record in college. With or without the help that can be given through psychotherapy, all of the other persons we have described *may* leave behind them the immediate attitudes that keep their lives from being as rich and productive as they might be. The tragedy is that they *may not*. Further development may bring not the stability and competence of increasing maturity but the suffering and waste of a full-blown neurosis or psychosis. We need to understand as well as we can how this comes about.

OBSTACLES TO HEALTHY DEVELOPMENT

The one factor that is found in cases representing most if not all of the major varieties of psychiatric illness is the presence at some period of the person's life of an unusually large amount of *anxiety*. We have all experienced this feeling often enough so that we hardly need to have the word defined. It refers to an acute but vague dread, a state of mind in which the person is overwhelmed by something like fear, but is unable to analyze what it is that he fears. It is probably the most intensely uncomfortable state of mind a human being can experience. (In Chapter 13 we have discussed some of its origins in early childhood and the ideas of Freudian psychoanalysts with regard to it.)

Because it is so uncomfortable, people unconsciously learn to defend themselves against the feeling in various ways. One of Freud's contributions was to identify and give names to many of these defense mechanisms, and his daughter, Anna Freud, [1] elaborated them in some detail. For example, *rationalization* involves making up "reasons" for a humiliating event or a failure, so that anxiety is not increased by a sense of personal inadequacy. *Projection* refers to the process of reading one's own unworthy motives into someone else's behavior and thus blaming the other person rather than oneself. *Reaction formation* is an attempt to get rid of anxiety-producing impulses by acting in an opposite manner. It has become common knowledge that the compulsively clean housewife is probably actuated by an unconscious wish to be messy, the puritanically virtuous man by an unconscious sexual drive.

Without cataloguing the long list of separate defense mechanisms about which one or another personality theorist has written, we can

[1] A. Freud. *The ego and the mechanisms of defense.* New York: International Univ. Press, 1946.

understand what it is that they serve to do. They keep the person from becoming aware of the threatening forces *within himself.* It appears now that it is chiefly these inner threats rather than outer dangers that are the important instigators of personality difficulties. We have seen in earlier chapters that for an infant to grow into an acceptable member of society, he must limit the expression of powerful drives. As development proceeds, he is always haunted by a knowledge that these forces can get out of control. This keeps anxiety alive. A certain amount of it is normal and natural and helps to channel his striving in acceptable directions. But too much of it, particularly at crucial developmental stages, can be paralyzing or completely disorganizing.

The differences between abnormal personality states and those that we all experience, then, seem to arise mainly from individual differences in *susceptibility* to such inner threats, and differences in the means that have been developed for *coping* with them. It is impossible to specify any one source from which individual differences come. They occur at all stages of development, from the very first. There is fairly clear evidence that there are hereditary determiners for some of them. Kallman [2] has for years been collecting evidence with regard to the way several different kinds of mental illness are distributed in families. The fact that identical twins are much more alike than pairs of people having any other kind of relationship points to some hereditary influence. Prenatal conditions and complications in the birth process may leave some persons more susceptible to stress from the beginning.

Early childhood is the period that has been most clearly seen as a source of chronic anxiety that may lead to various behavior abnormalities later in life. The baby during his first few months is especially susceptible to frustration. This means a state in which a strong need is not being met. We can visualize it as a massive obstacle in the path toward something greatly desired. The reason that the effects of frustration during infancy are more serious than those of frustration during later periods is that there is absolutely nothing the baby can do to help himself. An influential theory in psychology [3] held that *aggression* of some kind always occurs as a natural reaction to frustration. Since it was first proposed in 1939 the theory has undergone many modifications. Certainly not everyone reacts with open, aggressive conduct to the frustrations he encounters. But it may well be that stirred-up feelings with strong aggressive coloring feature largely in the anxiety that is an aftereffect of frustration, especially when it comes from neglect or bad treatment in infancy.

[2] F. J. Kallman. *Heredity in health and mental disorder.* New York: Norton, 1953.

[3] J. Dollard and associates. *Frustration and aggression.* New Haven: Yale Univ. Press, 1939.

The anxiety that has its origin in the second, third, or fourth years is likely to be related to *conflicts*. The socialization process inevitably brings conflicts between the child and the external authorities who are trying to guide him toward the control of his impulses. But more important as a source of basic anxiety are the conflicts between different aspects of his own personality. He comes to love and hate the same persons, and this *ambivalence* is very unsettling. When he has internalized the rules that have been taught him about what to do and what not to do, the rudimentary conscience that arises out of his wish to please those who are dear to him comes into conflict with strong impulses to carry out the prohibited acts. No child escapes such conflicts entirely, since he must be trained to go to the toilet, to keep away from dangerous places, and to show some consideration for other people's rights. If the training is especially severe and if drastic punishments or alarming threats are used to keep him in line, his chronic anxiety level will be higher than average.

Each succeeding period has its new sources of anxiety. The school years may bring devastating doubts about one's adequacy as a person. Illness, injury, or extreme danger situations are generators of anxiety whenever they occur. So-called war neuroses, for example, may occur in men who have shown healthy reactions to life up to this time if they are exposed to unusual or prolonged danger situations. It seems to be true, however, that stress situations occurring at later periods are not so devastating in their effects as those of infancy and early childhood. In cases where an adult shows an unusually anxious reaction to some misfortune, such as a serious automobile accident or the loss of a loved one, it is usually because old anxieties, long held in abeyance by defense mechanisms of one kind or another, are *reactivated* by the event.

People differ also in the resources they have for *coping* with anxiety. Here too there are perhaps sheer quantitative differences in "ego strength" arising from genetic determiners that are as yet little understood. Kallman, [4] in his investigation of the genetics of schizophrenia, found that it was necessary to postulate differences in an inherited *resistance* to the schizophrenic process, as well as differences in the predisposition itself, in order to bring his findings into line with genetic theory. But here too what happens at each developmental stage helps to determine individual differences in "coping" ability. Again, early stages, especially the preschool years, are especially influential, but there is abundant evidence from education and psychotherapy that at *all* stages, even in old age, individuals can learn better ways of coping with anxiety.

[4] *Op. cit.*

Differences in how well people handle their anxieties are not just quantitative, but qualitative as well. That is, different persons hit upon different means of keeping anxiety under control, and some of them work more successfully than others. Freud called attention to the pervasive importance of *repression,* which means essentially keeping oneself unaware or unconscious of the disturbing feelings. Many of the separate defense mechanisms, such as projection and reaction formation, serve the purpose of keeping anxiety-producing feelings repressed. Probably the majority of people make some use of repression as a way of maintaining equilibrium. "I won't let myself think about it." "I'll keep busy so that I don't have time to brood." How often do we hear remarks like this from persons undergoing some unusual strain?

Usually this course of action works well. The trouble with it, when the underlying chronic anxiety level is very high, is that if it is not *altogether* successful, a sort of vicious circle can be set in motion. The unconscious drives break through the wall of repression and affect the person's dreams, or lead to inexplicable symptoms. These alarm him still more, his anxiety level rises still higher and he uses up more and more of his energy in trying to patch up the crumbling wall of his defenses. But they cannot be made strong enough to control the ever-increasing anxiety. Thus a real neurosis may develop.

Defense mechanisms, or devices for keeping disturbing motives out of consciousness, are not the only resources the person has. His intelligence, his special talents, his skills, are all important assets. One of the most important developments in mid-twentieth-century personality theory has been the increasing emphasis on such *constructive* processes. An eight-year-old boy can learn to be *good* at many things instead of trying to silence his anxieties about his own inadequacies through boasting or making excuses. An adolescent girl can improve her appearance, learn social skills, and overcome shyness instead of developing a system of devious rationalizations to protect herself from the realization that she is a wallflower. Emphasis on individual assets that can be used in constructive ways so that anxiety will not increase to unmanageable proportions is characteristic of much applied psychological work, in child guidance clinics, in schools, in counseling centers, and in rehabilitation agencies.

VARIETIES OF MALADJUSTMENT—THE NEUROSES

The most basic distinction that psychologists make when they attempt to set up classification systems for behavior disorders is the line they draw between *neurosis* and *psychosis.* A neurotic condition is considered to be considerably less serious than a psychotic condition. But the difference between them is not just quantitative, but qualitative as well. In a neurosis, the patient is still in active communication with the external world. He is aware of his own suffering, concerned about his symptoms. Usually he can continue his work, though perhaps with a considerable loss of efficiency. The psychotic patient, on the other hand, is to a greater or lesser extent out of touch with the world of people's common experience. He may say and do strange things—things that are unintelligible unless one knows what his inner world contains. He may try to avoid all interaction with people around him and remain mute and motionless for long periods of time. He may be unable to organize his complex ideas, emotions, and attitudes into an intelligible total pattern, so that his behavior seems fragmentary rather than "all of a piece." He may act as though he no longer cares what anyone thinks of him.

In general, there is little tendency for a neurotic condition to become psychotic as time passes. It seems rather that these are two different patterns of reaction to psychological stress. Some individuals have a tendency toward one, some toward the other. There are, of course, all sorts of combinations of neurotic and psychotic symptoms that may occur in individual cases.

As indicated in the previous section neurosis can be thought of as an outgrowth of an unsuccessful effort to keep anxiety under control by the use of defense mechanisms. It takes many forms, depending upon personality and circumstances. Certain ones of these forms are common enough to lead to special diagnostic labels. In anxiety neurosis the patient is overwhelmed by the anxiety feelings themselves. He has periods when he feels an apprehension amounting almost to panic. Any of the physiological symptoms that would occur in an extreme danger situation may put in their appearance—heart palpitation, nausea, tremors, effects on bowels and bladder functions. (In Chapter 5 we explained how the autonomic nervous system produces such effects.) Such attacks perpetuate the "vicious circle" effect mentioned earlier, because the person worries so much about the fact that he could suffer such an attack for no apparent reason that the worry increases the supply of anxiety, thus leading to even more neurotic manifestations.

Other neurotic conditions center more around inappropriate patterns of defense against anxiety than around the anxiety itself. In *hysteria* the anxiety is converted into some physical symptom having no organic basis. Many of us have known chronic invalids whose disabilities were of this nature. For example, a young woman was engaged to be married to a man who lived next door to her and whom she had known since childhood. One day the man came home, bringing with him another girl whom he introduced to his amazed family as his wife. They had been married that day. When his jilted sweetheart was told of the marriage she was greatly upset, and in the midst of her tears she exclaimed, "I will never go there to call on her. Never!" A day or so later she was taken ill, and it was soon discovered that a paralysis had developed in both legs. The relationship here is fairly obvious. She would not go, hence it was necessary for something to happen that would make it impossible for her to go.

At first thought it seems as if the patient were just pretending to be sick, but in true hysteria this is not the case. The patient has deluded himself so thoroughly that to all intents and purposes he is as sick as he thinks himself to be. Of course there are many cases in which the illness is pure make-believe, and it is probable that in most instances the device, which is adopted more or less intentionally in the beginning, later progresses to a stage where it takes on a character of reality to the patient. The physical symptoms assumed by the hysterical patient cover almost the entire range of human diseases. Hysterical blindness, deafness, mutism, and cardiac disturbances are fairly common.

Cases of *amnesia* are also classified as hysterical reaction patterns, because in such cases the mental symptom of forgetting a whole period of one's life, or even one's own identity, serves exactly the same purpose as does a physical symptom like paralysis or blindness. It keeps the person from feeling intolerable anxiety.

Another sort of neurotic reaction pattern with a superficial resemblance to hysteria is the *psychosomatic* disorder. The realization that diseases like asthma, hypertension, and peptic ulcer often seemed to have emotional origins opened the way to rapid progress in our understanding of these and a great many other medical conditions. They differ from hysterical reaction patterns in that the organ in question *is* actually out of order. When we remember that anxiety is physiological as well as psychological it is easy to see why it is that if too much of it continues too long, some organ system of the body is likely to be affected. Painful as it is, a psychosomatic symptom can serve as a defense mechanism, in that it makes the individual's general anxiety seem more reasonable to him. It gives him something tangible to worry about. In general, however, such symptoms solve no problems, but rather set up the kind of vicious circle to which we have referred.

Another whole family of neurotic reaction patterns consists of the *obsessive-compulsive* conditions. The term *obsession* refers to a thought or idea that recurs constantly and cannot be dismissed. The term *compulsion* refers to some apparently meaningless act that a person has a strong impulse to carry out. *Phobias* also are classified here, the irrational fears that some persons experience for such things as closed rooms, high places, or open spaces. Such symptoms too seem to give a person a tangible basis for anxiety and thus keep it from being overwhelming. They thus serve as partial defenses. But like the other neurotic reactions, in the long run they tend to increase the amount of anxiety present rather than to reduce it.

For all neurotic disorders, therapy can be directed toward reducing the anxiety level, toward enabling the person to locate and face the real origins of his trouble rather than the symptoms that are only its disguises, or toward working out more constructive ways of coping with life's strains. Different kinds of therapy emphasize different approaches. Tranquilizing drugs, for example, reduce the present anxiety level without regard to its origins. Psychotherapy pays more attention to unraveling complex origins of the state of mind and replacing inadequate coping mechanisms with better ones.

VARIETIES OF MALADJUSTMENT—THE PSYCHOSES

Among the psychotic reaction patterns the commonest and the most serious is schizophrenia. [5] About half of the patients in our mental hospitals throughout the country carry the schizophrenia label. The disease often begins during youth (sometimes even in early childhood) and in many instances lasts throughout all the rest of life. (However, because of the efforts that have been made in the past few decades to find out more about this condition and to focus more therapeutic attention on patients who suffer from it, the prospects for an individual schizophrenic are much more promising than they used to be.)

It would be more accurate to use the plural noun *schizophrenias* rather than the singular noun *schizophrenia,* because of the great variety of reactions included under the term. There are almost as many ways of being schizophrenic as of being normal! The one thing they all have in common is a breakdown in the complex process by means of which an individual's inner world and his relationships to all the people and things around him are organized or *integrated.* He no longer operates as a coherent, intelligible personality. Thoughts, feelings, and actions proceed in directions of their own, apparently out of touch with each other and out of communication with those of other people.

[5] Probably no psychiatric term is more commonly misused in ordinary speech than this one. It means something far more serious than the kind of multiple personality many newspaper writers seem to think that it means. A person who leads a double life is a kind of neurotic of the hysterical type. The *split personality* of schizophrenia is a *shattered* or *fragmented* personality, not just one that is divided into two inconsistent parts.

Several main subtypes of schizophrenia have been described, but individual variations are more striking than diagnostic types. In some persons the main symptom is apathy, the loss of all motivation to achieve and to participate in human affairs. In others it is mute immobility. In still others peculiar grimaces and inexplicable rituals are in evidence. Some show a sort of general silliness, giggling for no reason, combining shocking or sorrowful remarks with totally inappropriate emotional expressions. Some develop delusional systems centered around plots, inventions, or strange mystical religions.

We are still a long way from a complete understanding of why schizophrenia develops in some individuals. Through the years, many research workers have preferred to focus their efforts on a search for some physical cause, some subtle difference in brain structure or body chemistry that would generate these abnormalities. Kallman's evidence mentioned earlier shows that in 86 per cent of the cases where one of two identical twins becomes schizophrenic, the other also contracts the disease. Where the twin pair is nonidentical, only 14.5 per cent are alike with regard to it. This enormous difference suggests that some kind of predisposition is inherited. Brain specialists and biochemists continue their attempts to find out what it consists of, so that we may be able to counteract it.

But many psychiatrists and psychologists are firmly convinced that the important origins of this breakdown of integration are often located in the person's life history rather than in his genes. In psychonanalytic terms, schizophrenic reaction patterns represent a *regression* or reversal of the developmental process. It is as if the person were trying to get back to the period of infancy (or even prenatal life) when he was not expected to take responsibility for himself and manage an intricate network of relationships to other people.

Probably when a great many more facts are assembled, schizophrenia will turn out to be a result of many causes varying somewhat from patient to patient. This seems the most reasonable conclusion in view of the many kinds of therapy that seem to help at least some patients to improve. Tranquilizing drugs, various kinds of shock treatment, group and individual psychotherapy, and reorganization of the patient's social surroundings in the hospital are all being tried. Each therapeutic method produces cures in some cases. Patients who do not respond to one kind of treatment alone may improve under some combination of treatments. There is much "trial-and-error" still going on in our attempts to change schizophrenic reaction patterns, but considerable progress is being made in our understanding of them.

There are many other special varieties of psychoses. Some appear to be exaggerations of normal mood changes. In a *depressive* state, a patient will be extremely sad, and all of his movements and mental reactions become painfully slow. A man in the grip of a psychotic depression may sit for hours with his head between his knees, bemoaning his guilt and worthlessness. Hospitalization is advisable in such cases to forestall suicide. Keep such patients alive and they usually recover even without treatment of any sort. Such things as electric shock can shorten the period of extreme depression, and psychotherapy can often head off future attacks. Some patients suffer from the opposite variety of symptoms, *manic* or wildly excited moods. These too are temporary. In some instances patients shift abruptly from depressed to manic phases and back again. The manic and depressive psychoses typically occur in middle age rather than in youth.

There are other psychotics whose only abnormality seems to be the peculiar ideas we call *delusions*. These are the *paranoids*. Sometimes the ideas are worked into highly complex systems expressing a high level of intelligence. Often they are harmless. The person who thinks of himself as an inspired but misunderstood religious leader and who devotes all of his time to working out the fine details of the new theology, cosmogony, and philosophy will not require psychiatric attention unless his inner voices begin to admonish him to kill those who stand in the way of the new gospel.

There are also many psychotic conditions that are clearly organic in their origin. Brain tumors, poisons of various kinds, infections that attack the nervous system, deterioration of brain tissue in old age— all these and many other conditions lead to psychosis. It is interesting to note that even in cases with a known organic cause, the particular set of symptoms a given person will develop depends to some extent on what his previous personality has been like.

NORMAL AND ABNORMAL REACTIONS

If there is one thing that our attempts to study and to help neurotic and psychotic patients have taught us, it is that there is no hard-and-fast line that can be drawn between the normal and the abnormal. Any one symptom that we examine resembles experiences we have all had. For example, all of us have at times been misled into thinking that we saw or heard something that was not there. Usually there was something there, but not the thing we supposed. Mistakes of this kind are known as *illusions*. Some illusions of visual perception are experienced under the appropriate conditions by almost everybody. They are normal illusions, resulting from the way the eyes work. A number of these illusions have been described in Chapter 14. Here is another one known as the "floating finger illusion" that you can easily try for your-

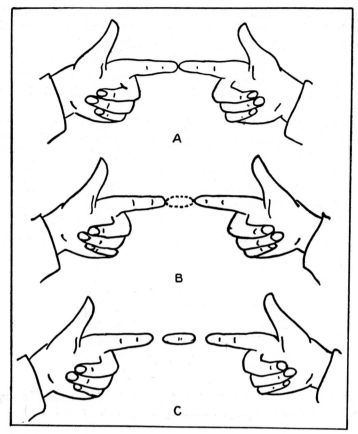

FIGURE 102.   The floating finger illusion. (From W. L. Sharp. The floating finger illusion. *Psychol. Rev.* 1928, 35, 171-173. Courtesy Psychological Review Co.)

self. It is due to the fact that you have two eyes which see things from slightly different angles. (See Figure 102.)

Choose a position where you can fixate the eyes on an object at some distance. Bring the tips of the two index fingers together at a distance of about eight or nine inches from the eyes and just below the line of regard. Although your finger tips are actually in contact with each other, they will appear to be separated by about two inches and to be connected by a third finger which completely fills the intervening space. Now if, while you continue to look at the distant object, you separate the fingers slowly, the third finger will at first appear to be floating in space between them. As the fingers draw further apart the third finger grows shorter and eventually disappears.

Illusions of this kind have attracted a good deal of interest among psychologists because of the light they throw on fundamental questions of perception. But in addition to these generally experienced illusions of perception, every one occasionally has illusions that are peculiar to himself and are chiefly determined by his organic state at the moment, by what he happens to be thinking about, what he is "set" to see or hear.

I am expecting a telephone call. The telephone is in another room from which I can hear the bell but not very clearly. Half a dozen times I stop what I am doing and listen, thinking that I hear it. My state of expectation makes almost any noise sound like the telephone call. A timid woman alone in the house hears burglars in every room. A superstitious boy ran shrieking frantically that he had been pursued by a tall white ghost that stretched out its long arms trying to seize him. The ghost was a pillowcase on the clothesline, blowing in the wind.

FIGURE 103. Jastrow's illusion. (From J. J. B. Morgan. *The psychology of abnormal people.* Courtesy Longmans, Green & Co.)

Much of what even normal people perceive is the result of what they are set to perceive. Show Figure 103 to a friend after having previously told him that you are going to show him a picture of a duck. Tell another friend that you will show him a picture of a rabbit and then show him the same picture. The chances are that the one who expected to see a duck will see a duck; the one who was prepared to see a rabbit will see a rabbit. Getting set to respond in a particular way is in reality the beginning of the act of responding in that way. Unless there is a fairly sharp interference, such as would come, in this case, from being shown a picture that could not be reasonably made to confrom to expectation, the activity will run along its appointed course.

The more intense the preparatory reaction, the more likely it is to override the obstacles caused by discrepancies between expectation and fact and to make the external evidence conform to the pattern set by the internal drive. Emotional states such as anger, fear, jealousy, or suspicion are preparatory reactions that may carry all before them.

The jealous wife sees infidelity in the most ordinary acts of courtesy shown by her husband to other women. The timid pedestrian sees a bandit behind every bush. The unduly self-conscious person thinks that everybody is looking at him and talking about him.

Illusions due to strong preparatory reactions are experienced by everybody, and when these reactions are not too grossly inappropriate to the situation that touches off the response, no one pays much attention to them. The city woman walking along a leaf-strewn path in the woods starts back at the sight of a half-hidden stick exclaiming, "Gracious! I thought it was a snake!" Here as in many other cases the phenomenon which Hollingworth called *redintegration* plays an important part. From a single feature one reconstructs a total situation. Something about the stick resembles a snake, and the woman, who in any case is prepared to see snakes, responds as suddenly and as strongly to this single feature as if the snake were there.

Illusions such as these disturb nobody as long as the "mistake" has an actual basis that other people can see. But when the intraorganic state dominates the situation so completely that the response occurs with no external conditions to justify it, we say that the person is suffering from *hallucinations,* which are a common symptom of schizophrenia. But there is really only a slight difference between the normal illusion and the abnormal hallucination.

The same could be said with regard to the unrealistic thinking of the paranoid, the dream states of the schizophrenic, or the exaggerated moods of the manic or depressive patient. There is no clear boundary between the "sane" and the "insane." The one merges into the other by imperceptible stages.

This kind of understanding of what would otherwise appear to be strange and frightening types of human behavior can do two things for us. In the first place it can give us a deeper tolerance, an attitude of kindness and concern toward the mentally ill. They have not been transformed into something less than human. They are still our kinsmen.

In the second place, it can increase our sensitivity to some of these less than adequate ways of coping with life at the times when they *originate.* We are beginning to realize that human personality in its development may learn to adjust to its immediate difficulties at the cost of future disaster. In paranoia, we see how the child who learns to compensate for his disappointments through daydreaming, who learns to project his wishes and phantasies into the external world until he sees in the behavior of others the things that actually exist only in his own mind, who learns to rationalize his failures by referring them to an imaginary system of persecution, may, as his responsibilities increase with adult life, take refuge in a series of delusions until he can no longer distinguish between fact and fancy. By so doing he has protected his self-esteem, but he has lost everything else. The hysterical person adopts a different device. He makes physical disability his excuse and protects his pride by a physical handicap that is always serious (otherwise it would not fulfill its purpose) and that often means chronic invalidism. Obsessive-compulsives, schizophrenics, and manic-depressives are all using methods they *learned* somewhere along the line. If they could have had a little more help at this crucial time with finding better ways of reducing anxiety and satisfying basic needs, the course of their lives might have been different.

Much progress has been made in finding ways to "cure" mental illness, or, to put the matter more accurately, to change patterns of adjustment. We hope for continued progress along these lines, but we also believe that in the long run prevention will be more important than cure.

SUMMARY

Examples of immature behavior can be found in many if not most adults. In some cases such modes of adjustment are habitual and keep the individuals from attaining the satisfactions of maturity.

The emotion that is at the root of serious abnormal states is anxiety, or fear without an apparent cause. It arises from sources within the personality, though it may be touched off by shocks or misfortunes. People differ in susceptibility to anxiety and in the means they have for coping with it. Such individual differences may come from heredity or from experiences encountered during any of the periods of development. The earliest years are especially influential.

Neurosis differs from psychosis in seriousness and in quality. The neurotic maintains his contact with the world and with other people and keeps his own life organized after a fashion. The major varieties of neurosis are exaggerations, either of anxiety states or of defense mechanisms used to ward them off. In psychosis, the patient's communication with other persons is cut off or distorted, and his own personality becomes disorganized. Hallucinations and delusions are common symptoms.

The most common and most serious psychotic condition is schizophrenia. It has a variety of manifestations all exemplifying disintegration of the personality. Other psychotic states include the manic-depressive conditions, paranoia, and the organic reactions.

Experimental work on illusions has shown how complex our day-to day perception of the world is. Abnormal symptoms like hallucinations and delusions are not totally different from common errors we all make. Understanding of abnormal psychology can help us accept and aid those who are mentally ill, and to head off undesirable developmental trends in children.

FOR FURTHER READING

MAY, Rollo. *The meaning of anxiety*. New York: Ronald, 1950.

In this book the concept of anxiety is examined very broadly with an eye to history and philosophy as well as psychology. It helps the reader understand a state of mind rather than abnormal symptoms, and helps him to think in terms of sound mental health as well as therapy.

The student with limited background in psychology may find some of the discussion overly technical and detailed. He will do well in this case to focus his attention on Chapter 1, "Introduction," Chapter 6, "Summary and Synthesis of Theories of Anxiety," and Chapter 7, "Case Studies Demonstrating Anxiety." It is here that the author's ideas find clearest expression.

CHAPTER 25

What is your estimate of the total number of serious crimes committed in the United States in the course of a single year? After you have made a guess, look at the figures in the first section of this chapter and see how close you came to the facts.

In what way is the social problem of crime and delinquency related to developmental psychology?

Is there any evidence to support the idea of a "criminal type"? What physical and psychological characteristics have been shown to be more frequent in delinquent than in nondelinquent children?

What is meant by a "delinquency area"?

What aspects of family situations are most clearly related to delinquency?

What are the implications for prevention and treatment of a "multiple causation" theory of delinquency?

Delinquency and Crime

EXTENT OF THE PROBLEM

DURING THE LAST WEEK of April, 1958, the newspapers of the country were devoting a great deal of space to the story of the murder of seventeen-year-old Michael Ramos, a leader of the King's Dragons gang, by sixteen-year-old Pedro Ramon Serra, the chief of the Egyptian Crowns gang. This was just one in a long series of not too different stories from cities and towns throughout the country. People who pick up their morning papers see headlines of this kind often enough so that they are shocked but not surprised by them. More and more people—fathers and mothers, teachers, policemen, citizens—are asking "Why?" What has gone wrong when teen-agers explode in senseless brutal violence? Who is to blame? What is to be done?

There is no question about the *fact* that this is one of the most serious problems our society must face. The FBI reports [1] show that in 1956 there was a total of 2,563,150 major crimes committed in the United States. "Major crimes" means such acts as murder, rape, larceny, auto theft, robbery from the person, and aggravated assault (assault in which deadly weapons were used in such a way as to be likely to cause permanent maiming or even death of the victim). Startling as it may seem, the figure of two and a half million crimes does not include minor delinquencies such as traffic violations, petty thievery, and the like. These are real crimes.

[1] *Uniform crime reports*, J. Edgar Hoover, U. S. Department of Justice. Washington, D. C.: 1958, *World Almanac.*

The situation is even worse than this total figure indicates. For one thing, the rate has been increasing in an alarming way. The increase in the number of crimes between 1950 and 1956 was 43 per cent, as compared with a population increase of only 11 per cent. The figures for the first half of 1957 indicated that the rate was still increasing. Furthermore, 46 per cent of the arrests in 1956 were of youngsters under eighteen. It is *juvenile* crime that is flourishing in spite of everything that is being done to combat it.

Such statistics are showing us more and more clearly that criminality is a *developmental* problem. Certain persons begin antisocial careers very young. Sheldon and Eleanor Glueck [2] found that almost half of their carefully chosen samples of institutionalized delinquents had shown the first clear signs of antisocial behavior before the age of eight. In 88 per cent of the cases, the delinquent pattern was well established before puberty. Crime is not something that erupts inexplicably during adolescence. There is also clear evidence that adult criminals are recruited from the ranks of the juvenile lawbreakers. [3] Seeing the problem in this way creates the proper framework for research on it. What we must try to understand is why some children take this direction rather than the one that society sanctions and approves.

ARE CRIMINALS "BORN" OR "MADE"?

An idea from an earlier period of criminological investigation that still crops up from time to time is that there is a "criminal type" of person, doomed by his hereditary deficiencies to live as a sort of perpetual exile from human society. Lombroso, whose writings were very influential at the beginning of this century, held that these true criminals tended to have an unusually large number of physical anomalies which he called "stigmata." By this he meant such things as a peculiarly shaped skull, an undeveloped or deformed nose, various types of dental anomalies, bodily characteristics resembling those of the opposite sex, unusual distributions of body hair, and so on. Lombroso thought that the criminal could be identified by means of such physical signs of degeneration, and that even the type of crime he was most likely to commit might be predicted on this basis.

[2] S. Glueck and E. Glueck. *Unraveling juvenile delinquency.* Cambridge, Mass.: Harvard Univ. Press, 1950.

[3] Fortunately the *majority* of juvenile delinquents do not become criminals but settle down into law abiding lives, when they get out of their teens. In a group studied by Wirt and Briggs (1957), for example, less than a fourth of those with court records before sixteen showed any reported law violation in the period when they were twenty to twenty-three years old. Delinquency is primarily a phenomenon of adolescence.

This theory was startling enough to capture the imagination of many persons and set them to gathering data for the purpose of testing it. These studies have generally yielded negative results. Goring, [4] for example, published in 1913 a study of 300 English criminals in which he found no evidence for Lombroso's ideas. The American anthropologist Hooton [5] revived the Lombroso theory in 1939, presenting measurements of large numbers of American convicts, and concluding that they *are* somewhat inferior physically to the general population of corresponding race and age. It is very difficult to control all of the social factors that complicate a study of this sort, however, factors having to do with which criminals are apprehended, what the attitudes of families and communities are toward different physical characteristics, and how good the nutrition and medical care is in families of different socio-economic levels. So, in spite of periodic revivals of the Lombroso theory, the conclusions are accepted by few if any reputable criminologists of our day. It seems highly unlikely that anyone is *predestined* to a life of crime.

It is quite possible, however, that inferior physique can be one of the predisposing factors in individual cases. The person with poor physical endowment often feels the need to compensate for his defects in one way or another. Many do so directly and effectively. They admit frankly to themselves and others that there are certain fields of human endeavor from which they are barred by reason of their constitutional handicaps. They therefore seek some occupation where their talents can have full scope and that makes little or no demand upon those areas in which they are deficient. Others, through blundering or unwise guidance, fail to make a successful adjustment of this kind, and in the absence of true compensatory behavior they resort to one or another of the mechanisms known as "overcompensation" but for which "pseudocompensation" would probably be a better name. The boy who recognizes that he is physically inferior to others may find balm for his wounded self-esteem through playing malicious tricks on other children, bullying those weaker than himself, or excessive boasting. Or he may attempt to buy the friendship of boys with whom he is unable to compete physically by providing them with all sorts of little treats. If he lacks the money to procure these honestly, he may resort to stealing. The child who steals in order to buy friendship is a familiar figure in every child guidance clinic. But the lad who begins by stealing for his friends soon extends his activities to stealing for himself, and so the pattern grows.

[4] C. Goring. *The English convict.* London: H. M. Stationery Office, 1913.
[5] E. A. Hooton. *Crime and the man.* Cambridge, Mass.: Harvard Univ. Press, 1939.

Interestingly enough, however, so far as juvenile delinquents are concerned, the careful research done by the Gluecks [6] has shown that it is the kind of physique we usually think of as superior or desirable that predominates. There is a strong tendency for male delinquents to be *mesomorphs* with the kind of muscular, well-co-ordinated bodies that we find in athletes and men of action (Sheldon's classification has been discussed in Chapter 17). Table X shows the distribution for the sample of about 500 delinquents and 500 matched nondelinquents used in the Glueck research. The differences are large and very significant.

TABLE X

DISTRIBUTION OF SOMATOTYPES IN DELINQUENT AND NONDELINQUENT BOYS

	Per Cent Delinquents	Per Cent Nondelinquents
Endomorphic Dominance (soft and round)		
Extreme Endomorphs	1.2	5.0
Endomorphs	2.8	4.8
Mesomorphic Endomorphs	3.2	1.5
Ectomorphic Endomorphs	4.6	3.7
Total Endomorphs	11.8	15.0
Mesomorphic Dominance (muscular and hard)		
Extreme Mesomorphs	23.2	7.1
Mesomorphs	16.9	12.2
Endomorphic Mesomorphs	13.3	3.1
Ectomorphic Mesomorphs	6.7	8.3
Total Mesomorphs	60.1	30.7
Ectomorphic Dominance (thin and slight)		
Extreme Ectomorphs	1.8	14.5
Ectomorphs	5.0	14.7
Endomorphic Ectomorphs	4.2	3.1
Mesomorphic Ectomorphs	3.4	7.3
Total Ectomorphs	14.4	39.6
No Component Dominance		
Balanced Types	13.5	14.7

Adapted from S. Glueck and E. Glueck. *Unraveling juvenile delinquency.* Cambridge, Mass.: Harvard Univ. Press, 1950, p. 193.

The most reasonable explanation of the relationship between physique and delinquency is not in terms of constitutional inferiority. It is rather that boys who are mesomorphic in build tend to have the temperament Sheldon calls *somatotonia*, a predisposition to action and

[6] *Op. cit.*

adventure. Thus their inner tensions, if they become serious, are more likely to produce aggressive violent action than some other symptom of maladjustment.

Inferior intelligence is another factor that is often invoked as a major determinant of crime and delinquency. Just as with inferior physique, there can be no doubt that intellectual retardation is a handicap that makes truly successful adjustment more difficult than it would otherwise be. There is the further fact that persons of limited intellect are for that very reason less able to look far afield and understand all the likely ramifications of their own acts. They have less insight into the rules by which society is governed and so are rather more at the mercy of chance circumstances than is the person who, because of his more highly developed judgment, is able to exert more control over the persons and events by which he is surrounded. Because of his shorter range of intellectual vision, he is somewhat more likely to adopt quick and easy ways of attaining satisfaction, and these are frequently not ways of which society approves. Although there are many persons of limited intellect who are as law-abiding as you or I, it is apparently true, as many investigations have shown, that the delinquent and criminal groups include a greater proportion of mentally backward and uneducated persons than does the general population. Table XI, for example, shows that the delinquent group includes more persons in all the below-average categories and fewer in all the above-average categories than the general population does. The average IQ for delinquents in this study by Merrill was 92.5 as compared with 101.8 for the general group. Obviously, however, we cannot *account* for delinquency on the grounds of low intelligence, since there are both delinquents and normals at all the ability levels. Low intelligence is a handicap, but it need not be a fatal one, as we indicated in a previous chapter.

The proportion of mentally diseased persons among the criminal group is not known. It is presumably higher than it is among the general population, a fact that you will not find hard to understand if you will review what was said about mental illness in Chapter 24. But the statement sometimes made by sentimentalists of the modern school that all delinquents and criminals are "mentally sick" is neither accurate nor helpful. The personality of the criminal has been stunted in its development, particularly on the side of his attitude toward himself in relation to society. His sense of values has become distorted through having selected the wrong goals. He needs re-education and guidance into fields where he can attain success by socially acceptable means.

Some criminals, however, are unquestionably the victims of genuine

TABLE XI

PERCENTAGE DISTRIBUTION OF IQ's OBTAINED ON REVISED
STANFORD-BINET TEST FOR 500 JUVENILE DELINQUENTS
IN ONE COUNTY, AS COMPARED WITH
TEST STANDARDIZATION GROUP

IQ	Percentages of Delinquents N=500	Percentages of Standardization Group N=2904	Classification
140 and above	1.0	1.3	Very Superior
120-139	6.8	11.3	Superior
110-119	9.4	18.2	High Average
90-109	39.0	46.5	Normal or Average
80–89	18.6	14.5	Low Average
70–79	13.6	5.6	Borderline Defective
Below 70	11.6	2.6	Defective

Adapted from M. A. Merrill. *Problems of child delinquency.* Boston: Houghton, 1947, p. 168.

mental disease. Many states have recognized this and have provided special institutions for the detention and care of the criminal insane. The number of inmates of such institutions is, however, a poor clue to the total proportion of mentally diseased among criminals, for there are many among the regular prison inmates who belong in this group. On the other hand, there are undoubtedly some inmates of these institutions who have used the plea of "temporary insanity" as a means of escaping more severe punishment and in hope that by later claiming a cure they might gain early release. Of those criminals who are diagnosed as suffering from mental disease, a large proportion are of the paranoid type. This is quite understandable when we remember the kind of systematized delusions from which the paranoid suffers. Manic-depressives make up the greater part of the remainder, and the crimes are usually committed while the patient is in the manic phase. The depressed phase is more likely to be marked by suicide than by homicide.

Thus the theory that most crimes are committed by people who from the beginning are "constitutional inferiors," "degenerates," or something equally sinister, has not stood up under careful investigation. Efforts to delineate a "criminal type" characterized by physical anomalies, low intelligence, or mental disease have not been successful. Criminal behavior is not instinctive but *learned.* And it is in following this clue that the greatest progress has been made toward understanding it.

THE SOCIOLOGICAL APPROACH

1. Neighborhoods

While we are still a long way from being able to predict accurately whether any individual child will become a lawbreaker, we can perdict delinquency *rates* with considerable success.

There is no doubt whatever that far more than a chance proportion both of adult criminals and of juvenile delinquents come from those poverty-stricken and crowded areas of our large cities that we refer to collectively as "the slums." Shaw,[7] in a monograph that has been much quoted, shows that when the addresses of all the boys passing through the juvenile courts of Chicago during a given period of time were plotted on a city map and the number from the various parts of the city was in each case reduced to a ratio of the total population of that area, the proportion of delinquents in certain sections was so vastly in excess of that in other sections that these regions might properly be designated "delinquency areas." In one such area, according to Shaw, no less than 28 per cent of all the male youths between the ages of seventeen and twenty-one years of age were arrested and arraigned before the Boys' Court on charges of serious crime during the three-year period, 1924-1926. "Delinquency areas" are likely to be found near the railroad yards and the manufacturing districts, in sections that are gradually being taken over by industry and where, consequently, such dwellings as remain are allowed to become run-down and dilapidated. The many saloons, poolrooms, and gambling houses are gathering places for undesirable characters of all kinds. In Chicago, Shaw was able to show that delinquency tended to center in the region of the "Loop" and decreased steadily toward the suburbs. Similar studies conducted in a number of other cities have confirmed Shaw's findings. These studies have also shown that many other municipal features are associated with the frequency of delinquency. It is most common in areas where there is the greatest concentration of families in receipt of public relief or who are known to social service agencies of various kinds. It is less common in parts of the city where there are public playgrounds than in those areas where there are none. The "geography of crime" is more than a catch phrase. It has become a field of serious investigation.

2. Families

Another factor that in dozens of studies has been found to be related to delinquency rates is the amount of training and guidance families

[7] C. R. Shaw. *Delinquency areas.* Chicago: Univ. of Chicago Press, 1929.

are able to provide. A large proportion of lawbreakers come from homes that have been broken by divorce or desertion or those where one or both parents are unable to handle parental responsibilities because of illness, mental retardation, emotional disturbance, drunkenness, or criminality. Table XII, from the Gluecks' study, shows the differences in proportions for these factors in delinquents and nondelinquents from the same kinds of neighborhood. The family conditions that breed delinquency have been strongly emphasized by all research workers in this area.

TABLE XII

PERCENTAGE OF FATHERS AND MOTHERS OF DELINQUENTS
AND NONDELINQUENTS SHOWING VARIOUS HANDICAPS

	Mothers		Fathers	
Condition	Per Cent of Delinquents	Per Cent of Non-delinquents	Per Cent of Delinquents	Per Cent of Non-delinquents
Serious Physical Ailments	48.6	33.0	39.6	28.6
Mental Retardation	32.8	9.0	18.4	5.6
Emotional Disturbances	40.2	17.6	44.0	18.0
Drunkenness	23.0	7.0	62.8	39.0
Criminality	44.8	15.0	66.2	32.0

Adapted from S. Glueck and E. Glueck. *Unraveling juvenile delinquency.* Cambridge, Mass.: Harvard Univ. Press, 1950, p. 101.

3. Schools

Another general factor that has been universally found to characterize juvenile delinquents is difficulty at school. The problem here is of a different sort, however, from the problem of inadequate homes and neighborhoods. It is not that the schools to which delinquents go are any poorer than the others, but rather that this particular group of boys and girls does not fit into the established order. They are almost *immune* to formal education. This shows in several ways. At all school levels, they are much more retarded in their knowledge of standard subjects like reading and arithmetic than they are in intelligence. They dislike school intensely and begin playing truant at an early age. They "act up" in school and are often recognized as behavior problems there before they begin to get into difficulties with the law. All the research workers who have studied delinquents have been impressed by this factor of maladjustment in school. What to do about it is a difficult question.

4. Gangs

One of the first of the social factors to be recognized as a source, or at least a concomitant, of delinquency was the juvenile gang and its activities. The study by the Gluecks [8] found that 56 per cent of the delinquents as compared with less than one per cent of the nondelinquent boys from similar surroundings belonged to these gangs. Delinquents seem to gravitate toward one another and to get satisfaction for their needs out of adventurous, often violent activity. Loyalty to the gang may be a far more important motive in a member of such a group than loyalty to a family that has failed him, a school that holds nothing for him, or the larger society whose standards he does not accept.

It is apparent that there is nothing criminal or abnormal about this loyalty itself. We have seen in an earlier chapter how useful the peer group can be as a socializing force in the development of children and adolescents. In combatting delinquency it is better to work with this tendency to belong to a group than against it. But to change the aims of the lawless juvenile gangs, or to replace them with other kinds of clubs and organizations is far from easy.

THE INDIVIDUAL DELINQUENT—
HOW DOES HE DEVELOP?

Since the universality of these social factors we have been discussing became apparent to students of criminology, the focus of research attention has shifted to another kind of question. If influences of this sort are so powerful, why do not *all* children living in delinquency areas and coming from poverty-stricken families become lawbreakers? Why do some of them stay out of lawless gangs and join boys' clubs at a neighborhood center instead? Why do some settle down in school to work hard and make good academic records? What differences can we identify in the way development proceeds for those who rebel against society and those who contribute to it?

During the 1950's there have been a number of well-planned studies in which groups of delinquents were compared with control groups of

[8] *Op. cit.*

nondelinquents who were like them in most of the factors known to be related to lawlessness. Much earlier than this, Healy and Bronner [9] had compared a group of delinquents with their nondelinquent siblings and found differences in the way they responded to what seemed like very similar external circumstances. Emotionally the delinquents were much more disturbed.

The later work has helped to clarify what these emotional attitudes so often encountered in delinquents are like. Glueck and Glueck, [10] in the major research study to which we have several times referred, controlled many of the external factors by equating nondelinquent boys with the 500 delinquents they studied on age, IQ, national origin, and type of neighborhood. There were still large and significant differences between the groups in many other things. The lawbreakers had poorer relationships with their families. While home situations for the boys in both groups were far from ideal, they were much worse, on the average, for the delinquents. The most striking differences were in the psychological *quality* of these homes, not the socio-economic indices. Table XIII shows the differences in the ratings for *cohesiveness*, the quality that holds families together, doing things as a group, and feeling some loyalty to one another.

TABLE XIII

DIFFERENCES BETWEEN HOMES OF DELINQUENT AND
NONDELINQUENT BOYS IN COHESIVENESS

Extent	*Per Cent Delinquents*	*Per Cent Nondelinquents*
Marked	16.0	61.8
Some	59.3	37.4
None	24.7	0.8

Adapted from S. Glueck and E. Glueck. *Unraveling Juvenile Delinquency.* Cambridge, Mass.: Harvard Univ. Press, 1950, p. 115.

Assessments of the boys by means of the Rorschach (ink blot) test and psychiatric interviews showed basic temperamental differences. Maladjustment in the delinquents showed up in activity, aggressiveness, and restlessness, rather than in anxiety, withdrawal, and depression. Delinquents are not *neurotic*.

Corroboration of this finding of distinct differences in the shape or direction that the attitudes of delinquent and nondelinquent persons

[9] W. Healey and A. F. Bronner. *New light on delinquency and its treatment.* New Haven: Yale Univ. Press, 1936.
[10] *Op. cit.*

take comes from a series of studies reported by Hathaway and Monachesi [11] in which the Minnesota Multiphasic Personality Inventory was administered to various groups in correctional institutions. This personality test is scored on a number of scales, each of them made up of items on which some special type of psychiatric patients differ from normal men and women. Consistently, for both male and female lawbreakers, the group scored high on the scales labeled *Pd* and *Ma*. The *Pd* scale had been intended in the first place to measure personality characteristics of the kind that lead to a psychiatric diagnosis of *Psychopath*. Patients of this sort act impulsively, show little or no remorse, and do not seem to be able to profit from experience. The *Ma* scale measures traits especially characteristic of *Manic* patients—enthusiasm, energy, overactivity.

Like the Gluecks' study, this indicates that delinquents are not neurotic. They are not burdened with worry, guilt, and remorse. In fact, there is some evidence from studies of total test profiles for these subjects that a higher than average score on the *D* (depression) scale is a favorable sign. A certain amount of anxiety can perhaps counteract impulsiveness and aggression and thus improve the person's chances to modify his antisocial attitudes under treatment.

One of the most novel and important features of this MMPI research was the testing of almost all the ninth grade students in Minneapolis in 1947-1948, a total of over 4,000 people. The aim was to obtain a personality picture of these boys and girls *before* the age at which lawbreaking is most frequent and serious, and then to compare those who subsequently became delinquent with those who did not. Two years later the investigators checked juvenile court records and compared MMPI scores for the groups. The same sorts of differences appeared, pointing to instability coupled with activity, aggressiveness, and impulsiveness, in the delinquent groups. Few lawbreakers have neurotic patterns of scores, but psychotic patterns are not uncommon. [12]

Some parts of this temperamental pattern are covered by the label *somatotonia*, which Sheldon has used for the vigorous, outgoing, adventurous tendencies that accompany mesomorphic body build. Thus there may be constitutional differences present from the beginning of life, that predispose some young people to hit back at life instead of suffering, or as the psychoanalysts put it "to act out." But since such a small proportion of mesomorphs go into criminal activity, this can be at best only a partial explanation. As Table X shows, about 31 per

[11] S. R. Hathaway and E. D. Monachesi. *Analyzing and predicting juvenile delinquency*. Minneapolis: Univ. of Minnesota Press, 1953.
[12] The distinction between these two main types of abnormality has been elaborated in the previous chapter.

cent of the nondelinquents in underprivileged neighborhoods are also mesomorphic, yet they do not break the law. Why?

One theory that is stimulating some important research is that of Gough. [13] He holds that what the delinquent really lacks, probably because of the handicaps he suffers as a child, is *role-playing* ability. He is not able to take the point of view of other individuals and groups, to sense how they feel about things, and to see himself as others see him. This theory has led to the development of another personality scale for measuring delinquent tendencies or their opposite, *Socialization*. This is one of the parts of the California Personality Inventory. This, like the MMPI, is designed to measure a number of different traits, but unlike the MMPI it is focused on different kinds of *normal* or even *above-normal* qualities in people. An impressive amount of evidence has been collected, showing that this Socialization scale does in fact differentiate in a very clear-cut way between delinquent groups and others.

But the most significant turn that this research has taken is to begin to analyze the qualities that make some boys and girls *immune* to delinquency even under considerable pressure to become delinquent. It is such *strengths* that Gough has been especially interested in bringing to light. Reckless and his associates [14] have studied what they call *insulation* against delinquency. Instead of using delinquent boys in the experimental group and nondelinquents in the control group, as previous investigators have done, they reversed the situation and used "good" boys in "bad" areas as the subjects they scrutinized most carefully. They asked sixth grade teachers in thirty schools in high-delinquency areas of Columbus, Ohio, to pick out the boys who were not and probably never would be lawbreakers. They gave these boys several kinds of tests, including Gough's scales for Socialization and Responsibility. The group averaged unusually *high* on these scales. They described themselves as law-abiding, obedient, strict about right and wrong. They were trying to live up to the expectations their families had for them. It is significant that the families of these boys were more stable than average, although they lived in the poorer sections of the city. Parents supervised the children's activities and took an active interest in them.

It is self-concepts of this sort that the authors believe serve as "insulators" against bad influences. It may be especially difficult for children to develop such concepts when their parents do not help

[13] H. G. Gough and D. R. Peterson. The identification and measurement of predispositional factors in crime and delinquency. *J. consult. Psychol.*, 1952, 16, 207-212.

[14] W. C. Reckless, S. Dinitz, and E. Murray. Self-concept as an insulator against delinquency. *Amer. sociol. Rev.*, 1956, 21, 744-746.

them, but it seems at least theoretically possible that other means of encouraging development of this sort may be found.

In another study of this type Wirt and Briggs [15] used specially chosen samples from among the boys Hathaway and Monachesi had tested in ninth grade. At the age of twenty-three, a considerable proportion of those whose personality test scores had indicated that they belonged to the active, impulsive, delinquency-prone group still had no court record of any sort. In general, these were the boys who came from homes above average in the occupational and educational scale. On the other hand, among those whose personality test scores had pointed toward anxious, neurotic reactions rather than delinquency, a minority had become delinquent. In general, these were boys from unusually unstable or inadequate homes. The study shows quite conclusively that both temperament and circumstances determine outcomes.

TREATMENT AND PREVENTION

Incomplete as the research evidence is in this field, it has already thrown light on doubtful issues with regard to policies and institutions. Ideas that once seemed reasonable now appear naïve and superficial When the work on delinquency areas first came out, for example, well-meaning community leaders concluded that the provision of playgrounds in congested areas would be a good preventive measure. Knowing what we now know about the deeper sources of antisocial behavior we are not surprised when we read that the delinquent children either avoided the supervised play areas because they preferred to roam the streets, or in some cases even used the facilities provided as places to congregate and formulate plans for lawless projects of various kinds! When the evidence of the important role played by the child's relationship to his parents became available, police departments here and there hit upon the idea of *punishing* the parents for the child's crime, thus forcing them to accept their parental responsibilities. We realize now why such methods cannot be expected to work. Complex and subtle emotional attitudes cannot be changed for the better by ten days in jail!

It is plain that so far as treatment of boys and girls who have already become delinquent is concerned, our attention needs to be focused on trying to change the person's self-concept and attitude toward the world. Even if we could eradicate completely the conditions that produced his unsound attitudes in the first place, the

[15] R. D. Wirt and P. F. Briggs. Factors in the development of delinquency. (Mimeographed report distributed by the authors.)

attitudes themselves would still remain and have to be dealt with. Neither the theory that crime is a sin that must be punished nor the theory that crime is a disease that must be cured by some kind of "social medicine" is adequate for the treatment of an individual. Crime grows out of an attitude or approach to life, and attitudes can be changed, though with great difficulty. The setting of clear definite limits on behavior that will be tolerated, the provision for deep personal relationships with understanding (but not soft) adults, the introduction of the person to alternative paths of life, so that he may find acceptable substitutes for the delinquent way—all these and many other facets characterize treatment methods that have a chance of working. Unfortunately both funds and personnel are often lacking, so that they cannot be put into effect.

In the long run, knowledge of how to prevent delinquency will be of more importance than treating it. The thing that research results now make it possible for us to do is to identify early in life the boys and girls who are *potential* lawbreakers, and concentrate our attention on them. These boys and girls, especially those from unstable or vicious homes, need to have adults other than their parents take an active interest in them. It is still far from clear how (or even *whether*) a concept of oneself as a steady, law-abiding, responsible person can develop in a child whose parents give him no help or guidance. But there do seem to be such cases. Some day we shall understand them better and be able to apply this understanding. And some day we may be able to head off the family deficiencies themselves.

Meanwhile the standard methods for ameliorating bad conditions can still be stressed—improvement of housing, more attention to individuals in school, better recreational facilities. Such things benefit all children in a community at the same time as they make for some reduction in the delinquency rate. Perhaps the most important outcome of all the work that has been done on crime and delinquency is our realization that we must take responsibility for the total pattern of life in our communities in order that all children may develop soundly. Crime prevention is but one aspect of a broader social awareness.

SUMMARY

Crime and delinquency constitute one of society's most serious problems. Statistics show that they are increasing at a rapid rate.

The idea that criminals are defective or degenerate individuals predisposed toward antisocial behavior by their hereditary defects no longer seems reasonable. Physical and mental defects may be predisposing factors, but they operate along with many others. Research shows that juvenile delinquents are more likely than not to be well-built, muscular individuals with the active, adventurous temperament that tends to accompany this body build. Mentally, delinquents average a little below the general norms, but they distribute themselves over the whole range of intelligence.

Sociologically-oriented studies have shown that certain kinds of neighborhoods and certain kinds of homes and families produce far more than their share of delinquents. Retardation in school and gang membership are very common among delinquents.

There have been several studies in which delinquents and non-delinquents from the same areas, matched for some of these gross handicaps, have been compared. Such studies have delineated a certain pattern of attitudes related most closely to emotional deficiencies in the children's homes. Another pattern of attitudes that has been identified seems to serve as an insulator against delinquency even under the pressure of many unfavorable influences.

REFERENCE—A CLINICIAN LOOKS AT DELINQUENCY

MERRILL, Maud A. *Problems of child delinquency.* Boston: Houghton, 1947.

Dr. Merrill considers many of the factors we have discussed in this chapter and reports a major study of her own, comparing 300 delinquent children with a control group. What the student will find most interesting in this book, however, is the way in which she endows these facts and figures with flesh and blood by describing with sympathy and understanding many individual boys and girls she encountered in her years of clinical work. To understand what these factors mean we must sense how they interact in the lives of real people. This book can help the reader to "get the feel" of these children's experience.

PART V

Implications

CHAPTER 26

Why is the study of human development important in the progress of psychology as a science?

If a society wished to encourage the best possible development of its individual members, what policies should it adopt?

How can parents provide for optimal development in their children?

What kinds of things can adults do to accelerate their own progress toward real maturity?

Stimulation and Encouragement of Optimal Human Development

SCIENCE AND HUMAN PROGRESS

PSYCHOLOGY IS THE SCIENCE of human experience and behavior. Its aim is to apply to the study of man himself the methods of controlled observation and experiment that have so greatly enlarged our knowledge of the world around us.

There is no question about the effectiveness of these scientific methods. We have only to look in any direction to see what they have accomplished. They have given us automobiles, airplanes, and earth-circling satellites. They have placed television sets in our living rooms and automatic dishwashers in our kitchens. They have made it possible for each of us to look ahead to a life that is many years longer than we could have expected had we lived in an earlier century. From birth to death there is hardly a moment when we are not making use of some product that science has made possible.

But it is very evident when we consider scientific progress that our knowledge of human nature has lagged far behind our knowledge of the rest of the natural world. The engineer who can turn rivers from their courses, who can transform the energy of a waterfall into light for a city hundreds of miles away, is baffled by a child's temper tantrum. The mathematician who attacks the most difficult problems without hesitation may be so unable to solve the riddles of his own personality that he must spend precious years of his life in a hospital for mental disease. Nations destroy each other because they do not understand each other. And with the coming of nuclear weapons, there is a real possibility that this lack of understanding may wipe out human life on this planet. Thus it seems to many observers of our time that progress in the human sciences has literally become a matter of life and death for mankind as a whole.

But many of those who are concerned about man's present predicament still have grave misgivings about psychology as a science. Experimental work with human beings must of course always be limited by ethical considerations. We cannot take a baby and operate on various parts of his brain to find out what will be the effect upon his behavior; we cannot deliberately take a group of boys from good families and put them to live in a delinquency area, while we remove another group of the same age from the delinquency area and place them in the homes from which our first group came. Even when experiments are likely to be beneficial, the difficulties do not disappear. We cannot, at will, take children out of the environment in which they have been reared and place them in foster homes whenever we have reason to think that the change would be to their advantage.

The chemist is free to try practically any experiment that seems desirable to him. He can vary his conditions at will. He can be sure that in the intervals between trials his chemicals are safely housed in their own bottles and jars on his laboratory shelves where nothing can happen to them. But the psychologist with human beings for his chemicals is in a very different position. Not only are many of the experiments that would add most to his knowledge completely out of the question, but he is forced to work with materials of whose individual idiosyncrasies he knows but little, whose nature is constantly changing with the passage of time, and which are being subjected to all sorts of unknown conditions during the hours when they are not with him. When we consider the complexity of the problems he is trying to solve and his very limited facilities for solving them, the wonder is not that the psychologist has made so little progress but rather that he has succeeded in finding out as much as he has.

But even more fundamental than the doubt about whether psychologists can hope to gain a truly scientific knowledge of human nature without being able to experiment freely on all kinds of problems is a conviction voiced by a considerable number of able and influential people that the scientific approach to human problems is basically *wrong*. It is often said that the aims of science are *prediction* and *control.* If we assume that psychology shares these aims with other sciences, then questions about how such control is to be exercised come to the fore. Who is to control whom, and to what end?

To both these objectives to scientific psychology—doubt as to its efficacy and opposition to its avowed aim—developmental psychology constitutes a kind of answer. The careful observation of processes occurring naturally has always been as much a part of science as experiments are. Just as medicine has learned much about the course of many disease processes without violating ethical principles rooted in reverence for human life, so developmental psychology is working out ways of discovering new things about human behavior and experience by observing individuals and analyzing situations. There is, of course, a wide range of experiments that psychologists *can* ethically carry out using human subjects, and a still wider range where animals can be used. But the observational methods of developmental psychology extend the range of psychological science far beyond the scope of any sort of experimentation.

The implications of developmental psychology for our thinking about the second issue—the question as to whether prediction and control are really desirable *aims* for human society—are still more significant. One who is concerned with growth and change inevitably comes to have a somewhat different orientation from one who deals only with mechanical relationships. It is important to remember that a garden is as clearly a product of applied science as is a factory. The goal toward which we strive can be thought of as the flowering of individual lives rather than as the fitting of inert parts into a predetermined pattern. It is possible to envisage a society in which each person is seen as both plant and gardener, cultivated and cultivator, a society dedicated to the optimum development of all of its individual members.

We are beginning to get glimpses of what such a society could be like. It would not be at all like the mechanistic nightmare of *Brave New World.* There would be a large measure of personal happiness, and this would make for more rewarding social relationships. Each person would be competent, productive, even creative, free to make the maximum contribution to the common good. And above all, each person would be a unique individual, prized for his own special qualities.

Such a description sounds utopian, almost as if from a world of hydrogen bombs and overwhelming anxieties, we had retreated to an island of golden dreams. But in spite of all the present threats and dangers, there are many evidences that we are actually moving in the direction of such a society. Throughout our democratic community,

ideas like this have shown themselves in many tangible forms—
agencies set up to help children and families, patient and increasingly
skillful efforts to rehabilitate the victims of illness and injury, special
kinds of education for the mentally deficient and for the unusually
gifted, individual and group therapy for psychotics and neurotics.
The ideal is very much with us, imperfectly as we have grasped it.
And it is this ideal that the scientific study of human development
serves.

GENERAL PRINCIPLES AND POLICIES

Even with the limited knowledge at our disposal now, we can see
what general policies would promote the development of individuals.
In the first place, we should try to insure that as many persons as
possible start life without serious hereditary handicaps. The study of
ways of improving the hereditary quality of the population is called
eugenics. After the genetic mechanisms of heredity turned out to be
vastly more complicated than the early geneticists thought they were
(see Chapter 3), some people lost faith that much could be done
about reducing hereditary handicaps. The trouble is, of course, that
what people inherit makes them differ in many ways, not just in
all-round quality. If we could breed human populations for intelligence, for example, this would not insure freedom from neurotic predispositions. There is no simple way of eliminating mental deficiency.
If we were to sterilize all feeble-minded persons of one generation,
it would produce only a small decrease in the proportion of such cases
in the next generation, because the majority of feeble-minded children are born to normal parents, some of them outstanding contributors
to society.

But with all these limitations on what can be done about improving
hereditary quality, there are many kinds of things that are possible.
Social and governmental policies that encourage the more intelligent
groups of people to have children, and the simplification of information
about contraception for the benefit of the dull and the defective who
really do not want children—such measures could be expected to
make small but in the long run significant differences in the average
intellectual level of the population. Furthermore, as we increase our
knowledge with regard to hereditary predispositions toward specific
difficulties, such as schizophrenia or epilepsy, for example, it becomes
possible for physicians to give their patients sound information about
the probability that the defect will occur in the children of any particular pair of parents. Special counseling services to deal with eugenic
problems have been set up in some places. Eventually, also, knowledge

of the actual mode of operation of many genetically-determined handicaps may permit us to counteract some unfavorable predispositions before they have a chance to affect development at all. Whatever can be done to improve the hereditary potentialities of its individuals constitutes significant progress toward the good society.

Another kind of policy clearly suggested by general developmental principles is the provision for each individual of what might be called the "raw materials" for development. It requires no knowledge of psychology to realize that in order to grow, a child must have food of the right kinds in sufficient quantity. What the scientific study of psychological development has added to this knowledge is an awareness that there are some intangible "raw materials" that are just as indispensable. The need for love and closeness to someone—the actual physical closeness that Harlow calls "contact comfort"—is perhaps as real as the need for food. Things to look at, listen to, handle, and struggle with can all be classified with the raw materials used in the developmental process. We are making some progress in providing these essentials for all children.

As we have seen in previous chapters, however, development includes much more than maturation. Learning is essential to it at all stages. This means that in order to improve its outcomes, we must try to make sure that appropriate learning situations occur at each developmental level. We must provide guidance and training in essential skills—from control of the bowels at two to control of an automobile at sixteen. We will often need to set up limits to the kind of behavior that is permitted, so that children will direct their efforts toward what must be learned instead of expending their energies in all directions. We should try to make sure that all children encounter a variety of persons they can use as models, so that the important learning that goes on by means of identification can occur. These are only samples of the many specific things we could do to maximize the learning components of development.

Besides furnishing these universal essentials, we need to formulate policies for the encouraging of individuality itself. We could accomplish this partly by reducing the pressures toward conformity in schools, social organizations, and communities. It would be necessary to make parents, teachers, and community leaders more fully aware than they now are of the wide range of individual differences in all kinds of human traits—physical growth rates, level and type of mental abilities, special talents, susceptibilities to disease, and hundreds of other specific things. We would need also to make available to developing human beings themselves more help with the making of the choices on which the shapes of their own individual lives will depend.

This calls for more counseling services for both children and adults.

As we have indicated in previous chapters, development is a matter of *activities* as well as inner forces or external influences. How a person responds to each situation that confronts him helps to determine the pattern of his life. Because situations are very complex, some choice as to the nature of one's response is usually possible. Often such choices are made unconsciously, so that we do not realize we have made them. Sometimes, as with occupations and marriage partners, they are more apparent. Counseling psychologists have come to realize that a chance to sit down in a quiet place, free from demands and distractions, and talk over one's situation with an understanding listener is often all that a person requires to enable him to set his choices in order.

As we understand the choice process better, it may be possible to help it along in many other ways. The eight-year-old boy who decides to collect stamps, the twelve-year-old girl who spends money she earned picking berries for a dress she wants very much, the sixteen-year-old high school student who joins the dramatic society rather than the glee club are all developing individuality through choices. It may well be that the saleswoman who helps a customer pick out a coat that really fits her self-concept as well as her figure, and the teacher who helps a student find a topic for a term paper that is really more meaningful to him than any of the other topics are fully as important as professional counselors in the stimulation and encouragement of individuality.

These, then, are the general policies we would follow if we wished to encourage individual development. We would take steps to minimize hereditary handicaps. We would provide both the tangible and the intangible raw materials human beings need. We would make guidance and training available for everyone. We would explore new ways of helping each person make the choices through which the pattern of his own unique individuality takes shape. All of these things we are now doing to a greater or lesser extent. They can serve as guiding principles in the working out of new policies in education, social work, and community planning.

BRINGING UP CHILDREN

Of all the influences that affect development, child rearing is by far the most important. If it were possible to give all children a really good upbringing, many social problems would be wiped out in one generation.

From the standpoint of social progress, no other occupation in which people can engage is so important as parenthood. Had all parents of the generation just past done their jobs thoroughly and well, the world would not be plagued by hatred and conflict. Men would not be tortured in concentration camps; children would not go hungry in a world that can produce an ample supply for all. Persons with dark skins would no longer be the victims of stereotyped attitudes but would be judged according to their own individual merits. Labor and capital would work together and no longer at cross purposes, the gangster cease to exist, and government be cleanly administered. Utopian? Yes, but a Utopia that could be brought much nearer realization in the next generation if concerted effort were made now. If preparation for parenthood were taken as seriously as preparation for earning one's living, if young people who expect to become parents would endeavor to fit themselves for the job by the same methods that have been found useful in preparing for their profession, much could be accomplished. It is true that not everything could actually be effected in the course of a single generation, and this for two reasons. First we have not enough information. We do not always know what is best to be done either generally or in the specific instance. Secondly, we are not starting far enough back. Training for parenthood begins with the birth of the parent. By the time the boy or girl reaches an age at which formal parental or preparental education begins, attitudes, habits, ways of thinking, and ways of doing that will play a highly important part in the life of the children that are to come have already been well established. But this is no excuse for not making a start with the present generation and doing as much as we can.

Many of the implications of research for child-rearing practice have been pointed out in previous chapters. A book like this is no place for detailed advice as to what to do about the multitude of specific questions parents face as their children grow. To spank or not to spank, to allow or prohibit teen-age dates on week-nights—such are the issues parents find most troublesome. Actually, there are no hard and fast answers to such questions. But we do know in a general way what children need. The important thing is that these needs be met. The specific methods and procedures vary from one culture to another and from one family to another.

The first and most basic requirement of every child is a *feeling of security*. This feeling has its roots in the personal relations of the people around him. The love of the parents for himself and for each other should be to him as immutable facts as the rising of the sun or the character of the elements. He must not be taught that this feeling has to be earned or that it can be altered by changing conditions. Under no circumstances should he be told that "Mother won't love you if you do that." Never should he have reason to question the nature of the tie that unites his parents. Family love, harmonious family relationships, provide the foundation on which the child's personality is erected. If these stand firm, the first essential is fulfilled.

The second need of the child is *opportunity for unhampered development*. This is not to say that he must not know restraint, that he be allowed to run wild without design or guidance. It means that restriction upon his acts shall not be imposed erratically or without reason, that he be allowed to make his own mistakes as far as this is at all consistent with reasonable attention to his health and safety—and these limits are much broader than many nervous parents think. It means that he shall be allowed to learn for himself, not expected to satisfy himself with the tales of other's experiences, even though they may be those of his own parents. He must be allowed to experiment widely in order that he may choose wisely. It means that he shall not be hampered by a false idea of his own place in the social world through thoughtless exploitation, by being constantly encouraged to "show off," or by unwise indulgence. It means the encouragement of initiative and independence, learning to do for himself and fend for himself. It means freedom from the hampering effects of fear by learning to meet situations that he is capable of overcoming, to avoid issues not worth a struggle, and to admit defeat honestly and courageously.

The third need is a *feeling of success*. The little child explores the world about him and tries out his abilities with a degree of zest and enthusiasm that later on is all too often lost when his self-confidence has been dampened by repeated failure and discouragement. Nothing can compensate for a loss of belief in one's own capacities. Every child faces the world with confidence at the start; the parent must see to it that that attitude is retained.

As the child grows older *his primary attachments must shift to the members of his own generation*. This shift is often hard for parents to accept. They feel that they must bind him closer to themselves. Whatever happens in these cases is unfortunate. If the parents succeed, the normal course of the child's emotional development may be stunted and deformed. He may fail to make the proper adjustments to his own group, marriage may be delayed or prevented, or, if it takes place, the parental relationship may still take precedence over the marital relationship, with unhappiness and misunderstanding as the result. When the parental efforts to hold the child fail, the consequences may be almost as unfortunate. The child resents their attitude; the parents feel that he is ungrateful; and the end is bitterness and disappointment. Wise indeed is the advice said to have been given by the oracle consulted by an anxious mother who wanted to know by what means she could retain her child's love. The answer was, "If you would hold him, you must let him go."

"Happiness first, all else follows." This is the slogan of one of our leading institutions for feeble-minded children; it may well be adopted as the first rule of every family. Happiness is the birthright of every child. As long as the child is happy he is not likely to go wrong. If unhappy, he will not make much progress that is worthwhile.

INCREASING EMOTIONAL MATURITY IN ADULTS

Because development continues throughout life, and because it depends at all stages partly on decisions the person himself makes, an adult who is willing to do some thinking and planning ahead can do much to accelerate his own progress toward genuine maturity. The principles to be applied have been discussed in previous chapters, but perhaps there is something to be gained by pointing out more explicitly the kinds of action most likely to be effective.

Finding one's niche in life. A large share of the adult life of most people is spent at work. We have seen that people differ greatly in the kind of thing they are best fitted by temperament and ability to do well. A good many people are unhappy because they have drifted into the wrong kind of job. The earlier in life a young man or woman is able to make the right vocational choice, the better will be his chances for future happiness and success.

It is highly unfortunate that the American tradition has tended to glorify the advantages of the learned professions and the "white-collar" types of job to such an extent that the great majority of young people hesitate to aspire openly to anything else. When questioned about their vocational plans, the number of high school boys and girls who state that they expect to enter one or another of these fields is vastly in excess of the number of possible openings. A good deal of future disappointment could be avoided if those who are unlikely to be able to carry out such ambitions could be induced to shift their aspirations to a more realistic level.

Learning social skills. How many unpopular people there are in the world! How many wallflowers at every party! One of the major causes of unhappiness is the inability of many people to win friendship, to find a place for themselves in the social world which they long to enter but which seems ringed about by invisible barriers that they are unable to penetrate, however hard they try.

This lack of social skill not only means lessened happiness for the person himself but also cuts him off from some of the most important avenues of service to others. Elsewhere we have indicated a number of principles that are useful in improving human relationships. Here we shall merely enumerate a few aids to social intercourse that any one who cares enough about the matter to make the necessary effort can master.

1. Learn to play. The person who can make a competent fourth at bridge, who can dance, swim, skate, play golf or tennis, who can build a campfire and cook a steak, drive a car or ride a horse will find himself in social demand on many occasions when another of equally pleasing personality but who lacks the special skill that is in demand at the moment will be left out.

2. Keep in touch with current affairs and especially with those topics that are of particular interest to the people whom you would like to have as friends. Do not get the mistaken idea that there is something sycophantic or charlatan-like in acquiring information along lines in which you have no strong personal interest, merely for its social value. One of the most charming women I know happens not to be particularly fond of reading but enjoys the companionship of a group of people who read a great deal. This woman subscribes to one of the leading literary reviews which she reads regularly. Then when the conversation turns to books, instead of having to remain silent she can say, "No, I haven't read that, but I did read a review by So-and-so who says that . . . ," and so on. Needless to say, this woman never misrepresents the facts. She does not pretend to have read the book, but her account of the review often serves the social purpose for which it was designed better than would her less expert account of her own direct impressions.

3. Be a good listener. People who are socially not quite at their ease often try to cover up their embarrassment by talking too much. Remember that the best host is not always the one who openly dominates the conversation but rather the one who is most successful in getting his guests to talk.

4. Overcome shyness by keeping your attention firmly fixed upon what is going on rather than upon yourself. Shyness and self-consciousness are almost synonymous. Don't let your thoughts wander back to yourself but give all your attention to other people.

5. Don't talk about yourself or try to force the conversation in the direction of your own interests. Find out what other people are interested in and talk about that. However, the rule does not apply to their purely professional interests, and this for two reasons. Most professional people do not enjoy talking shop during their hours of recreation, and few if any laymen are equipped to carry on a con-

versation of this kind at a level that will be anything but an unmitigated bore to the professional man. One might add that when the layman attempts such a conversation with, let us say, a doctor or a lawyer the latter may suspect an ulterior motive, that is, that an attempt is being made to secure professional advice or information free of charge. Better to talk about the other person's hobbies, his favorite recreations and personal interests. Lead him to talk about himself. Most people are only too ready to do so!

6. Have a reserve supply of good stories and jokes but don't insist upon telling them. Encourage other people to tell theirs but be ready to fill in awkward silences. Don't forget to laugh at other people's stories, even if you have heard them before.

Developing a backlog of interests and hobbies. No matter how many friends you have, there will be times when you are thrown on your own resources for enjoyment. Just as there are people who suffer from having too few friends, so there are others who are bored and unhappy whenever they are left alone. Every one, in addition to the things he enjoys doing in company, should develop additional interests and skills that will give him pleasure when he is alone. Reading is the great stand-by of many people. Some enjoy music; others painting or one of the various handicrafts such as wood-carving, metal work, or cabinet-making. Others collect coins, stamps, or newspaper clippings on certain specified topics; still others try their hand at amateur photography. Like other personal pleasures it will be found that hobbies of this kind have a social value as well.

Developing the kind of attitudes and mental habits that make for happiness. Not easy, you say? True, but here are a few rules that will help.

1. Learn to center your attention upon the present and the future, rather than the past. Worry over past mistakes is always useless. Plan how to avoid similar errors in the future, but don't cry over spilt milk.

2. Learn to accept inevitable facts. This includes things that have already happened and so cannot be changed. If you have made a mistake, admit it frankly, remembering that everybody does so at times and that it is chiefly by our mistakes that we learn. When conditions exist that are beyond your power to modify, don't waste time in dreaming about a Utopia that cannot be yours or in futile complaining or resentment about things as they are. Try to adjust your life in such a way that the unpleasant conditions will interfere with it as little as possible. Fill your mind with other things.

3. Maintain a bulwark of personal pride, or if you prefer, call it self-respect. Such an attitude is not to be confused with egotism, which is bland self-admiration with little regard to the facts. Self-respect sets

certain standards of conduct and achievement to which one must hold and that provide a strong anchor to leeward when things go wrong. True, personal pride can be carried to ridiculous extremes, and all of us need to check up on ourselves at times to make sure that we are not confusing pride in character with pride in reputation. But no one can be truly happy who lacks a reasonable measure of self-esteem, who is unable to say to himself with a feeling of justifiable pride, "This I have accomplished. To these standards I have held. This code I can claim as my own."

Perhaps it might seem to some readers that the foregoing recommendations place too much emphasis on personal happiness and self-development. If so, it is because the authors of this book are convinced that there is no contradiction between personal happiness and service to society. *Complete maturity of personality has been reached when the individual is able to combine the maximal degree of personal happiness with the utmost service to humanity that for him is possible.*

Neither the martyr-like person who sacrifices his own good for the assumed good of someone else or the ruthless climber who gets to the top of his business or profession by trampling on subordinates and rivals is a complete human being. Success fairly won, joy in work, rewarding relationships with others—these are things each of us can seek for himself *and* for his fellows. Self-fulfillment is not selfishness.

DEVELOPMENTAL PSYCHOLOGY AND SOCIAL INSTITUTION

It has often been noted that social policies and institutions change much more slowly than technology does. But little by little they do change, and take on the shape of the value structure of the society they serve. If the goal we have been stressing—the development of finer individuals—really becomes a guideline for us, we can use it in evaluating and modifying many of the institutions we have. It would be an impossibly large undertaking, far beyond the scope of this book, to carry out this kind of social criticism in any detail, but a few examples can be given.

Society must be prepared to handle breakdowns and emergencies in the lives of its members. Incarceration for lawbreakers, hospitalization for psychotics, are the means for doing this that we now take for granted. But are they really the best way to handle such crises? They do serve to protect society for a time from persons who might be dangerous to others, but in the long run they do not solve the developmental problems for the individuals involved. In our time we are seeing a great deal of what can be called social experimentation in these areas—the increasing application of probation and parole in delinquent and criminal cases, the provision of community mental health services as an alternative to hospitalization.

Long ago, we in America decided that society as a whole is responsible for the basic education of its members. At the time this chapter is being written (1958) we are going through a period of widespread public questioning as to whether the school system we now have is carrying out this responsibility in a satisfactory way. If we used the values that have been expressed in this chapter to help us analyze and modify our present educational institutions, it would mean that we would attempt to provide more diversified learning situations to promote and encourage individuality, in place of the predominant pattern of organization we now have—placement by age, one year spent in each grade, and a standard curriculum. Various kinds of changes of this sort have already been introduced.

The cultivation of our human garden is a complex endeavor. We must try to live our own lives wisely. We must pay special attention to the needs of children. We must take care of persons of all ages who have special weaknesses and problems, but we must also create social institutions to nourish and stimulate the healthy and the well-endowed.

Finally we must strive for an appreciation of individuality that is more than passive tolerance. Human society can attain its full richness of pattern only if the unique and special qualities of its individual members are really used and valued.

FOR FURTHER READING

Fromm, Erich. *The sane society.* New York: Rinehart, 1955.

In a series of books Dr. Fromm has been presenting a thoughtful critical analysis of man's life in modern society, the special strains and difficulties it involves, and steps that might be taken to improve our situation. This one is concerned especially with social institutions. Many psychologists do not agree with all of his theoretical ideas about personality organization, but they find his diagnosis and prescriptions good starting points for thinking and discussion. We need this kind of stimulation. For the creation of a "sane society" is our common responsibility.

A SELECTED LIST OF BOOKS
FOR SUPPLEMENTARY READING*

I. SOURCE BOOKS

BORING, E. G., and others (Eds.) *History of psychology in autobiography*, Vol. IV. Worcester: Clark Univ. Press, 1952.

CARMICHAEL, L. (Ed.) *Manual of child psychology*. New York: Wiley, 1954.

GARRETT, H. E. (Ed.) *Great experiments in psychology*. (3rd Ed.) New York: Appleton-Century-Crofts, 1951.

KUHLEN, R. G., and THOMPSON, G. G. (Eds.) *Psychological studies of human development*. New York: Appleton-Century-Crofts, 1952.

MARTIN, W. E., and STENDLER, C. B. (Eds.) *Readings in child development*. New York: Harcourt, Brace, 1954.

MURCHISON, C. (Ed.) *A handbook of child psychology*. Worcester: Clark Univ. Press, 1933.

II. GENERAL CONCEPTS AND IDEAS

ALLPORT, G. W. *Becoming: basic considerations for a psychology of personality*. New Haven: Yale Univ. Press, 1955.

ANDREWS, T. G. (Ed.) *Methods of psychology*. New York: Wiley, 1948.

BEACH, F. A. *Hormones and behavior*. New York: Hoeber, 1948.

BISCHOF, L. J. *Intelligence: statistical concepts of its nature*. Garden City: Doubleday, 1954.

BLUM, G. *Psychoanalytic theories of personality*. New York: McGraw-Hill, 1953.

BORING, E. G. *A history of experimental psychology*. (2nd Ed.) New York: Appleton-Century-Crofts, 1950.

CASSIRER, Ernst. *An essay on man*. Garden City: Doubleday, 1954.

CORNER, G. W. *Ourselves unborn: an embryologist's essay on man*. New Haven: Yale Univ. Press, 1944.

DIAMOND, S. *Personality and temperament*. New York: Harper, 1957.

FORD, C. S., and BEACH, F. H. *Patterns of sexual behavior*. New York: Harper, 1951.

FRANK, L. K. *Individual development*. Garden City: Doubleday, 1955.

FROMM, E. *Man for himself*. New York: Rinehart, 1947.

* This list includes those recommended at the close of each chapter.

FROMM, E. *The sane society*. New York: Rinehart, 1955.

FULLER, J. L. *Nature and nurture: a modern synthesis*. Garden City: Doubleday, 1954.

GESELL, A. *The embryology of behavior*. New York: Harper, 1945.

HALL, C. S., and LINDZEY, G. *Theories of personality*. New York: Wiley, 1957.

HARRIS, D. B. (Ed.) *The concept of development*. Minneapolis: Univ. of Minnesota Press, 1957.

HAVIGHURST, R. J. *Human development and education*. New York: Longmans, 1953.

HEIDBREDER, E. F. *Seven psychologies*. New York: Appleton-Century-Crofts, 1933.

HILGARD, E. R. *Theories of learning*. (2nd Ed.) New York: Appleton-Century-Crofts, 1956.

KLUCKHOLN, C., MURRAY, H. A., and SCHNEIDER, D. M. (Eds.) *Personality in nature, society, and culture*. (Rev. Ed.) New York: Knopf, 1953.

LANGER, S. K. *Philosophy in a new key*. Cambridge: Harvard Univ. Press, 1942. Reprinted in New American Library (Mentor Books), 1953.

LORENZ, K. *King Solomon's ring*. New York: Crowell, 1952.

MEAD, M. *Male and female*. New York: Morrow, 1949.

MILLER, N. E., and DOLLARD, J. *Social learning and imitation*. New Haven: Yale Univ. Press, 1941.

MUNROE, R. *Schools of psychoanalytic thought*. New York: Dryden, 1955.

NEWMAN, H. H., FREEMAN, F. N., and HOLZINGER, K. J. *Twins: a study of heredity and environment*. Chicago: Univ. of Chicago Press, 1937.

OGG, E. *Psychologists in action*. New York: Public Affairs Pamphlet, No. 229, 1955.

PFEIFFER, J. *The human brain*. New York: Harper, 1955.

PIAGET, J. *The psychology of intelligence*. London: Routledge and Kegan Paul, 1950.

PRESSEY, S. L., and KUHLEN, R. G. *Psychological development through the life span*. New York: Harper, 1957.

SCHEINFELD, A. *You and heredity* (New Ed.). Philadelphia: Lippincott, 1950.

SELYE, H. *The stress of life*. New York: McGraw-Hill, 1956.

SHELDON, W. H. *The varieties of human physique*. New York: Harper, 1940.

TANNER, J. M., and INHELDER, B. (Eds.) *Discussions on child development* (Proceedings of the World Health Organization Study Group on the Psychobiological Development of the Child). London: Tavistock. 1956, 2 vols.

TINBERGEN, N. *The study of instinct*. London: Oxford Univ. Press, 1951.

TYLER, L. E. *The psychology of human differences* (2nd Ed.) New York: Appleton-Century-Crofts, 1956.

WALTER, W. Grey. *The living brain*. New York: Norton, 1953.

WERTHEIMER, M. *Productive thinking*. New York: Harper, 1945.

WOODWORTH, R. S. *Contemporary schools of psychology*. New York: Ronald, 1948.

III. CHILDHOOD AND ADOLESCENCE

Association for Childhood Education (International) Bulletin No. 59. *Pictures of children living and learning.* 1951.

BARKER, R. G., and WRIGHT, H. F. *One boy's day.* New York: Harper, 1951.

BIBER, B., MURPHY, L. B., WOODCOCK, L. P., and BLACK, I. S. *Child life in school.* New York: Dutton, 1942.

BLOS, P. *The adolescent personality.* New York: Appleton-Century-Crofts, 1941.

BOWLBY, J. *Maternal care and mental health.* Geneva: World Health Organization, 1951.

CATTELL, P. *Measurement of intelligence in infants.* New York: Psychological Corporation, 1942.

DUDYCHA, G. J. *Learn more with less effort.* New York: Harper, 1957.

ERIKSON, E. H. *Childhood and society.* New York: Norton, 1950.

FENTON, J. C. *A practical psychology of babyhood.* Boston: Houghton, 1925.

GESELL, A., and ILG, F. L. *The child from five to ten.* New York: Harper, 1946.

GESELL, A., and ILG, F. L. *Infant and child in the culture of today.* New York: Harper, 1943.

GESELL, A., ILG, F. L., and AMES, L. B. *Youth: the years from ten to sixteen.* New York: Harper, 1956.

HAVIGHURST, R. J., and TABA, H. *Adolescent character and personality.* New York: Wiley, 1949.

HAYES, C. *The ape in our house.* New York: Harper, 1951.

HOLLINGSHEAD, A. *Elmtown's youth.* New York: Wiley, 1949.

JONES, H. E. *Development in adolescence.* New York: Appleton-Century-Crofts, 1943.

KELLER, H. *The story of my life.* New York: Doubleday, 1905.

KELLOGG, W. N., and KELLOGG, L. A. *The ape and the child.* New York: Whittlesey House, 1933.

LANDRETH, K. *The psychology of early childhood.* New York: Knopf, 1958.

McGRAW, M. B. *Growth: a study of Jimmy and Johnny.* New York: D. Appleton-Century, 1935.

MURPHY, L. B., and others. *Colin—a normal child.* Vol. 2. *Personality in young children.* New York: Harper, 1956.

PIAGET, J. *The language and thought of the child.* New York: Harcourt, Brace, 1926.

PIAGET, J. *The moral judgment of the child.* New York: Harcourt, Brace, 1932.

The psychoanalytic study of the child. Vols. 1-12. New York: International Univ. Press, 1945-1957.

RIBBLE, M. A. *The rights of infants.* New York: Columbia Univ. Press, 1943.

SEARS, R. R., MACCOBY, E. E., and LEVIN, H. *Patterns of child rearing.* Evanston: Row-Peterson, 1957.

Shirley, M. *The first two years: a study of twenty-five babies.* Minneapolis: Univ. of Minnesota Press, 1933, 2 vols.

Spock, B. *The pocket book of baby and child care.* New York: Pocket Books, 1946.

Terman, L. M., and Merrill, M. A. *Measuring intelligence.* Boston: Houghton, 1937.

Trager, H. G., and Radke-Yarrow, M. *They learn what they live.* New York: Harper, 1952.

Whiting, J. W. M., and Child, I. L. *Child training and personality.* New Haven: Yale Univ. Press, 1953.

IV. THE ADULT YEARS

Anderson, J. E. (Ed.) *Psychological aspects of aging.* Washington: American Psychological Association, 1956.

Burgess, E. W., and Wallin, P. *Engagement and marriage.* New York: Lippincott, 1953.

Cavan, R. S., Burgess, E. W., Havighurst, R. J., and Goldhamer, H. *Personal adjustment in old age.* Chicago: Science Research Associates, 1949.

Evans, J. *Three men.* New York: Knopf, 1954.

Gilbert, J. G. *Understanding old age.* New York: Ronald, 1952.

Lawton, G. (Ed.) *New goals for old age.* New York: Columbia Univ. Press, 1943.

Paterson, D. G., and Darley, J. G. *Men, women, and jobs.* Minneapolis: Univ. of Minnesota Press, 1936.

Roe, A. *The psychology of occupations.* New York: Wiley, 1956.

Scheinfeld, A. *Women and men.* New York: Harcourt, Brace, 1943.

Super, D. E. *The psychology of careers.* New York: Harper, 1957.

Terman, L. M., and Oden, M. H. *The gifted child grows up.* Stanford: Stanford Univ. Press, 1947.

Wechsler, D. *The measurement and appraisal of adult intelligence.* Baltimore: Williams and Wilkins, 1958.

White, R. W. *Lives in progress.* New York: Dryden, 1952.

V. PERSONALITY AND BEHAVIOR DIFFICULTIES

Buck, P. *The child who never grew.* New York: John Day, 1950.

Dollard, J., and others. *Frustration and aggression.* New Haven: Yale Univ. Press, 1939.

Fenichel, O. *The psychoanalytic theory of neurosis.* New York: Norton, 1945.

Freud, A. *The ego and the mechanisms of defense.* New York: International Univ. Press. 1946.

GLUECK, S., and GLUECK, E. *Unraveling juvenile delinquency.* New York: Commonwealth Fund, 1950.

HEALY, W., and BRONNER, A. F. *New light on delinquency and its treatment.* New Haven: Yale Univ. Press, 1936.

HORNEY, K. *Neurosis and human growth.* New York: Norton, 1950.

HORNEY, K. *The neurotic personality of our time.* New York: Norton, 1937.

HORNEY, K. *Our inner conflicts.* New York: Norton, 1945.

HUTT, M. L., and GIBBY, R. G. *The mentally retarded child.* Boston: Allyn and Bacon, 1958.

KALLMAN, F. J. *Heredity in health and mental disorders.* New York: Norton, 1953.

MAY, R. *The meaning of anxiety.* New York: Ronald, 1950.

MCKINNEY, F. *Psychology of personal adjustment* (Rev. Ed.) New York: Wiley, 1949.

MERRILL, M. A. *Problems of child delinquency.* Boston: Houghton, 1947.

O'CONNOR, N., and TIZARD, J. *The social problem of mental deficiency.* New York: Pergamom, 1956.

REDL, F., and WINEMAN, D. *The aggressive child.* Glencoe, Ill.: Free Press, 1957.

SARASON, S. B. *Psychological problems in mental deficiency.* (2nd Ed.) New York: Harper, 1953.

SHAFFER, L. F., and SHOBEN, E. J., Jr. *The psychology of adjustment* (2nd Ed.) Boston: Houghton, 1956.

SHAW, C. R. *The jack roller: a delinquent boy's own story.* Chicago: Univ. of Chicago Press, 1930.

WHITE, R. W. *The abnormal personality.* New York: Ronald, 1948.

WILSON, D. P. *My six convicts.* New York: Rinehart, 1951.

≫≫≫≫≫≫≫≫≫≫≫

Index

539

THE CENTURY PSYCHOLOGY SERIES

Richard M. Elliot, *Editor*

Kenneth MacCorquodale, *Assistant Editor*

The Century Psychology Series